FORT DONELSON'S LEGACY

FORT DONELSON'S LEGACY

WAR AND SOCIETY IN KENTUCKY AND TENNESSEE, 1862–1863

Benjamin Franklin Cooling

The University of Tennessee Press / Knoxville

Copyright © 1997 by The University of Tennessee Press / Knoxville.
All Rights Reserved. Manufactured in the United States of America.
First Edition.

The paper in this book meets the minimum requirements of the
American National Standard for Permanence of Paper for Printed
Library Materials. ∞ The binding materials have been chosen
for strength and durability.
🌐 This book is printed on recycled paper.

Frontis. Confederate Monument at Fort Donelson. Photo by
James Jobe, 1986.

Library of Congress Cataloging-in-Publication Data

Cooling, B. Franklin.
Fort Donelson's legacy : war and society in Kentucky and
Tennessee, 1862–1863 / Benjamin Franklin Cooling. — 1st ed.
p. cm.
Includes bibliographical references and index.
ISBN 0-87049-949-1 (cl.: alk. paper)
1. Fort Donelson (Tenn.), Battle of, 1862. 2. Fort Henry (Tenn.),
Battle of, 1862. 3. Civil-military relations—Southern States—History—19th century.
4. Tennessee—History—Civil War,
1861–1865. 5. Kentucky—History—Civil War, 1861–1865.
6. United States—History—Civil War, 1861–1865—Social aspects.
I. Title.
E472.97.C66 1996
973.7'32—dc20 96-10012
CIP

TO TWO "HEARTLANDERS"

Rudolf K. Haerle of Indianapolis and
Frank G. Rankin of Louisville who widened the author's
perspective on the Civil War in the Western Theater.

CONTENTS

	Preface	xi
	Acknowledgments	xix
One	Aftermath of Disaster: February 1862	1
Two	Asserting National Authority: Spring 1862	26
Three	Confederate Resurgence: Summer 1862	58
Four	Heartland Havoc: Late Summer 1862	92
Five	North to Kentucky: Autumn 1862	118
Six	Decision in Middle Tennessee: Late Fall 1862	145
Seven	Rebels Return to Fort Donelson: February 1863	176
Eight	Heartland Impasse: Late Winter 1863	207
Nine	Heartland Dynamics: Spring 1863	233
Ten	To Tullahoma and Beyond: Summer 1863	264
Eleven	Victories Blue and Gray: Autumn 1863	292
Twelve	Last Hurrah at Chattanooga: November 1863	318
	Notes	347
	Bibliography	377
	Index	391

ILLUSTRATIONS

FIGURES

Frontis. Confederate Monument at Fort Donelson	
Interior of Fort Donelson and Water Battery	2
Restored Dover Hotel, Dover, Tennessee	4
Railroad Bridge and Nashville Skyline	14
View of Nashville, March 1862	20
Railroad Bridge, Bridgeport, Alabama	29
Fugitive Slaves Coming into Union Lines	42
Colonel John Hunt Morgan and His Wife, Mattie	48
Colonel Adam Rankin Johnson	71
Tishomingo Hotel, Corinth, Mississippi	77
Colonel Tom Woodward	96
Sergeant Eugene Marshall	104
Morgan's Raiders at Paris, Kentucky	125
Impressing Contrabands at Church	127
Defending Kentucky, Fall 1862	131
Fight at Licking Bridge	136
Impressing Negroes to Work on Nashville Fortifications	147
Sketch of Fort Negley	151
Union Foraging Party	181
Guerrillas Burning Steamboats	189
Colonel Sanders D. Bruce	191
Fort Bruce and Vicinity	192
Colonel Abner C. Harding	194
USS *Fairplay*	199
Lieutenant Commander Le Roy Fitch	225
Commander S. L. Phelps	228
Guerrillas Destroying a Train	242
Wheeler's Attack on Supply Train near Jasper, Tennessee	308
Colonel Robert H. G. Minty	310
Railroad Bridge at Whiteside, Tennessee	323

View of Paducah, Kentucky	329
Knoxville Skyline from Fort Sanders	333
Chattanooga Skyline	334

MAPS

Strategic Situation in Late February 1862	23
Proto-Ruhr of Upper Confederate Heartland	31
Strategic Situation on the Eve of Shiloh, 1862	56
Strategic Situation in West Tennessee, July 1862	59
Vicksburg Campaign in Mid-September 1862	116
Forces before Invasion of Kentucky and Middle Tennessee, September 1862	121
Failure in Kentucky and Return to Middle Tennessee, October and December 1862	133
Vicksburg Campaign from Mid-December to Early January 1862–1863	174
Battle of Dover, February 3, 1863	196
The Union Fort Donelson	256
Tullahoma Campaign at the End of June 1863	268
Advance on Chattanooga, August 1863	293
Advance on Chickamauga, September 9 and 10, 1863	302
Siege of Chattanooga, October 1863	319

PREFACE

American military professionals have been enamored with the early-nineteenth-century Prussian theorist of war Karl von Clausewitz since their own unfortunate excursion in Vietnam. Notwithstanding his conventional themes that continue to mesmerize war colleges everywhere—war as an extension of politics, the trinity of war (political direction, the armed forces, and the popular base), the search for the enemy's "center of gravity," and friction, or "fog of war," as a negative "force multiplier"—Clausewitz's incomplete magnum opus, *Vom Kriege*, also touched upon a theme relatively new to conflict in his own time—the People in Arms. In Book Six, Chapter Twenty-Six, this great student of the French Revolutionary and Napoleonic wars briefly addressed the phenomenon unleashed by that era. His death in 1831 and the lack of an English translation available to the generation of American soldiers that fought their Civil War thirty years later do not detract from Clausewitz's prescient observations when applied to that war. The facts of the war bore out his contentions.

Clausewitz believed that a popular uprising should be generally considered "a broadening and intensification of the fermentation process known as war." The whole system of requisitioning, the enormous growth of armies resulting from it and universal conscription, the employment of militia, even the calling out of the home guard and arming the people ran toward the intensification of war itself in his age. He suggested that any nation that used this powerful new weapon intelligently would "as a rule, gain some superiority over those who disdain its use." Certainly neither Union nor Confederacy disdained its use.

Clausewitz further prescribed that it was wise to think of a general insurrection within the framework of a war conducted by regular forces and coordinated in "one all-encompassing plan." Clausewitz's conditions for an effective plan included the following: 1) the war had to be fought in the interior of the country; 2) it must not be decided by a single stroke; 3) the theater of operations had to be fairly large; 4) the national character had to be suited to that type of war; and 5) the country had to be rough and inaccessible due to mountains or forests, marshes, or local methods of cultivation. Population density was not a factor, argued Clausewitz, since there were always sufficient people for the purpose, and it mattered not whether they were rich or poor, although the latter were accustomed to hard, strenuous work and privation and were generally more vigorous and warlike. He could well have been talking about the hinterland of the American south and its yeomanry at the time.

Clausewitz further cautioned against employing militia and bands of armed civilians against the main enemy army—or against any sizable enemy force, for that matter. They were intended, rather, to operate in areas just outside the theater of war, where an invader would not appear in strength, so as to deny the invader those areas altogether. "Thunder clouds of this type should build up all around the invader the farther he advances" were the Prussian's captivating words. The people not yet invaded would be most eager to arm against the intruder, spreading their fervor like wildfire to their neighbors, even closing in behind the enemy force to threaten his line of communication and his very existence. The enemy's only answer to militia actions would be to dispatch escorts for convoys, guards to all stopping places, but, in effect, fanning the flames of insurrection by the very presence of such a response. Thus, these conditions would stimulate the courage and appetite for fighting along with the tension, "until it reaches the climax that decides the outcome."[1]

The master theorist enjoined that a general uprising should be "nebulous and elusive," with resistance never concentrated lest the enemy direct sufficient force against its core, thereby crushing it, taking many prisoners, and thus causing the people to lose heart and believe that the issue was settled. Yet, he said, there should be some concentration at key points—"the fog must thicken and form a dark and menacing cloud out of which a bolt of lightning may strike at any time." Insurgents should construct larger and better organized units along with parties of regular forces to make them look like a proper force and to enable them to undertake larger operations, particularly in the enemy's rear. Not only would they engage the enemy units thus dispatched to counter them, but also they might then "arouse uneasiness and fear, and deepen the psychological effect of the insurrection as a whole."

A commander could more easily shape and direct popular uprising by providing small units from the regular force for support. Without these units to give encouragement, local inhabitants "will usually lack the confidence and initiative to take to arms," Clausewitz argued. Not that regulars should be frittered away on secondary objectives or be too heavily saturated in an area, since they might dilute "the vigor and effectiveness of a popular uprising" by attracting too many enemy troops, by causing the inhabitants to rely too heavily on the regulars, or by their very presence taxing local resources via billeting, transportation, requisitions, etc. Furthermore, insurgent action was similar to all others fought by "second-rate troops," said Clausewitz. They commence full of vigor and enthusiasm, "but there is little level-headedness and tenacity in the long run." Defeat or dispersal of a body of insurgents would not lose much; still, the wise commander would not allow too much of this force to be killed, wounded, or made prisoner and thus dampen its ardor.

In Clausewitz's mind, one of the basic principles of insurrection always stood uppermost. He preached that seldom or never should this important strategic means of defense be allowed to turn into merely tactical defense. Therefore, defensive action involving insurgency had to be slow and calculated, entailing a definite risk, and should never be brought to a final defensive battle. No matter how brave a people might be or how warlike its traditions, no matter how great its hatred for the foe or how favorable the ground upon which it fights, he claimed that a national uprising "cannot maintain itself where the atmosphere is too full of danger."

For the defender, then, national uprising was a fuel to be fanned into major conflagration by distance, where sufficient air prevented smothering by a single stroke such as climactic battle. He prescribed that with the retreat of the army into the interior—no matter how complete the defeat of a state—the potential of fortresses and general insurrections had to be invoked. This strategy would fix or tie the enemy to dispersal of resources, thereby providing the time for the defending army to deliver a well-placed blow to the attacker.

Had Clausewitz lived to see the American Civil War, would he have judged his principles sound? Would he have regarded one antagonist as more skillful than the other at carrying them out? Alas, he died before the war's onset, and Europeans of succeeding generations focused upon different lessons from their study of the conflict. After all, Clausewitz himself admitted that this new type of warfare was not yet very common in his lifetime and that little had been said by those who had observed its rudimentary beginnings in Spain and Russia during the Napoleonic period. "We merely wish to add that strategic plans for defense can provide for a general insurrection in one of two ways: either as a last resort after a defeat or as a natural auxiliary before a decisive battle" formed his parting words on the subject. That the Civil War in Tennessee and Kentucky in 1862 and 1863 reflected his wisdom would surely have pleased Clausewitz. The war after Forts Henry and Donelson seemingly mirrored "the People in Arms" envisioned in his writings.

The theme of this work then is the symbiosis of war and society as the principal legacy of spectacular Union victories at Forts Henry and Donelson in February 1862. These twin battles on the Tennessee and Cumberland Rivers in Middle Tennessee might have ended the American Civil War, if they had been exploited properly by the Union high command. They were not, and instead these battles spawned a legacy of continued bloodshed that cut beyond armies and into the fabric of civilian society. The war after Henry-Donelson witnessed army-navy conquest of the Great Valley of the Mississippi, helped demythologize some of the South's foremost military/planter aristocracy and their world, and ultimately produced the Union leadership team that redeemed the trans-Appalachian West for the nation. But it also spawned civil resistance, guerrilla warfare, and devastation of property and culture in the southern heartland.

In the narrow view, the war after Henry-Donelson became one of distance and logistics, cavalry raids (dashing, sometimes useful, often overused and ill-used by both sides), and additional pitched battles from the Ohio river to the Gulf. These battles included Shiloh, Perryville, Murfreesboro, Vicksburg, Chickamauga, and Chattanooga, to name only the most prominent. Gradually, under national government oversight, the great western rivers reopened to commercial intercourse and communication—the lifeblood of nineteenth-century inland America. But social comity and political stability hardly accompanied such developments. Herein lay a less appreciated legacy. Political reconstruction, suppression of civil disobedience, and restoration even reform of cultural and economic institutions paralleled the operational demands of wartime.

In the first instance, the war in the West remained preeminently a river war after Donelson. As Major General William Tecumseh Sherman perceptively announced while moving east from Memphis to help relieve Confederate-besieged Chattanooga in the fall of 1863: "We are much obliged to the Tennessee, which has favored us most opportunely, for I am never easy with a railroad which takes a whole army to guard, each foot of rail being essential to the whole; whereas they can't stop the Tennessee, and each boat can make its own game." He never forgot those words, remembering them ruefully during his Georgia campaign the following year, when Tennessee cavalry wizard Nathan Bedford Forrest flaunted the last gasp of Confederate striking power in his rear. In the end, Forts Henry and Donelson bequeathed a continuation of professional soldiers' perspective, since, as historian Archer Jones contends, the Union's persisting strategy "became fundamentally a logistic strategy of occupying the country to weaken the Confederates by depriving them of recruits and agricultural and industrial resources." Lessons learned in the upper heartland in 1862–63 led both sides to resort to this so-called raiding strategy during the final year and one-third of the war.[2]

Nonetheless, the confluence of war and society formed an important second legacy. One historian observed recently that the fall of Forts Henry and Donelson set in motion a process that irrevocably altered southerners' way of life. Pointing to economic and cultural ramifications of those Yankee victories, Robert Tracy McKenzie quoted a Bedford County, Tennessee, planter who exclaimed in the spring of 1862 that God alone knew what would result from the war. Civil-military relations became entwined with the social and political process. What was clearly a people's war about defense of hearth and home (in southerners' eyes) was also a contest about government authority. Social issues concerning men's beliefs and their willingness to fight for them (even out of uniform) were entwined with economic self-interest. The use of a peacetime labor force for wartime activities soon prompted Federal government actions against property as well as against people's hearts and minds. Slavery's utility to the Confederate war effort (first evidenced by slave-built fortifications and resupplying activities encountered in the Henry-Donelson campaign) contributed to de facto Union army emancipation preceding any policy decision by the central federal government. Herein lay the basis for so much acrimony between heartland civilians and the national military occupation authorities during 1862 and 1863.[3]

Stubborn civilian opposition to Union invaders prompted oppressive military occupation, subversion of civil liberties, and confiscation of personal property in the name of allegiance to the United States—or to the Confederacy, for that matter, since some Unionist southerners resented Confederate intrusion fully as much as their secessionist neighbors opposed Yankee government. The full impact of this second legacy in civil-military relations lay suborned by the operational legacy until the summer of 1862. Then, officially sanctioned Confederate partisan rangers blazed the path for irregular warfare and popular uprising, suggesting a society in arms, not merely insurrectionary armies battling national counterparts. None of this reached full flower before 1864–65 (the subject of a succeeding volume). Yet, the pattern of civil-military relations becomes unmistakable during the immediate twenty-two months after Fort Donelson's surrender.

Such phenomena suggest that the primary thrust of the present book be military history, not social history. The events of the period were above all military in nature—dictated by necessity or until Union forces had either cleared Confederate opponents from Tennessee and Kentucky or had been swept back to the Ohio River in turn. With new Civil War orthodoxy focusing less upon operational brilliance and more on systematic application of military resources and the changing nature of combat, authors and readers cannot neglect southern society as it butted against the rush of armies and navies. The current vogue of seeking the origins of "total war" in American experience or clarifying the evolution of "hard war" as official policy frankly drives a more integrated approach to war and society than found in most Civil War "blood and glory" accounts. The undercurrent of social resistance and rebellion persisted long after Napoleonic-style warfare passed from the region. New studies by young scholars such as Stephen V. Ash and Mark Grimsley underscore that fact.[4]

Readers actually need look no further than the hoary Official Records to sense the disorderly matrix of the western war in this regard. Despite the historian's tendency to search for new and untapped sources, merely revisiting these published army and navy records will kindle new possibilities for appreciating the war in its holistic but unruly context. Modern chroniclers sometimes synthesize and paraphrase to the point of arcane generalization, and indeed we simplify the Civil War at our peril. Comprehending historical complexity suffers when modern historiography rejects confrontation with *wie es eigentlich gewesen est*—history as it really was. Failure to make this happen in these pages will be my responsibility alone.

This work, like those of Daniel Crofts and Michael Fellman, is a modest plea to revisit the upper Civil War South as an object of study. Here the personal antagonisms, the physical devastation, and the social effects of civil conflict were felt with special intensity—and beyond the limits of the principal battles. In the words of Clarksville, Tennessee, lawyer Joseph B. Killebrew: "We were where the waves advanced and retreated." Overlapped first by one side and then the other, after each change, "we had to govern ourselves accordingly." The greatest safety in those times, he concluded, was found simply in staying home. A Kentuckian veteran of War of 1812, Moses Wright, wrote a friend after the war that he had supported the Confederates "only from principle," bearing no private grudges or malice against any northerner who had been a brave soldier in the Federal army. But he quickly added that he entertained no "friendly feelings for those creatures from Kentucky and Tennessee who were in the Federal army."[5]

A portent of this wartime southern landscape where physical devastation was evident and loyalties were divided was but dimly evident when a young English journalist visited America in the spring after Fort Donelson. Edward Dicey, special correspondent for *The Spectator* and *MacMillan's Magazine*, supplied home readers with a lively account, later published in book form as *Six Months in the Federal States* (London, 1863). His observations of Kentucky and Tennessee especially captured the unfolding themes of war in the upper heartland. Battles did not command his attention; instead, politics and society did. Secession had received its first rebuff in Kentucky, he claimed, but a well-planned reconstruction policy was quite absent. Everywhere, he saw "tokens of the great insurrection."[6]

Dicey experienced Kentucky in May. If Louisville languished in commercial doldrums and monotony, Bluegrass hamlets sparkled by comparison, while lush croplands, and the absence of "shiftless slovenliness" that he saw in other slave states, made his Kentucky sojourn memorable. He supposed that every Kentuckian had a friend or relative on one side or the other; yet, happily, Kentuckians remained aloof from commitment to either side. The overpowering presence of slavery meant that, while loyal to the Union, Kentucky seemed equally wary of the triumph of either North or South. Its sentiments were drawn to the latter, he said, while its interests were drawn to the former. The result was that the state was "still halting" between allegiances.

Freedom of speech, yet evident in the Bluegrass at this point, greatly impressed Dicey. The open avowals of disloyalty and loathing of the Lincoln government he heard in every Louisville barroom stood in stark contrast to suppression of dissidence in Ireland, with which he was more familiar. But Tennessee proved different. News censorship and the required oath of allegiance were commonplace when Dicey had visited there a month before. The impact of Shiloh seemed less evident, as he focused on Nashville and its new military government. The capital was the most picturesque of American cities, he thought as he arrived on the Louisville and Nashville train, and he relished the neatly rowed streets and houses, shaded by lime and chestnut trees that blended out to the nicely appointed villas in the city's outskirts. The deplorable Confederate destruction of Nashville's prized suspension bridge caught his eye, of course. So too did the squalor of hotel accommodations, and Dicey sneered at a society where whites thought it beneath them to work and the blacks refused unless forced to do so. Overall, he characterized Tennessee's premier city as "still stunned by the blow of some great calamity." That calamity had been the fall of Forts Henry and Donelson.

Most of all, the Englishman thought it baleful that the Federal government and the North had not determined future policy beyond merely suppressing the rebellion. The only guidelines seemed to be a restoration of the status quo before the war. Still, this would do for the people of Tennessee, he thought. The appointment of East Tennessee slaveholder and United States Senator Andrew Johnson as military governor seemingly guaranteed no violent revolution for life and property in the state. Pacification would ride on the notion of winning back the people's allegiance. Dicey cited Johnson's speech to a Minnesota occupation regiment in which he assured them that abolitionism was not in the cards. The assemblage had cheered wildly, observed Dicey. In fact, the journalist embraced Lincoln administration dogma that the common folk of the South had been seduced and oppressed by an antebellum slaveowning oligarchy. If the Federal government could continue to guarantee property and safety, then recovery and reconstruction would occur by degrees.

Dicey pointed to certain unassailable facts. As long as the war lasted in their midst, upper heartlanders feared Confederate retribution should they embrace unionism. A reign of terror would attend the return of Confederate fortunes to Nashville and vicinity. Dicey believed that the sullen attitude he had seen in Tennessee had good cause. Fence straddling made sense to potential victims of harsh civil war in the Volunteer state, just as it did, for different reasons, in Kentucky. The battles that had been fought had not been decisive. Rather, the divisiveness of families caught in the middle made equivocation most advisable. Once the insurrection had been suppressed and order restored, thought Dicey, then southerners would acquiesce to the inevitable. Whether slavery might still prove an insuperable obstacle to union could not be answered, he supposed. He was positive, however, that the North would "suppress or remove this cause; rather than ever consent to disruption of the Union."

So, the military and social legacies unfolded both slowly and segmentally after Forts Henry and Donelson. The years 1862 and 1863 formed a pivotal first part of that legacy. Complex in converging detail, the period covered by this book portrays a transitional phase. Great armies oscillated across the upper Confederate heartland until the Union victory at Chattanooga. (They would return briefly and decisively in the autumn of 1864 for one last lurch toward gore and glory in the battles at Franklin and Nashville.) But, in 1862–63, the transitional phase was marked principally by policy change with respect to the populace of Kentucky and Tennessee. Union policy and practice evolved from conciliation to demand for unconditional fidelity to the national government and retributive punishment for continued rebellion.

As one recent reviewer of Lee Kennett's study of William T. Sherman's 1864 Georgia campaign observed, the author recognized the Civil War for what it was—not a joust by chivalric knights but rather a hard conflict between two societies and among members of the Southern society itself.[7] This had already become evident by 1862–63. The story is one of process, to be sure, with participants great and small pursuing countless agendas, but always with one goal in mind. That goal, for both the Union and the Confederacy, was control of the heartland—of Kentucky and Tennessee—but, most of all, of the people.

ACKNOWLEDGMENTS

An author always welcomes the opportunity to thank people for helping make a book possible. Those who have helped me include old friends Professor Allan R. Millett of Ohio State University and Professor Herman M. Hattaway of the University of Missouri at Kansas City, who commented upon drafts of the manuscript. Professor Archer Jones of Richmond, Virginia, James Gilchrist Barrett of Lexington, Virginia, and James I. Robertson of the Virginia Polytechnic Institute and State University blessed the original proposal. Among those individuals who graciously provided private research material were Lieutenant Colonel (Ret.) William E. Laybourn of Grand Junction, Colorado; Michael Klinger of Ft. Wayne, Indiana; Lon Carter Barton of Mayfield, Kentucky; Professor Edward M. Coffman of Madison, Wisconsin; Dr. Hunter Hancock of Lexington, Kentucky; C. L. Pollard of Water Valley, Kentucky; Frank G. Rankin of Louisville, Kentucky; Rudolf K. Haerle of Indianapolis, Indiana; W. E. Dorris of Lemoyne, Nebraska; Hunter B. Whitesell of Fulton, Kentucky; Ursula Beach of Clarksville, Tennessee; Walter T. Durham of Gallatin, Tennessee; Professor Richard Gildrie of Austin Peay State University, Clarksville, Tennessee; Professor Lonnie E. Maness of the University of Tennessee, Martin; James T. Siburt of Hermitage, Tennessee; and Roger Hunt of Rockville, Maryland.

Similarly notable for providing research support from their institutions were Paul Brockman and Alexandra S. Gressitt of the Indiana Historical Society Library, Indianapolis; Eric Austin of the State Historical Society of Iowa, Iowa City; Colonel Donald L. Armstrong, Kentucky Army National Guard (Ret.), Kentucky Department of Military Affairs, Frankfort; Mary Margaret Bell and James Russell Harris of the Kentucky Historical Society, Frankfort; Keith M. Heim of the Forrest C. Pogue Library, Murray State (Kentucky) University; James J. Holmberg of the Filson Club, Louisville; Patricia M. Hodges and Sue Lynn McGuire of Western Kentucky University library, Bowling Green; Gerry Reed of the Murray (Kentucky) Public Library; Steven Eric Nielsen of the Minnesota Historical

Acknowledgments

Society; Richard A. Shrader of the University of North Carolina library, Chapel Hill; Janie C. Morris, Linda McCurdy, and Patricia Webb of the Perkins Library at Duke University, Durham, North Carolina; Raymond Shook and Jill A. Hosmer of the Clarksville-Montgomery County Museum, Clarksville, Tennessee; Ann Alley and Wayne Moore of the Tennessee State Library and Archives; James B. Lloyd and William B. Eigelsbach of the University of Tennessee Library Special Collections, Knoxville (with whom the bulk of this book's research notes will be deposited to aid other scholars); and James Jobe of the Fort Donelson National Military Park, Dover, Tennessee, where the research files of my previous work, *Forts Henry and Donelson: Key to the Western Gateway*, will be supplemented by material from this book concerning subsequent battles at Dover and in the Fort Donelson area.

Of course, it is always pleasant working with the staff of the University of Tennessee Press, particularly for this volume, and I would like to thank Jennifer Siler, Tana McDonald, Kim Scarbrough, Meredith Morris-Babb, and especially Scot Danforth and June Hussey for patiently working through a complex manuscript. Finally, I wish to recognize my wife, Mary Anne, who has endured the struggle by initially placing this manuscript in the computer until such time as she could pass the baton to the author, only lately graduated from pen to electric typewriter to word processing. Naturally, mea culpa: any mistaken facts, interpretations, and acts of commission and omission are his alone.

AFTERMATH OF DISASTER: FEBRUARY 1862

It had already been a long winter for the sullen groups of men huddled around flickering campfires near the sleepy Stewart County seat of Dover, Tennessee. Yet, it was only mid-February. The frozen landscape and biting wind cut deeply into the bodies and spirits of the ill-clad Confederates about to be surrendered to their enemy. Battlefield success had crowned their efforts at Fort Donelson. The men were ready to renew the fray. Their generals were not. "We were thunderstruck," noted Lieutenant Flavel C. Barber of the Third Tennessee, adding that they had anticipated a desperate fight at daybreak, "but no one had dreamed of a surrender. . . . Thus passed away, Sunday, February 16," he decided, "the dreariest day I ever experienced."[1]

The plan had been to hold the fort long enough for the Bowling Green army to retreat, then whip the enemy back and get away, said J. A. Hinkle of the Thirtieth Tennessee. Discipline plummeted along with morale as the cold dawn broke over the camp and firing line. Some of the men pitched into barrels of whiskey and boxes of clothing sent forward from Nashville supply depots. Others disgustedly hurled their firearms and swords into the swirling floodwaters of the Cumberland River. It was a devastated garrison, declared Alexander Jackson Campbell of the Forty-eighth Tennessee, "who felt that an outrage had been committed in surrendering them."[2]

First Lieutenant W. N. Brown of the First Mississippi wrote Confederate president Jefferson Davis eighteen years later of "the mingled feeling of despair, desolation, and desperation brought upon us by this disappointment." Major Nathaniel Cheairs later called it "the most disgraceful, unnecessary, and uncalled for surrender" of the entire war. Still another Confederate, Hugh Gwyn, wrote: "in this surrender, we have lost the chivalry and flower of our whole army." Nevertheless, surrender was the fate of approximately fifteen thousand men under Brigadier General Simon Bolivar Buckner that Sabbath morning.[3]

First, Fort Henry twelve miles away on the Tennessee River had yielded to

Aftermath of Disaster

Interior of Fort Donelson and interior of Fort Donelson water battery. Harper's Weekly, March 22, 1862.

Yankee gunboats on February 6. Poorly situated on the flood plain and inundated by high water, the fort succumbed quickly to point-blank naval gunfire, although most of the garrison escaped overland to swell the ranks at Fort Donelson. They left behind a gory mess, as Ira Blanchard of the Twentieth Illinois described it: "Legs, arms and heads were scattered in all directions by the bursting of shell from the fleet." Captain J. A. Haydon of the Tennessee Engineer Corps, captured at Fort Henry, observed: "At least, we shall hear no more of Kentucky, Virginia, and Missouri only suffering from the absolute distress of actual conflict." In April during his subsequent imprisonment at Johnson's Island, on Lake Erie, he wrote perceptively that "the war will have reached every southern State both in the seaboard region and the exposed river regions."[4]

The fall of Fort Henry opened a river invasion route to Union forces as far as northern Mississippi and Alabama. Ten days later it was Fort Donelson's turn, and these twin river disasters would resound in bitterly hushed tones across the South for generations. Larger and more famous battles would eclipse the infamy of Forts Henry and Donelson, perhaps, but the gall of ultimate Confederate defeat by 1865 could be traced directly to those early, shocking setbacks in Middle Tennessee.

Public and government embarrassment about stupidity, culpability, and poor generalship seemed the only immediate response. Young Alice Ready of Murfreesboro penned in her diary on February 11 that the fall of Fort Henry was the third in a series of calamities that included the death of Nashvillian Felix Zollicoffer in January's disastrous defeat at Fishing Creek or Mill Springs, Kentucky. It was God's punishment "for our boastfulness," she decided, although claiming that these losses really strengthened her resolve. Erstwhile Kentucky Confederate governor George W. Johnson wrote his wife from Bowling Green just before its evacuation on February 15: "The South has now waked up." Before, he suggested, they would not believe that a southern army, however weak, could be defeated, and would do nothing to respond to Western Theater commander Albert Sidney Johnston's remonstrances. Perhaps, he continued, the twin defeats at Forts Henry and Donelson would lead to an honorable peace based on southern independence and reciprocal free trade. "If they have this effect, our disaster will be valuable to us," Johnson concluded.[5]

FORT DONELSON'S SURRENDER

The initial word came from a rebel staff officer's servant that the Confederate generals at Fort Donelson were planning surrender. There were three brigadiers in charge: Virginian John B. Floyd, Tennessean Gideon Pillow, and Kentuckian Buckner. A midnight council—more an *opéra bouffe* spectacle—had seen the fainthearted commanders pass command and then flee the post. Only Buckner remained, pale and sad, observed future *Confederate Veteran* editor and publisher Sumner Archibald Cunningham, who claimed to have seen him sitting by a campfire. By dawn, the Kentuckian requested a parley and appointment of commissioners to determine the terms of capitulation. The Union expeditionary commander, Brigadier General Ulysses Simpson Grant, shot back the uncompromising answer that would echo through the pages of history: "I have no terms but unconditional surrender. I propose to move immediately upon your works." By this time, rebel commissary officers had thrown open storehouses to the angry, cold, and hungry rebels. "Sugar was abundant and it was not unusual to see a barrel of whiskey with one heading burst out and buckets of the contents taken out, and large quantities of sugar put in," remembered Kentucky scout John M. Porter. "Many got under the influence of sweetened drams to a conditional extent," he added.[6]

Over in Grant's lines, the shouts of victory already resounded among the hills and valleys. Ira Blanchard recalled that comrades in the Illinois ranks threw off their hats and coats and "fell to whipping one another until their wind gave out, or their coats went to pieces." It was the first major victory of the war for them, he declared, and "the greatest day of rejoicing I ever saw." But, before long, acts of defiance appeared in rebel ranks. Color-bearers like Spencer Elkins of the Shelbyville Rebels in the Forty-first Tennessee and Andrew S. Payne of the Fourteenth Mississippi personally cut flags from staffs and hid them beneath their clothes to escape Yankee detection. Payne coveted the hand-painted shield of Lady Liberty with a portrait of Jefferson Davis in her right hand that had been the center of the Magnolia State's regimental banner. Jake, the rooster mascot of the Third Tennessee, and Frank, a mongrel belonging to the Second Kentucky, prepared to march off to prison with their masters. The pup had his own little haversack strung around his neck to carry scanty rations. At least one member of

Restored Dover Hotel, Dover, Tennessee, was the site of surrender of Fort Donelson. Courtesy of James Jobe, 1986.

the crestfallen garrison noted how suddenly liberated slaves seemed to be so impudent. Many of the blacks were from the local neighborhood of the twin rivers and sensed deliverance from bondage.[7]

So it was that Simon Buckner, having finished a morning repast of cornmeal washed down with black coffee in the company of an old friend, Indiana brigadier Lew Wallace (who had arrived early for the surrender), pushed back his chair and strode out on the porch of the venerable Bufford Hotel at Dover's upper steamboat landing to meet his old army friend Grant. However, the meeting proved perfunctory. Buckner just could not understand Grant's "ungenerous and unchivalrous terms." The two men would meet again over the next several days as the Federal commander tried to make amends for the necessary but hard doctrine of unqualified capitulation. Remembering Buckner's prewar kindness when Grant had been down on his luck, the victor proffered his erstwhile foe a small purse to help him in captivity. The proud Kentuckian brushed aside the gesture, leaving Grant with "tears rolling down his face" as Buckner went off to captivity. The two men would see one another again only when Grant sat in the White House years later. Meanwhile, the curtain of war slammed down between them. Grant's unconditional surrender dictum was a distinct omen for the weeks and months ahead. Chivalry was a thing of the past.[8]

Southern newspapers like the Memphis *Avalanche* proclaimed that "the conviction in our mind [is] that no surrender should have been made." Instead, "a little more patience—a little more suffering—would have secured us the most splendid victory." Candidly, there were those on both sides who were simply pleased that the winter ordeal had ended. James Drish of the Thirty-second Illinois enjoyed taunting the Virginia prisoners because Old Dominion spokesmen had proclaimed for months that they scarcely thought the Illinois men would fight at all. He admitted, "it was the hardest battle ever fought on the American continent," and his comrades' endurance was "wonderful they fought for three days with scarcely anything to eat and they had to lay down on their arms in the snows for three nights in succession without blankets." Lieutenant Charles Brown Tompkins's men in the Seventeenth Illinois thought Tennessee rather a rough climate for war, adding, they wanted to sing "farewell forever to old Tennessee," rather than "Uli, Oli, Ili, E, Soldiering down in Tennessee."[9]

Some malcontents surfaced among the victors, too. Medical Steward Edward P. Bishop aboard the USS *Carondelet* claimed that his mates had not received credit due for their role in the victory. He felt it could be traced to ill-will between flotilla commander Andrew Hull Foote and boat captain Henry Walke. He told home folks irately: "Commodore Foote showed the white Feather, for had all the boats of staid [*sic*] as us, the 14 of Feb would of decided it, instead of the 16th." The rebel water battery success against the Union gunboats at Fort Donelson on Valentine's Day notwithstanding, at least Grant's soldiers reassured their homefolk how northern battle losses were considerably less than reported in the newspapers. Only about 1,000 to 1,500 Federals had fallen, while the cost to the enemy probably was close to calculations by Confederate Jared Carl Frazier of the Forty-eighth Tennessee, who enumerated 200 killed, 1,190 wounded, 13,657 captured.[10]

Grant firmly believed that the surrender had avoided any further bloody combat. He boasted to his congressional patron, Illinois representative Elihu B. Washburn, that "our volunteers fought a battle that would figure well with many of those fought in Europe where large standing armies are maintained." He felt that this had caused profound effect upon the local community—the "effect of defeat, disastrous defeat." On February 23, he wrote his departmental commander Major General Henry Halleck's chief of staff that "a powerful change is taking place in the minds of the people through the state."[11]

RECRIMINATIONS AND FINGER POINTING

The victors simply shipped their hapless captives to months of incarceration in prison camps from the Midwest to New England. In prison the men of Dixie languished, nostalgic for home and freedom, keeping track of the progress of humdrum daily events in diaries and journals and hoping for foreign intervention and their own speedy release. Thwarted by northern censors from talking about the disasters (and politics generally), their letters spoke only of good prison treatment, their concern about spring crops and loved ones at home, and how they might acquire more luxuries and money to ease their plight. Captain George Triplett Moorman, aide to Brigadier General Bushrod Johnson, wrote to William Bayliss in Nashville from temporary incarceration at Louisville on February 4, asking about his missing camp chest, which had been left aboard the steamboat *John A. Fisher* when the prisoners departed Dover. He had put it aboard "for safety, it has my clothing, and papers in it, and I want you to go down to the *Fisher* and get it and take it up to your house, and keep it for me, until I send for it," the young officer instructed Bayliss. Such was the informality attending the whole POW business at this stage of the war. Time ameliorated even some of the ill-will and pettiness present among Confederates at Fort Donelson prior to the surrender. Colonel Alfred Harris Abernathy of the Fifty-third Tennessee noted in June how the friction between himself and fellow Clarksvillian Colonel James Edmund Bailey of the Forty-ninth Tennessee and other rival Clarksville officers at Fort Warren, Massachusetts, had abated, as all "have been more courteous and attentive." They studied Spanish and tactics, formed a reading and writing group, and enjoyed some more stirring game of exercise. Access to outside newspapers gave him a better opinion of Yankees than before, he also claimed.[12]

Captain John Henry Guy of the Goochland Light Artillery, imprisoned on Johnson's Island, Ohio, ensured that reading material was sent to his enlisted men in Union prisons elsewhere, and he, like a few of the young officers, kept detailed prison journals recounting experiences and reminiscences of the times. During the six months' incarceration, some of the prisoners fell victim to prison diseases or previous exposure from the battlefield. Some died; a few escaped prison; some sought parole. Most of them were ultimately exchanged in the autumn. A number (how many has never been calculated) returned to the ranks in reconstituted units. An equally uncalculated number simply went home to sit out the remainder of the war in local defense outfits or even guerrilla bands. Some probably evaded other military duty altogether.[13]

A few of the surrendered rebels actually escaped during the post-surrender confusion at Dover. Brigadier General Bushrod Johnson and Captain J. H. Anderson of the Tenth Tennessee simply hiked across the frozen battlefield and made their way to safety in Nashville. Others had more unique experiences. Artillery Lieutenant Thomas F. Perkins (a prewar student at Western Military Institute in Nashville) was confined with other officers in one of the two Dover hotels. His black servant had been allowed to pass in and out carrying provisions, and Perkins simply traded his uniform for the servant's homemade brown jeans. Perkins ostensibly walked past the Yankee guards, down to Grant's headquarters boat *Uncle Sam*, and boldly asked the general for a pass to go home, muttering something to the effect that he had had enough of war. Grant obliged him with the pass. Perkins quickly went through the lines and joined Colonel Nathan Bedford Forrest's cavalry, which itself had escaped dramatically across frozen backwaters just before the surrender. Perkins subsequently became a captain in the partisan rangers and a decided thorn in the side of Union occupation troops. Apparently he had not had enough of war after all.[14]

The irresponsible brigadier generals, John B. Floyd (together with his Virginia brigade) and Gideon Pillow (with small personal staff), escaped by water. Similarly, army scout John M. Porter and three comrades were shipped aboard a prison boat to St. Louis, where they convinced guards that they were merely citizens caught at the fort and exempt under a Union departmental commander decree that noncombatants were to be released. Within three days, the four were headed back upriver to Fort Donelson on a boat with a Yankee cavalry regiment aboard. "No oath of any kind was required and we took none," declared Porter. They remained aboard all the way to Clarksville, where they secured room and food (having only Confederate money), finally passing out of that now Union-occupied town disguised as woodcutters. Making their way back to the Bluegrass via Russellville, Kentucky, Porter and his party enjoyed their "furlough" before departing south to rejoin General Johnston's army in northern Mississippi.[15]

None of the Confederate generals involved in the twin rivers fiascoes escaped censure. Brigadier General Lloyd Tilghman was blasted for his dismal performance as Fort Henry commander, and erstwhile Kentucky Confederate governor Johnson wrote his wife from Bowling Green on February 15 that "if this vain and incompetent fellow had never been in command we [might] have held the heights of Covington [across from Cincinnati]." Ironically, Tilghman was a citizen of Paducah, Kentucky. But the ill-assorted lot of brigadiers that had yielded Fort Donelson received the brunt of southern ire. Floyd, senior commander at the post and a prewar Virginia politician as well as United States secretary of war, together with Pillow, a Tennessee lawyer-politician in uniform and his second-in-command, suffered most for deserting the beleaguered garrison. Called to account by the Confederates government, they were passed off to insignificant new assignments, but were not cashiered.[16]

The fact that Floyd and Pillow were retained angered Fort Donelson survivors like Colonel Roger Farquharson, commander of the Forty-first Tennessee in the fight. He wrote to a friend from imprisonment at Fort Warren in Boston Harbor in July that the people of Tennessee "have never yet had a full statement of all the facts of the criminal blunders at Donelson." He contended that the army and Buckner were made victims of the "incompetency or crime of Pillow or Floyd or both." Fort Donelson was no longer tenable after Henry's capture and should have been abandoned before Grant had been allowed to surround the position on the Cumberland. By the time the garrison had fought for three days and nights in frigid weather, the men were completely worn out by exposure and could not "muster one third the strength of any regiment for any duty whatsoever." His own unit counted scarcely 100 out of 575 at midnight Saturday night, most of them asleep standing up in the trenches. The Yankees had simply overwhelmed them with numbers, claimed this Scottish immigrant and Mexican War veteran.[17]

Buckner and Bushrod Johnson also bore some of the onus, although largely escaping the wrath of the southern press. Victory had been within the South's grasp during a brilliant counterattack—termed by one participant, S. A. Cunningham, as one of "the most persistent infantry engagements" of the war—on February 15. But all four generals had squandered the fruits of their success by misunderstanding, command bickering, and jealousy. Floyd had vacillated at a pivotal moment and yielded to Pillow's enjoinders to stand and fight another day. Buckner, whose dislike of Pillow dated to prewar political differences, suddenly buckled under battle fatigue and the knowledge that his defensive lines had been breached by Grant's swarming attackers. Pillow pleaded innocent to having caused any misunderstanding, while Bushrod Johnson (always a shadowy figure in the action) had simply remained out with the troops while important decisions were made in the council that ultimately decided the army's fate. It was a classic comedy of errors.[18]

By remaining with the army to share captivity, Buckner eventually achieved Confederate sainthood. Nobody at the time realized that the Kentuckian too had suffered faintness of heart and had actually urged surrender during the midnight deliberations. Cavalry chief Nathan Bedford Forrest, at least, had defied army doctors and scouts and stormed out of the trap with perhaps a thousand horsemen and infantry. He safely reached Nashville several days later. Meanwhile, Floyd (and some claimed Pillow too) had commandeered an arriving steamboat with a raw Mississippi regiment and a delegation of Maury and Giles County citizens bearing provisions for the garrison. Since the steamboat was unable to land the provisions (although, ironically, the Mississippians went ashore to be surrendered), something of a picnic attended the fleeing generals, Floyd's Virginian brigade (which he managed to evacuate), and the citizens as they subsequently steamed back upriver. As J. T. Williamson told it: "Shortly after leaving Clarksville, these citizens opened their baskets and boxes and jugs and bottles and spread a bountiful feast to the half starved soldiers. Oh, how we enjoyed it." Yet, back in Dover, quartermasters destroyed copious amounts of supplies that had never reached the nearby front lines during the fighting. All in all, it was an affair that did little credit to anyone on the southern side.[19]

As for Albert Sidney Johnston, the embattled commander of Confederate Department Number 2, cavalryman Thomas Black Wilson reminisced: "I think Gen. Johnston ought to have gone [to the twin rivers] himself, and all of [Major General Leonidus] Polk's men from Columbus [too]." Another soldier observed that "if old Johnston had have acted as he should have done, we could not only have sustained ourselves, but captured and killed all of the enemy and rid Tenn. of the foul invader." Instead of sending reinforcements, as Pillow suggested, Wilson continued, "Johnston was sitting up at Nashville drinking fine whiskey, and smoking cigars." Yet a third commentator from the ranks added bitterly: "The after effect [of Fort Donelson] has been yet more terrible. Nashville surrendered; army demoralized—in fact the glory of the cause almost obscured; true and firm hearts are fast giving way under this current adversity—and the worse management of the—Great Mogul—Albert Sidney &c. and now unless some great Military Chieftain rises in our midst to lead us on to victory, this great cause of 'Southern Independence' will be reduced to the mothering of a simple rebellion."[20]

Some commentators thought there had been alternatives. Colonel Farquharson claimed that every man north and west of Nashville should have been retired to the Cumberland. Johnston could have held Major General Don Carlos Buell's army, which was advancing south from central Kentucky on the Louisville and Nashville rail line toward Bowling Green, in check until the Donelson troops rejoined him. Then, the combined force (together with newly raised levies) could have held the Yankee advance until Johnston's second-in-command, General

P. G. T. Beauregard, accomplished some diversion northward from West Tennessee toward Paducah and Cairo. "In this way middle Tennessee might have been saved—although the Mississippi and New Orleans were lost," commented the Tennessee colonel. Farquharson's biased, embittered perspective was understandable. Johnston did have alternatives, and so did subordinates. But General Leonidus Polk (much less Beauregard) made no countermove against Union supply bases at Cairo or Paducah from his Columbus bastion on the Mississippi River in extreme southwest Kentucky, and the four brigadiers on the Cumberland frittered away similar opportunities to at least escape capture.[21]

Some of the most perceptive, if stinging, criticism came from E. M. Bruce, a Confederate congressional representative from Kentucky's Ninth District. Writing from Atlanta on March 11, he told President Davis that he had been with or near Johnston's army ever since the general took command, had been his admirer and defender, and still respected him as a man. But his errors "of omission, commission, and delay" had been greater than "any general who ever preceded him in any country." Johnston, in Bruce's view, had "inexcusably and culpably lost unnecessarily an army." Bruce claimed this was the almost unanimous judgment of officers, soldiers, and citizens, and was demonstrable by dates, facts, figures (all of which he failed to provide the chief executive), and the disastrous results. The congressman believed that the general could never reorganize and reinforce his army with any confidence.

The people looked only to the president, Bruce claimed, "as their deliverer, and imploringly call upon you to come to the field of our late disaster and assume command," as Davis had apparently promised if it became necessary. Such a step would be worth "a hundred thousand soldiers" throughout the Confederacy. If Davis would not come west, then the command should be given to Beauregard, Bragg, or Breckinridge, "or all will be irretrievably lost." Prophetically, the Kentuckian told the president, "We cannot survive the permanent loss of Tennessee and Kentucky for the war." Their loss would produce "great suffering for provisions and forage" as the inevitable and immediate consequence.[22]

Some southern firebrands, like South Carolinian Edmund Ruffin, rebuked Johnston's name in their private journals, and one Louisiana overseer declared that the "old ass" should be "hung for not making a Stand at Nashville." Predictably, the Tennessee congressional delegation (led by Senator Gustavus Henry, for whom the Tennessee river fort had been named), led the charge to relieve Johnston of duty. Writing Davis privately on March 8, all nine of them declared that a visit home by one of their number had netted the impression that Tennessee was very "dispirited and demoralized" on account of the disasters, with the deplorable feeling increasing daily. Whether rightly or wrongly, "confidence is no longer felt in the military skill of [Albert Sidney Johnston]." Admitting that such a condition might be "all wrong, foolishly wrong," the stubborn fact remained that his army had lost faith; it would not fight under him "with that alacrity" necessary to secure success. Even worse, the people of Tennessee "from whom our new levies must come, partake in the same feelings." The Tennesseans requested a new commander and asked the president himself to go west to restore confidence.[23]

Davis did not take field command in Tennessee. Instead, he looked to Johnston for self-redemption by deed. The general naturally explained his actions to his friend the president by letter. Short on details, the general was busy reorganizing an army at the very moment he had to explain defeat. He told the chief executive that he had sent most of his available fighting force from Bowling Green to reinforce the river positions. This had worked for a time, he observed, citing victory telegrams received from both Floyd and Pillow. Thus he had turned to the more daunting task of extricating Major General William Hardee's Central Army of Kentucky and the stores from Bowling Green. He claimed to have instructed Fort Donelson subordinates to save the army should the fort fall. Of course, none of this truly exonerated the Western Theater commander for errors in judgment. Johnston's headquarters correspondence book and other surviving documents suggest that he was caught off guard by the speed and audacity of the Union river advance and simply devoted too much attention to deterring a different threat.[24]

The threat of Buell's Army of the Ohio from Louisville was real enough. And it froze Johnston in place. "Our route lay over the hills and through the mud, over a common dirt or mud road, and sometimes no road at all," wrote William M. McKinney, a Union soldier at Munfordville on February 22. Therefore, Buell's movement was ponderously slow, but Johnston never appreciated that salient fact, nor apparently that the Confederates simply could be outflanked more quickly by Union control of the western waterways. The new technology of railroads mesmerized the generals in this conflict, and Johnston was no exception. The fact that he was poorly served by subordinates who either failed to follow discretionary orders about fighting the enemy on the Cumberland or to fortify Nashville properly made little difference. As senior commander, defeat was ultimately Johnston's responsibility.[25]

Johnston's sense of purpose was defused by his very presence at Bowling Green. He could rely only on the telegraph to orchestrate subordinates elsewhere when he chose not to take command personally on the rivers. At 9:30 P.M. on February 7, and 7:00 P.M. the next evening, and twice again on February 11 (first at 9:30 A.M. and two hours later at 11:15), Johnston's loyal chief of staff, Colonel W. W. Mackall, issued Floyd discretionary orders about how and where he should fight the Federals. At this point, army engineers Major Jeremy Gilmer and Captain George Sheliah were supposedly busily putting up defensive works at both Clarksville and Nashville. The hour was late, but Nashvillians still could not be persuaded to willingly send their slaves to build forts. Middle Tennesseans generally had been lulled by lucrative military contracts, the labor-intensive harvest season, and the reliance on Fort Donelson to defend them. Too late they began to seek avenues of self-protection, even as that fort lay besieged. Whether or not Johnston realized all this when he penned his responses to Davis's desire for a postmortem remain unclear. It was left to historians to decipher the chinks in Sidney Johnston's reputation.[26]

In Johnston's defense, he had been given too large an area to defend with too few resources. Arms, ammunition, clothing, and equipment were in short supply. Despite two congressional acts in December 1861 that called for purchasing and outfitting steamers as gunboats for the Tennessee and Cumberland Rivers, almost nothing had been accomplished with the allocated five hundred thousand dollars. Except for land fortifications, the rivers lay totally open to Federal invasion. Johnston's supply lines were either the rivers (upon which few boats plied due to northern owner withdrawal or lack of crews that had gone into the Confederate army the previous autumn) or tenuous rail lines running back hundreds of miles to main supply centers like Nashville and Memphis. His pleas for aid had met with bureaucratic deafness in Richmond.

Actually, neither the Union nor the Confederate government anticipated a long war, and both were ill-prepared to cope with demands of a multitheater conflict. Johnston turned to the upper heartland for succor, but, as former Confederate Commissary General Colonel Lucius B. Northrop admitted to President Davis seventeen years later, he had long doubted Johnston's ability to hold Bowling Green, and Northrop also believed that Nashville would be lost. At the time, Northrop had instructed his chief commissary officer in Tennessee not to ship anything but stores "for temporary use" to the Johnston's army at Bowling Green.[27]

Moreover, disease had reduced rebel ranks in camps and forts from the foothills of southeastern Kentucky to the great Columbus bluffs on the Mississippi. As Major J. T. Williamson of the Third Tennessee recalled, "At Bowling Green we had a great deal of fever of a very malignant type, and many of our stoutest and most robust soldiers died with it." Measles, mumps, typhoid fever, and pneumonia ravaged the ranks of youthful soldiers. Ignorance of germ theory, unsanitary living conditions, and unaccustomed mixing of humanity in the close confinement of camps and garrisons were responsible for the disease outbreaks. Parents warned their sons about imprudent eating and sanitary habits, and Williamson noted how homefolk plied the camps with "good things to eat and drink," for nothing was "too good for a soldier." But the hard work on fortifications and clearing fields of fire for artillery and musket took their toll in the dews and damps of late fall and early winter.[28]

A much-coveted doctor's certificate was all that would excuse a fellow from such debilitating work, noted Williamson. Still, the soldiers died like flies at places like Camp Beauregard in the Jackson Purchase section of Kentucky west of the Tennessee River. Spinal meningitis was the culprit there, attested to by today's small graveyard and marker atop a hill at the site near Water Valley, Kentucky. Even evacuation of the sick and infirm during Bowling Green's abandonment in February bordered upon the scandalous. John S. Jackman of the Ninth Kentucky penned in his diary that the sick were simply thrown aboard rail cars "like the commonest freight." Seriously ill soldiers were completely neglected, he claimed, and many died from want of any attention at all. No official was present to direct their removal, as all the medical personnel attended Johnston's retreating army. Frankly, it was a marvel that anyone stood to the colors at all given such conditions. A bedraggled, demoralized, unwell Confederate force streamed back from the Kentucky border. All winter it had been capable of feinting and sparring Fabian-like, but it was certainly unprepared to meet a foe on any sort of equal footing. Now this force seemed able only to retreat.[29]

The fact remained, however, notwithstanding such difficulties, department commander Johnston had never gone to inspect the critical link in his western defense line—Forts Henry and Donelson. However, neither had Leonidus Polk, a former Episcopal bishop whose jurisdiction covered those positions. The soldier-priest simply looked for a Union advance down the Mississippi, much as Johnston saw it coming via the railroad from Louisville. Moreover, southern officer gentry did not relish the task of suffering through frontierlike conditions on the twin rivers in order to personally attend to defense of that approach. Winter camp life was so much better at Columbus, Bowling Green, or other rear posts like Russellville, Clarksville, or especially Nashville. So, neglect crowned efforts to defend the Tennessee and Cumberland Rivers. Besides, nobody truly thought the Federals would attack in winter anyway.[30]

One young Confederate (known to posterity only as "Willie") wrote his sister from Bowling Green in late January that he anticipated no fighting there before the end of spring, and even then he thought that the enemy "is going around this place." Colonel Bailey of the Forty-ninth Tennessee wrote his wife in Clarksville from Fort Donelson on February 6 that his men were busy perfecting earthworks, that reinforcements could be expected momentarily, and that it was all "a mistake about the Yankees having so large a force." The twin rivers garrisons were nominally larger, he observed, but acknowledged ruefully, "owing to so many being sick, the effective strength is not so great." In short, overconfidence, neglect of the obvious weak point on the defense line, surprise at enemy capabilities, misjudgment of senior leaders, and plain bad luck lay behind the events of February 1862.[31]

There was another possible factor. The Confederates simply lacked the urge to go for their opponent's jugular at this early stage of the conflict. Johnston told Davis that he had sent roughly one-half of the Bowling Green army to hold the line on the Cumberland when Grant attacked. But Johnston's strategic intentions at that moment remained exceedingly fluid. He intended Floyd's force at Fort Donelson neither to annihilate the invader nor to be a forlorn hope. Rather, the men he sent to do the job were to act as a delaying force (although he never made that crystal clear to any of his brigadiers).

Apparently, at some point he intended consolidating the Donelson force with Hardee's Army of Central Kentucky coming from Bowling Green, and Brigadier General George Crittenden's force retiring from Chestnut Mound on the upper Cumberland in southeastern Kentucky. He requested that the Confederate government forward fifteen thousand arms that had run the blockade at New Orleans to Nashville. Yet, on Valentine's Day, he also asked the Western Department ordnance chief to rush five hundred thousand rounds of shotgun and musket cartridges to Fort Donelson. Such signals may only be confusing in retrospect, for they suggest that he considered a decisive battle would take place there, rather than before the capital. Still, such a battle was perhaps only a holding action to

Johnson. But, whatever his intent, four brigadiers of marginal capacity fought the critical battle for the upper Confederate heartland. How badly they bungled the mission was reflected simply in Johnston's 11:00 A.M. dispatch on February 16 to Beauregard at Corinth, Mississippi. It read: "At 2 A.M. today Fort Donelson surrendered. We lost all."[32]

Indeed, Johnston lost all—including, two months later, his own life. Only then was the criticism of Ruffin and others effectively silenced. The general's death that April afternoon at Shiloh, when Confederate victory once again seemed assured, vaulted Albert Sidney Johnston to the postmortem pantheon of southern "might-have-beens." Meanwhile, Johnston's decisions looked shaky. If Floyd, Pillow, Buckner, Johnson, and Tilghman had lost the twin rivers, Johnston was the man who had placed them there. As modern historians Larry J. Daniel and Lynn Bock have suggested, the fervor of anti-Johnston demagoguery while he was alive was blunted or suppressed merely because of Jefferson Davis's friendship for his favorite general.[33]

CONFEDERATE STRATEGIC RETREAT

Those seeking a silver lining to these winter storm clouds found solace in the fact that Johnston had orchestrated a masterful withdrawal from Bowling Green. Shortly after noon on February 13, he personally took the train south to Edgefield, where he confronted his various options. Then, with the news of Donelson's fall, he redirected concentration of all the columns at Murfreesboro, thirty miles south of Nashville. He now wired Richmond to send arms to the Rutherford County seat instead of Nashville. He also directed Captain D. P. Buckner not to destroy either army stores or the railroad bridge at Clarksville because such a course might endanger that city. Captain Moses Wright was to remove all ordnance equipment and stores to Chattanooga, with railroad transport impressed for the use of the army. Everything was done in extreme haste, and the intent of Johnston's actions was mainly to save military resources of men and materiel, not to defend the capital. Everyone feared a quick strike by the Yankee gunboats. Ironically, the evacuation went on unimpeded by the enemy.[34]

Johnston anticipated making his next move by February 20. He wrote Beauregard about consulting with Polk and proceeded with previous plans for a concentration at Corinth, Mississippi. He also sent a separate missive to Tennessee Governor Isham G. Harris, advising that the politician should bring "the whole strength of the State to their aid, in the time, and mode they suggest." He explained to Alabama brigadier Leroy Pope Walker at Tuscumbia that defense of the upper Tennessee Valley should be undertaken in cooperation with Mississippi brigadier James R. Chalmers at Iuka. Chalmers commanded the line from Memphis to that river.

Meanwhile, noting an absence of pressure from either Grant or Buell, Johnston rested his command, and recruited in the Nashville region. He also assured protection for supply dumps at Shelbyville and even sent a party of the Fifteenth Mississippi on thirty-five freight cars back to evacuate more supplies from then

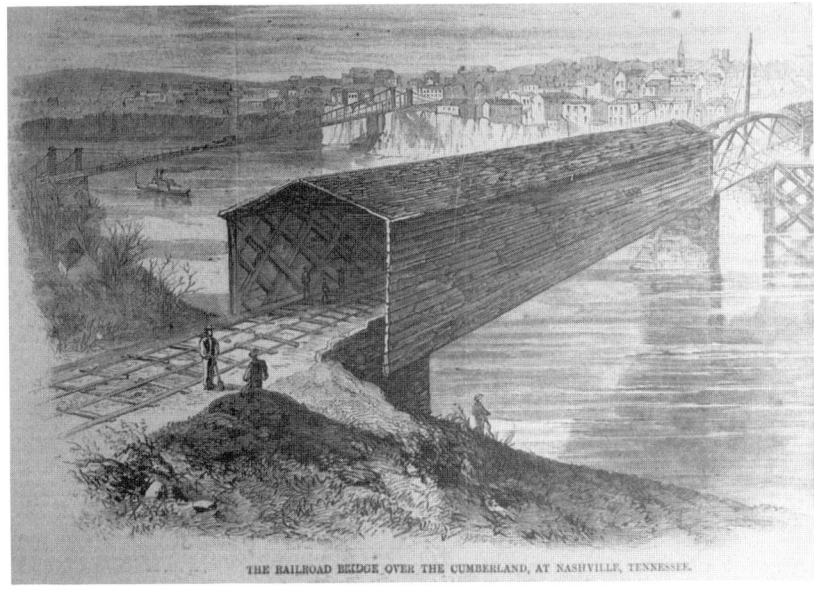

Railroad bridge across the Cumberland River at Nashville with a highway suspension bridge in the background. From Harper's Weekly, *March 8, 1862.*

unoccupied Nashville. Johnston additionally set in motion the staged withdrawal of his army farther south to north Alabama.[35]

Commissary General Northrop told Jefferson Davis in 1879 that he had greatly admired Johnston's ability to coolly save the stores at Nashville and Shelbyville, in contrast to General Joseph Eggleston Johnston's destruction of supplies during a similar retirement later that spring in northern Virginia. Indeed, Sidney Johnston directed the firm of Bruce and Company to impress wagons and teams in Patriot, Tennessee, to retrieve a quantity of pork to go south with the army. Cavalry colonels Jake Biffle and John Hunt Morgan helped crossload railroad cars across a flood-induced break at the Mill Creek bridge, and Captain Moses Wright was told to go on to establish his ordnance shops at Atlanta, Georgia. Floyd's Virginians would to cover Chattanooga in case the Yankees advanced in that direction.

Meanwhile, Brigadier General Thomas C. Hindman's party ensured bridge crossings farther south, while Colonel John Scott's Louisianians went back to burn all bridges between Columbia and Nashville should the Federals advance from that direction. Bedford Forrest continued to Huntsville, Alabama, on February 24 to recruit his command, and that same day, Johnston wired Richmond that, despite the severe storms, "this army will move on 26th by Decatur for the Valley of the Mississippi." It was in good condition and increasing in numbers, he said.[36]

Johnston and the army were safely behind the protective waters of the upper

Tennessee by early March. Colonel St. John Liddell left for Richmond on February 28, with dispatches including Floyd's and Pillow's explanations for the Donelson defeat. Johnston had saved the army; yet, in the end, he unwittingly sacrificed far more. A trail of destroyed highway and railroad bridges marked his line of retreat from Nashville south to Alabama (although not on the Murfreesboro to Chattanooga line, perhaps indicating his plan to use that axis as a means of eventually returning to Middle Tennessee). His evacuation of undefended Nashville had left that vulnerable city reeling in disbelief. "Our men are greatly annoyed at the reported surrender of Nashville," recorded chaplain George Eagleton of the Forty-fourth Tennessee, adding that there was "no foe there" as the disheartened army had limped away in the winter gloom. Nashville citizens were even more annoyed when their prized highway suspension and railroad bridges were dropped into the Cumberland by the retiring rebel army.[37]

Middle Tennesseans watched with sinking hearts and many unanswered questions. When would the army come back? What would happen to the agriculturally rich region and to the cottage war industries in towns and cities fed by the rich iron deposits farther north on the twin rivers? What about families that had provided the fighting men to protect southern civilization? As chaplain Eagleton penned in his daybook: "We have backed far enough. If we yield this grain growing state to the foe, where will we get bread for the army? If we yield this state with its important railroads and tributaries to the Ohio river, we only have built and surrendered the best avenues to the heart of the Confederacy." Thomas Black Wilson, a newly enlisted cavalryman, had another answer. Writing after the war, he suggested that Johnston's retreat caused the "loss of a great many men to the Southern Army who left ranks to visit their homes and not return, while large numbers in Kentucky and Tennessee who would have joined us stayed at home or went against us."[38]

EARLY STAGES OF UNION OCCUPATION

Survivors and spoils awaited the victors in the wake of Johnston's retirement. Yet, the Federal campaign languished as Yankee generals bickered, hesitated, and sacrificed momentum to the lack of command unity. Buell's army had spent the early winter encamped on the Green River in Kentucky. "The weather was bad; drills incessant, the boys dissatisfied and mutinous," recalled regimental commander John Beatty later at Bowling Green. "The flags and our spirits, therefore, drooped together in sympathy," and he added that soldiering no "longer quickened the blood and we began to doubt whether such a condemned, disagreeable country as we had about us was really worth saving at all." Fear of Confederate counterattack, a communication breakdown with other Union forces, petty jealousies over jurisdictional boundaries, prerogatives, and seniority—as well as wretched weather conditions—clouded Union success on the twin rivers, even as Buell's army moved ponderously overland coincidentally with Grant's river advance.[39]

Boredom and camp sickness took over in camps outside Dover and over at Fort

Henry while Grant's splendid host awaited new marching orders. James Drish told his wife that there were scarcely "250 men able to do duty" in his regiment. P. J. Snyder added that he had not "seen one well hour since the 10th of Jan. and do not know when I will" so long as the army kept feeding the men hard crackers and salt meat and kept them out in the wilderness camps. Drish believed that such conditions were fast destroying a splendid body of men, "something the rebels can't do themselves in a fight." Lethargy was hardly relieved by three- to five-day-old newspapers or by merely looking at "trees over one foot through" sliced by cannon balls and saplings filled with bullets that marked the passage and intensity of these soldiers' first battle. Something more was needed to break the campaign's impasse and the boredom for hyperactive youth in uniform.[40]

Rumors circulated about their next destination. Brigadier General Stephen A. Hurlbut told one soldier in early March that it would be Montgomery, Alabama, cradle of the Confederacy. Others claimed that rebel forces were marshaling from all over the South about fifty to one hundred miles up the Tennessee River in order to block Union passage into Alabama, but that Memphis on the Mississippi was completely clear of rebels, and that might be their destination. Additional rumors followed in the wake of Confederate evacuation of the Columbus bluffs, where Colonel Frederick Starring reported that irregulars or guerrillas might attempt to retake that post. Nobody suggested the same possibility for Forts Henry and Donelson. For the moment the men in blue worried more about camp fevers and the next campaign in Dixie.[41]

Union military authorities concentrated upon capturing or incapacitating specific military targets rather than consolidating control over the countryside and its inhabitants. Frankly, they were merely reflecting what historian Joseph L. Harsh terms a "national consensual mandate" both in official Washington as well as the northern home front that sought "to conserve the Union and the Constitution and to restore the status quo ante bellum." The iron industry in the twin rivers area already lay prostrate, owners and their slave work force dispersed. The Missouri Department commander, Major General Henry Wager Halleck, prodded Grant as early as February 8 to move past Fort Henry and destroy the Memphis branch railroad bridge at Danville as a distinct military target. The navy attended to the matter in due course. Clarksville and Nashville naturally provided attractive goals because of their importance as political urban centers and supply bases. Indeed, as for Clarksville, Flag Officer Foote, Grant's chief of staff Colonel Joseph D. Webster, and two of the gunboats made their way up to the city three days after the fall of Donelson.[42]

Foote's Jack Tars, in fact, stopped and burned John Bell's Tennessee Iron Works, about six miles above Dover, simply because its owner, a former Tennessee congressman and 1860 presidential candidate, had engaged in war work for the Confederacy. Bell claimed that he had no alternative to joining the Confederate side because of Confederate trade embargoes with the North, but Lincoln's call for volunteers after Fort Sumter apparently had driven Bell into the Confederate camp. Thinking to find other more positive Unionist sentiment along the river, the two boats pushed on to New Providence where they discovered an abandoned Fort Defiance and other works at the point the Red River emptied into the Cumberland just below Clarksville.[43]

Clarksville mayor George Smith and a delegation that included antebellum politician Cave Johnson (a friend of Foote's father) met Foote upon the gunboats' arrival. The group remonstrated with the Federal officers about Yankee intentions. Foote had no desire to issue any proclamation, but claimed that the town "was in a state of the wildest commotion from the rumors that we would not respect the citizens either in their persons or their property." Indeed, Clarksville had much to fear, since this thriving tobacco, iron, and commercial center had assuredly aided the Confederate cause and was quite demoralized by the sudden collapse of Fort Donelson. Residents had just witnessed the parade of dead and dying from that battle, and local nurses like Blanche L. Lewis hoped for quieter moments. They had barely had enough time to bury the fallen on the hospital grounds and pass other wounded upriver to Nashville before Foote's arrival. Teenager Nannie Haskins wrote in her diary that the people were running about, hospitals emptying of the walking wounded, and even Foote calculated that fully two-thirds of the five thousand inhabitants had fled at his approach.[44]

Certainly all the rebel soldiers had gone, leaving bulging supply warehouses and a smoldering but intact railroad bridge across the Cumberland. So, Foote issued the desired proclamation to quiet the overall situation. He promised protection to all "peaceably-minded persons" so that "they may in safety resume their business vocations." But, he stated forcefully, "all military stores and army equipment shall be surrendered" with nothing withheld or destroyed meanwhile. No secession flag or manifestation of disloyalty would be tolerated. Hoisting the national flag, Foote also humored Cave Johnson, who had pressed a letter into his hand containing a twenty-dollar gold piece to be sent to his son, captured at Donelson. "The Clarksville affair will do me credit," Foote wrote his wife.[45]

Suddenly, Grant also decided to visit the newly taken city. With Brigadier General John A. McClernand, Colonel William H. Wallace, two companies from the latter's brigade, and a regimental band, this second Union group went by boat for a day's visit. They discovered, Wallace told his wife, that Clarksville was "a beautiful village or town of 5 or 6000 inhabitants on the North side of the Cumberland," but nobody "except the negroes" welcomed them (one woman apparently displaying a British flag from her house in feigned neutrality). As had been the case with John Bell, the fall of Fort Sumter and Lincoln's call for troops to suppress the rebellion caused Clarksvillians to vote 651 to 1 (surrounding Montgomery County 2,632 to 2) to join the Confederacy. Sensing this Confederate loyalty from his reception, Grant took no chances. By February 22, he had dispatched Brigadier General C. F. Smith's division to take possession of the city and its stores of cannon, ammunition, and army supplies. "I have no special directions to give that won't naturally suggest themselves to you," he told his old friend, but cited orders "keeping the men from going into private houses and annoying the citizens generally." Within the week, both Grant and Foote and other Federal officers had traveled on to captured Nashville to see that city also. Then Grant returned to Fort Donelson to await further directions from Halleck.[46]

Grant promptly became involved with housekeeping chores that absorbed his stagnating army's time. The "rush of citizens," particularly the Sanitary Commission group, "who infested Donelson after its fall" seeking to care for wounded and sick irritated him. Scavengers after war trophies from this first major Union victory also earned his displeasure and resulted in press rumors that his army was in disarray and pillaging the countryside. Grant explained all this to Halleck and then moved quickly to resupply his army with fresh beef and await his next mission. Still, the issue of battlefield relics haunted Grant for months. He personally carried a captured pistol at Shiloh while many vindictive northerners sought public auction of all captured and liberated rebel property under provisions of the First Confiscation Act of August 6, 1861. Writing to Halleck on February 17, United States Marshall D. L. Phillips of the Southern District of Illinois noted the large quantity of merchandise, tobacco, etc., seized up the twin rivers, and declared venomously: "I want to see their last dollar and piece of property seized, it forfeited to the Government, and that such seizures shall issue to the benefit of the Government for which our best men have died." Halleck ordered all such property sent to St. Louis.[47]

Halleck could read between the lines on this issue. A hungry and vindictive soldiery had begun to forage the heartland countryside with questionable results for civil-military relations. Friction was unavoidable. The Union military had gone south fully intending to battle enemy soldiers, not woo a hostile citizenry. Official policy dictated exclusion of runaway slaves from camp, confiscation only of identifiable rebel property, and conciliation toward the civil populace. Naturally, the boisterous northern volunteers hoped that Tennesseans and Kentuckians could be persuaded to peaceably embrace the old flag and end the war. However, the army in the field often undid the best intentions of high-level policymakers in Washington and St. Louis.[48]

Sent out simply to find fresh provisions and pay for them with national specie, soldiers and their officers often tried to root out rebel supply caches and procure work gangs from local slaveholders under the guise that everyone south of the Ohio River was "secesh." Promised compensation hardly placated diehard Confederates or even closet Unionists. Until promulgation of Article 102 of the Articles of War on March 13, 1862 (which prohibited the return of fugitive slaves), slave exclusion varied with army and army commander despite a national policy that promised to protect private property of nonaggressive citizens. Buell not only blocked fugitive slaves from his lines but allowed masters to search for and reclaim their property. Halleck and the navy on western waters practiced similar strict interpretation of the exclusion policy. But Grant and others specifically used the First Confiscation Act to impress construction-gang slaves under the guise that they had helped construct the rebel forts. Before long, queues of protesting slaveholders in front of headquarters tents complicated the slave issue for commanders everywhere.[49]

One case in point at Clarksville commanded Grant's attention long after his expeditionary force steamed up the Tennessee River in late March. When Colonel Crafts J. Wright of the Thirteenth Missouri decamped at Clarksville, he personally carried off two young African Americans belonging to Mrs. R. W. Thomas, wife of the crippled local newspaper editor and mother-in-law to a former congressman who was a friend of McClernand and John A. Logan, two of Grant's politicians in uniform. Colonel Philip B. Foulke, left in charge at Fort Donelson, as well as a local citizen, J. M. Quarles, told Grant that Wright had made a general mess of things in a climate of "desperation," and that no less than two hundred men "had gone off to join the Confederate army" who would never done so "if protection to their property could have been afforded." Moreover, Mrs. Thomas's two slaves were mere tobacco stemmers, had done no war work, and were her sole support. Foulke thought their return would "cultivate a union sentiment" in the neighborhood as he cited Grant's own policy at Dover, which he considered to be more valuable "than a victory with arms." He further suggested that the Cumberland situation was quiet with "all satisfied, commerce and business beginning to move" and that, in a short time, "a large majority will wish to vote for the 'old union' again."[50]

Dealing with slavery was quite new for many Union soldiers. Captain Channing Richards of Wright's regiment recalled later how easy it was to forget the hesitancy of the national government to interfere in any way with that institution early in the war. It "seems marvelous," he noted, to think of both Congress and the president fearful of alienating loyal border state citizens or of stoking political dissension in the North over the issue of "the peculiar institution." Richards's own initial experience in dealing with slavery had come at Clarksville, where humanitarian motives, not legal methods, seemed the advisable way to address the issue. Destitute, displaced slaves could always find work with the post quartermasters or on the levee; after all, they had been used in the same way by the Confederacy, or had been used to help construct fortifications.[51]

Often, abolitionist officers like Richards used the device of employing slaves to ensure protection and freedom for the so-called "contraband," who quickly departed downriver with the first barge or steamboat. Subsequently, "as the struggle progressed," commented Richards, "it became more and more evident that the fate of slavery involved the fate of the Confederacy.... Observation, and the personal experiences of those brought into contact with 'the peculiar institution,' rapidly disarmed opposition to active interference, and military orders against aiding and harboring fugitive slaves soon became dead letters."[52] Still, as the northern invaders would learn as they moved deeper into Dixie, slavery and emancipation were incendiary and complicated matters.

NASHVILLE'S "GREAT PANIC"

Grant's twin victories sent shock waves through the state capital of Nashville. The appearance of Johnston's retreating army at Edgefield had created apprehension, but false telegrams proclaiming victory at Fort Donelson then had lulled the seventeen thousand residents of Nashville into a sense of security. They awoke confidently on Sunday, February 16, only to have their hopes immediately dashed when news of the surrender reached the streets and churches. Even then, how-

View of Nashville. Harper's Weekly, March 8, 1962.

ever, no Yankees appeared immediately, and it was Johnston's decision not to stand and fight for the city that caused what local lore always styled "the Great Panic" of the subsequent week.[53]

Nashville stood as the commercial and political centerpiece of a region. Annual commerce netted over twenty-five million dollars for her citizens. Sophisticated beyond most other southern cities, New Orleans and Charleston excepted, Nashville boasted fine residences, churches, and schools (including medical-education institutions second only to Philadelphia). Designer William Strickland's lofty capitol building dominated the downtown from atop its craggy eminence. Gas illumination of streets and homes and an ice plant reflected Nashville's sophistication, while her bustling commercial district sported business establishments and hotel accommodations, including the famed Maxwell House. A new suspension bridge across the Cumberland River linked railroads running north and south. The river itself offered a commercial artery without parallel.

Local architect Adolphus Heiman (who surrendered with his Tenth Tennessee unit at Fort Donelson) had designed many of the wealthiest homes, while outlying estates of the Overtons, Erwins, Acklens, and others symbolized the bountiful attractiveness of this section. Such was an environment ripe for complacency. Somehow, local defense and sacrifice had never appealed to Nashville planter or mercantile elites; both had made money on the war through lucrative government contracts. Nashville, like Clarksville, had rested its fate solely upon the solitary fort, seventy miles downriver at Dover. That faith had not seemed misplaced until that bright Sabbath morning.[54]

The fortnight of the battles at Forts Henry and Donelson had created bustle and electricity in the air at the capital. One Yale-educated, Mississippi-born staff officer who passed through the city on February 12 wrote his wife that the hotels, streets, and wharves teemed with people, but that they "seem very much alarmed," having until late "felt quite secure." Now they were beginning to form self-defense groups and "drill with quite a gusto," reported Henry Richmond Slack. All this gave way to a "reign of terror and confusion" and a city "thronged with people wild with excitement," church bells ringing as women and children left the various churches, "darkies smiling at the scene," and people running here and there "seeking a place of safety—a place to flee," noted Rowena Webster, a local girl. Chaplain Robert F. Bunting of Terry's Texas Rangers wrote home that he had never seen as much sorrow at public calamity as when news of Fort Donelson's surrender hit the city. Evacuation was on everyone's mind, with the threat posed by Yankee gunboats prompting the greatest fear. What ensued fully equaled the Henry-Donelson tragedy in terms of loss to the Confederacy.[55]

Both Johnston and Mayor R. B. Cheatham pleaded for calm. Yet bedlam reigned as families rushed to railroad depots to get away or made their way out of town by carriage, wagon, horseback, or even on foot. Perhaps only a thousand residents left in the initial surge. But businessmen emptied banks of their assets, Governor Isham G. Harris abdicated leadership by fleeing to Memphis with the state archives, and, before he departed, he issued a call for the legislature to reconvene at that river city on the Mississippi. V. K. Stevenson, president of the Nashville and Chattanooga Railroad, left hurriedly with his family on a private train, forgetting that he was a serving Confederate officer under military orders.

Arrival of the Fort Donelson wounded, and a score of Yankee prisoners, confounded the problems for authorities. Many of the ill and infirm were passed on to the welcome hospitality of matrons like Mrs. Andrew Ewen at "Beechwood" near Wartrace, farther south. Some even went as far as to Memphis hospitals. The blueclad prisoners, however, remained at Nashville awaiting deliverance. A. F. Gilbert of Company A, Seventeenth Illinois, recalled his incarceration in the Zollicoffer Hotel, where ladies like the wife of John Bell attended them. "Had my husband been elected," she told them, "this war would never have taken place." "For the first (and only) time, I most heartily agreed," said Gilbert, as he noted how two former French army surgeons saved any number of the wounded from needlessly cruel amputations. In fact, local citizens soon moved the sick and wounded Federals into schools and public buildings, hoping that acts of charity would secure favor when the enemy took over the city.[56]

Local citizens gathered at station stops on the rail lines to Chattanooga and Decatur, taking in the wounded or burying dead retrieved from the battlefield by friends or relatives. Washington Matthews at Columbia watched Governor Harris and Tennessee Adjutant General W. C. Whitthorne pass by on February 16, then the next evening helped bury a neighbor's boy, Anderson Davis, who had been mortally wounded in the head. Back in Nashville, passage of Johnston's forlorn troops across the suspension bridge from Edgefield, the general's unwillingness to defend the city, and consequent disintegration of law and order threatened real trouble until the crack First Missouri Infantry took up patrols through the streets at nightfall. The main army settled briefly into makeshift bivouacs just south of town, before later moving on to Murfreesboro, but few citizens looked forward to the week ahead.[57]

Buell's army failed to appear much before the following weekend. All during the intervening week, further confusion, rumors, and destruction of public morale and property continued. The arrival of the steamboat carrying Floyd and his Virginians, as well as a similar appearance of the bombastic Gideon Pillow, only added to the gloom. Forrest's cavalry clattered into town, proving that overland escape had been possible. Brandishing sabers and revolvers, they helped contain riotous mobs seeking food and supplies from government warehouses. Interspersed with heavy rain storms, the destruction of half-finished gunboats at the waterfront, and, finally, the destruction of the prized suspension and railroad bridges over the Cumberland, it was not a pleasant period.

Floyd had been left in charge of things at Nashville by Johnston. Military necessity was Floyd's excuse for destroying everything in his wake. But even the most ardent secessionists—Commissary General Northrop's praise for Johnston's management notwithstanding—thought this was needless waste as an estimated one million dollars in war materiel was lost to the Confederacy by the precipitous evacuation of the city. As the milling throngs in the streets thinned with the departure of the army (even local home guardsmen tramped southward with Johnston), residents realized that their next visitors would be Yankees.[58]

IMPOSITION OF A NEW ORDER

That second Sunday of Nashville's ordeal dawned bright and beautiful. Crowds gathered at the river, again looking for telltale signs of the invaders. Mayor R. B. Cheatham as well as state senator and former U.S. congressman George Washington Barrow eventually rowed across the river and prepared to surrender. They found only a lowly cavalry captain and returned with meager assurances that the Federal army intended no harm to the city and its inhabitants. Another encounter with a Union colonel later that day reaffirmed the pledge, but the northern soldiers made no attempt to cross the flooded river. The work of destruction and removal of Confederate property continued until the last grayclad stragglers scurried off to rejoin Johnston's ranks at Murfeesboro. The swirling waters of the now bridgeless Cumberland River and Union slowness saved both Johnston and Nashville from possible combat.[59]

The morning of February 25 brought the first sizable contingent of Federal troops, under the command of Brigadier General William "Bull" Nelson, to the city by steamboat. Buell's army finally had departed the Green River country on February 10, crossed the Big Barren River into Bowling Green six days later, and discovered that, as Colonel John Beatty declared, "the rebels burned a million dollars worth of stores, but in their haste to get away, left enough pork, salt beef, and other necessities behind them to supply our division for a month." Beatty and his comrades then had force-marched, "without wagons, tents, or camp

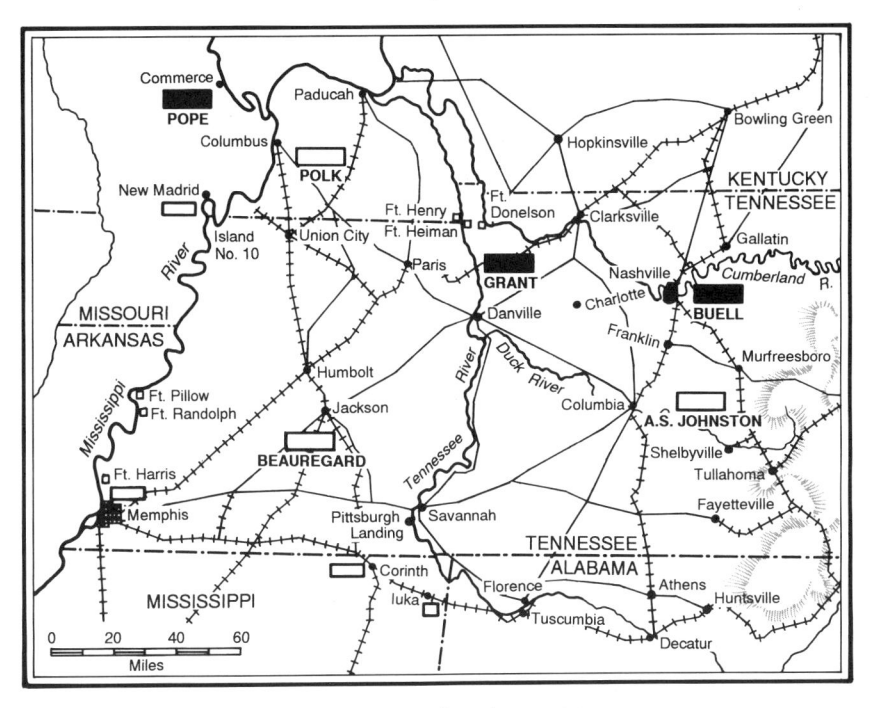

Strategic situation in late February 1862.

equipage," in the rain and found shelter during the night in tobacco houses, barns, and straw piles, the martial band also contributing much toward "keeping the boys in good heart." When the whole force reached the Cumberland at Nashville, they began the city's occupation in an atmosphere captured by an officer who wrote that, while the shoreline was black with citizenry, not a sound could be heard, not an American nor Confederate flag in sight, only "thousands watching with awe the steadily approaching army . . . dumb with apprehension." They meant business, proclaimed Lieutenant Colonel Horace N. Fisher, "and the people knew it."[60] The Unionists who had remained during the months between Tennessee's secession and this date emerged to embrace their deliverers, but they were few in number. Carefully retrieving an old American flag that had been given to him before a South Pacific cruise in 1831, retired Nashville sea captain William Driver presented it to a Union officer to raise over the capitol building. Dubbed "Old Glory" by Driver (an appellation thereafter applied to the American flag generally), it was seventeen feet long by nine and one-half feet wide and had a little anchor instead of a star in the bottom corner of the blue field. It was only fitting, observed the aged sailor, that this flag should replace "the damned Confederate flag set there by that damned rebel governor Isham G. Harris." But most Nashvillians seethed sullenly as they watched the introduction of a new order for their city.[61]

This new order was restrained at first. That was national policy anyway—conciliation designed to woo southerners back to the Union. Besides, Grant told his wife, Julia, "Sesch is now about on its last legs in Tennessee." Union officers softly approached questions about slaves, confiscation of strictly rebel property, restoration of county courts, and other civil matters. Buell also cautioned Washington, thinking (like Grant) that "a great change will take place speedily in the attitudes of the Tennesseans" both politically and militarily. He urged pursuit of "a lenient course" in terms of reconstructing general government, feeling that there was an abundance of reliable Union people "though for some time overpowered and silenced." In communiques to General-in-Chief George B. McClellan at the capital, Buell argued against appointment of a military governor for Tennessee, who would "do incalculable harm."[62]

President Abraham Lincoln, however, saw Union military success along the twin rivers in Tennessee as his opportunity to take the first step in political reconstruction. He wanted to allow loyal citizens a chance to speedily return to the Union. Believing that a civilian, not a professional soldier, could best restore Tennessee to the Union, the president disregarded Buell's advice and sent former Tennessee governor, congressman, and senator Andrew Johnson to take charge at Nashville. But Johnson went there as an army brigadier to underscore his role as military governor. Known as a staunch Unionist, this self-made tribune of the common man was determined to enforce "a civil government in conformity with the Constitution of the United States." Secretary of War Edwin M. Stanton also told Johnson that his mission included nominating district marshals, attorneys, a district judge, and authorizing "suitable persons" to raise loyal units for service in the Union army.[63]

Buell told Johnson on March 11 that he had seen and conversed with the most prominent Unionists in and around Nashville, and, while they were truly loyal, "the mass are either inimical or overawed by the tyranny of opinion and power that has prevailed or are waiting to see how matters turn out." He felt they would acquiesce when they saw that the new governor meant business. Still, he tactfully suggested that the politician not expect "to be received with enthusiasm, but rather the reverse," and he suggested that entry into the capital be "without any display." Indeed, when apprised of Nashville's animosity toward him, and of the possibility of bodily harm, Johnson responded by taking a special night train from Louisville much in the manner of Lincoln's disguised trip to Washington for his inauguration just a year before.

Both Lincoln and Johnson would become beleaguered government heads in their respective wartime capitals. They initially took office, in Johnson's words, "with the olive branch in one hand and the Constitution in the other." President and military governor both had the support and physical presence of the military to underwrite their rule. Yet, within weeks of their respective arrivals, both executives resorted to a full panoply of military and political power under the Constitution, not conciliation by the olive branch.[64]

For Andrew Johnson and others, the Union victory at Forts Henry and Donelson was but a prelude. Northerners like St. Louis's Sara Jane Hill believed that the twin river success "greatly heartened and encouraged the North," showing that in Grant it had a general equal to those of the South. Tennessee cavalryman Thomas Black Wilson, just then making his way south to join Johnston's retreating force, decided in retrospect: "I look on Fort Donelson as one of the most important battles of the war." The northern states had gained little renown in the War of 1812, since winning generals like Jackson, Harrison, and Scott had been southerners, he said. Nor had the Mexican War changed the picture, and in the early stages of the Civil War, the esprit of the southern army was the best, he claimed. Bull Run had encouraged the South and discouraged the North. If Fort Donelson had been a southern victory like Bull Run, thought Wilson, "it would have gone far towards ending the war." Again, the postwar South would live with dreams and might-have-beens at places such as Donelson.[65]

The early Union victories meant something entirely different to Stanton B. McGuire. Three-fourths owner and captain of the steamboat *J. H. Baldwin*, McGuire did not find Union success meant retrieval of that craft, which he had left tied up at Nashville the previous fall. It had been pressed into Confederate service after the Cumberland River had been closed by construction of obstacles in the stream, although McGuire had enjoined the master of transportation in the city, Andrew Hamilton, not to use his boat. Hamilton told Unionist McGuire to "shut up and say no more about the boat." Federal occupation of Nashville led to the *Baldwin*'s charter by the victors, and then it was seized as contraband by the United States marshal, because it had been employed in rebel service. In turn, authorities sold her for less than half her prewar value, and, at the very end of the war in 1865, Unionist McGuire still sought recompense from his government for losses. Victimized by both sides, McGuire represented yet another American caught in the cauldron of civil war. For him, too, Henry and Donelson was only a prelude to something else.[66]

For Confederate Tennesseans, like Pulaski resident Martha Abernathy, wife of a local doctor, February's events were shocking but not conclusive. Downcast with a spirit "which would quail in this hour of seeming defeat and disgrace," she penned in her diary on February 19, 1862. "O help me to bear the humiliation" of Nashville's loss, she wrote, although adding that she would rather see all that was dear in ruins and "know that my country is safe and free." Citing the words of one fallen Mississippi patriot that the South was a country to live for, to fight for, and if necessary to die for, she snarled, "Know you Yankee horde that I'll die before I'll vow obedience to your dictates!" Here, then, was a divided legacy that confronted the Federal government in the upper heartland after the capture of Forts Henry and Donelson.[67]

TWO

ASSERTING NATIONAL AUTHORITY: SPRING 1862

General Albert Sidney Johnston and barely seventeen thousand men from the Army of Central Kentucky retired to Murfreesboro after Fort Donelson's capture. Learning of that disaster while on the march, chaplain George Eagleton of the Forty-fourth Tennessee noted how "we shed many a tear for our unfortunate fellow soldiers, for our Country, our families, and our homes!" Another young soldier recorded making camp on the night of February 22, completely worn out, and "found our army in a good deal of confusion." Many of the men lacked tents or any kind of shelter, and "had to sleep out and take the rain." "Everywhere we are whipped," he announced dejectedly, "the people through the country seemed to be in a great panic." Ironically, the general still wired Secretary of War Judah P. Benjamin on March 5: "the forces are en route and in good order." But rainy weather, washed-out bridges, and the stigma of defeat hung over the column.[1]

The western defense perimeter of the Confederacy had crumbled. rebel forces from West Tennessee and northwestern Kentucky eventually withdrew all the way to northern Mississippi. Administrative personnel relocated to places like Chattanooga, Tennessee, where Dr. Samuel Hollingsworth Stout, for example, faced the challenge of establishing hospital facilities following precipitous evacuation of sick and wounded from Nashville. Aided by assistants, including Emily Todd Helm (wife of a Confederate brigadier and sister to Mary Todd Lincoln, wife of the president of the United States), as well as other soon-to-be famous southern matrons in white—Ella Newsom and Kate Cumming—Stout soon had nearly a thousand patients on his hands. Transported without care for eighteen hours in frigid weather in unheated boxcars and cattle cars without food, water, or attendants, they arrived in a settlement "little more than a village" with unimproved streets but six hotels that quickly became hospitals, despite filth and poor ventilation. Stout and his colleagues created a well-managed hospital center at Chattanooga until they were forced to evacuate in August of 1863.[2]

Spring 1862

Meanwhile, river garrisons above Memphis clung precariously to Island Number 10 and New Madrid, although Columbus, the poorly named "Gibraltar of the West," was evacuated on March 2. Massive blufftop gun positions and an anchor chain that stretched across brown Mississippi waters to impede Yankee boats passed into history. Two weeks later, J. Alexander wrote Confederate president Jefferson Davis declaring: "The probability is, without a change in the tide now against us, Memphis will soon be in the hands of the Lincolnites." With it would go a large portion of the section's cotton plantations, he lamented.[3]

Alexander pulled no punches with Davis concerning the loss of positions like Columbus and Fort Donelson. More than two months before, he had heard Mississippi cavalry colonel Wert Adams at Nashville proclaim that the city enjoyed little protection other than low water in the Cumberland and the wholly inadequate fort downriver. Alexander blasted Secretary of War Judah P. Benjamin, a Louisianan who might have known better concerning Yankee threats on western rivers, for being "entirely too slow in commencing to build gun-boats." Now, said Alexander, the secretary was "heartily cursed from one end of the country to the other," while the property taken and destroyed by the Federals on the Tennessee and Cumberland "would have built gun-boats sufficient to have protected all the rivers in the South." Loss of Columbus only confirmed Alexander's conclusion.

Confederates withdrawing from Columbus disabled the cannon and rolled ammunition into the river (where Federals recovered it later in the summer). They did not destroy the railroad depot of the Mobile and Ohio railroad, an ignominious cluster of buildings that constituted the hamlet, or an ingenious engine works used by the military to hoist river water up to the fortifications. Brigadier General William Tecumseh Sherman's arriving bluecoats marveled at the refuse of the abandoned camps (just as Grant's soldiers had found similar sloth at Fort Henry earlier). They had not been anxious to assault the place and were much happier settling down to make Columbus a Union base of operations.[4]

Elsewhere, Major General Don Carlos Buell finally occupied Nashville with fifty-five thousand men on February 25, while Brigadier General Ulysses S. Grant—soon to be promoted to Major General—accumulated another forty thousand at Fort Henry, succored his sick, and awaited orders for his next move up the Tennessee River. Divided command, petty jealousies between departmental commanders (Halleck and Buell), and general inertia now stymied the Yankee advance. Finally, in March, Missouri departmental commander Major General Henry Halleck persuaded Washington to give him overall command in the West. Unified command had been lacking for a year; whether or not it would make much difference now remained to be seen.

The men in the ranks simply delighted in the return of spring prior to their next move. "It seems like the eastern Yankees are afraid to fight, they are leaving all the fighting for us suckers to do," exclaimed southern Illinoisan H. R. Reckley from Savannah in West Tennessee in March. "We want to settle this war now in a short time," he added, recalling that there had been ninety-four steamers preceding his own transport, which had come up the Tennessee River with "troops enough on this river to whip the hole [sic] sesess [sic] army especially if they don't fight better than they did at fort Donelson." Regular army sergeant Arthur P. Carpenter of the Nineteenth U.S. Infantry told his family that soldiering in Kentucky and Tennessee was not "so pretty" as it had been at Indianapolis where he had enlisted. Carpenter and his comrades were "half starved, half frozen, and half drowned" in the awful mud of Kentucky. Often they were so hungry that they snatched up pieces of turnips and egg shells that lay along the roads and ate them, and the rain soon washed the dirt from their tanned and weather-beaten brows. They were quickly becoming veterans.[5]

The Confederate military reversals began to have their effect by mid-March. Domestically, Mississippi valley spokesman J. Alexander and A. Battle from Tuscaloosa, Alabama, wrote Richmond officials protesting the government's policy of destroying cotton and tobacco to deny those cash crops to onrushing Yankee hordes. Alexander pointed to the hardship for currency-starved cotton planters beset with the war tax and their personal expenses and lamented the lack of remuneration for their patriotic sacrifices. Battle, on the other hand, urged immediate firing of these cash crops. "Let the tower be pulled down at once and felt by Europe as well as America," he declared. Confederate agent Charles J. Helm in Havana, Cuba, noted pointedly that the recent reverses in Tennessee and on the seacoast of North Carolina, as "magnified by the Northern press," had created doubt in the minds of "our foreign friends here as to our ultimate success." Together, such spokesmen observed how Union armies and fleets would soon overrun the cotton states and destroy their crops "which will starve the people and Army and bring about submission to Lincoln," in Battle's words, unless some great victories were soon achieved by Confederate arms. Regrettably, Battle and others "can see no prospect of that."[6]

Actually, this lull in the fighting accommodated Johnston and his colorful deputy, General Pierre Gustave Toutant Beauregard, as they reconstituted the rebel army at Corinth. Here, declared postwar historian Thomas B. Van Horne, "the Memphis and Charleston and Ohio and Mobile railroads intersect, and thus form a railroad center which sustains relations to the Mississippi and Tennessee Rivers and the railroad system of the South, especially with the great road connecting these rivers and Richmond, Virginia." Halleck now pressed for a focused drive by Buell and Grant against that strategic point. The pair rendezvoused in the nick of time to save Union fortunes at Shiloh on April 6 and 7. Johnston lost his life, the Confederacy lost another battle, and Halleck subsequently took personal charge of a tortoiselike advance upon an evacuated Corinth. Buell found other demanding tasks for his command, including detachment of some thirty-five thousand men for railroad and garrison duties all over Kentucky and Tennessee, other expeditions to seize Cumberland Gap in southeastern Kentucky, and a sluggish advance toward Chattanooga in East Tennessee via the Memphis and Charleston line. North Alabama around Huntsville unexpectedly received a Yankee visit by late April, when Brigadier General Ormsby McKnight Mitchel's Third Division brought the sour taste of Yankee occupation to that locale.[7]

Spring 1862

Railroad crossing of the Tennessee River at Bridgeport, Alabama. National Archives and Records Administration.

A CHANGING FACE TO WAR

The Federal advance gave most young northerners their first taste of Dixie's diversity. Mitchel's men, marching south from Murfreesboro discovered great variation all over the region. Cotton fields disgorged plantation slaves, who flocked to see "the abolition army, the music, the banners, the glittering arms, and possibly the hope that their masters would be humbled," decided Colonel John Beatty, commanding the Eleventh Ohio Infantry. When the national troops entered Shelbyville in Bedford County at noon on April 4, they met wildly enthusiastic Unionists in this reputedly most loyal town in the state. One old lady clapped her hands and thanked heaven for deliverance. After a week of such favor, however, Mitchel's advance moved on through avowedly secessionist Fayetteville and eventually crossed the state line and took a position astride the Memphis and Charleston from Decatur to Stevenson, Alabama.

Mitchel's men missed the Shiloh carnage, but the effect of their capture of the east-west railroad, said Beatty, was that an important victory was won without "the shedding of a drop of blood." By mid-month they were chiding paroled rebels from Shiloh about being tired of soldiering and "goin' home on furlough," marveling all the more at the steady stream of African Americans from the plantations, commencing arrest of disloyal civilians while creating general turmoil wherever they went. Many in the Union army were sure that the end of the war was in sight.[8]

The swath of territory from the Ohio River to just below the Alabama and Mississippi line symbolized the extent of Union domination in the southern heartland that spring. The flat land between the Tennessee and Mississippi Rivers, the undulating terrain of Bluegrass Kentucky that carried south into the Central Basin or "Garden" of Middle Tennessee, then the upland plateau and eventually mountain country to the east would become familiar to the soldiers over time. Aside from the Ohio, Mississippi, Tennessee, and Cumberland Rivers, there were smaller streams of importance. The Barren and Green Rivers in Kentucky, the Harpeth, Elk, and Duck Rivers in Middle Tennessee as well as the various forks of the Obion, Forked Deer, Hatchie, and Wolf Rivers in West Tennessee and Clark River and Mayfield Creek in the so-called "Purchase" section of western Kentucky provided obstacles to movement and inviting defensive positions to the enemy. Crossing these terrain features were railroads and highways that not only further carved up the landscape but afforded economic and social links for the populace.

The major rail link of the region, the north-south Louisville and Nashville, had only been completed in October of 1859. Additionally, the Edgefield and Kentucky (designed to meet another road from Henderson on the Ohio River in order to serve the western Kentucky coalfields of the lower Green River country) and a so-called "air line" route from the L&N at Bowling Green, Kentucky, to Memphis (via the Memphis and Ohio line) provided incipient service between the Bluegrass and Tennessee. South of Nashville, the Nashville and Chattanooga and the Nashville and Decatur lines carried traffic to the indispensable east-west Memphis and Charleston Railroad that cut across the northern tier counties of Mississippi and Alabama to Chattanooga. West of the Tennessee River, the Mobile and Ohio coming south from Columbus, Kentucky—where a ferry carried goods and passengers on to the Illinois Central depot at Cairo, Illinois—the New Orleans and Ohio out of Paducah, as well as an unfinished line northwestward from McKenzie, Tennessee, and the Mississippi Central that met the Mobile and Ohio at Jackson, Tennessee, similarly enthralled Union and Confederate leaders. Of course, limited carrying capacities, rickety conditions, and the fact that the railroads were open targets for cavalry raiders offset their clear advantage in adding speed to logistical support of the armies. Still, such simple travelers' aids as Appleton's *Railroad Guide* must have caused at least a few staff officers on both sides to daydream about their potential for contributing to victory.[9]

These railroads stood as monuments to the construction fervor of the 1850s. Some of them were completed literally on the eve of secession or just afterward. Their peacetime intent had been to connect hinterland with water—rivers, Gulf, and ocean. None of the attractions of the "Iron Horse" could completely obviate the traditional value of steamboats. Hardly "trunk lines" or through service routes in the postbellum sense, the nascent southern railroads had been mere feeder lines to the water trade before the war. On the Mississippi, as well as the

Spring 1862

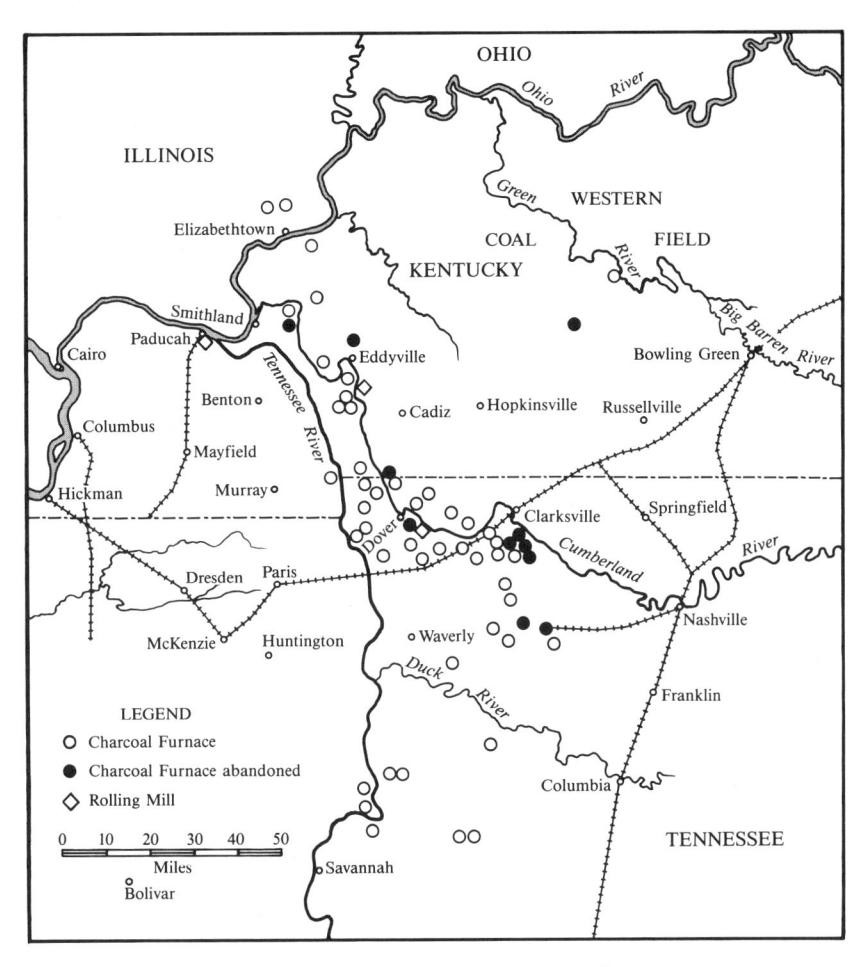

Proto-Ruhr of Upper Confederate Heartland.

Tennessee, Cumberland, Barren, Green, and Duck Rivers, rivermen had enjoyed an antebellum favor far surpassing the promise of railroads. Enterprising citizens on Kentucky's Green River had lavished time and treasure upon elaborate improvements like stone locks for year-round navigation. While the allure of coal and other minerals of that section had not been tapped completely at the time of the war, the potential was there, and agricultural as well as timber resources helped reimburse investors in the enterprise. Tennesseans, by comparison, were less inclined to internal improvements, but relied upon waterways just as much for trade. But such commerce ended with the announcement of war and the withdrawal of northern-owned steamboats from the streams.[10]

Civilian trade came to a standstill on land too. One of Johnston's staffers, Colonel Robert W. Wooley, noted that, during Confederate occupancy, "the [L&N] railroad was almost bare of transportation; the locomotives had not been repaired for six months, and many of them lay disabled in the depots" and could not be repaired at places like Bowling Green. Railroad officials, such as President V. K. Stevenson of the Nashville and Chattanooga, understood the problem, but despaired of easy solutions. Johnston's subsequent retreat left the line to Kentucky in a shambles, largely to deny it to Buell's advancing army. In fact, both sides jumped too quickly to destroy property in order to prevent its use by the enemy. The Union Navy either burned or otherwise disabled all the rivercraft of any size it encountered. Union and Confederate military appropriated or destroyed the enemy's materiel and a path of destruction generally had begun in the upper heartland in the days after the fall of Donelson.[11]

Certainly, the upper heartland's natural resources were sure to feel the stern hand of war. The famed riches of Middle Tennessee and western Kentucky provided a backdrop, and the image of "hog and hominy" hardly did justice to a full range of resources from grain, timber, tobacco, and livestock to corn, wheat, and even cotton. Iron manufacturing was a particularly hidden resource, vastly overlooked by both sides, as Stewart County in Tennessee and its neighbors of Trigg and Lyon Counties across the Kentucky line and the western coalfields to the northeast added minerals to the list of important resources for war making. Slaves, horses, and mules factored into the picture with mostly small to middle-sized farms and a handful of larger spreads of the one-thousand-acre to fifteen-hundred-acre range in the northern part of the region, steadily increasing in number as one moved south. Recognition of the implications of food, forage, and metals for a protracted war of attrition often eluded the contending armies as they moved through the area in the spring of 1862. Emphasis remained on the one decisive stroke to net quick victory and an end to the conflict.[12]

Ignorance of the Tennessee–Kentucky iron-mining and production region (a sort of "proto-Ruhr" of the Cumberland–Tennessee valley) outside the area and the iron trade itself was prevalent on both sides and not surprising. Few officials in either Washington or Richmond probably appreciated the iron region's war-potential. Too few people were conversant with J. P. Lesley's deft summary of the subject, *The Iron Manufacturer's Guide to the Furnaces, Forges, and Rolling Mills of the United States*, which he had completed for the American Iron Association in 1859. Otherwise, would southern leaders have so quickly relinquished the area to Yankee control in the winter of 1862? Similarly, Federal authorities might have been less anxious to condone or acquiesce in their soldiers' wholesale destruction of rebel iron-making facilities after the fall of Donelson.

Lesley had declared authoritatively that "[t]here is as yet but one principal iron region in the far west, that of western Tennessee and western Kentucky, with its peculiar ores and 45 furnaces, and six or eight forges." Production from these works exceeded all other southern manufacturers, including those in Virginia, in terms of pig iron, iron blooms, bar, sheet, and railroad iron. Moreover, the facilities were not that far from Quinby and Robinson in Memphis and T. M. Brennan in Nashville—specializing in farm implements, heavy equipment, and later munitions for the Confederacy. The war machinery of Dixie needed such iron for industrial, commercial, as well as military purposes. Yet, facilities were sacrificed almost without notice in February 1862, and the Federals further neglected their potential as they allowed the plants and forges along the Cumberland to rot in the wake of Grant's success. Of course, they represented rebel property, and perhaps lay too close to the fighting front to be worked during wartime anyway.[13]

As for the region's major cities and towns, few approached Nashville, Memphis, Clarksville, or even Bowling Green and Paducah as centers of prewar commerce and activity. Still, as county seats or neighborhood crossroads, places like Gallatin and Springfield north of Nashville, Waverly or Dover to the northwest, Paris and Union City beyond the Tennessee River, Mayfield and Murray in the Purchase, or Hopkinsville and Russellville to the east beyond the Cumberland were important. They were equaled by towns like Murfreesboro, Franklin, Columbia, Shelbyville, and Fayetteville farther south, or Paris, Jackson, and Henderson in West Tennessee. In profile, most of them probably resembled sleepy Waverly in Humphreys County, with its tree-lined dirt streets, a modicum of frame or brick houses, and a smattering of churches and businesses that formed around the square or other common meeting ground in the center of town.

Goods came to Waverly via freight wagons from Waverly Landing on the Tennessee River, and by public conveyance whether stagecoach or steamboat, as well as by a few buggies or farm wagons. Horses and mules complemented foot travel by residents. Men and women alike were expert riders, according to contemporaries. A hotel kept by Berry S. Bowen, commercial stores run by James "Calico Jim" Harris, D. H. White and Brothers, J. E. Mickley and Monroe Rogers, as well as Isaac Drake's tailor shop, the Pitts Brothers drugstore, Massey and Atkins saddle and harness shop, Ed and Dorsey Cowen's grocery and saloon, James McGee's wagon, repair, and wood shop were the principal places of business. Indeed, such establishments, along with the several blacksmith shops, lawyer James Harris, and Drs. Gould and Marable, provided a model for other hamlets and towns in the region. A "Waverly" might be found all over the upper Confederate heartland. Within a month of Yankee occupation, Waverly, Tennessee, became a partisan stronghold.[14]

The Upper South's principal asset, whether in peace or war, remained its people. Self-reliant and ardently independent by nature, Kentuckians and Tennesseans traced their forebears to Virginia and the Carolinas. Many kinsmen had gone on to populate lower Ohio, Indiana, and Illinois. Disciples of moderation in politics, they had championed Tennessee's native son, John Bell, or an erstwhile vice president, Kentuckian John C. Breckinridge, in the 1860 national election. Then, they spurned fire-eaters, such as Governor Isham G. Harris of Tennessee when he plumbed for a state convention to discuss separation in January 1861. Hardly countenancing secession at first, Tennesseans voted 69,772 to 57,708 against calling any convention on the matter, as well as 91,803 to 24,748 for Union candidates. In the state's midsection, Montgomery County went 1,611 to 389 for a convention but also 1,852 to 62 for Union candidates. Yet, as Daniel Crofts has so meticulously shown in his study of upper South Unionists in the secession crisis, the region changed dramatically in the wake of Fort Sumter.[15]

Republican President Abraham Lincoln's call for volunteers to coerce secessionist South Carolina's return to the Union struck a raw nerve with Tennesseans. Suddenly, they responded differently to their governor's colorful rhetoric that "in such an unholy crusade no gallant son of Tennessee will ever draw his sword." Actually, thousands of closet Unionists would, but not immediately. It was not necessarily a question of slavery, although most Tennessee households either owned or hired blacks in bondage. Rather, it was a threat—a challenge to a way of life, independence in principle, if not in fact—that motivated voters. For the moment, loyalty to the old flag collapsed as the total Tennessee vote for separation now stood at 104,471 to 47,183. Again, accordingly to Crofts, Lincoln's call caused Tennesseans to be "reluctant Confederates" no longer.[16]

Most northerners accepted Lincoln dogma that large numbers of southerners had been unwittingly drawn to secession by their state politicians and the slave oligarchy. According to this view, they would return willingly to the Union at the first manifestations of Federal authority. Yet, some astute observers believed that the tension of secession had hung over Tennessee for easily a year prior to the outbreak of hostilities. John Duling, from the village of Farmington in Marshall County, Tennessee, recalled later that a climate of change could be sensed well before the war. The local wagon spoke-and-hub factory had shut down, he said, the tannery had been closed, and general stores had begun to retrench with no infusion of new goods from the North. Military drill musters crowded out regular social affairs. Then Fort Sumter had incited "a universal uprising both in the North and the South." Every neighborhood had its rallying point, observed Joseph Buckner Killebrew, a slave-owning, sometime teacher at Clarksville's Female Academy. Women were as zealous for war as the men, and "there was a universal cry throughout the South for arms." Unionists were intimidated to leave their homes and churches. Some families split apart; for instance, Stump Shipp, Farmington's gunsmith, headed off to the Union army early on, while his brother Ebb joined rebel forces.[17]

Governor Harris's administration had begun to align itself with the Confederacy prior to actual secession. Words like "detestable," "insane," "aggressive," and "malignant" were attached to the Lincoln government before secession. Popular allegiances transferred totally. One former moderate, S. B. Morse, wrote to former governor William B. Campbell and rejoiced: "we are all one way in the river counties and that for secession and war." By June, Federal troops had invaded Virginia's "sacred soil" and blood had been shed, while coercion had commenced even in the loyal border slave state of Maryland. Tennesseans read about such events in their newspapers while their political propagandists ranted and raved. Secession came soon afterward, followed by state mobilization, commencement of the river forts, and the eventual transferal of some twenty-two regiments of infantry, two regiments of cavalry, ten companies of artillery, an engineering corps, and an ordnance bureau to Confederate control in the autumn. Defense of community and hearth against northern aggression united a people of previously divided sympathies.[18] As East Tennessean Oliver P. Temple observed sagely many years later: "Sympathy with friends and kindred became the bond that united the South." Tens of thousands who had no desire for secession, he suggested, did have sympathy for their neighbors and family. Avowedly, just as many northerners felt the same way. A year and a half later, many of those who harbored no particular desire for slave emancipation, nevertheless would have sympathy for their neighbors, kindred, and the common cause of Union. Many such Unionists, in fact, inhabited the mountainous section of East Tennessee.[19]

East Tennessee loyalists (or "tories" as they were styled by secessionists) became subject to Confederate intimidation, coercion, and oppression from the outset. Among East Tennesseans, 70 percent had voted against secession, and, throughout the summer and fall of 1861, they organized political groups and militia home guards and seized control of much of the region. Confederate officials dispatched two regiments, first to conciliate and then to suppress dissension. Like the Lincoln administration, only in reverse, both Governor Harris and Confederate president Jefferson Davis were convinced that East Tennesseans labored under unreasonable fears created by demagogic leaders, including native U.S. Senator Andrew Johnson.[20]

Conveying the Confederacy's conciliatory policy in East Tennessee was Brigadier General Felix K. Zollicoffer, soon to lose his life at Mill Springs, Kentucky, in January 1862. The Nashvillian was flabbergasted when East Tennesseans defied rebel authority, returned loyalist candidates to office in the August state elections, and then, encouraged by signs of imminent Federal invasion through Cumberland Gap, engaged in clandestine bridge burnings and other incendiary acts against Confederate communications in the region. To Zollicoffer, leniency had been "unavailing," and he believed that the East Tennessee counterrebellion should now be pursued to "extermination if possible." The result was a wave of arrests, summary executions, and imprisonments—in short a repressive policy that was only lifted by the first of the year when a Confederate government review suggested that only counterproductive results had resulted thus far. Still, many East Tennesseans—like residents elsewhere in the state—displayed an aversion to "national" governmental intrusion into their affairs whether from Washington or Richmond.[21]

Kentucky voters showed little inclination to follow Tennessee into the Confederacy. A border slave state (and, indeed, it would remain so longer than any other state) Kentucky's human ties to the South were more than offset by commercial and economic linkages northward. Still, secessionist spirits burned brightly for some Kentuckians, who felt betrayed by one of their own—Abraham Lincoln—and by his coercive actions. Indeed, a fleeting effort to establish a prosecession state regime at Russellville blossomed during Sidney Johnston's occupation in the winter of 1861–62. Lesser known was a secession movement in the so-called Jackson Purchase area in the western part of the state. Nothing came of either ploy, notwithstanding the Russellville experiment, which actually set up a rival state government and provided officials to the Confederate Congress. Certainly many Federal authorities came to believe that the whole state was an incubus for rebellion.[22]

The situation was rendered even more sensitive by the neutrality game played by Kentucky until September 1861. Both Federal and Confederate governments courted her favor; both sides finally violated her neutrality by moving military forces onto her soil. But the actions of rebel generals Leonidus Polk and Gideon Pillow in occupying Columbus, Kentucky, on September 4 precipitated the violation, unbeknownst to Richmond authorities. Officially, Kentucky's regular government reacted adversely and the Bluegrass state clung to a precarious Unionism. Kentuckians went south to enlist in Tennessee or form their own Kentucky "orphan brigade," while training facilities sprang up along the border and in Graves County in the Purchase section at Camp Beauregard. When the Fort Donelson disaster caused rebel withdrawal from Kentucky soil, 350–400 young southerners remained buried at that camp, victims of spinal meningitis, pneumonia, and typhoid.[23]

Bluegrass secessionists continued to support the southern cause in absentia with provender, with factories that produced brown or gray jean cloth, and by purchasing Confederate bonds in anticipation of deliverance. But, in fact, borderline Christian County was probably indicative of most Kentuckians' dilemma. Yeoman farmers in the northern part were Unionist; their wealthier neighbors on the Tennessee border sided with the South. Similarly, tobacco- and slave-rich Caldwell County in the "Black Patch" section of western Kentucky solidly rejected secession, despite prewar elections that failed to disclose strong Unionism either. Kentucky remained a patchwork of divided loyalties that promised disruption and unpredictability for both sides in the struggle.[24]

So, both Union and Confederate governments had their hands full with possible popular dissent all over the Upper South. From eastern Appalachia and the north Alabama sand hills to Weakley and McNairy Counties in West Tennessee, as well as to the north in Kentucky, "national" authorities wondered about peoples' loyalties. Even a Corinth, Mississippi, newspaper had opposed secession before being forced out of business. Such manifestations would strain the ability of a central government to do its job, and strain the patience and discipline of the opposing military professionals, whose missions would be directly affected by civilian loyalty and support.[25]

As in all American wars, some citizens tried to remain uncommitted and suffered their consciences accordingly. Killebrew, for example, had subscribed five hundred dollars to a Clarksville fund for arms purchase and had been made commissary general of a local regiment. But he had not gone off to war. Commissioned to raise a Kentucky regiment by President Jefferson Davis and then Secretary of War Leroy Pope Walker, he returned home to find that the Confederate advance to Bowling Green in September 1861 had cut off the flow of Kentucky recruits. He then decided that ill health, protection of his family lest his slaves rebel, and the fact that "I was not born a warrior," all gave good cause to sit out the conflict. "I cannot see how the giving of my life to the service of the Confederacy could have made the aggregate results of it as valuable as they afterwards became," he decided. "Its cause never had my full sanction or sympathy." Yet, he helped with the wounded from Fort Donelson.[26]

Many sons and daughters of the upper heartland remained skeptical of either side. They delighted when soldiers in blue or gray spared their properties a visit.

Spring 1862

A Logan County, Kentucky, farmer and Methodist circuit rider, George Richard Browder—like Killebrew a southern sympathizer and slave owner—also deplored violence and felt that he could not leave his family in the hands of slave protectors by going off to war. Josephine Covington enthusiastically wrote her father from Bowling Green on March 2, 1862, having hosted General P. G. T. Beauregard and other Confederate officers during their stay in town. But she expressed relief that army rabble like Benjamin Terry's fearsome Texas Rangers had destroyed only fence rails and timber during their occupancy of the place. She was even more uncharitable toward Confederate destruction of warehouses filled with pork and other supplies, the railroad depot, and other public structures when they left town. Of course, she was hardly any happier when Buell's "thirty dutch soldiers" ransacked her home while searching for food, "even taking women's and children's clothes to send to their own families, they said."[27]

One of Covington's neighbors, farmer L. C. Porter, more caustically termed the Confederate occupation of the Green River country "the most absolute tyranny under the name of a provisional government without even as much as consulting the people as to their wishes." He declared that confiscation of all firearms was not a ploy to help equip the rebel soldiers, but rather to thwart any chance of local civil resistance to Confederate authority. He believed that the southern military government proved "to be very distasteful to our people," for Confederate officers had purged the civil jurisdictions of judges, magistrates, and sheriffs who refused to embrace their cause. Porter was pleased, at least, that the high incidence of sickness in army ranks had not spread to the civilian populace.[28]

Federal authorities everywhere encountered the likes of Killebrew, Browder, Covington, Porter, as well as more ardent upper-class rebels like squire William G. Harding and his wife of Belle Meade plantation just outside Nashville. The soldiery found "secesh" wounded or captives who admitted that, in their locales, the prominent citizens had told them that their property would be taken from them and all would be lost unless they went to fight the Yanks, and that no man would allow that to happen if he had any pluck in him. Union assistant surgeon John Vance Lauderdale, aboard the floating hospital ship *D. A. January*, wrote home in May that "ignorant and unsophisticated" Tennesseans were motivated by such leaders, and he concluded that one great cause for the war was this determination of a few in the South to rule the many in this fashion. Illinois and Ohio recruits in the Seventh Kansas Cavalry found Purchase Kentuckians especially "very lazy" and in need of "a little Yankee enterprise." The task of returning any of these people to their normal lives and allegiances may not have seemed the primary mission to these soldiers in blue. Yet, there was more to civil war than merely winning pitched battles.[29]

The problem of securing the allegiance of these southerners loomed large in northern policymakers' minds. How best, then, to treat the portion of southern society not overtly secessionist? How to handle their property—farms, factories, businesses—and slaves? How might trade, local government, law and order, and domestic tranquillity be restored in the armies' wake? Soldiers and civilians alike were fully aware of the stakes. Midwestern politicians never flagged in pursuit of the trade issue, and soldiers at the top, like Halleck and Buell, directed subordinates to root out the fire-eaters but encourage accommodation with moderates and uncommitted alike in the spirit of reconciliation.

Countenance of slavery, protection of property, a "rose-water" policy toward southerners (as it was styled), and conciliatory indulgence of the citizenry all vied with Halleck's snappish comment, "let them take the oath of allegiance," when queried about what to do with rebel deserters at Paducah who wanted simply to return to quiet, civilian pursuits back home. Ulysses S. Grant informed Illinois Congressman Elihu Washburn in March 1862 that "East western Tennessee is being reduced to working order," since with the introduction of the "mails, trade, and the assurance that we can hold it, it will become loyal, or at least law abiding." Naively, perhaps, the victor of Henry and Donelson believed that "one week to them would be worse under the so-called Confederate Government than a year of Martial Law administered by this army." An accurate perception of the conditions in the upper heartland seemed clearly premature for Federal officials that spring.[30]

ISSUES AND ANSWERS

One student of the evolution of Federal policy toward southern civilians, Mark Grimsley, has decided that this conciliatory policy was based on three factors. They included the perceived nature of the rebellion (duping of the people by the slaveholder oligarchy), legal precedent (domestic and international law), and the inheritance of previous American military experience (from colonial through Mexican wars). This would seem to hold true, at least for top political and military leaders. Most certainly the Lincoln administration (as well as loyal opposition and other northern men of influence) thought the rebellion was spawned by a very small number of southern firebrands. The question of whether the Constitution or the laws of war took precedence in conducting the conflict also had major import, and the army itself counted one of its own, Henry Halleck, as the most recent published scholar of international law. But he was heavily influenced by Swiss jurist Emmerich de Vattel, and neither authority could have been widely read among a people thinking with passion, not reason, in 1860–61.[31]

The laws and usages of war seemed to reinforce the notion of conciliation, as did historical precedent. From colonial wars to the late conflict with Mexico (including Halleck's own analysis of Napoleon's disastrous experience with the Spanish people from 1808 to 1813), precedents pointed toward successful war confined to the battlefield. To the professional soldiers who populated America's upper ranks and set the rules of engagement, resolution on the battlefield was the hallmark of their trade. Past history demonstrated that such successful resolution made attacks upon the civilian society and economy unnecessary.

There was just enough recognition of the historical horrors of "people's war" to render it unpalatable to the professional military. If Vattel and Halleck both allowed for foraging among civilians and destroying their property, the army's senior leader in early 1862 did not. Lieutenant General Winfield Scott, old "Fuss and Feathers," had enunciated a set of rules in Mexico that had provided the model for the present policy in the occupied South. His General Orders No. 20 called for an "even-handed system of justice that sought as far as possible to preserve peacetime standards of order." His junior officers in Mexico, from Halleck, Buell, Grant, and even those now in Confederate gray, to George B. McClellan (soon to usurp Scott's position and prestige as general-in-chief) knew and understood that requirement. Like the impressions of politicians, those standards provided the soldiers a guide for the early occupation policy in the South. Scott would see to that.[32]

Ironically, the people themselves—through their manifestations in uniform, as northern volunteer soldiers—as well as the actual conditions in the field would alter Federal policy during the spring and summer of 1862. Change would come not in abstract terms, but rather through experience with the immutable facts about war and society in a combat zone. Grimsley, in fact, suggests that a policy of pragmatism eventually emerged even for some of Scott's surest disciples among western generals. Just as Buell and his cohorts remained steadfast to Lincolnite principles of a conciliatory policy in pivotal Kentucky, experience in turbulent Missouri in 1861 set a different direction in motion. Here, departmental chief Halleck at first emphasized the avoidance of damage to civilian property until guerrilla depredations against unionist civilians in the countryside and openly supportive secessionists in St. Louis changed his mind.[33]

Grimsley has observed that the legalist Halleck liked to keep matters orderly in his jurisdiction. Citizens who openly aided the enemy might expect to have their property taken through confiscation or contribution. Conversely, soldiers who preyed upon civilians could expect harsh punishment. The aim was to render the war between Union and Confederacy "a conventional military struggle as a far as possible" and "to keep civilians on the sidelines as much as possible." In sum, Halleck's soldiers supported unionists, punished secessionists, and expected "the remaining population to remain quiescent." This policy accompanied Grant's forces and others from the Department of the Missouri to Tennessee in the winter and spring of 1862. It would remain in effect until Halleck left the Western Theater to assume other duties in Washington in July.[34]

In the process, popular attitudes were made even more sensitive by the slave issue for field soldiers. In many ways, Federal policymakers poorly perceived the issue. Kentucky's 1860 population of 1,155,684 included 225,483 slaves, with an additional 10,684 listed as free colored citizens. But the state had more slaveholders (39,000) than any other except Virginia and Georgia. Key counties in the Bluegrass section as well as in the Purchase and along the Tennessee border were heavily slaveholding, and these areas provided the zone through which northern forces would march southward or find themselves engaged in occupation duty. By comparison, Tennessee had a slave population of 275,719 and an additional 7,300 free blacks, out of a total 1,109,801 residents, of whom scarcely 36,844 were slave owners. Middle and West Tennessee farms depended upon black labor. Given antebellum emancipation fervor, the delicate balancing act of Kentucky neutrality, and the general ignorance of the nuances of what those statistics meant for the men in the ranks, the slave question posed interesting dilemmas.[35]

Hoosier regular army sergeant Arthur B. Carpenter was hardly alone among the men in blue when he declared his willingness to fight for his country if necessary, but saw no point to fighting for the "stupid nigger." If emancipation was to be the policy of the nation, he declared, he did not care "how quickly the country goes to pot." Yet, slave owners became the target of military action, not because of morality or even politics, but rather because slaves as property quickly became identified with the Confederate war effort. Their liberation hurt the enemy slave owners who had caused the war. More important, in the soldiers' view, confiscation or simple liberation could shorten the war and save their own lives. There lay the crux of the issue as Grant, Buell, and Halleck moved national armies across the region.[36]

Washington policy clouded the issue. It had to do so. Conscious of keeping Kentucky in the Union at all cost, determined to enforce national law (under which slavery was legal) and conciliate southerners, the Lincoln administration's hands were tied. Yet, the armies of the Union felt no similar compunction. They resolved a basic policy conflict as well as the resentment and noncooperation from Kentuckians from the moment they entered that state. Whether or not the sight of victims of human bondage, the public notices of slave sales and enforcement of the Fugitive Slave Law, or tyrannical overseers and owners searching army camps for their chattel ultimately caused revulsion, the notion of rambunctious Yankee youth soon held sway: anything south of the Ohio constituted rebeldom and was fair game for liberation, destruction, and mayhem.

Buell, reputedly an arch-conciliationist among Union generals, wrote defensively to J. R. Underwood, chairman of Kentucky's military committee at Frankfort, on March 6, 1862, that his army was law abiding and that "it is neither its disposition nor its policy to violate law or the rights of individuals in any particular." However, Buell's army contained units like the openly abolitionist Twenty-second Wisconsin, which declared Kentuckians' "whole attitude proves clearly that the people of this state think more of a 10-stone contraband than they do of the whole Union" and ran slave owners out of their camp. Or, as another Union officer told a local slave owner at Bowling Green, raising his arm and in a most bombastic style: "what care I for your negroes, my business is to plant the stars and stripes" as he proceeded to shield the runaways.[37]

Aiding and abetting "contraband," as they were soon called, was a way to strike back at recalcitrant and unrepentant Kentuckians and, later, Tennesseans as well. Of course, in turn, such actions simply hardened property owner attitudes. As for policy clarification, Grant's adjutant, Colonel John Rawlins, issued General Orders 14 on February 26, 1862, which reiterated an earlier directive declaring that "the number of citizens who are applying for permission to pass through the camps, to look for fugitive slaves, proves the necessity of the order, and its faithful observance. Such permits cannot be granted, therefore the great necessity of keeping out fugitives." But slaves who been used by the Confederates to build fortifications or in any other hostile manner would not be returned to their owners. They would be employed by the Quartermaster Department for the good of the national government. Here was confusing adherence to the prewar Fugitive Slave Law, modified by military necessity (the presence of enemy civilians in camp was prejudicial to sound military policy), and tempered by strict enforcement of the confiscation act of July 1861 (which turned over ex-slaves who had worked on Confederate government projects to Union quartermasters for U.S. government purposes).[38]

Although passing slaves on to quartermasters was hardly a most humane act in emancipationist eyes, at least the slaves were tacitly free. Halleck clarified his own feelings in a note to Indiana governor Oliver P. Morton on February 25, declaring, "let the negroes go, if they wish it; if they prefer to stay they must be under military police and not allowed to go in and out of the Camp or barracks." A week later he again wrote the politician, "they can stay with their master or go where they please. If they select to stay, they will be under military control. If they wish to go, let them, but they must not return into camp or barracks." Colonel Crafts J. Wright of the Thirteenth Missouri wrote Halleck from Clarksville on March 24, 1862, that some thirty blacks had proved that they had worked on a nearby fort. According to Wright, "They are afraid to be left when we leave and want to go on this boat down the river," so he asked Halleck what he should do. Halleck answered the next day that "if free by act of Congress, let them go down in the boat, to where they will be safe."

Wright's provost marshal, Captain Channing Richards, noted that Wright had become aware of that act of Congress—the confiscation law of August 1861—only by reading a newspaper. Richards liberally interpreted the circumstances, as he found one friendly white resident who willingly smuggled him a roll or time book that contained a complete list of the slaves who had worked on the rebel fortifications. The man told Richards that "he wanted to help the boys get their freedom," but enjoined secrecy as to the manner in which his confidante obtained the roster, "as it might cost him his life if discovered."[39]

De facto army emancipation was made easier by open boasts of newspapers, like that of the Memphis *Avalanche* of April 3, which highlighted Confederate use of "negroes and fortifications" to block the Federals. In an editorial showing classic attitudes of the antebellum South, the newspaper proclaimed that "this war has developed an element of strength among us of the South, which may always be turned to account in like ways hereafter." Black men were now making all the fortifications, said the editor, working cheerfully and with even more success than southern soldiery. "If our troops had to do the drudgery of handling the spade, pick and axe in the way our negroes do, they could not drill as efficiently as they should." Under the present arrangement, "our negroes throw up our fortifications, and the soldiers prepare themselves for the duties of battle." The editor believed this division of labor might be extended to other duties like cooking, washing, and wood chopping; indeed, he insisted, "let our negroes be our hostlers" since they "are used to that duty at home." They made better cooks than "nine-tenths of our white men," and since at least "ten percent of the army is now employed in attending to that drudgery of a camp which our negro men

Fugitive slaves coming into Union lines. Sketch by Alfred R. Waud, Library of Congress.

can discharge better than our white men," the strength of the army would be increased "at least one-fifth, and that might turn the tide of battle in almost any contest." No wonder Federal commanders and troops felt little remorse in stripping southerners of slaves and believed emancipation to be a major element of their war effort.[40]

Resumption of civilian commerce and trade was another sensitive issue. Halleck, possibly more than Buell, realized that one path to reconciliation lay in reopening rivers, rails, and roads to commercial intercourse. Unofficial trade had been carried on during Kentucky's neutrality as "thousands of dollars worth of goods are daily smuggled through to Tennessee at great profit to the speculator and without much risk," noted Bowling Green farmer L. C. Porter. But the onset of combat stymied that trade, and U.S. Treasury agents rigidly enforced bans on commerce with insurrectionary states like Tennessee. Naturally, innocent civilians suffered most. St. Louis cotton factor Adolphus Meier wrote Halleck requesting the dispatch of confiscated cotton from Nashville so that his business would not suffer, while N. Ranny cited the general hardship for businessmen and labor attending any continued shutdown of commerce with points south of Memphis.[41]

Halleck moved to reopen unilaterally the twin rivers on March 3, only to encounter obstruction from Secretary of the Treasury Salmon P. Chase and his officials. Through Secretary of War Edwin C. Stanton, they pointed to the previous year's congressional prohibition about trade with rebellious states. But Halleck fired back that: "The order opening the navigation of the Cumberland, is not a commercial measure but a military ruse to get steamers into that river without disclosing the real object." Empty steamers would have tipped off Confederates to Buell's operational moves to aid Grant on the Tennessee River, he said. Obviously, the Union military buildup continued to take precedence on the rivers. But, soon, permits for commercial activity were issued again at Nashville, and trade reopened with St. Louis, Louisville, and Cincinnati. The first cotton shipment went downriver from Nashville on March 5, bound eventually for Cincinnati and consignment to merchant R. Moore.[42]

The conciliatory policy brought a measure of success, as shown by comments in the Memphis *Avalanche* on February 28. Citing a Clarksville report that nearly one thousand former slaves had made their way to Federally held Fort Donelson and Dover, the paper's informant observed "that the owners of the slaves, who can show that they are loyal Lincolnites, are permitted to recover their slaves, and that all others are contraband." Further, said the piece, the Federals treated Confederate prisoners courteously, and "their kind course toward the citizens, respecting private property, had a demoralizing effect on the people in that section." The Memphis editor then commented sourly that Union authorities "are just preparing to bind the people hand and foot" by extending such feelers of amity.[43]

Buell, more than Halleck, pursued the accommodation approach in Middle Tennessee. On February 26, he congratulated his men for restoring the national banner to the state capitol building at Nashville. Thinking that "thousands of hearts in every part of the State will swell with joy to see that honored flag reinstated in a position from which it was removed in the excitement and folly of an evil hour," Buell decided that the Tennesseans "will soon proclaim its welcome, and that their manhood and patriotism will protect and perpetuate it." Accordingly, he reminded his troops of rules of conduct in dealing with civilians. They were in arms, he suggested, "not for the purpose of invading the rights of our fellow-countrymen anywhere," but rather to maintain the integrity of the Union and protect the Constitution under which people had been prosperous and happy.

There were people, claimed Buell, "endeavoring to defeat these objects," but peaceable citizens would be protected and wrongs to persons and their property would be corrected, and the offenders punished. Of course, the order continued, compensatory appropriation of private property for military purposes was possible, but only the highest commander might exercise that authority. Soldiers were to avoid private and commercial property, and Buell promised to strip offenders of their "posts of honor" and place them in positions "where they cannot bring shame on their comrades and the cause they are engaged in."[44]

Like Grant, Buell also wrote Washington officials concerning conditions in Tennessee. "I have reason to hope that a great change will take place speedily in the attitude of the Tennesseans," he told McClellan on February 28, "in both the manner of the military and the political policy to be observed." He urged McClellan to press the Lincoln administration to pursue a lenient course in reconstructing "the machinery of the General Government out of material here"— the closet unionists or neutralists that Buell at least thought could be found in abundance.

Deferral to recommendations of the most reliable unionists in Nashville was advisable, Buell counseled. The time was not right for administering any oath of allegiance or even arresting individuals whose loyalty "is only doubtful." Rather, a liberal protection policy might reach "a class of persons who are not hostile to us although not warmly our friends." Still, Buell's chief of staff warned one general to have his officers on outpost duty remain "cautious and watchful and not expose themselves" by becoming separated from their commands thus courting harm "either by citizens or the enemy." Federal officials were quite aware that, conciliatory policy or not, both regular and irregular armed Confederates, and even secessionist citizenry, in the upper heartland could be deadly.[45]

Rumors concerning civil disobedience and the rise of irregulars in the Union army's rear surfaced in earnest by early March. Grant wrote Halleck from Fort Henry on March 11 that "there is a disposition to carry on a guerrilla warfare in Kentucky north of this point." His army was facing nothing formidable yet, he advised, but he was sending a few cavalry companies to Eddyville and thence to Hopkinsville to ferret out the troublemakers. Halleck wired back that he had informed Buell of the situation, but he also proposed withdrawing the Clarksville garrison since "the country north of the Cumberland belongs to his department, we cannot interfere without his request." As Halleck told Buell: "It is reported that secessionists about Hopkinsville and other places are endeavoring to organize guerrilla parties." Halleck would withdraw the Clarksville garrison, but he suggested to the Ohio department commander that the city's occupation by a cavalry regiment "could throw out parties to Hopkinsville and other places to prevent any such formations." Jurisdictional boundaries thus became an issue quite soon after Fort Donelson's capture. The partisan or guerrilla problem boded ill for the future.[46]

Grant's army also experienced civilian opposition and a residue of organized resistance in the vicinity of Paris, west of the Tennessee River. He sent a small expedition, which promptly got bloodied, to suppress the problem. As yet, none of this represented any hardened Confederate policy with regard to irregular warfare. Sidney Johnston had neither the time nor the inclination for this type of combat. He sternly advised that the organization of the army be preserved, and that all troops in the service had to be subject to the articles of war, as well as to "discipline and such organization as may be necessary to render ours an efficient army."[47] This was George Washington's Europeanized and professionalized Continental Army theme from the Revolution all over again. Johnston, like Washington—and even regular officers in Union blue—all reflected the professional soldiers' concept of historical precedent for fighting wars. To Confederate West Pointers, victory and independence had to be attained by besting an enemy on the battlefield.

Nevertheless, by the spring of 1862, a cause-and-effect relationship began to emerge in the West. Continuing resistance, recalcitrance, and the first murmurs of uncontrolled, unorganized popular violence against the advancing Yankee hordes suggested problems for the commanders on both sides. For Federals, the question was how to reintroduce occupied territory back into the Union while maintaining control over Confederate sympathizers in that land. For their southern opponents, the matter was whether or not to embrace this type of people's war. As Stephen Ash has suggested, some southerners under occupation at this time were undergoing "a crisis of faith."[48]

ENTER A MILITARY GOVERNOR

The arrival of East Tennessean and United States senator Andrew Johnson as the new military governor of Tennessee coalesced forces of opposition as well as support for the Union in the upper heartland. "Gov. Andy Johnson is here," exalted one of Buell's men in the Fifteenth Indiana, "and is putting his scheme of Military Government into practical operation." Like a rock dropped in a placid pool, Johnson and his brand of reconstruction reverberated beyond the confines of the state capital, however. Change was borne upon the presence of national troops, the hovering and tenacious question of oaths of allegiance, the slave and property problem, and partisan opposition. History has portrayed Johnson as a symbol of stern military government, suppressed dissent, and oppression of secessionist sympathizers. Johnson's avowal of uncompromising unionism, his defense of strong executive power, and his conviction (like Lincoln's) of the vitality of latent loyalism in his native state marked the man as a force to be reckoned with.[49]

Johnson's first public appearance at Nashville was conciliatory in tone. Echoing throughout his speech, however, was one salient point. "In returning to my native State," he claimed, "I offer the olive branch in one hand, and the Constitution in the other." Empowered by Lincoln to suspend the writ of habeas corpus and to establish all necessary loyal offices and tribunals, Johnson served at the president's pleasure or until loyal Tennesseans could reorganize a civil government in conformity with the Constitution. A Cincinnati newsman told his readers that Federal troop presence at the event was "almost hid by the brown jeans of the farmer." These were neither Nashville's finest citizens nor plantation lords, he added, but rather simple rural folk with a fair sprinkling of blacks.[50]

Within weeks, Johnson had moved to a seemingly more vengeful policy designed to purge Nashville's secessionist citizens from positions of influence. Thought control accompanied early reconstruction in the city. Johnson purged from office the mayor and twenty-one councilmen and aldermen and jailed seven clergymen, a college professor, and the state insane asylum director for refusal to take an oath of allegiance to the Union. As Federal troops moved beyond the capital region, the city became an embattled enclave. With Johnston's army far to the south, enemy military activity provided no immediate threat. But Nashville's secessionists always maintained hope of some sort of Confederate recapture of the "Athens of the South." For the moment, however, thousands of Buell's soldiers defended Johnson's city. The problem would come when they eventually left for more important undertakings.[51]

Like their eastern comrades who passed through Washington on their way to the Virginia battlefront, these western soldiers similarly frolicked in the glow of a capital city. Nashville's sights—William Strickland's classic capitol building, the tombs of Andrew Jackson and James K. Polk, as well as the increasingly tawdry commercial and red-light districts, and suburban palaces like Harding's Belle Meade mansion just outside of town—caught their fancy. To their officers and local unionists, these soldiers were well behaved and quiet; to local secessionists, they were rapacious and destructive to property and person. Ethie Eagleton, the wife of a chaplain in Johnston's army who was staying with her sister on a plantation outside Murfreesboro, felt that visits by Buell's men who stole chickens and looked for arms were bad enough, but imposition of civilian passes even for simple travel seemed ludicrous and onerous. A person could not even visit a neighbor or walk over her own farm, she complained, "this is freedom, is it?"[52]

Such anticonspiratorial devices suited Johnson's purpose. The soldiers' presence ensured security and cowed the locals. The rub would come when the main army moved on, and Johnson complained to Washington about leaving some means of protection and coercion at his command. The War Department shunted his pleas from Stanton to Halleck, or back down the chain of command to Buell. The latter had already promised the governor that he could draw on the local provost marshal for help. The governor, however, wanted more than a corporal's guard left to protect his base of authority.[53]

Buell naturally saw his role as closing with the enemy army, and thereby protecting Johnson and civil authority. Feeding and supplying his army, planning major operations, as well as more petty matters like removing the rebel obstacles in the Cumberland below Fort Donelson focused the soldier's attention. The rebellion would end only with defeat of the main enemy army, whether by Grant, Grant and Buell in cooperation, or some other major combination. Rumors that Beauregard had garnered twenty-five thousand fresh troops from Virginia and South Carolina to join Johnston at Fayetteville in preparation for a strike on Nashville greatly worried Buell.

So did orders from McClellan to "hold Nashville firmly." Buell felt the need to hold all "the country north of the Tennessee River, with Nashville as its center," since this would provide a secure base to permit government forces to operate in all directions. Evaporation of the Fayetteville scheme relieved Buell of that worry. With Brigadier General Ormsby McKnight Mitchel moving on East Tennessee via the railroads to the Alabama border and Grant fixing the rebels in northern Mississippi, it was difficult for him to perceive any immediate major Confederate threat to Nashville.[54]

When Buell's army moved south in late March, Johnson remained adamant about holding his city at all costs. He received permission to raise a sort of governor's guard, but got few recruits for the First Tennessee (Union) regiment. His span of control hardly extended beyond Nashville's limits, except where borne on the point of Union bayonets. Indeed, Johnson's success was tied directly to military operations. Once Federal troops converted the city into a forward base for further operations in Tennessee and beyond, then homes, land, and commercial structures were taken over, and Johnson benefited from such action, for it meant the presence of more Union soldiers.

Now, Nashville assumed a new role. Clergy and businessmen were driven from their places of occupation, and their properties were confiscated for hospitals, barracks, stables, and supply warehouses for the invading army. The inevitable arrival of the flotsam of war—clerks, con men, courtesans, and criminals—soon changed the city's face. The whole downtown took on the appearance of a tent city. Nashville, the symbol of Upper South civility, became a wartime beacon or target as a Federal political-logistical nerve center. Both sides would lust to control its central position in the upper heartland.[55]

GENESIS OF A CONFEDERATE RESPONSE

Confederate authorities still claimed control over areas now occupied by Federal forces, at least in principle. Tennessee's elected governor, Isham G. Harris, exercised a shrill yet potent presence at Memphis until he was swept away by Federal capture of that city in June. Back on February 19, he had issued a proclamation calling upon all able-bodied white males in the state to enlist regardless of age. He berated the rump legislature for not doing more to rebuild Johnston's army and steps were taken in March to conscript Tennesseans for the rebel army. Elsewhere, Major General Braxton Bragg, commanding on the Gulf Coast, had urged concentration as early as February to strike a single heavy blow in the West. Abandon all points except those of strategic importance, he said, assail the enemy where he was most vulnerable, and "Kentucky is now that point." Events got away from everyone, and the best Bragg could do was send an instructor team to help Johnston, eventually arriving with reinforcements only in time for the Shiloh battle.

Confederate strategy remained basically defensive, while southerners yearned for offensive action. Confidence in Johnston remained low. Lieutenant Colonel Robert C. Wood Jr., who had joined Wirt Adams's cavalry and was the grandson of Zachary Taylor, told Colonel Charles Ready's family at Murfreesboro that he had personally defended Johnston's actions long enough. He now berated the army commander for leaving Hardee "blind-folded" to bring up the rear of the retreat from Bowling Green, for taking no notice of the many and important dispatches sent to him, and for being "either a fool or a traitor." Johnston's actions were "not the silence of wisdom, but the wisdom of silence," he ranted. Daughter Alice Ready, after hearing Wood's diatribe, noted in her diary that it was a shame the South "must have leaders in whom no one has any confidence," but she added hastily that it would be presumptuous to say so. Still, Johnston "really does not seem to have the mind" to be a senior leader in the West, she decided. A thoroughly disgusted Ethie Eagleton added privately: "I am afraid that the generals in Middle Tennessee are not doing their duty," adding bluntly that Johnston and George B. Crittenden "are drunkards."[56]

Wood, Ready, and Eagleton were young, impatient, and unforgiving of inertia. Yet, the spirits of most Tennessee Confederates hung heavy, and they looked on northern authorities with open animosity. Itinerant Middle Tennessee preacher Jesse Cox recorded moods as somber as the rainy March weather, adding "with an enemy in our midst seeking to kill our sons and soldiers everything looks

Colonel John Hunt Morgan, CSA, and his wife, Mattie, shortly after their wedding. Courtesy of the University of Kentucky Library.

gloomy." Alice Ready deplored that they were now under Lincoln's rule, and more immediately under that of the abominable Andrew Johnson. She sneered at the military governor's vow to distribute fifty thousand stand of arms among "the loyal citizens of Tennessee." If she could feign loyalty to get a pistol to shoot him, she would do so with relish, she declared. Certainly, next to Johnson's arrival, the Confederate army's retirement caused the greatest pain in the region. It severed ties with the rest of the south for people like the Ready family. Still, declared young Alice, hearts remained true, since Middle Tennesseans were brave and "can submit for awhile to the reign of tyranny." The people would have to persevere "until our army can reorganize, receive reinforcements, and march back with flaunting banners, driving the enemy before them," she vowed.[57]

That was precisely what Johnston and Beauregard wanted to do as they gathered forces from all over the lower south. Some three hundred men from Colonel A. E. Reynolds's Mississippi regiment who had nominally surrendered at Fort Donelson, for instance, were discovered awaiting guidance in Tishomingo County and were banded into a new "war regiment" organized by Colonel Robert Lowry.

Beauregard secured plowshares for swords, as more than one Mississippi valley plantation and church sacrificed its bells for new cannon. The Creole general told a priest at Saint Patrick's church in New Orleans that such efforts would "rebuke with a tongue of fire the vandals who in this war have polluted God's altar." But it would take more than flowery words. Units like Colonel John S. Scott's First Louisiana Cavalry performed just as valuable a service by screening the army along the Duck River while collecting and forwarding government property as well as "straggling soldiers, a large number of whom are hourly comin' in," as Scott told Johnston on March 19.[58]

About the only aggressive Confederate moves during this period came from Kentucky Captain John Hunt Morgan's cavalry strikes against isolated Federal posts and his harassment of the enemy's advance. Morgan would emerge as more than just a Lexington hemp factory owner with glory in his eye. A veteran of the Mexican War and, like Brigadier General Simon B. Buckner, a prominent member of the prewar Kentucky state guard, his audacious raids back to the Bluegrass would soon stir the spirits of upper heartland residents everywhere.

Morgan and his men (whether scions of solid Bluegrass stock or newcomers from the rougher irregulars forming in the region), had been at this business since the previous September. Well mounted, always itching for action, they reflected the cavaliers of old. They had learned basic military skills in the militia and then honed them as Johnston's outposts in Kentucky. After the defeat at Donelson, they covered the retreat south and helped quell the rioting in Nashville. Positioned at La Vergne, between Murfreesboro and Nashville, in late February, they scouted the countryside, establishing knowledge of the locale and contacts with local citizens for future reference.

On February 26, Morgan and a dozen of his men disguised as Union troopers slipped into Nashville and brazenly burned the steamboat *Minnetonka* in the very midst of the naval flotilla. Escaping undetected, his merry band and Scott's Louisianans harassed enemy pickets, captured wagon trains, and wrought havoc with the railroad and telegraph line. Morgan himself courted the lovely Mattie Ready at Murfreesboro when he was not engaged in badgering the Yankees or in carrying out telegraphic banter with George Prentice, editor of the distant Louisville *Journal*. Prentice had accused Morgan and others of being mere bandits and wandering robbers. Morgan's men also cultivated a rivalry with Colonel John Kennett's Fourth Ohio Cavalry, whom they would meet on many a future battlefield.[59]

That Morgan and his men accomplished relatively little by their March antics was beside the point. The intelligence passed to Johnston probably proved the most meaningful military result. But, by flaunting Yankee prisoners like some medieval prize before the downcast Tennessee citizenry, they helped offset the bitter gall of recent defeats. "We were all of course very much excited and delighted," recorded Alice Ready when learning of one of Morgan's successes. "I could only give vent to what I felt by jumping up about two feet and clapping my hands, we had all felt the anxiety on his account." Yet, ultimately, Morgan's band had to depart, usually singing lustily "Cheer boys, Cheer," and vowing to return. In their wake, civilians had to brave the wrath of Union pursuers. Morgan got his superior officer's commendation and colonelcy for his derring-do. The people of the upper heartland received only bittersweet memories—of his coming, departure, and the relentless visits of the Federals thereafter.[60]

Federal authorities viewed Morgan's irritating forays as fomenting civil disobedience and beyond the rules of civilized warfare. Kennett told his superiors after one such March brush with the Kentuckian that "we are surrounded by treachery," for examined prisoners lied, and "many who take the oath of allegiance only do it to betray us." Local civilians were totally unreliable, and only the slaves proved dependable. None of this was very surprising, but given the high expectations of latent unionism, northern soldiers were caught off guard. Buell threatened to execute some of Morgan's men as outlaws, and the Kentuckian went under a flag of truce to Buell's headquarters to negotiate their release, only to find the West Pointer refused to deal with an officer of lesser rank. So Morgan threatened reprisals on Union captives. That put an end to the matter—no one was hanged—but the signs were clear. Federal military authorities were unprepared to either counter or countenance warfare outside the bounds of textbook military practices. Yet, such warfare directly impinged on how either side controlled the upper heartland over the coming months.[61]

OMENS ON THE TWIN RIVERS

Grant's force uncovered similar stirrings of resistance in his jurisdiction. Probing southward along the eastern bank of the Tennessee River shortly after Fort Donelson's fall, a blueclad column stirred local shotgun-wielding militia at Waverly. A few shots were exchanged, and the Yanks scampered back to the fort's safety. After learning on March 11 that the enemy had occupied Paris for the purpose of enforcing Harris's conscription order in Henry County, west of the river, Grant sent a weak column "to afford protection from being drafted."

White flags greeted men from the Curtis Horse (Fifth Iowa Cavalry), Fifty-second Indiana, and Captain Robert E. Bullis's St. Louis artillerists of Battery I, First Missouri Artillery, as they chased rebel outposts through Paris. A brisk firefight developed a mile west of town with Confederate Major H. Clay King's mounted troops (described by one Iowa officer as "a wild, marauding set [who] may never have heard of the laws of war, and utterly disregard the flag of truce"). Bullis was killed, and the enemy's strength caused the hesitant expeditionary senior officer, Captain J. F. Croft of the Curtis Horse, to retire back to the protected camp at Fort Heiman, leaving his dead and wounded behind.[62]

Captain Charles Cooper Nott, a sophisticated young New Yorker who penned letters to students of the North Moore Street school in Manhattan so as to educate the youth about military life and the war, was part of the Curtis Horse that went out several days later to retrieve casualties. Describing Paris's brick houses and churches to be "more northernly than I expected to find," Nott and his men quickly gauged the vagaries of local attitudes about the northern soldiers. Having already encountered several farm and mill families on the ride from Dover to Fort Henry who "are not surly but they do not smile," for they had "sons and brothers" among the Fort Donelson captives, Nott was somewhat baffled by Henry County residents, who professed unionism but were "secesh" according to local slaves.

Disappointed at the poor and neglected farmsteads and the backwoods timber dwellings, Nott also encountered various citizens claiming hardships from the war. "Do you know, sir, whether trade will be opened soon with the North?" asked one woman, as she regaled Nott with inflationary prices of fourteen dollars for a sack of salt, coffee at a dollar a pound, and new hand cards for weaving at ten dollars per pair. Confederates had already carried off the family's pigs, and she wailed about her son, "so ill and so young, he will die if kept a prisoner at the North," for he had not enlisted until they threatened "the drafting."[63]

Nott learned even more in Paris. He found two brothers who ran the local spinning mill and had emigrated years before from Massachusetts, but whose strong unionism had been repressed to avoid problems with local authorities. They owned slaves through their southern wives, but had readily cared for the Union dead and wounded, burying the former in the town cemetery. Still, one individual who had cared for Bullis's body shrank from open contact with Nott, for fear of being taken off to a rebel prison at Memphis once the Federals had departed. When the cavalrymen rode into town, "we seem to be riding up an avenue of staring, frozen images," neither smiling nor frowning, agreeing or disagreeing, but "having a vague, stupid look of frightened wonder, as though we were dangerous serpents escaped from a traveling menagerie, which they can see for nothing at the risk of being swallowed alive," Nott wrote. Once the soldiers conversed with the townspeople about the attractiveness of Paris, several Parisians stepped forward to assure their enemy that Union wounded had been well cared for.[64]

Country folk outside town proved equally mystifying. One couple who plied Nott with supper and hospitality told him how Tennessee authorities had forbade them to vote for the Union in the second election for a secessionist convention. The man stated that he could not abide President Jefferson Davis's doctrine of fighting until everyone was dead, as his wife proclaimed, "we were the most prosperous, happy people on earth, and we had better go back and be so again than be killed." She also chuckled that if everyone were killed off, then the southern girls would have nobody to marry but Yankees, "so the South would get to be the North in no time."

Within minutes of the conversation, Nott's senior sergeant brought word that local slaves claimed that this very couple had been out cheering the Confederate cavalry only the day before and that the husband had been seen chatting with rebel pickets shortly before Nott's arrival. The captain wondered if "the man had gone to raise a crowd of irresponsible countrymen, who will think it fine fun to kill us and capture our horses, and of whom Gen. Beauregard will say, he really knows nothing, they were not soldiers, and acted without authority." Nott, like thousands of his comrades over the next three years of conflict in the heartland, was left wondering if these civilians were merely trying to "survive" by transforming chameleonlike when either army passed through.[65]

Meanwhile, Grant's army finally moved upriver to the environs of Savannah, Tennessee. Temporarily left behind, some reinforcements, like young Will Kennedy, a musician with the Fifty-second Indiana, simply put out fishing lines to avoid boredom while awaiting orders to rejoin the main column. Also in the army's wake, other units were cast in a more permanent role in the captured region. Nott and his fellow Iowans established a pattern for garrisons left behind to guard the twin rivers. Scarcely a thousand men remained at Clarksville by mid-March (principally the Twenty-second Ohio and the Fiftieth Illinois), but there were some twenty-three hundred garrisoned at Fort Donelson, with similar numbers at Forts Henry and Heiman. Later in the month, Federal authorities realized the vulnerability of their lengthening lines of communication. A Former Louisville and Nashville Railroad official, J. B. Anderson, a Kentuckian with questionable sympathies, took charge of repairing the Nashville and Chattanooga line for Buell, and a line of railroad garrisons soon sprang up along the line in his army's rear also.[66]

Colonel Edward C. Williams's Ninth Pennsylvania Cavalry, for example, found itself stretched thin with four companies stationed at Springfield, two more at Gallatin, two more at Clarksville, two at Bowling Green, and one close-in at Edgefield, across the river from Nashville. A hard-bitten Indiana politically appointed general, Ebenezer Dumont, a Mexican War veteran with experience in western Virginia against Robert E. Lee the year before, commanded all the troops in and around Nashville, as well as those on the communication lines north to Munfordville, Kentucky. Similar forward defense perimeters, using infantry, artillery, and cavalry, were set up at Franklin, Murfreesboro, and even along the Harpeth and Duck Rivers as well as Rutherford's Creek. Like Fort Donelson/Dover, Forts Henry and Heiman, and Clarksville, they became strategic hamlets to guard against raiders and a salve to Buell's conscience, assuring him that his army was indeed providing protection to Governor Johnson. In reality, they formed a porous screen through which Morgan, Scott, and soon Colonel Nathan Bedford Forrest might slip with impunity. In retrospect, they better served the mission of population control than as a deterrent to rebel incursions.[67]

Federal authority tightened across Middle Tennessee in March and April. Prominent residents like Harding, George Washington Barrow, Josephus Conn Guild, and others were packed off to Yankee prisons by a paranoid Andrew Johnson. The forest of smokestacks on the river signaled stockpiling of army supplies in and around the city. New telegraph wires paralleled the L&N tracks northward from the city (and suggested inviting targets for partisans and raiders). The din and congestion of a revitalized downtown market and warehouse district marked the restoration of trade with the North—but with a twist. The trade was military, not civilian, in nature.

Yankee money poured in, but the populace remained resentful, even openly insulting, to the occupation troops. A reign of terror was the way secessionists characterized Johnson's initial sixty days in office. Carpetbaggers, wounded soldiers from Shiloh, countless skirmishes, and the vigilant (even oppressive) presence of the provost marshall's guard cloaked the city. Rumors of citizen uprisings disturbed many nights' slumber for everyone, and the shadows of Morgan's band in the neighboring countryside concerned Johnson and Dumont and frightened unionists and innocent soldiers on picket duty.[68]

In West Tennessee, Grant's column bogged down in the recriminations from Shiloh while his rear echelon commanders wrestled with leftover rebel property still present at Forts Henry and Donelson and Clarksville. Colonel Crafts J. Wright, for example, protested that "if we move away the property will pass into the hands of enemies unless others take our place." Furthermore, he argued, "the Railroad between the Rivers can be easily opened and even now passed over by Hand Cars," despite the fact that the bridge over the Cumberland stayed inoperable.

Grant rejected Wright's pleas, ordering things shut down, and by the next week he queried Colonel Philip Fouke at Fort Donelson: "Has the force from Clarksville yet moved?" A late discovery of one-hundred-thousand-dollars' worth of uncured bacon delayed matters, while Wright beat the bushes on every local farm, smokehouse, and city property trying to confiscate even more contraband property. Finally, Grant had enough and he directed Wright to rejoin the army. Grant heeded his warning, however, shipping Colonel Rodney Mason's Seventy-first Ohio (which had bolted for the rear at Shiloh) back to relieve Fouke at Fort Donelson and Clarksville on April 15.[69]

Grant told his wife, Julia, that he anticipated the last battle in the Mississippi valley would occur soon and that deserters coming through the lines seemed "heartily tired of the war." But he also noted that noncombatants were "worse rebels than the soldiers who fight against us." Confident always of success, Grant was now satisfied that his own rear area on the twin rivers was capably protected by Colonel William Lowe's cavalry and Mason's infantry. Buell could guard his own line of communications. Grant's vision pointed southward toward Mississippi. But West Tennessee, as well as the land between the Tennessee and Cumberland Rivers and the stretch of territory known as the Purchase in the northwest corner of Kentucky, would remain contested ground for both sides long after Grant's passage farther south.[70]

CHANCE CAVALRY ENCOUNTERS

Curiously, local secessionists urged Confederate cavalry commander William H. Jackson at Trenton in West Tennessee to avoid alienating their unionist neighbors for fear of bringing Federal down wrath upon them. They refused to supply him with provisions. Coping with the unionists was "one of the most delicate and perplexing problems," he admitted to his superiors. Still, he thought his numerical superiority over Union garrisons, which were clinging to various river posts, gave him control of the interior. Those garrisons even avoided heavy-handedness with local residents. One Tiptonville native wrote an imprisoned cousin at Sandusky, Ohio, on May 25 that the local blue-coats were more accommodating than he expected, and he awoke every morning to the "delightful sounds of the Yankee's drum and [was] lulled to sleep with the same." Still, like Ethie Eagleton, he too disliked having to secure a pass even to visit neighbors, and the dearth of servants, who had run away at the approach of northerners, rankled him.[71]

Elsewhere Nott and his Yankee companions remained skeptical of what favor they encountered. One man in little Como, Tennessee, near Dresden professed his belief in "the Union, the Constitution, and the Enforcement of the Laws" and doffed his hat. "We had seen so little patriotism in Tennessee that we doubted this," Nott wrote to the Moore school students. One detachment of Federals from Paducah invaded a circuit court session at Mario in Crittenden County, Kentucky, on May 13, and its commander directed Judge Wiley P. Fowler of Smithland and other court officers to take an oath to the Constitution. They refused, were arrested, and had to post bond to appear in Paducah. Such was the patchwork appearance of loyalty and honor in the upper heartland for the moment.[72]

Beauregard wanted his cavalry to raid Grant's line of communications, and on May 4 Jackson was joined by Colonel Thomas Claiborne at McKenzie's station en route to capturing Paducah with its supply warehouses. Claiborne's force numbered about 1,250 men, and he and Jackson headed for Paris, where some 250 to 300 outriders from Lowe's twin river garrison were busy trying to intercept the medical contraband trade out of Paducah. The Federal force under Major Carl Schaffer de Boernstein had left Paris, gone on toward Dresden, and then turned northward toward Mayfield. On the afternoon of May 6, Claiborne's superiors caught up with de Boernstein's column at Marshall Lockridge's mill and Obion River bridge on the Dresden–Mayfield road. Nearly half the Federal column was killed, wounded, or captured in the resulting melee. De Boernstein fell mortally wounded, and Nott barely escaped to Paducah with survivors. Learning of the disaster, Lowe set out from Fort Henry to intercept Claiborne, but the rebels escaped. All in all, both combatants learned a great deal about the region and its inhabitants; Claiborne noted numerous encounters with unionist residents, while Lowe reported that an additional regiment and battery might "easily hold and occupy the country for thirty miles back of the river" since there "are many good and loyal citizens in this vicinity," who should receive all possible assistance in the area.[73]

Ironically, the very day before Claiborne's striking success at Lockridge Mill, the Federals inflicted a similarly singular defeat of Morgan's horsemen east of Nashville in an affair styled the "Lebanon Races." With Bedford Forrest recuperating from a wound suffered at Shiloh, it devolved upon Morgan to carry the war behind Union lines. Morgan, now the darling of southern newsmen and ladies, as well as the bane of Union authorities, intended striking for his home in Lexington, Kentucky. Departing Corinth, Mississippi, at the end of April, Morgan checked with his loosely knit network of independent operators, including Champ Ferguson and Captain Willis Scott Bledsoe, before crossing the Tennessee at Decatur, Alabama, with about eight hundred men. He raised the flagging morale of Pulaskians in Giles County, Tennessee, on May Day. "Our spirits were low and our hearts faint for we felt that the iron chain of despotism was fastening upon us as time rolled on," wrote a local doctor's wife, Martha Abernathy, in her diary. Basking in the warm glow of ladies, "their faces expressive of the most intense joy and gratitude," Morgan subsequently gobbled up an arriving band of Yankee recruits and mostly unarmed infantry. He paroled the lot amid the adoration of the townsfolk.[74]

Morgan's departure the next morning, however, left Pulaskians at the mercy of Colonel Marcellus Mundy's rampaging Twenty-third Kentucky Cavalry. Abernathy described the subsequent three-day "reign of terror," in which Yankee horsemen ravaged the town and insulted its residents "on account of Morgan's enthusiastic reception." Mundy demanded that prominent citizens, like Abernathy's husband, remain at home. The doctor refused, and he, like others, was arrested and imprisoned because of his defiance. Still other residents, including William Martin, said Abernathy, collaborated with the newcomers. But she swore to teach her children about her husband's patriotism. Supported and comforted by refugees from Kentucky and her own friends in town, Abernathy's diary soon became a litany of invoking prayer along with oaths about the hated Yankees. The sort of scene would be repeated often in the coming months across a Union-occupied South.[75]

Meanwhile, Morgan moved on to Harrington and the nearby unionist Shelbyville. As Morgan's men burned cotton fields and savaged unionist merchants, one store owner styled them "the first organized band of horse thieves and store robbers that ever passed through the country." Little of lasting military significance was accomplished in Bedford County, but Morgan and Mundy both set the pattern for future intimidation of civilians. The Confederate raider soon skirted Murfreesboro's burgeoning garrison, but caused the Federals to shift their Franklin garrison, thereby inspiring rebel sympathizers in that quaint Harpeth Valley town. By nightfall on a dark and rainy May 4, 1862, Morgan's party reached Lebanon, east of Nashville, thoroughly fatigued and unprepared for the disaster that awaited them.[76]

As his weary men spread out to find comfortable billets against the storm, Dumont with some six hundred effective men of the First and Fourth Kentucky and Seventh and Ninth Pennsylvania Cavalry regiments swept down by surprise. Colonel Frank Wolford of the First Kentucky was wounded and captured, six of Morgan's men were killed with 150 or more captured, and Morgan's prize mount, "Black Bess," also fell into Union hands. Morgan himself escaped, but the rest of his proud command scattered across the countryside in rout. It was a brilliant Union victory, largely unsung by subsequent Morgan admirers. Still, Morgan was resilient and posed an enduring threat.[77]

Morgan recovered quickly, and he decided to restore confidence among his surviving followers by continuing northward against the L&N rail line, hoping perhaps to free some of the prisoners taken at Lebanon, who were rumored to be going north by train. Guided by the infamous ruffian Champ Ferguson and reinforced by several local militia (possibly partisan) contingents, Morgan avoided the Bowling Green garrison and moved in on the railroad at Cave City. Here he captured and burned forty-five freight and four passenger cars, destroyed a locomotive, extracted six thousand dollars from the local express agent, and cap-

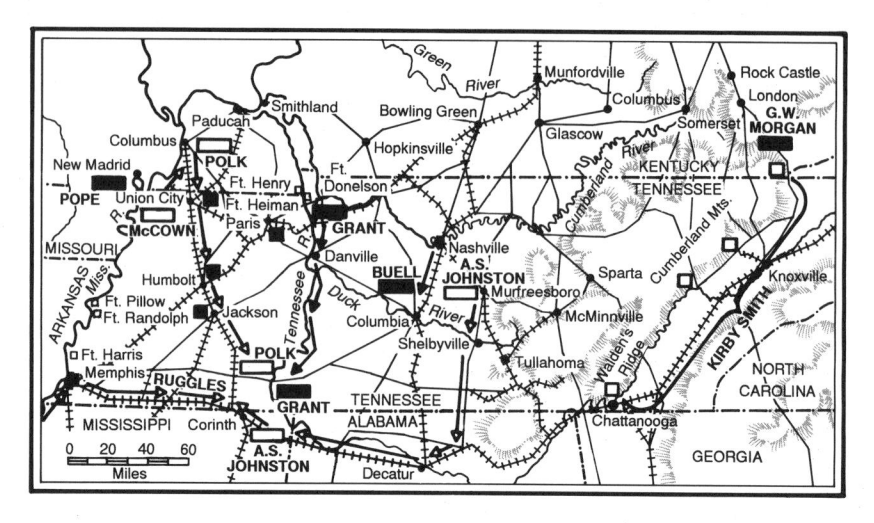

Strategic situation on the eve of Shiloh, end of March 1862.

tured a Nashville-bound express train with a party of Yankee army wives aboard. Southern newspapers played up this success, conveniently forgetting the Lebanon disaster, and little was said about how Major Thomas Jefferson Jordan's battalion of the Ninth Pennsylvania horse unit thereafter hotly pursued Morgan's band back across the upper Cumberland to Sparta.[78]

Morgan's audacity and publicity thoroughly irritated Union occupation and railroad officials. They strengthened station guards throughout central Kentucky and concentrated the rest of the Pennsylvania cavalry regiment in the Bowling Green sector against future raids. Governor Johnson was most chagrined that the Cave City caper dampened a planned unionist rally at Nashville. How could the governor overawe rebel citizens when Morgan's deeds suggested the imminent return of rebels to the region? Assistant Secretary of War P. H. Watson suggested the raiding would cease if men like Morgan were shot "without challenge as enemies of mankind." A perceptive Union brigadier, George Washington Morgan, calmly suggested that "Morgan's guerrillas" had to be caught before they could be shot.[79]

The little affrays involving Claiborne with the Curtis Horse and Morgan with Dumont at Lebanon and Cave City served notice for the future. They suggested new directions for the war in the West and pointed to exposed, soft areas behind the invaders that might be ripe for Confederate raiders. A prophetic message went home in the correspondence of Texas Ranger Benjamin Franklin Batchelor. Writing his father on April 17, young Batchelor noted receipt of orders taking him back to Tennessee after Shiloh. "The object of returning to the state," he said, "is to hold it as long as possible and harass the enemy on his rear." It was the inauguration, he supposed, of that guerrilla warfare that he had thought necessary all along to achieve Confederate victory, and about which he had written his father three months before while encamped with Johnston's forces in Kentucky. "Our armies are not large enough to cope with those of the enemy in regular pitched battles, hence we must divide our forces and try to surprise and whip them in detail," he claimed. The trip would be long and toilsome, he suggested, "but I shrink not from fatigue or labor or peril in times like these."

Writing again a fortnight later, Batchelor tried to bolster home-front spirits by declaring defeatist newspaper talk to be "twaddle," as "it seems to me our prospects have been brightening every day since the fall of Donelson." Grant's immense army and fleet had done considerable damage, "but they have been met with such stubborn resistance that they are badly crippled and have failed to accomplish the designs intended"; their splendid army was badly cut up at Shiloh and thus far checked in its progress. He insisted that if the war assumed a guerrilla-like character, as it probably would if more reverses attended both western and eastern battlefront, "then the North will only have begun a subjugation which twenty years could not effect, had our enemies the wealth to carry it on."[80]

THREE

CONFEDERATE RESURGENCE: SUMMER 1862

Weeks passed before Benjamin Franklin Batchelor and his Texas comrades returned to the now greening fields and woodlands of springtime Tennessee and Kentucky. Meanwhile, the succession of Confederate disasters had continued unabated in the West. The near victory at Shiloh and another surrender of a rebel army at Island Number 10 on the Mississippi River marred the month of April. Bloody Shiloh created more vacant dinner chairs across the South and took the life of the theater commander, Albert Sidney Johnston. But the loss of Island Number 10 was even more significant. Brigadier General William C. Mackall yielded another 7,000 men as well as three general officers and 123 heavy and 35 field guns. More important, his surrender further opened the Mississippi River to Union invasion. In words reminiscent of those uttered after Fort Donelson's fall, a former Philadelphian now serving in the First Alabama, Daniel P. Smith, suggested that "the universal feeling among the men and officers was, that the surrender was utterly uncalled for, and that the greater portion of the force could have been safely taken out while a few men held [the enemy in check]."[1]

How long would the military defeats and further retreat continue, southerners wondered. "Why not carry the war into Kentucky, or even [the North's] own territory, if we can?" A. Battle of Tuscaloosa, Alabama, wrote to Secretary of War George W. Randolph on April 29, 1862. Let them overrun the South, "as they will anyhow, shall we not more likely turn them from the South by sending our armies north?" Our struggle must be one of endurance anyhow, he added. The answer came in late May when Johnston's successor, General P. G. T. Beauregard, evacuated Corinth, once more leaving large quantities of supplies for the advancing Yankees. In actuality, Corinth had merely become a wet, pestilential death trap for thousands of wounded as well as able Confederate soldiers after Shiloh. Beauregard's evacuation fifty miles south to Tupelo probably saved the army to fight another day. Otherwise, dysentery and typhoid threatened to accomplish

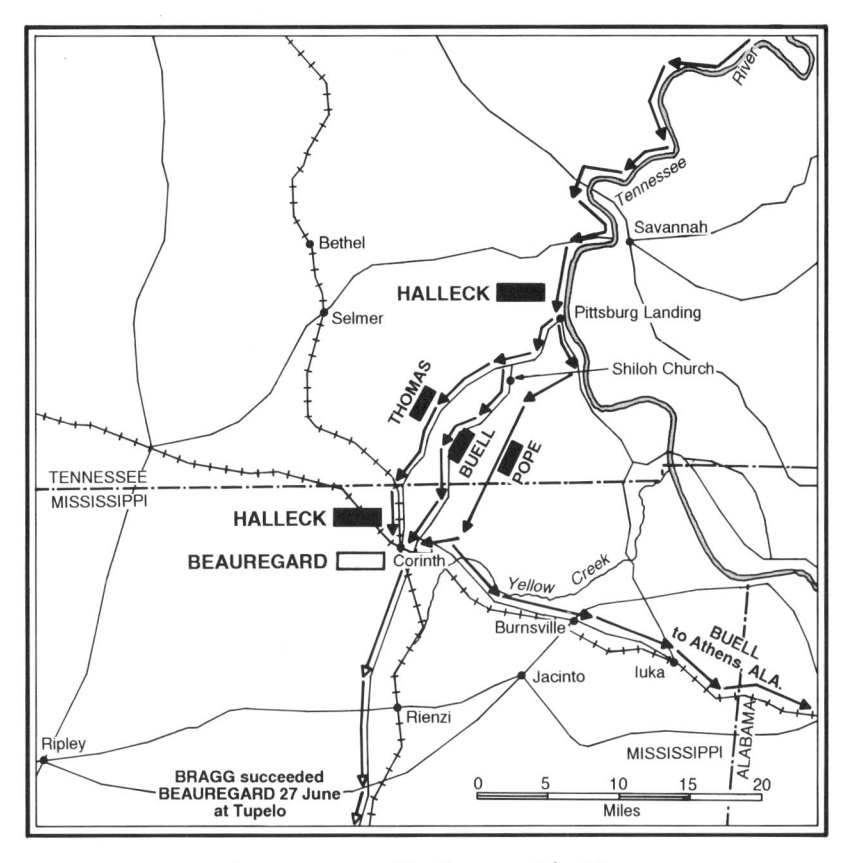

Strategic situation in West Tennessee in July 1862.

what Yankee bullets had not. As it was, many of Beauregard's men spent all summer recuperating from Corinth's unhealthy living conditions.[2]

Memphis fell to the Union navy the next month, and direct Confederate control receded south from the Bluegrass and Middle Tennessee to Alabama and Mississippi. The spirited rebel newspaper, the Memphis *Appeal*, took up new residency in Grenada, Mississippi. Union troops began to picket bridge crossings and crossroads, and occupy key towns and villages along the vital east-west Memphis and Charleston Railroad. Memphis citizens sullenly acquiesced to the arrival of the Yankees, much as Nashvillians had done several months before. But, given the North's demand for cotton, a lively business in this stored commodity soon sprang up all over West Tennessee as local rebel farmers found accommodation with enterprising northern merchants or their representatives. At least one West Tennessean observed that the high price of cotton (he claimed fifteen thousand dollars from his stockpile that had escaped the Confederates' destruction order) "in some degree helps us in our losses by the War."[3]

So captive Memphis and its environs quickly became a mecca for northern cotton agents, economically pressed locals, and an array of speculators. The city itself eventually rivaled Nashville for wartime transients and schemers. Moreover, it also became a Union supply base as well as administrative center for reintroducing United States control to the surrounding territory in West Tennessee and Arkansas. Leading the conquerors in this effort would be the hero of Donelson, Ulysses S. Grant, and his colleague William Tecumseh Sherman—a man termed insane earlier in the war for predicting that conquest of the South would require hundreds of thousands of men and vast resources.

THE RISE OF CIVIL DISCONTENT

By early summer, Major General Henry Halleck, overall Union commander in the West, had dispersed the immense army that he had collected to take Corinth, spreading it across the region to consolidate control. In July, he went to Washington as general-in-chief of all Union armies, leaving Grant in command of those forces in West Tennessee, with Sherman as a sort of proconsul at Memphis. As this pair attempted to concentrate enough military force to continue the conquest of the Mississippi valley over the succeeding months, they experienced what Grant admitted for himself was "the most anxious period of the war." Civil disobedience, rising guerrilla activity, and his own subordinates who bridled at conciliatory treatment of civilians—not to mention the relentless problem of slave refugees flocking to Union lines—all underscored that anxiety. Helping fan the flames of civil insurrection was the Memphis *Appeal*, which reported every Confederate triumph no matter how minor. Even a supposedly unionist successor *Appeal* in Memphis itself and the Memphis *Argus* were soon driven out of existence by Federal military authorities for incendiary and treasonous expressions during the period.[4]

Grant claimed in his postwar memoirs that the rebel counterattack at Shiloh had caused him to give up "all idea of saving the Union except by complete conquest." No longer would he order his troops to protect private property regardless of owner loyalty. Now, "I regarded it as humane to both sides to protect the persons of those found at their homes, but to consume everything that could be used to support or supply armies." But, apparently, as Mark Grimsley has suggested, Grant did not actually come to that feeling immediately after Shiloh at all. In fact, in letters to his wife, Grant held closely all summer to the opinion that again if southern civilians "could express their unbiased feeling untrammeled by leaders" and if they would stop thinking of the Federal war effort as abolitionist, then reconciliation was still possible. He deplored "negro stealing," as he termed blatant confiscation of slaves by emancipation-minded soldiers. But Grant's subordinates, including Colonel William P. Lyon, simply saw it as proto-emancipation—"where the army of the Union goes, there slavery ceases forever."[5]

On the other hand, Grant abandoned limited war with a "surprising speed and decisiveness" that summer, claims historian Brooks D. Simpson. Shutting down pro-Confederate newspapers like the Memphis *Avalanche* and replacing them with pro-Union sheets, assessing pro-Confederate civilians' property to compensate the army's losses to guerrillas, and declaring captured irregulars as beyond treatment as legitimate prisoners of war would all become Grant's new standard—with Halleck's complete accord from Washington. Grant told his wife in June that southern women and children were worse rebels than their soldiers, although he continued to threaten dire punishment for any of his soldiers who pilfered or destroyed private property. By July, he was actively entertaining the idea of "turning all discontented citizens within our lines out South," a notion that also met with Halleck's full concurrence.[6]

Indeed, "Old Brains," as the scholarly Halleck was dubbed by army colleagues, told Grant on August 2, 1862: "If necessary, take up all active sympathizers, and either hold them as prisoners or put them beyond our lines." It was "desirable that you should clean out West Tennessee and North Mississippi of all organized enemies," so "handle that class without gloves, and take their property for public use," especially "all the supplies you can from the rebels in Mississippi. . . . They should feel the presence of war on our side," was Halleck's conclusion. One irate Mississippian vowed that "henceforth our motto shall be, Blood for blood, and blood for property." As Simpson suggests, disobedient populace and guerrillas, not Shiloh, "toughened Grant to the notion of hard war." Grimsley terms Grant's policy "discrete, proportional severity."[7]

A more irascible Sherman came to the same opinions as Grant. He spent the summer "fighting off cavalry detachments coming from the south, and waging an everlasting quarrel with planters about their negroes and fences" (which his men apparently destroyed with abandon). "The well settled policy of the whole army is now to have nothing to do with the negro," he preached in support of the official exclusion doctrine of the moment. Slavery—whether enforcing it or smuggling slaves away—was not the business of the soldier, Sherman announced. His tenure at Memphis returned that city and neighborhood to some semblance of order. Overcoming the initial animosity of Memphians through the administration's policy of accommodation and conciliation, Sherman also uncovered mischief and exploitation. While building a fortified logistical and command base for future operations downriver, he faced smuggling and contraband trade, civil disobedience that escalated to open partisan warfare, and a reaffirmation of what he remembered from prewar experience with southerners—their devout commitment to disunion. Sherman became convinced that all the people of the nation had become the enemies of one another during wartime, and he hoped that the war's results would include extermination of the disloyal, as well as emancipation (which he personally disapproved of).[8]

Sherman's frustrations with the truculence and intransigence of southerners, and the blatant misuse of the cotton trade by locals to covertly help Confederate arms (especially irregulars), produced a response far different from official government policy. As he told Grant at Corinth on August 11, the cotton trade order from Washington was a travesty, and he would "move heaven and earth for its repeal," as it was fatal to their success. "If we provide our enemies with money we enable them to buy all they stand in need of," for "money is as much contraband of war as powder." But there was more.

The murdering of Federal soldiers in the countryside and the wanton attacks by guerrillas on river boats led to harsher measures under Sherman's reign, measures historian Noel Fisher has called "collective punishment" of the populace. Exiling disobedient residents, winking at soldierly plunder under the guise that it was done for the government's benefit, and destroying civilian safe havens for guerrillas became de facto policy. Privately, Sherman hoped to carry fire and sword into southern states until not one habitation was left intact, he said. On August 17, he wrote Grant that he believed in universal confiscation of rebel property and colonization of ex-slaves. He did not "exact the oath universally," Sherman told his friend, "but assume the ground that all within our lines are American citizens, and if they do any act or fail in any duty required of them as such then they can and will be punished as spies." The next day he ended a blunt dispatch to Halleck: "All the people of the South are now arming as partisan riders, daring not to be guerrillas." "Cump" Sherman (as his brothers and sisters had quickly dubbed him in youth, abbreviating his middle name) was not always sure there was much difference, and reprisals or war on civilians was the result.[9]

Curiously enough, Abraham Lincoln and his advisers also had begun to alter their perspective in the summer of 1862. Faced with military collapse in Virginia and antagonistic citizenry in rebel states, Lincoln shifted direction. Historians like James M. McPherson have concluded that administration actions during this period marked a "decisive turn toward total war." They attribute the move to increasing dissatisfaction of northern politicians, journalists, and civilians toward coddling the South, and to Major General George B. McClellan's unsuccessful Peninsula campaign to take the Confederate capital at Richmond. Not only would more manpower be needed to suppress the rebellion, but also the president sensed that confiscation and slave emancipation "could be used to fashion a tougher military response," in the words of another historian, Daniel E. Sutherland.[10]

The result included several appeals (both public and private) for more northern volunteers, passage of the Confiscation Act (defining slaves as property of "traitors" and hence "contraband" eligible for confiscation), and the Militia Act (allowing "persons of African descent" to serve in the military) on July 17, 1862. But Congress indicated that it would seize control of emancipation policy should Lincoln stumble in his resolve. So the president soon hinted to several cabinet confidants that he was now seriously thinking of a presidential decree on the issue. Clearly, then, the political climate was forcing policy change in Washington at the very moment that soldiers in the field (facing an incipient southern people-in-arms movement) were forging change in practice. The result was a harder war. Moreover, in Sutherland's view, the remarkable appearance of two new generals in the East, fresh from experiences in the Western Theater, also formed part of this series of events.[11]

Lincoln summoned Major General John Pope to command a new Virginia field army in late June, and he appointed Halleck as new general-in-chief of all Union armies three weeks later. Lincoln's moves were prompted both by the generals' successful conduct of war west of the Appalachians and the chief executive's desire to reconsider his policy toward civilians and the course of war in general.

Summer 1862

When, at the end of July, an Illinois congressman urged Lincoln to take more forceful military action to "maul the rebels," the president responded bluntly, "Tell the people of Illinois that I'll do it." Certainly, the two professional soldiers had the requisite experience to put down civilian insurrection and change the conduct of war, since they had dealt with growing civil restiveness in Missouri as well as Kentucky and Tennessee.

Moreover, Pope enjoyed the president's confidence as an old friend with familial ties to the Kentucky–Illinois locale. He had been with Lincoln on the newly elected president's inaugural trip to Washington the previous year. So, the commander-in-chief understandably endorsed a series of Pope's orders that identified this western general as herald of the new war policy. Pope's soldiers in Virginia could now subsist upon the country and had to give vouchers for confiscated property only to loyal citizens of the United States. Rebel Virginians would be held responsible for disruption of Union supply and communication lines and for attacks upon uniformed personnel. Those combatants not in uniform or part of organized Confederate units would not be covered by "privileges and immunities of warfare." Even nonparticipating civilians would be considered "evil-disposed persons," and sabotage of any railroad, wagon road, or telegraph would require civilians within a radius of five miles of the incident to be "turned out in mass" to repair the damage and pay the costs of those repairs "in money or in property." Civilians firing on Union troops would be punished by having their homes destroyed or all neighbors within a similar five-mile radius pay "an indemnity sufficient for the case." In short, perpetrators would be punished without recourse to court trial.[12]

Additional orders further reflected Pope's hardness. All southern civilians who refused to swear allegiance to the United States would be exiled from their homes to rebel lines. Exiles caught returning to their homes or anybody communicating with people within those Confederate lines would be shot. Moreover, Pope refused the common military practice of accommodating citizens requesting protection on the grounds that it wasted his troops energy and effectiveness "in protecting private property of those most hostile to the Government." As he had in the West, Pope heard reports about the increasing menace of spies, guerrillas, and bushwhackers within his Virginia sector of operations. He became determined to erase this threat before it impacted his plan of operations. In this goal, he had the full blessing of Lincoln, as on July 25, the president issued a public warning to anyone guilty of aiding, countenancing, or abetting the rebel cause would immediately cease or suffer forfeitures and seizures of their property. Needless to say, Pope's dictums prompted strong protests from the Confederate high command.[13]

Labeled a "miscreant" by Robert E. Lee, Pope prompted even stronger vituperation from Jefferson Davis. The Confederate president threatened retaliation against any captured Union officer from Pope's Army of Virginia. They would be denied their rights as prisoners of war. On the Union side Halleck as well as McClellan expressed shocked at the westerner's policy, and Pope (under proper tutelage from Washington), eventually backed away from enforcement. He condemned "acts of pillage and outrage" of his soldiery and reprimanded subordinates for condoning plunder of the countryside. Yet, in Sutherland's view, it remains difficult to adversely judge the Union soldiery for actions they took to be acceptable under Pope's July orders, for they were "not acting far outside the spirit of those orders." Pope's own tactical setbacks at Cedar Mountain and Second Manassas soon sent his star into eclipse. The new war policy of Lincoln and Pope gave way to McClellan's return to conciliatory measures for noncombatants. Nonetheless, the damage had been done: precedents were set, and retaliation threatened from the other side. Moreover, in the Western Theater, Lincoln countenanced Military Governor Andrew Johnson's belief that "the rebels must be made to feel the weight and ravages of the war they have brought the Country" by extending Pope's most stringent General Order Number 11 to Tennessee as a counter-subversive measure at the governor's request.[14]

Those southerners willing to take the oath of allegiance to the Unites States could remain at home and "pursue in good faith their accustomed avocations." Those refusing the oath would be escorted beyond Federal lines and told if they returned they would be considered spies "and subjected to the extreme rigor of military law." Any violator of the oath would be shot and his property confiscated for public use. Communication with anyone within Confederate lines was strictly regulated and violators here, too, would be treated as spies. Even the patient Lincoln had turned hard-nosed about the rebellion by the second summer of the war.[15]

RISE OF THE PARTISAN RANGERS

The period after Shiloh also witnessed momentous changes in Confederate government policy. In fact, they underscore historian Emory Thomas's interpretation of the Confederacy as a revolutionary experience. The very day after headlines announced the fresh casualty lists and Johnston's death, the Confederate House of Representatives introduced legislation with far-reaching ramifications. Eventually passing Congress after lengthy debate in mid-April, the two acts provided for the first manpower conscription in North America and for recruitment of so-called "Bands of Partisan Rangers." They complemented earlier measures that had authorized suspension of the writ of habeas corpus and a declaration of martial law by the president.[16]

Indeed, the movement to muster organized irregulars had enjoyed some fashion in Richmond even before the first battle of Manassas in July 1861. One official had actually directed their enrollment. But the opposition of the West Pointer in the Confederate White House, Jefferson Davis, and his coterie of advisers had scuttled the idea. Acting Secretary of War Judah P. Benjamin had continued that aversion when on March 29, 1862, he vowed that guerrilla companies would not be a recognized part of Confederate military structure. Then the exploits of independent warriors like John Hunt Morgan, Turner Ashby, and Jake Thompson captured public fancy. "Morgan fever" gripped a young nation seeking heroes and victories. The enemy must be conquered, proclaimed *De Bow's Review*, and by any honorable method. Partisan warfare seemed honorable, and so events in the field as conveyed through public acclaim now drove government policy.

Although some opposition to mustering irregulars surfaced in the Confederate Senate, where members feared its impact on implementing conscription (and justifiably so, as it turned out), the Partisan Ranger Act was passed on April 21. It reflected public dissatisfaction with the progress of the West Pointers' war.[17] The Partisan Ranger Act would prove to be one of the Confederacy's missed opportunities, but its failure was unforeseen at the time. Whether by companies, battalions, or regiments of either infantry or cavalry, these rangers could be received into the regular Confederate service, operate under army regulations, and were entitled to the same pay, rations, and quarters as other soldiers. Moreover, they could be further rewarded for any arms and munitions of war captured from the enemy—sort of incentive pay for action behind Union lines. The lure of fame, glory, and freedom of action would appeal to recruits, as would the idea that these men could remain in their home neighborhoods and avoid the vicissitudes of distant field service.[18]

As transmitted by army general orders, the Confederate War Department substituted the partisan corps for guerrilla service. Like Lincoln's professionals, Davis's generals also wanted to keep the war confined to regulated military operations and away from the civilian populace. But such aims stood in defiance of history. Whether termed partisans, irregulars, or guerrillas, the idea of such warriors was hardly new. Legalistic fine points had never been known to guide actual events in time of war. Dating from ancient resistance fighters and other unconventional combatants, such bands thrived in American colonial and revolutionary times. The Iberian campaigns of the Napoleonic era had contributed the very word *guerrillos* to the vocabulary. To Richmond officials, the more accepted and honorable-sounding term "partisan" made sense. For one thing, partisans, as authorized warriors, would maintain a semblance of order in a people's war and would evoke the actions of southerners' own forbears.[19]

Actually, experience with irregular or unconventional combat has formed a thread in the overall history of American arms, notwithstanding professional soldiers' eternal quest to confine combat to their own arena. Geographical and cultural conditions on the shifting frontier underpinned that tradition, particularly in the clash between settlers and native cultures. Native Americans were superb guerrilla fighters, and settlers eventually adopted their style of fighting. Settlers undertook this transformation reluctantly, since civilized Europeans and their descendants considered native warfare barbaric. Colonel Benjamin Church understood the value of Native American irregular warfare and so became (in Michael Pearlman's opinion), "Colonial America's foremost proponent of ranger operations." As early as 1722, so-called rangers helped pacify the Georgia frontier, while the famous Rangers of New Hampshire captain (later colonel) Robert Rogers conducted numerous raids during the French and Indian War, serving as a model for several Tory units in the American Revolution. Such patrols literally "ranged about" Virginia's frontier forts too, providing regional security as well as long-range reconnaissance and early warning. They sought to uncover and disrupt enemy raids before they could descend in full fury upon settlements. Indeed, this device blended well with two other elements in the diverse military culture of the Anglo-American colonies—volunteerism and the general repugnance toward time-consuming military service.[20]

Certainly the question of a standing army, a viable militia, and irregular warfare all played their part in the American rebellion against the English crown. Varying success with both undependable militiamen and George Washington's small, European-style Continental Army marked most of the combat. Washington himself had little patience for militia, although he drew upon the system to feed manpower into his standing army during the war. By both temperament and patrician background, he especially had little inclination to resort to the third of the triad—partisan warfare. More emphasis on this element might have produced truly horrid civil war in a society where one-third of the people were loyal to the English, one-third patriots for a new country, and the final third a swing weight of uncommitted souls.

Yet, it was just that element of partisan warfare that southern patriots had used with such telling effect in that struggle. So, embattled southerners returned to this heritage in 1862. Stunned by the failures of their conventional generals, politicians and the public looked for a fresh start. Mounted free-wheeling riflemen, hit-and-run tactics, and slashing assaults against pickets, enemy encampments, supply lines, and civilian "tories" were the lessons learned from Revolutionary War ancestors. For Civil War-era southerners, then, irregular fighting had a heroic and honorable tone. Moreover, it made sense. It offset Yankee numerical superiority in one's own backyard.[21]

Young southern blades seeking alternative service to conscription in 1862 looked foremost to their revolutionary ancestors as models. The legend of men like Francis Marion, Thomas Sumter, and Andrew Pickins spoke to the free spirit of the nineteenth-century frontier as well as being a rejection of European textbook military convention. Hardly anyone was alive in the 1860s who actually remembered Marion or the others. Their fame had been passed down through the family lore of transplanted Carolinians who settled Tennessee and Kentucky during the intervening years. Antebellum spokesmen leading the section toward secession had evoked memories of those guerrilla saints, while the romanticized tales of Sir Walter Scott and his Scottish guerrilla chieftain, Rob Roy, also stoked the fires of restless southern youth, male and female. American authors Beverly Tucker and William Gilmore Simms politicized homegrown characters in their novels as a means to oppose northern tariff and business aggression in this same period.

As historian Anne Norton has suggested, popular ideology in the South of the time bridled generally at any perceived abridgment of civil liberties ("the same doctrine which undergirded Nullification and Secession"), and transferred such paranoia to the ranks of its citizen soldiers when war came. Seeking alternatives to the blood baths of a conventional battlefield like Shiloh or to straitjacketing service under martinet officers, it was but a short leap of faith to remember swashbuckling ancestors who rode with the Swamp Fox and Gamecock. Many enlisted in the bands of Morgan, Forrest, and lesser-renowned partisan rangers who would battle Yankees on their own terms.[22]

That an element of brigandage lurked just beneath the veneer of this grassroots fervor escaped the paeans to these cavaliers of Dixie. Popular image easily lifted middle-class businessman John Hunt Morgan to the position of aristocratic knight of the Bluegrass. That Iberian guerrillas, Carolina frontiersmen, or even some of Bedford Forrest's rough-hewn men might have quibbled about such upper-class identification did not matter. Morgan, Turner Ashby in Virginia's Shenandoah Valley, and Jeff Thompson in Missouri provided models to assuage the pain of the Henry-Donelson, Shiloh, Island No. 10, and other disasters, even though irregular warriors had been in this war since mid-1861.

For instance, the Nashville *Union* reported on June 19 of that year that rebel cavalry had visited a cotton plantation owner near Smyrna, in Rutherford County, Tennessee, requesting that he burn his crop. He had refused, and they promptly murdered several of his slaves. Arrests were made in what, at that time, was more a civil than a military crime. East Tennessee had been ablaze with irregular warfare since the following November, and there were also increased irregular activities in the western part of the state, understandable since turbulent Missouri lay only across the Mississippi River.[23]

Curiously enough, the notion of irregular troops as part of Tennessee's military response had surfaced soon after secession. Governor Isham G. Harris received proposals to raise irregulars (or in two cases even "male free persons of color") from Theodore Harris of Pulaski in Giles County, A. O. W. Lattern of Jackson, S. J. Rudd of Gallatin County, Kentucky, B. B. Seat (a former Tennessean who had moved to Benham, Texas), as well as from several volunteers at Camp Zollicoffer and David Hubbard of Okolona, Mississippi. The general assembly actually empowered the governor to receive free African-American males between ages fifteen and fifty into military service at his own discretion. However, nothing was done at the state level concerning guerrillas as a natural offspring of the militia system. Lattern, at least, foretold that "If the people are armed, and have powder, ball and caps in their houses, ready for use, they will rise en masse and the whole country will be filled with armed men to repel the enemy at every point." As he observed sagely, no "more deadly and destructive antagonism" could be raised to repel invaders, and at "small expense to the state."[24]

Later, once Tennessee troops had joined Confederate service, the bishop-general Leonidus Polk, commanding at Columbus, Kentucky, on November 5, had authorized Len G. Paxon to "raise guerrillas" for scouting duty. Men responded from as far as Clarksville, Tennessee. A month later, a small expedition from Colonel Nathan Bedford Forrest's Tennessee cavalry regiment shot and killed a local unionist named Scott near Marion, Kentucky. Scott had led a band "sworn to shoot Southern men from their houses and behind trees," Forrest claimed. He had already lost several men from Captain J. D. Biffle's company to such action near Hopkinsville on October 14.

Scouring the Eddyville and Caseyville neighborhood from their base at Hopkinsville, Forrest's men thought they were "giving confidence to the Southern-rights men, and destroying the distorted ideas of Union men" who had expected the worst from the rebels. This intimidation, along with requisition of large quantities of cattle and hogs "under the auspices of the expedition," became trademarks of partisan warfare over the next three years. In fact, with Forrest and Morgan in late 1861 came the protean beginnings of independent mounted operations, unconventional warfare, psychological pressure, and confiscation of supplies regardless of ownership. Not without cause, a unionist shopkeeper "patronized" by Morgan's men at Harrington, in Bedford County south of Murfreesboro in early May 1862, considered them mere felons.[25]

Prewar feuds and other neighborhood quarrels (only some of which were based on political differences) also figured prominently in the rise of irregular warfare in areas like the Kentucky–Tennessee border on the Cumberland Plateau. Willis Scott Bledsoe, John M. Hughs, and Q. C. Sanders fought as members of conventional Confederate units at Mill Springs, Kentucky, in January, then left the Twenty-fifth Tennessee to operate on their own. They enflamed the border, occasionally joining raiding parties like those of John Hunt Morgan. Other shadowy characters included "colonels" James Bowles (a Louisville native) and Joseph T. Tucker, who likewise slipped in and out of formal association with Morgan. The infamous Champ Ferguson did likewise, when he was not carrying on his feud with Union guerrilla "Tinker Dave" Beatty in Fentress County. Beatty, in turn, represented the code of the mountains, carried over into the war. Because one local judge, Jefferson Goodpasture, had defended him in a prewar indictment, Beatty left this Confederate sympathizer and protector of rebel partisans alone.[26]

A brief truce occurred on this border sometime in March 1862. Initiated by a meeting known as "the winter compromise," drawn up by Goodpasture and unionist Elijah Kogier, border belligerents set aside their arms and raids upon one another. The lull ended, predictably, when regular campaigning resumed in April. Confederate Captain J. W. McNairy (together with Hughes and Bledsoe) undertook an expedition to Fentress and Clinton Counties in Kentucky to recover stolen property and retaliate against alleged unionist depredations. They battled Beatty and company near Romes Mill. Then, the bloodshed abated once more when Ferguson and Bledsoe went south to cooperate with Morgan in his May raid in Middle Tennessee. Action resumed in June, however, when Ferguson murdered Kogier without remorse. As he told a postwar jury in Nashville, Kogier "was a treacherous dog and richly merited his fate." Such was the guerrilla code in the Cumberlands.[27]

This type of conflict generally remained scattered and sporadic early in the war. Grant's warning about guerrillas forming at Eddyville, Kentucky, his dispatch of Lowe's men to protect unionists at Paris, Tennessee, and his report from Savannah, Tennessee that a prominent union sympathizer named Cherry had lost all of his cotton to rebel bands punctuated concern in March about such random lawlessness. On March 5, Lieutenant William Gwinn commanding the gunboat *Tyler* on the Tennessee River called his superior's attention to the unionist cast of two counties upriver near Savannah, thereby suggesting the possibility of exploiting civil dissent from established rebel authority in that area. Citing large popular majorities in both Hardin and McNairy Counties on the secession issue during the last election, he noted the constant cry from these people to "send us arms and a sufficient force to protect us in organizing, and we will drive the secessionists out of Tennessee ourselves." Such sentiments continued to fuel false hopes in Washington and were bitterly dashed as the year wore on. Buell's chief of staff, Colonel James B. Fry, wrote Major General George H. Thomas from Huntsville, Alabama, on July 11 that eighty or ninety "citizens from this country about 25 mile south have come in to enlist in our army." As many more were trying to get in "but prevented by the rebel cavalry and guerrillas." Even the slightest signal of Unionism seemed to fuel guerrilla activity that confronted professional soldiers in Middle and West Tennessee by mid-1862.[28]

Irregular warfare especially increased with the advance of Major General Don Carlos Buell's legions into north Alabama. Occupying the Huntsville area produced "the bitterest feelings" among the local populace, according to Brigadier General Ormsby McKnight Mitchel. These feelings quickly translated into irregular attacks on trains, telegraph lines, bridge guardposts, the capture of couriers, and even interference with sawmilling and Tennessee river traffic generally. One enterprising Michigan major converted a local ferryboat to counter the partisans until enemy gunfire near Gunter's Landing demonstrated the craft's frailty for such service. Such demonstrations of a militia war or civil resistance apart from the Confederacy's main armies held omens for the future war in the West.[29]

The Revolutionary spirit of Lexington and Concord could be seen in the June 19 proclamation in the exiled Memphis *Appeal* that declared that the enemy should not be allowed to advance farther. "Let them at every advance," said the newspaper, "meet with a deadly volley from every thicket." Every rifle and shotgun in the country should be requisitioned and every Yankee soldier taught that each step they made farther south "is made with hazard to themselves. . . . Even in the absence of any army," declared this rebel sheet, "it is within the power of the citizens of the country, by a judicious and well organized system of ambuscades and guerrilla warfare, to harass, terrify and hold the enemy at bay." Here was the doctrine of armed citizenry in defense of its home and civil rights against a tyrannical enemy. No wonder the newspaper boasted: "A people determined to be free will submit to any sacrifice and cannot be conquered." Such a contention remained to be proven, however.[30]

In retrospect, differences between regular troops, partisan rangers, and guerrillas would become blurred over time. Subsequent depredations committed in the name of the Union or the Confederacy by armed and mounted (or dismounted) men in various garb and under varied conditions would become indistinct to the popular press, regular military officials, and especially the citizenry. Outlawry and brigandage by deserters, freebooters, bushwhackers, or jay-hawkers—all titles became interchangeable—would break down finely constructed legal walls designed to keep the war civilized. Pillage, murder, and torture (and possibly occasional rape) would be committed in the name of partisan or guerrilla warfare. Each side blamed the other for such atrocities, and perhaps both sides freely committed them. In an area fought over for three long years, the niceties of who belonged to which army or in what capacity came to matter little to the populace. But, in the spring of 1862, all was hope and glory, as the mounted knights of the Confederacy—whether regular or irregular—seemed to southerners to offer an appropriate way to stop the invader.

HEARTLAND PARTISANS IN ACTION

Recruiting of partisan units under the ranger act took time. The lure of such duty caused some youth to evade conscription and affected general army recruitment just as earlier critics had predicted. The conscription act required all white males between eighteen and thirty-five (raised to forty the next year), to serve for three years. Those already in the ranks as twelve-month volunteers would receive a thirty-day reenlistment furlough and a fifty-dollar reenlistment bonus. They could reorganize their units and elect their own new leaders. Or they could allow their term of service to expire, be mustered out, and face conscription. Or they could join a partisan unit.

Those options blunted criticism for a while. Within the rebel armies, "no complaint or murmuring was made at this arbitrary proceeding," claimed Captain Thomas B. Wilson, a Davidson County resident with the First Tennessee Cavalry. "The only injustice done was that the officers who failed to be reelected were let off and got out of the army entirely," he said. Wilson felt that they should have been conscripted as others were, but he probably failed to realize that some either ended up in a partisan band or went home to serve with a local defense unit. In any event, measures like the partisan act, or subsequent exemptions for certain categories of manpower, caused leakage to the West Pointers' carefully crafted veteran ranks. Those leaks would affect war and society in Kentucky and Tennessee during the coming months.[31]

With principal Confederate forces in the West stymied after Shiloh, the conflict became a "war in the shadows" in which rebel horsemen garnered most of the honors. As the men of Morgan and Forrest (recovered from a wound suffered at the close of Shiloh) fanned out across northern Alabama, Mississippi, Tennessee, and eventually even Kentucky, attacking Federal outposts and supply lines, such movements provided a catalyst for opposition to Federal occupation. Although no pattern became immediately evident, partisan bands began to congeal around local charismatic leaders bent upon mischief. They were naturally aided by a friendly populace.

Illustrative, if not necessarily indicative, was Adam Rankin Johnson, one of the better-known and respected Kentucky partisans. Son of a Henderson doctor and his wife (both unionists), Johnson had brothers on both sides during the war. He had passed the prewar years on the Texas frontier, where he learned firsthand the harsh brutalities of Indian warfare. After joining Forrest's command at Hopkinsville in 1861, Johnson and Robert M. Martin served as Forrest's most trusted scouts at Fort Donelson. Johnson escaped from that debacle in the company of Brigadier General John B. Floyd, witnessed the panic-stricken evacuation

Colonel (later Brigadier General) Adam Rankin Johnson, CSA, 1863. From Johnson, The Partisan Rangers of the Confederate States Army *(Louisville: George G. Fetter, 1904).*

of Nashville, carried dispatches from Sidney Johnston to Governor John Lubbock in Texas, and missed Shiloh. But he returned to Forrest's command in time to resume scouting duties thereafter. Attached to Major General John Cabell Breckinridge, Johnson and Martin received orders to return home and "bring out all the Kentuckians you can to serve as Southern soldiers." With that, Johnson launched an independent career, eventually leading to formation of the Tenth Kentucky Partisan Cavalry.[32]

Johnson and Martin experienced great difficulty recruiting anyone at first. Older men (many of whom like Captain Andy Ray were busily organizing their own bands), told Johnson point-blank: "What we want in Kentucky is a leader, and when one comes I will be willing to follow him, and could bring a good company to back him." A Federal amnesty policy and local hero worship by the fair sex also kept a number of ex-Confederates from returning to hardships of military service. Johnson then resolved "to make the Yankees run these stay-at-home Confederate soldiers out of the country." With only two companions he set about "kicking up a rumpus" by attacking the Union provost guard in his home town of Henderson on June 7. Local citizens considered Johnson and his comrades merely outlaws until Johnson told a newsman that the three were all Confederate soldiers. Recruits suddenly flocked to his standard as the newspapers spread word of his deeds. His recruiting agents went into Henderson, Daviess, and Union Counties with instructions to secure men for picket duty on the important roads where they would demand passports from citizens and foster the impression that various large and organized bands of Confederate partisans existed all over the western part of the state.[33]

Federal retaliation was swift as Louisville authorities sent a mounted regiment to Madisonville with instructions to destroy the houses of all citizens giving aid and comfort to these rebels. Johnson, in turn, gathered his recruits and routed this Yankee force in their camp near Madisonville, pursued them to Henderson, captured the town, and raised a Confederate flag atop the courthouse. Johnson and his men subsequently crossed the Ohio River and attacked Newburg, Indiana, in July using the ploy of two ersatz cannon (made from stovepipes) to overawe local home guards. From then on, Johnson was known as "Stovepipe" Johnson because of the fake cannon.

The effect of Johnson's actions was electric. Blueclad troops rushed to the affected river line as well as to posts along the Louisville and Nashville Railroad. Since Henderson was a major tobacco market, news of its capture found its way to the editorial pages of the *London Times*. "The price of that weed suddenly rose," noted Johnson. His force netted five hundred stand of arms, and, more important, recruiting moved ahead at a brisk pace. One of Johnson's earlier recruits and later Major Frank Amphilias Owen observed after the war, "soldiers, like other men, worship a rising rather than a setting sun." And "Stovepipe" Johnson was certainly on the rise as he now called his enhanced command "the Breckinridge Guards." Later, his men became the Tenth Kentucky Partisan Rangers.

Other guerrilla parties congealed during that summer of 1862. Like Johnson, Captain Ellis Harper of Lebanon, Tennessee, had been at Fort Donelson, and he had escaped after five months of subsequent imprisonment. He had gone home intent upon taking the Union oath of allegiance, but had been dissuaded by friends, who noted that as an escaped prisoner he was a wanted man. Harper stayed in hiding until he was recruited into Morgan's cavalry, but later operated more under Forrest than under the Kentuckian. T. Alonzo Napier, originally from Benton and Hickman Counties, had also been taken at Fort Donelson while commanding Company I of the Forty-ninth Tennessee. Sent with other junior officers to Johnson's Island, Ohio, he escaped on April 26 and returned home to organize what became styled "Napier's cavalry," which raised havoc in the district west of Columbia toward the Tennessee River. Jacob Biffle, Duncan Cooper, and Thomas J. Williams (all of Maury County) also recruited bands, as did Lewis Kirk of Lawrence County. W. W. Faulkner claimed West Tennessee and the Purchase area of Kentucky as his haunts. Even more notorious was Dick McCann, while to the east, closer to the Cumberland Mountains, reigned the infamous Champ Ferguson.[34]

Portions of the Federal Ninth Pennsylvania Cavalry, operating out of the Bowling Green–Scottsville–Glasgow area of south-central Kentucky, managed to temporarily clean out the nest of another partisan, Captain O. P. Hamilton. But his Celina, Tennessee, lair near the state line remained something of a guerrilla sanctuary, with Hamilton and parties slipping in and out for active operations.

This area also lay in a corridor through which Confederate raiders often passed northward into the Bluegrass. Colonel E. C. Williams, commanding the Pennsylvania horsemen, told his superior, Brigadier General Jeremiah Boyle, at Louisville that if he could take his whole re-armed regiment into the Tompkinsville, Kentucky, neighborhood "I feel confident that I can be of great service in driving out the robbers and restoring peace and quiet to that afflicted district." But at this point, more important tasks kept the thin line of blue defenders closer to the rail lines, and Williams's regiment soon found itself dispersed in parcels throughout the area from Tompkinsville westward as far as Madisonville in Hopkins County. They became ripe targets for Morgan's main force of raiders.

The partisan activity that developed in the late spring and summer from Kentucky to northern Mississippi and Alabama established patterns. Where partisan units could hit Federal supply and communication lines on defined military missions they did so. But often they focused more on political action—intimidation and harassment (sometimes pure deviltry and grudges or family feuds)—directed at punishing unionists and neutrals. Champ Ferguson, for example, had started killing unionists as early as November 1, 1861, more for personal and psychopathic reasons than any real military passion. Border strife on the Kentucky–Tennessee line simply escalated by March and April, when Pennsylvania and Kentucky Union cavalry rode search-and-destroy missions as far east as Cumberland and Clinton Counties in Kentucky, while Ferguson and Hamilton, as well as Morgan's men and others, ranged almost everywhere.[35]

By July, the guerrilla pestilence spread far more evenly across Middle and West Tennessee. Brigadier General James S. Negley, commanding at Columbia, reported at least two companies under Napier had formed the cadre of a regiment in the vicinity of Charlotte and Centerville (west of Columbia in Hickman County). Hardly a day passed that they did not commit some depredation on the railroad by stopping trains and pulling up rails. In June, Negley had fined local landowners "near whose property the telegraph wire was cut," a practice followed quite generally by Union commanders everywhere at this time. Even Buell finally told him not to confine his cavalry to defense but to "put a little life into it and destroy the marauding bands that hover around you." Negley then decimated Napier's band in a pitched battle at Kinderhook on the old Natchez Trace on August 17, thus eliminating both Napier and another group led by a partisan named Anderson. Yet, such triumphs were usually temporary.[36]

Negley noted that other bands easily eluded his pursuing parties. Cooper's group simply removed its headquarters to Persimmon Branch, six miles west of Ashland, while another group under Jake Biffle found haven some five miles south of Ashland. Tom Williams's contingent nested at Buffalo Creek, eight miles southwest of Henryville, Tennessee. Negley remained confident that when his Third Kentucky Cavalry was completely mounted, then it could strike at those guerrilla strong points. "These sudden dashes frighten many of the scoundrels back to their home," he contended.[37]

Nonetheless, even Stewart County (supposedly well under control of the Fort Henry and Fort Donelson garrisons) was thrown into turmoil by guerrilla seizure of guns at Tennessee Ridge (between Dover and Waverly) in late July. Meetings of "all peace-loving citizens opposed to guerrilla warfare" brought out some 175 unionists but few secessionists, and rumors circulated that guerrilla parties were secretly forming in that rural county. That same month, a picket party from the Twenty-third Minnesota of Murfreesboro's Yankee garrison was attacked "by a party of men, supposed to be citizens of the neighborhood" and all five of the party killed or wounded. Colonel William P. Boone, commanding the Gallatin garrison, rounded up a company of ninety guerrillas who were blatantly engaged in drilling in an old field between Gallatin and Hartsville only forty miles from occupied Nashville. Random but steady violence and increasing guerrilla activity accompanied the rising heat of summer.[38]

Even in Negley's tightly held Columbia—where he practiced enlightened but firm control to the extent of fitting out a special prison "into which many rabid rebels found their way"—guerrillas openly molested his stockyard just outside town. He admitted that "guerrilla parties are increasing rapidly west of this, strongly aided by disloyal citizens." Every day, he received intelligence about their intention to destroy the railroads and bridges, a threat exacerbated by heavy rains and floodwaters. In fact, the very next day, guerrillas caused a railroad wreck and by the end of July, he noted "guerrilla parties numbering in all about 300, are organized and preparing for some movement in the western portion of [Maury] and Hickman Counties." Similarly, from Pulaski, Brigadier General Speed Fry reported that guerrilla bands were organizing "in almost every direction," allowing that "we could now disperse them without much trouble, but if they are allowed to become thoroughly organized, we will be annoyed by them." Higher authority sympathized, as Buell had requested more cavalry from Secretary of War Edwin M. Stanton on May 12. "The warfare has already assumed a guerrilla character in Tennessee, and it is to be renewed in Kentucky by marauding bands organized in the State, assisted by a few rebel troops," he advanced.[39]

Conditions were as bad in West Tennessee and the Purchase section of Kentucky, where every citizen seemed to be as devout an enemy as any soldier clad in gray. Every farmer was a night rider that preyed on unionists in army blue and mufti alike. Ira Blanchard said that when his Twentieth Illinois entered Jackson, they found "a fine wealthy town, but terribly bitter against the 'northern hordes.'" The place had furnished a full regiment to the rebel army, he continued, and "we could see nothing but malice depicted on every countenance." His comrades were covered with dust and perspiration, so the town ladies "gathered up their skirts, turned up their noses and skipped away with the utmost horror at the sight of animals," he chuckled. However, the African Americans in town were more responsive, greeting their liberators with "De Lor bless you all," in Blanchard's words.[40]

Before long, Blanchard and company were busy rebuilding the Columbus and New Orleans rail line, and then patrolling it against partisans, while indulging freely in the spoils of local plantations and making off with young slaves for personal servants. The major rub was the partisans, however, since here as elsewhere, Federal commanders lacked the requisite cavalry to hunt down the partisans, and Grant's response was an increasingly stricter one. On July 3, 1862, he issued General Order Number 60. Military commanders who suffered material losses to guerrillas could seize a sufficient amount of personal property from people in the immediate neighborhood who expressed sympathy with the rebellion. After all, the people themselves had responsibility to suppress this system "being so pernicious to the welfare of the community where it is carried on." Thus, the government might be remunerated for all loss and expense of collection. Furthermore, those guerrillas without organization and uniforms would not receive treatment as legitimate prisoners of war.[41]

Two weeks later, Brigadier General Grenville Dodge reported from Trenton on the Memphis and Ohio Railroad that "the guerrillas are pressing me, and I am using all my cavalry force against them." Two days later he noted having nine hundred effective cavalry, "with the worst guerrilla county to take care of on [this] line of road." All of his force were out on countersweeps, he noted, since "the guerrillas are determined to give us work." Brigadier General I. F. Quinby, commanding the District of the Mississippi at Columbus, Kentucky, advised Grant on July 20 that reports reaching him had rebels capturing Clarksville and moving on Fort Henry with six hundred to eight hundred men. "Guerrila [sic] bands are forming through Western Kentucky and Tennessee, and unless they are promptly attacked and dispersed they will give us great trouble."[42]

Similar complaints reached Buell's headquarters from subordinates, like Ormsby Mitchel, in north Alabama. This area had become even more distressed than Tennessee with the appearance of Yankee troops in the spring. Astride the direct railroad route eastward to Chattanooga, the blue-coated troops had devoted great care and attention to controlling that line. At some points, however, they had gotten out of hand. The occupation of Huntsville on April 11, followed by the much ballyhooed "Sack of Athens" by Colonel John Basil Turchin's unruly Eighth Brigade on May 2, not only prompted much controversy but also led to mounting civil disobedience, as well as counterresponses by partisans. The situation soon became a revolving door of violence and accusations. Forty-five Huntsvillians claimed $54,689 in damages done by rampaging Federals. Mitchel rebutted all charges but admitted that such action "seems to have produced among rebels the bitterest feeling." Under the conciliatory policy in official fashion at this stage, Turchin was eventually court-martialed, Mitchel relieved (ostensibly for trafficking in cotton), and the Union rank and file were much demoralized by a confusing policy that seemed to allow hostile attacks by populace and guerrillas but gave soldiers no recourse to retaliation.[43]

Mitchel had written to the secretary of war on May 1: "This campaign is ended, and I now occupy Huntsville in perfect security, while all of Alabama north of Tennessee River floats no flag but that of the Union." Yet, within a month, his dispatches to Washington were filled with tales about guerrilla depredations, and he told Buell: "There is but one way of ridding the country of guerrilla bands, and that is to turn out against them a sufficient force of cavalry to pursue and utterly destroy them, with orders not to return till the work is ended." Mitchel advised Stanton on May 19 that "The most terrible outrages—robberies, rapes, arsons, and plundering—are being committed by lawless brigands and vagabonds." He wanted to punish all those found guilty by hanging them. The War Department responded three days later on May 22 by allowing him "to inflict the extreme penalty of military law upon persons guilty of the crimes specified in your telegram and upon those guilty of irregular or guerrilla warfare." Now it was up to the men in the field to track them down and exterminate this pestilence. And that is just what Union commanders attempted to do all summer.[44]

Both sides seemed quite ready to resort to the black flag of no quarter when on August 5, Captain Frank Gurley (whom the Federals declared a guerrilla, but who was apparently an enrolled member of the Fourth Alabama Cavalry) murdered the very popular Colonel Robert L. McCook, who was riding ill in an ambulance somewhere between Decherd, Tennessee, and New Market, Alabama. McCook's Ohio troops, many of them incensed German Americans (already well known for their rough treatment of civilians during service in western Virginia in 1861 and later in Middle Tennessee), wreaked vengeance up and down that part of the Tennessee River valley for miles. Of course, they never found the perpetrators, for they "had disbanded, and members appeared as citizens, until ordered out by the commander for another raid." Mrs. Mary Ione Chadick, wife of a Cumberland Presbyterian preacher at Huntsville, jotted in her diary that when the Yankees eventually evacuated the town later that month, Gurley immediately returned, arrested slave dealer and hotel proprietor James Hickman as a collaborator, and received a hero's welcome. He was "literally crowned with the wreaths of ivy and flowers," she beamed.[45]

Federal commanders came dangerously close to abrogating the unwritten rules of warfare at this point and completely losing control over the population. When Indiana colonel Abel D. Streight sought to lead an expedition into the Alabama hill country to the south in order to rescue unionists and recruit them to the Union army, fears of persecution and retaliation by their secessionist neighbors blocked his success. But, at the same time, Union conduct itself worked against reconciliation. Nearby Jackson County, which was actually unoccupied and supposedly the last place in the state "to acknowledge allegiance to the Southern Confederacy" was devastated by vengeful Union troops. The loyal editor of the Jacksonville *Republican* commented sullenly that between Huntsville and Stevenson the countryside was desolated, slaves run off, and railroad facilities destroyed so that "at their departure," the Federals actually "left fewer Union men than they found."[46]

Such actions provided grist for secessionist complaints against the invading vandals. Mrs. Chadick's diary from April to August is a chronology of Federal arrests, searches and seizures, insults to women, and convalescing Confederate soldiers, burnings, and disruption. "We are all prisoners of hope," she confessed on April 28, looking daily for saviors like John Hunt Morgan or Department of East Tennessee commander, Major General Edmund Kirby Smith. The wife of Confederate Alabama senator C. C. Clay seemed utterly shocked that Mitchel and others would confiscate her property or that the senator's aged father, a former Alabama governor, would be arrested and relegated to home confinement dur-

Tishomingo Hotel and railroad station, Corinth, Mississippi. National Archives and Records Administration.

ing Union occupation. Nothing so graphically illustrated the wide gulf in understanding between military and civilian in the upper Confederate heartland that spring and summer. Yankee soldiers and southern civilians (regardless of political preference) stood a chasm apart on the code of war. It hardly helped when midwestern northern volunteers acted irresponsible. Vett Noble of the Fourteenth Michigan recounted how he and a comrade, straggling from their regiment, would stop at any house about dusk and call for supper. "We would eat supper, lodge & get breakfast," he told his mother, then ask the homeowner what the bill was, and "tell them to charge it to Uncle Samuel, say good morning and leave."[47]

By August 23, General Dodge could report having taken nine hundred shotguns and five hundred rifles from guerrillas and citizens. Still, just three days before, Grant had wired Halleck in Washington that guerrillas were becoming so active in West Tennessee that a large mounted force was needed to suppress them. Could he not receive more cavalry? Stanton replied typically that horses were being procured to mount two additional regiments and that manpower levies would go in part to Kentucky and Tennessee. Even then, Union horsemen at this stage of the conflict were poorly trained and indifferently equipped—and most were certainly badly deployed.[48]

Static infantry garrisons proved no match for fast-moving, brigade-size raiding forces employed by the rebels in the wake of Morgan's late spring success. Moreover, the Federals had little chance for successful interception of partisan bands either. What maturing Federal units like the Second and Fifth Iowa, Third and Fourth Kentucky, and Seventh and Ninth Pennsylvania Cavalry gained was a sort of tactical training at the hands of Morgan, Forrest, and the elusive irregulars. The very lack of horsemen, teamed with dispersal of the armies to occupy territory and reconstruct the inhabitants, deterred Union advances all summer. Confederate leaders could thank the partisan rising for that.

THE GERM OF COUNTEROFFENSIVE

Federal authorities faced more than an emergent raider-partisan threat in the summer of 1862, however. Halleck's dispersal of his vast army after Corinth opened the way for a Confederate military renaissance. Thus, General Braxton Bragg, who succeeded an ailing and insufficiently aggressive Beauregard in charge of Department Number 2 following the Louisianan's evacuation of Corinth, sensed strategic possibilities for a massive counterstroke. Middle Tennessee seemed especially ripe, as Forrest reported the populace of that section had become intensely hostile to the enemy.

The proper objective appeared at first to be Nashville. Such a move would certainly force Buell to withdraw from north Alabama and the approach to Chattanooga. It might even cause Grant and yet a third Union general in the field, Major General William S. Rosecrans, to divert their forces from West Tennessee and northern Mississippi to assist Buell. Indeed, Bragg wrote Major General Sterling Price, the Confederate commander in that sector, on August 2 that with Grant diverted "the road is open for you into Western Tennessee." In turn, Price communicated with Brigadier General Earl Van Dorn commanding the Mississippi River at Vicksburg, proposing that the two cooperate and "move irresistibly through Western or Central Tennessee and advance our armies concurrently into Kentucky." That ever-present Lorelei of borderland Kentucky appeared anew.[49]

Information from Morgan and his second-in-command Basil Duke also suggested that "nothing is wanted but arms and support to bring the people [of Kentucky] into our ranks, for they have found that neutrality has afforded them no protection." Thus lured again by dreams of glory and the notion of possibly wintering on the Ohio River, Major General Edmund Kirby Smith at Knoxville very quickly fell prey to the Kentuckians' blandishments. By early August, he had convinced Bragg of the attractiveness of bypassing Nashville and moving directly to the Bluegrass. Richmond authorities agreed that interdepartmental cooperation was vital, but everyone wasted time late in the summer negotiating that coordination. Frankly, little could be done until Bragg laboriously moved his army across to Chattanooga anyway, ensured its protection, then mustered sufficient arms to start northward; moreover, the Confederate command had to wait until Van Dorn and Price could get their own act together.[50] Not that the sluggish Federals showed much energy in countering Confederate plans. They were bogged down in countering partisan threats to supply lines.

Cessation of partisan ranger recruitment, in order to ensure enforcement of the conscription law, further delayed Confederate maneuvers and may have actually cost the leadership an invaluable tool for permanently obstructing Union offensive operations. Nonetheless, Bragg confidently predicted the Federals would retreat, and by late August he urged Price and Van Dorn to speed up their plans and actions. This pair concurred on an ultimate goal of Paducah, Kentucky, but then proceeded to haggle over the more immediate objective of defeating Union forces around Corinth and Iuka, Mississippi.[51]

Bragg wired Price on August 27 that Smith, reinforced by two brigades from Bragg's army, had turned Cumberland Gap and "is now marching on Lexington, Ky." Buell's long line of communications back to Louisville could now be outflanked. "If Kentucky be as ripe for the move as all representations indicate, it must involve the abandonment of Middle Tennessee by the Federals," claimed Smith. Delay would only lose "the golden opportunity," since autumn would find "her people powerless and a large army between us and the waters of the Ohio," he noted. The anticipated return of Brigadier General Simon Bolivar Buckner and other Kentuckians from their post-Donelson imprisonment would be invaluable, for "[Buckner's] name is a division in any movement on Kentucky." Moreover, the conscript law could be applied in Kentucky and also would cause thousands of East Tennesseans to "to stand shoulder to shoulder with defenders of the Confederacy." Those who ran away "will be a happy riddance," Smith felt. Indicating complete agreement with Bragg, Smith told Jefferson Davis: "It is a bold move, offering brilliant results, but will be accomplished only with hard fighting, and must be sustained by constant re-enforcements."[52]

Smith's words received reinforcement when Union Kentucky brigadier Jeremiah Boyle issued an order telling the families of all men in Confederate service from that state or who intended to live in the Confederacy to leave the Bluegrass by September 1 or face imprisonment or expulsion. The Confederate commander in northwest Virginia, Brigadier General Humphrey Marshall, added to the urgency by sending word that the ultimate insult to southern chivalry was also taking place in Kentucky—women were being imprisoned. "It is our moment of trial, and unless we strike our friends must be overwhelmed," he declared, but he admitted quietly: "I may overestimate the importance of Kentucky to the welfare of the Confederacy."[53]

Smith seemed to be dictating strategy (although possessing the smaller of the Confederate columns) as Bragg promised to begin his advance into Middle Tennessee, "ignoring the enemy's works at Stevenson, Alabama, Murfreesboro, Tennessee and elsewhere." Smith countered by suggesting that "before I move far into Kentucky, Forrest with his cavalry [should] be ordered to destroy the railway bridges north of Nashville, which are not guarded, as then Buell could not possibly fall back rapidly, enough to interfere with me." Then, he caught the essence of coordination difficulties with Bragg: "The nature of the country and distance between us of course renders [Bragg's] marching up in time entirely impracticable."

Preparations for the great crusade accelerated as partisans were directed to disrupt affairs in north Alabama and Tennessee. Ordnance officers received orders to push arms repairs and collection, while paroled and exchanged officers and men from the disasters at Forts Henry and Donelson, Island Number 10, and Madrid Bend were to "be restored to their old companies and regiments." They would be reorganized and distributed to rendezvous at Tupelo, Mississippi, and Chattanooga. Bragg especially wanted "Kentuckians and Tennesseans as a general rule" to report to Chattanooga. Exchanged Kentucky brigadier Lloyd Tilghman, who had surrendered Fort Henry, returned to the army in charge of the rendezvous camps, while Richmond sent Buckner to East Tennessee to lend his appeal to the Kentucky invasion as Kirby Smith had wanted.[54]

Even the Kentucky delegation in the Confederate Congress entered into the spirit of the moment, pointing out how Union authorities had suppressed Kentucky political sentiment at the ballot box and now governed the state by bayonet. They urged that native sons John C. Breckinridge, Buckner, and Humphrey Marshall lead the advance so as to restore Kentuckians' confidence in the vitality of the Confederate movement. Then, by the last week in August, Kirby Smith had experienced his first difficulties as he advanced across the Cumberland range into Kentucky. Union brigadier George Washington Morgan stubbornly refused to yield Cumberland Gap. The Confederates had to circumvent that obstacle as well as overcome the animosity of southeastern Kentucky mountaineers, many of whom "bushwhacked" the advancing rebel column. Smith informed Richmond that he would push on to the more favorably disposed Bluegrass region at Lexington, but "should we not be largely supported by the loyal citizens of Kentucky, the maintenance of our position will depend upon the movement of General Bragg's column and the arrival of reinforcements from East Tennessee."[55]

Bragg assured Price at Tupelo, Mississippi, on August 27, that Buell had certainly fallen back from the Memphis and Charleston "and will probably not make a stand this side of Nashville, if there." The Federals were fortifying the capital but with Kirby Smith reinforced by two brigades from Bragg's Army, "we shall thus have Buell pretty well disposed of," leaving Sherman and Rosecrans (i.e., Grant's force) to Price and Van Dorn. Bragg was "satisfied that you can dispose of them, and we shall confidently expect to meet you on the Ohio and there open the way to Missouri." Rhetorical bombast, or impossible dream aside, Confederate military commanders appeared confident that their three-pronged counteroffensive would succeed. No doubt the Confederates were on the move; Kirby Smith's ten to twelve thousand men had moved into Kentucky; Bragg's approximately thirty thousand moved toward Middle Tennessee; the Price–Van Dorn wing of twenty-five thousand pressed northward toward West Tennessee. Much depended upon their timing, their coordination, and their opponents.[56]

Buell's forty-five-thousand-man Army of the Ohio had delighted Washington authorities by getting on the "direct line to Atlanta," so that "Smith must abandon East Tennessee or be captured," as he boasted to Halleck on June 11. Accordingly, Halleck told Military Governor Andrew Johnson ten days later that "the enemy is driven out of West Tennessee," while East Tennessee would soon be clear of the rebels, "and the regeneration" of the state was "not far off." Only rebel horsemen seemed capable of uncontrolled action, as they undertook thrusts behind vulnerable Union supply lines. With thirteen hundred horsemen, Morgan penetrated north and east of Nashville and exploited the dishevelment of his native Kentucky. Forrest's three-regiment brigade went into Middle Tennessee directly "to delay Buell's movement until Bragg's columns may make their appearance." After much negotiation and foot dragging, Bragg and Richmond authorities had accommodated one another in a plan to leave the Mississippi valley properly protected while Bragg moved to Chattanooga, a transfer that took weeks to accomplish because of the South's rickety rail lines and roundabout river routes. Meanwhile, the long Union lines of communication provided inviting targets for rebel horsemen.[57]

UNION LOGISTICS, POLITICS, AND SUMMER DOLDRUMS

Neither army could put together an advance during the height of the campaigning season. Bragg's experience with logistical delays in shifting wagons and artillery from Mississippi equated with Halleck's and Buell's frustrations at receding water levels in the navigable rivers and the overstretched rail supply system. The armies postured and countermarched to little purpose, it seemed. Union soldier W. E. Patterson suggested from northern Mississippi that the summer had been nothing but one big trek until his unit settled near Jacinto in mid-August. They had occasionally heard from Sterling Price, he declared, "but he did not cultivate a close acquaintance." Their nearest neighbor and friend was a secessionist gentleman named Davenport whose two sons were in the rebel army. "We guarded his property, devoured his fruit and confiscated two or three of his juvenile negroes," Patterson observed dryly. Others, like Tighlman Jones of the Fifty-ninth Illinois, helped gather cotton bales at Iuka, Mississippi, while several enterprising Yankee merchants who followed the army encouraged local girls to "use northern prints and hoops to adorn themselves with."[58]

Basically, Patterson and Jones were both simply defending supply lines. Supplies were essential to the armies' success, and foraging or local procurement could not substitute for reprovisioning from a distant base. Civil War armies required a massive buildup of supplies before launching major operations. Railroads and rivers conveyed Federal supplies to forward distribution points, but wagon trains had to take food, forage, and ammunition to the troops. Emergencies naturally prompted adjustments, but, as Buell's chief of staff Colonel James B. Fry put it to Louisville chief quartermaster Colonel Thomas Swords on June 29, the supply lines had to be prepared "at all times for the present to transport forage and rations at the rate of 200 tons a day, and these supplies must be sent forward in the proportion of one pound of subsistence stores to three and a half pounds of forage," and this exclusive "of extra stores, like clothing, ordnance, etc." It had not helped that two hundred wagons had been idled "because their drivers went off and could not yet be replaced," Buell told Halleck on June 12. Logistics was a tall order for men still learning the trade of large-scale warfare at this stage.[59]

Yet, key officials worked wonders. J. B. Anderson, Buell's railroad repair chief, engaged crews to rebuild burned-out bridges, wrecked rails and ties, as well as to rehabilitate or acquire rolling stock and locomotives. Colonel William P. Innes's First Michigan Regiment of Engineers and Mechanics spearheaded the work, refurbishing the Nashville–Decatur and part of the Nashville–Chattanooga lines in record time. Enemy partisans and cavalry kept his crews under constant pressure and cut the railroad and telegraph lines almost as quickly as the Federals reconstructed them. The answer to these depredations seemed to lie in some better type of bridge protection, and Buell set his chief engineer, Captain James St. Clair Morton, to the task of designing proper defenses. Morton, a hard-working thirty-six-year-old army regular, renowned for his flowing locks and beard, designed octagonal log stockades for each bridge crossing, from which small garrisons might fight any raider. The eighteen-hundred-man First Michigan engineers, plus future garrison troops and even local slaves, then went to work cutting timber and constructing the positions. Eventually, these strong points stretched south from Elk River to north Alabama, and, by the first of August, the rail defenses were virtually complete for most of the line back to Nashville.[60]

The flimsy bridge stockades alone proved inadequate. Mounted interception and rapid transport of reinforcements by rail were the key to defense. But, as in everything that summer, limited resources of manpower, horses, and equipment stunted the effort. Buell might demand quick action of Morton, but every garrisoned strong point sapped main army strength from the principal mission. Supply and logistics bedeviled Union military operations, even though everyone worked the system of men and machines to its limits. Senior generals never quite understood this problem. Buell continued to badger his subordinates about closing a twenty-mile gap in the Nashville–Decatur line that forced vulnerable wagon trains to keep two hundred to three hundred tons of forage and supplies moving daily to troops farther south. At the same time, ever testy union supply personnel constantly complained about receiving barely a tenth of their requisitions. The answer given usually involved "a deficiency in rolling stock" on the Louisville and Nashville Railroad.[61]

The war's progress became measured in poundage not mileage, as army quartermasters failed to find enough railroad equipment, wagons, or shallow-draft boats to accommodate what appeared to be the voracious appetite of Buell's army. Buell tried to explain this to Halleck on July 11 and encountered increasing pressure from Washington concerning his inertia. He still hoped to accomplish his mission of advancing on Chattanooga without unnecessary delay and in a manner "neither to jeopardize my army nor its honor nor trifle with the lives of loyal citizens betrayed to the vengeance of their enemies by a promised protection and hurried abandonment." But consumption of one hundred thousand pounds of daily rations required allocation of five hundred wagons, and subsistence for the army's animals from a landscape "already exhausted of supplies" took sixty more wagons. Three hundred additional wagons were necessary "for service in the interior." Buell ordered repair of the Green River locks in Kentucky and told Swords to ship as much forage as possible by that stream to Bowling Green as well as via the Cumberland to Clarksville. Laborers would then reload aboard railroad cars for the trip farther south.[62]

Everyone played with statistics. Chief of Staff Fry pointedly told Louisville supply personnel that since the L&N, the Cumberland River, and the Green River were all "open to us," then "if we don't get supplies it can only be our own fault."

Supplies were to be stockpiled at Nashville, government business was to be systematized on the railroad, and order brought from chaos. Still, supply was not the only irritation for field generals that summer. The Virginia and Trans-Mississippi Theaters had also slowed in stubborn fighting. President Abraham Lincoln wanted twenty-five thousand men sent east from Tennessee until Halleck reminded him on July 5 that either the Chattanooga expedition would have to stop or any hope of holding West Tennessee would have to be abandoned. "I must earnestly protest against surrendering what has cost us so much blood and treasure, and which, in a military point of view, is worth more than three Richmonds," he told the commander-in-chief.

Washington officials backed off when Halleck wrote Secretary of War Edwin Stanton from Corinth, Mississippi, on July 1, pleading that western generals counted but sixty-five thousand effectives against seventy-five to eighty thousand rebels and that they had to repair and guard three hundred sixty-seven miles of railroads between front lines and the rear. Halleck had also informed Lincoln that "for the last week there has been great uneasiness among Union men in Tennessee on account of the secret organizations of insurgents to cooperate in any attack of the enemy on our lines." Any loss on the part of Union forces "will be followed by insurrection in Tennessee and Kentucky" and even greater difficulty pacifying those states than encountered in Missouri. To some degree, the fog of war between Washington and the West cleared a bit when Halleck went east to replace Major General George B. McClellan as general-in-chief.[63]

Moreover, politician Andrew Johnson remained a thorn to the generals. He never ducked an opportunity to tell either Halleck, Buell, or Lincoln how his needs had been neglected. Colonel J. F. Miller's 3,537-man protection force at Nashville seemed insufficient to him. Actually, Johnson was particularly peeved that Buell had ordered Colonel Lewis D. Campbell's Sixty-ninth Ohio into the field. The Tennessean had personally helped raise the regiment in Columbus, Ohio, and Stanton had personally allocated this unit to Johnson. Professing belief in God and Christianity to the celebrated Ohio preacher-colonel Granville Moody one day, Johnson barked, "but I'll be damned if Nashville shall be taken." By August 1, the governor had reputedly "changed his ideas in regard to treating rebels with lenity [sic]." Now, he believed that "they must be made to feel the burden of their own deeds and to bear everything which the necessities of the situation require should be imposed on them." So he continued to barrage the administration with complaints about his defenseless condition. The ever-present threat of Confederate raids and the generally unsettled condition of the region around the state capital kept civil-military relations on edge all summer. But Halleck had already told Stanton pithily back on April 26 that the Union armies were the politicians' first line of defense and that time did not permit the army to hunt disloyal civilians. "We are now at the enemy's throat, and cannot release our grasp to pare his toe-nails." Apparently the toe-nails, not the enemy's throat, bothered Johnson.[64]

In truth, Governor Johnson's troubles with western army professionals concerning the defense of Nashville paralleled those of Lincoln and Stanton with eastern generals concerning the defense of the city of Washington. The civilians needed the comfort of nearby military protection to assure their power and authority in seats of government. Only a strong garrison could provide that protection, while men like Halleck, Buell, and McClellan viewed their field armies as sufficient deterrents to the enemy. They could ill afford what they considered tertiary missions, whether such missions involved protection of cities, counterguerrilla operations, or even suppression of civilian dissidence. Of course, Nashville contrasted with Washington as a bastioned city at this point. Fortifications for the Tennessee capital would come, but resolution of this fundamental difference in the handling of Union military forces remained unresolved for much of the war. It certainly was not close to solution in the spring and summer of 1862, and Johnson's badgering only enflamed relations between senior men in uniform and politicians.[65]

Johnson kept busy with other political-military chores during this period also. Under heavy guard, he attempted to spread unionism in heavily secessionist Middle Tennessee towns like Murfreesboro. The town was rapidly becoming a Union supply base, but its citizens never gave up hope of deliverance that summer. He occasionally tried to coerce Confederate captives in the local penitentiary to recant and take the oath of allegiance. One such captive, Rufus Howell Cook, had been captured while convalescing from the rebel army at his home in Jackson County, Alabama and shipped to Nashville. Cook, like others, refused the oath of allegiance and actually escaped thanks to local secessionist ladies, who brought food (and a hacksaw) to the prisoners. Johnson was more successful with other captives, who preferred a Yankee oath to death in a dank cell.[66]

Johnson also welcomed news from Lieutenant Colonel Thomas C. James of the Ninth Pennsylvania Cavalry that Clarksville, another county seat and secessionist hotbed, seemed to be showing a resurgence of unionism. But the hardbitten East Tennessee politician complained to Halleck and Washington about Buell's indifference to the actions of Provost Marshal Stanley Matthews of Nashville and Assistant Adjutant General Oliver D. Greene, who blocked the governor's confiscation of rebel colonel Adolphus Heiman's home (Heiman was in prison at Johnson's Island resulting from his capture at Fort Donelson). Johnson also protested that Tennessee Union troops, recruited to redeem the eastern part of the state, had been placed under Buell's command rather than assigned to a loyalist like former governor Alexander Campbell, and he let Lincoln know about his ire in no uncertain terms.[67]

The long-suffering president predictably chided Johnson gently on July 11. "Do you not, my good friend, perceive that what you ask is simply to put you in command in the West?" he asked. Such would never do, said Lincoln, adding that he doubted Johnson truly wanted that anyway, but merely control "in your own localities." Still, that would disrupt other arrangements with the army, so why not simply have a conference with Halleck to iron out differences? He passed the suggestion on to the general, observing that "Governor Johnson is in great trouble and anxiety about a raid into Kentucky," and he reminded Halleck that "the Governor is a true and valuable man—indispensable to us in Tennessee."

But Lincoln knew that no conference would take place; Halleck was coming east. So that left Buell as the principal negotiator with Johnson, and the president made an error in judgment if he thought those two could resolve their differences.[68]

Still, the War Department made a good-faith effort to paper over the political-military difficulties in Nashville. Part of the problem was the dabbling that soldiers and politicians did in each other's domain at this time. Both Buell and Johnson involved themselves with confiscation of civilian property under the guise of military necessity and punishment of the truly disloyal. For instance, Buell's chief of staff wrote to one Nashville citizen, N. E. Alloway, about the V. K. Stevenson property, which had been seized "for the wants of the government." Stevenson, president of the Nashville and Chattanooga Railroad, had been very active in Confederate military affairs under Sidney Johnston and had fled south to continue such service. He had conveyed the house to Alloway "after the rebel army had commenced to evacuate Nashville, and when it was quite plain that the city would thus fall into our hands," said Buell's chief of staff, "and thus the transaction was void." Governor Johnson, likewise, used property seizures as a device to intimidate rebel sympathizers remaining in the city, so there was much working at cross-purposes during the early months following Union occupation.[69]

Johnson finally received permission in June to raise two Tennessee cavalry regiments for three years' service or the duration of the war. Less than a month later, escalating pressure from Confederate raids led the War Department to broaden Johnson's authority to include raising additional units, even infantry. The governor, who never forgot that his original charter had included "an adequate military force for the special purpose of a governor's guard," gradually constructed his own personal army by approving Tennessee West Pointer Alvan C. Gillem as recruiter and commander of the First Middle Tennessee Infantry (later the Tenth Tennessee). Drawing upon yet another proviso in his charter that permitted an expenditure of up to ten thousand dollars "for the purpose of organizing a Home Guard," Johnson supervised establishment of a military company, the Nashville Union Guards, to defend Nashville. Before long, he succeeded in ridding the city of Matthews and Greene and, by fall, even of Buell himself. For the moment, in July and August, everyone on the Union side braced for a sudden Confederate resurgence.[70]

FORREST RETAKES MURFREESBORO

Bold appearances by Forrest and Morgan and a partisan raid on Clarksville underscored Johnson's concern even more poignantly than his communiques to Washington. The two Confederate cavalry wizards descended almost simultaneously upon portions of the Federals' long line of communications. It was a prelude to the coveted Confederate counteroffensive in the West. Fry had alerted Union brigadier Morgan at Cumberland Gap on July 12 that "The rebel Morgan had advanced into Kentucky and reached and burned Lebanon; is advancing on Danville, and threatens Lexington and your line of communications." But it would soon be Buell's own line that received the greatest jolt. The dearth of cavalry in Kentucky made it difficult to check raiders there, and Fry told Morgan that everyone was on his own. Indeed, telegraph wires hummed in the Bluegrass with panicky communiques from Jeremiah Boyle and others about John Hunt Morgan. About this same time, Forrest appeared in Middle Tennessee, thus setting the whole region on edge.[71]

Morgan's escapade lasted from July 4 to July 28, as some 850 troopers from his old Second Kentucky, a composite battalion of Texans and Tennesseans under Major R. M. Gano, Lieutenant Colonel R. M. Nix's First Georgia Partisan Rangers, and two mountain howitzers accomplished what has been called his "First Kentucky Raid." Indicted for treason for a second time in his home state on June 19, Morgan may have simply felt challenged to test Federal control of the state before that control solidified. This raid featured stock tools of Morgan's style—swift-moving light cavalry, dismounted envelopment against enemy roadblocks, information derived from a friendly populace, as well as use of the telegraph to baffle pursuers, thanks to George Ellsworth, the lighthearted wire operator who rode by Morgan's side.[72]

The ghosts of Sumter and Marion rode with Morgan's men, a lusty, devilish crew with storybook fashion. The column knifed westward from Knoxville, took some casualties from unionist bushwhackers atop Walden's Ridge, then turned north at Sparta. At Tompkinsville, Kentucky, they captured most of Major Thomas J. Jordan's battalion of the Ninth Pennsylvania in a fair fight. Morgan's exploits attracted followers: independent companies under captains Bledsoe, Hamilton, McMillan, and Ferguson were picked up along the way. The raiders were opposed mostly by home guardsmen and even a scratch detachment of Cincinnati firemen with a brightly burnished twelve-pounder.

Actually, nobody posed much of an obstacle as Morgan's band covered over a thousand miles in twenty-four days, riding through Glasgow, Lebanon, Harrodsburg, and the heart of Kentucky, winning friends and drawing crowds of happy bystanders who lined town squares and roadsides. Thousands of weapons, hundreds of horses, and quantities of other supplies reputedly fell into their hands before Union authorities mustered stronger pursuit. Morgan then turned southward from Cynthiana and the road to Cincinnati and beat a hasty retreat back through Paris, Winchester, Richmond, and less hospitable southeastern Kentucky to Kirby Smith's sanctuary in East Tennessee.[73]

Both Morgan and Forrest had a military mission and a political one. The Kentuckian's aim was to dislocate Federal control over his home state while also disrupting Buell's supply far to the rear. The Tennessean's principal goal was to capture the Union supply base at Murfreesboro, but the goal also had political implications inherent to Confederate recapturing of Middle Tennessee. Buell advised Brigadier General William "Bull" Nelson, whom he soon sent to grapple with the mounted raids: "We have an object in Tennessee of far greater importance to the Union and to Kentucky than driving Morgan out of Kentucky." Forrest underscored the political implications of that statement when, having left Chattanooga on July 9, he soon met with exiled elected Tennessee governor Isham G. Harris at Altamont and Beersheba Springs en route to Murfreesboro. Harris's interest in Forrest's mission undoubtedly related to returning to power at Nashville should Bragg's army recapture the capital later.[74]

As he recovered from his Shiloh wound, Forrest remained an undetermined factor in the war's equation. A Memphis slave trader in peacetime, he was as representative of West Tennessee as Morgan was of the Bluegrass. He organized a new brigade of cavalry around Colonel John A. Wharton's Eighth Texas (Terry's Texas Rangers), Colonel W. J. Lawton's Second Georgia, another mounted battalion from the Peach State, and a rump contingent from the old First Kentucky, now led by Lieutenant Colonel Thomas G. Woodward. All of them were well aware of his reputation for willingness to engage in hand-to-hand combat with the enemy.[75]

Forrest's fourteen hundred troopers (and their African-American servants, according to one Federal commander) completely surprised the Murfreesboro post at dawn on July 13. Quartered in several separate camps around town with no coordinated command, several of the blueclad units nevertheless put up a fight. Rebel bravado and Forrest's experience won the day. He had implored his new comrades the night before to mark his birthday by showing courage. They did more than that, liberating the secessionist town, the railroad depot, and capturing about twelve hundred men of the Ninth Michigan, Third Minnesota Infantry, a detachment of the Seventh Pennsylvania Cavalry, and a four-gun Kentucky battery. Over five-hundred-thousand-dollars' worth of government stores, a transport brigade of sixty wagons, three hundred mules, and one hundred to two hundred horses, plus a stretch of the railroad and telegraph line fell into rebel possession. Much of the booty was consigned to flames by Forrest's jubilant men.

Happiest of all were the nearly four thousand residents of the town. Not only were one hundred and fifty prisoners freed from the town jail (several of them were spies, due to be hanged that day), but also a newly mustered-out chaplain of the Forty-fourth Tennessee, George Ewing Eagleton, was able to retrieve and destroy a copy of his oath of allegiance from Yankee headquarters. He had openly aided the raiders in their assault and feared retribution from the enemy. Indeed, many local secessionists like Eagleton left town with their families when they discovered that Forrest and his men were simply riding through and not establishing a permanent presence.[76]

Union authorities were aghast at the rebel's audacity. The surrender seemed to be a mystery, noted Jesse B. Connelly of the Thirty-first Indiana, attributing the attack planning and leadership to local citizenry. Some of the Confederates told their prisoners that, if one more assault had been stopped, the whole operation would have collapsed. Men like Connelly tended to criticize the post commander, young and untried Brigadier General Thomas T. Crittenden, a Kentucky-born Missouri lawyer and son of the old moderate politician and author of a prewar compromise designed to avert the war, John Crittenden. They blamed him for not expecting an attack in the midst of enemy country.[77]

Forrest, like Morgan, soon faded into the countryside, and then he moved to McMinnville for a short rest. The Federals reoccupied Murfreesboro with a vengeance. "Bull" Nelson led the retribution. He was "an overbearing tyrant," according to Rutherford County residents like William Henry King, as Nelson drew upon the family's four slaves to dig fortifications to prevent a recurrence of the Confederate mischief. But Federals met William Henry King's father's stubborn resistance. Old James Moore King was a veteran of Andrew Jackson's victory at New Orleans in 1815, and he defied these new invaders with similar ardor. King informed the requisitioning team that he would as soon erect a gallows to hang his own sons upon as consent to sending his slaves to construct fortifications to fight Confederate soldiers who were his friends and their sons. Accordingly, the Yankee answer was wholesale foraging on the King property: thousands of bushels of corn, livestock, demijohns of brandy, and widespread plundering brightened Yankee cooking pots for many months. Retaliation against civilians who supported partisans and raiders became the norm. Union soldier John Berger's simple statement to his homefolk from a campsite four miles south of Murfreesboro in September said it all—"we lived off of the country mostly on the march."[78]

Despite this northern retaliation, Morgan and Forrest had severely dislocated Buell's timetable. Nelson quickly used the rebuilt railroad to move large bodies of troops north and south of Nashville in pursuit of an elusive enemy. But his command was made up mostly of infantry and was utterly useless against mounted columns moving at high speed. "Old Monitor," as some of his men called him, promised no quarter for marauders, and Tennessee unionist cavalry received special license to prey on their neighbors in gray. Hoosier Jesse B. Connelly approved of the tougher policy, too, especially when they rode after partisans at McMinnville, for these men had not waged "honorable warfare." Still, Forrest and Morgan were neither guerrillas nor partisans but regular cavalry. Forrest continued to roam the capital region for a fortnight, defying the Federal units that were lumbering around with a three-hundred-pound Nelson while chasing rumors, sightings, and pleas from higher authority to "destroy Forrest if you can." They could not, and the pursuit slackened by the end of July. Forrest still threatened the area.[79]

Buell set to fortifying more posts and river crossings and reconstituting the Murfreesboro base for operations against the Middle Tennessee raiders. He also sought to explain all this to Washington. His message of July 22 was not very optimistic, for the enemy, he said, had thrown a large mounted force, made up of both regulars and irregulars, upon his lines of communication and "the embarrassment from this is great." Small guard posts had been totally inadequate; yet, the alternative of larger ones would soon disperse his army. Nashville was again threatened, but "whether really in danger or not its security is a matter of too vital importance to be left in jeopardy." More mounted troops were needed, as he explained vaguely: "I am compelled to ascribe the greater part of our annoyance from guerrilla bands to the spirit of hate and revenge which has been inspired in this quarter by an unwise policy and personal wrongs."[80]

Pressure mounted once more against Federal garrisons across the region. Guerrillas redoubled their efforts against the rail line to Decatur, forcing Negley at Columbia to strengthen bridge guards and dispatch search-and-destroy missions into the interior. Far to the northwest, Adam Johnson's partisans rode from their Union County, Kentucky, stronghold seeking active cooperation with Tom Woodward's band from Forrest's command. An ever-jittery brigadier Jeremiah Boyle in Kentucky and Governor Johnson at Nashville fussed about the uproar to Washington. Boyle incurred Buell's displeasure by using the L&N for his own movements to corner Morgan at the expense of supply trains bound for the main army. Boyle was new to his Kentucky command, having been appointed only on June 1 as a reward for recruiting success the previous year. Buell and Halleck remained unruffled for the most part, and Morgan's desultory destruction of the Salt River bridge and some spur line facilities in Kentucky were more irritating than truly harmful. Most of what Morgan attacked supported Union authorities in that state, not main army operations against Chattanooga.[81]

Nevertheless, Morgan succeeded admirably with the political part of his assignment. "The people of Georgetown also welcomed us with gladness and provided my troops with everything that they needed," he waxed enthusiastically on July 16. Many citizens simply turned out to see the phenomenon of this homegrown cavalier and his men. Some four hundred recruits appeared, offsetting battle losses incurred during the expedition. Still, whether or not latent secessionist sentiment truly burned in Kentucky breasts that summer can never be answered with certainty. More likely, Kentucky animosity at Boyle and other heavy-handed Federal authorities prompted the response to Morgan. Persecution of nonaligned and states' rights citizens had been building ever since Boyle had issued a June 9 order requiring the hated oath of allegiance and posting of bonds for future good conduct. The alternative was imprisonment, and Kentuckians reacted accordingly—they seemingly embraced Morgan and the Cause.[82]

Actually, the Lincoln administration raised little protest at what transpired in Kentucky. In fact, the administration further fueled the fires of discontent by announcing a plan to compensate emancipation of slaves—hardly calculated to win friends in slaveholding Kentucky. Then Boyle's resolute provost marshals and vindictive home guardsmen's enforcement of oath taking and military disruption of civilian courts, as well as Boyle's inflammatory statements, all played to Morgan's perception that his home state was ripe for Confederate redemption. By August, blueclad soldiers actively interfered with the election process in counties across the state, and everything pointed toward a secessionist renaissance. The only trouble was that the curiosity and frolic of Morgan's arrival may not have accurately reflected the depth of civilian commitment to any rebel alternative.[83]

One Kentuckian was not only displeased with Union control, but he also remained apprehensive of the ultimate result. Farmer and Methodist circuit rider George R. Browder of Logan County on the Tennessee border north of Clarksville expressed shock at Boyle's interference with civil rights, arguing that "the constitution prescribes no oath to private citizens or persons not in the official employment of the Government." He searched his conscience and concluded, "I think we will have dark days in Kentucky, and it will be long perhaps before the war is over." He decided to "suffer many things that are even painful to me," noting an increase in guerrillas, and how "there is indeed a prospect of troublous times before us."[84]

Kentucky will again be "the dark and bloody ground," he jotted in his diary on July 12, for guerrilla bands were hovering over the state, with enmity growing deeper and hatred intensifying as the unionists increased their intolerance of secessionists. Noting how Woodward's band was reportedly on the march for Hopkinsville at mid-month, he declared his fear of those "small bodies, called urellias [sic], coming in and scouring the county, and yet not in force enough to hold it." They would accomplish nothing more than to enflame hatreds and damage crops and other property. "I fear guerilla warfare more than the shock of vast armies in battle array," he claimed, for the irregulars "are never still—life, liberty and property are not safe an hour."

Another Kentuckian, Thomas H. Clay, wrote Lincoln from "Mansfield," near Lexington, on July 24, suggesting that, while Morgan would be disappointed in the number of recruits, "almost all the Federal troops had been withdrawn from the State, and it required some days to collect a sufficient force of cavalry to pursue him and act offensively." Other unionists had requested Clay to ask the chief executive for two regiments of cavalry on the line of the L&N and two more on the line from Lexington to Cumberland Gap. "As this guerrilla mode of warfare appears to have been generally adopted by the rebel authorities, it is absolutely necessary that in some mode it should be counteracted," Clay said. Confederate horsemen had indeed raised levels of Union apprehension, and seven new cavalry regiments soon joined the national colors in Kentucky alone.[85]

Buell excitedly ordered a speedup in railroad defense construction, and even sent engineer Morton back to fortify Nashville on August 6. The general wanted only small works for four to six companies and from two to four artillery pieces. But they were to command the principal roads and other prominent points, and they were to be beyond musket range of houses and other sharpshooters' havens yet close to the city. The earthworks were to be simple and practical "so that they can be constructed with the greatest promptness and occupied immediately by a small force." Expansion into a full-blown defense system might take place later. For the moment, Buell and Morton looked to denying the city to raiders like Forrest. The main Confederate armies off in East Tennessee hardly posed a threat. Morton also designed protection for the state capitol as well as the city's bridges.[86]

When Morton tried to requisition slave labor from the local gentry, he received no more cooperation than his Confederate counterpart, Major Jeremy Gilmer, had the previous fall and winter. Slave owners certainly did not want their slaves exposed to emancipationist Yankees in blue. So the work proceeded slowly at first. Intercepted Confederate correspondence indicated that Nashville might not be the rebel target after all, but Federal authorities could never be sure. They pressed ahead, diverting men and resources toward strengthening their span of control, from bridge crossings on vital supply routes to the bases at Murfreesboro, Nashville, and elsewhere. Morton hired Nashville civilians as teamsters, wagon masters, laborers, and hospital attendants and especially impressed "teams, carts, negroes and all the spades, picks and chopping axes of the neighborhood." Even Buell worried that the initiative had returned to the rebels.[87]

Indeed, the Confederacy had made a stunning recovery from the disasters of winter and spring. Morgan, Forrest, and the partisans disrupted railroad traffic, surprised and captured numbers of Union soldiers, and derailed both Buell's advance on Chattanooga and expansion of Federal political control over more of Middle Tennessee. Their audacity forced the fortification of Nashville and other towns. Grant had to detach two divisions to help Buell defend the capital region. Moreover, Buell had to concentrate his cavalry to pursue Morgan and Forrest, further exposing his lines of communication. Major General Alexander McCook figured that it would take fifty thousand troops merely to keep open the Memphis and Charleston Railroad against rebel incursions.[88]

Faced with widespread civil opposition, Buell, Johnson, and even Grant and Sherman additionally confronted a new threat from mounted rebels (aided by friendly citizens). National authorities simply could not complete the task of conquest. Stunned and embittered, they recoiled and awaited developments. What the future portended remained unclear, as sultry August passed to the dusky haze of a heartland autumn. But "collective punishment" of the populace had been definitely introduced by Union army commanders like Sherman, Grant, and others as part of the new way of suppressing the rebellion.

FOUR

HEARTLAND HAVOC: LATE SUMMER 1862

Confederate horsemen dictated the pace of war in the West as the hot, dry summer of 1862 dulled the ardor of both armies. Assistant Surgeon John Vance Lauderdale aboard the *D. A. January* told his brother on August 6 that he understood Memphis had hosted a unionist meeting but that rebel guerrilla activity was upsetting loyalists all the way southward from Iowa and Illinois. Taking the oath of allegiance did not seem to mean much to the immoral secessionists, he suggested. Our military "must be more severe" with the border men especially, with broader application of fire and sword leading to "thorough work of exterminating" the guerrillas. It might sound severe, he offered, but the disloyal must either leave the country, join the national forces, or commit unconditionally to the Union cause. Even to this noncombatant, the war had taken a sterner tone.[1]

Partisans certainly roamed Tennessee and Kentucky. Colonel William W. Lowe, the local commander at Forts Henry and Donelson, told higher authorities on July 27 that R. B. Griffin, a telegraph operator on the line back through Kentucky to Smithland, had warned of 150 or 200 partisans hovering around tiny Eddyville, waiting to attack the town. "Most of the Union citizens have taken to the woods," said Lowe. He dispatched "all that could be spared" to assist in their defense since "the small force here is inadequate to the demands." Headquarters sent support, including an artillery company, aboard the *I. Raymond* that succeeded in capturing three or four guerrillas plus several dismounted cannon, which, according to Lauderdale, "are all safe now in our hands, and will be put to a better use."[2]

Still, "guerrillas infest the Green River counties," Brigadier General Jeremiah Boyle informed Major General Don Carlos Buell's Louisville headquarters after a skirmish at Russellville on July 29. In Tennessee, Brigadier General James Negley wrote the secretary of war from Columbia on August 11, claiming that his Kentucky and Tennessee cavalry had successfully terrorized the bands of Napier and Anderson near Kinderhook once more, and three days later had had a brush with

Williams's guerrillas near Mount Pleasant. Captain W. E. Worth of the Rock Creek, Kentucky, home guards reported taking sixty-six partisans near Mammoth Cave on August 17. He apologized to the secretary of war for sending his report out of channels, but his men had been in service eleven months with no pay, mounts, or firearms (except the common musket), and he wanted to sell forty-three captured mounts to procure sidearms and reimburse his men for their trouble in chasing guerrillas.[3]

Indeed, resources remained a constant problem. While mounts could be procured in northern Kentucky or Ohio, distributing them effectively to newly recruited as well as veteran units took time. There were constant battles for priority between Buell's main army needs and subordinate commanders like Boyle or the garrison commander at Cumberland Gap in southeastern Kentucky, for instance. Underscoring the crisis were two additional Confederate mounted attacks on Federal bases at Clarksville and Gallatin, Tennessee, on August 18 and 22. These brazen displays served as a further prelude to the larger Confederate counteroffensives planned for early autumn.[4]

GALLATIN AND CLARKSVILLE

Brigadier General John Hunt Morgan's attack on Colonel William Boone's Union garrison at Gallatin was distressingly swift and destructive. Well recounted by later historians, from Louisville Boyle simply said that "Morgan surprised Colonel Boone at Gallatin, Tenn.; captured his whole command and freight train. Not a man lost; not a gun fired." The raiders then methodically blocked the nearby railroad tunnel. As Morgan's own brief report to Knoxville departmental headquarters declared: "The tunnel and trestle work between Bowling Green and Gallatin were set fire to; totally destroyed. The bridge between Nashville and Gallatin blown up and 40 cars burned. A large quantity of Government stores were destroyed. Over 100 horses taken." The effect of all this was a deluge of explanatory Yankee paperwork, and it took over a month to clear the tunnel and repair the bridges. Moreover, just the day before, Morgan had captured one of his dedicated pursuers, Kentucky colonel Richard W. Johnson, and some of his command nearby, seriously crippling Federal deterrent capacities in this sector.[5]

This time, Morgan's raid had a military purpose rather than a political one. His command continued to range along the railroad toward Nashville for the next week or so, beating off Federal pursuers and even threatening the newly reconstructed railroad bridge across the Cumberland into the state capital. Secessionists everywhere suddenly spread rumors that the city would be retaken and that Governor Andrew Johnson would be hanged. Johnson had already indicated that, if this happened, the rebels would find only smoldering ashes upon which to resurrect the city. Off in southwestern Virginia, Brigadier General Humphrey Marshall enthusiastically wrote Richmond about Morgan's success: "He says Kentucky only wants the presence of Confederate force to revolt, and urges immediate action."[6]

Federal officials soon adjusted their supply route to Nashville. Morgan's wrecking of the Gallatin tunnel forced them to establish a new railhead ten miles to the north at Mitchellville. Wagon trains and civilian stagecoaches then had to navigate a winding road through Tyree Springs and Goodlettsville. Here were inviting targets for guerrillas, especially Major Dick McCann, a Davidson County farmer and sometime battalion commander under Morgan and Basil Duke. Alternate water and rail routes through Clarksville to the Edgefield and Kentucky Railroad might help offset Morgan's achievement, despite low water in the river and questionable conditions on that rickety rail line. It remains unclear whether the Confederates realized all this when they struck at Clarksville itself four days after Morgan's foray. Yet, these two assaults on Buell's line of communication facilitated Confederate generals Braxton Bragg and Edmund Kirby Smith's passage to Kentucky. The Union commander, however, remained preoccupied with withdrawing his army from north Alabama and consolidating his position before Nashville.[7]

The Clarksville caper, in comparison to Gallatin, has remained shrouded in obscurity, possibly because it involved lesser-known partisans than the popular Morgan or Bedford Forrest. As this pair hammered away at the outskirts of Nashville, Lieutenant Colonel Thomas G. Woodward, a diminutive Kentuckian and West Pointer, received orders to clear the lower Cumberland of Yankees. Clarksville and Fort Donelson provided the targets. While Donelson proved impossible to capture, Clarksville fell with the same ease as Gallatin had. In the process of cooperating with Colonel Adam Rankin Johnson's First Kentucky Partisan Rangers, Woodward's command surprised and captured six companies of Colonel Rodney Mason's Seventy-first Ohio, which garrisoned the Montgomery County seat. This action inspired renewed hope among local secessionists and briefly raised the Stars and Bars again over Clarksville's streets and homes. It was a breathtaking—if fleeting—moment in that city's wartime history.[8]

Woodward and his men were no strangers to the locale. Despite Woodward's childhood in New England, he had settled as a lawyer in Christian County, Kentucky, after the Mexican War. He raised the Oak Grove Rangers in April 1861, which became part of Colonel Ben Hardin Helm's First Kentucky Confederate Cavalry, until the unit's enlistment expired in June 1862. Woodward then linked up with Forrest and actually may have been on a recruiting and quasi-political mission when he rendezvoused with Johnson's men and another group under H. Garth at Hopkinsville, Kentucky. Together they then rode southward, reaching Clarksville on August 18.[9]

Clarksville had suffered for its unabashed secessionism. Virtually shut down following Grant's winter victories, the city government struggled on until June. Local trade foundered as the tobacco industry closed down, and nearby iron forges and rolling mills lay in ruins. The Federals took over warehouses and other buildings for their needs, while residents like D. H. Kennedy went south to help the Confederate government. Those civilians who stayed behind (including Kennedy's stalwart wife, Sarah Ann) monitored their neglected city and rural properties, nursed a clandestine mail service across the battle lines, and harassed the new Federal garrison in word and deed. A local farmer, John "Nick" Barker, who lived near Dunbar's cave, kept particular track of the activities of "Link cavl.," as he styled them in his diary. "Andy Johnson arresting our citizens for expressing opinions," was a typical entry. Little wonder that residents welcomed Woodward and Johnson as they swept into town.[10]

Of course, Colonel Mason and his Buckeyes had other things on their minds besides a truculent citizenry. While responsible for reinstituting national laws and government at Clarksville, their principal function was to facilitate Buell's resupply. The storage space available and the relationship of river and rail rendered Clarksville attractive, although low water in the Cumberland by mid-August hardly justified trying to bring supplies upriver. Still, with the L&N shut down because of Morgan, the river route took on new importance. At any rate, Mason's post remained an important cog in the Federal logistical network servicing Yankee operations throughout Tennessee and north Alabama. Besides, the garrison also served to suppress secessionism in the area.[11]

Mason recognized his exposed position to some extent. He had written Governor Johnson at the end of July suggesting that "there is no doubt the wealthier part of the population is distinctly disaffected and the humbler classes the reverse." He noted how hard it would be to raise any of the governor's desired cavalry in the area, but that local partisans had no trouble securing plenty of horses. He wanted Johnson's permission to "possess and occupy" local mounts to help comply with the order to raise loyal Tennessee troops. His infantry never made counterguerrilla sweeps in the countryside, and his eleventh-hour plea for aid from both Nashville and Buell's headquarters blended with equally futile cries from other local commanders all over the upper heartland. Furthermore, Mason and his command labored under a cloud and may accordingly have received little attention at headquarters.[12]

The reason for the Federal lack of faith in Mason was simple. The Seventy-first Ohio had been badly battered and routed at Shiloh. Grant immediately sent the regiment to lighter duty, guarding telegraph lines and supply dumps at Clarksville. Some observers attributed the ill-luck to Mason's personal cowardice; others to a high casualty rate (137 of 510 men in the battle). Four companies were deposited with Lieutenant Colonel George W. Andrews at Dover, where they began constructing "a small fort . . . the old fort of the enemy being greatly too large for my small force to occupy." Using several leftover rebel cannon that Colonel Crafts J. Wright and the Thirteenth Missouri had not sent north as Grant had ordered earlier, Andrews told superiors that he could "defend and hold" his new post against any force that "could in the then condition of the country, be brought against it." But Andrews became almost independent from his parent unit and lost touch with the regiment to some extent. The chain of command was confusing as these Ohioans all remained within Grant's jurisdiction, but labored for Buell's purposes and received no recognition from either headquarters. It would seem that neither Mason nor Andrews (nor Lowe at Forts Henry and Heiman, for that matter), paid heed to reports of rebel attacks on the railroad closer to Nashville. As young Minnesota sergeant Eugene Marshall in Lowe's command wrote his sister on July 22, the capture of the Third Minnesota at

Colonel Tom Woodward, circa 1862. Courtesy of the Clarksville-Montgomery County Museum, Clarksville, Tennessee.

Murfreesboro by Forrest had caused another good scare, "but it is gradually dying away."[13]

Disaster struck Mason's command on a bright but somewhat cool morning of August 18. As at Murfreesboro, the Federals were dispersed all over town. The colonel received word just before 9:00 A.M. that the enemy was in the vicinity. As a special team of rebels rode into the city to personally capture him, Mason mounted quickly and made his way from his downtown headquarters to the regimental encampment at Stewart College. Here Andrews (who apparently just happened to be upriver from Donelson on business that day) and the company officers struggled to get the men into hastily dug rifle pits designed to ward off such an attack. The Federals claimed scarcely 250 officers and men fit for duty, with thirty-six more on special stable, commissary, and quartermaster assignments in town. An additional thirteen were off working the telegraph line survey, and twenty-two more had gone upriver as steamboat guards. By comparison, Woodward and Johnson brought some eight hundred men, who were well equipped with revolving carbines and a battery of light artillery, according to Union after-action reports. Local secessionists claimed the Confederates had fewer men and poorer arms than that.[14]

Whatever the truth, Woodward and Johnson bluffed Mason and Andrews into surrender within minutes. Not a shot was fired, and Mason was amused at having himself photographed alongside a dapper Woodward, resplendent in huge cavalry boots with jangling Mexican spurs, a dark gray hunter's shirt, and a narrow-brimmed corduroy hat. Weighing all of 110 pounds, even Woodward's saber seemed too big for him, and Mason joked about showing people back home what a "runt" his captor was. "We had no hope of reinforcements, and no possibility, with the Cumberland and Red Rivers on three sides of us and an enemy indefinite in numbers in front, to retreat," claimed the Ohioan.[15]

Union officers were dumbstruck by what they saw literally paraded before them by the victorious rebels, plus an estimated one thousand citizens, although they never caviled at the surrender decision. The elated populace flocked to witness Yankee humiliation, while youthful, exuberant Nannie Haskins colorfully recorded in her diary that when the Confederates came dashing in with their old horses, dirty clothes, and all sorts of arms, they had no band and not even a bugle or flag to show. "But, 'fight was in 'em.'" and they "tuck the place and the Feds" with "all their blue broadcloth and brass buttons." Elderly Mrs. Bringhurst went forward to lower the Union flag. But Woodward halted her and turned to Mason for that dubious honor, telling his adversary later that since he respected his own flag, he presumed the Union officer did likewise.

Later that afternoon, or early the next morning, a local belle, Tennie Moore, presented a silk banner to Johnson with the explanation that it had been sewn "for a band of heroes" who had left the "lovely little city to fight for their beloved country," but the Federals had prevented its delivery. Despite Yankee searches, an old slave had hidden it securely until this new presentation to another band of heroes "has rescued us from the hateful bondage of these bluecoated Unionists." Everyone cheered (except Mason and his men).[16]

Woodward's Confederates took possession of the provost marshal's office, the commissary stores, and the post office, and captured the steamboat *Fisher*, just then coming upriver. They unaccountably threw corn and oats into the river, but held a public auction for other stores. They respected private property, although Adam Johnson claimed seizure of "several thousand wagons," five hundred firearms, and one-million-dollars' worth of army stores all told. Woodward also ordered his quartermaster, local Montgomery County lawyer and farmer Thomas L. Yancey, to retrieve forty-five bales of cotton from the riverbank between Clarksville and Nashville. It went to auction and eventually was shipped by another Clarksvillian, Andrew Hamilton, to parties in Cincinnati and New York. This action landed Yancey in jail when the Nashville customshouse surveyor, Colonel George W. Ashburn, claimed to own the cotton and prosecuted Yancey, who by that time had left Confederate service and taken the oath of allegiance to the Union. Elsewhere, Woodward and Johnson prevented Clarksville civilians from hanging their postmaster, port collector, railroad engineer, and telegrapher.[17]

The raiders also paroled Mason and his Seventy-first Ohio. When Grant heard about it afterwards, he ordered the parolees to Benton Barracks at St. Louis for lengthy rehabilitation. The unit's subsequent story proved controversial. Lieutenant Colonel Andrews, either seeking to gain a regimental command for himself or merely trying to purge the incompetent leadership, secured all of the officers' signatures on a document explaining the disaster. But he never added his own, and within weeks Mason and the others (but not Andrews) had been cashiered. Military Governor Andrew Johnson argued that "the conduct of Col. Mason's 71st Ohio at Clarksville is not only humiliating but disgraceful in the extreme," and he told Buell that he hoped examples would be made of these soldiers since "there must be more efficiency imparted to this Army in this part of Tennessee, or we are doomed to meet with reverses that will retard and protract the War if not in the end to result in the loss of Tennessee."[18]

A somewhat perplexed Buell inquired of Major W. H. Sidell at Nashville on August 20: "What became of the garrison that was at Clarksville? How strong was it?" Between the exploits of Morgan, Forrest, Woodward, and Johnson, Buell's line of communications lay in disarray and his timetable was disrupted. By seriously damaging the tunnel near Gallatin and capturing its protective force, hovering on the fringes of the state capital, capturing the Clarksville post, and destroying the Red River railroad bridge on the Edgefield and Kentucky line near that city, Confederate raiders had all but regained the advantage in the upper heartland.[19]

With restored morale among southern sympathizers and a renewed spirit in army ranks, a resurgent rebellion beckoned in Tennessee and Kentucky. Writing from Chattanooga on August 15, 1862, Lieutenant Colonel M. Jenkins told his father bluntly: "all [here] believe that Tenn and Ky will be under the Shield of the Confederate flag before Christmas." The entire army seemed to be in a "most prosperous and flourishing condition." Enough troops were in the field to achieve the South's independence. The South now had the spirit to avenge the foul wrongs that had been heaped upon it by the North, "and she will have vengeance, cost what it may." There was no use in talking about southern submission, Jenkins claimed, for that was impossible: "the south will fight for half a century before she will give up." He ended his epistle with the hope that the portion of Tennessee that now lay within Federal lines "will prove to the Yankies [sic] that they are not submissionist if they are in the hands of the Federals."[20]

PARTISANS ON THE LOOSE

Confederate forces controlled the lower Cumberland valley for three weeks following their capture of Clarksville. New recruits flocked to the colors, and armed citizens even helped sever Union rail communications. Still, many citizens knew that Federal retribution would be swift and sure. Local planter James Buckner Killebrew recalled later that soon after sowing his autumn wheat, he and a black helper and a neighbor took his wagon and mules and carried bacon, whiskey, and salt southward to sell within Confederate lines. Moving via Charlotte to Williamsport near the old Natchez Trace crossing of the Duck River in Maury County, he met a former college mate from Alabama and sold his goods for $1,750 in South Carolina currency. The trio returned home, avoiding capture by wandering bands of irregulars as well as Union soldiers, and exchanged $800 of the state money for $400 in gold, which his wife wore around her body in a money belt for the duration. At least Killebrew had been able to spirit away goods that he knew the incensed Federals would confiscate when they returned to Clarksville and vicinity.[21]

As was predictable with the transitory control exercised by raiders and partisans, Adam Johnson's band soon moved northward to Madisonville, Kentucky, reinforced by two of Woodward's captains, Sam Taylor and Al Fowler. He had planned to attack Union-held Dover after capturing Clarksville, but word of a counterguerrilla sweep by brigadiers John Foster and James M. Shackleford (who had earlier commanded a Kentucky Union infantry regiment at Fort Donelson) led him to protect his own lair. Meanwhile, the Union navy dispatched shallow-draft gunboats to reaffirm control of the Ohio River shoreline. Skirmishes resulted at Madisonville on August 25 and September 5, Unionville on September 1, and Henderson, where Johnson captured the opposing force on September 14. None of the Federal moves dislodged the irregulars as newspapers and rumor mills exaggerated Johnson's exploits so that "mere mention of our names inspired fear in the hearts of the Federals," Johnson claimed after the war.[22]

A Logan County preacher and farmer, George R. Browder, suggested in his diary on August 11 that "the excitement in the country is keeping up by rumor more than actions." Recruits joined Johnson, Woodward, and other irregulars because they promised to meet the enemy in their home neighborhoods rather than on some distant battlefield. Yet, unionist retaliation and sentiment also affected partisan enlistments, and Browder (as much pro-South as he was pro-neutrality) deplored the resulting government repression, confiscation of horses and foodstuffs, agitation of the slaves, and general mayhem resulting from all this. Complaining did no good, he groaned on September 4, for Federal authorities rampaged "in our fields carrying off our horses and mules without pay, insulting our wives and daughters if they remonstrate & imprisoning peaceable citizens contrary to the constitution." So, he quietly ministered to the spiritual needs of his congregation, and spent September 9, "all day cutting, hanging & housing tobacco." Life went on despite Woodward, Johnson, Garth, the Yankees, or the war.[23]

A Federal crackdown now developed all over the upper heartland. Officers at Tuscumbia, Alabama, received instructions on August 6 to seize cotton, slaves, and other property of people hostile to the national government. Anyone of any age or gender who displayed hostile words and actions could be exiled beyond Federal lines and have their property taken, their homes burned, and their crops and livestock given over to the needs of the army. A ever-fidgety Grant, faced with guerrilla depredations against his long rail line in West Tennessee, noted many tales of harassment of unionists in his area, and, unfortunately, some Yankee units, like the Seventh Kansas Cavalry, had already begun to retaliate indiscriminately. Veterans of the rough, bloody border fighting in Missouri and Kansas, the Jayhawkers transported their attitudes and style east of the Mississippi in the summer. They made a joke of "rose water" relations with civilians as they marched through West Tennessee en route to the Mississippi line.[24]

Led by the hard-bitten commander, Lieutenant Colonel Daniel R. Anthony, the Kansans' actions produced a litany of theft and insult to civilian friend and foe that became a familiar one at headquarters. Brigadier General Robert B. Mitchell, Major General William S. Rosecrans, Grant, and others tried to tame the Kansans and relax tensions with southern civilians, to no avail. Fighters like the Seventh Kansas stood at the forefront of carrying the Civil War in a direction toward total war, mixing idealism for emancipation and punishment for treason with self-seeking mayhem, long before generals like William T. Sherman elevated such practice to high policy. At this point, however, Sherman told an assistant quartermaster at Memphis that "we have nothing to do with confiscation" but only with possession of those abandoned rebel homes and businesses in the city. Once property courts had been reestablished then they, not the army, would execute the law, including the confiscation act. Until that time, every opportunity "should be given to the wavering and disloyal to return," he announced solemnly. Clearly army policy left room in principle for exercise of either conciliation or retribution at the local level. Meanwhile, the troops, observed historian Bruce Catton, spent their days rebuilding and guarding miles of track and bridges, garrisoning city and rural posts, and basically awaiting the rebels' pleasure.[25]

August skirmishes in West Tennessee included those at Meriwether's Ferry on the Obion River in Dyer County on the sixteenth and two days later only six miles from Dyersburg itself. In both cases, Brigadier General Grenville M. Dodge's Mobile and Ohio Railroad guard force clashed with raiders entering the area from Kentucky and Missouri, seeking to escape conscription, he thought. More threatening were confrontations at the end of the month near Bolivar, Medon and Toone's Stations, and Britton's Lane near Denmark. The appearance of regular Confederate troops under Brigadier General Frank Armstrong now suggested the opening rounds of more serious fighting between Union forces and the armies of Price and Van Dorn as part of the autumn offensive.[26]

Dodge caught the essence of Confederate plans when he wired a Columbus, Kentucky, subordinate on August 29: "From all the information I can obtain there is some movement in contemplation in West Tennessee by the rebels. They are massing all their cavalry; have drawn in all their guerrilla bands, and everything is very quiet." The calm was broken as Armstrong's sixteen hundred men, reinforced by eleven hundred more under Brigadier W. H. Jackson, soon had West Tennessee Federal garrisons in a panic, virtually besieging many of them, like the one at Bolivar. A completely frustrated Grant wired Halleck late on the evening of September 10: "With all the vigilance I can bring to bear, I cannot determine the objects of the enemy. Everything threatens an attack here, but my fear is that it is to cover some other movement." He enumerated the possibilities—to prevent Union transfer of reinforcements to Kentucky, to cover a Confederate countermove against New Orleans, or to cover a similar advance against Buell to the east.[27]

Armstrong's success, like that of Woodward and Johnson, brought out latent secessionism west of the Tennessee River. News of Confederate presence spread like wildfire, claimed Captain Thomas B. Wilson, riding with the First Tennessee Cavalry under Armstrong. The locals met their heroes with wagons of melons and peaches at every road fork. These were the first bona fide Confederate troops to enter the region since Shiloh, and, while doing little more than dislocating Grant's plans just as Woodward, Johnson, Forrest, and Morgan were doing to Buell, they stimulated recruitment and strengthened civilian resolve against Union oppression. But, as was the case with Woodward and Johnson, this enthusiasm dissipated when Armstrong and Jackson also departed, leaving only a residue of bitter retaliation and further instability in the neighborhood.[28]

Affairs remained off balance for weeks, especially on the Tennessee and Cumberland Rivers. With Johnson and Woodward in the neighborhood, it seemed that even the river forts were threatened, and rumors had the intrepid Morgan clearing all of western Kentucky of unionists. Lowe wired Grant from Fort Heiman, the very day Clarksville fell, that it was probably all just a "scare" but that guerrillas seemed to be organizing everywhere and that reinforcement might be advisable. Major James H. Hart, left in command of the "rump" portion of the Seventy-first Ohio at Fort Donelson, was even more adamant about needing help. But he vowed to defend the place until forced to surrender. Everyone seemed spooked when one of Lowe's patrols stumbled upon a tiny rebel group midway between Forts Henry and Donelson on August 23. This meeting caused major search-and-destroy columns to be launched against what was rumored to be "a large party." Indeed, that party was Tom Woodward's force, replete with cannon and bent upon retaking Fort Donelson and Dover. On August 23 and 25, it appeared that Woodward just might succeed.[29]

When Adam Johnson went back to Kentucky, Woodward moved west to harass Federal positions on the Cumberland. Reports later numbered Woodward's force at 335 cavalry, 450 infantry, and a lone six-pounder cannon. His appearance on August 25 began at 1:30 P.M. and promised a repeat of Clarksville. Again he hoped to bluff the Buckeyes into surrender without a fight. But Major Hart was in no mood to repeat the embarrassment. Besides, he apparently had a portion of Lowe's Fifth Iowa Cavalry to stiffen resolve. When he put Woodward's proposal to his own subordinates, they all declared, "fight them." So, Hart told the Confederate that his men would fight until "hell froze over" and then "fight them four days on the ice." Woodward got the message even clearer when the Ohioans and Iowans shot to pieces an ill-advised mounted rush by his men, at no loss to themselves. Peter Fowler, a civilian telegraph operator at the fort, and a young female camp follower were among those wielding weapons in the affair. Some observers thought that Lowe appeared in person with a relief force and, during an impromptu parley, bluntly told Woodward that he had fifteen minutes to get beyond Union picket lines. Yet, Lowe's own report claimed that "the affair ended before my command got in—about sundown."[30]

Woodward's attack left "the village of Dover mostly destroyed by fire during the attack," observed Minnesota native Eugene Marshall, who was serving with Lowe's Fifth Iowa Cavalry out of Forts Henry and Heiman. Hart himself claimed to have fired on several buildings to prevent their use by the rebels. The Federals asserted they had taken the Confederate commander's horse, saddle, and pistols and ascribed a loss of five to ten men killed and wounded and four horses captured by the enemy. At any rate, the stout defense forced Woodward to withdraw with little to show except the campfire story that one telegraph repairman had been captured west of the fort and the line had been ripped down, thus isolating the garrison from Smithland, Kentucky, for the next few months. One of Woodward's men even intervened on the line at some point, in the style as Morgan's famous prankster, George Ellsworth, and answered a Union query as to his identity with the words "Confeds are now whipping hell out of the Yankees in Fort Donelson and will be down your way soon and catch you."[31]

This time, however, the joke was on the rebels at Dover, "and of this I am right glad for it cost too much to be surrendered lightly," observed Colonel T. Lyle Dickey, a former Illinois judge, who led the Fourth Illinois Cavalry in Grant's victory at the place. The members of the decimated Eleventh Illinois (which had also fought at Fort Donelson in February) agreed when they arrived as reinforcements from Paducah on August 30. Their number, which had shrunk to 250 from the original compliment of 800 men, joined the remnants of the Seventy-first Ohio, the Thirteenth Wisconsin, and Captain James P. Flood's Battery C, Second Illinois Light Artillery in throwing up earthworks to protect the town and keeping "an eye out for guerrillas." The Illiniosian soldiers revisited the enclosed mass grave of their comrades from the first battle, peered at the farmhouse hospital that still contained February's smell of gunpowder and blood, and the now dusty, overgrown field of strife on Dover's outskirts. They vowed to defend this sacred ground. The partisans sent word that they were going to take the place, recorded Captain Henry Dean of the newcomers, "but we have 'heavy doubts' to the contrary."[32]

Lowe started after Woodward the next day. But his 120 troopers proved inadequate, as they learned quickly in a brisk firefight at nearby Cumberland Iron Works. Lowe lost nineteen men in quick succession, thanks largely to rebel captain W. B. Allbright's ambushing of the advancing Federals with the lone cannon. Nevertheless, the Iowan reported cheerfully to Grant on September 2 that "all is going well; am almost ready to mount a punitive expedition to recapture Clarksville." but he also admitted that he needed a "small amount of secret service money" to pay informants and spies who were guiding his efforts in this guerrilla-infested country. Indeed, civilian informants were indispensable for antiguerrilla operations. When Confederate sympathizers like farmer Nick Barker could gloat in his diary that the rebels had defeated "the Links at the Rolling Mills," as he termed the Lincolnites or Yankee cavalry, then Lowe needed more substantial means for wooing neutrals as well as potential dissidents.[33]

Even Major General Horatio Wright, commanding the Department of the Ohio at Cincinnati, diagnosed the situation correctly as he wrote Halleck on August 29: "Kentucky is in a much worse condition than I had been led to believe. Guerrilla bands and recruiting parties parade the State under the very noses of the civil and military authorities, and thus far it has been next to impossible to put down for want of a mounted force." It was no different in Tennessee, causing Halleck to urge Grant to "take all possible measures to put down Guerrilla operations on the Tennessee and Cumberland Rivers," regardless of strict jurisdictional boundaries. Clarksville had to be retaken and occupied as soon as possible, Halleck directed. But Grant was already ahead of Washington on that one. He had already assigned the task to Lowe.[34]

FEDERAL RETRIBUTION

Lowe regained control of the supply line of the Cumberland when Woodward went north to help Johnson and to intimidate the civilians in the counties just over the state line. Admittedly, the Iowan first complained to Grant about his inadequately armed and equipped men and wondered if he could even retake Clarksville. The enemy had been strengthened by materiel they had captured there on August 18, and Union sergeant Marshall, for one, felt that "it is certainly cruel to take [his unit] into action so poorly armed" with nothing more than pistols and sabers. Requisitions had been returned consistently with the scrawled note, "there are no cavalry arms in this department."[35]

So Lowe urged Grant to wire Washington directly for support. Nevertheless, Lowe's Fifth Iowa, which had changed its name from the "Curtis Horse" in June, already resembled the infamous Seventh Kansas now in northeastern Mississippi. Both units included hard-bitten, rough-hewn, cock pit–fighting veterans of rough-and-tumble combat against insurgents. They were anxious to get on with the task of cleaning out rebels and were fast becoming the Union's best counterguerrilla forces. They fit well the change from a conciliatory policy to a pragmatic, even hard war one.

The Iowans actually hailed from all over the Midwest, and they brooked little nonsense about "obeying orders from imbeciles and drunkards and suffering petty annoyances from men for whom I have not the least particle of respect," as Eugene Marshall put it. Schooled in garrison, patrol, and search-and-destroy duties since arriving on the twin rivers at the time of the February victories, by August "we have done nothing but enact the part of scare crows to the enemy lying in camps and trying to make the rebels believe that if we were once among them we should be most terrible adversaries to contend with," according to Marshall. Guarding the telegraph line, overseeing a hostile countryside, and "living on Corn bread and bacon with coffee extemporized from wheat or corn meal or something of that kind" made up their daily existence. Very capable of defying higher authority's orders to turn slaves out of camp (largely because the common soldier discovered how versatile the contraband were for cooking, cleaning, and other camp shores), Lowe's men marveled that "the people along this line between the Cumberland and Tennessee Rivers are generally poor and have but little at stake as regards slavery but the prejudice in its favor is very strong and they will hardly tolerate any interference with it."[36]

Dutifully they had escorted Governor Johnson's minion, the politico-colonel Ethridge Rogers of the Eleventh Tennessee (Union), as he stumped the Paris neighborhood in West Tennessee, noting how Henry County differed so greatly from neighboring Weakly in its secessionist sentiments. They captured and

Sergeant Eugene Marshall, USV Fifth Iowa (Curtis House) Cavalry, circa 1861. Courtesy of Duke University Special Collection Library.

unaccountably let escape an avowedly rebel doctor who openly preached the rising of guerrillas. They stood guard in small, inadequately protected picket posts among unfriendly civilians, much as Lieutenant Charles C. Nott and his command had done earlier in the spring. And, as John Edgerly of the Eighty-third Illinois wrote a friend, they regularly captured guerrillas, some carrying "three-barelled guns" while pilfering local farmers' chicken coops and sweet potato patches and welcoming escaping slaves to Union lines. Then, Lowe confidently brought his command across from Forts Henry and Heiman to clean out Woodward and Johnson east of the Cumberland River.[37]

Lowe concentrated his strike force to retake Clarksville. In addition to the eight companies from the Fifth Iowa Cavalry, consisting of six hundred men, that encamped in the valley between the ruins of Dover and the old Confederate water batteries, Hart's four companies of the Seventy-first Ohio were joined by six more from Colonel T. E. G. Ransom's veteran Eleventh Illinois. Eight companies of the Thirteenth Wisconsin, which had railroad guard experience on the Mobile and Ohio in West Tennessee, two guns of Flood's battery, and a similar section of Battery H of the same Illinois artillery under Captain Andrew Stenbeck, and the newly minted Eighty-third Illinois (which upon arrival divided its companies as garrisons between the forts, thus freeing the old regiments for Lowe's tasks) completed the force. All together, the Hawkeye colonel numbered 1,030 men and four cannon under his command when his column splashed across the drought-stricken Cumberland on the morning of September 5. His own men had been up early expecting pay. They received marching orders instead.[38]

That very day, the manager of the Nashville telegraph office, C. Dwyer, informed Buell's chief of staff that the party he had sent up the Edgefield and Kentucky Railroad the previous week had found downed wires at the Red River crossing, three hundred barrels of unattended flour at Ford's station two miles beyond, and had met a similar crew coming from the Clarksville–Bowling Green line without incident. "They saw no enemy, and believe there is no enemy in the country," Dwyer added, confirming that classic statement about conditions in the upper heartland: "the secesh attend their farms in the day time and go bushwhacking at night." Indeed, Lowe encountered nothing until close to Clarksville. A dispatch arrived from Grant informing him that he need not retake Clarksville just then, but the Hawkeye was determined to complete his assignment.[39]

Lowe's column encountered more determined opposition between Woodlawn and New Providence and finally pitched into Woodward's men at New Providence on September 6 and at Riggins' Hill the next day. Rebel hunting rifles and double-barrel shotguns proved no match for the disciplined infantry and Flood's six-pounders. As Ransom's foot soldiers went in with "bayonets at the charge" against Woodward's irregulars posted behind a split-rail fence at Riggins' Hill, Flood blasted the position. One hundred and twenty shots lopped off one rebel's head, another's legs, and the arms and part of the chest of a third man. Woodward's force scampered off, leaving behind seventeen dead, forty wounded, perhaps fifty to sixty captives. Only two of Lowe's column were injured, one because he fell off an artillery limber moving into position.[40]

Lieutenant M. T. Patrick's two companies of Iowans interrupted the partisans' vain attempt to burn the Red River bridge between Clarksville and New Providence. This enabled Lowe's force to quickly take the city. But, once in town, Ransom's Illini became particularly unruly. They ransacked a dry goods store and haphazardly began destroying public goods (probably Federal property left over from the earlier surrender). Their irate colonel rode among them using the flat of his sword to get them back into the ranks, and Lowe soon slapped an ironclad rule on "the town [which] was said to be a very hot bed of secession." Private Robert McConnell of the Seventy-first Ohio noted how Union officers forced residents to provide both supper and breakfast for the victors. "We left them with the understanding that if we had to go back we would burn the town," he noted.[41] Quartermaster Sergeant Josiah Conzett of the Fifth Iowa remembered that the citizens generally stayed out of sight, the women refused to flirt ("which we were all willing to do"), and nobody got up "any Parties or Dances for us or even Invite any of us to Dinner." That did not bother the troopers, however, since "at dinner time, we went into the first house any of us came on our Tour of Inspection of the Stores in the City and Set down at the table with them." Naturally, said Conzett, they raised no objections, but how welcome "we were and what they thought of us their faces plainly showed." Strict orders prohibited "wanton and personal outrage," and there was none, but otherwise the Iowans operated on the principle of "to the victor belong the spoils." Conzett remembered his brother returning to camp with a pair or two of new shoes wrapped in four or five yards of black silk. "That is only a faint showing of what the good people of Clarksville Tenn contributed to the comfort of the 5th Iowa cavalry," he concluded. "We never after were very popular around there," Conzett chuckled.[42]

Lowe destroyed two hundred and fifty boxes of commissary stores, removed yet another two hundred boxes of stores as well as one thousand bales of hay, forty horses, and three wagons, and "also brought with me several Union families who were afraid to remain in the place." A crestfallen Nannie Haskins noted pungently in her diary that "the Jayhawkers came from Fort Donelson on a thieving expedition," adding that they carried off a great many blacks and horses, including her favorite gray, named "Stonewall Jackson." It had been a present from her father, and "I thought a great deal of him because he was all my own." She wished she had given him to Tom Woodward, her hero, and the thought of her beautiful horse in the hands of the Yankees rankled the seventeen-year-old for months to come. Needless to say, Clarksville's support of Woodward and Johnson had cost the town dearly when the Federals returned.[43]

Lowe felt inadequate to reestablishing any permanent presence at Clarksville. He left promptly at 10:00 A.M. on the ninth and returned to Fort Donelson over roads so dusty that Eugene Marshall commented, "it was often impossible to see the third man in front or to see our knees through the dust as we rode." Lowe's men, however, left a wake of devastation worthy of Sherman's later march through Georgia. As one Illinois soldier put it, "during the whole time we were gone we lived entirely off the country through which we marched." Upon reaching home base at Fort Donelson and Fort Henry, "a dirtier lot of men you never saw, but we lived freely as we had all the peaches and applies we could eat, and chickens and turkeys are now very scarce on the road." McConnell told his wife how his comrades had robbed grocers and watchmakers, with one man liberating eighteen watches alone in the unnecessary pilferage. "We lived off the Citizens from here up there and back again," he gloated, claiming the expedition had stolen all the fowl, pork, beef, mutton, sweet potatoes, and roasting ears that the men could eat, as well as feed for about eight hundred horses. It was a real letdown to return to garrison "living on Sheet Iron Crackers and Sow Belly, and Coffee again."[44]

Lowe's men were obviously angered by citizen intransigence. Eugene Marshall spoke of "250 citizens" (probably considering them partisans) who had brazenly helped Woodward and Johnson capture the city, while Lowe himself claimed knowledge of at least sixteen civilians. Slaves informed Wisconsin soldiers in the column that they knew that "many citizens came home and changed their clothes after the fight [at Riggins' Hill] before we got them" and that the inhabitants had been terribly bitter toward the bluecoats. So, the situation the Federals left in their wake must have been appalling. In any event, aggrieved citizens penned a remonstrance directly to Grant on September 17, recounting the atrocities of slaughtered livestock, stolen horses and slaves, looted stores, etc.[45]

"From Sunday noon until Monday noon, a reign of terror, kept alive by every species of outrage, was established in this city," claimed the correspondents. Given pardonable exaggeration of these Clarksvillians, Lowe's visit symbolized "a series of outrages, robberies and insults upon the citizens without regard to sex or condition, which we believe to be without parallel ... in the present war and unknown to the civilized warfare of modern times." Mrs. Sarah Kennedy wrote her absent husband about "all sorts of Devilish deeds, excelling anything that I have heard during the war." She thanked God that "the advent of the Northern Demons" had lasted only a day, for in her view they were too cowardly to remain longer. The citizens' letter to Grant went unanswered. Instead, a Yankee reign of terror descended over the whole Cumberland Valley.[46]

Possibly viewing themselves as avenging angels, Colonels Lowe and Abner Harding of the Eighty-third Illinois operated almost in defiance of directives Grant had issued in July against "marauding, pilfering, and any unauthorized and unnecessary seizure or destruction of private property." The Clarksville citizenry even sought redress from the Richmond government, and the populace met on October 17 under the gavel of local first citizen and former United States Senator Cave Johnson to prepare their letter to Confederate officials. The Reverend B. M. Taylor and William Hume carried the petition to the Confederate capital, a petition that alleged that "marauders from the Northwest" had committed daily "the most gross outrages upon our citizens." Citing their defenseless condition, since locally raised units like the Fourteenth, Forty-ninth, and Fiftieth Tennessee regiments had been committed to battle elsewhere (the latter pair had surrendered at Fort Donelson), the Clarksvillians pinned despicable acts directly upon the Yankee colonels and their men.[47]

Pillage and insults regardless of age and sex, wanton destruction of the Woods, Lewis & Company rolling mill, theft of 240 slaves, arrest of rural parsons and intimidation of their congregations by confiscation of parishioner horses and carriages—these outrages were cited specifically. The country along the line or march was devastated for thirty miles "on both sides of the road," complained the aggrieved southerners. But, striking at the most sensitive of Confederate issues, Cave Johnson alluded in a covering letter to the fact that the twin rivers section "can and will furnish an immense quantity of provisions for the Confederate armies," if they could be made secure from the visits of those "jayhawkers from Iowa and Northern Illinois." He referred specifically to the immense corn crops ready for harvest, and no less than fifty to sixty thousand barrels of flour from local mills.[48]

President Jefferson Davis and Secretary of War George W. Randolph were shocked by the Clarksville situation. They immediately put a price on both Lowe's and Harding's heads, calling them common felons. The notice went accordingly to Braxton Bragg, but nothing was suggested to him about dispatching a protective force to the area. Either Richmond was lax in this regard, or, by the time Bragg became aware of Clarksville's plight, he was too far into the autumn campaign to help out. Lowe and Harding continued their oppression, the partisans lurked in the background, but no permanent Federal force returned to occupy Clarksville before December.

Confederate reliance upon partisans or even on Woodward's small and quasi-irregular command had proven dubiously successful at best. Basically, the lack of manpower for both the main armies and neighborhood partisan groups prevented Confederate exploitation of obvious Federal occupation weaknesses and resulted in undue suffering for southerners left behind Yankee lines. Jefferson Davis's own orders that all men enrolled in partisan groups after July 31, 1862, should be transferred to conscript status did not help either. Western generals particularly were cautioned to report what measures had been taken to disband the partisan corps, thereby sending mixed signals to professionals like Bragg and others that guerrilla activities held little official sanction and would play little importance in any joint operation for overcoming the invaders.[49]

Woodward, Johnson, and the partisans continued to apply pressure along the twin rivers all fall. After capturing Clarksville, but failing to repeat the victory at Dover, Johnson returned to southwestern Kentucky, surprised a Hoosier unit encamped there, and bested Colonel James Shackleford's Eighth Kentucky (Union) at Geiger's Lake on September 3. He then traveled southward once again, allowing his second-in-command, Lieutenant Colonel Robert Martin, to range at will in the direction of Owensboro. Woodward, Adam Johnson, and their lieutenants had contact with the Federals all over the region. Young John Edgerly of Company D, Eighty-third Illinois, wrote a friend on September 20 that patrols seeking deserters had uncovered shotguns and other firearms instead, as well as local livestock, all of which had assisted the partisans in their endeavors. "We are daily behind breastworks waiting for the rebels to attack," he noted, as rumors had six or seven hundred partisans near Fort Donelson. None came, although various encounters in mid-September caused Lowe to dispatch Harding and his infantry "out after Woodward with a fair prospect of overhauling him." But infantry chasing cavalry was never a fair prospect, as Lowe should have known. The partisans kept some rear-echelon Federals pinned down and away from reinforcement of major army operations.[50]

TOWARD A GUERRILLA POLICY

Federal authorities encountered similar problems in West Tennessee. One counterguerrilla sweep surprised Colonel Faulkner's command encamped in broad daylight near Dyersburg, Tennessee. These raiders had been ordered to burn all cotton west of the Tennessee River to prevent it from falling into Federal hands. They were also engaged in recruiting in the Purchase section of Kentucky when the bluecoats surprised them. Later in October, Faulkner would be captured just days after a botched partisan assault on the Union garrison at Island Number 10.

Success often eluded the Federals, however. Colonel Frederick A. Starring went downriver by boat from Columbus in the early fall with the Seventy-second Illinois Infantry and Company D, Second Illinois Cavalry, landed at Fort Pillow, and moved inland. Apparently his Illinois horsemen spent more time plundering civilians than carrying out its mission, and unhappily alienated some unionists in the area. They even murdered a convalescing Confederate officer at his house, but accomplished little against the elusive partisans themselves. Starring commented, "I deem it almost impossible to capture or catch the guerrillas of Tennessee, Missouri, or Kentucky with infantry." The enemy partisans were well mounted and kept themselves apprised of all Union movements "by regular system or sort of pony express, sending work, signalizing [sic] their neighbors, signs on trees, bushes in the roads, &c." Unless they had superior force and all the advantage, he added, "they manage to keep out of the way or scatter and become peaceful farmers and citizens until the danger is past."[51]

Federal authorities moved to counter this increasingly irritating type of warfare. In Middle Tennessee, Governor Johnson authorized William B. Stokes, a former U.S. Congressman and erstwhile provisional Tennessee army officer under Confederate colors before seeing the light of unionism, to raise a battalion of cavalry. Cumberland Gap commander George Washington Morgan similarly commissioned local unionist William Clift to raise the Seventh Tennessee (Union) Cavalry for counterguerrilla work. Union volunteer cavalry under Colonel Edward C. Williams and Major Thomas Jordan busily swept the Tompkins–Celina area. Williams failed to prevent Jordan's capture when Morgan knifed up through this corridor headed for Kentucky the following month. Generally, the Federals could not keep up with the irregular activity on the Tennessee–Kentucky line eastward to the Cumberlands. Captain George W. Carter's Company A, Fourth Tennessee Cavalry (Confederate)—its commander was the son of a blacksmith from Spencer in Van Buren County, Tennessee, and was known throughout the region as a pugilist—spent most of its service battling Union home guards in the shadow of those mountains.[52]

One of Buell's quartermasters whined that the organized irregulars gave the Confederates an advantage over the Federals. The guerrillas could be easily supplied by their families, he claimed, because of their knowledge of the country. He estimated that ten thousand cavalry would be required to protect the five-hundred-mile line of communications stretching from Louisville to Huntsville, Alabama. Obviously at this point Buell's subordinates were very conventional, determined to adhere to established rules of warfare, including resupplying rather than living off the country. Moreover, Colonel Marcellus Mundy of the Twenty-third Kentucky cavalry commanding at Pulaski in this period later told an army commission investigating Don Carlos Buell's conduct of affairs in Kentucky and Tennessee that Federal authorities could not "expect any demonstrations of loyalty from the people there unless we can assure them of protection against the rebel armies and guerrillas." So it seemingly mattered little if the Yankees lived off the country at this point anyway.[53]

In late September, Grant reorganized his District of West Tennessee into the Department of Tennessee with four parts. By early October Major General Edward O. C. Ord's Second Division embraced the country northward to the Kentucky line. Major General William S. Rosecrans's command straddled the Tennessee–Mississippi line, and, like Ord, he focused primarily on railroad protection. Another division under Brigadier General Isaac F. Quinby (later commanded by

Thomas A. Davies) was a purely logistical command, covering former districts of Cairo and the Mississippi and included Forts Henry, Heiman, and Donelson. Quinby counted 281 officers and 5,962 men with 56 heavy and 8 field guns—many of whom were tied down in counterinsurgency work against the partisans. Ironically, the honor of Grant's February victories kept these latter positions in his jurisdiction rather than more logically aligned with Buell, for whom the streams these divisions guarded served as major supply lines. Finally, Major William T. Sherman commanded a fourth division, headquartered at Memphis and embracing "all territory south of the Hatchie [River] and west of Bolivar occupied by our troops."[54]

A perceptible change in attitude manifested itself among both Union soldiers and political leaders in the upper heartland by late summer. Perhaps they partially reflected the government's hardening attitude, alluded to in the previous chapter. But, locally, Major General William Tecumseh Sherman, commanding at Memphis, was one Union general whose disposition assumed harsh if not sinister overtones concerning guerrilla depredations in his jurisdiction. He might oppose wanton foraging by his men as contrary to discipline and order. Neither was he for wholesale emancipation in principle. But, like Grant, Sherman followed Halleck's direction, focusing any retribution strictly upon the slave-owning classes as directed military punishment. Attacks upon lines of communication, ambushes of garrisons and patrols, and harassment of unionist civilians were bad enough, but when guerrillas attacked unarmed, commercial steamboats on the Mississippi, that was quite another matter. Union retribution could prompt guerrilla retaliation. But when the packetboat *Eugene* was fired upon in September near Randolph, some twenty-five miles north of Memphis, Sherman ordered an Ohio regiment to lay waste to Randolph as an example to the local populace who either had aided, abetted, or, in some cases, perhaps even constituted guerrilla forces.[55]

After considering that many Memphis rebel families resided comfortably in the Union-occupied city and that they, plus regular Confederate authorities, openly sanctioned such warfare, Sherman decreed on September 27—three days after the destruction of Randolph—that some ten families would be expelled with only three days' notice and required to distance themselves at least twenty-five miles from Memphis for each boat fired on in the future. Sherman temporarily relented when one Arkansas partisan chief threatened to hang ten captured Yankee soldiers for each evicted family. But, before long, he returned to his threat of "collective punishment." Finally, on October 29, he ordered the S. P. Bankhead family out of town because some "are in a guerrilla band" that fired upon steamers *Continental* and *J. H. Dickey* and their actions had a tendency "to restrict commerce and lessen supplies at Memphis," according to the Provost Marshall. Similarly, the spunky Mrs. Elizabeth Avery Meriwether was among the first banished because, she believed, her husband was in the rebel army and she had stood up personally to Sherman's bullying manner. She nurtured a profound hatred for this Yankee general until her death in 1916. It certainly found ample expression in her recollections, penned when she was ninety-two years old.[56]

Sherman was fanatical about two things: law and order, and the symbolic nature of the great Mississippi River as the essence of nation and Union. His exposure before the war to vigilantism in California, to Jayhawkers and Free Soilers in Kansas, and northern abolitionists led him to suspect any threat to social order. As a professional soldier he resented the untidy nature of irregular warfare, but as a midwesterner (in the same spirit as Lincoln, Grant, and others from that section), free navigation of the nation's rivers represented the lifeblood for farmers, tradesmen, and commercial interests and had to be maintained against any depredations.

Sherman had long since declared openly: "Let all the people understand that we claim the unmolested navigation of the Mississippi River, and we will have it, if all the country within reach has to be laid waste. . . ." To fellow general John A. Logan, he claimed that to secure the safety of the Mississippi, "I would slay millions. On that point I am not only insane, but mad. . . ." He threatened to shoot a thousand thirty-pounder Parrott guns into even helpless towns, "or wherever a boat can float or soldier march," for every steamboat fired upon. Whether or not the general realized that the Mississippi's closure to the Gulf had led to increasing Midwestern trading with the east via railroads, thus rendering the river route to the sea moot, Sherman was determined to root out lawlessness and civil unrest as it affected both military and commercial activities in the Mississippi Valley.[57]

One of Sherman's most colorful statements soon appeared in an October 4, 1862, letter to his friend Grant. Declaring that the local populace had begun to realize that the Northwest "intends to fight to the death for the Mississippi River," he avowed "this is my hobby, and . . . I am daily more and more convinced that we should hold the river absolutely and leave the interior alone." Detachments there could be easily overcome and really did little to convert the people to unionism. "They cannot be made to love us, but they can be made to fear us, and dread the passage of our troops through the country," he avowed. Sherman doubted that the army could change the hearts of those people in the South, "but we can make war so terrible" that they would realize that no matter how brave and devoted to their country, they were still mortal and should exhaust all peaceful remedies before flying to war. Still, the seeds for this sentiment had been planted long before autumn in Sherman's heart.[58]

Nevertheless, Sherman remained somewhat indulgent of local trade in the Memphis area. He told Grant on October 9 that "farmers have come in gangs, representing their determination to fight guerrillas and carry out to their suffering families the clothing and groceries necessary to their existence." Still, such trade usually helped either the main rebel armies or the irregulars—or both, as surely Sherman must have known. Yet he, like the Lincoln administration generally, or Buell as an example in Middle Tennessee, thought that farmers and property holders "may realize their dependence on other parts of our country, and also realize that a state of war long continued will reduce them to a state of absolute ruin." Partisans did more harm to the Confederacy than the Union, he claimed, "for they in their wants and necessities must take meat and corn, and will take it when and where they please, of friend or foe." The consequence "is that the farmers and planters begin to realize that they have to submit to be plundered by these bands of marauders, and are getting heartily tired of it." Yet, he was aware of the dangers of smuggling and misuse of his benevolence, and he recommended prohibition of all trade to all districts "until the military commander notifies the Government that the rebellion is suppressed in that district. . . ." Such an approach contrasted sharply with policies of others in the upper heartland.[59]

In Kentucky, for example, Brigadier General Jeremiah T. Boyle's relentless determination to suppress dissidence via "arrest for opinion's sake" (as critics claimed) reached a veritable fever pitch. Here, the danger was even more clear than in Memphis. The border states forever seemed to flirt with possible secession. Secretary of War Edwin M. Stanton alluded to it ever so briefly in mid-August, but by then literally hundreds of people had been ensnared and thrown into jail on charges of disloyalty. As in Nashville, clergy were singled out because of their position as spokesmen in the community, but even women and children felt Boyle's wrath. The momentum of terror did increase after the Confederate autumn offensives, but Lincoln administration pronouncements concerning confiscation, emancipation, and a general paranoia about traitorism fueled Boyle's actions even before that. Washington might urge caution, but Boyle's moves found great favor with Tennessee governor Andrew Johnson, who had urged his fellow brigadier as early as August 4 to expel and put to the sword all traitors who persisted in opposing the national government. Treason must be made odious, Johnson announced repeatedly, with traitors punished and impoverished—a sentiment openly in conflict with the conciliatory "rose water" doctrine of protecting citizen property for even those in rebellion.[60]

Conflicting policy pronouncements meant confusion for men in the ranks. Sergeant Eugene Marshall of the Fifth Iowa Cavalry on the twin rivers wrote to his sister in late September that he and his men had been on twenty-hour counterguerrilla sweeps, stopping to eat at various farms and isolated houses. "[W]hen we are out on a scout," he declared, "we live off the enemy now, we have given up the principal of guarding rebel property." Mitchel Andrew Thompson, a soldier of Company B, Eighty-third Illinois, at Fort Donelson recounted his conversation with one local unionist and scout during Lowe's expedition to Clarksville in September. When Thompson queried the man about why his fellow unionists did not enlist in the northern army as the guide had done, the Tennessean set him straight immediately. What would become of their families, he asked, for the unionists were among the poor rather than the elite of the locale. The latter were all rebels so that the poor unionists could only guide and scout, and rely upon "you of the north to conquer our enemies for us."[61]

The guide thought Federal authorities were suppressing the rebels in a completely erroneous fashion. Guarding mansions of the rich, while husbands and sons were in the rebel army, was intolerable, he contended. Suggesting that an underlying class struggle was part of the heartland's civil war, this native son, at least, argued that "You must reduce the rich lordling that is engaged in the rebellion to poverty—cut and slash until there is nothing left that he can recover himself with." The country was ruined anyway, he told Thompson, so it would hurt no worse to divest the scoundrels of all property. Thompson replied that when a recently enacted congressional confiscation act took effect, the army might do just that. "I wish to God you had done it a year ago," was the lanky Tennessean's only rejoinder.

The measure to which Thompson referred strengthened the hand of retributionists. The so-called second Confiscation Act, signed by Lincoln on July 17, 1862, provided for emancipation for slaves of all those who supported or aided the rebellion, as well as seizure of other property like land and houses. But the act applied only to seceded states, not the border states. In fact, other moderating provisions held for returning fugitive slaves from the border states whose owners could prove their loyalty to the government. Still another provision called for gradual, compensatory emancipation, which Lincoln hoped would induce Virginia and Tennessee back into the Union.[62]

Calculated to clarify the vagaries of the policy for army officers encountering refugees and runaway slaves, a preliminary emancipation proclamation pronouncement of late September, which took effect on January 1, 1863, was a double-edged sword. It appealed to abolitionists and their Radical Republican allies in Congress and, together with confiscation, helped hard-line officials and soldiers operating south of the Ohio and Potomac Rivers. Lincoln's additional September 24 proclamation, suspending the writ of habeas corpus and providing for military trial of "all Rebels and Insurgents, their aiders and abettors within the United States," added statutory authority to what the men in blue were already effecting themselves. Of course, not everyone in national uniform agreed with those policies. But enforcement of these acts rode with officers like Anthony, Boyle, Lowe, Bruce, or Harding, backed by the higher authority of Sherman, Grant, Acting Rear Admiral David Dixon Porter, and the politicos in Nashville and Washington. Enforcement of these acts formed "all-out" war. But, as Mark Grimsley advances, to the fighting man all-out war meant a struggle "waged against the delicacy of protecting Southern property," while to his officers, it was "a battlefield-oriented conflict with foraging and destruction of property playing ancillary roles."[63]

Frankly, the men in blue delighted in stricter enforcement, whether directed toward suppression of partisans or punishment of wicked slave owners who had perpetrated the war. Private Tighlman Jones of the Fifty-ninth Illinois asked his father what he now thought about the confiscation bill and employment of African Americans by the United States under the Militia Act of July 17, 1862. He quickly answered that he liked it "just well enough to spend the rest of my three years carrying it out to the limit." There had been too much leniency shown rebel property while the owners were away in the Confederate army, he contended. Even taking a peach or apple "was a cruel offense," but no longer, Jones observed. His new brigade commander, Brigadier General R. B. Mitchell was a hard-liner, which suited the Illinois soldiers.[64]

Indeed, even the United States Navy entered the counterinsurgency activity.

When the heavy gunboats of Flag Officer Andrew Hull Foote transferred their spring operations from the twin rivers to the Mississippi, only the 86-ton USS *Alfred Robb* remained behind to police the Cumberland and the Tennessee. Built in Pittsburgh, she had been a Confederate transport until captured by the USS *Tyler* at Florence, Alabama, on April 19. By summer, she sported two 12-pounder howitzers and was soon joined by yet another converted rebel boat, the 38-ton *General Pillow* (her name was apparently retained on Union rolls), with similar armament, and the *Little Rebel* (161 tons, same battery) that had been captured as a Confederate cotton-clad ram at the battle of Memphis on June 6. Commodore Charles H. Davis, commanding the Mississippi flotilla, assigned Lieutenant (later Lieutenant Commander) Le Roy Fitch as executive and gunnery officer for this light squadron on August 21. Under the overall direction of Commander and Fleet Captain Alfred M. Pennock, Fitch took two of his craft up the Tennessee on August 23 and was plagued, as the navy would constantly be, by low water and the shoals at the mouth of Duck River. Then he rushed back to Paducah on September 4, after hearing that the city feared immediate attack.[65]

Rebel irregulars focused Fitch's attention by jumping the army transport *W. B. Terry* when she ran aground on August 30 at the Duck River shoals. Some two hundred members of Captain T. Alonzo Napier and Captain James B. Algee's gangs overcame two six-pounder cannon and a seven-man gun crew plus ten sharpshooters from the eighty-first Ohio, forcing Master Leonard G. Klinck to surrender. After dumping the boat's coal into the river to lighten her ballast, the rebels used her to ferry them across the river, then sent the civilian passengers and crew unharmed into the country, while setting Klinck and his officers adrift on a raft to float back to Fort Henry. Army officials were aghast at the news.

The steamers *Skylark* and *Callie* had suffered similar fates the previous week and, like the *Terry*, they had been burned when of no further use to the irregulars. Grant blamed the "connivance of the captains or Treasury agents," while pursuit from army garrisons at Forts Henry, Heiman, and Donelson accomplished nothing. As Marshall opined, the perpetrators had crossed the river or dispersed to their homes, so the cavalry scooped up fewer than fifteen captives. Fitch, at least, got two other gunboats, the *Cordelia Ann* and the USS *Fairplay* out of it. The refitted 162-ton *Fairplay* carried four twelve-pounder howitzers, and in early September it began patrols on the Ohio River "as guerrilla raids had become very annoying along that river, too."[66]

Aside from occasionally stopping at Ohio towns like Uniontown and Shawneetown, Kentucky, to extract loyalty oaths and bonds for good behavior, Fitch's boats also sent landing parties to chase irregulars with varying degrees of success. He conveyed released Fort Donelson prisoners downriver for exchange at Vicksburg, Mississippi, and encountered problems similar to those the army faced with regard to refugee ex-slaves, with many going aboard the flotilla as coal heavers. St. Louis and Cairo boat yards busily constructed and re-outfitted more craft for the Mississippi squadron, building both light draft vessels for the upper rivers and the heavier battle wagons for use against rebel forts in Mississippi and Louisiana. Fleet Captain Pennock pointedly told naval constructors: "The guerrillas are at nearly all points on the Ohio and Tennessee Rivers, and the need for armed boats is extremely urgent."[67]

Pennock told Commodore J. B. Hull at St. Louis that these gunboats could be mosquito craft, lightly armored only on the hurricane deck and topside. Inevitable delays and labor squabbles attended the preparation of antiguerrilla boats, but, finally, on September 25, Naval Constructor Edward Hartt sent word of the 12:40 P.M. departure of USS *Brilliant* (227 tons) and USS *St. Clair* (203 tons), soon to be mainstays of Fitch's effort since both the craft drew only one foot, ten inches of water fore and two feet, four inches aft. First Master Charles G. Perkins took charge of the *Brilliant*; Master Jacob S. Hurd commanded the *St. Clair*. Both boats carried two twelve-pounder rifles and two twelve-pounder smoothbore howitzers apiece.

The transfer of the western gunboat flotilla from army to navy control on October 1, 1862, forced the sea service to reexamine its policies concerning the growing guerrilla threat. Porter took over the Mississippi squadron and quickly decided that "the guerrillas were very troublesome and were firing on unarmed vessels from the river banks and at places not occupied by United States troops, when the steamers stopped and allowed themselves (I think) to be robbed." Large quantities of goods were being shipped intentionally from St. Louis and landed for trade in the Kentucky and Tennessee interior, he thought. The war would never end as long as such free trade continued. Therefore, he imposed a blockade of all points not occupied by the army or covered by a gunboat. He also ordered retaliatory measures to stop the irregular warfare taking place throughout his jurisdiction. Incidents continued, however, and Porter soon found himself resorting to Sherman-like tactics, destroying one Arkansas hamlet because guerrillas had ambushed a passenger boat and killed a civilian.[68]

Fitch did not have to go that far, but the capture of the *Hazel Dell* on the Ohio by Adam Johnson's band prompted his swift retribution. Fitch imposed a thirty-five-thousand-dollar tribute (Porter actually wanted ten times that figure applied) upon Caseyville and vicinity in Union County, Kentucky. This was precisely the way that army commanders handled partisans and the local populace in Tennessee, and he particularly singled out local troublemakers Philip Acker, William Pemberton, and J. M. Scantlin, while residents who had fed and sheltered Johnson's men received special attention. Unionists naturally escaped the levy. Fitch also shut down ferry traffic with the Illinois and Indiana shore from Paducah upriver. He confiscated all scows, flatboats, skiffs, and other craft and notified the public that anyone sending or selling any goods across the river without official signature would be arrested.[69]

When low water shut down his gunboat operation, he transferred boat howitzers to mail boats for their protection. He told his superiors that this arrangement worked well, "for guerrillas on several occasions made so bold as to present themselves on the banks and hail the steamers in, but receiving rather unexpected and severe lessons from the howitzers, soon learned to let vessels pass unmolested." Davis praised Fitch's work to Secretary of the Navy Gideon Welles on October 2, and Porter liked his subordinate's hard-nosed approach so much that

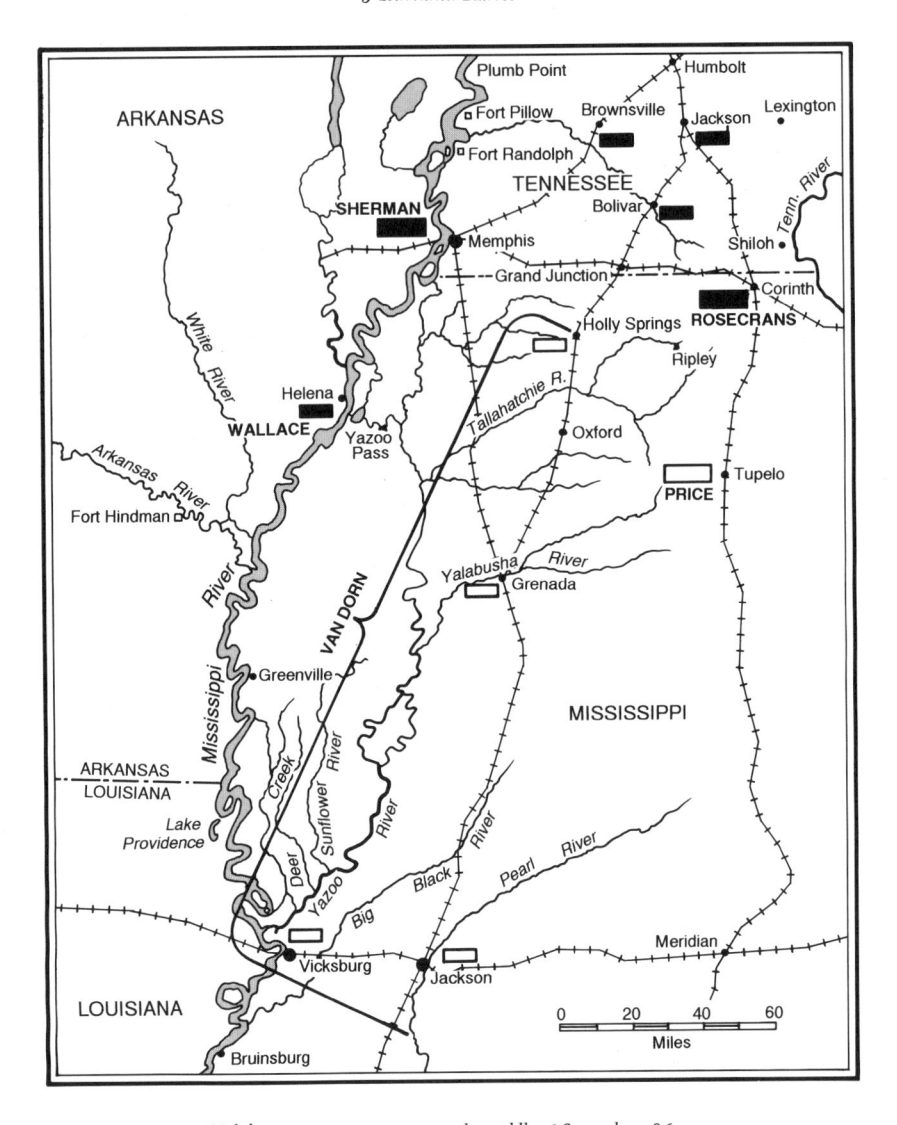

Vicksburg campaign situation in the middle of September 1862.

he expected him to transfer his protection of loyalists to the Cumberland and Tennessee Rivers as soon as he finished cleaning up the Ohio. "This is the only way of putting a stop to guerrilla warfare," he told Welles late that month. "Though the method is stringent, officers are instructed to put it down at all hazards," adding that he anticipated organizing a naval brigade (comprising one thousand infantry, one hundred cavalry, and a full artillery battery) from army troops for rapid deployment against partisan bands along the riverbanks of the West. That, however, would await action later in the fall.[70]

By late summer, cavalry raids and partisan operations had all but stymied the promising Union offensives of the spring. As soon as Generals Buell, Halleck, Grant, Rosecrans, and others embraced the new technology of the "iron horse," their opponents proved how vulnerable the railroads were to mounted raids and irregular attack. The Union generals also learned that mounted warriors posed equally disturbing interruptions to pacification and reconstruction activities. Destruction and intimidation became weapons in the Confederate arsenal that helped offset the Yankee success on the main battlefields. Union army and navy units found themselves increasingly drawn into this nasty, mostly inconclusive style of warfare. Lacking training manuals and textbooks on the art and science of irregular warfare, they improvised and turned increasingly harsh in response. Rebel retaliation followed like a revolving door in an unceasing cycle of bloodshed and violence.

If Union authorities won the battles, they were losing the pacification war at this point. Every time Union soldiers lost their patience and preyed upon innocent civilians, as Starring's men had done in West Tennessee, the task of the occupier became more difficult and the role of the guerrilla much easier. On the other hand, the situation began to change as unionists began to make their way into Federal ranks. In West Tennessee, McNairy County "tories" Fielding Hurst and Stanford L. Warren organized the Sixth Tennessee Cavalry (Union), and the number of such loyal units would grow despite persecution and unbridled retaliation by both sides as the war progressed. Generals like Grant and Sherman, who were held in place until a logistical buildup permitted regular campaigning, necessarily had to be infuriated by the long-term harassment and delays. Suppressing partisans and the contraband trade, tolerating cotton exchange, and supporting incipient unionism all took time, and they were part of bringing national authority to such a large area. Moreover, by September and October, the principal Union and Confederate armies had rejoined battlefield bloodletting once again. Cavalry raids and partisan incursions had been the prelude. Now they became sideshows to the main events.[71]

FIVE

NORTH TO KENTUCKY: AUTUMN 1862

Captain Andrew Jackson Campbell of the Forty-eighth Tennessee stared across the muddy, tepid water of the Mississippi and Ohio Rivers where they merged at Cairo, Illinois, early on September 7, 1862. He jotted in his pocket notebook: "The scene here this morning beggars description." Only recently freed from Johnson's Island after being captured at Fort Donelson, he now leaned on the rail of the old steamer *Choutan* and awaited its departure downriver for the prisoner-exchange point of Vicksburg, Mississippi. Campbell saw five other steamboats anchored in midstream with upwards of ten thousand prisoners aboard. Gathered from prisoner camps all across the Midwest, these were the survivors from Forts Henry and Donelson, Island Number 10, and other battles and skirmishes in the West. They had braved the intervening months of poor rations, inadequate shelter, underweight clothing, and, above all, boredom. Many of them were still sick.[1]

Some of the prisoners, like Thomas Rawlings Myer of Company F, Forty-first Tennessee, still bitterly remembered "the deep humiliation" to which they had been subjected by great crowds of onlookers who had flocked to various railroad stations along the route to Camp Morton, Indiana, back in February. Their faces and clothes grimy with the dirt from Fort Donelson's trenches and powder smoke from the battle "afforded our Northern brethren great amusement," which only intensified "our deep humiliation and mortification." Only some Catholic nuns in Illinois, and later at the prison camp itself, had offered succor, particularly to the ill, he noted.[2]

Camaraderie, prison yard games, and the insuppressible resistance to Yankee authority had sustained them through the ordeal. A few might chuckle at the tale of a tiny band at Camp Butler, Illinois, which had discovered a cache of unused muskets and had clandestinely burnished them to a new brightness in order to escape: they had then "escorted" fellow prisoners past militia guards to freedom. But the rest had languished until news of the prisoner exchange arrived in August. "We all felt lighthearted at the prospect for Dixie," Campbell noted in his diary on August 27.[3]

Far to the east in Virginia, a similar group of prisoners also moved toward repatriation. Fewer in numbers, these Union captives also had been taken at Fort Donelson and had been carefully shipped upriver prior to the surrender. Lieutenant James Vernay and a handful of wounded men of the Eleventh Illinois left aboard the very steamboat that had conveyed Brigadier General John B. Floyd and his Virginia brigade away from the doomed post. Vernay and company secured their freedom back with the fall of Nashville. Other Illini, however, like Lieutenant Nathaniel C. Kenyon of Company D, had suffered months of ignominious transfers from Nashville to Tuscaloosa, Alabama, then to Atlanta, and finally to Richmond. The guards "appear to be as afraid of unarmed Yankees as though they were monsters that possessed supernatural strength," he observed at one point.[4]

Indeed, years of antebellum nurturing on a litany of horror stories about Yankees had produced that conditioned response. And so, Confederate treatment of these early war captives equaled the reputedly callous handling that Federal guards accorded southern scions at Alton, Camp Douglas, Camp Chase, Johnson's Island, and elsewhere. Now, in September, these bluecoats awaited release at Aiken's Landing, Virginia. Once home or back in the ranks they were determined to exact retribution on the Confederacy. Indeed, their tales helped inspire confiscation, intimidation, and slave liberation as their brothers in blue moved farther into Dixie.

Returning to Campbell's story, the train ride from Johnson's Island to Cairo had been cramped and tedious. But, astonishingly, the dearth of guards permitted the prisoners to roam freely at every station stop, seeking food and drink. Citizens in southern Illinois openly cheered the transiting rebels. Campbell found the Irish Americans to be far more sympathetic to the plight of the south than their German-American counterparts. Finally, the trains arrived in Cairo, disgorged their passengers, who discovered personal baggage had been rifled by Federal authorities and sent south separately. But all was forgotten as the POW flotilla, carefully shepherded by two gunboats, pushed off on September 8.

The trip downriver witnessed more wild enthusiasm by southern ladies (the men were conspicuously absent, Campbell noted) on the Tennessee shoreline, although Memphis seemed a city of the dead. Restive to the point of rioting, some of the boys found lager beer kegs below decks and led the guards on merry chases around the craft. Finally, by September 16, the Henry-Donelson prisoners stepped ashore at Vicksburg amidst rain and mud. At least they were "relieved of the hated presence of the Yankees once more."[5]

Freedom proved disheartening, in some ways. High prices, lack of recognition for the returning patriots by the Vicksburg populace, and the obvious impact of the war upon that city bothered Campbell. His old regiment passed muster by September 28, although "the way we are treated on our arrival throws a damper on the enthusiasm of the troops," he observed. After being moved inland to a collection point at Jackson, the troops underwent reorientation under exchanged

Kentucky brigadier Lloyd Tilghman, captured at Fort Henry, before being assigned to Major General Sterling Price's army in northern Mississippi. They numbered perhaps as many as fifteen thousand men (according to a Tennessee brigadier, also exchanged and awaiting assignment at Oxford, Mississippi). Campbell went along as a newly minted major. Aside from the rounds of more drill and rehabilitation, he found time to analyze rumors and study the newspapers, as everyone learned about Bedford Forrest's maneuvers in the Nashville suburbs. The city was surrounded and threatened, but not taken, and Campbell wondered: "will they fool around until the place can't be taken, or will they take it before reinforcements arrive?" Several days later, he jotted despairingly in his diary: "Middle Tennessee is again to be overrun by the Vandals," and "my home is to be laid waste and desolated by them," while he and his follow Tennesseans were away and unable "to strike the dogs down."[6]

THREE REBEL OFFENSIVES

Notwithstanding Campbell's concern, whatever the intensity of Federal oppression in Tennessee and Kentucky that summer and fall, ardent friends of the Confederacy never lost hope. When Nashville *Union* editor S. C. Mercer, a Kentucky unionist brought in by Military Governor Andrew Johnson and paid from U.S. government funds, sneeringly ran the romantic poem about John Hunt Morgan entitled "Hero of the West," his action immediately prompted an irate reply from its author. It had been written, she rejoined, "for a little girl to sing when Morgan does come," and she assured the editor that "'John Morgan' will certainly come and Mercer as certainly will have to get away." In fact, the poem's final phrase said it all for anguished civilians—"John Morgan, 'Thou Invincible'— Return and Set us free." Yet, Morgan did not redeem Nashville, and the poem's author had to be content merely venting her ire at the Yankee editor "upon a sheet adorned by the Goddess of Liberty, with her face and arms blacked and the American flag marked out with ink."[7]

Defiance was double-sided. When a mysterious fire consumed a city block in Pulaski, Tennessee, on the night of September 20, local citizens were amazed that neither Union soldiers nor their "loyal" negroes lifted a hand to help contain the blaze. Twenty-one houses were burned and fourteen men thrown out of work, penned Martha Abernathy in her diary. She claimed the whole affair resulted from lax garrison control over prowling African Americans. But the soldiers jokingly attributed the conflagration to rebels "to make a light to fight us by." The town was a wreck, and Abernathy wondered about the reaction "of our brave-hearted Southerners, whose homes are in this town and county, when they return and witness the works of a hostile foe in our midst." Unrepentant as ever, she wrung her hands at news of the confiscation act, due to become effective on September 25. This act would cause the men still at home to take the oath of allegiance to save their property, while those in Confederate service "will have to fight for theirs if they get it." Meanwhile, their families would suffer intensely, while returning

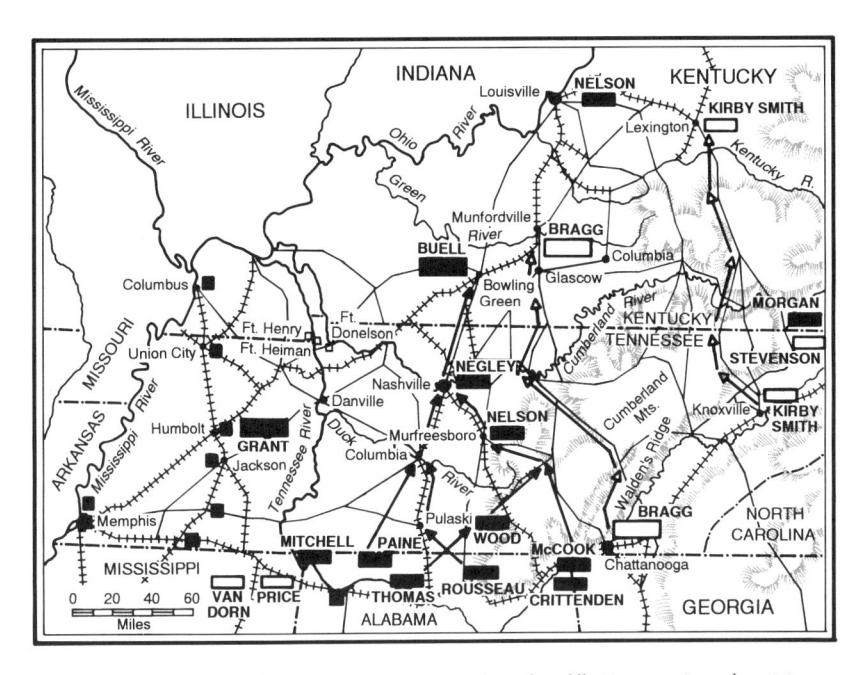

The deployment of forces before the invasion of Kentucky and Middle Tennessee, September 1862.

husbands would "see their children begging bread." She implored God to save them from utter destruction.[8]

Of course, news of home front persecution raised the dander of those men in gray. After noting published accounts in Cincinnati newspapers that Federal agents "are forcing Morgan's friends to pay for the acts of their favorite chieftain," Morgan personally declared in mid-August that he would now retaliate against unionists, people hitherto spared in his destruction of government property. "For every dollar exacted from my fellow citizens, I will have two from all men of known Union sentiments, and will make their persons and property responsible for this payment," he declared. Blaming the "vindicative and iniquitous proceedings of our Northern foes," he vowed to "induce them to return to more human conduct." In fact, such Federal oppression, in part, caused Confederate leaders to seek redress through military counteroffensives. Of course, other sound political and military reasons also existed for such moves. Again, effect and countereffect could be found underlying the antagonists' actions in the upper Confederate heartland.[9]

General Robert E. Lee's invasion of Maryland, the Smith-Bragg attempt to "liberate" Kentucky, and the Price–Van Dorn maneuvers in northern Mississippi—and even some advances into Missouri—all aimed at carrying the war northward in the fall of 1862. Foreign recognition, recruitment of fresh manpower, acquisition of supplies, and securing Kentucky and Maryland politically were the principal motives of the Confederacy. So, too, was reopening trade with the Midwest (on Confederate terms). Richmond, in fact, sent directions on September 24 that, as soon as military commanders approached or entered Union-held territory bordering the Mississippi River or its tributaries, they should issue proclamations assuring the populace "of the free navigation" of the river in accordance with a February 25, 1861, act of the Confederate congress. Not only had this been an inflammatory issue in the Great Valley during the Secession Winter of 1861, but also it now threatened popular support of the Lincoln administration north of the Ohio.[10]

None of the Confederate offensives lacked for zeal or purpose. But all of them died within six weeks—in Maryland at Antietam on September 17; in northern Mississippi at Iuka on September 19 and at Corinth on October 3 and 4; and at Perryville, Kentucky, four days later on October 8. It was almost as if Ulysses S. Grant had been prescient when he wrote his wife, Julia, on September 14: "You will see the greatest fall in a few weeks of rebel hopes that was ever known." They will have made a bold effort, he continued "but it is a spasmodic effort without anything behind to fall back on." He felt that when they did begin to recede, "all resources are at an end and rebellion will soon show a rapid decline." Grant remained a little too overconfident on that point.[11]

Borderland ambivalence, stubborn Yankee resilience on the battlefield, and poor command coordination would doom the rebel offensives. Confederate failures meant that both Kentucky and Tennessee would remain the dark and bloody ground of skirmishes, raids, partisans, and sanguinary battles well past the changing hues of autumn. None of the four principal rebel generals misperceived the goal of wintering on the Ohio. But difficulties in communicating with one another to coordinate their efforts and in subordinating personal desire for glory to teamwork as well as changing circumstances on the ground befell each column. For example, uncertainty about how to incorporate the returning prisoners into the armies, the embarrassing reappearance of Brigadier General Gideon J. Pillow at Mississippi army headquarters—without a command but full of ideas and promises—and horrendous battlefield judgment at Iuka and Corinth quickly bedeviled Price and Van Dorn. Moreover, misreading Bluegrass signals underscored the Bragg—Kirby Smith reverse.[12]

Confederate Kentuckians, from division commanders John C. Breckinridge and Simon B. Buckner to cavalry cavaliers Morgan, Duke, and Adam Johnson, all thought their personal, unabashed dedication to the Cause mirrored that of oppressed kinsmen at home. Certainly, troopers like John M. Porter, riding with Morgan, saw the offensive as a chance to relieve friends and relatives from the likes of Union brigadier Jeremiah Boyle and his "tory" Kentuckians. But mere raids and partisan activity could not accomplish that feat. Only a major army victory and the installation of a pro-Confederate state government at Frankfort as well as a permanent military presence would accomplish that end. Just such a permanence seemed quite possible in the autumn of 1862, if the people flocked to embrace their deliverers. Indeed, dreams of grandeur and political success flickered across the minds of many in the Confederacy at this time, and the consummate macro-planner of them all, General P. G. T. Beauregard, was one person always prepared with a scheme.[13]

While convalescing in Mobile, Alabama, Beauregard wrote Confederate Adjutant/Inspector General Samuel Cooper on September 5 that, once rebel arms stood on the banks of the Ohio, then the Cumberland and Tennessee Rivers should be refortified. Only this time, the site should be the more sensible location near Eddyville, Kentucky, where the streams were only about a mile and half apart. Kentucky's neutrality had made an occupation of this region impossible in the fall of 1861. As a result, the twelve-mile gap between Forts Henry and Donelson had proved fatal. Now it could be different, for a strong fieldwork could be constructed on a commanding elevation at Eddyville for a garrison of about twenty-five hundred or three thousand men. They could hold out (with ample provisions and ammunition) against a large army. The guns of this work and a series of riverbank batteries armed with eight-, nine-, and ten-inch cannon could be constructed, bearing directly on obstructions placed in both of the rivers.[14]

Of course it was pure fantasy—it had not worked at Henry-Donelson, so why should it work now? Undaunted, however, Beauregard also advocated building a fort near Louisville for the command of the Ohio and the local canal, which he "would destroy . . . as soon as possible so completely that future travelers would hardly know where it was" in retaliation for Yankee vandalism in attempting obstruction of Charleston and Savannah harbors. Another fort, built at Covington, could cover the perceived logical waterborne move by Confederate arms on Cincinnati across the river. In all, Beauregard saw the value of controlling waterways, but repeated the illusion that static shore defenses offered the solution. It was Columbus, and the twin river forts all over again. Naturally, it was a premature plan. At some point a copy of the scheme fell into Don Carlos Buell's hands, so the Federals knew all about it anyway.

Beauregard and Knoxville, Tennessee, commander Major General John P. McGown passed the idea directly to Bragg. But Richmond authorities also entertained notions of returning to river defense. Lieutenant Colonel Jeremy F. Gilmer, an engineer bureau chief and former designer of the twin river defenses, sent a subordinate to Bragg on September 26 with instructions "to make a reconnaissance of the Cumberland and Tennessee Rivers, with a view to an early occupation of the best points by fortifications commanding obstructions in their channels." It was a replay of the previous autumn, although some of the lessons of Henry and Donelson were reflected in Gilmer's instruction to Captain Edward B. Sayers to site any new works on elevated ground; further, he pointed out that "land defenses in rear of each river battery should have sufficient strength to resist a storming party, thus forcing the enemy to a regular investment."[15]

In addition, self-sufficient storerooms, magazines, and bomb proofs would support the artillery units, as would criblike, stone-filled dams placed in rows across the rivers to provide permanent barriers that would not be susceptible to the whims of river currents and freshets. Pilings and steamboat hulks would increase the strength of the position. All of this, of course, would depend much "upon the occupation of the country by our troops," said Gilmer, as well as upon establishing limits within which the proposed defenses should be located, the strength of garrisons that could be spared by Bragg, availability of armament, and the duration anticipated to hold out against attack. Again, as had been the case with Beauregard's plan, the "lessons learned" pointed backward not forward in terms of military reality after seven months of Union success. Still, possibilities existed.

Richmond naval authorities also joined in this planning, and they came up with a more improbable scheme than even Gilmer's. Secretary of the Navy Stephen R. Mallory directed Captain Samuel Barron, C.S.N., to construct ironclad gunboats for western rivers. Barron went to Tennessee from his naval billet at Charlotte, North Carolina, carrying drawings for a side-wheel ironclad, expressly devised to receive engines and boilers that might be obtained from river boats. He was to procure such a craft "within a certain stipulated time, which must be as brief as possible." Penalties and bonuses for delivery over or under contract would amount to two hundred dollars per day. Rolled iron plate, "if we can get it," would provide the material for fabrication, since railroad iron would be imperfect against shot, but might suffice if no other proved available. Most of all, however, "our roads should not be denuded of rails if we can avoid it." One Florence, Alabama, resident volunteered the suggestion that his city should be the construction site, but Mallory told Barron, "should we get possession of Nashville, that city would doubtless afford greater facilities than you could find elsewhere upon either river." Yet, timing was everything, and much depended upon the ultimate success of Kirby Smith and Braxton Bragg in conquering Kentucky.[16]

Many Kentuckians remained ominously apathetic at first. One Louisville observer wrote his wife from the Galt House on September 1 that matters were in a sad state and getting worse. Louisvillians, he thought, equated both Lincoln and Davis with the Lord or Devil as circumstances dictated, and they were "just as impassive or undisturbed as if nothing were the matter." Then, this mood changed as swarms of rebels under John Hunt Morgan swirled through the middle part of the state, gathering supplies, recruits, and raising mayhem in advance of the main Confederate forces. With bank deposits flowing back to Louisville for safekeeping from Lexington, Frankfort, and dozens of smaller towns, Kentuckians realized a way of life was threatened, businesses disrupted, and their trades and fortunes, possibly even the placid existence beyond the war zone, lay in jeopardy. Suddenly, river towns from Louisville to Cincinnati echoed to the beat of drums, pick, and shovel in preparation for the rebel onslaught. The tone turned solemn, even testy, as unionists and neutrals both wondered why elected officials and the army seemed to be doing so little. But some people were taking action. Fort Donelson veteran Colonel James Shackelford and others organized the Eighth Kentucky Cavalry at Russellville on September 8, mustering 1,248 men within weeks after the date authority was given.[17]

Kentuckian J. B. Cochran asked militia brigadier Ben Finnell at Louisville why "a few straggling parties of rebels can ride over this country with pleasure." Even unionist sentiment was waning, he claimed, for the government seemed willing to abandon loyal citizens to the mercy of the enemy. He also wondered why three

Morgan's Raiders at Paris, Kentucky. Sketch by H. Louvie. From Mottley and Campbell-Copeland, eds., The Soldier in Our Civil War *(New York: Stanley Bradley, 1885), 1: 372.*

or four cavalry regiments were "doing nothing under the walls of Louisville," while there would be no more expense to the government to scour the countryside and keep the rebels beyond the Kentucky River at least. As examples of "the real military genius now prevalent about Louisville and the wonderful strategic talent that is evidently bent on taking good care of itself," he suggested, "a constant stream of rebel recruits out of the city itself" passed through Shelbyville en route to the southern army. How long would this last?[18]

Nobody had answers. A portion of Shackelford's cavalry under Lieutenant Colonel Benjamin Helm Bristow tried to corral Adam Johnson's partisans harassing Madisonville and Hopkinsville. But everyone awaited the return of Buell's army from Tennessee. While Kentucky simmered, Buell tarried, reluctant to truly abandon his drive on Chattanooga. Then he pulled back slowly, screening rebel moves by a line of observation through McMinnville. Ever sensitive about his Nashville supply base, he slowly concentrated at Murfreesboro by the first week in September. His harassed supply personnel struggled to relocate the immense baggage and supply trains back from Stevenson, Alabama, via Tullahoma, Shelbyville, and eventually to Nashville and beyond. The Union forces rapidly back-peddled, so fast in some cases that they spared neither unionist nor even personal crops of individual slaves, like Harry Pendicord, who leased a field for himself near Fountain Head, Sumner County, Tennessee. He laid a claim for its loss to the United States government *twelve years later.* Meanwhile, Kentucky officials had to handle the preliminary defense of the state, although Buell eventually sent

Brigadier General William "Bull" Nelson back to provide a steadier hand. Even that proved an illusion when Kirby Smith's ten thousand stalwarts coming north out of the Cumberland Gap region smashed through Nelson and his untested force of levies at Richmond, Kentucky (twenty miles southeast of Lexington), on August 30. For the moment, only Nashville was safe.[19]

SAVING NASHVILLE AND LOUISVILLE

The Tennessee state capital now became the Union's sticking point; the thorn was Andy Johnson. The governor concerned himself foremost with symbolism and imagery, and Nashville was the key to Union restoration in Tennessee in that regard. Buell worried most about his army, its logistics, and doing something about the enemy army. To him, Nashville and Kentucky both could be protected best by his army on the offensive. Buell advised Johnson, on the same day Nelson's force was annihilated at Richmond, that he intended to fall back to Nashville mainly to secure his line of communications. Johnson replied patiently the next day that he doubted Bragg would attack Nashville "unless induced to do so by a retreat of our forces." A heated exchange between the two men developed over the next few days as Buell followed Bragg northward. Johnson vowed to see the city destroyed rather than given up. Buell declared that he, not Johnson, commanded, and added that the city would be "left as he found it." He allowed that he had never considered Nashville to be of any military significance and that it could have been abandoned three months before. This led to the Johnson-Granville Moody prayer session, alluded to in chapter 3, and Johnson's complaint to Lincoln the next day about Buell's perfidy.[20]

Johnson hit the president's raw nerve, suggesting that Buell never had intended nor ever would redeem East Tennessee, the president's pet project. Buell had sufficient strength to do so, but instead of moving promptly to defeat the enemy, he sought a defensive position in Middle Tennessee that sacrificed all unionist interests elsewhere. Johnson believed that the general feared for his own safety and that his army was a "kind of body guard" to protect and defend him without reference to unionists' plight elsewhere. Johnson also repeated various rumors about Buell's disloyalty. Indeed, said the governor sarcastically, the general could not have done any more than he was now doing to accomplish the goals of ridding Tennessee of good unionists and establishing a successful Confederacy. It was a bitter message that Johnson sent to Washington.[21]

Buell, of course, had dispatched his chief engineer, Colonel James St. Clair Morton, to help Johnson fortify the city, the capitol building, and the bridges across the Cumberland. But it was slow work, with few slave owners willingly providing a labor supply. So, African Americans were dragooned from church meetings, hotels, barbershops, and livery stables and handed pick and shovel to work for their new masters. It would be months before they received any pay for the work; other blacks, who were impressed into service as teamsters, cooks, and nurses during the crisis, were no more successful at being paid. Food and shelter proved inadequate, too. The railroad bridge was fortified against all but distant

Impressing the contrabands at church in Nashville. From Fitch, Annals of the Army of the Cumberland *(Philadelphia: J. B. Lippincott, 1864), 665.*

artillery bombardment; Fort Negley and the capitol were rendered secure "against any attack except regular approaches and investment." Other individual forts remained isolated from one another and provided little more than a framework for the type of integrated fortification system that engineers liked to execute as part of their professional specialty. Nothing was complete about Nashville's defense when Confederate troops again roamed the precincts of the capital region. But, like Confederate Forts Henry and Donelson, the defenses of Yankee-occupied Nashville were constructed by black laborers.[22]

Johnson's prayers and rantings aside, Nashville's streets buzzed with rumors of Yankee evacuation. Major General George H. Thomas sent word from McMinnville that captured letters indicated Bragg was moving on Murfreesboro, but Buell demurred from any countermove that would tax water and food supplies and might not even discover the Confederates. Buell and his chief of staff, Colonel James B. Fry, both adamantly denied any intent to leave Nashville defenseless. Dispatches to Halleck at 1:55 P.M. on September 2 and from Bowling Green, Kentucky, twelve days later reiterated that fact. Unwilling to be stampeded by a politician in uniform, Buell toured the sparse defense lines of the city and designated unit positions in case of emergency. Like Major General George B. McClellan and the Army of the Potomac, which was charged with defending Washington, Buell preferred to maneuver against his foe rather than conduct a static defense of a city. Both the generals and their political masters had understandable points of view. For Lincoln and Johnson, Washington and Nashville were political symbols that had to be defended. For Buell and McClellan, however, enemy armies provided the true focal point. At any rate, both Lee and Bragg soon solved the issue, as each moved past the capitals and into the border states, which, after all, were their targets anyway.[23]

Ironically, Nelson, Boyle, and Department of the Ohio commander Major General Horatio Wright seemed to have better intelligence than Buell about the whereabouts of Smith and Bragg. They plied Washington with all sorts of information, but little trickled down the railroad to Nashville. Only on September 3 could Buell wire Wright "at Cincinnati or elsewhere" that he had heard about the reverses in Kentucky, and "I need not tell you that the security of Louisville above all other points is of the most vital importance to our position in Tennessee." It should be protected at all costs, he noted. Kentucky was now in a panic, the War Department was not even sure about Buell's location, and everyone assumed the general had verged on evacuating Nashville entirely. Halleck hinted at the administration's dissatisfaction with Buell's slowness and at his possible dismissal. Finally, on September 10, Buell wired Lincoln directly that "cut off effectually from supplies, it is impossible for me to operate in force where I am," but that he would endeavor to defend Nashville, drive the rebels out of Kentucky, and still hold his line of communications. Perceptively, he suggested that Bragg's "movements will probably depend on mine."[24]

Anxious demands for reinforcements echoed across the West and on to Washington. But Grant, for one, had his hands full with cavalry raids under rebel brigadiers Frank C. Armstrong and John P. Villipegue, who were preparing the way for the Price–Van Dorn operation. Buell finally got his men marching northward from Nashville in what observers called a vast parade of animals, soldiers, and camp followers. Such a host darkened the sky with dust clouds, proclaimed elated Nashvillians as they viewed the Yankee exodus. Surely their deliverance was at hand. Such hopes were dashed on September 7, however, for Buell had left Thomas behind to organize the defense of the city. Trooper James W. Daniels of the Fourth Ohio Cavalry recorded in his diary that no doubt "Pap" Thomas would make a desperate resistance, if not a successful one, for the city.[25]

Other soldiers were not so sure about the city's security. Bergun H. Brown, a Hoosier serving in a Nashville hospital, wrote home that he scarcely knew what to think about the army's retirement, for it seemed that once more the Union cause was getting the worst of the bargain. Withdrawal was a great mistake, in his view, and he thought the generals' blundering bordered upon treason. Superior Union forces could easily prevail over the rebels, if properly led. He regretted that all the miles of fortifications and stockades protecting railroads would be given up and eventually have to be reconstructed when the Federals returned to Middle Tennessee, as they most certainly would. Loyal Nashvillians, he concluded, would have felt more secure if Buell had remained, but many in the army openly distrusted the general.[26]

Buell wired Halleck on September 14 that he could retain but a nominal hold on Nashville. He believed that "there is not for the present an organized force to come against it," unless it was Price. Correctly, as it turned out, he pronounced that the real danger lay with unification of Bragg and Kirby Smith astride the army's line of communications in Kentucky. Given such comment, it probably came as a surprise only to Johnson when even Thomas's force pulled out, leaving scarcely five thousand men with eighteen field guns and some heavier pieces to defend the state capital. But, sputtered Johnson, "a portion of Bragg's forces were lingering about Carthage and the Cumberland River," and they would be induced to attack the city as soon as Thomas left. Johnson pointed out that Thomas had noted "a large force of the enemy is near Nashville awaiting an opportunity to attack it." Brigadiers James V. Negley and John M. Palmer could do the job, Buell answered, for they had specific instructions to post their men with twenty days' rations at each fort, the capitol building, and the railroad bridge and "fight to the last extremity." Frankly, Buell contended, "If Bragg's army is defeated Nashville is safe; if not, it is lost."[27]

As it turned out, the Federals who remained at Nashville were on their own for almost two months. Whether or not they were truly besieged is conjecture. Certainly many soldiers and newly arriving civilians in the city thought Brigadier General John Hunt Morgan had them surrounded all summer. Yet, most of them, like Bergun Brown, kept busy (when not anticipating an attack) by examining Nashville's sights, such as the six-million-dollar state capitol building, now bristling with bulwarks and siege guns but still resplendent with marble floors, magnificent stairways, stone railings, and niches for statues that had either been removed or else never purchased in the first place. He climbed to the cupola from which flew the Stars and Stripes and looked down upon cotton bales blockading the streets. By October, however, Brown would declare "this deserted hole" had been cut off from all outside communication. Still, it was not quite a siege.[28]

Naturally, many civilians in the Nashville area welcomed Buell's departure. Around the periphery of the city could be seen increasing signs of the Yankees' wanton pillaging. Elizabeth Harding, mistress of the lovely Belle Meade plantation, across the road from the Nashville and Northwestern's unfinished right-of-way, wrote Johnson on September 14 about conditions. She complained about overrequisitioning by commanders like Colonel William B. Stokes of the First Middle Tennessee Cavalry and of blatant robbery by hordes of scavengers in blue uniforms. Her letter was a classic recital of depredations not only against crops and livestock, but also against prized exotic animals, stone fences, and other destruction for which her husband, William, eventually claimed thirty-two thousand dollars in damages when he returned from a northern prison. She asked Johnson "to mitigate this monstrous evil," for she had upwards of 150 people dependent upon her for support during the coming winter.[29]

Ironically, after Buell's departure, Johnson also received unionist citizen complaints about Confederate partisan and guerrilla depredations in addition to those lodged by Confederate sympathizers against the main Federal army. Maury County teacher George W. Blackburn wrote to ask for an audience and money since the guerrilla bands of Captains Duncan B. Cooper and John G. Anderson had run local unionists like himself ragged after the departure of the army. Cooper, formerly with the Fifty-first Tennessee and captured at Fort Donelson, had been exchanged, and, rather than returning to army ranks, he had organized a company of partisan rangers to preserve his devotion to the Cause. Neely's Bend just east of Nashville was a den for guerrilla activity. So, while Johnson's docket showed little surcease from a continuous parade of solicitations for relief from prisoners, parolees, and bail bondsmen collecting tribute from known secessionists to ensure good behavior, the wave of guerrilla actions that followed Buell's retirement northward increased the governor's anguish and frustrations. Meanwhile, the race for the Ohio River assumed an accelerated pace.[30]

FOOTRACE TO THE OHIO RIVER

Bragg's cavalry touched down on the Louisville and Nashville at Cave City and Proctor's Station, intent upon retarding Buell's use of the line without totally destroying it in case the Confederates needed the road for some reason. The main Confederate advance overwhelmed the reinforced Union garrison at Munfordville on the Green River on September 17, and Bragg stood in a good position to offer Buell a decisive battle for Kentucky. Whether or not it could have occurred at this point remains moot. Adam Rankin Johnson declared later that here was Bragg's fatal mistake, for he felt confident that if the two armies had met at the Green River, as Bragg intended ("or as he declared he intended"), the Confederates could have crushed the Federal army, and with the aid "of many thousand assured recruits it could have held the State." But Bragg obligingly moved off the railroad to seek resupplying, to make a rendezvous with Smith, and to install Governor Richard Hawes in the Frankfort statehouse on October 4, "while the enemy's guns were heard during the inauguration."[31]

Buell outnumbered Bragg by varying estimates ranging from twenty-five thousand to thirty thousand men. But Bragg held the initiative. The Confederates' northward march—with Terry's Texas Rangers in the lead—most assuredly caused havoc. Alanson Rynam of the Sixty-eighth Indiana recorded how his unit evacuated Lebanon Junction in haste, destroying everything in sight that might be used by the onrushing rebels. He noted almost gleefully that the African-American laborers cavorted in discarded army uniforms before skedaddling back toward Louisville. A fellow Hoosier, Alva C. Griest of the Seventy-second Infantry, filled his diary with comments about the confusion and endless marching and countermarching. He refused to believe that Bragg ever intended to confront the siege guns and fortifications at the Ohio River city.[32]

The rapid Union retirement to Kentucky also wrought havoc on Buell's service support elements. Captain Samuel Bruch, who handled the military telegraph chores, recounted that from mid-August through the first of October, "all the lines in the Department of the Cumberland were entirely abandoned on account of the retreat." Equipment and operators went back to Nashville, while surplus operators accompanied the army to Kentucky, assigned two men to a division. Guerrilla infestation prevented all attempts to keep the lines open to Nashville or anywhere else, as some of the operators were captured and paroled, but were robbed of money and other valuables, including some of their instruments. Ex-

Defending Kentucky, Fall 1862. National Archives and Records Administration.

cept for those in Bowling Green and Nashville, "all offices were at one time closed," Bruch commented.[33]

Quartermaster personnel claimed similar difficulties. Captain Theodore C. Bowles of the Sixth Brigade, Second Division, recounted a year later that, after a delay of two or three weeks at Bowling Green, a "celebrated train of nearly 2,000 wagons commenced its march for the Ohio River, moving via Litchfield, Kentucky, leaving the contending forces far to the right." Divided into three sections, each one in the charge of an assistant quartermaster (with six hundred wagons alone in the rear section), the train made an inviting target for Confederate raiders. Yet, Bowles reached the Ohio at West Point on October 4, "and at noon on the 5th was safely in Louisville, having accomplished a distance of 140 miles in seven days and a half, without the loss of a mule or wagon wheel." In fact, he noted that it took seventeen and a half days to traverse the divisional trains from Bridgeport, Alabama, on the Tennessee River to Louisville on the Ohio—a distance of 360 miles by the route taken. Ironically, the Confederates captured Bowles and a farrier's workshop train three days later at Lawrenceburg while they going south to aid Brigadier General Joshua Sill's division.[34]

Jesse B. Connelly of Company 1, Thirty-first Indiana, claimed that the race for Louisville was a rugged trek from the beginning, "and we on the long line." After night marches, half-rations, and sometimes no rations, not to mention brackish water that never quenched the hikers' thirst, Connelly and his comrades were only too glad to reach the Ohio and encamp on the island formed by the canal around the falls. They spent the first day in the river, he reported, trying to find "the man under the dirt and dust." His sunburned comrades quickly dubbed newcomers from recently recruited midwestern units as "band-box soldiers." Yet, these were the reinforcements Buell would have to use to fight Bragg and Kirby Smith. One of the novices was William B. Miller of the Seventy-fifth Indiana, who readily admitted that his new clothing and glittering accoutrements drew the veterans' derision.[35]

Relaxation and liberal partaking of beer and Kentucky bourbon soon restored Connelly's unit. The German-American Ninth Ohio, which had suffered greatly from the "blood-red disc" of a sun and from the sand that had filled their mouths on the march up from Tennessee, found the water from suburban wells too full of minerals to their taste when they got to Louisville. They found "better water and excellent beer" when they got downtown. However, Alva C. Griest of the Seventy-second Indiana detected a nasty undercurrent of distrust and dissatisfaction in the ranks. The soldiers suddenly believed that Buell was either a traitor or a coward because he should have whipped the enemy before this point, commented Griest.[36]

PERRYVILLE AND BEYOND

Buell took charge of a sizable but disgruntled force of rejuvenated veterans as well as Wright's levies. Louisville had been saved. An aroused citizenry had flocked to the barricades there and at Cincinnati, and gunboats "paddling up and down the river just waiting for something to do" gave an air of preparedness, noted James H. Jones of the Fifty-seventh Indiana. Reinforcements, including Brigadier General Gordon Granger's division, had arrived from Grant's army. Nevertheless, Washington remained unhappy with the slowness of heartland commanders. Halleck wired Wright on September 25: "There must be more energy and activity in Kentucky and Tennessee, and the one who first does something brilliant will get the entire command." The government, he explained, seemed bent upon applying "the guillotine to all unsuccessful generals." This might seem unduly harsh, voiced Halleck sardonically, but, as in the French Revolution, "some harsh measures are required." Finally, Halleck sent Colonel J. C. McKibbin west with orders to replace Buell with Virginian George Henry Thomas unless Buell "could be found in the presence of the enemy preparing to fight at battle, or if he should have gained a victory, or if General Thomas should be separated from him so as not to be able to enter upon the command of the troops operating against the enemy."[37]

Halleck's confidential order also held that the army should detach itself from the interminable supply trains that had slowed its movements in the past. In a tone suggesting drastic deviation from the conciliatory "rose water" policies of the past, Halleck now told to Thomas: "you can subsist your army on the country passed over, paying or receiving for supplies as directed in general orders." The administration's move caused mixed signals in Louisville. Thomas begged off assuming command, telling Halleck at the end of October that "this order reached me just as General Buell had by most extraordinary exertions prepared

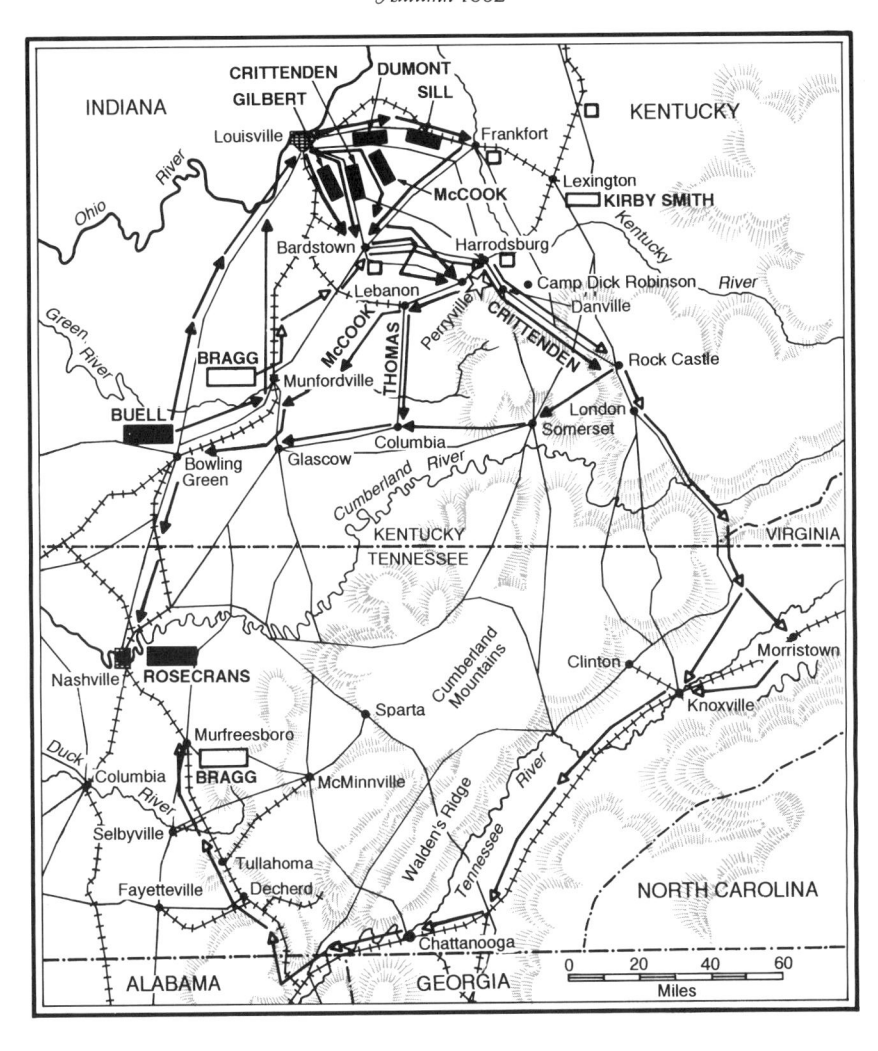

Situation following the failure in Kentucky and the return to Middle Tennessee, October and December 1862.

his army to pursue and drive the rebels from Kentucky." At the time, Kentucky unionists also wired Washington protesting a change in commanders just when their favorite son, Brigadier General William "Bull" Nelson, had been murdered by fellow Brigadier General Jefferson Davis over a personal slight of honor, which "caused regret and something of dismay." The War Department backed off for the moment, despite McKibbin's observation that great dissatisfaction existed within the ranks about Buell, and "there is no probability of a fight within a week."[38]

Buell, heeding the warning signals, advanced cautiously from Louisville with upwards of eighty-seven thousand men within the week. None too soon, suggested Arthur B. Carpenter of the Nineteenth U.S. regular infantry to his father on October 5. All the old veterans were discouraged—over a year they had endured fatigue and hardship and now "we are just where we started." The sooner peace was declared the better, he announced; recognize the South—"we have no men capable of carrying on a successful warfare." Plagued by heat, dust, and lack of water, the Federals plodded after Bragg and Kirby Smith, as newcomers in the ranks like William B. Miller began to see firsthand the effects of war on the Kentucky landscape. Destitute refugees and inhabitants contrasted with his comfortable home back in Indiana. Frequent halts attended the movement, as the soldiers anxiously searched for water. Finally, Union and Confederate forces stumbled into each other in an encounter over water holes at a hamlet known as Perryville on the Chaplin River in Boyle County south of Frankfort and Lexington.[39]

The day of the battle, October 8, was dry and hot, the contenders only a portion of both armies. The result was a bloody tactical success for the Confederates, but a strategic victory for Buell when Bragg began his retreat back to Tennessee that night. By taking time to place a Confederate governor in power at Frankfort and trying to coordinate with Smith, as well as undertaking the futile task of recruiting reluctant Kentuckians to the Cause, Bragg had surrendered the initiative to the stolid Buell. To historian Grady McWhiney, Bragg's greatest liability throughout the invasion had been a divided command, "for which Jefferson Davis was responsible." The Confederate general realized too late that he faced overwhelming odds as more of Buell's men concentrated against him. Whatever the cause, Perryville had saved Kentucky for the Union.[40]

Notwithstanding the reports of unionist oppression, the Bluegrass failed to respond to southern trumpets. Perryville was almost anticlimactic, in that respect. Bragg was already withdrawing when the battle cost him thirty-four hundred men. Buell had won the footrace to Louisville, and the northern part of the state stood solidly under control of Union bayonets. Bragg frittered away an opportunity for a solid victory in favor of political solicitation. The epitaph for the autumn invasion was written not on gravestones of the fallen, but rather in the wagon loads of weapons that Bragg carried into Kentucky to arm the new recruits, and which remained in those wagons when he returned south.

Nobody seemed content with the result. Bragg told his wife that there was no reason to linger to fight for "cowards who sulked in the dark and held back their allegiance" until the men in gray whipped those in blue and then turned to protect them. In his view, "the love of ease and fear of pecuniary loss" were the sources of Kentucky's duplicity. Kirby Smith understood the problem just as well, having complained to Bragg on September 18 that the Kentuckians "are slow and backward in rallying to our standard," for "their hearts are evidently with us, but their blue-grass and fat-grass are against us." None of the Confederates quite understood that Kentucky economic interests now pointed as much to the north and east as to the south, and sons of the Bluegrass greatly feared becoming the battleground for both sides in the war.[41]

Frankly, Bragg may not have used some of his resources to best advantage.

Partisan leader Adam Johnson had been escorted to the general's quarters by his old commander, Bedford Forrest, early in the campaign. Bragg told the young Kentuckian to return home, collect his partisan rangers at Hopkinsville, and screen Buell's left flank and hinder any escape of the enemy down Green River. Johnson had hustled back to his old haunts and with handbills called for followers to rendezvous at Camp Coleman between Hopkinsville and Russellville. Reputedly, some twelve hundred men had appeared, and together they proceeded to burn the Red River and Licking Creek bridges, thus carrying out Bragg's instructions, according to Johnson. But Bragg failed to use Johnson's force closer to Louisville, where he most needed their kind of irregular action to disrupt Buell's race to the Ohio and subsequent advance to Perryville. Isolated by Bragg's rebuff in the Bluegrass, Johnson had to disperse his band quickly when Federal counterguerrilla sweeps by Bristow's portion of the Eighth Kentucky Cavalry subsequently rendered untenable his corner of Kentucky. Again, West Pointers saw only limited utility to the partisans, with predictable results.[42]

On the other hand, as Bragg declared in his final report, he and Smith had redeemed northern Alabama and much of Middle Tennessee, as well as reclaiming Cumberland Gap. They had erased no less than twenty-five thousand Federals from the chess board, captured over thirty artillery pieces, hundreds of wagons, horses, and mules, seventeen thousand small arms, and two million cartridges. Grady McWhiney points out how one commentator subsequently decided that it was one of the "most extraordinary movements in history," while five Union generals (who subsequently investigated Buell's actions during the campaign) opined: "History of military campaigns affords no parallel to [Bragg's] army throwing aside its transportation, paying no regard to its supplies, but cutting loose from its base, marching 200 miles in the face of and really victorious over an army double its size." Bragg himself noted that his army had subsisted for two months off the country and procured enough material in Kentucky to clothe the army. Still, the main prize had eluded the Confederacy once more.[43]

Buell also admitted that his army had not accomplished all that he had hoped. Yet, "composed as it is, one half of perfectly new troops, it has defeated a powerful and thoroughly disciplined army in one battle and has driven it away baffled and dispirited at least, and as much demoralized as an army can be under such discipline as Bragg maintains over all troops that he commands," he wired Halleck on October 16. This was not enough to most unionists. Even north of the Ohio, there was displeasure at Perryville's result. Governor Oliver P. Morton of Indiana warned Lincoln about midwestern disgust with the indecisive outcome of Buell's work. Pursuit proved dilatory; thoughts of annihilating the enemy were absent. No wonder Morton proclaimed: "Nothing but success, speedy and decided, will save our cause from utter destruction," since to the northwest "distrust and despair are seizing upon the hearts of the people."[44]

Buell's army was in no shape for rapid pursuit, and so the rebels departed almost in peace. Bragg's army left Bryantsville, where the general had hoped to secure much-needed food, and headed for Cumberland Gap by October 13. Morgan retired circuitously via Lexington, Versailles, Bardstown, and on through

Fight at Licking Bridge in Cynthiania, Kentucky, between Federal troops and Morgan's Raiders, July 18, 1862. Sketch by H. Louvie. From Mottley and Campbell-Copeland, eds., The Soldier in Our Civil War *(New York: Stanley Bradley, 1885), 1: 372.*

Elizabethtown, Morgantown, Rochester, and eventually to Hopkinsville. Partisan Tom Woodward hosted a confab with Morgan at Camp Coleman as local citizens brought in wagonloads of provisions for the raiders. Morgan wanted Woodward to join him. But Woodward and Adam Johnson conducted independent operations. The likelihood that they would remain very long under regular Confederate operational control was slim.

Captain John M. Porter reported the Hopkinsville sojourn as pleasant, free of inclement weather, and filled with examples of men who were sobering up after a whiskey binge. Here, too, brigade newspaper editor Captain R. A. Alston unleashed a scathing denunciation of Yankee depredations in the border region following Clarksville, Tennessee's reoccupation in September. Alston declared in his *Vidette* that the Federals had stayed a week harassing women, robbing and pillaging, and that Morgan's men had felt constrained to arrest local unionist officials because of such activities. He also suggested that Brigadier Jeremiah Boyle, the Kentucky slave-owning, unionist lawyer who ruled the District of Kentucky with an iron hand, had proved neither a good strategist nor tactician.[45]

Unionists like Elizabethtown farmer S. Haycroft irately noted for posterity that Morgan's men had done the same kind of pillaging and robbing as they rode through, and they demanded action and protection. Grant, from Jackson, Tennessee, told his new Columbus, Kentucky, commander, Brigadier General T. A. Davies—a West Pointer, engineer, and prewar New York City merchant—to draw upon Colonel William Lowe's twin river garrison to clean Morgan out of southwestern Kentucky. Together with Boyle moving in from Bowling Green, Davies managed to mobilize a twelve-hundred-man column (only two hundred were mounted, however) and respond to Grant's directive, all the while protesting insufficient manpower. Grant merely told him that he doubted that Morgan had superior numbers. Besides, he said, "if Morgan is there he will likely run," as "it is not his policy to fight, but to plunder and interrupt our lines of communication as much as possible." This perception proved true, for Morgan soon retired to Middle Tennessee, well ahead of his pursuers. Adam Johnson temporarily accompanied Morgan southward, bent upon going to Richmond, he claimed later, to ensure proper recognition for his partisans. He never got there, but received President Jefferson Davis's blessing at Murfreesboro in December (endorsed but not dated by Secretary of War George W. Randolph).[46]

The Confederate departure from Kentucky nonetheless left an aftertaste of dissent and partisan activity. Unionist Daniel A. Brooks wrote John Finnell of the Kentucky military board at the end of the month about being aboard the USS *General Pillow* when it shelled some three hundred guerrillas two miles back of Caseyville in Union County. "In God's name," he wailed, "how long are the Loyal Citizens of Union, Crittenden, Hopkins, Caldwell, Trigg, and Livingston Counties to submit to Secesh Outrages; are we never to have any protection thrown around us, have you any influence with the powers that rule, if you have Save us from ruin and destruction of property." He noted that he had spent time recruiting and raising money and then was told that if he took command of the unit, it would be "gobbled up and the government will loose the arms etc." If relief did not come soon to the 120-mile strip from Henderson to Smithland, he claimed that "there will not be horses left in the country to make a crop the next season and all the pork and beef will go where it went last winter to feed the rebels."[47]

Brooks threatened to join a unionist guerrilla outfit "and drive the Southern robbers from my county or sacrifice my life in defence of my country." Thus, the Confederate invasion of Kentucky created confusion and dislocation. If Bragg and Kirby Smith had lingered and better integrated Adam Johnson, T. G. Woodward, and other partisans with the main force operations, such confusion could have been exploited for months. Properly handled, such moves might well have kept Federal authorities from quickly returning to major operations in Tennessee and Mississippi, and might even have eventually wrested control of the Bluegrass state from them. But, since Confederate regulars held such dim perceptions of the partisans' value, Woodward and Johnson, among others, were left to their own devices in northwest Tennessee and south-central Kentucky. True, the partisans were independent operators and may not have contributed that much to the main offensives anyway. The shadow war continued, but Kentucky remained in the Union.

EXIT A GENERAL AND A POLICY

Grave doubts persisted about Buell's combativeness. He issued a general order on October 26 that declared all rebel recruits from Kentucky would be regarded as prisoners of war and merely sent to Vicksburg for parole. Similarly, any civilian caught helping or abetting Confederate forces in the state would likewise go to Vicksburg, but was forbidden to return. To many unionists, this merely shifted the problem temporarily, leaving their enemies free to campaign against the Union from afar. Both Ohio department chief Major General Horatio Wright and Kentucky district commander Boyle bridled when the order specifically exempted indicted persons and those already awaiting trial and stated that no new arrests would be made merely on suspicion or with insufficient evidence of guilt. Both officers felt that imprisonment at Camp Chase, not transport to Vicksburg, was the answer.[48]

Even Halleck joined the stir, telling Wright that he had always advocated "a vigorous and strong policy" because "domestic traitors, who seek the overthrow of our Government, are not entitled to its protection, and should be made to feel its power." Claiming that this policy had netted favorable results in Missouri, Halleck felt that it had caused secessionists to join Union ranks, "which, after all, is the very strongest lever to apply to them." He wanted to protect the innocent and prosecute the disloyal so that they might suffer for the difficulties they had caused others. "Let the guilty feel that you have an iron hand" and "don't be influenced by those old political grannies, who are only half way Union men, and who are ever ready to shield and apologize for traitors." Late the following month, Halleck again counseled Wright: "You know the practice of our Government is to listen to the representations of civilians, especially politicians, who think they know much better than our generals how military affairs should be conducted." He admitted to releasing "some of the worst traitors in [Kentucky]" while commanding in the West, all because of the blandishments of so-called unionists. He feared that "local influence in Kentucky" had induced Wright to adopt "a policy not sufficiently rigid."[49]

Many of Buell's soldiers also had grave doubts about the way their commander had handled the campaign. Tighlman Jones of the Fifty-ninth Illinois vociferously condemned Buell in a letter home as "not sound" and as "a betrayer of the trust that his country has given him," for he had aided the rebellion by giving the enemy a chance to take arms, clothing, cattle, horses, mules, pork, and other articles "back safe to their rendezvous at Chattanooga." Rumors circulated freely in camp, said James Connelly of the Thirty-first Indiana, that Buell purposely held back two corps so Bragg might escape with his army and the large amount of plunder that he had gathered and that he had conferred with Bragg privately in Perryville the night after the battle. And many men believed such talk, he added. Civilians along the rebels' retreat route later reported such complete demoralization among the hungry and fatigued southerners that the Federals could easily have bagged the lot, he observed. The implication of disloyalty, cowardice, or plain inefficiency hung over Buell's conduct after Perryville, and the army resented a cold chase without proper shoes or food, so that "the prize of the Rebel army had slipped through our fingers."[50]

In fact, Connelly's regiment had tramped far to the east in search of the enemy, settling finally upon destruction of a vast salt works at Manchester in the mountains as their only solace. Shoveling salt into the local creek (after leaving just enough for the populace) was not what the Hoosiers considered a victory. Connelly, for one, thought that it was not the soldiers' fault that "the Rebel army went out with fuller hands than when it came in." The Ninth Ohio fared somewhat better. "Chasing Bragg zigzag," they ended up seizing a distillery near Lancaster, Kentucky, whose owners "had been pointed out to us as Rebel sympathizers." Rewarding, indeed, given conditions under which they labored daily. The unit's chronicler later reported, "the area not only flowed with milk and honey, but also overflowed with whiskey." Nonetheless, "we suffered many hardships, that, if even necessary, produced no tangible results," he concluded about Buell's actions in the Kentucky campaign.[51]

Sergeant Arthur Carpenter, who missed Perryville because of chronic diarrhea, mused from a Louisville convalescent barracks about the interminability of the war due to misgovernment and corruption in Washington by "fops and light brained scoundrels." The country was ruined and past the "meridien [sic] of its glory," he groused; the South was as strong as before. "She will never submit—never be conquered," he whined after Buell's failure to pursue and destroy the battered forces of Bragg and Kirby Smith. Kentucky lieutenant colonel Benjamin Helm Bristow also wondered whether there was enough "power and generalship in the government" to stop Confederate incursions into his state. "These things have been tolerated long enough," he wrote his wife on October 22.

Indeed, Washington officials decided that it was time to replace Buell. Influential Kentucky railroad magnate James Guthrie lobbied hard for the general's retention, but to no avail. Lincoln wanted a change, and midwestern governors as well as congressional radicals all wanted vigorous prosecution of the war not just against rebel armies but also against civilians. Governors Morton of Indiana and Richard Yates of Illinois wired Lincoln bluntly on October 25 that Buell's removal "could not have been delayed an hour with safety to the army or the cause." The War Department tapped Major General William Stark Rosecrans to replace Buell on October 24, much to Grant's relief, since he and "Old Rosy" (as his soldiers styled him) had never quite seen eye-to-eye in West Tennessee. Only Pap Thomas was displeased, for "although I do not claim for myself any superior ability, yet feeling conscious that no just cause exists for overslaughing [passing over] me by placing me under my junior, I feel deeply mortified and aggrieved at the action taken in this matter," he wrote Halleck on October 30. Affronts to Civil War generals' honor could be boundless.[52]

A special investigative commission, chaired by Major General Lewis Wallace (another Fort Donelson veteran), met in November in Cincinnati and took evidence not only about Buell's conduct of the campaign, but also about what historian Kenneth P. Williams called the general's "unwillingness to harm the Confederates." The commission dismissed quickly the question of Buell's loyalty, as well as the charge of "what is familiarly known as the conciliatory policy" towards the disaffected. "Whether good or bad in its effects," they noted, "General Buell deserves neither blame nor applause for it because it was at that time understood to be the policy of the Government." He had violated no orders on the subject, because there were none, said this committee of the general's military peers. Nonetheless, the group listened attentively when Colonel Marcus Mundy of the Twenty-third Kentucky explained how he had followed Buell's conciliatory orders when in command at Lebanon and Pulaski, Tennessee. His testimony provided distinct evidence of the disparities in how Federal troops carried out government policy during the Buell period.[53]

Mundy claimed that his conciliatory policies at Pulaski had been praised by ex-Tennessee governor William P. Campbell and had protected citizens not only against the enemy but also against marauding Union teamsters and other camp followers. Mundy had issued an order against any depredations and made it stick. He had welcomed the rural population to visit town so that he might converse with them and convince fence sitters and pseudo-rebels to renounce secession. Like Lincoln and others, Mundy remained convinced that most illiterate and ignorant Tennesseans had been duped by stump-speaking politicians, so he "counseled" the unrepentant about taking the oath or leaving the area for Confederate territory. "Having relieved the community of these men that they were afraid of, there was no longer any hesitation in declaring their Union sentiments," and Mundy concluded that 80 percent of all the men in his jurisdictions had returned to their loyalty for the Union.[54]

Mundy claimed that he had distinguished between the loyal and disloyal not upon "mere questions of sentiment," but rather from "their course of conduct and conversations." He had instituted a commission that assessed the disloyal for damages to unionists suffered when Morgan rode through the town, for example, and Mundy avowed this procedure found such favor with Andrew Johnson that the governor himself embraced the model for his own actions. "We cannot expect any demonstrations of loyalty from the people there unless we can assure them of protection against the rebel armies and guerrillas," he contended. Those Pulaskians who were disposed to come out openly for the Union had told him that they feared they would be marked and destroyed by the rebels for doing so. "If they were to incautiously develop the Union sentiment," the Kentuckian concluded, and they lacked protection from the national government and its army, "it would be to seal their doom."[55]

Mundy also declared that Buell's vindictive punishment of Union officers, such as that suffered by Brigadier General John B. Turchin for the famous plundering of Athens, Alabama, earlier in the year, had soured the army on its commander. Brushing aside judge advocate Major Donn Piatt's attempts to bar such discussions from the hearings on the grounds that higher authorities deplored such wanton acts, Mundy agreed that such free-bootery damned Federal psychological efforts to win back the affections of the populace. Plundering only led to Confederate retaliation, and, as evidence, he told about hangings of local unionists by guerrillas in reprisal. No doubt Buell was following strict War Department and administration policy, but that policy had become unpopular among the men in the ranks and their officers. Hence, Buell, with his conciliatory attitude, no longer retained the confidence of his army, a fact confirmed by his lackluster performance against Bragg in Kentucky.

The questions of conciliation, depredation, resistance, and reprisal must have all seemed distinctly circular to the commission. Which came first and where did it all lead for military purposes? Nashville quartermaster J. D. Bingham testified concerning the hardships of sending supplies by water or rail from Louisville during those last frantic, heat-ridden weeks in August and September before Perryville, and he outlined the reception accorded his agents when they sought food and forage in the countryside around Nashville. Notwithstanding the requirement for taking the oath, these purchasing agents offered good Yankee dollars, said Bingham. But the people were afraid to sell to Union agents, "for the reason that the guerrillas had threatened the destruction of their property if they were detected furnishing any supplies to the troops of the United States," he observed. Although Bingham did not say so, the result was simply confiscation and plundering as Buell's troops passed northward to pursue Bragg. Certainly civilian accounts of the period corroborate this fact, and they were the victims either of guerrilla reprisal or of army robbery. Generals like Buell were incapable of quashing either phenomenon.[56]

Buell's departure, in effect, meant the end of a particular policy to war and reconstruction in the upper Confederate heartland. To many, his approach had been almost "Machiavellian in effectiveness." Winning respect and popularity among southerners ultimately cost Buell his command, for he had lost them among his soldiers. The winds of change blew colder and harder, as officials like Boyle in Kentucky, Johnson in Tennessee, and Halleck in Washington took hold. Political unrest in the North and fatigue with the pace and lack of progress at subduing the rebellion forced Lincoln's hand. As the Union and Confederate armies moved back to the killing grounds of Middle Tennessee for more fighting, conciliation gave way to sterner treatment of "secesh" sentiment and civil disobedience, fanned as they were by continual intimidation either by rebel guerrillas or Federal heavy-handedness. Washington added a loud "amen" to the Tennessee military governor's exclamation at the height of his feud with Buell over protecting Nashville: "My God save my country from some of the Generals that have been conducting this war."[57]

FAILED CONFEDERATE HOPES

Bitterness also hung over the retreating Confederates as they made their way through an early winter snowstorm to East Tennessee. Their generals still had a lot of explaining to do in Richmond. Price and Van Dorn had come nowhere near to closing on their target in the northwest corner of Kentucky. In fact, they had never gotten out of northern Mississippi. Bragg and Kirby Smith had badly misjudged any "rising" in the Bluegrass, and everyone wondered why. Only Commander Samuel Barron, the naval officer sent from Richmond to build gunboats on the recaptured rivers once the offensives had succeeded, truly reflected the ultimate ramifications of the missed opportunity. Writing his chief on the final day of October: "The repulse of the army of General Van Dorn and the retreat of General Bragg render it altogether inexpedient to attempt at this time the construction of gunboats on either [the Cumberland or Tennessee] rivers." Tennessee Confederate governor Isham G. Harris and Brigadier General Nathan Bedford Forrest concurred in this conclusion, he noted, and the only available river boat machinery seemed to be aboard two dozen steamboats laid up on the Yazoo River in Mississippi. The cost of purchasing and transporting that machinery to a place of greater security for constructing boats "will involve an immense amount of labor and expenditure of money."[58]

Barron was as dejected by the prospects as everyone else in Confederate gray. There would be no return to hegemony over the western waterways of the South. The Kentucky Lorelei had eclipsed even the more practical goal of simply reestablishing Confederate control of Tennessee. Now, as Van Dorn wired feebly to Richmond in late October, the situation was more desperate. Not only had his and Sterling Price's botched efforts cost men and resources, but, as one East Texas cavalryman, Lon Cartwright, observed dejectedly after Van Dorn's bloody rebuff at Corinth, the Yanks could well boast of victory: "our troops were whipped." Indeed, the autumn of 1862 may well have been the high tide of Confederate dreams, stopped not so much by superior enemy resources as by the Confederacy's own generals' bungling. Moreover, the failure of the generals' offensives meant that Union armies could pour southward into Mississippi, threatening anew Confederate control of the river route to the sea.[59]

Few southerners were talking about a western offensive with the end of the active campaigning season in 1862. The Confederate failure to annihilate George B. McClellan in Maryland and Buell, Grant, or Rosecrans in the West ultimately doomed Confederate dreams of seducing border states out of the Union. But the military failure to undertake more modest goals, such as attacking and capturing Federal political-military nerve centers like Washington, Nashville, or Louisville, may have been the costliest blunder of all. Loss of such practical as well as symbolic points could have caused the Union to fall like a house of cards. But the Confederacy opted for more sweeping territorial gains.

So, too, the failure of Confederate generals to establish some form of permanent presence or occupation of neighborhoods and regions, which were then more or less controlled by the partisans, caused the populace to question rebel resolve. Citizens could hardly be expected to embrace the Cause when such raiders were transitory—and Lee and Bragg were little more than expanded versions of Morgan, Forrest, or Wheeler as far as permanent occupation was concerned—and likely to be followed by reassertion of iron-fisted Yankee control. As for Bragg, to his credit, his actions had maneuvered the Federals out of Middle Tennessee and north Alabama and, to a large extent, had blunted their movements in the Mississippi Valley by implication. Van Dorn and Price had been badly bested in northern Mississippi, but had established a second river bastion at Port Hudson, Louisiana, for defense of the Mississippi. Moreover, Buell's threat to the strategic logistical center of Chattanooga and the gateway into Georgia remained blocked for a whole year.

As Professor Lawrence L. Hewitt has asked, can it then be denied that Bragg's invasion of Kentucky prolonged the war? He quoted one contemporary Tennessee matron, Betty Ridley Blackmore, as declaring emphatically upon Bragg's return from Kentucky that, when the war was impartially evaluated, this Confederate general should be awarded the praise of having "done more with his men and means than any other general with equal resources." Still, the answer to Hewitt's question may lie in a slightly different context and should be placed outside the traditional framework of comparison between Bragg and Lee. Politically sensitive facts are overlooked in the usual analysis, not withstanding lack of battlefield decisiveness.[60]

In his most recent study of the Kentucky campaign, James McDonough provocatively concludes that the sum of events in 1862 suggested that the Confederacy "strategically, was in a very precarious situation," even that quite possibly it had lost the war, "unless the Federals lost the will to prosecute it." Indeed, here was the crux of the matter. Despite McDonough's fatalism, the Maryland and Kentucky campaigns suggested another possibility. To many observers at the time, it seemed that rebels could still come and go at will, regardless of the odds or tactical decisions reached at Antietam or Perryville. The virtually unharassed Confederate retirements from both Maryland and Kentucky underscored this fact. Moreover, the recapture of Cumberland Gap in Kentucky, the capitulation of Union garrisons at Harpers Ferry in Virginia and at Munfordville, Kentucky, and the annihilation of "Bull" Nelson's blocking force at Richmond in the Bluegrass lead one to conclude that the Confederacy still retained plenty of resiliency if not ascendancy.[61]

Therefore, the contemporary impression of many northerners, southerners, and Europeans (albeit not necessarily Marylanders or Kentuckians, perhaps) was that the Confederate retained a certain kind of invincibility. Retreat and strategic defeat, however, became overriding post-hoc measuring sticks, as subsequent generations sought desperately to place these events into an overall explanation for the ultimate collapse of the Confederacy. The abiding embarrassment lay not in the fumbling actions of both armies and their commanders in the autumn of 1862. Rather, it rested with the Confederacy's singular inability to redeem lost territory and to stabilize control, and thereby securing inhabitants' loyalty.[62]

Nonetheless, different contemporary lessons had been learned from the autumn operations than those gleaned by historians. The unit chronicler of the Ninth Ohio suggested that foraging, as much "forced by necessity as driven by desire," had become a way of routine as his unit traversed the vast region in pursuit of Bragg and Kirby Smith. Despite all that had been "beautifully said and written" in orders, everyone realized now that south of the Ohio, "we not only faced enemy troops but were also on enemy soil." They began, however reluctantly, "to see and treat the inhabitants as enemies." If they had gained nothing else but this knowledge during the Kentucky campaign, he claimed, then "the profit was considerable."[63]

Indeed, sometimes "the knowledge" went too far. The influx of new midwestern regiments as a result of Bragg's invasion of Kentucky—some imbued with abolitionism, all possessed of feverish patriotism, and none impressed by vacillating Kentuckians anxious only to make money from selling supplies to their deliverers—created a tempestuous situation. Tempers soon flared, especially concerning slavery. This new wave of soldiers in blue, like their earlier comrades that spring, clashed with the values they found below the Ohio River. They even fell into arguments and pitched battles with fellow U.S. soldiers from the Bluegrass. As Colonel Smith D. Atkins so bluntly explained from Mount Sterling on November 2, his Ninety-second Illinois seemed doomed to a cold winter "*guarding* a little sesesh hole that is too *cowardly* to guard itself, and our priniciple [*sic*] business is, expected to be returning niggers." He told a friend back home that, while loyal and anxious to do his duty, he could not "conscientiously force my boys to become the slavehounds of Kentuckians and I am determined I will not."[64]

Atkins's determination led to a civil suit against him for "stealing niggers" (as assisted flight and sheltering the freemen was termed in the South), while conditions worsened on the issue. Republican Thomas T. Davis from upstate New York wrote Secretary of State William Henry Seward that "everything [is] very much unsettled" in Kentucky, as "designing men on both sides" were misrepresenting to the common folk what Lincoln's Emancipation Proclamation was all about. He, like Kentucky brigadiers Marcellus Mundy and Jeremiah Boyle, preached conciliation and nonobstruction of civil law in the state. Their immediate superiors, like Horatio Wright and Quincy Gillmore, echoed the official exclusion policy once more, with little resolution of the issue in sight. Much of the problem centered on the large number of fugitive slaves from the deeper South, who had accompanied Buell's army northward in September. Sorting out the refugees from loyal Kentuckians' slaves would stymie Union army and Kentucky civil officials long into the following year.[65]

SIX

DECISION IN MIDDLE TENNESSEE: LATE FALL 1862

Tennessee returned to center stage following the Kentucky campaign. Eviction of the Federals, now commanded by Major General William S. Rosecrans, became the top priority for southern strategists. Conversely, protection of the Nashville base and the vital Louisville and Nashville line of communication returned to top priority for the Federals. Confederate and Union civil-military fortunes west and south of the Tennessee River also vied for attention as did the Mississippi Valley. In addition, "Old Rosy" immediately felt the same pressure from Washington as Buell had endured concerning prompt movement to East Tennessee.

Soon the new commander of the old XIV Army Corps, renamed Army of the Cumberland, also began to sound like an echo of his predecessor. Rosecrans wired General-in-Chief Henry Halleck on November 1 that he understood Bragg was making "forced marches to Nashville." Movement through southeastern Kentucky to East Tennessee was quite out of the question, "for want of adequate transportation for so great a distance," he claimed. Rosecrans viewed the situation as had Buell—return to the railroad umbilical, give a token nod to Governor Andrew Johnson's concern for his state capital, and then move on with the war. This would be his army's theme for winter campaigning—concentrate at Nashville but aim for Bragg's army, while generals Ulysses S. Grant and William T. Sherman drove on fortress Vicksburg.[1]

Actually, Middle Tennessee had witnessed conflict even as Bragg and Buell sparred in Kentucky. Bragg and the small group of hapless, exiled Tennessee politicians like Isham G. Harris never let Buell completely forget Nashville's vulnerability. While writing to Confederate secretary of war George W. Randolph on August 15 about arresting and returning all southern soldiers absent without leave to their commands, the elected governor declared that "little can be done until we have regained possession of the middle division of the State." He trusted that the autumn offensive would accomplish this goal "within a very short time."

But Bragg had feinted and dodged off for the Bluegrass, leaving Brigadier General James Negley and Nashville's defenders unmolested. Or so it seemed until other Confederate generals Samuel Jones and John C. Breckinridge became torchbearers for a new crusade.[2]

TARGET NASHVILLE

Jones seized the initiative in the matter. The forty-three-year-old West Pointer and old army artillerist from Powhatan County, Virginia, aggressively pursued his mission as East Tennessee commander in Bragg's wake. He used partisan rangers in north Alabama and in Tennessee in the absence of any regular force. He told subordinates on August 27 to employ partisans against the Duck River railroad bridge at Columbia and believed that local citizens were so loyal they would burn the bridge themselves if they thought it served the Cause. By late September, Jones alerted Bragg to Buell's movements, reported that there were reputedly ten thousand African-American laborers employed on Nashville's trenches, and conveyed rumors that "the people of Middle Tennessee are reported rising en masse." If Kentuckians would join the movement, he claimed, "I cannot see how the fortifications at Nashville will save Buell's army."[3]

Still, Jones chafed at his main assignment, which was merely to transfer reinforcements from Mississippi—including four thousand exchanged prisoners, some of whom had been Henry-Donelson captives—to bolster Bragg's invasion force. He wanted personally to capture the capital. Ordered from Chattanooga to Knoxville by the War Department, Jones informed Bragg at the end of September that he still hoped "headquarters of the base of operations would soon be moved to Nashville." Further, he told the army commander that he was forwarding Colonel J. T. Morgan's Alabama cavalry to cooperate with Brigadier General Nathan Bedford Forrest, who was supposedly within five or six miles of the Tennessee capital. Indeed, Bragg had ordered Forrest back to Murfreesboro on September 25, both to recruit two new cavalry and four infantry regiments and "to operate against the enemy wherever found, but especially at Nashville, Clarksville, &c., cutting off supplies, capturing trains and harassing them in all ways practicable." Forrest brought with him only four companies of his old regiment. Sam Jones was to provide the logistical support.[4]

Suddenly, Nashville shone anew as a beacon for Confederate hopes. Harris wrote Sterling Price to ask him when his army might appear before the city. Middle Tennessee "can forage and subsist your army," he decided, promising all aid within his power. Jones then sent Lieutenant Colonel H. Maury's Thirty-second Alabama and Captain S. L. Freeman's Tennessee battery to Tullahoma, feigning a major advance from Chattanooga. On October 4, he advanced this diminutive force to Murfreesboro and La Vergne "to reconnoiter Nashville, cut off scouting parties, and in every way harass the enemy and watch the opportunity to drive them out of Nashville."

Confused Confederate communications at this point interrupted a promising drive. On September 23, Bragg ordered Jones to establish a District of Middle

Late Fall 1862

Impressing Negroes to work on the Nashville fortifications. From Fitch, Annals of the Army of the Cumberland *(Philadelphia: J. B. Lippincott, 1864), 665.*

Tennessee at Murfreesboro for the purpose of directing all military operations from north Alabama to the Kentucky border (including the forwarding of recruits and conscripts to the main army) and to press on and capture the state capital. This directive obviously conflicted with War Department instructions sending Jones to Knoxville, a fact Jones quickly pointed out to Adjutant General Samuel Cooper in Richmond on October 5. "As far from having a force at my command with which to capture Nashville," he noted, "I have not men enough to occupy and guard the most important points in the Department of East Tennessee." He quickly added: "I have regarded the fate of Nashville as dependent on the campaign in Kentucky," and "if we are successful there, as I trust we shall be, Nashville must I think fall into our hands with little or no opposition."[5]

Meanwhile, Forrest set up a recruiting rendezvous at Murfreesboro and enjoyed a brisk influx of young Tennesseans. Fifty-six-year-old militia brigadier S. R. Anderson, a longtime Nashville resident, concentrated seventeen hundred of his own raw levies at nearby La Vergne. Forrest soon counted a total of three infantry and two cavalry regiments with three batteries. But he did not anticipate Federal brigadier John McAuley Palmer's eighteen-hundred-man sortie on October 7, which routed Anderson's command with heavy losses. Palmer eventually withdrew back to Nashville, hotly pursued personally by Forrest. But the mortifying spectacle of fleeing rebels became more galling when Jones claimed he could send no additional reinforcements to Forrest and suggested that the cavalryman retire to Tullahoma, "and farther, if necessary." By this point Jones had persuaded the War Department that he should exercise overall command of the area between the Tennessee and Cumberland Rivers.[6]

Negley's troops, supported by Captain St. Clair Morton's forts, deterred Jones and Forrest while Buell's army fought Bragg. Yet, Nashville's defenders came close to starvation. As one Hoosier told homefolk in early November: "No tea, coffee, sugar, beans, rice or even bacon—and by the way not enough soap to make lather to shave [a] chicken nose." Cut off by rail, inhibited by low water in the Cumberland, and intimidated in turn by the rebels just outside the city's gates, Negley's men tightened their belts and waited. The railroad would reopen in November, observed convalescing Bergun H. Brown of the Twenty-ninth Indiana in the city, for "the sulking secesh" to try their hand at new destruction. But he thought that interrupted communications caused local unfriendly citizens more distress because it compelled the garrison to forage, "which is one of the most devastating features of the war."[7]

Brown painted a colorful picture of long wagon trains, winding their way into the countryside and returning with every imaginable commodity from cellars, granaries, chicken coops, and cattle pens around Nashville. Despite Forrest's efforts, starvation now stared the populace, not Union soldiery, in the face, with "the wealthiest farmers living on little more than milk and bread," said Brown. It was a vicious cycle, for such foraging only incited more hatred, resistance, and expectations that southern arms would drive the hated oppressors from the heartland. Yet, in a landscape stripped of sustenance, neither the local populace, supportive partisans or cavalry, nor even the invading enemy had much alternative at this point.[8]

Stopping these Federal foraging parties temporarily became the primary mission for Confederates around Nashville. Jones, writing Bragg on October 12, admitted that the Federal garrison was possibly stronger than previously thought. Still, he hoped to gather ten to twelve thousand men to take the city, which was especially important with the Confederate repulse at Corinth on October 3 and 4 impacting upon Bragg's success in Kentucky; Jones also told Bragg that he was retaining all reinforcements under Kentucky political general John Cabell Breckinridge for work in Middle Tennessee. He and Forrest gathered as many stragglers from Kentucky as they could find over the next week, while Jones personally attended to suppressing East Tennessee opposition to the hated Confederate conscription laws.[9]

In some ways, East Tennessee held nearly as much importance as the rest of the state to the Confederacy. While often regarded as relatively insignificant strategically, the region included the main railroad connecting the Deep South with Virginia. Moreover, East Tennessee not only guarded the approach to Georgia, but its mountains offered a sort of reverse "covered way" via Cumberland Gap into Kentucky—similar to the same geographical benefit provided by the Shenandoah Valley for invading Maryland and Pennsylvania in the East. Then, too, East Tennessee unionism struck at Confederate pride of cause and allegiance. If Edmund Kirby Smith had not been able to end dissent, perhaps Jones could, especially when Richmond had told him that his chief duty there "will be execution of the conscript law." That would send a signal of Richmond's "determination to force East Tennessee to function as part of the Confederacy," as well as to suppress dissent. Generally speaking, Davis and his administration wanted to reduce the number of unionist dissidents either by forcing them to leave East Tennessee for Kentucky or by bringing them into the ranks of the Confederate army.[10]

Jones tried to duck strict enforcement of the conscription law by negotiating with prominent unionist leaders. He was under the impression that the unpopularity of the President Abraham Lincoln's preliminary emancipation proclamation, suspension of the writ of habeas corpus, imprisonment of rebel dissidents, and his calls for troops without congressional mandate were anathema to the East Tennesseans. While several, including T. A. R. Nelson, wavered, the majority of radical loyalists did not, fearing too much, states historian Noel Fisher, from the untrustworthy Confederate authorities, "who confiscated their property, drove them into military service, and killed their friends and burned their homes." So, Jones's conciliatory policy got nowhere (as neither had Lincoln's "rose water" treatment of southerners earlier), and by mid-October Davis clamped down by withdrawing Jones's ability to enforce martial law and demanding enforcement of the draft and suppression of dissent. As Fisher emphasizes, the Confederate government (like Washington) never realized that the groundswell of opposition among these southerners was due to more than just "demagogic and unprincipled" secessionists leading them astray. Above all, however, Richmond saw East Tennessee as a generator of resources, and Confederate government officials needed to maintain order in a region vital to coordinating the war effort elsewhere.[11]

That elsewhere included Middle Tennessee and the Mississippi valley. So, Breckinridge assumed command at Murfreesboro on October 28, styling his force the "Army of Middle Tennessee," and moved Forrest forward to La Vergne. Together the force numbered about sixty-five hundred men of all arms. Breckinridge, like Jones and Forrest, felt that more could be done to reassert Confederate control in the capital region. But his force hardly approached his opponent's reputed twenty-five thousand men (including five thousand cavalry and forty cannon). Indeed, at this point, the Confederates may have been capable of little more than an open, ranging warfare practiced by Forrest and Morgan. Partisan action worked better in snatching pickets, frustrating foraging parties, terrorizing black laborers, and preventing Union depredations against the country folk. But, taken together, their mere presence gave secessionists inside Nashville great hope for deliverance, and skittish unionists, officials in Johnson's administration, and even soldiers in the garrison cringed with every exchange of shots in the suburbs.[12]

Fighting escalated as Negley kept columns probing beyond the city's outskirts, gaining experience and confidence. A small action on November 5, 1862, could be called "the first battle of Nashville." Whether or not Breckinridge or one of the cavalrymen actually originated the plan, the idea was that Forrest would fix Negley's defenders on the south side of the city while Morgan dashed into Edgefield across the river to destroy railroad facilities and rolling stock. A recently completed pontoon bridge of old ice barges as well as the railroad bridge across the Cumberland provided inviting targets. "Remember the primary object is for Morgan to destroy the cars and locomotive," Breckinridge admonished Forrest. He knew the Tennessean desperately wanted to take the city, but the Kentuckian feared the consequences of raw troops assaulting fortified positions.[13]

Indeed, elements of Forrest's command, such as the Fourth (Starnes), Eighth (Dibrell), and Ninth (Biffle) Tennessee Cavalry, plus J. T. Morgan's Alabamians and Lieutenant Colonel A. A. Russell's partisans, supported by Freeman's and Franklin Roberts's batteries, all needed further seasoning. Still they would be supported by Breckinridge's infantry—returned veterans of the Fort Donelson fighting, now reorganized into brigades under the command of Roger Hanson and J. B. Palmer, themselves supported by Rice E. Graves's battery. Morgan's two hundred horsemen (Negley falsely estimated ten times that number) had much more experience with their particular type of mission.

Both columns moved into position for their coordinated dawn attack on November 5. Things went well for the Confederates at first. They drove Negley's pickets back on the main defense line, and Breckinridge's infantry surged forward from the vicinity of the lunatic asylum. However, they bogged down when they came under fire from heavier Union positions. The fighting became more general as Negley sent two maneuver columns of his own to clear the Franklin and Murfreesboro road sectors. Just then, sounds of John Hunt Morgan's attack echoed across the valley of the Cumberland, and orders arrived from Breckinridge (ostensibly at Bragg's direction) to suspend the operation south of the city.

Forrest kept on skirmishing until mid-morning in order to cover the retiring infantry, although Negley claimed that his men pursued the rebels to within five miles of Franklin later that day. North of the river, John Hunt Morgan ran into heavy resistance from Colonel Robert E. Smith's Sixteenth Illinois and destroyed only eight freight cars and an old railroad building at Edgefield. Losses on both sides numbered fewer than one hundred. Interestingly, African-American workers working on fortifications atop St. Cloud's Hill requested weapons to defend themselves, but Union officials allowed them only a symbolic stand with picks, shovels, and axes. These were probably the same ex-slaves who had been impressed while at church services and marched off to do the "blue man's" labor.[14] Interestingly enough, some nine hundred black men still labored on forts for the beleaguered city—mostly "at no wages," reported St. Clair Morton, the army's chief engineer on the project.

Two of Forrest's postwar biographers claimed that Nashville's recapture held such clear moral, political, and military attraction that Richmond authorities "surely ought to have initiated measures to insure the operation." Lieutenant Junius Holloway of the Fifth U.S. Cavalry—only recently released from captivity—claimed that his informants told him that Forrest intended to capture and burn the capital city since so many of its inhabitants were perfectly willing to help. Holloway, however, thought it more probable that Breckinridge merely wanted to let his troops visit their friends, obtain clothing, and carry off all the provisions in Middle Tennessee, without holding Nashville.[15]

Fort Negley, Nashville, Tennessee, as drawn by sketch artisit Ira H. Blakeslee, 1863. National Archives and Records Administration.

Morgan later galloped back from Edgefield to ambush part of Rosecrans's army returning from Kentucky on the turnpike north of Gallatin on November 8. He caused little discomfort to the main body of forty-five thousand veterans, and these troops soon filed into well-beaten fields, bare pastures, and the shrinking woodlands around the city. Bragg wired Cooper the next day that Morgan had destroyed large quantities of railroad equipment and facilities and that Forrest's "brisk skirmish" had unsettled Negley's garrison. He announced that the enemy "is reinforcing, our forces are moving up," and he would depart Knoxville for the front. With the passage of autumn, the contenders gathered anew for what everyone assumed would be the conclusive battle for Middle Tennessee. But, so far, rebel arms—army, raiders, and partisans—had been unable to retake Tennessee's capital.[16]

RECUPERATION AND RECOVERY

Federal intelligence indicated that Breckinridge might pull back from Nashville. He had gathered provisions and suffered the discontent of his Tennessee and Kentucky troops. These men were ready to return home because of Buell's lenient policies, according to former captive Holloway, who had briefly met Breckinridge during his detention. Breckinridge had supposedly told him that Buell's policy had hurt the South far more than Union armies, and that Tennesseans particularly implored their sons to return home, since "General Buell would not incarcerate them in a prison, as they supposed." Bragg, meanwhile, had his work cut out for him if he intended a decisive blow at Nashville.[17]

Fissures had developed between Bragg and his principal generals, Kirby Smith, Leonidus Polk, and William J. Hardee. They lacked confidence in his leadership. Then, on November 24, Richmond added to the problem by attempting to unify western Confederate command under General Joseph E. Johnston (ironically, as much President Davis's enemy as Bragg was the chief executive's friend). Johnston's task was to coordinate the movements of Bragg, John C. Pemberton in Mississippi, and Theophilus Holmes in the Trans-Mississippi. Johnston tried to secure the Holmes's cooperation, but to little avail, and within a week rebel strategic policy again lay in a shambles; Secretary of War George Randolph resigned in disgust at Davis's interference.[18]

After returning from Kentucky, Bragg set out to reorganize, re-equip, and instill discipline and order in his army. He intended to rekindle an offensive spirit in this "Army of Tennessee." His thirty thousand men traveled back to mid-state via the creaky East Tennessee and Georgia and Nashville and Chattanooga Railroads. "For the first time in the war have we had to complain of a want of men to handle our arms," he wrote the war department from Knoxville on November 3. He reduced the number of extra-duty personnel, established parolee camps, and temporarily reprieved deserters to induce them back to the ranks. He attached cavalry brigades under Brigadiers Joseph Wheeler and John A. Wharton to two army corps. Examining boards weeded out disqualified, disabled, and incompetent general officers.

Moreover, general orders issued at Tullahoma on November 8 tightened discipline as a result of rumored depredations against civilians along the transfer route. Straggling and "the entering of houses of private citizens" would not be tolerated, while "private property must and shall be protected" so as to win back the confidence of Middle Tennesseans. A week later, General Order 146 prohibited "consumption of grain by distillation" since distilleries were speculating wildly with profits from the "great evils of drunkenness" as the army passed by. Bragg even allowed barefoot men to be transported by wagon or rail, as the general wrote Samuel Cooper from Chattanooga on November 12, that his army was rapidly closing on Middle Tennessee. While outnumbered by the similarly concentrating enemy, "our hopes are strong and our troops very confidant," Bragg suggested. He was most solicitous of the citizens' well-being in his new operational area.[19]

While he wisely sought to restrain the partisan ranger corps whose marauding and impressment of horses disturbed Middle Tennesseans almost as much as the actions of the Yankees, some of Bragg's changes prompted further dissension among the officer corps. The Wheeler and Wharton promotions caused Forrest to seek a temporary leave of absence and prepare to undertake an independent assignment elsewhere. Morgan returned, avowing fealty to Bragg, but he was restless at being reined in by the new cavalry arrangement. Bragg declared that Forrest and Morgan, with brigades of some twenty-five hundred men each, were "to act as partisans," a service "for which and which alone, their commanders are peculiarly and specially suited." But this order left many other irregulars without the explicit protection of the Confederate military; they now could be declared guerrillas and bandits by the Federals. The discipline-conscious Bragg was more interested in stabilizing his army, with enjoinders about "remembrance of Richmond, Munfordville, and Perryville," than in fully utilizing the rich potential of combined action by his army, partisan rangers, and local irregulars.[20]

Bragg finally got down to business at Murfreesboro by the end of October. While reporting scarcely 30,649 effectives in the ranks on November 20, he had informed Adjutant General Samuel Cooper on November 12 that "should the enemy move out of his entrenchments at Nashville, we will soon fight him." Admitting Van Dorn's and Price's costly experience with frontal assaults against an entrenched enemy in recent battles, he continued: "To assail his strong works, garnished with the heaviest guns and defended by numbers superior to my own, would be an act of imprudence, to say the least." If the war department decreed that it be done, he would undertake such an attack, "as I have troops ready to dare anything their leaders may order." But he would prefer to await the Federals, while his cavalry exploited Rosecrans's long line of communications. "The whole of Middle Tennessee south of the Cumberland is tributary to us, and we are drawing immense supplies of subsistence, with considerable amounts of clothing, leather, &c. from the region just vacated by the enemy," claimed Bragg.[21]

Furthermore, Bragg informed Davis two days later, the populace (with few exceptions) "are loyal and true, having once felt the yoke of Abolition despotism." A rich fall harvest flowed not only to his army, but also was sufficient to supply other commands, although limited transportation hampered shipment to storehouses beyond the reach of the enemy. Still, the general warned, "we are now gleaning the country, and many of these articles, especially salt meat, will not be reproduced during the war." He mentioned sending a thousand men and three thousand muskets to Pemberton. But to send any additional men, Bragg told Cooper on November 21, "would require evacuation of Middle Tennessee." Rosecrans was superior in numbers, and the immense supplies that had been gathered would be lost in the process. Yet, by December 1, Bragg could report his force at 46,784 officers and men, and the total rose to 51,036 effectives ten days later. Obviously, stragglers and reinforcements were swelling the ranks of his "Army of Tennessee."[22]

Bragg argued that a planned raid by Forrest beyond the Tennessee River would help with the defense of the Mississippi (an idea he reiterated to Pemberton as well). What he did not say openly was that moving Forrest "south of the Cumberland and west of Nashville" and into West Tennessee to operate against Grant's railroads and supply system would also keep the troublesome cavalryman out of Bragg's way. The general had little faith in the efficacy of mounted warfare other than his suggestion that "with a fine battery of rifle guns, [Forrest] will destroy their transports on the rivers." Strangely, Bragg did not explicitly mention that mission in Forrest's orders of November 21.[23]

Confederate instability in the Mississippi valley brought President Davis west again in December. Senator James Phelan of Mississippi had written him about a civilian population wallowing "in listless despondency" and engaged in draft dodging. "It seems as if nine tenths of the youngsters of the land whose relatives are conspicuous in society, wealthy, or influential obtain some safe perch where they can doze with heads under their wings," said the senator. Davis stopped at Murfreesboro on December 12 and 13, delivered a stirring stump speech about patriotism and anti-abolitionism, and urged the soldiery to fight until death, holding Middle Tennessee "at all hazards" until Grant could be whipped in Mississippi, according to intelligence passed on to Union general Rosecrans, which he dutifully transmitted to Washington superiors on December 15. Preholiday spirit gripped the army, with local belle Mattie Ready preparing to marry her *beau sabreur*, John Hunt Morgan, and blue and gray alike making ready for a festive Yuletide.[24]

"We lived like lords" was the way Kentuckian Gervis D. Grainger in Bragg's ranks phrased it, as a clandestine operation from home brought in food and clothing for the forlorn "orphans," as the Bluegrass troops were styled. Unfortunately, the puritanical Bragg saw great mischief in all this and issued orders curtailing the merrymaking. "The country for miles around our military stations is full of officers and soldiers visiting, loitering, and marauding," stated his general order. The army had quartered itself on the local populace, "claiming as a right that they should be entertained," and such actions "are denounced as highly pernicious to the discipline and efficiency of the army." One suspects, however, that the relaxed mood of the veterans continued as long as possible.[25]

RAIDS, CIVIL DISCONTENT, AND MAYHEM

President Davis chose at this point to unilaterally order a full division from the Army of Tennessee to help Pemberton. Bragg and Johnston both protested that the men should come from Holmes's department, but to no avail. Major General Carter Stevenson's units departed for Mississippi, and Kirby Smith used this as a convenient moment to return to his independent stance in East Tennessee. All of this portended ill should Bragg's army be called to battle. But he was lucky. For the most part, December merely passed with cavalry raids and skirmishing as the major activity in the upper heartland.

On the Union side, Major General Alexander McCook arrived in Nashville early on the morning of November 7 and immediately reported to Rosecrans that he had found "everything all right," with the troops "in excellent fighting order, and ready," wanting nothing but "sugar and coffee, shoes and blankets." By the time the army commander set up headquarters there two days later, the men in blue had already spread out to every hamlet and town as a sort of cordon defense around capital region's outer perimeter. Hoosier Bergun Brown pronounced that the "siege" of Nashville, had been tough, but that it had passed "and a new page commenced in this raging conflict." Indeed, this new page would find Morgan, Forrest, and partisans all testing Federal positions across the state of Tennessee.[26]

Bluecoats literally swarmed across the region to protect both the L&N Railroad lifeline and its repair crews. A Michigan mechanics and engineers regiment fabricated replacement bridges at Edgefield, and the industrious Yankees developed a system for quick fixes that often repaired Morgan's damage in short order. The Kentucky cavalier found easier pickings on the picket lines where, as at Cage's Ford on the upper Cumberland, he seduced the Thirty-first Ohio into capitulating on November 22. Confederate harassment of courier stations on Stones River and Forrest's mauling of the Fourth Ohio Cavalry in another fight prompted Negley to issue instructions to use "extreme caution in operating against Forrest's cavalry" for they were "constantly moving, and are always watching for an inferior force and ready to remove from an equal one." Such hit-and-run attacks and the constant fear of snipers and bushwhackers took their toll.

Rosecrans issued a general order on November 14 stating that "the general is pained to learn that many soldiers have sought and allowed themselves to be captured and paroled by the enemy to escape from further military duty, and in order to be sent home." Rosecrans wired Halleck that he anticipated major fighting "on the table land near Tullahoma" and wanted gunboats run up the Tennessee River to protect his extreme right flank. But he worried most about dispersing his forces, weakening Kentucky, and leaving telegraph and railroads untended.[27]

Kentucky remained especially vital to Rosecrans's line of communications. He approached Ohio departmental commander Major General Horatio Wright about sending a force of two cavalry and an infantry regiment to Russellville to clean out the southwestern part of the state for "it is a granary of supplies for us" (he might have added, for the enemy, too). Wright ordered Colonel Sanders D. Bruce with parts of the Ninth Michigan, Seventeenth and Twenty-eighth Kentucky infantry units, as well as the Fourth and Eighth Kentucky Cavalry, "to clear of rebels the country lying between Green River and the Cumberland, and the Louisville and Nashville Railroad from Muhlenberg, Hopkinsville, and Lyons—put a stop to contraband trade in that region."

Wright directed increased protection for railroad lines in central Kentucky also. Jeremiah Boyle's western Kentucky district increased unit sweeps from Owensboro to Smithland on the Ohio River line, declaring such "ought to be ample to secure all that portion of State from the raids of the enemy, and from the depredations and outrages of guerrillas, and, if kept on the alert, will no doubt prove to be so." Wright told Boyle that this latter force should operate south and east in conjunction with Bruce "to break up the bands said to infest the countries of Todd, Christian, and Trigg, and the tier of counties lying north." This was Johnson and Woodward country, and an area that had not been brought completely under Union control at this point.[28]

Moreover, Rosecrans envisioned fortified posts stretching from Monticello on the upper Cumberland to the Nashville region as an effective barrier to Morgan's traditional routes into Kentucky. He intended to fortify Carthage and Gainsborough, Gallatin, and the L&N, and he put a ten-thousand-man garrison in Nashville's forts. Still, he recognized that "I may require all of my spare forces for the fight." Rosecrans even asked Wright for more men. The Ohio department commander responded that he had sent every spare soldier to either Tennessee or Mississippi. Furthermore, he argued that winter weather would soon shut down any rebel threat to Kentucky anyway. Wright felt that a mutually agreeable arrangement of forces strung out from Bowling Green, Columbia, Jamestown, Burkesville, Somerset, Big Hill, and Crab Orchard would do the job. Besides, large-scale garrisons could not be maintained efficiently along the river line until the Cumberland contained enough water to sustain resupplying efforts. Bruce went to Bowling Green, and Colonel E. A. Paine moved into a similar command slot at Gallatin. Their names would surface often as the months passed.[29]

Aside from this "cordon sanitaire" of fortified posts, Federal officials were hammered by civil-military questions long after the fall invasions subsided. Kentucky unionists pressed for government remuneration for losses suffered during the Bragg-Smith venture. Wright refused to specifically assess disloyal elements, as he also listened to complaints about "abduction of their slaves" by the unionists. Equally charged were comments from citizens tapped by provost marshals in August "for the purpose of defraying the expenses for subsisting the Home Guards they had enlisted to assist them in discharging their duty." Nobody wanted to bear the costs for much of anything in this war, it seemed, and official correspondence fairly bristled with indiscriminate plundering of the citizenry by the provost marshals in Henry, Madison, Montgomery, Clark, Nicholas, and Bourbon Counties. Colonel Henry Dent, the state provost marshal, noted that the Confederates had stripped these very same counties of everything they could find during the autumn invasion. Such *quid pro quo* irritated sensibilities of both unionists and secessionists in still festering Kentucky.[30]

Wright also tried to allay Ohio Valley fears about further rebel incursions. But he told Ohio senator Thomas Ewing (who was, incidentally, Major General William T. Sherman's father-in-law) that he lacked the strength to prevent partisans from crossing a frozen Ohio River to strike at the Buckeye state in winter. At the same time, Lieutenant Commander Le Roy Fitch's mosquito naval squadron was stymied by low water from interdicting the flourishing contraband trade near Uniontown. Rosecrans, too, worried that low water might cause partisans to obstruct the Cumberland supply route, as Wright offered to have Bruce's men remove the old 1861 rebel obstructions near Cadiz and Eddyville, a feat actually accomplished by December. But, in all, Federal authorities seemed to make little progress in controlling the vast region stretching far to the rear of Rosecrans's army.[31]

The Louisville *Weekly Journal* added its own complaint on November 11 when the editors told readers that the agriculturally rich Green River country "has been almost entirely neglected by the Federal authorities from the commencement of the rebellion to the present moment." The area had been completely abandoned to the rebels the previous winter when they held Hopkinsville, Russellville, and Bowling Green, said the paper, and the northerners had departed the region with the promise to return, which they had not done, despite loyal unionist pleas to the government for help. "We frankly confess we cannot understand why these things have been permitted, with the large forces we have had in Kentucky," the editor noted in disgust. Citing Woodward's recruiting efforts in Christian and Todd Counties during the summer, Adam Johnson's escapades, and the accretion of some two thousand men for Morgan as well as the partisans, the newspaper proclaimed that nothing had been done to prevent those enlistments. Preparations to drive the rebels from the state had been very dilatory anyway, and Bruce's counterguerrilla sweeps seemed inept and frustrating.[32]

The *Journal* editor especially singled out one inept mid-October expedition that was sent to break up Woodward's camp near Hopkinsville. Eleven hundred Federals had bungled the attempt to ensnare four hundred partisans because the Federal commander stopped to parole rebel pickets who, in turn, heralded his approach when set free. Then, the commander proceeded to shell the woods, which broke up the camp, but, as farmer-minister George Richard Browder mentioned in his pocket diary, "the federals fired on vacant air!" Then the Federals proceeded to Hopkinsville, closely followed by Woodward. They stood in the streets all night, awaiting attack, even though townspeople offered to guide the column out to find Woodward. Naturally, the wily partisan never appeared, and the bluecoats soon returned to normal guard duty at Bowling Green.[33]

The newsman wanted more aggressive action. He advocated establishing a post at Allensville, midway between Russellville and Clarksville on the Memphis branch of the railroad, in order to close a gap in the dispersed cordon defense. Let a Kentuckian—someone who knew the countryside and the sort of men with whom he would have to deal in the neighborhood—command such a post with a single regiment, he argued. Loyalty would then be protected, and treason could be punished as "the guerrillas must and will be driven from the region, for men of nerve and energy will be placed on their track to hunt them down." The Green River country would be reopened to the arts of peace and its long-suffering people would again able to realize the blessings of law and order. On the benefits of that point, local residents might agree, even southern sympathizers like George Browder.

If Union generals could not figure out what was wrong with their counterguerrilla operations, the men in the ranks often had their own ideas. Corporal Mitchel A. Thompson of the Eight-third Illinois at Fort Donelson noted that "after the twelve-day scout" by Brigadier General Thomas Ransom into Kentucky, a sharp brush with Woodward near Hopkinsville was fine, and gave the men their first taste of combat. But marching some two hundred miles with thirteen hundred mostly infantry (and mostly from the Eighty-third) only to emerge scarcely forty-five miles from Fort Donelson and net only twelve to twenty-two dead rebels (at a cost of three to six Federals) was not accomplishing much.

Thompson did not see any sense in moving through the countryside against well-mounted Kentucky guerrillas when "we are encumbered with our heavy teams and artillery wagons and cannot go every place where cavalry can, so that they can escape us." The enemy knew every footpath and friendly neighbor in the region, he observed. Thompson's prescription lay in concentrating major army against major army in a battle to the death, then allowing those men who had volunteered for national government service from guerrilla-ridden districts to return home and put down what he declared were bands of thieves and robbers. As he added sagely, some six hundred men had gone into Union ranks from the Hopkinsville area alone, and, "if they were at home now and drilled as well," they would put down the plundering Woodward and company without trouble.[34]

The boundary between Rosecrans's and Grant's departments on the twin rivers offered a corridor for rebel intrusion like that through Tompkinsville, southeast of Bowling Green. Further, the area lying just to the south and west of Clarksville, in Dickson County, became a guerrilla sanctuary, with Charlotte and Waverly as especially troublesome nests. Roads from both Nashville and Columbia traversed this area, and they permitted a flourishing contraband trade with Confederate-occupied territory south of the state capital. Active patrolling and plenty of complaints from local Federal commanders had done nothing to clean out such an incubus. Men in units like the Eighty-third Illinois stationed at the twin river forts complained about illness reducing the ranks "to living skeletons," lack of pay, and infrequent mail deliveries from home. The little town of Dover was almost nonexistent, thanks to the combat of the late summer. Virtually every surviving dilapidated building in town—even sheds, cellars, and garrets—now served as stables or as hovels for refugee contraband slaves, declared one Illinois soldier, Stephen McBide, in late November. "Many Rebels are coming in and taking the oath," he believed, for "fear of starvation . . . the whole country both in Kentucky and Tennessee is ruined and the common class of people are regard[ed] on both sides of the question [of secession or Union]." Nobody was happy these days, he claimed, "but the Tarnell Nigger [sic] is flourishing and they certainly are the filthyest set of human beings ever was the good ones stay with their masters and the bad ones run away and cram in on the Union troops for support." Every house in town was full, including cellars, garrets, stables, and sheds, he said, with "more a'coming daily."[35]

Converging columns from Forts Heiman and Donelson swept through from October 22 to 25, attempting to catch Napier's band at Waverly. Several sharp skirmishes ensued between the partisans and Major E. C. Brott's portion of the Eighty-third Illinois, a section of Flood's battery, and some of William C. Lowe's Fifth Iowa cavalrymen under Lieutenant Colonel Matthewson T. Patrick. Actually outnumbered by the southern irregulars, the Federals nevertheless killed twelve and captured fifteen of the partisans, destroyed twelve barges and boats on the nearby Tennessee River, while losing six of their own killed and wounded. But, as always, the Federals then retired to their forts, leaving partisans to infiltrate back into the area without much intimidation.[36]

Rosecrans became apprehensive, especially about his downriver flank, and on November 15, he sent Colonel W. P. Carlin's brigade on a wide counterguerrilla sweep from Edgefield Junction toward Clarksville and thence back in the direction of Harpeth Shoals and a planned rendezvous with a similar expedition under Negley. Carlin's Twenty-eighth Illinois and Lieutenant Colonel David McKee's Fifteenth Wisconsin trudged through the countryside for five days on their hundred-mile swing. They never made contact with Negley, but did snare fifty-six guerrillas, one hundred small arms, eighteen horses, and twenty mules. The porousness of the Union defense line became abundantly clear during a late November intrusion by Woodward's gang via Harpeth Shoals and Clarksville.

Telegraph wires sang with Union efforts to coordinate a triangular intercept of this group from Bowling Green/Russellville, Springfield/Edgefield, and the twin river forts. Once more, however, it was infantry against cavalry, even though Bruce's men now traveled by wagon. Bruce remained skittish about Woodward's estimated twelve hundred to three thousand men and six cannon, and he decided that Woodward's movement was part of some larger Confederate plan for a major drive into Kentucky by Morgan and Forrest. Yet, he mustered enough nerve to push the enemy ten miles beyond Clarksville toward their Charlotte lair by the first of December. Civilian Sarah Kennedy in Clarksville wrote her exiled husband that the Yankees behaved well this time as they passed through the city, foraging only for corn, hay, and an occasional home-cooked meal.[37]

The Edgefield column under Lieutenant Colonel John S. McClelland unaccountably failed to join Bruce, but made its own ninety-seven-mile sweep "to Harpeth Shoals or Clarksville, to intercept a force said to be at Trenton, Todd County," in Kentucky. This body contented itself with capturing three wagon loads of whiskey together with the owner, his teamsters, and $3,080 "of Confederate bills, in sheets." They also brought off five hundred bushels of wheat, 150 bushels of corn, sixteen barrels of flour, and five barrels of salt, twenty or more prisoners (some of whom they paroled; others were released for lack of evidence), twenty horses, ten mules, and six guns. All of the property was taken "from persons known to be disloyal," with receipts given, McClelland declared, and "most of the property taken belongs to men serving in the rebel army." He further noted that the roads leading from Robertson County to the Cumberland "bore evidence of being much used, and, from information received from citizens, large supplies of provisions and other supplies have been sent south through these routes." The southern portion of Robertson County and the northwestern portion of Cheatham Counties, McClelland decided, were "avowedly disloyal."[38]

Although Rosecrans ordered similar expeditionary sweeps from the Charlotte Pike and toward La Vergne from Nashville to keep rebel raiders at bay, even as late as December 13, Military Governor Andrew Johnson told the general that he had "positive information" that Confederates were hauling salt and other provisions from Clarksville by way of Charlotte in Dickson County and that a company of partisans was organizing in Cheatham County near the Harpeth narrows. Not a week before, Bruce had reported that a "number of returned soldiers," mostly partisans, had turned themselves in; moreover, active abettors of those partisans "are being made to feel the power of the Government, and indemnify Union men for the property stolen or destroyed by paying for the same in cash." All of this took place north of the Cumberland along the state line, and Bruce avoided leading punitive expeditions across the Cumberland from distant bases at Bowling Green and Russellville merely to clean out the Dickson County sanctuaries. Indeed, the river became a virtual boundary between the Union army and the partisans.[39]

Rosecrans worried as much about military infiltration of his rear via this corridor as he worried about the continuing contraband trade that was aiding Bragg from this section. Colonel W. W. Lowe sent word from Fort Henry on December 9 that the understood Morgan, with three thousand men and four pieces of artillery was near Port Royal in Montgomery County (near Clarksville) while raiders Napier, Forrest, and Woodward were concentrating near Waverly "with a view to divert attention from her and [Fort] Donelson." Morgan would move against the fort, not to take and hold the Union post at Dover, but "to secure stock and Government stores and arms." Rosecrans thus warned Bruce (in Russellville), Boyle (in Louisville), Richard Granger (in Bowling Green), and Gordon Granger (in Lexington), as well as Grant's twin river garrison commander, to watch for Forrest's concentration at Columbia on the Duck River as a jumping-off point for mischief in Kentucky. Frankly, the Army of the Cumberland commander wanted McHenry's Seventeenth Kentucky to garrison Clarksville permanently so as to "nearly close the line, and prevent contraband trade in that direction," but also to deter aggressive northbound movement by main force rebels.

But Bruce protested against any such permanent post for Clarksville. His scouts contended that Forrest was preparing two to four thousand men for a raid into southern Kentucky through Palmyra to profit from rebel sympathizers, who would supply him with all types of provisions. "Rebels expect to feed Bragg's army from this part of Kentucky this winter," Bruce observed, and he feared being outmanned by Forrest. Moreover, Woodward and another partisan named Triplett had joined Forrest, although apparently most of Woodward's men had gone home, refusing to sign on for three years' service. Forrest had taken their horses and arms. Then, on December 20, Bruce confirmed that the southern Kentucky foray had been abandoned, as had a rumored assault on Fort Donelson. Federal movements may have thrown the Confederates off balance. More likely, however, Forrest's planned movement into West Tennessee simply averted the crisis on the Cumberland for Rosecrans and his subordinates.[40]

Both blue and gray apparently moved freely through the Clarksville area in this period. Bruce reported that the Confederates were there on December 12. Local civilians Sarah Kennedy and Nick Barker both noted the Federals' burning of the upper Red River bridge at the city to prevent their escape several days before. She added that the Yankees had now maliciously destroyed the pump and chain of the town's cistern at the square, for "they seem to have a particular spite at Clarksville, 'the secesh hole,' as they call it." Finally, Bruce reluctantly moved his entire three-thousand-man force in to occupy the city on Christmas Day. Higher command wanted him to put the place "into defensible condition and hold it," thereby closing the gate to the Kentucky border.

A startled populace found itself again subjected to the bayonets of an occupation force, with the Yankees demanding oaths of allegiance and arresting holdouts from the steps of homes and churches. When the local Methodist preacher invited the Union chaplain to preach, his congregation stayed away from church in droves. Mrs. Kennedy thought the Federals were preparing to receive Morgan and Forrest, but admitted that Bruce's men had orders not to molest private residents. The newcomers fanned out to forage in the countryside, leaving the townspeople to organize a private aid society to help their local poor, who had been ravaged by the war.[41]

MORGAN, HARTSVILLE, AND THE CHRISTMAS RAID

Rosecrans and his commanders remained baffled about Confederate intentions until at least mid-December. Rumors suggested that Woodward and his men were at Murfreesboro, that Confederate money suddenly had been rejected as legal tender in the Charlotte neighborhood, and that no blockade of rivers or railroad seemed in the offing. Bruce doubted that his twelve hundred infantry, two hundred cavalry, and four artillery pieces at Russellville, plus five hundred cavalry at Hopkinsville, could stop any determined drive by main-force Confederate cavalry. Then, disaster struck at the very opposite end of Rosecrans's overstretched river line. In the isolated sector east of Nashville, posts like Gallatin, Hartsville, and Carthage stood ripe for the plucking. Major General George Henry Thomas had responsibility for this area, and Rosecrans sent sufficient warning that Morgan's raiders seemed to be loafing around in civilian dress unmolested by Union forces. Union troops needed to make the acquaintance of "settlers" in the areas and arrest intruders. Above all, "who ever cannot give a good account of themselves shoot or hang to the nearest tree," said headquarters. Overlooked in the rush to investigate infiltrators was Colonel Absalom B. Moore's isolated brigade at Hartsville. It gained instant notoriety when, on the morning of December 7, it was annihilated by Morgan in a lightning raid on the unit's camp.[42]

Bragg gave Morgan specific orders on December 1 to operate on "the enemy's line of communications in rear of Nashville," assailing guards, capturing and destroying trains, bridges, depots, trestles, and, "in fine, harass him in every conceivable way in your power." He was to "do everything to prevent the enemy from foraging north of the Cumberland River, and especially toward Clarksville," and he was to communicate and coordinate with Forrest. Prevailed upon by his men to secure more modern firearms than double-barreled shotguns as well as fresh mounts, Morgan convinced Bragg first to authorize independent action against the isolated Hartsville garrison. So, while Generals Joe Wheeler and Benjamin F. Cheatham created a diversion on the south side of Nashville, Morgan dashed in upon Moore's hapless Federals at daybreak.

One Confederate likened the hoofbeats of the southern strike force to "the roar of a mighty wind as it tore through some unbroken forest," adding that it was wonderful, inspiring, and indicative of power, strength, and numbers. The Federals thought so, too, as they put up only a short fight before surrendering en masse—fifteen hundred to two thousand of them, along with supplies and several pieces of artillery. Southern morale surged with the news. Confederate Kentuckians like Richard Bean found pleasure in just relieving enemy officers and men of winter clothing and sampling victuals still warming over breakfast fires;

then the Confederates escaped back across the Cumberland before a Union relief column arrived from nearby Castalian Springs.[43]

Thomas and other Federal officers painfully explained the disaster to both Rosecrans and Washington officials. Bragg, meanwhile, gloated over Morgan's success, the actions of Wheeler and Cheatham, and the capture of a Union supply train by Alabama cavalry near Corinth in Mississippi. Rosecrans tried to focus Lincoln's attention on the fact that he lacked adequate cavalry to cope with the Confederate horsemen. But Washington leaders brushed all this aside, pointing to the culpability of Moore and his subordinates. Rosecrans wanted to relieve the Illinoisan from service outright but, like Rodney Mason at Clarksville in the late summer, reassignment proved to be Moore's ultimate fate. Meanwhile, Morgan's men rode back to Murfreesboro in high style with their booty. Their chief proudly presented his new bride, Mattie, with the captured prisoners as a wedding present. Morgan seemed like some medieval prince returning from the Crusades.[44]

Historian Kenneth P. Williams termed Hartsville one of the boldest and best-executed minor operations of the war. It was truly breathtaking. But Morgan's modern biographer suggests that the achievement should be placed in the context of the reopening of the Big South tunnel twelve days before and the resumption of regular traffic on the railroad supplying Rosecrans. Federal forces no longer depended upon a tortuous wagon road or had to await sufficient water in the Cumberland to be resupplied. Thus, neither Hartsville nor Morgan's subsequent "Christmas Raid" into Kentucky had quite the impact accorded them by Morganphiles. Luck and jerry-rigged logistics kept the Army of the Cumberland alive, although the psychological impact of Morgan's actions threw Yankee commanders and men off balance.[45]

The statistics alone that accrued from Morgan's Christmas foray into the Bluegrass proved impressive. This deep five-hundred-mile romp from December 22 until January 2 netted eighteen hundred prisoners, a hundred and fifty Union casualties (to but twenty-six of their own), and two thousand feet of destroyed railroad bridges (especially the magnificent twin trestles at Muldraugh's Hill north of Elizabethtown), plus other depots, water stations, and L&N facilities. Four hundred men of the Seventy-first Indiana yielded Muldraugh's Hill, and Captain Tom Quirk's scouts claimed the honor of actually setting fire to the trestles. Morgan's favorite telegrapher and prankster, George Ellsworth, again wrought havoc with blueclad pursuers by tapping their communication lines and misleading pursuit. Adam Johnson's four hundred riders also went along, and he claimed later that his small party had actually stymied Yankee pursuit by counterattacking at Lebanon, Kentucky, thus enabling Morgan's main body to ride through unscathed. Morgan had made Johnson's presence viable only by adhering to Bragg's desire that freewheeling partisans be carefully integrated with regular cavalry units. Johnson still preferred his independent roving in home counties.[46]

Despite advance intelligence, Rosecrans's three-thousand-man railway protection brigade under Brigadier General James Steadman proved totally ineffective. Several times individual guard units were caught napping, as in one case when bridge defenders were engaged in close-order drill outside their specially constructed stockade. Further, Boyle's garrisons in central Kentucky were not positioned to be of much help. Intimidating civilians rather than intercepting raiders was their duty anyway. Elizabethtown farmer S. Haycroft thought Morgan's men were simple horse thieves, and he pointed to their rifling of that town's stores for boots, shoes, and even material for a new dress for Mattie Morgan as evidence. The raiders eluded pursuit by Colonels John Marshall Harland and William A. Hoskins, as well as by Brigadier General Joseph J. Reynolds, although one rear-guard action at Rolling Fork resulted in the wounding of Basil Duke, Morgan's second-in-command and brother-in-law. Four days after Christmas, Indiana governor Oliver P. Morton urged Wright at Cincinnati to hustle bridge repair crews to fix the Muldraugh spans since Rosecrans depended upon the railroad for his lifeline. In all, the L&N was shut down for another five weeks, causing southern hearts to beat anew with dreams of redemption.[47]

Morton also advocated mounting more Union units to counter Morgan's style of warfare. "Unless this is done speedily," the politician urged Secretary of War Edwin Stanton on December 29, "roving, predatory warfare will instantly destroy our communications and wear out our armies." He also suggested sending "Rosecrans' supplies by way of the Cumberland and by Green River and Bowling Green." Boyle at Louisville and Brigadier General J. M. Tuttle at Cairo, together with other rear commanders, received orders to speed resupply by water. Wright also alerted naval Captain A. M. Pennock and Lieutenant Commander Le Roy Fitch "to render any aid you can," particularly in the conveying of supply boats. Meanwhile, railroad superintendent J. B. Anderson pushed repair crews to reestablish the rail line. Local commanders, like Bruce at Clarksville, were told to "gather provisions and forage, not only for yourself, but for the army at Nashville." Once again the vicious cycle began—supply route interruption followed by local foraging, succeeded by civil disobedience and rising partisan activity, followed ultimately by harsh retribution.[48]

FORREST IN WEST TENNESSEE

December saw similar cavalry raids against Union forces that affected Federal commanders' logistics in West Tennessee. Even more strategically important than Morgan's activities, Nathan Bedford Forrest's fifteen-day excursion against Grant's supply lines and Earl Van Dorn's similarly audacious raid on the supply base at Holly Springs, Mississippi, not only disrupted Federal control of the region, but also forced abandonment of the winter overland campaign against Vicksburg. Likewise, Forrest thwarted Andrew Johnson's intention of holding elections in West Tennessee. Again, the Federals had plenty of advance warning, including enjoinders about Forrest's concentration at Williamsport west of Columbia and about Bragg's overall restiveness in Middle Tennessee.

Grant, Rosecrans, and Admiral David Dixon Porter shared this information between them and with their subordinates, but possibly without the sense of urgency necessary to prompt preventive action. Then, too, Forrest's anticipated threat to the line of the Cumberland diverted attention. From the railroad in northern Mississippi back to Columbus, Kentucky, garrisons reacted hesitantly to this unclear threat. Coordination of these dispersed garrisons proved particularly inept, hampered also by a basically hostile populace. So, Forrest, like Morgan, achieved a major raid with only minor setbacks and losses.[49]

Forrest had seethed with unhappiness about Wheeler's elevation to top cavalry command. Hastily, he prepared a fresh brigade of some two thousand to twenty-five hundred men for a planned strike at Grant's line of communications. Bragg saw this as a good way to help Pemberton in Mississippi, for he could not detach infantry to attempt a crossing of the Union-controlled Tennessee River. Still, Forrest's units were newly formed, poorly clothed, and badly armed, despite their chief's constant harangues to Bragg to correct the problem. At this point, however, the army commander looked to the Yankees to supply Forrest's needs.

Forrest was on his own. First, he had to find a way to cross a nearly mile-wide river in the face of possible gunboat intervention; then, he had to enter Federal-occupied territory before striking the railroads. Friendly civilians were the cavalryman's best hope, since, after all, this was home territory for many in his ranks. Local procurement, enemy captures, and raising the level of popular participation in anti-occupation activities had become standard operating procedure. At one point, a local supplier provided Forrest with five hundred thousand shotgun and pistol percussion caps out of his own stock.[50]

Departing on December 11, Forrest added Napier's 450 partisans at Magdeburg, then crossed the river at Clifton northwest of Waynesboro. Rosecrans had alerted Grant two days before Forrest's departure, and the general asked Porter, in turn, to send gunboats to intercept the raiders. Porter demurred, claiming the two boats working the river could not get above "Cuba Ford," and communiques passed back and forth between army and navy leaders, wasting time without result. Even Halleck and Secretary of the Navy Gideon Welles got into the act, but Forrest slipped across unscathed, and it remained for Grant's soldiers to brace for Forrest's onslaught. With Grant's sights set squarely downriver and his own cavalry actively wrecking rebel railroads in Mississippi at this time, West Tennessee garrisons could hope for little succor from his direction.[51]

Grant had also had his share of non-operational problems that fall. The practice of widespread foraging that had originated in West Tennessee spread throughout the Western Theater by the close of the year. This did not mean that men like Grant or Sherman necessarily condoned "plundering and house-burning" or "gross acts of vandalism"; such a policy would only serve to drive southerners to implacable hostility. But rebel railroads or facilities, including grist mills, became legitimate targets, and soldiers often let flames spread to ancillary structures, even houses. Reprisals against civilians, except for guerrilla activities, remained contrary to official policy. In fact, to help unionist families in the coming winter, Grant ordered foragers to leave two months' supply of provisions. Such pragmatic policy, however, did little to stop guerrilla irritations, contraband trade, cotton speculation, or political disruption.[52]

Local commanders, like Major General Stephen A. Hurlbut at Memphis, misled politicians, including Andrew Johnson, about West Tennessee's readiness for Union reconstruction. He told the military governor on November 2 that the general feeling of the people in that section was "to submit to the constitution and the law" to discourage partisan warfare and to move quickly back under civilian control. Johnson wanted elections for representation in Congress as soon as possible. But William T. Sherman's words to the U.S. Commission in Memphis on the November 14 suggested that most of the local elected officials in that city still thought Tennessee law had higher authority than the U.S. Constitution. States' rights and secessionist opposition remained high. "No law of Tennessee, in conflict with the law of the United States, is the law, and if any lawyer or judge thinks different, the quicker he gets out of the United States, the safer his neck will be," said Sherman bluntly. Many citizens flatly disregarded this suggestion.[53]

The fact that West Tennessee remained unreconstructable at this stage was evidenced by the authority Richmond granted Confederate Colonel R. V. Richardson on September 6. Richardson was charged with raising a partisan ranger unit based at Galloway's Switch in Fayette County east of Memphis. He later claimed control over all of Tipton and Fayette, as well as parts of Haywood, Hardeman, and Shelby Counties. His First Tennessee Partisan Rangers relentlessly skirmished with Union columns from Fort Pillow, Trenton, Humboldt, Jackson, Bolivar, Memphis, as well as Corinth, Mississippi. Yankee commanders, like Colonel Thomas W. Harris of the Fifty-fourth Illinois, boasted that they could easily clean out hotbeds of traitors such as the one in Troy, in Obion County southwest of Union City, if given the opportunity. "This will be a pleasure to me, as I have done so once before," he gloated. But Richardson kept the area in an uproar as his troops captured Henderson's Station on November 25 and fought sharply the next day with the Seventh Illinois Cavalry at Somerville. This partisan force added greatly to Forrest's capability several weeks later.[54]

By mid-December, Halleck informed Assistant Secretary of the Navy Gustavus V. Fox that word from West Tennessee had Bragg's whole army "moving down the Tennessee River with the probable intention of occupying some point or points on the east bank in order to interrupt navigation." But Fox did not take the bait, which was designed to pry more gunboats from Porter. He merely informed the general that the navy had everything under control since five steamers had been re-outfitted for counterguerrilla service, "and vessels go up and down those streams without molestation." Grant also swallowed the Bragg rumor and could not fathom why Rosecrans was not moving to block their mutual adversary. It appeared that Grant was diverted at times by such matters as "the Jews, as a class violating every regulation of trade established by the Treasury Department and also department orders." He listened too easily to anti-Semite Kentucky brigadier Jeremiah Boyle, who insisted that Paducah Jews were secessionist and were engaged in smuggling for and helping the partisans. Grant ordered all Jews "as a class" from the district within twenty-four hours. Thus, Grant seemed quite content to allow subordinates to eradicate what, by December 18, he was telling Porter were five to ten thousand raiders under Forrest and Napier.[55]

Brigadier General Jeremiah Sullivan, a prewar lawyer with experience as a naval midshipman who had raised two Indiana regiments for the Union, now succeeded Hurlbut as Jackson district commander. He received the lead role in holding the rebels at bay. Railroad engineer and surveyor Brigadier General Grenville Dodge assisted as Corinth district commander, and Colonel William W. Lowe on the twin rivers was told to move fifteen hundred of his men by water to cooperate with this pair. Porter admitted his gunboats were musket-proof but not cannon-proof, and he advised Grant that low water prevented coordination. Everyone moved rather sluggishly, preferring to ensure the safety of their jurisdictions rather than aggressively seeking out the raiders. Grant had to prod them to action in the end.[56]

Le Roy Fitch, in the USS *Fairplay* out of Evansville, Indiana, did his best for the navy. Having just transferred his interdiction efforts from the Kentucky's Green River to the Cumberland, the lieutenant commander was catching his breath when Porter's orders arrived. He rushed to block Forrest's line of retreat just as Grant's land commanders began to feel Forrest's wrath. The Confederates mauled one after another of the railroad garrisons before ripping up the Mobile and Ohio line from below Humboldt to beyond Moscow, just north of the Kentucky state line. They began their assaults with Colonel Robert G. Ingersoll's eight hundred Federals near Lexington, capturing two or three steel Rodman guns, hundreds of horses, scores of wagons, and at least three hundred arms (largely Sharps carbines, which were badly needed by the shotgun-wielding rebels). Feinting at Jackson, they hit Trenton, Humboldt, and Union City, twisting rails from their ties, and leaving unscathed only the Forked Deer River bridge along a smoke-filled line of march between Jackson and Trenton.

Intersecting railroads, like the Memphis and Clarksville and McKenzie–Union City routes, also received heavy damage. Brigadier General Thomas A. Davies, prewar civil engineer and merchant in New York, and now responsible for thirteen million dollars of property as Columbus, Kentucky, district chief, wrote Grant two days before Christmas that a parolee had said that, among Forrest's thirty-four-hundred-man column, "most of them are unreliable troops; some hand-picked men." Whether unreliable or hand-picked, they all proved more than adequate against Grant's lethargic garrison troops, although Forrest occasionally ran into opposition.[57]

Such opposition came from an unexpected source. Forrest's capture of Trenton, for example, produced Sara Jane Hill, the wife of a Union engineer and officer who was off on assignment, leaving her with a young son, an ailing sister, and an entrepreneurial brother at the garrison town. Forrest's men swept in, captured teamsters, wagons, and battered defenders of a small fort. Mrs. Hill and her sister cheered the Federals from the hotel, amidst shot and shell, and then watched the Confederates mistreat the prisoners and ransack what was an otherwise normally secessionist town. After being saucy to a group of Forrest's younger officers, Mrs. Hill found herself hauled before the great Wizard himself. The interview went poorly, as Mrs. Hill declined to take any rebel oath, tongue-lashed Forrest to his face, and feared physical abuse when she chided him about his treatment of women, children, and POW's. "You will leave this town more rapidly than you entered it when you learn the Union army is coming," she declared pluckily. He ordered her confined to the hotel. Later, when his men left town, she aided a sick Union prisoner who was haltered and tied to the back of a buggy driven by a slouching rebel. When the victim pleaded for water and the driver sought it for himself, Sara Hill brushed the rebel aside brusquely, saying, "the blue before the butternut with me."[58]

Forrest also discovered a stronghold of unionism around Dresden in Weakley County. It was very painful to hear southern-raised people speak against the South, and a loathsome and disgusting sight to see a southerner in Federal uniform, said H. L. Huggins, a veteran of the raid. He tried to dismiss these appearances of Union sympathy by suggesting that it was not love of the Union, but rather "some bad purpose," like pillage, robbing, or just antagonism to those whom they hated for their prewar prosperity which compelled his fellow Tennesseans to embrace the Yankee cause. Nonetheless, Grant's rear lay in a shambles by Christmas day as rumors now had the raiders knifing eastward across the Kentucky line to hit Rosecrans's supply line beyond the twin rivers.[59]

Stray bands kept Hurlbut bottled up in Memphis, leading one Federal to observe "there is a general stampede here; several hundred cavalry hover around the city, threatening to enter," as they "saucily sent in flags of truce . . . to reconnoiter the position of things." Capture of the city would be very disheartening, he thought, and dangerous to Union forces throughout the region, as well as "inspiriting to our foes." One rebel scout gloated in a report to Pemberton that the Yankees had reported Memphis under assault and had begun withdrawing their forward units everywhere. It certainly did not help Grant when yet another Confederate column under Major General Earl Van Dorn surprised his Holly Springs base on December 20, destroying between $500,000 and $1,500,000 in supplies. The post commander, Colonel R. C. Murphy of the Eighth Wisconsin was subsequently cashiered.[60]

Fretful Federal leaders chased false signals all over the region between the Tennessee and the Mississippi Rivers. Downed telegraph wires hampered coordination. Everyone acted independently, as Fleet Captain A. M. Pennock, for example, sent the USS *New Era* from Cairo to stiffen Columbus resistance with its twelve-pounder and 180 rounds of ammunition. Still, signs of panic multiplied daily. One young artillery captain at Island Number 10 fired indiscriminately at every boat on the Mississippi until he was reprimanded by superiors. The unstable Davies sent a Wisconsin officer and some men down from Columbus to spike the heavy guns and needlessly destroy six hundred rounds of ammunition on the island for fear they would fall into rebel hands. The defenders of Hickman, Kentucky, similarly sweated to heave sixty-four-pounder naval guns into the river. Suddenly, everyone from Tuscumbia, Alabama, to New Albany, Indiana, wanted gunboat help.[61]

Steamboats conveyed Lowe's pursuit column as far upriver as Lexington on the Tennessee River, but low water and reports that Dodge had now joined the chase from the south caused the Fifth Iowa Cavalry leader to return to base.

Reports circulated that his own posts were under attack and that Paducah was threatened. One of Lowe's frustrated troopers, Sergeant Eugene Marshall, wrote home disgustedly that he had waited under orders for eighteen days and then chased ghosts because of faulty intelligence. Lowe's unwise departure enabled Forrest's column to slip southward back toward the Clifton crossing. Forrest himself remained unruffled by the possibility that the Federals might catch up, and he constantly prodded his anxious young troopers with the confident claim, "we'll whip them," acting as though "there was no problem to solve, no particular danger to face."[62]

Indeed, Grant's subordinates spent more time talking about cornering the enemy than actually doing so. Brigadier General Clinton B. Fisk, a prewar merchant, miller, and banker from Coldwater, Michigan, as well as an avowed abolitionist who neither drank nor swore, was perfectly convinced that he could hunt down "the brigand Forrest" and that "we could defeat or skedaddle the entire rebel horde." The thirty-four-year-old brigadier had been sent to help out at Columbus by Major General Samuel R. Curtis in Missouri, and Fisk lost little time in castigating the nervous and easily frightened Davies. Brigadier General Sullivan also told Grant on December 29 that he had Forrest in a tight place, but that he might escape due to a lack of cavalry. Lowe could have provided that edge, as Sullivan assumed the navy was busy upriver destroying Forrest's means of ferrying his command back across the Tennessee to safety.[63]

Sullivan fought Forrest on the last day of December at Parker's Crossroads near Clarksburg in Carroll County. At first, the Confederates pummeled part of the Federal pursuit under Colonel Cyrus L. Dunham. Then Sullivan arrived unexpectedly just as Dunham prepared to surrender. Three hundred Confederates fell—Napier among them, as he was mortally wounded while stepping "upon an elevation in front to reconnoiter more fully the enemy position"—cut down in an eleventh-hour assault by Colonel John W. Fuller's brigade. Forrest rose to the challenge, supposedly enjoining his men to "charge them both ways" when his staff asked him what to do. Most of his men escaped, brushed past one final roadblock, and secured their hidden flatboats opposite Clifton to make an unopposed return crossing. Men, recruits, and booty were safe, despite twelve long and anxious hours at the riverbank. Forrest now enjoyed an actual surplus of five hundred rifles as well as eighteen blankets and knapsacks. He reported to Bragg that "we have worked, rode, and fought hard, and I hope accomplished to a considerable extent, if not entirely, the object of our campaign as we drew from Corinth, Grand Junction, and La Grange about 20,000 Federals."[64]

Sullivan's dilatory pursuit of Forrest after the battle, in fact, caused Colonel John I. Rinaker of the 122d Illinois to term him the "Genius for Tardiness." Van Dorn's northern Mississippi raiders who had taken Holly Springs—hearty riders from Missouri and Texas as well as Tennessee and Mississippi—also slipped away unscathed, and even the guerrillas around Memphis faded untouched into the shadows. Together, they had caused Grant untold hardship. Bragg reported to Richmond that Forrest's results "have been most brilliant and decisive," adding that "he has received my thanks, and deserves the applause of the government." Grant withheld comment until his postwar memoirs, but his wartime dispatches reflected that Forrest had effectively stymied any mid-winter advance on Vicksburg that depended upon a single rail line for resupply. Grant's chief critic and rival at the time, Major General John A. McClernand, put it most succinctly: "The golden moment for the reduction of Vicksburg was allowed to pass unimproved."[65]

Not only had the raid tied down fourteen thousand Federals, but also it had caused the Union navy's primary function to shift from contraband interdiction to chasing land raiders. Grant had to change his base of operations from Columbus and the railroad to Memphis and the river. Meanwhile, Forrest's men secured needed material and psychological uplift, thereby vindicating Bragg's faith in raiding as a supply acquisition technique. Despite bitter winter weather, the Confederates had killed, wounded, and captured fifteen hundred Federals (including four colonels). They had taken several artillery pieces, eleven caissons, and thirty-eight wagons with teams. Preacher-farmer Jesse Cox, living near Franklin, recorded the good news simply in his diary: "Forrest, Starnes, and others went all over west Tennessee, took many towns, and prisoners, and a vast quantity of Army stores." Forrest and Van Dorn together gave the Confederate high command in the West a powerful new tool for countering the Yankee threat.[66]

Forrest's role in disrupting Johnson's political plans was possibly even more crucial to restoration of the Union. Fighting took place within sight of polling places in the ninth and tenth districts, and a sheriff of yet another district yielded his writs of election and gave bond to the rebels that no election would take place. Alvin Hawkins of Huntington, the unionist candidate for Congressman in the ninth district, fled the state to avoid assassination, although he later appeared in Washington to unsuccessfully claim a seat in Congress based upon securing some nineteen hundred votes (out of a voting population of eighteen thousand). But Calvin S. Ezell, coroner of Gibson County, who certified Hawkins's election, noted that most of Dyer County was so infested with guerrillas as to render dangerous the holding of an election.

Therefore, on the day before Christmas, Hurlbut listed Madison, Haywood, Hardeman, Fayette, and Shelby Counties as areas in which "a fair expression of the popular will cannot be had." Postponement to January 20 led to additional delays at Grant's request, and the subsequent change to March of 1863 netted only worthless, fragmented returns. West Tennessee remained unready for unionist redemption. Secessionism was not rooted out, and Forrest's intervention with Confederate troops underscored the point. In any event, loyal Tennesseans stood to gain since Lincolnite emancipation would not come to the Volunteer state.[67]

Ironically, as Mark Grimsley has detected, Forrest's West Tennessee raid, as well as a similarly spectacular destruction of Grant's forward base at Holly Springs, Mississippi, on December 20 by Major General Earl Van Dorn, actually had one salutary effect for Federal forces. While Grant, like other professional soldiers, largely regarded foraging as an ancillary means for his men, their retreat from Oxford (sixty miles inside Mississippi) provided wider potential for living off the land in the future. Northern Mississippi was blessed with surplus food at this time, and Grant's soldiers feasted during their retreat. "We gathered great stores of corn, fodder, beans, rye, and salt, cattle, sheep and hogs, with a little sugar," wrote Colonel Manning F. Force. His men were delighted with such "short rations." So Grant concluded "that we could have subsisted off the country for two months instead of two weeks without going beyond the limits designated." He later credited the retreat from Oxford in December as inspiration for his decisive march against Vicksburg in the spring.[68]

ON TO MURFREESBORO

The Morgan and Forrest raids of December kept both Union military and political officials off guard in the heartland. Federals encamped around Nashville anticipated a big battle. Still, nothing happened. Except for chasing raiders, partisans, and moonbeams, the monotony of camp life was broken only by orders to entrench each camp and station. Obscure posts from Castalian Springs to Gallatin and Carthage realized that axes and spades were terribly important "to keep the Rebs from getting in our rear." The mood was solemn also off to the northwest at Fort Heiman, where Sergeant Eugene Marshall and his Fifth Iowa troopers constructed winter quarters from old river barges. He wrote a married sister in North Bridgewater, Massachusetts, to disregard newspaper reports that the twin river forts might be attacked, for the "rebels in this quarter" were neither armed nor equipped with the means to make a successful attack.

Indeed, the fifteen hundred guerrillas of Woodward, Johnson, and Napier who lay "within fifty or sixty miles of us," observed Marshall, lacked camp equipage or stores and had "no uniform or clothes except what they brought from home or have stolen since." Their arms were no better than double-barreled shotguns so that a line of bayonets "is their abomination," he boasted. A squadron of cavalry armed only with revolvers and sabers "inspires them with a very wholesome fear." Still, chasing them "thousands of miles" to little purpose seemed senseless when the sight of a few cavalry uniforms "scatters them irrevocably amongst the people." In his view, their only purpose was to "harass the country stealing from Union men & cut off stragglers & small detachments of our men." Marshall had grown tired of the war entirely, and he yearned for some station where the lives of men who had enlisted for better purpose were not "frittered away by imbeciles, cowards, and traitors." The static camp life and inclement weather seemed to breed mistreatment by the officers, war department orders were disobeyed with impunity, and he wanted to get on with winning the war and ending the rebellion.[69]

The onset of winter clearly sapped the spirits of many young Federals. Sickness, rain, mud, and the ritual of burying the dead and cleaning up battle sites like Hartsville after each rebel visit all took their toll. "War in its worst phase," declared William B. Miller after his Seventy–fifth Indiana helped police the destroyed Hartsville site, which left flotsam of 76 Federal and 58 Confederate dead, plus 112 wounded for hasty care. "No mark of any kind designated the place where 'some body's darling' is left to rot," said Miller as he turned away from burying comrades without coffins; only handkerchiefs or coat flaps shielded dead faces from covering dirt. Northern civilians, like Mrs. John Lewis Ketchem, a Hoosier wife and mother, left comfortable hearth sides to contribute in hospitals at Munfordville, Pilot Knob, Gallatin, and countless other places. Supplies continued to enter the area at a premium cost, yet all around lay crop-laden fields. With Nashville prices bringing a dollar per pound for coffee and potatoes at three dollars a pound, John A. Berger of the Twenty-ninth Indiana wished that home state farmers could bring their produce south to sell to the soldiers for "they could get what they are worth." James H. Jones of the Fifty-seventh Indiana thought that he had never seen better corn than that grown in the Cumberland bottoms out near Andrew Jackson's Hermitage. "But, the army is feeding it out in a hurry," he suggested.[70]

Another Hoosier left a colorful picture of foraging when he told his homefolk about long Union wagon trains moving into the country with four men to a wagon as loaders, two or three infantry regiments and artillery accompaniment, with even more foot soldiers in the rear of the column. Thus formed, "we march out several miles—sometimes to the line of the enemy—drive into a good corn field—form the regt's in line around the teams and commence loading—which takes but a short time—then the main body of the force is thrown in the rear and again we are off," he recounted. Most often, this activity passed uninterrupted by the enemy. More troublesome was the attendant unlicensed looting, despite headquarters' attempts at suppression. When Alva Griest's commander in the Seventy-second Indiana declared that looters would be punished by being paraded in camp with barrels over their heads, this was a policy that would have to change before the war ended, said the young Hoosier. "We must make [the populace] feel the horrors of war by confiscation," he advocated. He wanted the soldiery to take all rebel property needed for good use whenever found, so that the people would soon "cry enough and will be eager to come back into the Union, and a better and wiser people." Eugene Marshall would have agreed. "I am tired of seeing aid given to the rebels [sic] by officers whose duty it is to do differently," he complained to his sister in mid-December.[71]

Apparently, Demon Rum reared its ugly head just as desertion plagued both armies during this interlude. Tighlman Jones of the Fifty-ninth Illinois noted the tension caused by a treacherous enemy constantly menacing picket lines and camps—"they keep us in hot water, it seems as though our officers are never going to learn duty before whiskey." Colonels and captains were so drunk, he suggested, that they "did not know their ass from a musket." He had given up all hope of ever reinstating Federal authority over the South as long as "our army is commanded by drunken sots." He attributed much of the problem to John Morgan and his peers, who "can out-general us in every move." Like Eugene Marshall, Jones's enthusiasm had gone sour. In fact, both sides needed action. The Illinois soldier recounted how rumors had suggested that smallpox was rampaging through Confederate ranks at Murfreesboro and that deserters told how a good many of the Middle Tennessee soldiers there "swear that they will never leave the state [to fight]."[72]

Indications of the war's harsh turn could be found in direct exchanges between the opposing generals at this time, too. The Harding–Lowe treatment of Clarksville in September still festered in Braxton Bragg's correspondence with Rosecrans. "An extended and uniform system of unparalleled and savage warfare," he termed it, to which Old Rosy answered that the Davis government's order putting a price on the two colonels' heads was "inhuman and barbarous," since neither had been accorded a fair hearing. He pointed out, in turn, that the people making the complaints "have been following the savage and disgraceful system of guerrilla warfare, the effect of which is to breed robbers and murderers, and to carry war and desolation into peaceful communities." The two generals sparred back and forth about pillage, arresting noncombatants, and convalescing soldiers, but more or less agreed that wanton house burning as well as guerrilla terrorism was wrong.[73]

Bragg cited his own conduct in the Kentucky campaign as exemplary; he had ordered his army to avoid persecuting unionists. But Rosecrans clung doggedly to his demand that irregulars wear "some badge to distinguish them from the citizens," to which Bragg replied that "a defensive war conducted by a people repelling the invasion of their homes is naturally accompanied with less formality than an offensive one" and promised to pursue the campaign further without being deterred "by the ill-grounded charges of improper warfare." With regard to distinctive garb or badge, said Bragg, "whenever you will afford us the facilities to obtain the requisite material, we shall be most happy to make the desired change." Rosecrans later issued orders reprimanding officers "who permit their men to kill stock, burn rails, and seize forage." But that was useless; necessity imposed its own code of conduct on the men.[74]

Frankly, the tone of both armies was as bleak as the weather. "I am wet, muddy and in no amicable humor at the root of a giant oak solitary and alone," young Alva C. Griest confided to his diary on Christmas Eve. Having just come off picket duty, he marveled "in what a novel manner I am celebrating it here." He coped with a rushing stream, made formidable by continuing rain and a wind roaring among the trees atop a rocky bluff, while in front of him a serpentine road wound through forest and swamp. All was hidden for this anxious and depressed Hoosier warrior, as his reveries were broken by quick flashes of lightning, followed by explosions from the "artillery of heaven" to dispel the gloom. The next day was little better, for, after coming off fifty-five hours of steady picketing without relief, he was faced with orders to move at 6:00 A.M. the following day "for some point, not yet know where." Unbeknownst to Griest, it was the big push—to overcome boredom, starvation, and the enemy. The destination was Murfreesboro, and a New Year's date with Bragg. It had taken Rosecrans most of the month to muster resolve to pursue one more battle before the onset of winter.[75]

Union General-in-Chief Henry Halleck finally sent Rosecrans a blunt message on December 4: the president was very impatient "at your long stay in Nashville." Union procrastination gave Bragg time to supply himself "by plundering the very country your army should have occupied." If "you remain one more week at Nashville," warned Halleck, "I cannot prevent your removal." But the army commander tarried until after Christmas, complaining about lack of supplies, poorly shod and equipped soldiers, and a cavalry that lacked good horses. And Rosecrans had good cause—Louisville and Nashville railroad president James Guthrie had written him on December 8 that the delivery of freight at Nashville had "disappointed our expectations" following reopening of the road after Bragg's fall expedition to Kentucky. But continued cavalry destruction of fuel woodpiles, water tanks, trestles, and other facilities, unreliable repair crews, and tunnel rebuilding continued to be a handicap. "We did not expect to deliver 100 car-loads of freight daily; that amount is beyond the capacity of our motive power and rolling stock, but expect soon to deliver 70 to 80 cars daily, namely, when we have a supply of wood and water," he told the general.

However, Halleck's grumpy wire of December 5 surfaced the administration's true concern about the Tennessee situation. Some positive sign of Union repossession of the region was needed prior to the return of the British parliament in January. "Tennessee is the only State which can be used as an argument in favor of intervention by England," stated Halleck. Rosecrans had been expected to recover quickly all the lost ground by mid-December, "so that it would be known in London soon after the meeting of Parliament." A victory or the enemy's retreat prior to the tenth "would have been of more value to us than ten times that success at a later date." Now, affairs stood at "the very turning-point in our foreign relations."[76]

Finally, the Army of the Cumberland plowed southeastward toward Murfreesboro just after Christmas. Heavy marching orders, three days' rations, a soaking rain, and mud attended the march. Rosecrans at least reasoned that, with Morgan and Forrest off on raids, he could safely assail his adversary's main position. The two armies soon locked in combat during dark, dreary weather that replaced nearly two weeks of previously clear skies and balmy breezes. Some forty-seven thousand men in blue and about thirty-eight thousand in gray clashed on the final day of December, as well as two days later, in the major battle for Middle Tennessee that both sides had anticipated for months. The cedar brakes and flat fields along Stones River just north of town were the scene of momentary rebel success, followed as always by the Confederates' inability to smash the Yankees' final position. Bragg was stunned by casualties that approached ten thousand men; Rosecrans suffered thirteen thousand killed, wounded, and missing in the stubborn contest. Joe Wheeler demonstrated that he, too, could ride around the Union army, catching Rosecrans's supply trains and nearly effecting a Union disaster. But, in the end, southern dash and élan again could not overcome Federal resolve. Bragg fell back toward Shelbyville, leaving the battered and bleeding Rosecrans in possession of both the field of battle and the capital region. His own army was too worn down to mount effective pursuit.[77]

And so, one year ended and another began in battle. The Pyrrhic Union victory at Stones River (or Murfreesboro) offset failures in Virginia and Confederate recovery of the port of Galveston, Texas. European intransigence over recogniz-

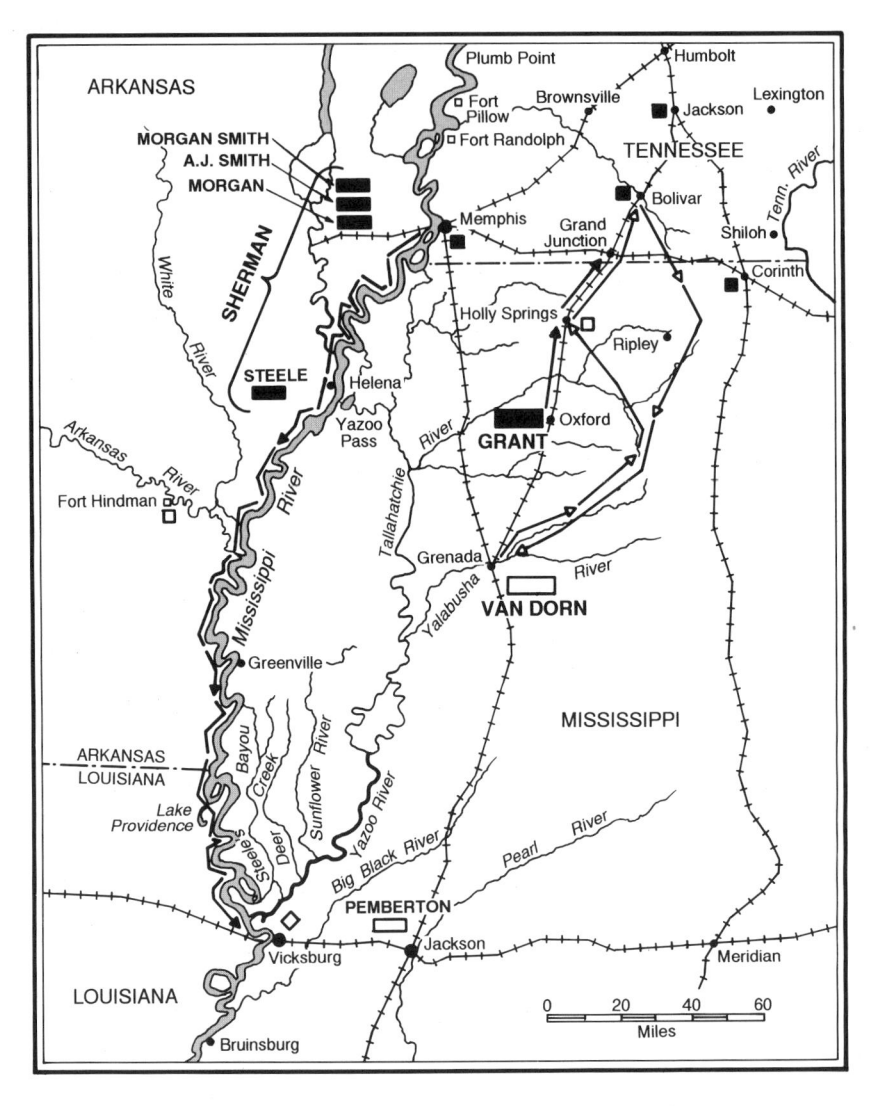

The Vicksburg Campaign from mid-December to early January 1862–1863

ing the Confederacy wavered anew, and Lincoln rejoiced at the New Year's success. Midwestern restiveness over the reopening of the Mississippi receded temporarily, although "copperhead" disloyalty still lurked just beneath the surface of politics north of the Ohio. Northern males increasingly dodged conscription, and the long casualty lists sapped the war's glamour and patriotism for the home front. Lieutenant Colonel John F. Beatty of the Third Ohio provided a gallowslike humor that reflected the attitude of many soldiers at the time by singing lustily outside his Nashville tent just two days before Christmas: "we are going home, we are going home, to die no more." At least Rosecrans had given the Union a victory of sorts by the end of the month. As the unit historian of the Ninth Ohio observed later, Rosecrans's forces as deployed between Louisville and Nashville were "stretched excessively thin." Nowhere strong enough, having too many commitments and positions to hold, lacking sufficient cavalry, this army could never be concentrated overwhelmingly for combat. "This attenuation," the Ninth's historian thought, kept it from pursuing the foe "when he retreated from the battlefield." Many problems still faced a successful Yankee resolution of the war.[78]

Major General John A. McClernand, an Illinois congressman in uniform, was quick to point out many of these problems to the administration. In a scheme to take his waterborne strike force and capture Vicksburg with the administration's blessing, he advanced a proposition that many Federal officers in the West openly advocated—more mounted units. Rapid movements could retard the foe's advance, cut his communications, destroy his trains, and harass his every step—the very things the Confederate horsemen seemed so adept at doing to the northerners. Augmented by mountain howitzers, such mounted riflemen as McClernand envisioned could rapidly pursue a retreating foe and constantly distress him.[79]

As if rubbing salt in the wound of Confederate cavalry successes during the year, McClernand wrote Secretary of War Edwin M. Stanton that "if an example was required to illustrate the soundness of these views I might refer to the success of the enemy in capturing our forces at Murfreesborough, in Tennessee; in overrunning Kentucky, and in signalizing these frequent raids by the spoils torn from peaceful citizens." Indiana governor Oliver P. Morton added his pitch on the very day of Stones River, claiming the government simply needed to mount more of its units to counter Morgan and others. Lincoln, Stanton, and Halleck knew this, and the issue would stand high on next year's agenda. Wheeler's success in the new year as well as his role at Stones River underscored the point.

SEVEN

REBELS RETURN TO FORT DONELSON: FEBRUARY 1863

A recuperating Captain Alexander Jackson Campbell of the Forty-eighth Tennessee sat musing in his diary at a private hospital in Port Hudson, Louisiana on the last day of 1862. The year "comes to a close on this bright, bracing, beautiful day after witnessing many tragic events," he observed. It had been an eventful year with the destinies of "the chivalrous" South hanging in the balance. The young nation, he felt, had been covered with the deepest gloom; the stoutest hearts had yielded to despair. Now prospects seemed brighter than at any previous moment in the momentous struggle. While "rejoiced and light-hearted," he still mourned the many valuable lives lost, the many desolate firesides, the widowed and the orphaned. "Oh, how long is this to continue," he wondered, adding, "may the next twelve months be fraught with fewer trials and troubles to the Confederacy and to myself is my prayer." Indeed, Campbell's prayer for himself was answered with his death on May 29. Having returned home on furlough, he was simply weakened by months of prison camp debilitation. For him, the war was over; for the Confederacy, 1863 would continue the recitation of trials and troubles.[1]

Despite Campbell's optimism, others realized that the situation had changed relatively little once the smoke cleared from the Stones River battlefield. General Braxton Bragg's mangled Confederates limped away from the field in a pouring rain on January 3, unpursued by an equally battered Union foe under Major General William Rosecrans. Pursuit of the defeated could be only furtive at best. The destruction and the post-battle fatigue simply immobilized everyone. Still, wrote Dunbar Affleck to his homefolk in Texas, "I can't understand why Bragg retreated from Murfreesboro—he had the Yanks completely whipped, and if he had followed them up, they could not have made another stand between here and Nashville." There, "we could have starved them out," claimed this member of Terry's Texas Rangers. Instead, "we are in full retreat for Miss[issippi], I suppose."[2]

Nashvillians were frustrated that redemption had been so close, yet remained so far. "Must we abandon all hope of Nashville [being retaken]?" queried Harriet Ellen Moore, as she noted that Yankee wounded (and some captured rebels, too) filled that city's churches. Faith in the Cause sagged anew, much as it had after earlier defeats. Even in south-central Kentucky, preacher-farmer George Richard Browder suggested that "the most intense and increasing anxiety to know the truth pervades the public," but was pleased that "most of our boys passed safely" through the terrible holocaust. Stones River seemed another bad dream for those seeking southern independence. Meanwhile, Bragg's army slumped into winter quarters along the Duck River many miles to the south.[3]

Civilians like Browder and Samuel Haycroft, a former Kentucky legislator and lately clerk of the Elizabethtown, Kentucky, circuit court, returned to their daily pursuits, far from the combat zone. Browder shrugged off the ferocity of war, "although the prospects of the South [seem] gloomy enough." He tended to the spiritual needs of his community, but he was puzzled by the contradictions his flock manifested. He shook his head at fellow Kentuckians who deplored Union president Abraham Lincoln's emancipation proclamation and who, while delighting in the growing anti-administration subversion north of the Ohio, nonetheless celebrated Federal military victories. "Consistency is a jewel," he concluded sardonically. Haycroft, a confirmed unionist, wrote in his journal that Indiana, Tennessee, and Ohio troops had camped on his land in eighteen-inch snow in early January. More important to his personal happiness, however, was the birth a month later of twin grandsons, a gift of his daughter amidst the strain and stress of wartime.[4]

Pride lay at the cause of the nation's ruin, Browder proclaimed boldly, "and all the scourge that war had brought seems to have failed to humble us." War, war, oh dreadful war, he wailed. Who could foretell its horrors, he added, the nation was doomed and ruined. Alluding to news coverage of the government's authorization to enlist 150 regiments of black soldiers, Browder thought that "the war is to be brought into Ky, Tenn, and Mississippi and we look for greater horror and outrages," since the rebels would raise the Black Flag of no quarter for African Americans caught in uniform, "and this may lead to cruel and bloody retaliation." People were troubled indeed as confusion and uncertainty accompanied passage into the second year of war in the upper Confederate heartland.[5]

WINTER OF UNCERTAINTY

Of course, the portents of the future seemed clear enough to some people. Major General John A. McClernand, a driven man who chafed at subordination to fellow Illinoisan Ulysses S. Grant, was convinced that he knew how to end the war and never stopped sending his ideas to Washington. Occasionally, they had merit, including those he passed to the president in September and again in November. Blockade of the Mississippi by the rebels "has left to the people of the Northwest but one outlet for their immense surplus of grains and livestock, and that by the lakes and railroads alone to the East," he trumpeted. Onset of winter would close those channels, and leave midwesterners at the "discretion of exclusive monopolists." High freight rates threatened people's livelihoods, while eastern capitalists profited handsomely by owning the railroads and manufacturing establishments. He felt those men actually welcomed continued closure of the traditional Mississippi trading outlet. But further delay in reopening the river "will seriously complicate our national troubles by adding yet another geographical question to the one already undergoing decision by force of arms."[6]

McClernand cited an earlier era when Spain controlled the Louisiana outlet to the Great Valley. He suggested that "already there are those who are beginning to look beyond the pale of Federal authority for new guarantees for the freedom of the Mississippi River." A new party might appear that would be favorable to Confederate recognition in return for treaty or union of the Midwest and South. Midwestern resentment would be whipped up by demagogic appeals designed to array them against easterners "upon pretended ground that the latter are in favor of continuing the war and the blockade of the Mississippi; as a means of fostering the interest of their trade, their manufactures, and their capital invested in both." McClernand, seeking to lead the crusade to reopen the Mississippi, clearly saw how political and economic necessity applied directly to military goals for the coming year in the West. The upper Confederate heartland would certainly be affected as a consequence.

Then, too, Tennessee Military Governor Andrew Johnson informed President Abraham Lincoln soon after the Stones River victory that the battle "has inspired much confidence with Union men of the ultimate success of the Government, and has greatly discouraged rebels, but increased their bitterness." If the rebel army could be expelled from the state, and "Union sentiment developed without fear or restraint, I still think Tennessee will be brought back into the Union by decided majority of popular vote." Here was Clausewitzian theory incarnate, with all its elements: war as an extension of politics, political direction, the armed forces, and the popular will. However, eviction of Braxton Bragg's army was one thing; renascent unionism quite another. The truth of Johnson's assertion awaited another two years for confirmation.[7]

More immediately, the policy of cleansing that region of rebellion was turning the area into a scene of perpetual conflict. Raiders and partisans had filled the void left in the wake of departing Confederate armies from March until September 1862. They had wrought havoc with Federal lines of communication and occupation efforts. Accordingly, Union military and civilian authorities failed to suppress rebellion as the ever-present butternut irregulars kept alive the torch of secession in Tennessee and Kentucky. The names of Forrest, Morgan, Woodward, Adam Johnson, Napier, McCann, and others supplanted those of Bragg, Polk, Beauregard, or Joe Johnston in local vocabularies during the period. For the Federals, the raiders' names individually inspired both fear and hatred. Collectively, they provided a different kind of war for combatants and noncombatants alike.[8]

Both armies now preyed upon the landscape and its people. If the raiders, partisans (the two often acting in concert), and their Federal pursuers kept the region in a turmoil, so too did the main armies themselves. It was more like Europe of the Thirty Years War or Napoleonic era. Plunder and confiscation assumed new meaning. Major General William Tecumseh Sherman had told Louisville *Journal* editor George D. Prentice on November 1 that he had frequently asserted that southern military rather than northern military officers "were the first to take the slaves of loyal masters and wagons and horses of our people" in Kentucky. Long before fugitive slaves had been encouraged to enter Union camps, slaves had been impressed by rebel authorities to work on fortifications at Bowling Green, Columbus, and the twin rivers forts. "My opinion," said Sherman, "is that the adherents of the Southern cause have instituted principles of warfare that when applied to themselves, will be destructive of material interest, and if we retaliated they are estopped [sic] by their own practice."[9]

Sherman bluntly wrote Miss P. A. Fraser and Miss Valeria Hurlbut of Memphis in late October and early November, rebuking them for their consternation over his expulsion order of rebel civilians in response to guerrilla attacks on the river steamboats *Catahoula* and *Gladiator*. He argued that Confederate authorities "must know and feel that not only will we meet them in arms, but that their people shall experience their full measure of the necessary consequences of such barbarity." If such authorities embraced Partisan Rangers as part of their army and did not disavow their action, then "they shall not live with us in peace." Union troops would not chase perpetrators aimlessly through canebrakes and swamps, but "will visit punishment upon the adherents of that cause which employs such agents." His temper rising, Sherman trumpeted: "[W]e must stop this, and no measures would be too severe." The "absolute destruction of Memphis, New Orleans, and every city, town and hamlet of the South would not be too severe a punishment to a people for attempting to interfere with the navigation of the Mississippi." Misplaced kindness to these guerrillas, their families, and adherents "is cruelty to our people," he added, noting that those exiled accordingly should welcome such opportunity to be "going to their own husbands and families." To the recipients of his written wrath, Sherman suggested: "Would to God ladies better acted their mission on earth; that instead of inflaming the minds of their husbands and brothers to lift their hands against the Government of their birth and stain them in blood, had prayed them to forbear, to exhaust all the remedies afforded them by our glorious Constitution, and thereby avoid 'horrid war,' the last remedy on earth."[10]

Indeed, Sherman informed General-in-Chief Henry Halleck as well as colleague Rear Admiral David Dixon Porter later in November that new northern recruits "come full of the idea of a more vigorous prosecution of the war, meaning destruction and plunder" and that they required "hard handling to prevent excesses." A resident unionist element had also been aroused, he asserted, and rebel cotton burning as well as their practice of taking corn, fodder, and supplies from country people had shaken the latters' faith in Confederate authority. In short, contended Sherman, albeit prematurely, "we have really made a substantial beginning of the conversion of the people to our cause." A significant number of heartlanders would not have agreed. Certainly those in Kentucky would have demurred: anger at Lincoln's emancipation proclamation "rose to a high tide," despite the state's exemption from the pronouncement, questions lingered about the necessity for presidential departure from his avowed policy that if those in rebellion simply laid down their arms and returned to the Union, "they would be protected in all their rights by the Constitution," including possession of slaves. Here then were the seeds of misunderstanding and distrust that would confront Union authorities even in supposedly unionist territory during the coming year.[11]

More rigid views attended unrepentant rebels like young Harriet Ellen Moore living with her family at Edgefield, just across the Cumberland from Nashville. She greeted the new year with morbid thoughts of "how many new battle fields will be made, new victories won, and new graves formed?" Listening to the distant rumble of the guns at Stones River, fifteen miles away, she trembled with joy "when we think that our foes may be driven from our homes and our southern friends once more reinstated in their rightful domains." We "long for deliverance," she wrote in her diary, and particularly from the onus of Lincoln's proclamation. A rural attorney from Springfield, Illinois, she scoffed, "assumes the responsibility to set free 4,000,000 of contented and happy slaves belonging rightfully to the south." Two of the family servants had left at the first sign of Yankee troops, but had since returned; "the rest seem perfactly [sic] contented." Whether or not this white southern girl accurately judged the African-American sentiment cannot be determined. What she did judge accurately was continuing resentment and opposition to Union rule in occupied sections of the Upper South.[12]

The Union Army of the Cumberland took to its winter camps in the Murfreesboro region with little thought of Black Flags, slave insurrection, or precisely what its presence meant to the population. Suppression of rebellion, but more important survival remained uppermost in the minds of its soldiery. Rosecrans's camps straddled the various turnpikes to Bradyville, Manchester, Shelbyville, Liberty, and Lebanon, as well as Franklin. Rear battalions moved up to La Vergne, to be supplanted by others formerly stationed farther back at Gallatin and other locations north of the Cumberland. General orders reorganized the army from three grand divisions (patterned after Major General Ambrose Burnside's similar ill-fated scheme with the Army of the Potomac in the East) into three army corps. Murfreesboro itself became a vast hospital and rehabilitation center, while those who were less seriously wounded were sent to Nashville and beyond.

Despite restoration of rail service to Louisville in December, Morgan's Christmas raid again put the L&N out of commission until February. The onset of frigid winter deprived the Union army encamped at Murfreesboro of resupply via the Cumberland. Dependent upon the horribly frozen and rutted local roads of Middle Tennessee, it was hard even to move supplies from the forward base at Nashville. Before long, a familiar picture reappeared. Yankee foragers began stripping neighborhood farms once more. Colonel James Moore King's place just outside Murfreesboro again suffered heavily, perhaps because King had shoul-

Return of a Union foraging party. National Archives and Records Administration.

dered an old 1812 musket and aided Brigadier General Joseph Wheeler's action at La Vergne during the Stones River battle. When Bragg pulled out of the area, the Federals descended with a vengeance upon King's six thousand pounds of bacon, over one hundred hogs awaiting slaughter, large numbers of cattle, sheep, and horses, plus a corn crop with an annual yield of twenty thousand bushels ripe for the taking.[13]

Similarly, the unit chronicler of the German-American Ninth Ohio recounted how his regiment, with two companies of the Thirty-fifth Ohio, two cannon, and over twenty wagons, had gone to Hartsville on January 6 "to plunder two mills that we believed supplied the rebels regularly with flour." Meeting farmers on their way to those mills with wheat, the Buckeyes relieved them "of their burdens and sent them home with about a tenth of what they carried when we stopped them." At the mills themselves, they found enough flour and wheat to return with full wagons to camp. The raid was made all the more interesting when some of the young bluecoats turned "first-class millers for the occasion" and ground additional flour on the spot. Moreover, the expedition delightedly recaptured one of its old regimental drums, a rebel flag having been painted over its original insignia.[14]

Some of Rosecrans's men celebrated their previous year's victory at Mill Springs, Kentucky, and then suffered through a mid-January rain and snow storm that caused the Cumberland River to rise thirteen feet in twenty-four hours. The water then froze on January 16, forcing many in the Ninth Ohio to seek refuge in the city itself. Still, said their spokesman, "our occasional duty on patrol was not hard," the weather soon cleared, they found a new, more accommodating campsite, and "with the sun in our favor, patrol and fatigue were much easier."

Rosecrans spent the winter fortifying Murfreesboro, attempting to resuscitate his army, and, according to one commentator, inflicting "the greatest possible restraint to the enemy north of Duck River, and the greatest possible injury south of that stream." The elaborate fortification at the Murfreesboro base easily equaled the autumn construction effort at Nashville. A huge earthwork went up on the high ground straddling Stones River about a mile and one-half northwest of the courthouse. It was "the largest enclosed earthen fortification built during the war," claims Lenard E. Brown, who has studied the project. Constructed under the professional oversight of Army of the Cumberland chief engineer James St. Clair Morton, it enclosed 200 acres and measured over 2,300 yards in circumference. Called "Fortress Rosecrans," it comprised a series of so-called lunettes linked by a continuous line of earthworks with an abatis of felled trees and brush outside to entangle would-be attackers. Four inner enclosed redoubts mounted artillery as a final line of defense if the outer works were breached. A cross-shaped blockhouse as well as a magazine completed the fortress. Designed as a refuge for the army after defeat and protection for the army's supply base, the fortress also served as a means of controlling the railroad and highway that ran through the work. Whether or not a full army of 50,000 men or more could have crowded into such a work in the event of an emergency—and survived for an anticipated two or three months—remains suspect. However, the 14,600 feet of rifle pits, lunettes, redoubts, etc., would certainly present "a formidable face to an attacker," in Brown's words.[15]

Rosecrans's men worked on these fortifications (as well as camp protection) between January and June. Rotational brigade labor groups moved the earth under tutelage of the army's Pioneer Brigade. All of this kept an idle soldiery employed (when not otherwise engaged in patrols, foraging, and drill) while offsetting sickness, boredom, and desertion that plagued the Army of the Cumberland that winter and spring. Four steam-powered sawmills provided timber for fortification revetments, blockhouses, magazines, warehouses, quartermaster and ordnance depots, wagon parks, and corrals—all in support of the construction effort. Ironically, Fortress Rosecrans would never be tested by Bragg's main army. But the complex would provide sanctuary for convalescents and other light-duty troops in the coming months. Moreover, the works gave their namesake a sense of security both for his troops in winter encampment as well as for their eventual advance against the enemy.

Halleck reported later that, after Stone's River, "the enemy took position at Shelbyville and Tullahoma, and the winter and spring were passed in raids and unimportant skirmishes." Unimportant though they might have seemed to this Washington bureaucrat, they were real enough for the soldiers and civilian populace directly affected by them. The month of January, noted Captain Marshall

P. Thatcher of Company B, Second Michigan Cavalry, "began our memorable Tennessee campaign—reconnaissances, skirmishes and fights occurring almost daily," many over the forage trains. Rebels captured such a train near Murfreesboro on January 21, and an infantry skirmish occurred at Woodbury three days later. Brigadier General Nathan Bedford Forrest's horsemen brazenly assaulted a Union railroad train at Mill Creek bridge just south of the state capital on January 26.[16]

Some incidents were far more controversial. Brigadier General Robert M. Mitchell formulated a directive to the Eighty-fifth Illinois to obliterate the house and property of partisan chieftain Dick McCann because his band had destroyed a Union construction train on the Nashville and Chattanooga line. The inhuman Yankees, noted Harriet Ellen Moore in her diary, had ousted McCann's wife and family from their property on short notice, declaring that life in a stable was quite "good enough for a secesh's wife," but that they did not intend to leave her even that much. Citing McCann as a regularly commissioned Confederate officer, Moore noted, "this act will not be forgotten." The Union probes extended outward in all directions from Murfreesboro and Nashville, but keyed on the southbound rail and roadways. Confederate partisans and cavalry kept control of the sparsely settled neighborhood to the south and west from the Cumberland to Duck River.[17]

A similar standoff situation could be found with Rosecrans's counterpart in West Tennessee, Major General Ulysses S. Grant. In trying to recover from Forrest's December strike and shift his Vicksburg operation from an overland to a river approach, Grant reported an aggregate force of 132,164 officers and men available for this new operation at the end of January. But nearly half that number remained pinned down by the threat of enemy raids and partisan activity. Major General Stephen A. Hurlbut's XVI corps protected the West Tennessee and Purchase area of Kentucky, with additional separate cavalry brigades and a XVII army corps detailed especially to rear area security. Always far too optimistic about his subordinates' capabilities for such missions, Grant purged the hesitant Thomas A. Davies from his Columbus command and replaced him with an equally inept brigadier, Alexander Asboth. But at least he teamed up more able commanders like Brigadiers Jeremiah Sullivan at Jackson and Grenville Dodge at Corinth, as well as Colonel William W. Lowe at the twin rivers forts, with navy efforts in counterguerrilla operations. Working together, army and navy units tried to destroy flatboats and ferrying craft, reestablish stockades at key points, and chase rumored rebels still lurking in their vicinity.[18]

Grant's December reverses endangered the Freedman's camps of Chaplain John Eaton at Grand Junction and Corinth; many of the ex-slaves were pulled into Memphis to spend the winter. Grant also ordered heavy ordnance stripped from positions on the east bank of the Mississippi where they might fall to partisan leaders like Colonel R. V. Richardson. Similarly, he wanted all contraband trade to be stopped and cotton exports to be carefully controlled in and out of Memphis. He feared that rural secessionists were gaining not merely the staples of life but also first-class Federal arms and equipment, which they then passed to partisans and main-force raiders alike. As for the ubiquitous guerrilla bands, Grant told Hurlbut on January 3 to exile to the south ten families of the most ardent local secessionists for every raid or attempted raid by irregulars. He intended to "make it the interest of the citizens to leave our lines of communication unmolested." There would be little in northern Mississippi to support such outlaws in a few weeks, he assured Halleck. Two weeks later, he issued a general order that stated bluntly that any guerrillas or southern soldiers caught in Federal uniforms would be considered spies.[19]

Assistance to the Union military occasionally came from isolated, singular Tennessee unionists, like Dr. W. T. Belisle of Jackson. He had provided Grant with information on several occasions just before Shiloh. But, too often, innocent civilians, whatever their sentiments about the rebellion, fell prey to notorious Union ruffians like the Seventh Kansas Cavalry. This band evoked the ire of one unionist and former Tennessee congressman, Thomas Rivers, for its rambunctious visit to his hometown of Somerville in Fayette County after the Holly Springs debacle. Rather than chasing Van Dorn, noted Grant in acting upon Rivers's complaint, the horsemen had deviated to plunder Somerville and also New Albany, Mississippi. Grant told Brigadier General Charles S. Hamilton, West Tennessee district commander, on January 20: "Their present course may serve to frighten women and children and helpless old men but will never drive out an armed enemy." In addition to units that preyed on the helpless in a cowardly way, Grant had a few units, like the 109th Illinois (raised the previous summer in southern Illinois), which flatly refused to fight. These men abhorred Lincoln's preliminary emancipation proclamation and thought they had been supplied inferior arms. They had a high desertion rate and were apparently eager to surrender. Some of their number had actually defected to local secessionists near their camps south of Holly Springs, which caused Grant to order confiscation of their arms. He convened a courts-martial, which led to cashiering the officers and transferring the men to the Eleventh Illinois.[20]

Frankly, Grant worried most about a return of a main force under Forrest, P. D. Roddey, and Earl Van Dorn. Local informants told the Union commander that Roddey had raised the old steamboat *Dunbar*, which had sunk the year before after the fall of Fort Henry, and was attempting to re-outfit her. So, Grant asked the navy to make a river sweep and destroy this potential menace, as well as to interdict rebel cavalry movements from Clifton southward into Alabama. Grant's January communiques rang with alarm about threats from Van Dorn and about brigade commander W. H. Jackson's six-thousand-man raid on the Memphis and Charleston Railroad, which his subordinates should be on guard to hold "at all hazards." Such warnings would become the winter theme for both Grant in West Tennessee and Rosecrans to the east as they waltzed to the tune of rebel cavalry and partisans. Still, many of his soldiers actually remained oblivious to such disturbances. Ira Blanchard of the Twentieth Illinois noted that his regiment countermarched back to Memphis after the abortive Mississippi move in December to enjoy blithely "many of the privileges of a great city." They attended churches, theaters, and other places of amusement (presumably even brothels, since Memphis was now beginning to rival Nashville in that regard). They passed much of the time "during our sojourn here in pleasantness and peace," he recalled.[21]

ATTENTION TO LINES OF COMMUNICATION

Rosecrans and his generals realized that Bragg might return to the proven tactic of disrupting Federal plans by attacking lines of communication. The Army of the Cumberland's support area was vast. Encompassed by the Department of the Ohio under Major General Horatio G. Wright at Cincinnati, some sixty thousand officers and men were spread across the Bluegrass trying to hold strategic points like Bowling Green, Munfordville, Lebanon, New Haven, and Henderson, as well as Clarksville, Tennessee. These places alone contained fifteen thousand garrison troops of Brigadier General Jeremiah T. Boyle's District of Western Kentucky. With the Louisville and Nashville Railroad blocked, the Federals turned by necessity to river resupply where possible. Boasting a depth of twenty-five feet during the winter, the Cumberland River particularly could serve the needs of its namesake field army.

As Grant turned his attention to similarly using the Mississippi River approach against Vicksburg, so Rosecrans looked to the Cumberland to succor his men after Stones River. Thanks to wise heads in Washington, this force was not split up merely to support Grant's major effort in the West. In administration eyes, Rosecrans could take advantage of Bragg's diminished numbers and "drive him back into Georgia," thus rescuing loyal East Tennessee, "an object which the Government has kept constantly in view from the beginning of the war," said Halleck. "I therefore urged General Rosecrans to take advantage of this opportunity to carry out his long-projected project," Halleck later reported, "informing him that General Burnside would co-operate with his force, moving from Kentucky to East Tennessee." But this goal required preparation. The Confederates could be depended upon to test those preparations.[22]

Wretched winter weather and poor road conditions, swollen streams, as well as hovering gray horsemen kept the Union buildup off-track. The army commander requested navy Captain A. M. Pennock at Cairo to provide gunboat convoys for army supply vessels plying the winding, narrow, eighty-five-mile Cumberland from Smithland to Nashville. The navy naturally claimed that it was overcommitted, which was true given Grant's demands on the Tennessee and Mississippi Rivers. Boats were needed for the main operation against Vicksburg, but also for counterguerrilla and barrier operations on the upper Tennessee. Moreover, said Pennock, at least one of his craft had smallpox aboard. Grant, still smarting from Forrest's and Van Dorn's rebuff in December, wanted Pennock to find and destroy "large numbers of flat-boats and other craft for crossing the Tennessee River hid away at the mouth of streams" emptying into that river. Pennock was also apprehensive about the *Dunbar*. The naval commander tried to duck Rosecrans's convoy request by claiming Congress had transferred the gunboat service to navy control back in October, and now his orders came from the rear-admiral in charge on western waters. He promised to forward Rosecrans's request to Porter before the latter departed downriver with Grant and to dispatch any spare boats up the twin rivers with directions to cooperate as much as possible with the army.[23]

Frankly, the navy was not enamored with convoy duty in hostile waters. Still, Rosecrans would not be denied. He offered to supply crews for new gunboats and asked: "why can not common boats be procured and barricaded, and armed and sent up the river?" He pressed his case in Washington, and the navy finally agreed to reinforce Pennock's flotilla with two hundred recruits from the army's forts around the nation's capital. Secretary of the Navy Gideon Welles rebuked Pennock directly: "It is expected that the Mississippi Squadron will cooperate with the army on every occasion in which its cooperation is required and can be extended, and in an emergency such as that now on the Cumberland and Tennessee Rivers that every exertion will be made to meet it." On January 24, he told Pennock that it was imperative that gunboats be sent to protect transports on the twin rivers. So, the naval officer dutifully deployed the light draft gunboats USS *Brilliant, St. Clair, Fairplay, Alfred Robb, General Pillow,* and *Silver Lake,* as well as the timberclad *Lexington,* on such duty.[24]

No matter what Welles had told him, Porter wrote Pennock four days later, "you will take every opportunity to write to these army officials and inform them that you have no information to give them concerning this department, and that General Halleck has no control here; also, that I dispose of the force under my command." In the admiral's view, the army's "own blundering gets them into difficulty." Still, such interservice spats had little place given the exigencies of guerrilla warfare on the rivers. Halleck wrote Rosecrans disgustedly on January 30: "We anticipated and predicted that just at the time and place where we most needed these boats there would be no co-operation." The best hope, he said, was for Rosecrans to continuously press Porter to keep his boats on the rivers, while the general-in-chief would keep the pressure on the navy department in Washington. "I have no doubt that there is every desire for cordial co-operation," he suggested, "but it is very difficult to effect when the parties have different objects in view and act entirely independent of each other."[25]

General Wright at Cincinnati joined the dialogue with the navy, pressing for commitment of an ironclad to smother enemy field guns that might accompany rebel attempts to impede river traffic. Rosecrans, too, urged additions to the flotilla "by purchase, adaption, or construction." But he shifted his concern to other aspects of improving the overall situation. First, he sought clarification of command arrangements for the Cumberland and Tennessee Rivers forts. He assumed they now belonged to his department due to transfer when General Order 168 had established new jurisdictional boundaries on October 24, 1862. Halleck and Rosecrans then argued about the forts being part of Grant's reward for their capture, until the latter suggested this was confusing and embarrassing now that the Cumberland was "my line of water communication." Their "maintenance and police surveillance [roles] are essential to my lines of communication and the control of the contraband trade," he contended, and "they ought to be under my command." Halleck finally relented, transferring Forts Henry and Donelson to Rosecrans on January 25, with Fort Heiman following as "an appendage to Fort Henry" on February 4.[26]

Old Rosy continued to press his luck in Washington despite a lingering lung infection. He tried to raid rear areas, even north of the Ohio, for surplus manpower. He sought to establish an elite battalion in each brigade composed of valorous officers and men, equipped with the best weapons, and mounted for rapid deployment. "We must bring down all the cavalry available, and add to it the mounting of brigades of infantry, for scouting and expeditionary purposes," he cautioned. Rosecrans correctly discerned that Confederate superiority in his region lay with mounted forces. Why should the rebels control Middle Tennessee with impunity because they had more cavalry, he asked correctly. He wanted "to annihilate the military power and exhaust the resources of the rebels," and this would involve using the rivers and a repaired Edgefield and Kentucky as well as completed Nashville and Northwestern railroad line to the Tennessee River to effect control over the region. He envisioned immediately occupying key towns like Franklin, Columbia, Charlotte, and Waverly and turning them into strategic hamlets.[27]

Rosecrans's scheme sounded brilliant. At one and the same time, alternate lines of communication would be provided, guerrilla sanctuaries in the quadrangle bounded by the Cumberland, Tennessee, and Duck Rivers (with the Nashville–Chattanooga Railroad on the other leg) would be cleaned out, and Federal occupation could begin the process of political, economic, and social reconstruction. Yet, amassing the resources to carry out the plan would take time, and it would compete with the other theaters of operation. Halleck pointedly asked: "will not the occupation of so many points as you propose between the Cumberland and the Tennessee Rivers greatly weaken your main army and expose the garrisons of the points occupied to capture?" If these were fortified towns, strong enough to "resist a coup d'main" noted Halleck, it would be different. Nothing was said about Rosecrans's advocacy of railroad repair or construction.[28]

Rosecrans found Ohio departmental commander Wright suddenly more cooperative. Wright promised to send Brigadier General Gordon Granger and fourteen thousand men (twenty infantry units, four cavalry regiments, and four artillery batteries) from central Kentucky. Rosecrans requested two additional brigades, two batteries, "and all your cavalry, with the pack animals and saddles." He had in mind debarking this force at Clarksville with ten days' rations "to sweep the whole country from the Tennessee River to [Murfreesboro] between the Cumberland and Duck Rivers." Carrying 120 rounds of ammunition per man, he explained to Wright, "I think by concert of action we can 'put [the Confederates] up a spout.'" If Wright could handle Kentucky, said Rosecrans on January 24, then "If I cannot whip them with what you send me, I will give it up." The rub would be in getting this force promptly positioned via the river. At this point, matters went critical on the Cumberland line.[29]

CONFEDERATES RETURN TO THE CUMBERLAND

Affairs on the lower Cumberland began warming up soon after the first of the year. Sergeant Eugene Marshall of the Fifth Iowa Cavalry wrote his sister in Bridgewater, Massachusetts, from Fort Henry on January 22 that he saw little danger from the rebels. His regiment had "followed the enemy some thousands of miles but it seems as if it was always at a safe distance." The war was the "greatest humbug of the age and must remain so while men are retained in command who have everything in the way of position, Money etc. to lose by the close of the war." They were reckless adventurers with little stake in ending conflict, he argued, with no inducement to carrying on the war vigorously, for that only meant that they "must retire into comparative obscurity when the war is done." Suddenly rebel activity changed the situation dramatically in the land between the rivers.[30]

A guerrilla force cut up a wagon train between Forts Henry and Donelson in early January. Six guards were killed as well as a man named Spaulding, the guerrilla leader. Two weeks later, Colonel William W. Lowe, senior commander in the region, sent another expedition from Fort Henry to Waverly in eighteen inches of snow to break up the partisan stronghold. Colonel Abner C. Harding's Eighty-third Illinois had visited the place in the fall, but this time the cavalry captured a major, two captains, a quartermaster, and eight enlisted men—all from different rebel units. This diversity of unit affiliations should have alerted the Federals that something more than mere partisans were in the neighborhood. Rumor had Forrest moving in the direction of Fort Heiman from West Tennessee, and this sent soldiers and freedmen back to strengthening the earthworks. The presence of the USS *General Pillow* in the river seemed reassuring until a detachment rode into Fort Heiman on February 1 from a scouting mission in Benton County, Kentucky. They reported a surprising number of Forrest's men roaming that area, a full month after their parent units supposedly had retired from the West Tennessee raid.[31]

Yankee complacency was upset further by appearance of a larger enemy force on the Cumberland closer to Nashville. This force resulted from Bragg's January 7 directive to his cavalry commanders to harass and check the Federal advance, to raid and forage "on the enemy's flank and rear," and to maintain a presence in the region to inspire secessionist civilians. Bragg counted scarcely twenty thousand effectives in the ranks, he claimed, and loyalty among his own generals was wanting after the singular lack of success with the Kentucky and Stones River ventures. Theater commander Joseph E. Johnston regretted Bragg's "falling back so far" to the Duck River line, but Johnston visited the army in late January and thought things were well in hand. He and Bragg tried to devise ways to recruit the army up to strength, as well as trying to keep Rosecrans off balance in the meantime. Bragg directed the ever-controversial Gideon Pillow to lead a Volunteer and Conscript Bureau sweep of various Tennessee counties below the Duck River for deserters, skulkers, and others liable to the 1862 conscription laws.

Guerrillas burning steamboats on the Cumberland River. From Fitch, Annals of the Army of the Cumberland *(Philadelphia: J. B. Lippincott, 1864), 664.*

Pillow's patriotic zeal proved quite effective. Meanwhile, Wheeler's horsemen undertook to disrupt Rosecrans's tenuous line of communications.[32]

Captain Joseph G. Vale of the Seventh Pennsylvania Cavalry, with Colonel R. G. H. Minty's famous mounted brigade, once rather ungenerously suggested that, all through the war, upon suffering a defeat or failing to accomplish some chosen goal the western Confederates "got up a side show, to amuse their people and delude them into the belief that the rebel cause was in the ascendancy." So it was in January 1863 when Wheeler took the lead in harassing Rosecrans. His actions would garner him a second star and congressional accolades in Richmond. Having reconditioned his horses in Lincoln County on the Alabama line, Wheeler moved his column to the Cumberland in bitter cold and snowy weather. The Confederates then jumped a boat column at Harpeth Shoals, midway between Clarksville and Nashville, on January 13 with brilliant results. Disregarding a hospital flag aboard the steamer *Hastings*, they riddled the boat, along with the *Trio* and *Parthenia*, with gunfire, then proceeded to swarm aboard to rob and rough up the 212-odd wounded as well as others aboard. Telegrapher Peter Fowler escaped such indignity by feigning death.[33]

Wheeler allowed a chaplain, M. P. Gaddis of the Second Ohio, and a surgeon, Luther D. Waterman of the Thirty-ninth Indiana, to convey the paroled *Hastings* downriver with the promise to burn the cotton aboard when she reached Louisville. Union authorities later prevented that from happening. Then the rebels captured another small gunboat, the USS *Siddell*, an old ferryboat supposedly mounting a single gun. The frolicsome southerners placed her hapless commander, Lieutenant William Van Dorn, backwards upon a mule, a coonskin cap on his head, and declared that "they were going to keep him as a specimen of Yankee bravery." Van Dorn's head "is not worth shucks" around Nashville, reported navy surgeon William Howard. Inasmuch as the USS *Brilliant* and other craft had run the gauntlet scant hours before the *Siddell*, claimed Howard, Van Dorn should have fought his way through.[34]

Rosecrans was aghast at the "inhuman violations of the rules of civilized warfare by the rebel authorities" in the *Hastings* affair. But his protests had little effect on Wheeler, who was busily wreaking havoc on the Cumberland. Forty volunteers from D. W. Holman's partisan ranger battalion swam the cold river in a driving rain on one occasion to ignite a supply dump near Ashland. Frightened guards fled, thinking Wheeler's whole command was at hand. On January 17, the same group caught the steamer *Mary Crane*. They consigned her contents of seventy-five barrels of prized, parched coffee to the swirling river (much to some individual rebels' disgust, for they relished that delicacy). Other brushes continued all month, and even the heavily gunned USS *Lexington* was set upon on January 29. Harpeth Shoals and Palmyra became the rebel choke points for river traffic, and, in the absence of military action, gunboat convoys became the device for running this gauntlet. As Howard cryptically described one such passage to his wife: "Lexington in advance, 64s [gun caliber]—then 5 transports, 'Fair Play,' 24s and 12's—then 5 transports 'St. Clair,' 24s and 12's—5 transports—'Brilliant,' 24's and 12's 5 transports—'Silver Lake,' 24's and 12's—5 transports, and 'Robb'—12's."[35]

The navy accordingly pushed through more convoys than Wheeler's men could effectively block, with steamboats lashed together in pairs to prevent stragglers. Gunboats hovered at the foot of the shoals, while steamboat crews crossloaded freight to lighten the craft just enough to pass over that obstacle and continue on to Nashville, returning later to retrieve the stores left ashore under close guard. It was hard, time-consuming work. Naval officers like Howard noted that civilians along the river (and especially in Nashville) were "bitter secesh," as the navy sought additional help from the army to counter Wheeler and the partisans. Wintry weather, however, largely kept the Federal soldiers confined to garrison and provided local commanders like Colonel Sanders D. Bruce with excuses merely to use the Cumberland as a convenient barrier to any Confederate thrust north of the river.

Bruce had returned a permanent Union garrison to Clarksville in December. His Seventeenth and Twenty-eighth Kentucky Infantry, 102d Ohio Infantry, two battalions of the Eighth Kentucky Cavalry, and the First Tennessee battery—scarcely three thousand effectives in total—clamped a lid once more upon that avowedly secessionist city. Ex-slaves were put to work improving the old Confederate Fort Defiance, which was now renamed to honor Bruce, at New Providence. The Kentuckians (who local farmer Nick Barker thought should have been garbed in rebel gray, not nationalist blue) also took over local mills—a sure way to gain popular compliance by affecting civilian food supplies. Together, they

Colonel Sanders D. Bruce, Twentieth Regiment, Kentucky Volunteer Infantry. The Roger D. Hunt Collection, United States Army Military History Institute.

wanted no part of battling main-force Confederates from Bragg's army in frigid weather on the Cumberland at this point.[36]

Such measures pointed to the importance of denying local support for partisans. But unclear administrative arrangements hindered more positive cooperation with fort garrisons to the west, while distance and inclement weather also played a role. Nonetheless, by early February, Granger's Army of Kentucky reinforcements were en route to reinforce Rosecrans. The twenty-eight-steamboat convoy carried starry-eyed recruits, who were critical of the absence of "beacon lights of civilization," such as churches and schoolhouses along the river. By the time the trip was over, the new men were profoundly tired after twelve days and nights aboard cramped river craft. It was all a race against time, however. Rumors held that upwards of seven thousand Confederates were moving toward Clarksville, "boasting they would take one hundred Federal transports, there being but two gunboats in convoy," as Rosecrans's controversial police chief, William Truesdail,

FORT BRUCE AND ITS VICINITY.[3]

Fort Bruce (formerly Defiance) at Clarksville, Tennessee. From Lossing, Pictorial History of the Civil War *(Hartford: T. Belknap, 1868), 2: 232.*

put it. At Fort Henry, Lowe debunked such news as a ploy to lure Bruce out of Clarksville so that John Hunt Morgan's men might make a dash into that city. Naval leaders like Pennock at Cairo, Lieutenant Commander Samuel Phelps of the *Lexington,* and convoy chief Lieutenant Commander Le Roy Fitch from Smithland contended they could stop anything Wheeler threw against them. But, at that very moment, Wheeler, Forrest, and Wharton were massing to shut down river traffic completely by recapturing old Fort Donelson—or more accurately, the new fortified hamlet of Dover nearby.[37]

THE SECOND BATTLE FOR DOVER

Sleepy little Dover must have been a "smart little town" in antebellum days, decided one Ohio soldier after viewing it for the first time in February 1863, and Illinoisian Stephen McBide added that the "nice little town" on the Cumberland had numbered some three thousand inhabitants before the death and destruction of two battles. But now "the indications of any degree of prosperity were extremely poor." Originally encircled by Confederate outworks during Grant's investment of Fort Donelson the year before, it had been buffeted since the summer of 1861, first by the rebel presence, then by that of the Yankees. It was presently a strategic hamlet; home to Colonel Abner C. Harding's Eighty-third Illinois Infantry, Captain James H. Flood's Battery C, Second Illinois Battery of four twelve-pounder rifled guns, as well as Captain Henning von Minden's Company G, Fifth Iowa Cavalry. Lure of the town itself had caused its occupation. The abandoned Confederate fort was less attractive, with its unburied battlefield offal, for residual policing of the old Confederate supply caches and patrolling the countryside against partisans. It was at Dover, rather than the old river fortification, that new battles would take place.[38]

Harding's men were fairly green, having been mustered at Monmouth, Illinois, only the previous August. Issued their Springfield muskets, the recruits had been put aboard a train to East Burlington, then sent by steamboat to Cairo. On August 28, they had moved upriver to Fort Henry, and, a week later, several companies marched overland to Dover. Subsequent months of drill and illness (at one point 150 of the regiment were hospitalized) completed the transition from civilian to military life. The highlights included an occasional guerrilla chase, and they had been called out against Morgan and Woodward, venturing to Garretsburg, Kentucky, on October 6. Flood's artillerists, while in service from August 1861, had only served in the Cairo or Columbus districts before moving to Dover and Clarksville after Grant's victory. Von Minden's Iowa horsemen, who had actually been recruited in Minnesota in 1861, had campaigned in Missouri as well as West Tennessee before going to the twin rivers. They were the most veteran of the lot, although all the units felt perfectly at home harassing rebellious civilians, braving foul weather, water, and food, and surviving in the field.[39]

These maturing young Federals survived the permeating stench of rotting horses and mules, which had been improperly buried from the Fort Donelson fight. In fact, human remains and other relics of the battle still surfaced around Dover. Generally, the men were bored, and mostly stood around watching boat traffic when not drilling. "It would open your eyes to see so many gun boats and transports plowing these rivers with all kinds of Army Stores," William H. Dorris of the Eighty-third Illinois wrote his wife. War was expensive, he concluded, but "drawing the money from Uncle Sam's Jacket to carry it on now" would speed the return of peace. Over at Fort Heiman, Robert McConnell of the Seventy-first Ohio searched the Tennessee River shoreline for shells from which to fashion heirloom trinkets, and he gathered bullets, shell fragments, and other relics to be sent home. He especially delighted in securing Tennessee tobacco and a pipe for his wife. He also fumed that the Clarksville fiasco in September had denied his regiment's rump companies under Major James H. Hart their pay for months. He told his wife in November: "Hum Bugged into this But they Cannot Hum Bug me any more, for if the regiment were to be disbanded or paid off, not a 'Corporals Guard' would be left there in ten days."[40]

Harding's men, at least, remained more resolute. Back in September, when chided by a group of partisans about his state's possibly joining the Confederacy, Mitchel A. Thompson of the Eighty-third Illinois had piped up that his regiment had taken only three weeks to be recruited after President Lincoln's call for 300,000 men to suppress the rebellion, and plenty of loyal recruits were set to follow their example. All in all, most would have agreed with Sergeant Major Thomas J. Baugh, who wrote his wife from Dover on the last day of January that "the rebellion don't amount to much here."[41]

Colonel Abner C. Harding, Eighty-third Illinois Infantry, USV. Library of Congress.

Not that the men necessarily admired their leaders. Private Joseph A. Latimer wrote home in early October that Harding "would be no military man if he knew by heart all the military books in the land." Later, he scoffed at the colonel's recent creek dunking while riding on reconnaissance after which he had quickly canceled the whole operation. "Then he hardly ever goes out on drill but what he gives the wrong command," said Latimer. Another soldier concluded that there were greater soldiers than Harding and cited rumors that he ought to resign because he was no drill master. Still, added this Illinois soldier, Harding would "stick with us through thick and thin," suggesting that miscues had been made, but "we were greenhorns at the business," and the officers had not yet learned their trade.[42]

Abner Harding, born to an old line Connecticut family in 1807, had migrated to Utica, New York, studied law in Pennsylvania, and gone west to Illinois in the 1830s. An accomplished politician, he had served as a delegate to the 1836 Pennsylvania constitutional convention, a similar gathering ten years later in Illinois, and served in that state's legislature in 1849 and 1850. A staunch abolitionist and Lincolnite, he had enlisted as a private, then helped raise a company of cavalry as well as the Eighty-third Infantry. In his mid-fifties and suffering from declining eyesight by the time of the war, Harding, like other Illinois politicians in uniform, did not shrink from a fight. He prepared his Dover defenses with some care. Like Lowe, his translation of abolitionist fervor into confiscation actions while in uniform had caused Confederate authorities to put a price on his head. This fact only further fueled his determination to stand up and battle the onrushing rebels when Wheeler and Forrest came into view about dinnertime on February 3.[43]

Naturally, Harding, Lowe, and Bruce all knew that they might come under enemy attack at any time, notwithstanding conflicting intelligence and naval overconfidence. On February 2, Harding telegraphed his superior, Lowe, that some nine hundred rebels under Forrest seemed to be upstream at Palmyra, interdicting river traffic. Harding proposed mounting a combination landborne and steamboat reconnaissance using a company of his Eighty-third infantry aboard the *Wild Cat* in conjunction with Von Minden's cavalry. Apparently, the cavalry started out smartly the next morning; the steamboat lingering at the Dover landing. Absence of key company commanders and other personnel, who were off at Paducah securing artillery ammunition or escorting regimental sick to Cairo, undercut Harding's position. Then, just before the midday meal on February 3, disturbing news arrived that advancing rebels had surprised and captured all but four men of von Minden's company on scout eight miles to the southeast at the Cumberland Iron Works. The cavalry commander had apparently given his half-frozen men permission to warm themselves in a nearby house and had not posted proper guard. The four escapees alerted Harding to the coming peril, and he sent out skirmishers and prepared the post for attack. He also ordered telegraph operators Peter Fowler and William A. Thayer to wire Lowe at Fort Henry requesting help. Lowe immediately replied that he was coming, but that it would take time since he had to ferry most of his men across the Tennessee from Fort Heiman. Nobody knew precisely what enemy force was charging down upon them.[44]

Enjoying the initiative, the Confederates nevertheless also lacked proper intelligence of the Federal position and strength at Dover. Frankly, some of their leaders sought to avoid a confrontation altogether, or so legend has it. Joe Wheeler, however, had been dissatisfied with results thus far attained on the Cumberland. Before returning to base, he sought a more significant success by striking at the Dover garrison and trying to shut down river traffic more soundly. The prospect of prisoners, food, and booty also beckoned, as did the chance to avenge the Fort Donelson disaster of the year before. A permanent presence was out of the question for the Confederates, although reoccupation of the old fort and its water batteries by the three or four thousand rebels and their six brass field guns seemed an attractive alternative to the Palmyra and Harpeth Shoals sites. Altogether, it was no whim of the force commander alone that carried Confederates back to Dover, notwithstanding Forrest's subsequent supporters.[45]

Wheeler's party labored under some important handicaps. There was certainly a shortage of ammunition and rations. Forrest's brigade averaged but fifteen rounds per man and only forty-five rounds for four cannon, despite three weeks

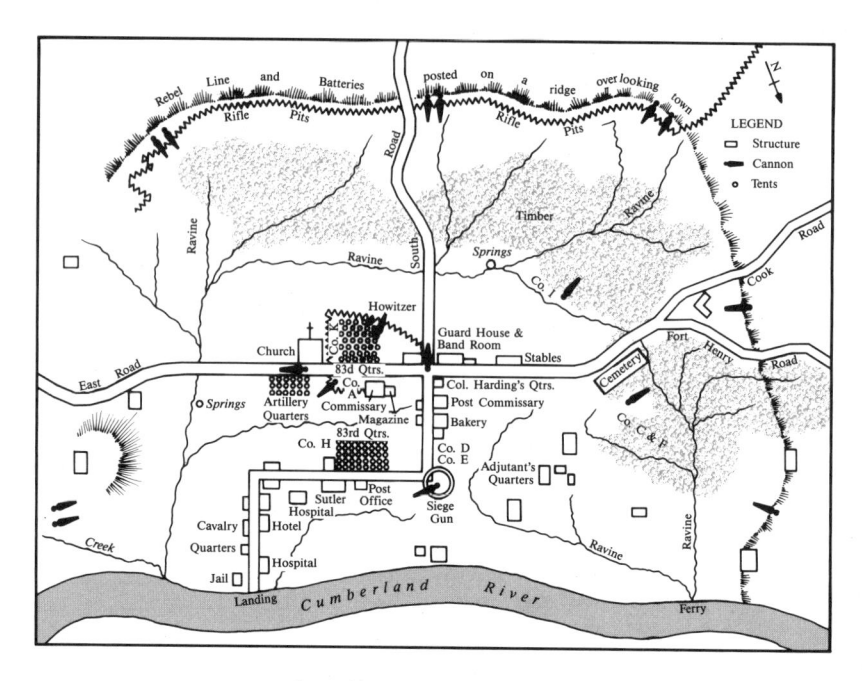

The Battle of Dover, February 3, 1863.

of preparation at Columbia following the return from West Tennessee. Brigadier General John Wharton's brigade likewise had only twenty rounds per man and fifty rounds for the two field pieces of Captain B. F. White's Tennessee artillery. This caused Forrest pause, but not Wheeler. New supplies could be had at Dover, and Wheeler was not daunted by reports of an enemy intercepting column closing in from Franklin. So Wheeler brushed past Forrest's hesitancy, perhaps rekindling the latter's resentment over Wheeler's appointment as Bragg's cavalry chief. In any event, Forrest called aside his aide-de-camp, Captain Charles W. Anderson, and brigade medical officer Dr. Ben Wood and requested: "If I am killed in this fight, will you see that justice is done me by officially stating that I protested against the attack and that I am not willing to be held responsible for any disaster that may result?" Forrest's plea came on the morning of February 3, 1863; his troopers, along with the rest, already pounded along the snowy road toward Dover.[46]

Guided by a friendly African American, Wheeler's men had easily bagged von Minden, and they expected similar success with the main Dover garrison. After all, had not the Yankees been intimidated into surrendering all over Middle Tennessee and Kentucky on the mere appearance of rebel horsemen? This time it was different, however. Harding, despite less than an hour's warning, disposed his six hundred to seven hundred men to meet ten times that number of the enemy. Flood's battery of six-pounders and an ex-Confederate thirty-two-pounder siege gun from the old water batteries (apparently never shipped north, despite Grant's

{196}

instructions, the previous spring) were located in earth works, either at the armed camp of the Eighty-third or in a special redoubt fabricated from bricks of the destroyed courthouse at the town square. Harding repositioned the field artillery as the enemy disclosed its intentions, and he sent some of the infantry with one cannon to the northwestern corner of the town at the old graveyard to guard the Fort Henry road. The only problem was that the Confederates held the higher ground to the east, south, and southwest upon which the 1862 rifle pits were still located (although they faced the opposite direction), and they poured a punishing artillery fire onto the Federal positions. Deep ravines and scrub growth on all sides between the two contending forces provided a natural obstacle to attack.[47]

Harding tried to send another telegram to Lowe, but the rebels had cut the line by this time. So, he dispatched three riders by a circuitous route, assembled all noncombatants in the hamlet aboard two steamboats at the landing, and sent them off downriver. One of the boats, the *Wild Cat*, bore orders to seek out any gunboats and speed them to relief of the besieged post. Meanwhile, Captain John McClanahan's skirmishers from the Eighty-third Illinois had been pushed back, and, by two o'clock in the afternoon, the three or four thousand Confederates with their six field guns had thrown a cordon around Dover and prepared to mount an assault. "They came in from the east and west round to the west," claimed John B. Whitcomb to his brother later, "and planted their guns as they went around." Forrest took the right flank position next to the river, an advance that would carry the Tennessean back into Dover on a road in reverse of his famous exit just before the 1862 surrender. He occupied a crescent-shaped ridge facing town from the south and southeast, about level with the town square. John Wharton, on the other hand, occupied somewhat lower ground "between the (old) lines of Fort Donelson and a graveyard on an eminence," which was occupied by Harding's second in command, Lieutenant Colonel A. A. Smith, and one of Flood's guns.[48]

Before launching his assault, Wheeler sent Harding an ultimatum. Signed by all three Confederate generals, the note called for an immediate and unconditional surrender of the fort with all forces, stores, etc. "If you surrender, you will be treated as prisoners of war; if not, you must abide the consequences," Wheeler's note declared. Harding, while untried in combat, was not impressed by the ultimatum. He surely remembered the price on his head. So, he shot back tersely: "I decline to surrender the forces under my command or the post, without an effort to defend them." Following this exchange, Wheeler ordered an immediate attack via a synchronized move by both Forrest and Wharton at 2:30 P.M. Meanwhile, Wharton sent the Eighth Texas Cavalry to block the approach from Fort Henry and any Union reinforcement of Dover. A three-inch snow lay under the feet of friend and foe alike.[49]

As the preparatory barrage lifted shortly after 2:00, Wheeler rode toward Wharton's brigade to begin the assault. He assumed that the accurate Confederate battery fire had largely suppressed Harding's dispersed artillery pieces (young Whitcomb claimed that the Federals only used five of seven available cannon) and discomforted the supporting infantry. The Confederate leaders did not realize that Harding had withdrawn his foot soldiers to a ravine behind the courthouse square to protect them from the enemy guns. At this point, Forrest interpreted their return to the armed camp and rifle pits as an escape attempt. Disregarding Wheeler's assault schedule, the Tennessean delivered a reckless charge, the head of which was literally blown to pieces by the unsilenced Union artillery supported by withering musketry fire. The unsuspecting horsemen spread confusion when Forrest himself went down as his mount was hit. One rebel sergeant managed to get all the way to the thirty-two-pounder redoubt and yelled, "God damn you, surrender," to which the gun's commander replied, "we will," then touched off the piece, which, according to one observer, "blowed the carcass out of the skin of the Rebel's horse," put seven grape shot through the man himself, and cleared a path through the whole attacking body. With such ferocity, little wonder that Forrest's veterans retired in disorder, leaving Forrest to make his own way back to the ridge on foot.[50]

Wheeler greeted Forrest's return and declared that Wharton had been unprepared to advance and that a new time for a coordinated attack would have to be arranged. Forrest reorganized his men and watched the Federals return to their rifle pits and readjust their positions. He then prepared a new assault, this time on foot. Supported by renewed enfilading artillery fire from his own guns, Forrest now forced Harding's defenders back to the redoubt and effected a lodgement on the east side of the town. Lieutenant Colonel Frank McNairy of Nashville, a volunteer for the fight, was killed, scores of other officers and troopers cut down, and Forrest lost a second mount as he and about a dozen companions rode to within thirty yards of the enemy parapets and fired at the defenders. But Harding's men made good use of every cover, including cellars of Dover dwellings, and the Confederates ran short of ammunition. Their attack stalled. Harding was everywhere, sword in hand, encouraging his men. When, late in the fight, Harding shifted some of his companies to the river's edge to replenish their own cartridge boxes, the irresolute rebels took this as a flanking attack to capture their horses and filtered back in droves toward the original ridge positions.[51]

Forrest was whipped even before Wharton finally launched his attack. It, too, ran into determined resistance, this time from Lieutenant Colonel A. A. Smith and his men. Smith's men fought first in the graveyard and subsequently, like Harding's men, from Dover cellars. Still, the rebels captured one brass twelve-pounder before their ammunition gave out. (Companies C and F of the Eighty-third Illinois were unable to bear the hot Confederate fire and, with all the artillery horses shot down, were unable to draw the piece to safety, according to John Whitcomb.) Then, Smith's galling return fire convinced the Rebs that the Yankee defense was too tough in this sector. Only the Fourth Georgia Cavalry and Malone's battalion continued fighting the Union men at this point, as Wharton's force also retired from its assault by dusk. Both sides milled around under a bright moon.

A chilly winter evening settled in, and the wounded suffered without relief as sporadic firing prevented either side from going to their aid. McClanahan on the Federal side and Holman among the rebels had been wounded, and Harding

USS Fairplay *(1862–65), "Tinclad Number 17." Photographed on the Western Rivers during the Civil War by Bell and Sheridan, Franklin Street, Clarksville, Tenn. Courtesy of the U.S. Naval Historical Center.*

"could now distinctly see along the whole extent of ridge encircling our encampment long lines of rebels, mounted and dismounted, apparently preparing for some new method of attack." But the plucky Illinoisan "felt secure," he recalled in his report. Wheeler and company sent a second demand for surrender about 8:00 P.M., boasting of having committed only a third of their force to the fighting. Harding again declined, answering in turn that he had only engaged one-fourth of his men. "When a bursting rocket seen many miles down the river announced [to] the beleaguered regiment that reinforcements was [*sic*] at hand," according to Alabama cavalryman Robert A. McClellan, the posturing and the fighting petered out. The Confederates concluded that the garrison was too strongly posted, little suspecting that Harding was about out of ammunition.[52]

Indeed, nightfall found two Federal relief columns approaching Dover. Despite Harding's anxious telegrams to Lowe, it was not the army that first came to the help of the beleaguered garrison. Almost by accident, Fitch and eight of his gunboats were on the lower river, convoying a large fleet of transports, when they were met about twenty-four miles downstream from Dover–Fort Donelson by the *Wild Cat*. Fitch pushed ahead with his gunboats, leaving the transports to make their way unattended to Dover, and encountered still another steamer just below the fort that brought "the intelligence that the place was entirely surrounded and could hold out no longer." Fitch and his flotilla came into view at Dover about 8:00 P.M., and found that the army was nearly out of ammunition, was entirely surrounded by overwhelming numbers of the enemy but that Harding was still holding the Confederates in check. "For a minute or so I was at a loss as to where to begin, as I could not get a word from our forces, the enemy then holding the ground between them and the river," recalled Fitch. He quickly "let off a gun up the ravine to give them encouragement by letting them know that assistance was at hand."53

As the moon shed illumination, one of the garrison's officers came to the riverbank and provided fire direction for the gunboats. Their heavy guns deluged shot and shell upon ravines, graveyard, and the valley beyond where the Confederates had their horses. Fitch's position "gave us a chance to rake nearly the entire length of this line," as the shaken troopers broke and ran from their positions. Fitch kept the gunboats *Alfred Robb* and *Silver Lake* below the town to prevent the Confederates from returning to carry off their wounded, while the *Lexington, Fairplay, St. Clair,* and *Brilliant* moved above Dover and shelled the roads leading out to the east. Then the *Lexington* and *St. Clair* followed the river a short distance, shelling the woods to "harass and annoy" Wheeler and Forrest's forces as much as possible. Naval gunfire thinned by 10:00 and ceased altogether an hour later.

Fitch claimed great accuracy, "and it is certainly very gratifying for us to know that [the enemy] force was cut up, routed, and despoiled of its prey by the timely arrival of the gunboats, and that Colonel Harding and his gallant little band were spared to wear the honors they had so fairly won," Fitch concluded in his battle report. Ironically, the one Confederate bright point in the otherwise dismal affair apparently came on the river. Young Texas Ranger Samuel Maverick, out of San Antonio, became so irate at the way the battle was going that, at some point in the lengthening twilight, he jumped into the icy Cumberland and swam out to set fire to a hay-laden barge jettisoned from one of the gunboats or steamers. This act netted Maverick a lieutenancy of the scouts later on.54

It was past midnight before any of Lowe's reinforcements completed the icy twelve-mile trek from Fort Henry. Harding's messengers had finally reached the Tennessee River post about mid-afternoon, and two signal cannon alerted those contingents to cross over from Fort Heiman. Yet, the crossing took two hours to accomplish, and when Lowe finally left, some of his men were still out on picket duty, unaware of the emergency. His force also included infantrymen of the Thirteenth Wisconsin, the rump contingent of the Seventy-first Ohio that had escaped the onus of Clarksville (rankers like Robert McConnell still feared the return of Colonel Rodney Mason's "Miserable Cowards"), and three guns of Steinbeck's Battery H, Second Illinois Light Artillery, plus four companies of Lowe's Iowa horsemen. Together, they moved as quickly as possible over the wretched roads. By this time, too, news of the attack had reached Bruce at Clarksville and Rosecrans's Murfreesboro headquarters. But only Lowe could immediately help at Dover.55

Lowe's relief column, led by Colonel William P. Lyon of the Badger regiment, stumbled onto Terry's Texans about five miles west of Dover and suffered an abrupt rebuff for about two hours. Finally, after deploying his infantry as well as cavalry, Lyon watched the Texans melt into the woods. Able to move more quickly now in the bright moonlight, the Federals passed through abandoned campfires of enemy pickets about four miles from the old fort. Signs indicated that perhaps six hundred or seven hundred rebels had warmed themselves before makeshift fires. Then the Federals assisted Steinbeck's gunners negotiate the steep grade just outside the old outworks and then again on the edge of Dover. It was nearly 3:00 A.M. before a weary relief force picked its way through the dead bodies strewn about the streets of town where "everything was confusion," according to Iowa trooper Eugene Marshall.[56]

Losses proved very heavy for the numbers engaged on both sides. Discrepancies typically abounded, with Federals admitting to eleven to sixteen killed, forty to sixty wounded, and some forty to sixty captured. Flood's prized twelve-pounder, a caisson, quantities of blankets, and some firearms were also lost. Holman's partisans especially delighted in exchanging Yankee firearms for their old double-barreled shotguns and obsolete muskets. One Texan also noted that "there were a great many stolen niggers in the fortifications" who came out of the woods as soon as the Confederate artillery opened, and he claimed the expedition made off with fifty men, women, and children as well as one hundred Federals in uniform. Harding and Lowe admitted only thirty freedmen lost. On the Confederate side, Wharton reported seventeen killed, sixty wounded, and eight missing. Forrest admitted losing roughly 25 percent of his command (including Lieutenant Colonel Frank McNairy), and Federal estimates of Confederate losses pointed to totals ranging from one hundred and sixty to two hundred killed, six hundred to eight hundred wounded, and forty to fifty captives, with many of the wounded left at the Cumberland Rolling Mill and houses along the retreat route.[57]

Federal land pursuit stopped eight miles from Dover at the rolling mill, while the gunboats prowled farther up the river in search of the defeated rebels. One soldier in the Seventy-first Ohio noted that "they could find two or three dead and four or five wounded in every house" all the way back to Dover, reputedly including partisan Tom Woodward, who had been shot through both hips, and was captured about four miles from town. Late in February, Fitch, returning from a trip up the Tennessee as far as Florence, Alabama, told superiors that a doctor in that city had told him that his two sons at Columbia, Tennessee, mentioned Wheeler's and Forrest's return there and "that the rebel loss in that attack was 800 or 900 men, 200 killed, one hundred and eighty-odd wounded, and some 400 or 500 missing." Of course, many of those missing may well have been partisans who simply faded into the countryside and went home to weather the winter before hearth not campfire. Fitch also noted that he had enrolled two prisoners taken at Clifton, Tennessee, who had been conscripted but never been sworn to service, and who now wanted simply to join the Union navy.[58]

RECRIMINATIONS

That night, the cold, tired, and hungry grayclads bivouacked about four miles from Dover. Frostbite attended many of them, and Frank Batchelor of Terry's Texans claimed that his comrades took the cold better than the natives of the region. "The weather was bitter cold and the troops suffered very much," was the way the unit historian of Napier's battalion remembered it after the war. The men's mood was as bleak as the weather. Federals canvassing the neighborhood thereafter were told of the despondency and discontent in the rebel ranks. Many of the raiders were upset at not being able to retrieve dead and wounded comrades as was apparently customary. Forrest was supposedly so upset at discovering that there had been only a mere seven hundred Federals in the Dover garrison that "he threatened to shoot the informant as too great a liar to live." Robert Anderson McClellan thought that the expedition could have whipped Harding and recaptured Dover and Fort Donelson if "we had all charged on horseback." But Batchelor simply wrote home subsequently that they had all been "fairly whipped," so nobody should pay any attention to glorious newspaper accounts that would undoubtedly "color up our backout until it will seem we were called off from the Yankee entrenchments out of pure pity for them." As one of the Confederates captured in the fight recalled laconically years later: "If Joe Wheeler had listened to Gen. Forrest we wouldn't have been on our way to prison."[59]

Daylight on February 4 found the Confederate cavalry column making its hazardous way southward to Columbia. Half-hearted pursuit by Lowe and Harding netted stragglers and cleaned out the immediate neighborhood around Dover. A stronger interception effort came from Brigadier General Jefferson C. Davis, who marched westward from Franklin with about fifteen hundred cavalrymen from J. T. Morgan's and R. H. G. Minty's commands "through a chilling snow-storm, and over almost impassable roads." After taking some thirty prisoners at Bon Aqua Springs, just south of Charlotte, Davis learned that Wheeler and Forrest knew of his coming, and had turned westward to avoid confrontation. Since enemy couriers probably frequented every town in the section and flew ahead of the Federals to warn to rebels, Davis found only southern conscript officers hard at work, trying to fill Bragg's depleted ranks. "Most of the inhabitants are disloyal; what few Union men I met were afraid to proclaim it, and therefore, worthless to us." Nonetheless, he boasted that, but for his worn-down men, ill-shod horses, and the wintry weather, "I could have beaten him badly and captured many prisoners."[60]

At least one Confederate general officer voiced the same impression about his side. Lieutenant General Leonidus Polk, in command at Shelbyville, urged Major General Earl Van Dorn "in the field" on February 8 to unite with Wheeler and make a combined attack on Davis, both front and rear. Nothing came of that scheme, for Van Dorn was still too far away to the south. But at least Wheeler and Forrest escaped, finally finding sanctuary at Centreville on the Duck River. Even then, they had to wait several hours until volunteers swam across the icy waters to secure the ferry and bring it back to transport the jaded troopers to the other side. Finally, on February 17 the half-frozen expedition finally went into camp at Columbia, as consolidation of various units proved necessary after the loses at Dover. Holman's partisans merged with Douglas's battalion to form the Eleventh Tennessee Cavalry, while Cox's and Napier's bands were similarly consolidated as the Tenth Tennessee Cavalry. Departure of Russell's Fourth Alabama for another assignment robbed Forrest of one trustworthy unit.[61]

The Federals remained in an exultant mood at Dover. The Confederates had "met with a defeat for once," observed David A. Fateley of Company A, Thirty-third Indiana, who arrived two days after the battle as part of Gordon Granger's riverborne reinforcements en route to Nashville. "The 83d done bully fighting," he added. Hamlin Alexander Coe of the Nineteenth Michigan, another member in this column, added: "I hear everyone is frantic with joy over the victory." Indeed, the action had been one of the most desperate of the war, chimed Eugene Marshall, who had come over with the Fifth Iowa Cavalry, and "no better fighting has been done by any troops than was done there," with the Eighty-third Infantry and Flood's battery having made for themselves "a most splendid reputation" in this action. But Marshall quickly suggested that, without the timely arrival of the gunboats, it would have been different since "the enemy force was too strong," even when the garrison was reinforced by the Iowans. Zeboim Carter Patten of the 115th Illinois pronounced solemnly, "It seems a great wonder the fort did not surrender." Lieutenant Commander Le Roy Fitch agreed, noting that his officers and men "claim the honor of dispersing [the enemy] and saving Fort Donelson." Lieutenant Charles Alley of Company C, Fifth Iowa Horse, put it more poetically: "Thank God for his goodness to us, surely the race is not always to the swift nor the battle to the strong." Robert McConnell of the Seventy-first Ohio declared, "the whole battle looks like a miracle—there surely was a stronger hand than that of Mortal Man had hold of the battle—why just look at it—six hundred men with six pieces of artillery holding off and whipping seven thousand men with eleven pieces of artillery for seven hours."[62]

As the steamboats conveyed Granger's column to Dover by noon the next day—many raced one another under forced draught—some twelve to fifteen thousand Federals could now be counted either afloat or on land in the immediate area. The acrid smell of burnt gunpowder still hung low over the river, yet some of the soldiers aboard the steamboats found "the fumes of sulphurous smoke were a bit exhilarating to our sense of smell," as their boats passed through it. Large numbers of the newcomers flocked to see the fresh battlefield and stared wide-eyed at the unburied rebel dead before they went into shallow graves at the cemetery where the Eighty-third had stood its ground. The newcomers eagerly gleaned details of the fight from the participants. Several of the victorious Federals recounted stories of rifling the pockets of the slain and securing such trinkets as fifteen hundred Kentucky dollars, gold watches, and a thousand dollars in Confederate scrip, and taking buttons from dead rebels' coats. They viewed Harding's two-story, frame headquarters, which was riddled with bullet holes and had suffered splintered timbers from shot and shell. One soldier observed a shell that had hit a stable, passed through a horse, and exploded among a flock of geese. "Non-combatants were also suffering the horrors of war in all its details," he decided. Navy surgeon William W. Howard from the USS *Brilliant* claimed one house on a hill that was occupied by the attackers "was so full of holes, that it was difficult to tell where the doors and windows were and this is no exaggeration." He also called attention to one bluecoated marksman's feat of picking off a rebel sharpshooter by simply putting his own minié ball through the house to catch the enemy soldier in the eye and blowing out the back of his head. Such was the fascination of the uninitiated with their first battle scene.[63]

Certain veterans in Granger's force found that a different experience awaited them at Dover. One brigade commander had been a company commander in the Eleventh Illinois during the first battle at Fort Donelson. Now, taking his staff with him, he rode out to visit the long grave of his former comrades in the Eleventh Illinois. The site lay almost two miles from the landing, and a light snow was falling as they all sat silently astride their mounts with heads uncovered in respect for dead comrades. The last stray remnants of rebel partisans in the area suddenly directed several shots in their direction before melting into the woods. "It was a remarkable incident," observed the unit's historian years later. That an officer of the Eleventh regiment, on returning to the battlefield almost a year after the first battle in a snow storm like that of 1862 should find the ground once more covered with freshly slain unburied dead, by the grave of slain comrades in the previous battle, and "should listen to the rattle of Rebel musketry" struck him as more than ironic.[64]

Men and events moved on within days after the second memorable encounter at Dover. Lieutenant Charles T. Clark of the 125th Ohio penned in his diary that it was safe to predict that few "will every again visit a battlefield just after the conflict from idle curiosity." Thoroughly sobered newcomers from Granger's force climbed back aboard their transports to continue their upriver trek to Nashville. Soon, other thoughts intruded—how much clearer the Cumberland River was than her sister the Tennessee, the high banks and rocky outcroppings along the former, the flotsam and debris of hay bales and other evidence of Wheeler's destruction of supply boats, the steamboats *Connelston* and *New York*, racing ahead of the forty-boat convoy while the troops stood aboard under arms anticipating a guerrilla attack that never came.[65]

Marshall's company of the Fifth Iowa went out to repair the telegraph line and met more of their Curtis Horse colleagues coming from Fort Henry, for everyone now wanted to have a shot at the rebels. He noted that "such had been the excitement in camp that when we were reunited it was found that the sick and lame had turned out until we had more men than we had returned to duty in several weeks." Everyone gaped at the prisoners—"a most motley collection"— many of them were locals well known to the garrisons. Many of the dead had been stripped of boots by their threadbare colleagues, but Marshall paid respects to five of the dead rebels as "big stout looking men," all of them, including the officer, "dressed in jeans." Apparently the only rank designation worn by the dead Lieutenant Colonel McNairy was a green sash, so nondescript were the lot. Having seen enough by the morning of February 5, and no longer needed on the Cumberland, Lowe's men returned to policing the valley of the Tennessee.[66]

Federal leadership quickly discerned the invaluable lesson from the Dover affair. The high ridge position behind the town had afforded the enemy a chance to enfilade Harding's fortified camp. "We were shelled out of our quarters quick," said Mitchel A. Thompson, and "compelled to take shelter in ravines on the north side of the town next to the river," where they were comparatively safe from fire.

After the battle, Harding and Lowe learned from Murfreesboro headquarters that Sterling Price and Earl Van Dorn might be moving with new forces against the Cumberland line and that "we would do well to fortify ourselves as strongly as we could to resist them." All hands, from soldiers to freedmen, teamsters, and other noncombatants set to work on a new site—"Searborrow Heights," or Scarborough Hill, about midway from the now demolished town and the old fort. Since it was covered by deep hollows running down to the river on two sides, Thompson noted that the position could not be commanded by other hills. Huts and other facilities would be located inside the new Fort Donelson, with two thirty-two-pounder cannon on the two wings and a "Colt Howitzer" in between. Like Harding's fortified post in town, the new Fort Donelson faced the hinterland, not the river, which had offered "but slight protection from an attack by land," Thompson wrote his wife later in February.[67]

This second wintry defeat of the Confederates on the Cumberland had an even more lasting effect on their effort in the West. The immediate retreat from the battlefield introduced a dissonant note into command relations. The celebrated controversy between Forrest, Wharton, and Wheeler developed in a little house by the roadside, where the three brigadiers tried to warm themselves the night after the battle. Wheeler sat before a roaring fire, trying to prepare his after-action report. Wharton sat opposite him, and Forrest lay prone between them, his feet warming to the blaze. Interrupting Wharton's verbal account, Forrest roared: "General Wheeler, you know I was against this attack. I said all I could, and should against it—and now say what you like, do what you like, nothing'll bring back my brave fellows lying dead or wounded and freezing around that fort tonight." Citing his friendship for and claiming no disrespect to the younger man, Forrest told Wheeler to put one thing in his report to Bragg. "Tell him," he said, "I'll be in my coffin before I'll fight again under your command." He then offered Wheeler his sword. Caught off guard, Wheeler mumbled that he would assume blame, and declined the Tennessean's sword.[68]

But Forrest made good on his promise, and the Confederacy would suffer from this permanent estrangement of two of her most successful warriors. Formation of two cavalry divisions later that spring found Forrest subordinated to Earl Van Dorn, with similar friction. Acting independently, he achieved great results; when he was a subordinate, he was less effective. The Wheeler-Forrest controversy quickly reached the southern press, as the exiled Memphis *Appeal* championed its West Tennessee hero in a December issue, while other southern publicists rallied to Wheeler's cause. The imbroglio between the two commanders' supporters simmered after the war, although the two generals became friends until death.[69]

As for the men in gray, they had seen the last of the scene of two or even three humiliations on the Cumberland—all within a year of one another. Whether or not Confederate units could have wrested control of Dover and Fort Donelson from the Federals remained moot. Pennsylvania cavalryman Joseph Vale best explained it after the war. While Bedford Forrest was the Confederacy's best cavalry general, said Vale, he "never would work in a double team; unless, indeed, it was hitched up tandem, with himself in the lead." At the battle of Dover, with

Wheeler in command, "the team balked from the beginning." As for that battle, Columbus district commander Brigadier General Alexander Asboth told his superiors succinctly three days later, "at Fort Donelson, the Rebels were handsomely whipped." Harding, soon to be promoted to brigadier general for saving Dover and Fort Donelson, would go on to Congress after the Civil War. But, more immediately, when he reported to Rosecrans at Nashville following his promotion, he was greeted by the Army of the Cumberland commander, who exclaimed: "Why I expected to see the defender of Donelson as a young, big six-foot rawboned powerful man, but here he is a short stumpy old wrinkled up man." Harding chuckled, but as one of his men, Mitchel Thompson, wrote to his wife: "I shall never have another word of disapprobation to say against any of our officers, for they all acted with the utmost coolness and presence of mind, never became hysterical or confused. . . ."[70]

The second (or perhaps third, depending upon who does the numbering) battle of Dover receded into history, scarcely noticed by Cause-conscious southerners, and only slightly remembered better by northern survivors or their descendants. At the time, Edgefield, Tennessee, resident Harriet Ellen Moore, the future Mrs. Thomas Porter Weakley, wrote in her diary only that the Nashville *Union* had carried a dispatch of the rebel repulse with 150 killed and 60 captured, including McNairy. George Richard Browder, much nearer the sound of the guns in southern Kentucky, made not even the briefest notation of any battle in his own diary. Rather, on February 14, 1863, George Dick, as he was known by his neighbors, wrote: "Twelve months ago to day I was horrified by the booming thunder of boats and batteries at the fearful battle of Fort Donelson." Then he was quickly diverted to more pressing matters—a messenger had called this preacher to the bedside of a dying cousin. Daily duty crowded from view the earth-shaking events of the battlefield. Hardly anyone noticed that once again the Confederate military had lost an opportunity to wrest hegemony on the Cumberland from the Yankees.[71]

EIGHT

HEARTLAND IMPASSE: LATE WINTER 1863

Attitudes hardened in the winter of 1863. President Abraham Lincoln's formal emancipation of slaves aimed not only at human bondage, but also at the Confederacy's breadbasket. Without a secure labor force represented by the "peculiar institution," the whole social and economic fabric of the South would unravel, taking with it all hope of independence. But emancipation was only a beginning for some northerners and carefully avoided by Tennessee military governor Andrew Johnson and his slaveholding unionist friends, who even caused the Lincoln administration to exempt their state from total enforcement. As Major General William Tecumseh Sherman stated in his March 12 letter to Governor David Tod of Ohio, the South was more formidable and arrogant than she had been two years before. The Union lost far more by having an insufficient number of men in the field than from any other cause. "We are forced to invade; we must keep the war South until they are not only ruined, exhausted, but humbled in pride and spirit," said the general. The general was espousing a philosophy of war, a policy statement fast becoming an act of faith.

Basing his opinion on prewar associations with Braxton Bragg, P. G. T. Beauregard, and other "extreme Southern men," Sherman suggested that the whole white male population of the region was now arrayed against the Union, one way or another. The countryside, population, and character of the enemy were perfectly suited to dashes upon Federal lines of communication. Dismissing "copperhead quabblings," as he called them, or northern sedition (which "the South spurns and despises worse than we do"), Sherman told the Buckeye governor that he never pretended to "foresee the end of all this, but I do know that we are yet far from the end of war." The hard-bitten Sherman advanced that even the "poltroons who falter and cry quits" could usefully help out and raise the food the army needed, but they should never claim a voice in the councils of the nation. Since the first hostile shots of the war, the northern people "have had no option," declared Sherman, "they must conquer or be conquered. There can be no [middle] course." It was no longer an open question—"we must fight it out."[1]

THE CIVIL PROBLEM—RESTORATION OF ORDER

The upper heartland lay in the bitter throes of winter. Sarah Kennedy thought her beloved Clarksville "looks like desolation itself" and that "all its glory has departed." "Poor old Rutherford County," such devastation, wrote Mary Cheatham, wife of a prominent Nashville physician to her sister, Mattie Ready Morgan, wife of the rebel raider, on February 20, adding, "the people have been robbed of everything. . . . We don't see the bright side here, Mattie"; it was "nothing but gloom," with horrid prisons, with "few really nice things" in the city as "our old merchants have nothing." Even Yankee pins had replaced English ones for women's finery. Harriet Ellen Moore, living with her family at Edgefield, across the Cumberland from Nashville, recorded in her diary on Tuesday, January 28, that the city's gas works had been shut down for a week due to lack of coal. She hardly realized that, thanks to Confederate general Joe Wheeler's interdiction of the Cumberland supply route and John Hunt Morgan's blockage of the railroad, citizens and Yankee occupiers alike suffered from that shortage. With wood commanding twenty dollars a cord, everyone had resorted to candles for illumination. All the churches, except the Catholic church, had been given over to Stones River wounded. Moore noted how significantly the city had changed since the previous September. Every "handsome house in the city with a few exceptions [was] occupied by Yankees or Negroes."[2]

Busying herself with Sir Walter Scott's *Waverley* romance or a surprising abundance of frilly cloth material for dresses (in contrast to a "scarcity of articles such as medicines"), young Harriet rejoiced at every tale of Confederate success. The family dodged Yankee bridge guards and detectives and carried on with sardonic humor. She suggested the irony of the Federals celebrating George Washington's birthday in Nashville (with "3/3 coldness among the bystanders," her father told her), since "this is sheer impudence as Washington was a rebel and a slave holder." Similar dissident thoughts could be found in educator John Lindsley's diary; he noted that, since the city's masters were "unable to conquer, they endeavor to exterminate a people."[3]

Extermination came close to Military Governor Andrew Johnson's idea for dealing with the rebel populace. But hundreds of Union club members testified to chinks in Nashville's disloyalty. Similar equivocation could be found in the countryside, especially when the Confederates as well as the Federals raided people's property. Isaac T. Renaeau, a Cumberland plateau native, wrote the governor about hundreds of rebels "some say they [are] part of Morgan's men, some again say they are Forrest's" who were stealing horses at Albany in Clinton County, Kentucky, a "downtrodden, oppressed, misused but loyal county" northeast of Nashville. No county in the state had as many brave sons in government service, he avowed, but asked that his name be kept secret for fear of reprisal. Still others continued to waver, their sympathies basically Confederate yet fearing to take that stance in occupied Union territory. Such was the case with Todd County, Kentucky, preacher-farmer George Richard Browder.[4]

Browder recorded that he had openly helped care for a sick slave who had been abandoned by the Union soldiery after he escaped from a local slave owner's factory. Browder deplored both emancipation and the new conscription law that Lincoln signed on March 3, compelling all able-bodied white males between ages twenty and forty-five "to take up arms at the call of the war department with few classes excepted." Such would produce a revolution in the North or "pour overwhelming and irresistible thousands and legions upon the Southern rebels." Most of all, it "will be the breaking up of thousands of happy homes and drive thousands of men into rebellion who would otherwise stay quietly at home," he thought. "I am positively a peace man," he reasserted in his diary. While the clergy had no exemption, he was fully resolved not to take up arms for either side, although his father had gone south to the Confederacy. Meanwhile, throughout his neighborhood, irregular bands skirmished with authorities, the Shaker town depot burned, and a train on the Russellville–Clarksville rail line was destroyed in escalating violence.[5]

Just what Johnson could do about affairs in Kentucky was anybody's guess. But southern unionists across the region looked to him as the defender of the faith. Asserting his own power in the face of rebel enemies in the countryside was fully as important as challenging Union generals like William S. Rosecrans, who might scoff at this civilian politician with one-star rank. The governor naturally had an agenda that included organizing loyal Tennessee units and appointing their officers, forming a personal defense force, and suppressing a burgeoning contraband trade as well as checkmating Rosecrans's meddlesome Nashville police chief, Colonel William Truesdail. But, above all, Johnson needed to reestablish a form of civil government through elections and reinstitution of a court system.

It did not help when letters poured into the military governor's office about unruly soldiers from the 105th Illinois and Eleventh Kentucky who were terrorizing the good citizens of Springfield in Robertson County. Moreover, Tennesseans had terrible difficulties in securing reimbursement for "requisitioned" items during the unceasing army foraging operations. Johnson was expected to do something about these things. How could a man who had taken an oath to support and protect the Constitution and all the laws of the land look on in silence while officers commissioned by the government tolerated such mischief, wondered farmer Daniel P. Braden about the Springfield incident.[6]

Braden raised a point fundamental to the whole history of Anglo-American civil-military relations back through the years. "I had rather See this continent Sunk and a wide Ocean remain whear [sic] it onst was than to See a military central Consolidated Despotism Spread over this Onst happy land of Washington," he proclaimed in rural simplicity. Then, too, the perpetual eviction of Nashville merchants to provide warehouses for army supplies added to the image of oppression, especially when it struck at Johnson's friends like Hugh Douglas. This

Nashvillian had already lost two houses and was threatened with eviction from a third "for ordnance purposes." So the governor minced no words in telling Rosecrans that such transgressions by the troops "have done and are still doing great damage to our cause," the effect of which "is most decidedly adverse to a restoration of a correct public sentiment." How could Johnson win over the hearts and minds of the uncommitted, much less unreconstructed citizenry, when the army practiced unlicensed mayhem?[7]

What was evident by early 1863 was a power struggle between military and civilian authority for reconstructing the upper heartland. Certainly their motives for doing so were different. One was political; the other related to combat operations. The Lincoln administration probably erred in failing to issue prompt, clear-cut guidance to both parties concerning areas of overlapping authority and mission when Johnson was first appointed governor of Tennessee. But maybe such clarity was impossible, since the distance from Washington to Nashville or the Ohio Valley made it most difficult to know the local situation. So each official (in mufti or army blue) interpreted the national strategy as he saw fit when it came to the task of reconstruction.

Johnson, for instance, listened to plaintive cries from Memphis unionists that "the progress of unionism here is not so rapid as could be wished." Restoration of civil courts seemed premature to men like Benjamin D. Nabers, since Memphis indebtedness to New York interests might be called on in any civil suit, but local debtors could hardly recover damages from Mississippians who owed them money in turn, since those parties were cut off by the war itself. However, Brigadier General Jeremiah Sullivan debunked this notion at Jackson, for he declared that his own district entirely clear of all rebels and argued that, by appointing judges and opening all courts, Johnson would do more to restore the loyalty "than all the military power of the Country." Still, the general's brother, a Memphis lawyer, stood to gain from such a move, and people everywhere told the governor that all important appointments should be given "to old Citizens in preference to Strangers." In Memphis, still run by the army and an Illinois political hack in uniform—Stephen A. Hurlbut—the governor's influence remained limited. Carpetbaggery in uniform preceded that in mufti for much of war-torn Tennessee.[8]

Johnson left Nashville in March for an extended political swing through the North. He sought support for his state's unionism. His reception in the Midwest, Pennsylvania, and New York was wildly enthusiastic, so he must have been buoyed in spirit by the time he reached the nation's capital. Here, he pressed for authority to raise northern troops for special duty in Tennessee and, in turn, was urged to recruit soldiers from ex-slaves in the Volunteer state. He most certainly conveyed displeasure with Rosecrans's policies and actions and his own clear lack of authority to administration officials. In response, he secured from Lincoln and Secretary of War Edwin M. Stanton not only authority to recruit troops in the North, but also to exercise powers to restore "to the people of Tennessee their civil and political rights under the Constitution of the State of Tennessee." With the president's endorsement, Stanton told the military governor to exercise whatever powers seemed necessary and proper to effect the republican guaranty clause of the Federal Constitution.[9]

More specific guidance accompanied Johnson home to Tennessee. In a directive issued on April 2, he was empowered to "impose taxes for the support of the poor, for police purposes, and purposes of his government generally." He could impose exactions upon all disloyal persons "for the support of the wives and children of those who may have been expelled from the country or who may be in the rebel service." He could further impose exactions upon "all who have contributed to the rebel service by money, by property, or by the use of their slaves," in an amount to be determined either by Johnson or an appointed board. Finally, he could "extend to the taking possession of property and collecting rents for property or hire of slaves owned by persons who are within rebel lines." On April 18, Stanton finally gave Johnson formal written notice of his duties.[10]

Johnson was now told to establish his headquarters as military governor in Nashville—which he had actually done the year before—and to occupy all public buildings there, as well as "the public commons and public property" throughout the state. He could further take possession of and occupy all vacant and abandoned buildings and property belonging to "persons engaged in the rebellion" both in Nashville and elsewhere in the state. He could likewise take control of "all abandoned lands and plantations," leasing them for productive use (and he was charged with keeping strict accountability records for war department purposes). This latter provision also extended to abandoned slaves; they were to be registered on labor rolls for use in work upon fortifications and other public works. The governor was also to take measures to secure employment and reasonable compensation for other laborers ("of whatever age or sex") and to furnish clothing and subsistence from quartermaster's and commissary stores for the support of the poor and destitute—again keeping strict accounting records for the Washington bureaucracy.

As historian William C. Harris has suggested, Johnson would return home in late April "elated with the results of his trip." He had helped bolster sagging northern morale and determination, and he had stymied challenges from compromisers and opponents of Lincoln's conduct of the war. Moreover, he had secured a clear view of his own mandate for Tennessee. However, it remained for General-in-Chief Henry Halleck to translate this arrangement clearly for Rosecrans and his military subordinates in the heartland. Actually, Rosecrans had a point when he told his superiors that Nashville was "at once a camp, a garrison, and a great depot," and he had felt obligated to "put and keep it under a species of martial law." So, Halleck counseled Rosecrans about legal differences in civil and military jurisdiction, civil and military crimes, and the fact that Tennessee, like Kentucky and Missouri, had duly organized civil authority to effect civil law. Such guidance would have seemed odd to Johnson, had he known about it, since he was really the military governor, not a popularly elected one. But Halleck was even then deeply engrossed in the scholarly ramifications of occupying enemy territory. Therefore, he preached that police matters must be left to civil officials, while provost marshals should look solely to military matters.[11]

True, said Halleck, any "non-combatant inhabitant of a country militarily occupied, who robs military stores and munitions, burns store-houses, bridges, &c. used for military purposes, or, as military insurgent, bears arms and takes life, may be tried and punished by a military court." But he felt that Johnson and Rosecrans really labored "with an eye single to the general good" and that there "need be no serious conflict of authority in Tennessee." To Halleck, they both aimed "for the accomplishment of the same great and patriotic purpose—the redemption of Tennessee from the oppression of the Confederate oligarchy, and the restoration of her loyal citizens to the rights which they have heretofore enjoyed under the Constitution, and to the protection which is afforded to persons and property by the glorious flag of the Union."

Why not place Johnson "in command of the troops in Nashville, and thus harmonize the civil and military authorities there?" Halleck asked Rosecrans. After all, the governor was a Union brigadier. Old Rosy evaded that one, although he continued to suffer Halleck's harassment all spring about avoiding intimidation of citizens; in one case, some Frenchmen in the city had been forced to take the oath of allegiance and post bond for good behavior. "Such an order is deemed unnecessarily rigorous in regard to foreigners who quietly pursue their ordinary avocations and take no part in the war," said the top Union general. So Rosecrans's dictum would be modified, "as to give no cause of offense to friendly powers."[12]

Even before his trip, Johnson had issued a confiscation proclamation on February 20 in line with Federal acts of the previous July. It was now bolstered by the additional authority about abandoned property and preventing fraud in insurrectionary districts. Secretary of the Treasury Salmon P. Chase consulted with Johnson about reopening trade in line with revocation of Lincoln's August 1861 prohibition against trade in insurrectionary states. Johnson responded by stating bluntly that desperate unionists were along the twin rivers "to procure the needful supplies of the prime necessaries of life" (perhaps a thinly veiled attempt to steer such trade toward supplier and friend Allen A. Hall). But the military governor had no firm means of carrying out his will in the countryside. Rosecrans hobbled Johnson's efforts to form a state militia or police to underscore his enforcement powers. That was the army's job, in his mind. In reality, the governor's control extended no further than the bayonets of the Army of the Cumberland.[13]

Alternatives surfaced, however. B. F. Cloud Smith of Gallatin wrote Johnson in early February, requesting authority to raise a regiment of "independent scouts" for either national or state service in troublesome Cumberland Plateau counties like Wilson, Smith, DeKalb, Macon, and Putnam. The state needed such a group, he claimed, patterned "on the Guerrilla order" to meet and rid neighborhoods of robbers that infested them in Confederate garb. Such local defense corps would be as familiar with the countryside as the bandits. Such a corps, said Smith, would enable Johnson "to set to work the machinery of the civil department of the state and restoring law and order and aid us perhaps in being represented [in] the congress of the United States." By this time, the governor also faced renewed pressure to put African Americans in uniform.[14]

Mobilization of ex-slaves for military as well as labor service appealed to some

Americans. Lincoln applied his seductive talents to enlist Johnson to raise "a negro military force" during his Washington visit. The country, he claimed, "now needs no specific thing so much as some man of your ability, and position, to go to this work." Adjutant General Lorenzo Thomas would report from Memphis in April that Hurlbut seemed excited about organizing six artillery companies composed of freed slaves. Later, in June, brigade commander Edward M. McCook suggested informally to Secretary of War Edward M. Stanton that "[a]ll my experience during more than twenty months' service in Kentucky, Tennessee, Mississippi, and Alabama has tended to impress me with both the wisdom and necessity of fighting the rebellion with its own weapons and knocking away its main support by destroying slavery," as he advocated enlistment of black soldiers. Their keen sense of locality and familiarity with their native regions made them invaluable as scouts as well as raiders, he said. But Johnson hung back from such a task for fear of possibly alienating loyal, slave-owning Tennessee voters.[15]

The president looked to Johnson as "an eminent citizen of a slave-state, and himself a slave-holder" to do the job. Here was the "great available, and yet unavailed of" force for restoring the Union, Lincoln told Johnson on March 26. He hardly contained his own enthusiasm for "the bare sight of fifty thousand armed, and drilled black soldiers upon the banks of the Mississippi, would end the rebellion at once." Such thinking was premature in theory as well as fact, and Johnson certainly was not ready for it any more than the rest of the divided nation. He was too bent upon securing a promised governor's guard, as two days later the war department authorized him to raise ten infantry and cavalry regiments and ten artillery batteries, as well as a separate brigade for the governor's exclusive utilization. As he wrote resignedly to wife Eliza on March 27: "things do not look in Tennessee at this time as we would like to see them; but [we] must take them as they are."[16]

Personal tragedy struck the Johnsons within the week when their eldest son accidentally fell from his horse and was trampled to death at the military camp of the Tenth Tennessee (Union) where he was an assistant surgeon. Neither parent attended the funeral; consultations with the president and war secretary stood at a sensitive point and the distance was too great. Later they would return to a Nashville that was changing daily with the military presence. Johnson now had to contend with Rosecrans, African-American recruitment, and civil matters, such as the dispute over excise taxes between Tennessee and Kentucky distillers. But the city itself had become a cesspool of turmoil, prostitution, and underworld districts—"Slabtown" and "Smokey Row" claimed victims by the score. While justice-hungry citizens howled that decency needed restoration at the Tennessee capital, the military standoff had caused this malaise.[17]

THE MILITARY PROBLEM—SECURING THE VICTORY

Johnson's words to Lincoln on January 11, 1863, that the Pyrrhic victory at Stones River had inspired confidence among Tennessee unionists and conversely discouraged the state's rebels was a new call for action. Yet, both battered armies in fact relished the lethargy of recuperation and inactivity that came with winter. From January through May 1863, they proceeded to eat up the riches of the district between Nashville and the Duck River. Meanwhile, to the rear of Nashville and before Rosecrans's front lines to the south, a different sort of war carried on in the absence of the clash of the armies.

Once Wheeler and Bedford Forest had been thrown back from the line of the Cumberland in February, Colonel Sanders Bruce, for example, reported only minor insurgency activities near his Clarksville base, but "the country is clear" with "no danger on river." Scouting missions and foraging activities continued unabated by the men in blue and gray. Rosecrans had sufficient manpower to handle eventualities involving protection of his supply lines, even as Bragg and his theater commander Joe Johnston determined that they would be the target of Confederate horsemen come good weather. For the moment, however, "all quiet on the Cumberland" seemed an appropriate if temporary refrain.[18]

Brigadier General Gordon Granger's so-called Reserve Corps provided a maneuver force for coping with threats to Rosecrans's rear. "After perils by land and water, negroism and abolitionism, worthless quartermasters, and vexation of every kind and description," Granger wrote Rosecrans on the very day that Dover came under attack, that his steamboat column had finally left Louisville with twelve thousand men and four six-gun batteries. Seven Michigan cavalry companies went overland, as the Louisville and Nashville railroad had reopened two days before. Naval convoys shepherded Granger upriver to Nashville. Still, it took ten hours to travel the 185 miles by rail; longer for Granger's riverborne contingents. Granger apologized to Rosecrans for not stopping to clean out the guerrilla-infested countryside south of Clarksville. Transportation problems once again thwarted one of Rosecrans's pet schemes for better ensuring his rear against raiders and guerrillas. Besides, nobody really wanted to chase insurgents in mid-winter.[19]

Counting Granger, Rosecrans statistically tallied nearly 100,000 officers and men with 35 heavy and 254 light guns for his Department of the Cumberland. Of this number, 23,637 men with 29 heavy and 53 light guns made up rear garrisons. Major General Horatio Wright added 37,182 officers and men plus 8 heavy and 39 light cannon from the Department of the Ohio to the figures. Rear area commanders from Robert B. Mitchell at Nashville to W. T. Ward at Gallatin, Bruce at Clarksville, and Colonel William W. Lowe on the twin rivers, as well as Brigadiers Quincy A. Gillmore in central Kentucky and Jeremiah T. Boyle in western Kentucky all had more than sufficient numbers for occupation and rear area protection. Granted, the convalescents and static garrison troops that manned these areas were never first-rate contingents when it came to a stand-up fight. Moreover, they too had to be clothed, fed, and sheltered just like first-line troops. However, they stood ready to intimidate civilians, chase irregulars, and support authority as required.[20]

Army needs clashed with civilian desires concerning use of this manpower. Rosecrans wanted fighting men as well as supply guards; Kentucky and Tennessee officials desired uniformed squads to counteract public unrest and the guerrilla threat. Congress accordingly authorized "the raising of a volunteer force for the better defense of Kentucky" on February 7, and Boyle was directed to aid Governor T. E. Bramlette in raising, organizing, and equipping this force. A twenty-thousand-man state protection force would oversee loyal Kentucky. But, as some like Brigadier General James B. Fry, the provost-marshal general, feared, recruitment for this new contingent might retard other mobilization efforts across the state. It would require arms, equipment, uniforms, and training. Of course, the ever-worrisome thought that arming African Americans might also be included at some point also distressed Kentuckians. Such issues would ferment over time. In the winter of 1863, the main problem was how to organize home guards for reconstructing heartland states without wholesale disruption of recruitment for Union field armies. Ironically, it mirrored the same problem the Confederacy faced with regard to its partisan rangers.[21]

Kentucky authorities worried constantly about forays by native son John Hunt Morgan, partisans like Tom Woodward and Adam Johnson, or raiders from western Virginia or East Tennessee. There was always the possibility of a strike by Forrest or Wheeler from Middle or West Tennessee or by Major General Earl Van Dorn from Mississippi. Indeed, intelligence indicated that the greatest immediate threat to Federal control seemed to come from that more southerly direction. Telegrams from Hurlbut constantly called for naval support because of such imagined threats to his Memphis position. But more resolute commanders, like Dover post commander Colonel Abner C. Harding, downplayed any immediate action by Van Dorn, while the Jackson district commander contended that the rivers were too high to cross and the Confederate general had "lost at Columbia all his corn and quartermaster's stores, and is now foraging." A small conscripting force might be active, but Union commanders generally decided that neither Van Dorn nor anybody else would be so foolhardy as to attempt a return to the line of the Cumberland in mid-winter.[22]

Nonetheless, rumors about Van Dorn's arrival from Mississippi kept Harding's men busily building the new Fort Donelson as well as patrolling for guerrillas. The Eighty-third Illinois lost its overage but beloved senior captain, J. B. McClanahan, to wounds suffered in the Dover fight, and his body was taken back to Warren County, Illinois, in a metallic coffin by his son. Amateur construction "experts," like Sergeant Eugene Marshall of the Fifth Iowa Cavalry, "inspected" the new fort and pronounced that it still left defenders exposed to hostile fire from distances of one hundred yards or less. But patrols out on the telegraph line to Clarksville were what usually preoccupied men like Marshall. This line lay on the south side of the Cumberland via Tennessee Ridge, right on the edge of guerrilla country. The Hawkeyes saw few rebels, but they commented about the destitute countryside, their own war weariness and desires for furloughs, and expressed shock that some of their number would actually desert to the enemy in order to secure paroles and hence be furloughed to go home. Many had begun to decry both secessionist and abolitionist alike, and particularly the policies of the Lincoln administration.[23]

The garrison soldiery predictably experienced a winter of discontent, wondering openly just what they were fighting for. Their patrols toward partisan strongholds at Charlotte and Waverly found houses lacking glass windows, inhabitants unable to read or write, and meager crops like corn, sorghum, or occasional cotton patches providing livelihoods for a region where everything "was made on the farm." "This is dixie with a vengeance," declared Marshall, where ignorance, poverty, and licentious drunkenness proved the norm. The Iowans' mission now included capturing "notorious characters" and denying horses to the partisans and keeping the peace along Will, White, and Hurricane Creeks in the so-called "coaling lands" where timber had been cleared before the war to fuel now abandoned Randolph Furnace and Cumberland Iron Works. "The danger from Guerrillas on the river appears to be pretty well over now," Marshall thought, somewhat prematurely, in mid-March. But steamboats now passed without convoy escort, so that, by early March, Rosecrans even ordered Forts Henry and Heiman abandoned and leveled and troops concentrated at Fort Donelson in order to counter an expected attack by Van Dorn from the south.[24]

Abandonment of the Tennessee River forts might have been occasioned by a massacre of twenty-eight men of a scouting party rather than any return of peace to the area. Soldiers like Marshall and Robert McConnell of the Seventy-first Ohio applauded Rosecrans's decision. They hated conditions at Henry and Heiman, although the situation was no better at Dover. Some of the men occasionally could get away upriver to Clarksville, and William H. Dorris of the Eighty-third Illinois was surprised "to see a nice town so near to Dover." Dorris even found distant relations—albeit secesh in sympathy—living there, and was roundly feted by his kinfolk despite his enemy uniform. "I should like to live here if it was not a slave state," he concluded. Other soldiers lacked such opportunities and were disgruntled; on the other hand, Fort Donelson commander Abner Harding simply claimed that "Fort Henry was untenable by high water" anyway.[25]

Time hung heavy for the troops; mail delivery was slow, and newspapers, like the traitorous Cincinnati *Enquirer* and Chicago *Times*, were banned from camp by army headquarters. Mitchel Thompson of the Eighty-third reported that a school for slaves or "contraband" was progressing nicely, but everyone took note of the high incidence of disease and illness that decimated the ranks. McConnell complained bitterly about living on "sow belly" and "Michigan Singles" (hardtack), while drinking "Cumberland River coffee," so no wonder so many soldiers took sick. At least he spoke with pride of nearly three thousand men and fourteen cannon now adorning the new Fort Donelson. He vowed personally to help fulfill Rosecrans's challenge to the garrison to hold an enemy in check for six hours and "he will send us all the help we need."[26]

Brigadier General Alexander Sandor Asboth, the fretful Columbus, Kentucky, commander, was less pleased with abandoning the Tennessee River forts. It threatened his control of the Jackson Purchase section of western Kentucky. The entire Tennessee line "from Duck River to Heiman, as well as the Kentucky and Tennessee State line, are uncontrolled," he wired Hurlbut excitedly on March 7. Asboth had served with Major General John C. Fremont in Missouri and had been wounded at Pea Ridge, Arkansas, the previous March. Originally a refugee freedom-fighter from Hungary, Asboth was something of an eccentric character. He had also inveighed against transferring the river forts from Grant to Rosecrans, and, on March 11, he again told Hurlbut bluntly: "I consider Heiman one of the most important points in the range of my district," inasmuch as it controlled the river, the state borders, "and all the country toward Paducah and Columbus." The distant Rosecrans hardly understood Fort Heiman's significance, and Hurlbut had his doubts; Asboth always appeared rattled, so people discounted his advice.[27]

At last Hurlbut allowed Asboth and Lieutenant Commander James H. Shirk to investigate affairs at Forts Henry and Heiman with the gunboats *Tuscumbia* and *Brilliant.* The pair found Fort Henry predictably inundated by floodwaters, but no sign of any rebels. None of the earthworks had been leveled, as Rosecrans had ordered. But there were no signs of Confederates either. So, Asboth left the Third Minnesota, the 111th Illinois, two artillery pieces, and two cavalry companies under command of Colonel Chauncey W. Griggs to hold Fort Heiman. The joint army-navy team continued upriver, destroying or confiscating flatboats as far as Perryville, Tennessee.

Asboth also told Hurlbut on March 14 that he planned further temporary posts for Mayfield and Murray, in addition to those already at Clinton and Benton, Kentucky. He felt comfortable in countering rebel irregulars under a Major Blanton who were conscripting and organizing resistance in that area. Since a telegraph line had been cut for miles, the next few weeks brought rumors that twelve thousand Confederates were within twenty-eight miles of Dover and that there was well-armed southern infantry with large wagon trains "just over the hills to the south." At least the twin river garrisons were prepared, as the local telegrapher tapped out "we are ready again for a fight" once his wires were restored.[28]

The crux of the twin rivers problem lay with the fact that these streams formed an administrative seam between Rosecrans and Grant. Grant was preoccupied now in cooperating with Acting Rear Admiral David Porter's naval squadron against Vicksburg. Like Rosecrans's forces, his paper strength looked impressive—128,850 officers and men, 64 heavy guns, and 277 light guns. But, more than Rosecrans and his subordinates, Grant's rear echelon commanders—Hurlbut, Asboth, and Brigadier General C. S. Hamilton in West Tennessee and northern Mississippi absorbed on paper a staggering 99,790 officers and men, as well as the bulk of the heavy guns and a large percentage of the light artillery. With this number, they had enough to seal off entry across the Tennessee–Mississippi state borders to raiders and partisans. But needing frontline manpower so desperately, Grant ordered Hurlbut and the others to break up workshops and railroad garrisons and rely on the river line of communications, shipping all surplus troops downriver to Vicksburg as soon as possible. Hurlbut thought Asboth's regarrisoning of Fort Heiman improper and ordered him to take those troops back to Paducah. Nevertheless, under orders from the secretary of war, Halleck directed reoccupation of the fort at the end of March and assigned the post permanently to Grant's jurisdiction.[29]

Guerrilla nests in both Middle and West Tennessee accordingly enjoyed a charmed life. Colonel R. V. Richardson's partisan stronghold at Somerville, east of Memphis, rivaled Waverly or Charlotte as a sanctuary. Arkansas, too, provided safe haven for irregulars, who constantly raided steamboats on the Mississippi. These irregulars led the Federals to level their hometowns in the hope that they would soon tired "of their fun of burning boats," said Hugh Bay of the Eighty-ninth Indiana stationed near Memphis. They did not stop their harassment, apparently, although Grant thought Hurlbut and the others, with the navy's help, could handle the problem. Grant was more concerned with the open trading out of Memphis, where cotton was exchanged for clothing, food, and even weapons that went immediately into partisan hands. "Cotton on the brain" was the way Grant characterized the lucrative intercourse that lined pockets of Yankee officers ready to profit from their tour in the war zone. A vicious triangle of cotton, unscrupulous military carpetbaggers, and rebel civilians as well as irregulars insured unceasing turbulence in Grant's rear areas.[30]

GUERRILLAS AND A CODE OF WARFARE

Grant's evolved thinking on guerrillas at this point surfaced in a heated exchange with Confederate generals Carter L. Stevenson and John C. Pemberton in late February. Admiral Porter had ostensibly signed an undated order declaring that persons firing on unarmed steamboats would be treated as "highwaymen and assassins and no quarter will be shown them." Suspected individuals would also be kept as prisoners of war in close confinement. "If this savage and barbarous Confederate custom cannot be put a stop to," read Porter's dictum, "we will try what virtue there is in hanging." Similarly, anyone caught pillaging houses along the Mississippi, levying contributions, or burning cotton would similarly receive no quarter. The Confederate generals protested vehemently, promising retaliation. Here, then, was an unresolved legal question for field commanders, and the time quickly approached when some sort of codification of laws of warfare might be in order.[31]

Semantic differences between "partisan," "guerrilla," or "raider" remained moot for field generals like Grant or Rosecrans. Disavowing that Porter had departed from any rule of civilized warfare, as Stevenson and Pemberton contended, Grant pointed to depredations by southern citizens in defiance of those very rules. "These are persons who are always in the guise of citizens and on the approach of an armed force remain at their homes professing to be in no way connected with the army, but entitled to all the indulgences allowed non-combatants in a country visited by an opposing army," he observed. These same people were always ready to fire on unarmed vessels or sometimes capture or murder Union soldiers passing through their locale. All people engaged in warfare "must have about them some insignia by which they may be known, at all times, as an enemy" to entitle them to treatment as prisoners of war. Even then, "their hostilities must be carried on in accordance with the rules of civilized warfare," he declared. Grant repudiated retaliation unless perpetuated by the rebels themselves.

"I have yet to hear, for the first time, of such a course securing any alleviation from the hardships necessarily produced by a state of war," he added.[32]

Rosecrans's situation in Middle Tennessee was slightly different. He and his subordinates discovered a more deeply divided populace around them than existed in West Tennessee and Mississippi. When Major General Joseph J. Reynolds, a former West Point classmate of Grant, took a column from his First Division of the XIV corps to the Auburn neighborhood east of Murfreesboro in early February, he found a mixture of unionists and secessionists living cheek by jowl with one another. So long as the powerful Confederate Army of Tennessee stood unvanquished only sixty or seventy miles to the south along the Duck River, uncertainty prevailed in this unsettled land. Reynolds's men found "the property of loyal men despoiled, that of rebels protected," with aged men and women left destitute if loyal to the United States, and youth conscripted into rebel ranks regardless of political persuasion. It was truly a society left unprotected and in disarray with Bragg's retirement from Murfreesboro. The secessionist element held the forage, animals, and provisions, much of which, in Reynolds's opinion, could be redistributed to the unhappy unionists, or even used to supply the Army of the Cumberland. If there were guerrillas about, it still was nothing like the country to the west, and beyond the Tennessee River.[33]

Reynolds's solution to what he found suggested that "the only effectual mode of suppressing the rebellion must be such a one as will conquer the rebellious individuals now at home as well as defeat their armies in the field." Either task left unaccomplished, he admonished in a dispatch to headquarters on February 10, "leaves the rebellion unsubdued," a sentiment readily endorsed by his immediate superior, Major General George H. Thomas. Reynolds's solution to taking care of those tasks lay in despoiling "the rebels as the rebel army has despoiled the Union men." Banish rebels from the country; make it safe for unionists to return. Let these unionists "feel that the country is once more in their possession instead of being possessed by their oppressors." Aid them in its possession for a while, argued Reynolds.

Thomas, in turn, told Rosecrans bluntly that conciliatory policies had failed miserably. Kentucky and Tennessee were both in the same condition. "We shall be compelled to send disloyal people of all ages and sexes to the south, or beyond our lines," however regrettable the necessity. Secession had "so degraded their sense of honor that it is next to impossible to find one tinctured with it who can be trusted." Rosecrans dutifully forwarded such observations without comment to Washington. There, Halleck and other administration officials, including Lincoln, had been pondering the issue of status and rights of participants in the war for some months. The general-in-chief had been in close touch with Dr. Francis Lieber, a German immigrant jurist at Columbia College in New York City.

So Halleck replied knowledgeably, if somewhat bureaucratically to Rosecrans on March 5, suggesting that "no additional instructions from these headquarters are deemed necessary," since the Army of the Cumberland had already been urged to procure subsistence, forage, and transport whenever possible in the occupied South. In approving the Reynolds-Thomas strictures for "a more rigid treatment of all disloyal persons within the lines of your army," he told Rosecrans that he could enforce all "laws and usages of war, however rigid and severe they may be," unless some prohibited by congressional act, regulation, order, or other instruction. Generally, however, the field commander had to be the judge of when "a more lenient course is of greater advantage to our cause."[34]

The owlish Halleck then proceeded to draw distinctions that Rosecrans might follow. First, he suggested, the "truly loyal" neither aided nor assisted the rebels, but favored the Union side, and should not be subjected to military requisitions generally, but rather paid or otherwise "fully indemnified" for any requisition of their property. A second category included "non-combatants," who were presumably in league with the Confederacy, since there "can be no such thing as neutrality in a rebellion." As long as this group committed no hostile act and its members plied their "private avocations" at home, it could escape molestation, confiscation, and requisition "except as a military necessity." Federal military protection could be extended to them as long as they did not take up arms or aid and abet the rebels. "They incur very serious obligations," and any deviations meant they "are war rebels, or military traitors, and incur the penalty of death." Even people furnishing information to the enemy would be considered spies, since, said Halleck, "our treatment of such offenders has hitherto been altogether too lenient."

Finally, the Union's top general bore in upon people who openly and avowedly defied the occupying army, but who did not actually take up arms for the Confederacy. "While claiming to be non-combatants, they repudiated the obligations tacitly or impliedly incurred by the other inhabitants of the occupied territory," he decided. These people incurred all the obligations of the second group, but could be treated as prisoners of war and subjected either to confinement or expulsion as "combatant enemies." He left it to Rosecrans to determine the proper course, but "we have suffered very severely from this class, and it is time that the laws of war should be more rigorously enforced against them." Naturally, such matters pertained to military status and military offenses under the laws of war, not to civil offenses incurred under the national constitution and the laws of the land. Rosecrans therefore could decide "where it is best to act with rigor and where it is best to be more lenient," and the war department would not burden him with minute instructions. "A broad line of distinction must be drawn between fiends and enemies, between the loyal and the disloyal," for the "laws and usages of civilized war must be your guide in the treatment of all classes of persons of the country in which your army may operate, or which it may occupy," Halleck concluded.

Just such a codification of the laws and usages of war appeared within a month from the war department. One student of Union policy toward southern civilians, Mark Grimsley, contends that Halleck "was almost certainly guided by his inside knowledge of a major War Department policy statement then in the works." Known to posterity as "Lieber's Code," it was drawn up by a War Department panel of which Lieber was the sole civilian and principal author. It went to the field on April 24, 1863, as General Orders Number 100, "Instructions for the Government of Armies of the United States in the Field." Halleck and Lieber had been communicating for months on the philosophical and legal questions posed by the war and enunciated in this order. Lieber had also provided the general with an essay on guerrillas that Halleck distributed five thousand copies of to the army. No doubt Halleck replied to Rosecrans in early March based on what he and Lieber had worked out up to that point.[35]

In any event, General Order Number 100 established ground rules and clear enunciation of ethics of conducting war, according to historian Frank Freidel. Others see the orders as a concise and careful rendering of international legal theory and practice up to Lieber's time. Declaring from the outset that "to save the country is paramount to all other considerations," the panel defined the key point of military necessity as "those measures which are indispensable for securing the end of the war," and thus "admits of all direct destruction of life or limb or armed enemies, and of other persons whose destruction is incidentally unavoidable in the armed contests of war." The orders deemed it unlawful "to starve the hostile belligerent, armed or unarmed" even though starvation might lead to speedier "subjugation of the enemy"; they also forbade "poison in any way, or wanton devastation of a district," or any act of hostility which would make the return to peace "unnecessarily difficult." Retaliation could never be used as mere revenge, but only as a means of "protective retribution," after careful inquiry into the real occurrence and character of the misdeeds. Killing the enemy was not the object in itself, said the panel, but rather destruction of the enemy in war was a means to achieve peace. Therefore, unnecessary or revengeful destruction was unlawful.[36]

Careful perusal of the 10-section, 157-article document lay beyond the capability of most of the army, although distribution in the field through its publication in the Chicago *Tribune* ensured that it would be "read by all General Grant's forces," said Cairo post commander Brigadier General N. B. Buford. Certainly four of those articles should have prompted the attention of those in the ranks. They treated military necessity, unarmed citizens, private citizens, and the "forcing of subjects of the enemy into the service of the national government." They did not mention guerrillas or partisans. Articles 81 and 82 did, and therefore probably mattered most to the common soldier facing sentry, patrol, or punitive sweeps through hostile countryside.

The subtle difference between "soldiers armed and wearing the uniform of their army, but belonging to a corps which acts detached from the main body for the purpose of making inroads into the territory occupied by the enemy" (partisans) and "men, or squads of men, who commit hostilities, whether by fighting or inroads for destruction or plunder, or by raids of any kind, without commission, without being part or portion of the organized hostile army, and without sharing continuously in the war, but who do so with intermitting returns to their homes and avocations, or with the occasional assumption of the semblance of peaceful pursuits" (the order called them "highway robbers or pirates") surely meant little to the Union troops who actually encountered them.[37]

Such legal niceties meant a great deal to the panel in Washington, and Confederate authorities blasted the document as propaganda and argued that it gave too much latitude to men in blue. Precisely what impact General Orders Number 100 actually had upon Civil War soldiers has never been very clear, though it was subsequently incorporated into the dogma of codes of conduct for modern armies. However, from April 1863 to the end of the war, its existence lent authority to how the Federal military further subjugated the South. Halleck also imparted his ideas to both Rosecrans and Burnside, which he had "formed from my own experience in Missouri and Tennessee," but he allowed interpretation of those ideas and the codification via General Orders Number 100 "to vary at different times and in different localities." Whatever the mission of those generals or of Grant and Sherman, "getting another blow at the rebels" was uppermost in West Pointers' minds. Guerrillas and upper heartland reconstruction remained tertiary unless they intruded upon major operations via raids, supply-route interdiction, or political intimidation, which siphoned off manpower resources from the main effort against Confederate field armies.[38]

ARMY-NAVY COOPERATION ON THE RIVERS

Mindful of rivals like Major General John A. McClernand (and of McClernand's contention that midwesterners' wanted the Mississippi River reopened to trade), Grant simply intended to get on with his main mission of capturing Vicksburg and its defenders. Halleck had told him on March 20 that "The great object on your line now is the opening of the Mississippi River, and everything else must bend to that purpose." The eyes and hopes of the nation rested upon Grant, in Halleck's view, and reopening that river would be of more advantage "than the capture of forty Richmonds." Halleck had learned the lesson well during his period in charge in the West. Now, guerrillas and cavalry raiders must be rendered inert by commanders behind Grant's main line. Garrisons left behind would become more important as instruments of political control rather than as logistical shields once the focus shifted again to operations on the Mississippi River.[39]

It was different for Rosecrans in Middle Tennessee. River resupply offered only an alternative to the railroad lifeline. There simply were not enough riverboats available to serve as principal suppliers for both Grant and Rosecrans. Foraging, in fact, had to "rescue us from want" for a while, and the Army of the Cumberland's commander feared rebel cavalry under Morgan, Wheeler, Forrest, Wharton, Buford, and others. Their employment "will endeavor to strike our flanks or rear, isolated posts, and control the subsistence and population of the country," he claimed. Indeed, Confederate numbers would swell from eight thousand at the end of January to more than double that number by spring as Bragg sought to strengthen the cavalry arm as his strike force. In fact, Dunbar Affleck of Terry's Texas Rangers wrote home on March 5 that "we have now in this army over thirty thousand cavalry." How much longer they would stay in Tennessee he did not know, but "we have eaten out the country where we have been," and every forage party that went out did so knowing they would have to battle the Yankees over foodstuffs," said Affleck. Aware of the supply problems, Rosecrans aimed "to move [Bragg's army] up near us, and then fight them."[40]

Captain Alfred Lacey Hough of the Nineteenth United States Regulars perceived Rosecrans's point: "I think Rosecrans argues that they must attack us, or fall back as the country is exhausted of supplies." He added that Old Rosy would "trust to the army in Kentucky to take care of them, if they pass us" on any major raid. Yet, the Bluegrass had already been tapped to send men forward. What Rosecrans wanted was simply more time to prepare and more resources, since, in his mind, the fatal errors thus far in the war derived from lack of solid preparation by impatient leaders, who were then "afraid to move when all the means were provided." Rosecrans aimed at changing that, and Washington could but hope that, when the time came, his high-sounding goals were executed with the same sense of purpose. To accomplish his long-term goals, however, he needed reliable supply from his Louisville base. Like Grant, Rosecrans also depended upon the navy's help.[41]

At first, Rosecrans demanded full command and control over naval vessels plying the Cumberland. Lincoln demurred when he read the general's request of February 11. He did solicit promises of cooperation from his war and naval secretaries. Frankly, Rosecrans's requests had begun to wear thin upon the administration. Still, as the general quickly pointed out to the president on March 16, Stanton had wired him after Stones River: "Anything you and your command want you can have." So far, in Rosecrans's view, Washington had turned a deaf ear to his requests. In turn, cost-conscious and resource-shy bureaucrats at the capital simply could not comply with all Rosecrans's requests, and they wondered why the smooth joint-service relations on the Mississippi between Porter and Grant could not be duplicated on the upper rivers. Above all, they wanted Rosecrans to begin his offensive with the first spring blossoms.

Rosecrans, however, contended that he needed more horses, better cavalry arms and equipment, control over all aspects of his communications, and, above all, more time, ever more time. He worried about reports of rebel gunboats being built along Caney Fork, off the Cumberland, above the state capital. He fretted about reputed Confederate earthworks under construction to block the Tennessee River at Clifton off to his right flank, and about rebel rehabilitation of a sunken steamer, the *Dunbar*, farther up that stream. The general saw no reason why naval commanders A. M. Pennock and Le Roy Fitch could not easily eliminate all these threats, while also intercepting Earl Van Dorn's cavalry column as it crossed the Tennessee en route from Mississippi to assist Bragg. But Rosecrans's suggestions amounted to procrastination in the War Department's eyes.[42]

Rosecrans also viewed the navy as a sort of long-range raiding force in the rebel rear, offsetting the grayclad cavalry that preyed on his own line of communications. In all naval commanders lacked resources to handle all their missions on four rivers—the Ohio, the Mississippi, the Tennessee, and the Cumberland (as well as tributaries). Frankly, Porter's operations on the lower Mississippi commanded the greatest allocation of his resources. But contraband commerce interdiction, deep raids behind enemy lines via the rivers, and combat patrols on northern portions of the streams, as well as convoy duty for resupplying the army stretched the navy very thin. Local army commanders, like Sanders Bruce at Clarksville, always wanted three or four gunboats simply to patrol between Fort Donelson and Nashville. Fortunately, the army did not see Porter's scathing communique to the secretary of the navy of February 23 wherein he declared: "General Rosecrans is very exacting, and at times imperious, forgetting what is due the Navy Department, which is straining every nerve to carry out the wishes of the War Department."[43]

The pressure of having to safely convoy over one hundred steamers and many barges to Nashville without loss and successfully rescuing Dover (which the army "did not think proper to make an adequate acknowledgment"), as well as the presence of some fifty thousand idle soldiers around Nashville who "do nothing to keep open the line of communication between that city and the mouth of the river," irked Porter. Clarksville, Fort Donelson and Dover, and Eddyville, "if properly fortified would break up rebel raids below Nashville." The admiral was distressed to find an army of twenty-nine thousand on the river doing nothing so that, referring specifically to Granger's passage, "I have to protect the whole line of river against the guerrillas, and am called on to send a gunboat to convoy 10,000 troops, with abundance of artillery." As Porter saw it from his perspective far down the Mississippi below Vicksburg, nothing had been done by the army in the upper heartland, and "the rebels are allowed to roam about and erect batteries on the river which the gunboats have to silence." Secretary Gideon Welles smoothed Porter's ruffled feelings by assuring him that the government valued the vigilance, energy, and efforts of the whole naval force on western waters.

Nonetheless, Rosecrans had a point. He had achieved unity of command over the land garrisons protecting his river supply line, but not over the navy. Therefore, the general found it difficult to maintain open and safe navigation. This joint-service issue dissipated as Fitch and Rosecrans developed closer relations over time. Meanwhile, separate army and navy actions on the upper Tennessee helped alleviate the strained situation for the Army of the Cumberland. Colonel F. M. Cornyn's West Tennessee district cavalry caught the tail end of Van Dorn's column near Tuscumbia, Alabama, on George Washington's birthday and captured prisoners, artillery, horses, and mules. The main Confederate body still crossed the river safely and joined Forrest and Wheeler in Middle Tennessee. But Federal arms were beginning to nip at rebel supremacy in the region.[44]

Soon, the gunboats USS *Lexington*, *Fairplay*, *St. Clair*, *Brilliant*, and *Alfred Robb* chased the rehabilitated *Dunbar* above Muscle Shoals and effectively neutralized her threat on the Tennessee River. They also attacked guerrillas along the stream near Tuscumbia. Another army group, under Captain Frederick C. Adamson, crossed the Tennessee on a flatboat and surprised and captured a guerrilla camp near Clifton, burning that pesthole to the ground. Fitch reappeared in time to cover the soldiers and carry prisoners back to Paducah. They also assisted thirty-

Lieutenant Commander Le Roy Fitch, USN, at the Navy Yard, Pensacola, Florida, after December 1870. Courtesy of the U.S. Naval Historical Center.

five or forty unionist families to relocate in the north. Fitch thus opened communications with Corinth district commander Brigadier General Grenville M. Dodge and generally supported land operations in the area. Rosecrans counted his flanks as secure by March, although Confederate activity never abated completely between the Tennessee River and Nashville.[45]

Fitch considered "the guerrillas along the Cumberland had become pretty well thinned out" by this point. He had added the USS *Silver Lake* and *Springfield* to convoy duty. Rosecrans still pestered about the inadequacy of such service, and sharpshooters on the banks kept heads down aboard craft going upstream. Fitch shuffled resources back and forth between the twin rivers, and his reports to Porter in mid-March detailed operational and navigational problems that on-the-job training provided for his officers and seamen. Fitch's descriptions of the Tennessee and Cumberland Rivers graphically explained operational hazards confronting the flotilla and provide a clear picture of the ebb and flow of riverine operations at the time. Had he forwarded copies to army headquarters, then Rosecrans might have better appreciated the challenges of western waters.

The Cumberland averaged about six hundred feet in width "inside of the trees," while her sister stream was over double that size, observed Fitch. Furthermore, the Cumberland frequently rose and fell with such rapidity that "a difference of from 8 to 12 feet in twenty-four hours is of no uncommon occurrence." Both rivers had navigational obstacles at Harpeth Shoals on the Cumberland, about 160 miles from the Cumberland's mouth and 35 miles below Nashville; and at Duck River Sucks on the Tennessee River about 134 miles from the confluence of that river with the Ohio. The "Sucks" was "very dangerous, in consequence of the channel being very crooked and the current setting so strong over the rocks." These obstacles were ideal battery sites, said Fitch, for the river banks on the Cumberland "are generally very thickly wooded with heavy hills overlooking the banks," while those of the Tennessee, by contrast, "are mostly flat and overflow at high water, with high hills back from 1 to 2 miles."

Fitch also noted that the Cumberland became very narrow and crooked above Nashville, and the boats frequently had to lower smokestacks. They still suffered structural damage from overhanging tree branches on runs up to Carthage. Since "everything above Nashville seems quiet," he saw no reason to keep boats there except by necessity. Palmyra, between Dover and Clarksville, and Beatstown or Betsy Town landing at Harpeth Shoals were more infamous guerrilla nests. The navy had burned or destroyed all the stores or houses near those shoals. Fitch included a tabulation showing that "very few loyal citizens" resided at Paducah and that while a unionist cluster of three houses stood at New Portland just above the Clarksville–Memphis railroad bridge upstream, basically "there are now few loyal citizens above Fort Henry."[46]

So Fitch and his little squadron aggressively performed their convoy and counterguerrilla responsibilities throughout the winter and spring. He told Porter on March 21 that things were so quiet on the Cumberland since his burning of Betsy Town that he was spending most of his time on the Tennessee, "as that river, though quiet at present, will need very strict watching." Indeed, within a week he had a joint landing team clean out a guerrilla hangout on the Dillahunty plantation near Savannah. Led by Lieutenant Colonel Chauncey Griggs and Acting Volunteer Lieutenant Martin Dunn, USN, they visited a factory said to be "run on shares with the country people" the material from which went indirectly to the aid of Confederate soldiers through their friends at home. Fitch refused to destroy the facility, but removed its machinery to the *Lexington*, thus crippling the cottage operation. He took twenty-five bales of cotton from the plantation, despite Dillahunty's professed loyalty, since he "had no papers to prove it; has never been molested by guerrillas, and, in fact . . . was at the time raising a guerrilla company." The expedition visited several other points before returning to Fort Heiman with the cotton, one thousand pounds of bacon; corn, fifteen horses, twelve mules, two wagons, and eight captured cavalry carbines. It was a typical haul from such forays.[47]

Fitch told Porter that refugees informed him that everyone upstream from Fort Henry "must be either disloyal in sentiment or actually engaged in the rebel cause." The secessionists permitted no one with "sentiments the least loyal" to remain at home or cultivate their farms. Having transported sixty-six refugee families out of the area, Fitch expressed surprise at the number of "applications of conveyance" from young Tennesseans fleeing Confederate conscription. He gave orders not to let them pass, but rather to enlist them in gunboat or land service. "If they love the Union better than rebellion now is the proper time to show it," he announced, adding that they must take sides one way or the other. This procedure netted thirty or forty men for Dodge's cavalry and eight to ten recruits for the gunboat service. "I deem it high time that some of these loyal refugees were showing some proofs of their loyalty," he reiterated. Earlier, Fitch had stated that his men had found so many dead guerrillas with the oath of allegiance in their pockets that he was forced "to believe no man living with these guerrillas, though he had taken the oath forty times."[48]

Affairs soon warmed again on the Cumberland in Fitch's absence. At 10:30 P.M. on April 2, Acting Volunteer Lieutenant J. S. Hurd was roughly handled by guerrillas at Palmyra as his USS *St. Clair* and *Fairplay* convoyed coal barges and supply boats upriver. The rebels—possibly Tom Woodward's men—opened fire from their Parrott rifle and a smoothbore gun atop a high bluff and with small arms fire from the hamlet itself. Hurd had disobeyed Fitch's orders about convoy lineup: "instead of having the towboats (the slowest) in the lead, the most valuable cargoes in the most secure place, and the swiftest boats in the rear, as was my custom, and as I had always enforced," complained Fitch, and he noted further that the result was that Hurd's "very slowest boats were in the rear, the most valuable boats in the front, and would, of course, receive the first fire." Thus, *St. Clair* bore the brunt of the rebel ambush and had to drop out of her river duties and return to Cairo, Illinois, for repairs. Then Acting Master George W. Foutty, a popular shipboard officer, died at the Fort Donelson hospital on May 10 from wounds incurred in the fight. When news of his death reached Pennock at Cairo, he telegraphed Fitch: "Go ahead and whip them out on both rivers."[49]

Fitch did just that with a vengeance at Palmyra on April 5. Fitch sent a landing party ashore under Acting Master James Fitzpatrick with orders "not to allow his command to remove or pillage a single article," but to burn Palmyra to the ground. "I was opposed to wanton destruction of property," he explained to headquarters, "but in this instance I deemed it justified, for it was one of the worst secession places on the river, and unarmed transports had been fired into from doors and windows of the houses." In his formal report the following November, Fitch wrote that "the summary manner in which the people of Palmyra were dealt with had a very good effect, for I do not think there has been a steamer molested on the river since." The Jack Tars pursued the partisans to Harpeth Shoals and, aided by Bruce's garrison, dispersed the troublemakers, although irregulars returned to harass river traffic at placed like Gallatin, upriver from Nashville, by the end of April.[50]

By this time, sailors and soldiers alike had become ruthless toward bushwhackers. Acting Surgeon William Howard of the USS *Brilliant* wrote his wife on April 5, seething with anger about the *St. Clair* episode and deploring the gunboats as "man traps" because of their feeble protection against small arms and because they seemed absolutely worthless against cannon fire. As for burning Palmyra in retaliation, "it made a sweet sight, and we will act the same with any and every place that opens a gun upon our boats." They had been too lenient, in Howard's view, for every town harboring rebel sympathizers should burn. Howard thought that as the gunboats spared sympathizers, they jeered at the navy's mercy, but now

Commander S. L. Phelps, USN. Photograph of an engraving by C. Burt. Courtesy of the U.S. Naval Historical Center.

they would feel the union navy's iron hand. There was no such thing as a fair fight, he said, since "they hide in the bush, shoot and run" then "we open on where we suppose them to be, and pray that we may have killed a few." An obviously embittered Howard, for one, vowed that if it were left to him, "I would make this accursed Reb country a howling wilderness, and trust in the goodness of the Lord that it might be peopled by a better race in the future."[51]

Questions of water depth, availability of boats, and the sporadic encounters with shoreline rebels all became standard for the brown-water sailors. Men like Howard became callous to the vicissitudes of shoal water. He wrote his wife in mid-May that working heavily laden coal and hay barges upstream was an endless round of off-loading and reloading around the shoals for even the gunboat sailors. "We make our headquarters now at Fort Donelson," he added, "and the Lord only knows when we shall see a civilized place," as he took a gratuitous swipe at the "precarious style of living" whereby country people supplied butter, eggs, and potatoes, as well as chicken, at exorbitant prices to the fleet. Other letters suggested that Howard and his fellow gunboat officers yearned for cleaner sea duty with the blockaders, or even service with Porter at Vicksburg. Instead, they remained stuck with upper heartland army support.[52]

Ever the professional, Fitch aimed at perfecting certain details of his duties. "It has always been my aim to have the means of communication and terms of meeting between the boats on [the Cumberland] and the Tennessee River so perfect that at a moments warning I can, in case of necessity, concentrate the entire force at any one point," he wrote Porter on April 6. Happily, this was now possible, he added. Arrival of Lieutenant Commander S. L. Phelps soon permitted reorganization of the upper river squadron into two divisions. Phelps took charge of the Tennessee River duties with the gunboats USS *Covington, Queen City, Argossy,* and *Emma Duncan* (later USS *Hastings*). The *Hastings* quickly received her baptism to guerrilla action at Green Bottom on April 24, in a manner reminiscent of the *St. Clair.* Fitch retained his boats for Cumberland work, and most of this buildup traced to Porter's efforts on behalf of his overworked subordinates. As the admiral told Welles on April 12: "I have and shall still continue to reinforce the vessels on the upper rivers—Tennessee and Cumberland—as the necessity for them diminishes below [on the Mississippi]."[53]

There were now ("or will be soon," Porter told the secretary of the navy on April 12, 1863) twenty-three vessels on the Tennessee (including those of the so-called Marine Brigade, a sort of amphibious counterguerrilla outfit with its own boats, landing parties, etc.). Fourteen of craft carried a total of ninety-seven guns, many of them of heavy caliber. Porter planned similar strengthening for the Cumberland division, for "now that we are getting a fair quantity of vessels, I shall be able, by drawing first from one division, then from another, to satisfy all demands." Phelps specifically requested two of builder Samuel Eads's twin turreted gunboats that drew only about three and a half feet of water, with hulls a quarter-inch-thick iron, six-inch revolving turrets, and armored decks. "Though not a proper one to place under the fire of heavy batteries," he said, they "would be very effective in operation on the [Tennessee], being of light draft, and much more efficient in contending with guns in position than the light drafts." Porter endorsed short-term loan of the "first turreted boat that comes down the Tennessee" but reminded his subordinate that he still had the USS *Eastport*, a sturdy 570-ton ironclad ram mounting six 9-inch smoothbore and two 100-pounder rifles that had been captured from the rebels by Phelps near Cerro Gordo, Tennessee, the previous winter and converted to Federal use. Besides, said Porter, "I have other work for you when the Tennessee falls."[54]

Phelps's boats made their presence felt all the way to Eastport, Mississippi, the highest navigable point at that stage, given the dropping water level. At Linden, in Perry County, Tennessee, Lieutenant Colonel W. K. M. Breckenridge and fifty-five men of the First West Tennessee Cavalry (carried across the Tennessee River by the gunboats) jumped a rebel party on May 12 and captured five officers, thirty soldiers, ten conscripts, fifty horses, and two wagons and then burned quantities of arms and supplies found in the courthouse that had served as a rebel supply depot. Phelps rejoiced that West Tennessee unionists had finally mustered a force of their own rather than relying on northern units for salvation. Breckenridge's men "are Tennesseans [who] are perfectly familiar with the people and country, and are admirably calculated for this kind of service, while the colonel himself is just the man," Phelps told Porter. He urged more responsibilities for this group, including organization of another sort of Marine Brigade—a three-hundred-man battalion that could be transported by flatboat up and down the river for counterguerrilla operations. Such a force could easily clean out Confederate buildup at Waverly and the mouth of Duck River, he observed.[55]

Phelps looked to destroy such buildup with gunboats on the Tennessee and the Cumberland while the army pinned down Confederates against the Duck River. He supposed that, with the advent of spring, a decisive battle was at hand, as he passed along Fitch's impression that the Confederates seemed to be "doing something" at the Duck River shoals where a combination of those natural obstacles plus a shoreline with "eligible locations for batteries" promised trouble for the navy. Phelps decided, however, that Middle Tennessee, not the Tennessee River region, portended major action in the near future. However, should Braxton Bragg and his army prevail in the struggle, he envisioned an attempt to reestablish their control of that river. "Secessionists report that the plan is to recapture Fort Henry, and to fortify also at Carrollville," he warned his superiors on May 14.[56]

All that lay in the future. In truth, both Union and Confederate armies desperately needed succor in their winter camps from the Harpeth to the Duck. If newly arriving cavalrymen under Van Dorn imagined a land of milk and honey—"a full ration of ham for all—even the privates"—once they crossed the Tennessee headed north from Mississippi, supply personnel were less sanguine. Indeed, Bragg's own commissary officer, Major John H. Walker, had told him late in February that the area could provide less than a month's food and forage and that an alarming crisis would engulf the army by summer if something was not done very soon. By June at the latest, he warned, "the catastrophe may be upon us and the terrible truth made public: 'No meat for the armies of the Confederacy.'" There were two solutions, he said: either procure from the north via cotton trading, or "make this army large enough by reinforcements to drive out Rosecrans and take Kentucky and hold it." Bragg and his department commander, General Joseph E. Johnston, endorsed the latter view, vowing "to return to Kentucky in the spring." At the same time, Rosecrans intended holding out until he could he could resume his own offensive. Wright (who was succeeded by easterner Ambrose Burnside in March) had like goals for East Tennessee. All told, Union plans rested upon quick resupplying by land and water and maintenance of rear area quiet to ensure that effort.[57]

From January through the early spring, Fitch, subsequently reinforced by Phelps, plied upper heartland waters with mosquito squadrons in support of the army. Colonel John Beatty, a young Ohio volunteer officer, may have been a trifle optimistic when he recorded in late February that with a thoroughly fortified supply base at Murfreesboro (containing provisions for at least a month) and "now that the Cumberland is high" and the railroad reopened from Louisville, "any amount of supplies may be brought through." It was not that simple. The army needed a unified effort by land and river to sustain forty to fifty thousand men, in addition to horses and mules and civilian retainers. In the end, the navy may well have provided the edge.[58]

Not only did the navy clear the rivers of irregular flatboat and contraband traffic, confiscate cotton "in a country infested by guerrillas, [that] was likely to go into the rebel army," punish rebel partisans, and extract unionist refugees, the flotilla also effectively refuted army claims of inadequate convoy support by its deeds, not irresolute wrangling and bickering. As Fitch reported the following November, "during my operations on the Tennessee, there were always gunboats enough left on the Cumberland to give convoy through to Nashville regularly twice, and occasionally three times a week." That was certainly sufficient to enable Rosecrans and the Army of the Cumberland to survive to fight another day. By spring, both blue and gray had begun to brush away winter cobwebs and prepare to resume active operations. No decision had been reached as yet in the heartland, but then survival, not decision, preoccupied both armies that third winter of the war.[59]

Behind the Union armies now lurked a different kind of warfare. It was described brilliantly on March 7 by Henderson, Kentucky, district commander Colonel John W. Foster to his superior Jeremiah Boyle at Louisville. The counties between the Green and Cumberland Rivers in Kentucky "are now in a comparative state of peace," he stated. Only small bands of guerrillas and "returned rebel soldiers" committed depredations, and they could be hunted out by his troops and not be allowed to concentrate. This season of the year was unfavorable for guerrilla operations "as the leaves and undergrowth do not now afford a hiding place, and the weather is too unpleasant." But he pointed to the previous fall and the upcoming springtime as higher threat periods.

Foster recalled how Adam R. Johnson and Thomas G. Woodward had been driven out of this country. Johnson had attached himself with Morgan and Woodward with Forrest, on the condition that both would be permitted to return in the spring with their followers and other soldiers, "and stir up the people anew to take up arms." Foster cited recent reliable information concerning the truth of this intelligence, and he argued that "the families and friends of those who are in the Southern army confidently expect their return, and they secretly boast that the whole country down to the Ohio will be in their power."[60]

Foster doubted that any large body of Confederates could infiltrate his jurisdiction. But small armed bands could get through, since "their friends and sympathizers are almost one united body from this region all the way through Tennessee to the rebel lines." However much he and other officials might deny that fact, "it must be borne in mind that this part of the State and Southwest is almost all rebel in its sympathies." Confident that he could easily counter Johnson and Woodward, Foster had but four companies of cavalry, and his preponderance of infantry "will be almost useless against the guerrillas." His command was thoroughly acquainted with the countryside, its roads and byways, and the character of the guerrilla warfare, he told Boyle, and he was anxious to meet the threat, But the irregulars, if they returned in considerable numbers, "will meet with a hearty welcome, and will be harbored and cared for by the people." Southern generals knew and appreciated this fact and wholeheartedly embraced the scheme "to permit them to return, to annoy the rear of the army and distract our forces."

Foster closed his missive with the request that mounts should not be delayed, "for in six weeks from this date I anticipate an active campaign in my district." Even Ohio department commander Wright endorsed sending him fifteen hundred horses for one regiment, and then wrote Halleck's chief of staff George W. Cullum in Washington at mid-month: "I have sent off, from time to time, as they were needed in front and were prepared for the field, the troops of the department, till there was left only enough to protect the State of Kentucky from inroads of the enemy in the winter season, while the roads were nearly impassable and the rivers so swollen as to be impracticable for any large force." At the present time, then, only six thousand available men in the Central District could "keep off raids upon the most fertile portion of the State, to protect its line of communication, and to cover the city of Cincinnati. In western Kentucky the numbers engaged in guarding the railroad from Louisville to Nashville, the line of communication of General Rosecrans' army, and in keeping down guerrilla bands, with which that part of the State is infested, and in covering the river frontiers of Indiana and Illinois, was, by the last return less than 9,000 effective men," he continued.

The bottom line, to Wright at least, was that "this number is too small for the real security of the State." His solution was twofold. A defense could be achieved by closing all entrances to the upper heartland "by taking up a line just within the edge of the blue-grass country," where use of interior lines could shift forces to meet an identified threat. But Wright claimed that "The true system undoubtedly is to combine with the defensive an offensive policy of raids, which shall annoy and distract the enemy." Wright, the departing commander on the Ohio, had but recently celebrated Brigadier General Sam Carter's successful New Year's strike into East Tennessee. Now, he was proposing exactly the plan that Union arms would follow that spring in trying to counteract the Confederate threat to the upper heartland.[61]

NINE

HEARTLAND DYNAMICS: SPRING 1863

Nashville "is the nicest place I ever saw, the roads are paved all over the town and the pike to there," one Federal soldier, G. H. Gates, wrote a friend on February 10, 1863. Fortifications and contraband camps also caught his eye, with tents and hospitals lining the roads into the city. His unit's camp was situated on deceased Lieutenant Colonel Frank McNairy's nine-hundred-acre farm with its cedar rail fences. Mostly concerned about having black teamsters handling wagon trains for the army, Gates could not "stomach the ladies here they eat snuff and chew tobacco and smoke," but were dressed "in the nicest style." Yet, everywhere devastation dominated Federal soldiers' accounts of Middle Tennessee in early 1863. Alanson R. Rynam of the Sixty-eighth Indiana mentioned miles of burned fences surrounding Nashville and wealthy mansions worth ten and twenty thousand dollars stripped of their beautiful shade trees by ravenous horses, mules, and wood-starved soldiery. If not for the nicely painted gateposts and macadam carriage driveways, he observed, one would hardly suppose that these homes had been enclosed by fences at all. He noted one particular owner who had purposely plowed his graceful lawn to prevent the hateful Yankees from encamping anywhere near the main house. It was poor satisfaction, Rynam sneered, "but it is all they can do." Other Hoosiers felt greater remorse. Having decimated groves of cedar, quaking asps, weeping willows, poplars, and fruit trees on the last day of January, Alva C. Griest of the Seventy-second Indiana believed he "was doing wrong all the time we were at it." But he decided that such was "the effect of war, ruthless war."[1]

The country between Nashville and Murfreesboro was hit especially hard. Rynam told his wife in late March that one short letter could not do justice to the desolation. Still, most residences had escaped unless they had served as guerrilla sanctuaries. Rynam cited the case of partisan Dick McCann's place near La Vergne. The raider's destruction of a Union supply train had led to retributive obliteration of this ringleader's farm. The secesh had found that war was a "very expensive luxury," and it was sure to ruin somebody, Rynam contended. The worst thing was that the innocent had to suffer along with the guilty. And suffer they did that winter and spring, despite the fact that a year earlier most of the young Federal invaders had been enamored with the lush region.[2]

Franklin was "a very nice town," replete with a female college and pleasant grounds, several churches, a courthouse, and "in time of peace, a thriving little city," noted Sergeant Frederick Nathan Boyer of the Fifty-ninth Illinois, soon to secure his lieutenancy. He even found an old family friend named Shy living in the area, who, together with a neighbor and his lovely granddaughter, were supposedly confirmed unionists and willing to socialize with the newcomers. They, like others, may have been what Griest termed tories ("those who call themselves Union and yet favor the Rebels"). True, the soldiers noted that the college yard had been "very much destroyed by the Rebel Cavalry having camped in it," and the longer they remained in the neighborhood, the certainty of greater property damage by both armies. Alfred C. Willett's 113th Ohio had made short work of garden fences for firewood when it had arrived in late February, and Zeboim Carter Patten of the 115th Illinois noted in his diary on February 22 that ever since the boys got to Tennessee, they felt "they had free license to take whatever they wanted." America had escaped this kind of ruin in the past. Now, as the armies of William S. Rosecrans and Braxton Bragg vied with each other for control of the region, the civilian populace felt the full fury of civil war. War in the upper heartland by 1863 embraced two societies—one civilian and the other military—with their forced cohabitation.[3]

LIGHTS AND SHADOWS OF WINTER ENCAMPMENT

Murfreesboro became a fortified town, a forward supply dump for the Army of the Cumberland. Having seen heavy fortifications at Fort Donelson and Bowling Green, observed James H. Jones of the Fifty-seventh Indiana on April Fool's Day, "they are small works by [comparison]." Fortress Rosecrans, just north of town, commanded the area with heavy cannon and shellproof magazines as well as personnel shelters. The town itself had lost fully one-third of its prewar population of fifteen hundred people. Comparing the place to a cardinal amid the drabber fowl of the air, Jones declared, "the red bird has now lost her feathers." Wheeled vehicles, marching men, and the hooves of horses and mules had chewed up town streets, accustomed to the lighter tread of upper-class carriages. Everyone moved at a rush, along sidewalks brimming with crates, barrels, and other military paraphernalia. Like Nashville, splendid properties now resembled brickyards, with the old stubs and shrubs that may be seen in "some old dedning [deadening]," observed Jones. Like at Franklin, every stick had been converted to stockades or consigned to ashes.[4]

Military authorities spared no structure at Murfreesboro in their search for suitable hospital, supply, or administrative facilities. They even erected bakeries to provide soft bread occasionally, noted William B. Miller of the Seventy-fifth

Indiana, illustrating the army's wide range of support facilities. Every eminence brimmed with a fortification, and even the elevated Rutherford County courthouse was ringed with artillery like the state capitol at Nashville. The courthouse also became a signal station. Some of the soldiers expressed concern for the plight of local inhabitants; others, like Miller, kept their distance. He considered the populace here as "doeless" as everyone else in the south, dependent upon their slaves, and "lazy and ignorant." The chronicler of the German-American Ninth Ohio observed quietly that president Lincoln's Emancipation Proclamation, issued New Year's Day, had ruled out compromise and had complicated matters considerably.[5]

Indeed, matters were very complicated for the two societies living together. Nothing better illustrated that point than the situation of the Carter family at Franklin. This was the very family whose property would become the center of a firestorm at the zenith of the battle of Franklin eighteen months later. With three sons away in Confederate service, family patriarch Fountain Branch Carter had only watched helplessly as the first Yankees filed through town en route to Shiloh the year before. A few abusive comments from the townsfolk went with them, but after Stones River the Yankees were back in force and there to stay. These new Yankees built Fort Granger, north of the Harpeth River, to control the highway and railroad bridges, and they cleared fields of fire by stripping timber from Carter land all the way from the river to his house, about two miles to the south. On the other hand, Ralsa Rice claimed that his company of the Twenty-fifth Ohio helped the family gin its cotton.[6]

Notwithstanding Rice's comment, the sixty-eight-year-old Carter would claim in 1865 that Union soldiers had destroyed over 2,000 board feet of timber, and, all told, damages to livestock and property at their hands would reach $20,000 by war's end. Only a quarter of that figure actually came from the battle-related destruction of 1864. Family members eventually got only $335 in restitution from an unimpressed Federal government, and they received this money only long after Carter's death in 1871. If Rice was correct, Carter ostensibly secured other benefits from his enemies in 1863; whether or not the cotton ginned by Ohio soldiers was actually sold for Carter's profit or merely confiscated by the government is unclear. What is clear is that one of Carter's sons, Tod, a war correspondent for the Chattanooga *Daily Rebel* who wrote under the name "Mint Julep," regaled his readers with lurid tales of dastardly deeds of "the abolitionists," gleaned from "conversations with several intelligent and creditable gentlemen from Williamson County," his homeplace.[7]

While Tod Carter rendered blistering accounts of pillage, destruction, and rapine, Union officers proclaimed adamantly that the people "shall not raise another crop." Calling for retributive justice, Carter declared that when the men of the country were torn from their homes to fight for the Confederate government, then that government should take some retaliatory steps to protect helpless families from the hands of "the incendiary and the ravisher." Was Carter's account true or merely impassioned propaganda? Certainly Rynam wrote his wife back home in Indiana that they lived well on the rich rebels in the vicinity of

Franklin, liberating chickens, hogs, and other livestock by the droves, despite their general's posting guards to protect against such pilferage. Since this town was reputedly the first to raise the flag of treason in the state, Rynam wanted to wipe out all such places. He hoped that she would not think him too hard on the secesh, but "I started out to do them all the harm I could and intend to do so." Ironically, it was young Carter who would fall mortally wounded within sight of his father's house in the following year's terrible battle. Here were two incompatible societies, military and civilian, thrown together by the exigencies of war.[8]

In the winter and spring of 1863, the tent and hut cities of both armies in Middle Tennessee epitomized military societies hibernating for the winter. The monotony of drill and inspection, fatigue and picket duty, skirmishes with lice and fleas, bouts with laziness and drunkenness (getting "cornerd," as one Illinois soldier put it), trying to keep camps clean, and battling "abominable Tennessee mud" often proved more daunting than the enemy for both sides. The Ninth Ohio actually welcomed brigade drills since "unproductive reconnaissance was especially disappointing when foraging was not included." Members of Company A, however, set up a woodworking shop in a rural cottage near Triune, crafted chessmen ("turned and finished beautifully"), and enjoyed brisk sales. This same enterprising regiment of music-loving German Americans recruited a regimental band from home, and their officers made up the difference in pay between that of the common soldiers and the musicians.[9]

Alanson Rynam regaled his wife in mid-March about beautiful spring days, and he thought it seemed more like some huge picnic to see so many cooking fires, small groups playing quoits, jumping, wrestling, and cavorting about. When the frolicking got out of hand, discipline could be the result. Still, physical abuse or drumming out of the regiment was reserved only for extreme cases. Every rumor of success or failure in Virginia or before Vicksburg rippled through camp, while Tighlman Jones of the Fifty-ninth Illinois commented: "We enjoy the works of various authors, take the papers, talk politics, advising each other about Old Abe's black foot pads," referring derisively to the emancipated slaves. Jones and his mates concluded "to let him do as he pleases as we can't hinder him."[10]

Everyone grew restive as the months passed. Henry Vincent of Battery D, First Ohio Light Artillery, wrote his hometown sweetheart in early May about the pretty girls of Nashville, who, while not liking Yankee officers, still flirted "with a good looking coat and shoulder straps." They particularly delighted in handing flowers to rebel prisoners, squads of whom were brought in every day, he claimed. These men were "the greasiest, dirtiest set of cutthroats that ever went unhung," and the female secesh sympathizers bowed and smiled at the traitors most sweetly when they thought the Federal officers were watching. Vincent felt that the order for all Confederate sympathizers to take the hated oath of allegiance to the Union within ten days would "put a stop to all this."[11]

Future American president Benjamin Harrison and his Seventieth Indiana squirmed at the "sheer madness" of trying to keep the Louisville and Nashville Railroad protected on what he called "the least honorable of any duty." He devoted much of his time to brigade-school training and background study in preparation for what he considered more pivotal to a soldier—the day of battle. Not all of his brother officers agreed with such diligence, however. Major James A. Connolly of the 123d Illinois found more pleasurable the George Washington's Birthday celebration in Nashville with its speeches by fiery preacher William G. Brownlow of East Tennessee, former New York senator Daniel S. Dickinson, Kentucky brigadier Green Clay Smith, and others. The stirring refrains of the "Star Spangled Banner" as sung by a Nashville glee club prompted him to write home: "if we could whip traitors as easily as we can sing songs and pass resolutions, what a glorious thing it would be." He felt very proud to be a member of the United States army, he said. Ironically, this was the very celebration scoffed at by Edgefield civilian Harriet Ellen Moore and her father.[12]

Military parades for the general officers often provided relief from these winter encampments. The "plain, strait" William Stark Rosecrans was very popular with his men because he had a word for every one of his boys and liked to talk with them. Still, Hoosier William B. Miller suggested that one such gala for corps commander George Henry Thomas, division chief Joseph J. Reynolds, and brigade leader John Wilder was a nice show "but I got tired of marching" (a sentiment echoed by one of Van Dorn's cavalry during a Confederate grand review at Spring Hill on April 8). Miller also concluded that his unit could make more fuss over a few hours of duty than they would a day's work at home. He believed that some of his comrades had come to Tennessee only to lay about, not realizing they were paid by the government to work. Most of the men derived more pleasure from cards, ball playing, Sunday preaching, and visiting friends and relatives in nearby regiments, and especially mail call. But Lieutenant Jesse B. Connelly of the Thirty-first Indiana happily recounted that the hard work had paid off.[13]

Connelly's camp was laid out systematically, with streets brushed clean, and shrubbery out in front of each row of tents. Some thought that scene had the appearance of a "palatial country seat [rather] than a military encampment." Tighlman Jones concurred, describing camp grounds that were "swept clean and the temporary cedars look as fresh and green as if they were still part of the parent tree." The men enjoyed the best of health, with plenty to eat and wear, he concluded. Still, death and disease surrounded them, and Hoosier Joseph Vanmeter observed from Murfreesboro on April 6 that the average of sixty deaths per week was carrying off the men "pretty fast." Spring warmth and the smell of fresh vegetation and overturned earth restored health and spirits. Some of the men, like Rynam, vowed to return after the war and seek their fortunes on Middle Tennessee farmland.[14]

If one thing incensed the Union soldiers, it was reports of malingering and "copperhead" traitorism at home. The encouragement these people received from northern Democrats helped prolong the war, suggested William B. Miller in April. Rynam agreed, telling his wife that if the copperheads were not allowed to kick up a fuss, then the war would soon end, but even if they did, "I for one want to go home to clean them out." Corporal Frederick Pettit with the One-hundredth Pennsylvania at Middleburg, Kentucky, quite agreed. There was no mistaking the army's loyalty, Rynam claimed, as there was no difference in loyalty between soldiers who had been Democrats and Republicans; indeed, there was not much difference between them on any question concerning the war. Procurement from the rebellious populace of the South could support the army for a few months, and by then "a United North would crush the monster in a short time." Exiled Ohio copperhead congressman Clement Vallandigham passed through the lines later that spring. Shunned by the men in blue, he was feted by a few Confederate generals, like Williams S. Hardee and Leonidus Polk. Officially, the Lincoln government welcomed his departure; that of Jefferson Davis tolerated his transit through the Confederacy.[15]

The Union soldiers viewed with interest the government's Enrollment Act of March 3, 1863, which promised to conscript every white male age eighteen to forty-five (unless unfit or entitled to an exemption). One Ohioan felt that it was "certainly not a sign of a speedy termination of the war!" More pleasing, to the Buckeyes at least, was a law passed in their state that made absentee soldier balloting possible since, as that same Ohioan declared, "a blow with the ballot was not less important than a stroke of the sword." In late March, Rosecrans promulgated a general order that created light battalions and rolls of honor of "the elite of the army" to be used for important and dangerous missions. To belong was "a post of credit and esteem" and promised veterans promotions to the noncommissioned officer corps as well as encouraging them to wear a red ribbon as symbol of the honor. Short-lived as it was (the War Department objected to organizing light battalions from the rolls of honor), Rosecrans saw this device as a way to record and reward the best soldiers of all ranks in an army corps and "to promote the efficiency of the service." In reality, it was more a device to counter rebel raiders and guerrillas in the absence of any increase in the Army of the Cumberland's cavalry arm. Still, it did build esprit for a soldiery experiencing many doubts about home front support and loyalty.[16]

On March 10, Lincoln issued a presidential proclamation of amnesty for any returning deserter. Many had wanted to return before, declared the chronicler of the Ninth Ohio, but could not reach their units without a pass. Some had accordingly enlisted in other commands, so anxious were they to again display their patriotism. Indeed, younger soldiers on both sides once more professed great readiness for battle. Memories of Stones River tempered such enthusiasm among wiser heads. Older hands looked to armies elsewhere to complete the work of vanquishing the foe and ending the war. The operations of the Army of the Potomac in Virginia provided the all-absorbing topic, since the fate of the Confederacy would be decided by the results of those movements, pronounced Lieutenant Connelly.[17]

Confiscation of goods, particularly horses, reached a crescendo by spring as Rosecrans's officers sought to mount more infantry and improve the cavalry arm. Jesse Cox, a seventy-year-old farmer and preacher living near Franklin, repeatedly recounted from January through June how Yankee foraging parties and horse-stealing groups had ravaged his place. This unrepentant rebel stood up to them and called them rogues, often coming under threat of bodily harm for his impertinence. A local scion and wounded captive, William B. Gordon, wrote home from a Federal hospital later in July that he was sorry to hear that "the feds took all of the Negro men and horses, including old buggy horses, but suggested there is one consolation; they are too old to do them any good." This argument impressed few Federals, however, as one young officer sardonically told a Tennessee plantation mistress: "Madam, we have not seen or heard of a *young* horse since we started out."[18]

Local secessionists decided that this was all a ploy to keep citizens from raising crops "for fear the Confederates will finally reap the benefits." Twenty-year-old Edgefield native Harriet Ellen Moore thought that "many persons in the midst of gardening and farming operations are left without a single or perhaps one horse to make their food for the coming year." As she watched one Federal officer (apparently a family acquaintance from before the war) supervise destruction of the lovely timber around the family property, she suggested that this was one of the characteristics of the Yankees—"they enter without form or ceremony." Foraging and such devastation that had developed from need when Confederates blockaded supply routes in and out of the Nashville region increasingly became standard operating procedure for Union soldiers. Jesse Cox bewailed that "it seems that the Yankees will take every thing that I have got," as he prayed that God would give grace and strength "to bear it with sufficient fortitude and resignation." Matters got so bad on Colonel James Moore King's wealthy plantation near Murfreesboro that this War of 1812 veteran simply left and took up arms with the Confederacy. King was a slaveholder, but also a prewar Whig and was originally an opponent of secession. Federal harassment and spoliation settled his allegiance for all time. Tales of Yankee depredations became part of family lore for generations.[19]

Aside from the irritation and inhumanity of it all, the sight of vast Federal foraging parties of two hundred wagons or more—accompanied by foot and mounted escorts—surely displayed the power of the national government to these besieged southern civilians. The army was stripping this country of everything, James Henry Jones of the Fifty-seventh Indiana jotted in his diary. The boys, noted both Jones and Frederick Boyer, liked to ransack sawmills and feed mills, in particular, tearing structures down to the rafters in pure mischief. Robbing local barnyards, corn cribs, and cold cellars of contents also gave great pleasure. Amos C. Weaver wrote home on March 6 that he had a slight touch of dysentery from eating too much fresh ham, but he reveled in it, claiming that seven hundred wagons had gone out and been loaded twice with secessionist corn. "This is taking corn on a large scale," he said gleefully. After a particularly successful raid on McMinnville and other hitherto Confederate controlled areas, Rynam told his wife in early May that they had taken all they could from the secesh, in some cases leaving "them almost destitute." Confessing that he did not "fancy this style of warfare," as in some instances it left families with small children to suffer and "for my part I am too merciful to do it, but if I come across a rich old slave owner then I can." He added that his group had discovered a poor, starving family in a log house, with children clad only in sack cloth that hardly covered their nakedness. He pointed out that his unit had given them something to eat and had placed a guard around their house to keep them from being harassed by thoughtless soldiers.[20]

Frankly, the boys in blue quickly grew cynical about some of the small Tennessee towns they visited on these foraging trips. Alva C. Griest noted on March 4 that they had passed through tiny Reedyville, but strained to see anything more "than a dilapidated old blacksmith shop, and a barn," although perhaps the town was "hid behind a stump some place, so that I could not see." These first expeditionary hikes of the season usually left roadways strewn for miles with castoff blankets, overcoats, and other heavy gear. The Ninety-second Illinois chaplain did his good deed for the regiment by retrieving such flotsam and returning it to camp. His packhorse resembled a traveling pawnshop; his reward for those yet-chilly nights was "gratitude that was visible on every face." Chaplain W. W. Lyle of the Eleventh Ohio suggested that the winter encampment at Carthage had little of note about it except an occasional rumor of a large attacking force on its way to attack the post, which would give "some little variety and zest to camp conversation." Rebel Dunbar Affleck, stationed with Terry's Texas Rangers at Fairfield, Tennessee, wrote home gleefully that whole Yankee regiments "are deserting every day," but that was wishful thinking. Overall, Rosecrans's men were simply building confidence while scavenging the neighborhood before the opening of the campaign season.[21]

Southern soldiers, like Colonel Arthur Manigault's South Carolinians, never had sufficient clothing, so they particularly welcomed the warming rays of spring. Some Tennessee cavalrymen, like Sergeant Newton Cannon, could slip home to farms located between the armies and get fresh clothing and revive their spirits. Similarly, Van Dorn's Texas cavalrymen foraged around Spring Hill, declaring that "the best folks in the world live here in Tennessee," as they were often plied even with warm beds and liquor to relieve the monotony of picket duty. But most of the rebels suffered through the snows and damp of a Tennessee winter, enjoyed occasional rabbit hunts, band concerts, amateur theater performances, and a profound religious revival that swept through their Army of Tennessee. Affleck, a Texas Ranger, noted on one occasion that a large ball took place near Wartrace, but only for officers, and that, except for corn meal and bacon, the enlisted men "have to give in the country for extras" like chicken at one dollar each, eggs fifty cents each, butter seventy-five cents a pound, and turkeys two-and-half dollars each. "We have to buy them or our camp fair [sic] will make us sick," he declared. Affleck thought he could stand it through the war, "then my turn will [be] one for some good living." By April, he and his comrades were also ready for a new season, a new campaign, and new adventures.[22]

Willie Presley wrote his wife back in Prattville, Alabama, on March 11 from a camp at Middletown in Bedford County, Tennessee, not to expect to see him very soon, as Bragg had canceled all furloughs until July "unless Yanks happened to shoot me and cripple me then I might get off home." Nearby skirmishes had netted some prisoners, and Union soldiers, singly and in pairs, seemed willing to desert, claiming "they are not fighting for what they volunteered to fight for . . . they say they will not fight any longer to free the negroes." The Yanks were "getting very tired of the war," in his opinion. But young Willie was far more concerned with conditions at home; after learning that his wife had lost both sows, he advised that raising four or five hogs every year "would be of great help to you for if this war lasts it will be almost impossible to buy pork at any price and molassas will be very scarce and hard to get as long as the Yanks have such a strong hold in Louisiana and hold New Orleans."[23]

South Carolinian Isaac Alexander wrote his sisters from Shelbyville on April 18 that everything was being put in readiness for the great struggle "which cannot be far distant." He thought that "this will be the Theater of war," not Virginia or Mississippi. As the southern host stretched from their winter somnolence, much stock taking occurred. Many of the men deplored the carping criticism of Bragg by "editors, civilians, and those who do not face the enemy." They worried about the undercurrent of dissent among senior generals like Polk, Hardee, Simon Bolivar Buckner, and others. Brigadier General St. John Richardson Liddell was also numbered among the intriguers (when he was not enjoying the warm hospitality of hosts Colonel Andrew Erwin and his wife near Wartrace). At least Liddell's men gainfully helped local Bell Buckle farmers harvest winter wheat and rye and plant the corn. But Alexander thought Bragg was a much-abused individual, despite his heavy-handed discipline and other odd traits. The commander had outgeneraled Buell in Kentucky and saved his army, said Alexander, a distinct slap at Albert Sidney Johnston's mishandling of affairs in the winter of 1862. Furthermore, thought the young South Carolinian, the present theater commander, Joseph E. Johnston, had pronounced Bragg and his army to be a solid fighting force and supported his leadership. Still, these troubling undercurrents coursed Confederate ranks as they welcomed the redbud and dogwood of spring in Tennessee.[24]

The lights and shadows of army life that winter reflected two societies in contest for subsistence and survival. For soldiers, it was a battle against the vagaries of weather and the yearning for home tempered by a patriotic call. Soldiers also wondered about the uncertainty of the future; a future that promised battle and death, but did not promise where their next meal might come from. For civilians, future uncertainty was just as real, only the battles were more personal in nature. Could Tennesseans (or for that matter Kentuckians) endure and survive the presence of oppressive, insatiable hordes of foragers in their midst? Only on occasion could local citizens share the spectacle of Forrest and Van Dorn; on April 8, for instance, they paraded their six thousand horsemen in review at Spring Hill. More often, however, civilians were concerned with safeguarding corn cribs, cattle pens, and their daughters, who attracted the eyes of rascally rebels bent upon mischief.[25]

COMBAT MINUETS BETWEEN BLUE AND GRAY

This is not to say that the late winter and early spring lacked for activity between blue and gray. Official reports, dispatches, and soldier writings all convey a

Guerrillas destroying a train near Nashville. From Fitch, Annals of the Army of the Cumberland *(Philadelphia: J. B. Lippincott, 1864), 674.*

mottled picture of combat activities during the first six months of 1863. In contrast to stagnant encampments were the almost continuous skirmishes attending foraging and reconnaissance activities. Historian Douglas Hale has likened the period's activity to that of boxers, stalking each other warily, jabbing, feinting, and parrying, or pummeling each other "until one adversary or the other backed off to gather strength, await a point of vantage, and begin probing the opponent's defenses all over again."[26]

In a typical case, Colonel Sanders D. Bruce reported from Clarksville in late May that his men had returned from a three-day scouting mission with eight prisoners. They had destroyed three flatboats and all was now quiet on the Cumberland. The rebels (or someone else) had "destroyed a small trestle on the railroad, ten miles from here, last night." As Brigadier General John Beatty, one of Rosecrans's brigade commanders put it, only "slight affairs occur, which are magnified into serious engagements; but really [are] nothing of importance." He cited a February exercise of the 123d Illinois in which a reputedly fierce combat took place with large casualties and three hundred stand of arms captured. In truth, laughed Beatty, the Federals had not taken time to actually count the dead and "the arms taken were one hundred old muskets found in a house by the roadside."[27]

The war was certainly real enough, however, for those soldiers involved with bushwhacked or "guerrilled" trains along the 185-mile stretch of railroad between Louisville and Nashville, or the additional thirty miles to Murfreesboro on the

Chattanooga line, equidistant to Franklin on the Tennessee and Alabama route. The portion of the L&N between South Tunnel and Franklin, Kentucky—and four miles farther at the so-called Negro Head Cut—witnessed almost constant fighting. Increased train guards and roving patrols from Bowling Green never stopped the incursions against wood and mail trains. Blockhouses and other fortified posts only partially deflected raiders in gray and butternut. This twilight war only got nastier with the passing weeks. When members of John Hunt Morgan's force set fire to a wagon train loaded with forage near Murfreesboro in late January, "negro teamsters [were] tied to their wagons and shot and then left to burn to death." Atrocities multiplied almost daily, so let the enemy beware, warned Alva C. Griest of the Seventy-second Indiana. Although they could not retaliate in kind—"God forbid that we should wish to," Griest added—the guerrillas would one day meet with a just vengeance from the outraged Union soldiers, he penned in his diary on January 23.[28]

Yet, occasional lighter moments accompanied even counterguerrilla activity. Coming off one punitive strike in April, Hoosier William B. Miller recalled that crossing chilly Stones River into camp prompted the unit quartermaster to dole out "rot-gut" whiskey as a fillip to the men. Some of the boys took a double portion, he recounted, "and was patriotic the rest of the way to camp." They were not drunk, he stated, but wading the river "made them seasick." As historian Kenneth P. Williams later suggested, the whole period seemed comprised of these "episodic weeks and a famous raid" and nothing more. Still, the work of blue and gray soldiers, variously attired partisans, and the omnipresent black hulks of the Union navy's gunboats as well as army transports on the rivers set the tone of military operations in the period. The principal area of contention in Tennessee stood roughly between Murfreesboro, McMinnville, Columbia, and Spring Hill—a bitterly contested "no-man's land" in a way, as Bragg deployed his cavalry to shield against Federal moves. The Federals, in turn, tried to keep the rebels at a respectful distance. But this was only at the front, for all over the upper heartland, from Middle Tennessee to the Bluegrass, both sides sparred relentlessly with each other to no decisive result.[29]

Lincoln's formal emancipation proclamation of January 1 added impetus to guerrilla activities in Kentucky, even though the measure did not apply to that state. Units like Benjamin Bristow's Eighth Kentucky Cavalry continued to act in concert with other contingents, trying to purge the region of guerrillas. But intense animosity between many Kentucky Union regiments and those from states north of the Ohio concerning emancipation and runaway slaves had eased slightly since its zenith in the autumn. Many of the northern emancipationist regiments were moving to the front in Tennessee or Mississippi, and Kentucky slave owners as well were left to fume about native son Lincoln's threat to their property, but they also had to worry about continued thievery and destruction with every Confederate or guerrilla mounted raid. Victor B. Howard has indicated that the majority of the soldiers now stationed in Kentucky basically favored emancipation, if only as "an emotional response that reflected anti-Southern sentiment." They left the political issue to unionist slaveholders and their legislators in this election year. On the other hand, civil authorities and Union Kentuckians, like Colonel Marcellus Mundy, now commanding the post of Louisville, continued to badger higher military authority about the fugitive slave issue. As Mundy phrased it: "I'm ashamed to find so many officers disposed to debase the noble principle for which we are battleing [sic] and degenerate it into a mere negro freeing machine." So, on April 28, the commander of the Department of the Ohio decreed that, in the spirit of Lincoln's January proclamation, nobody could interfere with Kentuckians' recovery of their slaves, but any blacks freed by other "war measures of the government were indeed free."[30]

Elsewhere, in Middle Tennessee, it was Wheeler (with John A. Wharton) and Forrest (joined in late February by Major General Earl Van Dorn's reinforcements from Mississippi) who held the key to southern fortunes. They stood ready to rebuff Federal overtures via the rail corridors south. Forrest and Van Dorn (plus various partisan bands) anchored Bragg's left flank between Columbia and the Tennessee River; Wheeler held similar sway on Bragg's right. Hamlets from Liberty to Auburn, Rover to Triune, with Yankee-held Franklin as a convenient target, became flash points. The seemingly endless scouring of the countryside for food, forage, and intelligence of the enemy provided the pretext. The Confederates added conscription of local males to this equation, and Alanson Rynam thought that prisoners taken in a March 25 scrap near Franklin were a "hard, ragged looking set of fellows," with some of them pleased to be captured as they were conscripts with little interest in the rebel cause.[31]

Areas behind the lines north or west did not escape this activity either. Major Hans Mattson led four infantry companies of the Second Minnesota and two of the Fifteenth Kentucky Cavalry on a scouting patrol through Henry, Benton, Carroll, Weakley, and part of Decatur Counties west of the Tennessee River and on both sides of the Big Sandy River in late May. They encountered small bands of partisans (no more than fifteen on any occasion), and their success was measured by destroying two large flatboats, seven large skiffs, and six canoes, mostly at the mouth of Duck River. They captured Confederate mail and several regular as well as guerrilla officers. They found a large recruiting station and an adjacent camp of four hundred to six hundred men nearby; this force consistently sent small parties across the Tennessee River to "gather up recruits and steal horses, and otherwise annoy the loyal citizens." Similar operations in Kentucky ferreted out collaborators and spies. Such search-and-destroy operations never completely obliterated the threat, but contained its growth unless augmented by regular contingents from Wheeler or Forrest.[32]

The threat from Confederate horsemen sent greater jitters through Federal ranks at every turn. Jesse B. Connelly, for instance, was almost always "stampeded" by Morgan's imagined horsemen in his reveries, and other frightened Yankees (even some at Rosecrans's headquarters) worried constantly since Morgan's men knew every cow path and local resident in their sector. Were these southerners in Ohio and as bitterly hated by the populace as the residents of Kentucky and Tennessee despised the national troops, said Buckeye brigadier John Beatty, then "it would be an easy matter indeed to hang upon the skirts of that army, pick up stragglers, burn bridges, attack wagon trains, and now and then pounce down on an outlying picket and take it," just as the rebels were now doing. Colonel Tom Woodward and 160 of his Second Kentucky partisans might chase double their number of blueclad horsemen for miles south of Franklin in one mid-February brush, but that was merely part of a larger scheme whereby 10,000 to 15,000 Confederate cavalry, aided by wintry weather and overall supply problems, effectively kept the whole Army of the Cumberland at bay until blossom time in Middle Tennessee.[33]

Eventually, Rosecrans sent out his own infantry and cavalry teams. They left weekly from the Murfreesboro–Franklin baseline, with the result, as seventeen-year-old Bromfield Ridley of Morgan's cavalry reminisced later, that the Federals disturbed "the pleasure of our dreams." They were "sometimes raiding for forage; often trying to intercept, and then receding, at times driving us and then being driven." This cat-and-mouse game produced skirmishes at places like Bradyville, Woodbury, Eagleville, Petersburg, Bear Creek, Unionville, Rover, Spring Hill, Richland Station, College Grove, Salem, Triune, Milton, or Vaught's Hill in Tennessee and Hazel Green, Mount Sterling, Paris, and other spots in Kentucky. Colonel Roy S. Cluke's rebel Eighth Kentucky Cavalry from East Tennessee and Brigadiers Humphrey Marshall and John Pegram from southwest Virginia also kept Kentucky authorities on edge for weeks as they raided the eastern part of the state. They captured garrisons, destroyed a million dollars in property, and defied bad weather, wretched provisions, and sickness. Worst of all, they convinced Department of the Ohio generals, like Wright, Quincy Gillmore, and Wright's newly arrived successor, the ill-starred easterner Ambrose Burnside, that this might truly be the long-anticipated new invasion by Braxton Bragg. No doubt it seemed like an emergency.[34]

THE WORK OF THE WIZARDS

The actions of Cluke, Morgan, Wheeler, Forrest, and Van Dorn kept the whole Federal program off balance. These raiders were truly wizards in the saddle. Cluke, in fact, successfully roughed up the Mount Sterling section of Kentucky from mid-February until late March, preying upon local farmers and stock raisers, most of them unsympathetic to the Confederate cause. The ever-flappable Union brigadier at Louisville, Jeremiah Boyle, wired Rosecrans on February 25 that the "rebels can cross Sahara, if necessary," while Governor James F. Robinson seemed equally shaken, suggesting that "the wilting and withering effect" of Lincoln's proclamation upon unionist sentiment meant that any new invasion would receive "aid and countenance" far beyond that accorded to Smith and Bragg the previous autumn. A rather inept Gillmore at Lexington also bungled some of the countermeasures, as rumors abounded that even Morgan and Forrest were joining Marshall, Cluke, and Pegram in a major strike into the Bluegrass. Union authorities greatly inflated their numbers, calling for Rosecrans and even Grant to return seasoned troops to counter the threat. Saner heads prevailed eventually, when Wright pointed out that Cluke had barely seven to eight hundred men.[35]

Pegram's threat was slightly more formidable. But Boyle, Gillmore, and other commanders finally got their wits about them and pushed this rebel cattle raid back across the upper Cumberland River by the end of March. Colonel J. S. Scott's First Louisiana Cavalry (which had scouted for rebels on the twin rivers prior to Forts Henry and Donelson the year before) stampeded when recrossing at Somerset, after a little affair at Dutton's Hill on the thirtieth, and Pegram lost most of his booty, including several hundred of the purloined cattle. Southern leaders were embarrassed by the defeat, but Burnside also felt chagrined at his own command's timidity in countering the raiders. He asked Washington to authorize organizing twenty thousand Kentuckians for one year's service and to transfer the remainder of his own IX army corps from Virginia. Along with the two field army commanders, he was especially concerned about shielding Rosecrans's left flank and rear. General-in-Chief Henry Halleck hedged on the reinforcements and merely advised the hapless Burnside on March 23 that he might invade East Tennessee, occupy mountain passes to deter rebel incursions from that quarter, or concentrate all available troops in central Kentucky for various defensive duties. None of this advice helped Burnside very much, but then, as the Rhode Islander's latest biographer suggests, Halleck made a habit of obfuscation so that he could place blame for failure squarely on his subordinates.[36]

On the other hand, the pesky rebel raids and continuing harassment of wealthy Kentucky farmers may have actually helped the Federal cause in the Bluegrass. Frederick Pettit, one of Burnside's newly arrived easterners in the IX corps, felt that the vast majority of Kentuckians now stood square for the Union. The citizens encountered by Pettit's One-hundredth Pennsylvania around Lexington were very friendly and courteous, he wrote home. "They have a warm side for Pennsylvania" but did not like New Yorkers, Michigan soldiers, "and Yankees." In mid-April he reported that Kentuckians around Camp Dick Robinson hailed his unit "as the defenders of their homes," having suffered for their loyalty at the hands of the Confederates. But he admitted that were many soldiers in Union blue "who disregard all law and plunder the property of friend and foe alike" and are "a great nuisance in the army."[37]

The Kentucky situation, of course, did not compare with Rosecrans's difficulties because of Forrest and Van Dorn. The arrogant, West Point trained Van Dorn and his rough-hewn Tennessee subordinate Forrest badly mauled and captured most of Colonel John F. Coburn's small reconnaissance force at Thompson's Station on the Tennessee and Alabama Railroad south of Franklin in early March. The seesaw contest was witnessed by the hamlet's female population, who alternated loud cheers with wailing when the rebels advanced or retired under stubborn Yankee fire. Only two Federal regiments ultimately escaped, while the bulk of the prisoners suffered a grueling fifty-three-mile march to Shelbyville with nothing to eat but raw meat and spoilt crackers, according to Samuel Coble of the Eighty-fifth Indiana. Apparently such privation left no permanent mark on some prisoners; Lieutenant William R. Shafter gained notoriety years later as the three-hundred-pound commander of the American expeditionary force battling Spaniards in Cuba. Ironically, that 1898 campaign would find the old Union nemesis in Middle Tennessee, "Fighting Joe" Wheeler, back in national blue. He accidentally enjoined his U.S. troops attacking Spanish positions to charge "the damned Yankees."[38]

Forrest's men soon discovered another such prize among Rosecrans's Middle Tennessee supply facilities. A large concentration of mules at Nashville and a stockaded supply dump at Brentwood (where highway and railroad passed through the Overton Hills between the capital and Franklin) beckoned to his troopers. A nearby railroad bridge over the Little Harpeth River also looked inviting. Van Dorn, Forrest's superior, ruled out the mule raid, but Brentwood was too good to pass up. Forrest and Colonel Jake Starnes struck this cache on the morning of March 25, capturing Lieutenant Colonel Edward Bloodgood's garrison without resistance. They soon duplicated this feat at the railroad bridge, taking 740 more prisoners. Green Clay Smith's mounted Kentuckians later caught portions of the rebel rear guard at supper and netted thirty-three captives of their own. But Thompson's Station and Brentwood demonstrated what Union brigadier John Beatty recorded disgustedly in his diary: "The rebels succeed admirably in gathering up and consolidating our scattered troops." Indeed, they did, as upwards of 2,500 more Yankees were paroled or marched off to prison camps as a result of these Confederate achievements.[39]

Van Dorn and Wheeler received division commands in reward for their winter and spring services. The brigades of Wharton, Morgan, and James Hagen went to Wheeler; Van Dorn acquired those of George B. Crosby, Frank C. Armstrong, and J. W. Whitfield. But Van Dorn and Forrest nearly came to blows over the Mississippian's misperception that Forrest sought only newspaper headlines and glory. The thin-skinned Van Dorn apologized, but the Army of Tennessee was not big enough for both of these officers. Forrest was too freewheeling and testy to work under West Pointers like Wheeler, Van Dorn, and Bragg. He and Van Dorn continued to operate from the Spring Hill neighborhood like two male dogs, wary of each other and jealous of the other's prerogatives. Command and personality difficulties bedeviled the principal western Confederate army at all levels.[40]

An embarrassed but now thoroughly alert Federal command slowly increased the capabilities of its own cavalry under leaders like Major General David B. Stanley, Colonel Robert H. G. Minty, Major L. S. Scranton, and others. More men and horses, better equipment, greater experience as a fighting force eventually led to improved balance between Union and Confederate mounted arms. While "the common verdict" among some rebels was that foes like Kentucky amateur Green Clay Smith "displayed little stomach for fight," they gradually lost ground to blueclad veterans in standup contests. Static garrison troops might crumble before the Confederate wizards, but not so the front-line units. And the Federals particularly concentrated upon destroying John Hunt Morgan's command.[41]

The Kentucky cavalier certainly came out second-best at Milton, or Vaught's Hill, northeast of Murfreesboro on March 21. Clashing head-on with a well-posted infantry brigade under Colonel Albert S. Hall, Morgan lost almost one-third of his force. Running out of ammunition may have saved the Kentucky cavalier further discomfort, inasmuch as Minty's riders arrived to help the embattled Union infantry just in time. "This was a hard fought fight," reminisced Bowling Green lawyer turned rebel captain John M. Porter, "and I dare say every man of Morgan's command who took part in that battle at Milton will remember it as long as he lives." The defeat surprised observers on both sides, increasing southern suspicions that Morgan's fighting abilities had somehow waned (Samson-like) in the wake of his Yuletide marriage to Mattie Ready. A more cynical Beatty still thought that reporters probably contributed to the "brilliancy of this affair," for it was always safe "to accept with distrust all reports which affirm that a few men, with little loss, rout, slaughtered, or captured a large force." But others, like William B. Miller of the Seventy-fifth Indiana, believed that Morgan tried to play the same game he had at Hartsville and found the Federals wide awake this time and did not "want them as bad as he thought he did."[42]

Rosecrans's men had an additional opportunity to pick at Morgan's reputation on April 3. They routed the Confederates from a strong defensive position at Snow Hill near Liberty in DeKalb County. Defense was not Morgan's style anyway. Yet, several weeks later, Major General Joseph J. Reynolds, anxious to avenge missed opportunities to corner Morgan during the Christmas raid, penetrated Morgan's McMinnville lair with 6,600 infantry, cavalry, and artillery. He nearly caught both Morgan and Mattie, and thought for a while that he had actually done so. The "noted guerrilla" Dick McCann briefly fell into the attackers' hands also, leading John Samuel Henry of the Thirty-seventh Indiana to conclude that "it is generally believed that they hung him—he had shot and hung so many Tennesseans and they would only be doing God's service in stretching such a one's neck." However, these celebrities escaped, and Reynolds's men contented themselves with 380 other prisoners, ripping up railroad track toward Manchester, destroying a cotton factory and other mills in the area, and confiscating 200 bales of cotton, 30,000 pounds of bacon, as well as large quantities of sugar, rice, whiskey, and other goods. Alanson Rynam, for one, relished the cotton factory's demise since the rebels had used it to make "their everlasting butternut cloth." While he was unhappy that Morgan had escaped, Reynolds still claimed that this district had been cleared of all forage and subsistence useful to the enemy.[43]

Wheeler wisely withdrew Morgan's demoralized command and sent it northward into Wayne County, Kentucky, for recuperation. The raiders returned on April 26, refreshed and strengthened to some twenty-eight hundred troopers. Before long, their commander (prompted by a desire for redemption) again chafed for one of his freewheeling jaunts toward the Ohio at the expense of Yankee reserves. Meanwhile, Wheeler found personal time to pen a cavalry tactics manual and propose a deep strike against Louisville. For the moment, Bragg's headquarters kept him focused on raiding the railroad closer to Nashville. His capture of a troop train at Antioch station on April 10, like Forrest's Brentwood success, sent shock waves through the state capital. Meanwhile, off to the southwest by a few miles, Van Dorn attempted his own ploy, pushing forward the outer Confederate defense perimeter to the Harpeth River. This time, however, Confederate arms were unsuccessful.[44]

Van Dorn chose the same day as the Antioch strike to pitch into Major General Gordon Granger's eight thousand men at Franklin. Bragg, hearing rumors that the Federals had evacuated this pivotal town, dispatched Van Dorn's force of some thirty-seven hundred troopers to reconnoiter the situation. They were not enough to overwhelm a defending force supported by fortress artillery, and certainly not inclined to withdraw as Granger was looking to avenge Thompsons Station and Brentwood. Advancing boldly, even rashly, Van Dorn's men were beaten back from an attempted crossing. Stanley's blueclad horsemen splashed across the Harpeth east of town and threatened the rebel flank until they were stymied in turn by sharp fighting. Forrest's favorite battery commander, young Captain S. L. Freeman, was cut down (murdered after he had surrendered, claimed his comrades), and his guns were lost when riders of the Fourth U.S. regulars struck his column before they had taken position. "This fruitless affair," as two of Forrest's biographers later termed it, ended with the cannon retaken, the Federal counterattack rebuffed, and Van Dorn retiring back to Spring Hill, sobered by the fact that the northerners were too strong for any permanent southern lodgement at Franklin.[45]

Freeman's mates mourned their leader's death—he was "a brave and gallant officer," dutiful and dedicated, trained in the law, and supposedly being groomed to become Forrest's artillery chief. They would return with Forrest on June 4 to assault Colonel J. P. Baird's Eighty-fifth Indiana, which had been left to garrison the town. Once more, Fort Granger's guns north of the river and Granger's dispatch of reinforcements from Triune stopped the attackers. Meanwhile, at some point that spring, Van Dorn became involved in a tryst with a local Spring Hill doctor's wife. The physician shot him dead on May 7, and Forrest took charge in his place, pending Bragg's general cavalry reorganization. As for Federal reaction to the steady round of action, Alfred C. Willett of the 113th Ohio wrote his sweetheart after the Franklin affair, "we are fortifying here all the time."[46]

YANKEE COUNTER RAIDS

At some point, Federal authorities in the heartland realized that they too could mount cavalry raids in the rebel rear areas. First, there had been the daring early winter foray by Brigadier General Samuel P. Carter, nominally a naval officer from East Tennessee, who led a strike force from Kentucky into his home neighborhood over the New Year's week. The 470-mile round trip (authorized by Department of the Ohio commander Major General Horatio Wright) left 10 miles of destroyed railroad, thus breaking the vital Confederate link between Tennessee and Virginia, wrecked bridges across the Holston and Watauga Rivers, and ruined large quantities of military goods, including telegraph equipment, rolling stock, food, and weapons. Some 400 prisoners were taken—many of them North Carolina conscripts averse to Confederate service in the first place. Rebel officers complained that the Yankees had stolen every horse in upper East Tennessee. Military engineers estimated that Carter's men had inflicted $50,000 worth of damages in scarcely 24 hours. East Tennessee unionists were encouraged to bushwhack rebels on their own. Halleck enthusiastically drew everyone's attention to Carter's "daring operations and brilliant achievements," which were "without parallel in the history of war." At any rate, historian William Piston thinks that Carter's raid most certainly caused Rosecrans to "draw inspiration" for a raid of his own.[47]

Civil War cavalry student Stephen Starr termed Carter's strike "the first long-distance raid staged by the Union cavalry." Carter also thought that his success sparked "a new spirit of enterprise" in the blue horsemen generally, which soon led to counterpoise for the rebel activities of Cluke, Pegram, and lesser-known Captain P. M. Everett in the region. In June 1863, Colonel William P. Sanders would lead fifteen hundred cavalrymen on a ten-day jaunt that destroyed three long railroad bridges, a saltpeter works, as well as large quantities of supplies. Three cannon, two hundred boxes of artillery ammunition, and over five hundred prisoners likewise fell into Federal hands. But, frankly, neither Carter nor Sanders—no more than Confederate cavalry wizards—caused permanent damage, even though their intent was pure destruction of facilities useful to the opposing military. This stood in contrast to the summer moves north of the Ohio River by Confederate captain Thomas Hines and those of the fabled Morgan, where the intent was more political although no less destructive.[48]

Certainly all of these raids proved disruptive to respective army operations. But Union strikes increasingly reflected government intent to destroy rebel property, raise unionist spirits in an affected area, and disperse or destroy southern military units encountered in the particular operation. Union authorities determined to work directly upon Bragg's own line of communications or Lieutenant General John C. Pemberton's northern Mississippi supply base. Colonel F. M. Cornyn's cavalry from Major General Stephen A. Hurlbut's XVI corps area in West Tennessee additionally struck into north Alabama, seeking manufacturing facilities in that sector. Indeed, Confederate rear echelons were stretched thin to counter Cornyn's moves, although Brigadier General James R. Chalmer's 1,200 to 1,500 regular Confederate horsemen and Colonel R. V. Richardson's partisans, in turn, were sent to threaten Memphis in this tit-for-tat shadow-boxing game.[49]

For a while, at least, the Confederates outplayed both Rosecrans and Ulysses S. Grant at this game. Fear of the vaunted rebel horsemen tied down over 60,000 rear area Federals as well as 130 heavy and 121 field guns in Grant's sector alone. Protection for Corinth and Memphis districts, as well as separate posts like Paducah, Clinton, and Hickman in Kentucky, or Fort Pillow and Island Number 10 in Tennessee, pinioned blueclad forces in place. A separate cavalry division of 3,873 officers and men operated out of Memphis solely against West Tennessee partisans. Colonel Chauncey W. Griggs had the Eleventh Illinois, Third Minnesota, and two companies of the Fifteenth Kentucky Cavalry tied to Fort Heiman, while the Dover/Fort Donelson garrison provided more emergency reserves in that sector. While the numbers seemed out of proportion to the partisan threat, generals like Hurlbut, Samuel Asboth, and others always worried about more serious raiders. So, under the guise of maintaining control over local populations in West Tennessee and the Purchase section of Kentucky, these subordinates thwarted Grant's repeated directives to move manpower forward for the Vicksburg operation or ravaging northern Mississippi in turn.[50]

Confederate officials were just as torn between countering the main Union armies and launching their own raids at the enemy's rear. Colonel George C. Dibrell's reliable Eighth and Thirteenth Tennessee Cavalry contained Cornyn near Florence, Alabama, but Pemberton and Bragg clashed over returning Van Dorn's troops to bolster northern tier defense along the Alabama and Mississippi line with Tennessee. On April 11, theater commander General Joseph E. Johnston warned that "should Grant's army join Rosecrans," then Pemberton might have to "cross the Tennessee near Muscle Shoals to move into Northern Mississippi and West Tennessee" in a massive raid that foretold John Bell Hood's ill-advised move in the autumn of 1864. Of course, Johnston misread Grant's preoccupation with the line of the Mississippi. But such misreading, in turn, kept the Confederates themselves off balance. Meanwhile, southern newsmen excoriated "the notorious ruffian" Cornyn for his "ruthless, inexcusable works of desolation." They failed to realize not only that their own partisans cause similar havoc, but also that the "flames of burning fences, granaries, meat houses, stables, and mansions that for years had been the scenes of a boundless hospitality and domestic comfort" were now identified by at least some of Lincoln's generals as the very infrastructure of rebellion, hence fair game for destruction.[51]

The Federals launched their most serious mounted raids in April 1863. One was the highly successful and sensationalized expedition of Colonel Benjamin H. Grierson across the length of Mississippi, which was memorialized by Hollywood actors John Wayne and William Holden in the 1959 movie classic, *The Horse Soldiers*. The second, just as spectacularly *unsuccessful* raid was that of Colonel Abel D. Streight, which aimed at interrupting Bragg's supply line north of Atlanta and destroying manufacturing and warehouse facilities at Rome in north Georgia. Streight, the energetic and courageous commander of the Fifty-first Indiana Infantry, had wanted for over a year to return to unionist Alabama hill country. Now he intended to run some nineteen hundred mule- and horse-borne midwesterners and two unionist Tennessee cavalry companies (actually recruited in those Alabama hills) circuitously via the Cumberland and Tennessee Rivers and then overland from a starting point in the Florence and Tuscumbia, Alabama, area. He failed miserably. Part of his problem was timing, and another part was the type of mounts provided by Union quartermasters. But a third element was Bedford Forrest, sent by Bragg to annihilate Streight's operation. In contrast to Grierson's raid, the operation involving Streight's "Independent Provisional Brigade"—or what was derisively styled "the Mule Brigade"—went down as one of the great mistakes of the war.[52]

Departing Nashville by boat in early April, Streight's men battled diseased and unruly mules during a training exercise at "the heap of black and charred ruins" that had been Palmyra on the Cumberland, and then during a similar sojourn at Fort Henry. Possibly twelve hundred of his men were actually mounted when they all went up the Tennessee on April 17. Then they fell in with one of those irregular outfits that always seem to spring ersatz-like during wars, in this case, the so-called "Mississippi Marine Brigade." It seems that Grant had suddenly determined that "everything portends an attack" on Rosecrans with follow up by cavalry and a raid from northern Mississippi into Middle Tennessee as well as West Tennessee. He accordingly had asked Admiral David D. Porter, the Mississippi squadron commander, for help, and the navy sent this Marine Brigade—a new, amphibious counterguerrilla unit of some fifteen hundred combined infantry, cavalry, and artillery, carried on specially outfitted transports, with its own supporting gunboats. The self-contained contingent was commanded by an energetic and highly independent brigadier, Alfred W. Ellet.[53]

Ellet was a prickly prima donna who had stormy relations both with Porter and even his own brothers and nephews who were also involved with the brigade as well as an earlier venture called the Ram Fleet. His men had been recruited from army hospitals from St. Louis to Cincinnati and from Louisville to Nashville. The force had great potential, but like Streight's command, it carried with it the seeds of its own undoing. Mules were not its problem this time, but rather family feuding, interservice rivalries, and incipient brutishness that made the unit as politically unpalatable as the guerrillas and outlaws it hunted during its seventeen-month existence. None of these problems was necessarily apparent when it left Greenville, Mississippi, on April 4. But problems surfaced when Ellet failed to stop at Memphis to pay his respects to Hurlbut, and when he lost more time at Cairo, Illinois, repairing his transports, rams, and support vessels despite a tight schedule. Linkup with Streight occurred none too soon.

Ellet's duties included convoying Streight's empty boats to Fort Henry, helping the army officer round up horses and mules and embark them to move upriver, and, finally to escort and protect the whole expeditionary force to Streight's initial point of departure for the overland raid. Then, Ellet's command would begin its own work of destroying ferry boats, mills, lumber, and other war materiel as well as launching a strike of its own up the Duck River to stop rebel traffic serving Bragg's army. Porter had cautioned Ellet not to dissipate his strength. Above all, he was to cooperate with Grenville Dodge's column moving from Corinth to cover Streight's movements on Florence and Tuscumbia, as well as help Porter's own gunboats, which the admiral was sending to help on the Tennessee River.[54]

Ellet's flotilla of rams, marine boats, transports, and Commander Le Roy Fitch's gunboats USS *Lexington, Covington, Queen City,* and *Argossy* finally steamed ponderously upriver on April 17. They soon uncovered unionists huddled in temporary shelters on the river banks where three hundred guerrillas had herded them from their homes and burned their property. These victims waved handkerchiefs anxiously as the fleet approached. The sight "was pathetic and deeply touched the hearts of all who beheld it," declared Marine Brigade historians after the war. Still, the fleet could not get above Eastport, Mississippi, where the deep water played out. Dodge's column had already left the vicinity, skirmishing vigorously with local rebels, thereby underscoring Hurlbut's confidence that his men could whip anything on the west and south banks of the Tennessee. The Memphis general was less sanguine that Rosecrans could do as much on his side of the stream. Actually, at this point, Hurlbut was too busy exiling rebel families from the city and recruiting loyal West Tennesseans to worry much about Streight, Rosecrans, or anybody else. His own heavy-handed Seventh Kansas Cavalry continued to win few friends in West Tennessee; in fact, it alienated the population still further in that area.[55]

Streight's complex timetable came unraveled when Bragg's headquarters sensed the unusual Union activity on the rivers, inadequate water depth above Eastport forced the gunboats back, and Ellet himself broke off to raid into the countryside at Savannah and Clifton. He accomplished little except to uncover numerous women and children—their men absent in the rebel army—trying to eke out an existence and aghast that "so many men in our great Yankee armies could be absent from home without leaving farms untilled, business prostrated, and families in want, to the north," commended Marine Brigade captain C. G. Fisher. The brigade ambushed and annihilated Major Robert M. White's Sixth Texas Cavalry at the mouth of the Duck River on April 26. But none of this helped Streight.[56]

In fact, mounting Confederate counteractivity throughout the region led Fitch to tell Porter on April 30 that, while he had seen few enemy actually crossing the river all month, "it is reported that Van Dorn is at Waverly with his whole force," preparing to attack Fort Donelson "or try[ing] to blockade this river or the Cumberland." Other random "collisions" (as Assistant Surgeon William Howard of the USS *Brilliant* quaintly dubbed battles with local partisans) attended the period. The steamboat *Emma Duncan*, for instance, was jumped near Green Bottom bar. Meanwhile, Ellet's unpredictable party back at Fort Henry was outfitting barges to carry unionist refugees downriver to safety. By May 7, both the brigade and the gunboats had been chased from Hamburg, Tennessee, back to Cairo, not by guerrillas, but by receding water levels. Brigade veterans spun wonderful postwar reunion tales of the Duck River fight, but Ellet and Fitch left Dodge and Streight battling alone in north Alabama without naval support.[57]

Indeed, Federal inability to provide proper diversion undermined Streight's mission. His valorous but doomed column kept just ahead of Forrest's pursuers as they raced toward the mountains of north Georgia. The jaded bluecoats were cornered just short of the Georgia line on May 3 and forced to surrender. Low on ammunition, food, and rest, Streight's men gave up on the very day that Grierson rode safely into Baton Rouge. Hurlbut told Grant that Streight had wasted too much time in preparation and that Dodge's prolonged fighting had alerted the Confederates. Grant, never one of Rosecrans's admirers, fairly gloated when wiring Washington: "Grierson has knocked the heart out of the State [of Mississippi]." By contrast, one of Rosecrans's cavalry commanders, Brigadier General David S. Stanley, merely commented grimly: "Streight ran through the enemy's lines on what he called a raid—at any rate, a fool's errand—and turned over to the Confederacy three excellent regiments of men, with their horses." Expanding the figure to four regiments and one hundred loyal Alabamians, "who were liable to be shot if taken prisoner," said Stanley in even less charitable postwar memoirs, the "contemptible fizzle" left nothing to show for the effort "but the vainglory of the charlatan Streight."[58]

Stanley's uncharitable comments actually hid a more positive result of the fiasco. Streight's foray unnerved many Alabamians, like Governor John Gill Shorter, who quickly badgered the Davis administration in Richmond for better protection. Protesting conscription of manpower for the principal armies when his state's border lay open to Yankee raiders, Shorter recited a litany of railroad depots and shops, ammunition and ordnance factories, farms, and warehouses that supported the Confederate war effort. "The recent raids through Alabama and Mississippi afford mournful and conclusive evidence," he proclaimed, that the only way to protect such infrastructure was to organize local defense troops and equip them for home protection rather than dispatching them to some distant army. While the governor wanted them as "a nucleus to rally around in case of invasion," the Davis government and its generals had other ideas about protecting this valuable part of the heartland. Their idea hinged on their own raids against the Federals' rear.[59]

Streight's raid had diverted Forrest from his role in Middle Tennessee, although earning Forrest "great demonstration and rejoicing by the citizens" of Rome, Georgia, recalled M. H. Clift, one of his men. Feted everywhere as he took the train to report his success to Bragg in person, even that general promised the Tennessean a second star and implied that Forrest would assume command of his army's entire mounted force. Just where Wheeler fit into that scheme escaped notice. Forestphiles subsequently contended that their hero declined the honor in deference to fellow Tennessean Gideon Pillow, whom he thought "could better fill that position." Such a contention seems ludicrous, given Pillow's performance at Fort Donelson, as does Pillow's contention that Forrest and Brigadier General W. H. "Red" Jackson had "asked to be placed under my orders" in late April. Yet, it seems no more implausible than Bragg offering command of his cavalry to a non–West Pointer in the first place, and Pillow's biographers do not dismiss the episode out of hand. The upshot, however, was that Van Dorn's cavalry went permanently to Forrest, although Bragg bowed to pressure and sent Jackson to help Pemberton, leaving Forrest with only Brigadier General Frank C. Armstrong and Jake Starnes as brigade commanders for duty in Tennessee. Forrest quickly sent them against Gordon Granger's command near Triune throughout much of June.[60]

Forrest's counteroffensive included briefly reentering Franklin on June 4, – freeing prisoners from a local jail, and narrowly escaping harm himself, thanks to a Federal officer whom Forrest had treated kindly during his capture of Murfreesboro the previous year. Union reinforcements arrived, including the Second Michigan Cavalry wielding Colt repeating carbines. Armstrong's force scattered in the melee, losing a new Texas battle flag in the process. Captain Marshall P. Thatcher of the Wolverine regiment recalled that one cocky rebel officer had enjoined his men to "cut down the cowardly sons of bitches," only to have his wounded horse pin him to the ground. "Oh, boys," he yelped at the hovering Yankee captors, "where's your ambulance? Help me out, I'm hurt." His unsympathetic listeners replied bluntly: "help yourself out and be damned to you! We've got something else to do besides waiting on blow-heads like you. Learn to keep a civil tongue in your head, will you!" Continued fighting in the vicinity did not deter the Union paymaster from making his rounds, and some of the Yanks frankly decided to escort a supply train out of the area simply because in case of a major rebel offensive, "we wanted a clear field, not encumbered with a helpless wagon train."[61]

Meanwhile, Starnes rode around various defenders, intending to demonstrate before Nashville, and succeeding, at least, in burning the partially reconstructed railroad bridge just south of Brentwood. Forrest's younger brother Jeffrey gained notoriety by making off with some 400 cavalry horses and fattened cattle as trophies from another affair at Triune on June 11. The nearby David McCord and John A. Jordan houses sustained damage from gunfire in the fray. Most of the skirmishing remained relatively innocuous, however, with the 125th Ohio recalling one instance when artillery exchanges preceding an enemy cavalry charge stopped it before it even reached the skirmish line. In some of these brushes, neither Union infantry nor Brigadier General Robert B. Mitchell's First Cavalry Brigade could quite handle the aggressive southerners. Then, on June 13 and 14, Forrest himself fell prey to a nasty knife and pistol altercation with one of his own lieutenants. The general killed the aggrieved junior officer but was himself rendered unable to fight for several critical weeks. By this time, however, orders had come to evacuate Spring Hill and retire to Shelbyville. Indications of a major Union advance provided the first signs of major summer offensives.[62]

SIGNS OF A CHANGING LANDSCAPE

In January, Rosecrans had written Halleck: "This war must be conducted to annihilate the military power and exhaust the resources of the rebels." He had then sent Streight's expedition against Bragg's line of communication without appreciable result. Old Rosy would not repeat the raiding strategy. He now settled down to build his strength slowly to strike Bragg directly by late May or June. Rear echelon commanders across the upper heartland received orders to reinforce the Army of the Cumberland. Veteran counterguerrilla fighters, like Colonel William W. Lowe's Fifth Iowa Cavalry, were wrenched from months of destroying rebel property and hunting partisans and sent to join the main army. Some of their noncoms on the twin rivers had written Military Governor Andrew Johnson seeking commissions to organize and command African-American companies from "a great many blacks here that is willing to engage in the service of their country." But orders arrived on June 5 to begin the overland hike to join the Army of the Cumberland. The troopers, for the most part, were elated.[63]

The customary counterguerrilla sweeps to Waverly and Charlotte, as well as into Kentucky toward Hopkinsville and Cadiz, were over for men like Marshall. No longer would these midwesterners need to worry about railroad protection between Russellville and Clarksville when low water in the Cumberland forced

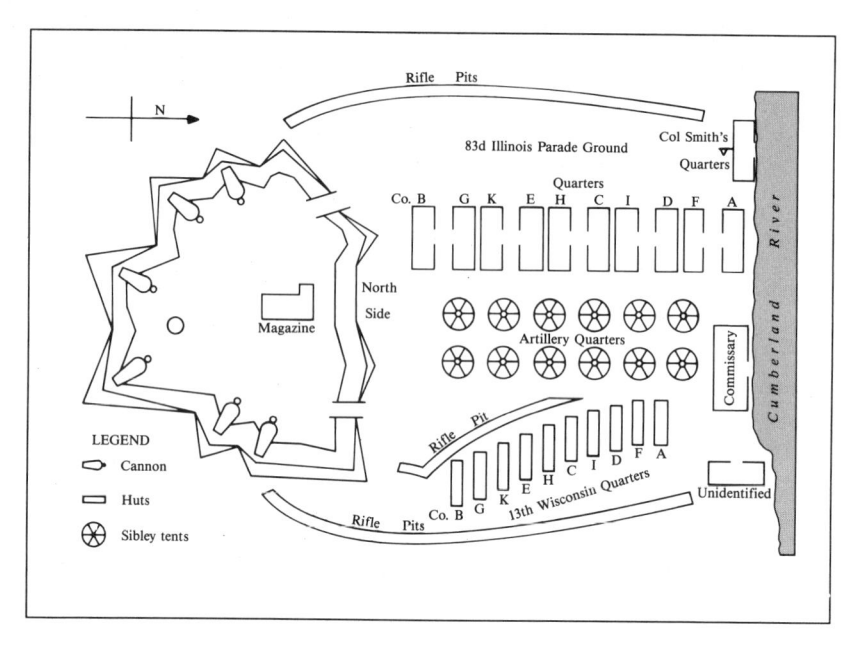

The Union Fort Donelson.

resupplying operations back onto land. After a farewell tour of the new Fort Donelson (with its twelve- to fifteen-foot deep dry moat surrounding eight- and ten-foot high earthen parapets, crowned by three or four thirty-two-pounder cannon for protection), these men decided that, in Sergeant Eugene Marshall's words, "this is intended as a permanent military post in the event of peace." But they would not be there to garrison the place. They would not be around to see the eventual national cemetery situated on the very site of the Union Fort Donelson.[64]

Passing through Clarksville, the Hawkeye cavalry noted that the city was strongly garrisoned by Bruce's command. Even a fortification bearing his name commanded the confluence of the Cumberland and Red Rivers. The macadam turnpike to Nashville produced more new sights, including lush, rolling countryside and an occasional tasteful residence that had escaped war's destruction. The stately capitol building (despite being festooned by cannon and barricades) caught their attention at Nashville, as did the forts and camps that stretched into the distance. At Murfreesboro, Marshall noted that observers commented enviously about the unit's fine horses and expressed surprise that the Iowans were mustered at full strength. Marshall decided that his regiment had done as much or more than any regiment there and was as well equipped as any. Despite being so near the front, the new campsites seemed fairly quiet with nothing foretelling danger. Forage proved scarce, so they had to graze their mounts. But affairs had been far more hectic in guerrilla country at Dover, thought Marshall.[65]

Rumor had the Confederates, not the Union army, advancing, and one day

William B. Miller's Seventy-fifth Indiana went on the Manchester Pike in anticipation of the enemy. It proved to be only Confederate cavalry thrown out as a feeler, and the Federal cavalry drove them back. Several days later, he declared that it was "getting monotonous to prepare for battle every day and no Rebs to fight." Washington and Nashville authorities must have wondered about that also. Both Lincoln and Johnson had been exceedingly anxious for Rosecrans and Burnside to advance; both generals stalled, pleading the need for more time, with Rosecrans unceasingly requesting more mounted troops. The threat of copperhead dissidence and subvention of conscription north of the Ohio, well as the impending elections in Kentucky, caused Burnside pause. He had declared martial law for a week in late March in parts of Kentucky, due to unrest and partisan activity. Then, on April 13, he issued a stringent General Order 38 promising to hang anyone aiding and abetting enemies of the United States. He targeted correspondents and carriers of secret mail, secret recruiting agents, persons intending to pass through Union lines to join the enemy, persons within those lines in Confederate service, all people giving protection, sustenance, or clothing to the enemy, or those spying for the Confederacy.[66]

Burnside also suggested that "treason, expressed or implied" would not be tolerated. Enforcement of the order proved difficult in nominally unionist territory like Kentucky or north of the Ohio. Precedents for such an extreme order existed, including Lincoln's own pronouncement on the issue in January, Burnside's earlier experience in secessionist North Carolina, and Halleck's evolving thoughts on how to treat the civilian population, together with Lieber's code published as General Order Number 100. Burnside was privy to all of them, yet his order met with a storm of protests when his heavy-handed enforcement attempts began. Neutrals like farmer-preacher George Richard Browder greatly feared for such subversion of civil liberties. Still, Burnside claimed that, because he and his soldiers should not say anything that might weaken the army, so civilians—and particularly the press—must be under similar prohibition. The idea of capital punishment for such offenses foundered with the banishment of Clement Vallandigham. But such civil issues certainly impeded Burnside's prompt attention to military matters, like an East Tennessee offensive.[67]

In sum, Burnside's order had the desired effect. Shocked Kentuckians flocked to Federal military headquarters at places like Russellville and Clarksville, Tennessee, to take the hated oath of allegiance to the Union. They went "swearing that they 'do it of their own free will, without any mental reservation whatever,'" sarcastically wrote Browder. They posted bonds for good behavior ranging from two to five thousand dollars, and unionist informants prowled neighborhoods looking for recalcitrant residents. Banishment south or vagrancy seemed the only alternatives to signing the oath, and Browder noted raiders from both sides burning houses, haystacks, and barns, while running off slaves or livestock as a result of this turbulence. Unionist John M. Wilkinson of Cadiz in Trigg County wrote his uncle on May 12, deploring the "possessing" of all the horses and mules by government troops, which deprived honest farmers of the means to tend spring crops. "Such conduct on the part of *Our* military is to be greatly deplored," he sputtered. Elizabethtown, Kentucky, resident Samuel Haycroft told how one guerrilla party had stopped a freight train and stolen its cargo of horses on June 13, while four days later, Browder jotted in his diary that trigger-happy Union horse thieves had gunned down a young man by mistake on a village street; moreover, they often disturbed church gatherings while seeking to take the congregation's mounts.[68]

Robbers seemed to be plundering villages and country stores at will in Browder's area of Kentucky. To this man of God, "swearing, drunkenness, and thriftless indolence are vastly increasing in the land." Wilkinson, while deploring government horse stealing, nevertheless approved of whatever was necessary to end the war. "The language of every *True Patriot*, of every lover of the best government the world ever saw," and of every man anxious to suppress "this 'most wicked of all rebellions'" should be prepared not just to deny sustenance to the rebels capable of bearing arms, but to "take the last morsel of bread from the mouths of females and infantry rebels, too," said the confirmed unionist. He also noted how several of his uncle's slaves had run off, but, apparently tiring of their freedom, had voluntarily returned and "of their own accord" replaced the "'inhuman yoke of human bondage' on their necks" once more. Browder also admitted how insolent and indolent his own slaves had become, and how he had to whip any number for disobedience. Many in Kentucky and elsewhere in the region desired peace. But they wanted no part of a conflict to overthrow slavery. They recoiled from the loss of civil liberties, yet expected the government to suppress rebellion and root out the disloyal. The inconsistencies of such thinking mirrored many heartlanders by mid-1863.

The increasingly oppressive Union rule in Tennessee was easier to rationalize, although many people there did not think so at the time. Brigadier General Robert B. Mitchell's Nashville garrison of two to three thousand men actively cooperated with Colonel William Truesdail's army police and Provost Judge John Fitch's office to stamp out spying, contraband trading, and oath evasion. Incarceration without trial, deportation beyond Union lines, and imprisonment in the North marked the Nashville story. As the city filled with "25 cents per day Yankee laborers," the residents cringed at the new rules and regulations. Enforcement of the oath requirement had lagged until late April; then the military suddenly clamped down hard. Citizens expressed their indignation and shock, but to no avail. "It is indeed humiliating to bow to this despotic rule," wailed Harriet Ellen Moore, as she prayed that God would make the travesty temporary, but wondered if the comely homes, fair meadows, and bright groves of her home state would ever be reclaimed by "those to whom it rightly belongs."[69]

Moore sensed the changing complexion of Nashville due to the influx of refugees, entrepreneurs, and wartime flotsam of humanity. She asked herself if it was all worth it. While she recognized that her father's accommodation to Yankee rule permitted him to visit his properties in Kentucky, she also noted how impossible it was for her eighty-year-old grandfather "to go in and swear allegiance to the government he so heartily detests." Moreover, she bridled at the suggestion that women should have to do so too. Obviously, families could ill afford to abandon homes and property to go south where lodging and food were scarce and friends or relatives would censure them for becoming vagrants. But for the distaff side to bow to oath taking was unconscionable to Moore. She procrastinated even past the May 5 deadline. Finally, begrudgingly, she went off to "become 'ironclad.'" Even then, when the administering Union official chided this "little Rebel" and read her the oath, Moore claimed that she "did not hear more than two or three words as I fixed my thoughts very intently on some other subject."[70]

Oath taking with silent reservations notwithstanding, masses of Tennesseans made the move to fulfill that obligation during the first half of the year, claimed the Nashville *Daily Post*. The rival *Daily Union* proclaimed wildly in early May that "Nashville may be regarded as a loyal city." Perhaps so, for life in this occupied southern city conveyed a picture of dodging detectives (including "women, not ladies" in Harriet Moore's quaint differentiation) and Union troops, being elbowed by rough laborers, conmen, and African-American freedmen, all drawn to work at Union forts and supply facilities or on the docks and in warehouses, somehow all connected with the war effort. Saloons and brothels abounded, and Nashville's gas lights came on again as a private stock of coal found its way upriver among the military supplies.[71]

Accommodation with the enemy suppressed the true rebel feelings still harbored by surviving Nashvillians. Theatrical entertainment vied with reopened churches for patrons, while hospitals competed with businesses for critical space (if any could be found among the Union army establishments). The city's schools remained closed, however, and on June 23, Military Governor Andrew Johnson appointed a commissioner for abandoned property "owned by persons who are within the rebel lines." Stagnating trade took an upward swing as soon as treasury agent W. P. Mellen arrived from Washington, and traffic in civilian goods resumed, subject to "military necessity." The earthworks surrounding the capital still guarded against enemy attack, but the old secessionist Nashvillians who remained still hoped for some sudden dash of redemption by Forrest, Morgan, or even a partisan.[72]

Union authorities thought they saw a change out in the hinterland also. Just after Forrest's attack at Brentwood, Lieutenant Zeboim Carter Patten interviewed some of the Confederate prisoners and pronounced them "to be a very gentlemanly set of men and many intelligent." He discovered a surprising number ready to admit that they and "the majority of the army are willing to return to their former allegiance if they can be guaranteed their rights under the Constitution." These men blamed leaders on both sides for "misrepresenting the public sentiments." Similar views came from Brigadier General Joseph J. Reynolds's latest survey of civilian attitudes, conducted just after the McMinnville victory over Morgan. He now claimed to find three distinct classes of Tennesseans, with only the wealthy still "with a few noble exceptions, decided rebels."[73]

The tone of the wealthy, pro-secessionist class had been "quite defiant" when Reynolds submitted his earlier observations in February. "They were determined to persevere in their rebellion until they secured their rights." Since that time, however, they had lost vast amounts of property in animals and forage to both armies. Further, their slaves had run away to become Union teamsters, and this fact alone had freed Federal soldiers for further foraging and destruction in an endless round of punishment for this class, claimed Reynolds. Frankly, this pressure had changed the tone of the wealthy, so that they had seen their mistake and now admitted to being duped by the politicians. "They are now anxious to take the non-combat oath, give bonds, and stay at home," he decided. Yet, they posed a threat whenever Confederate troops ventured back into the area. Then they aided and abetted the visitors. His answer was to ban the wealthy class *en masse* beyond Union lines and ensure an end to their influence and their presence.

Reynolds found a second category to be "those of medium means or well-to-do," who seemed better intentioned but with little influence. They had evolved into loyal citizens from "wavering men" and now desired to take the oath and pursue their ordinary avocations. Many had watched their own sons be conscripted into the rebel army, he contended, and they "would desert that service" and return home if their fathers were placed in a better position politically, and if their oppressors (the wealthy planter class) were sent away so that there would be no one to return them to onerous Confederate service. Reynolds believed that this second class deserved the national government's protection, as did the third, poor class, which was totally loyal, but had no influence whatsoever in the community, thus no stake in society and little property. This last group had been subjugated all their lives, and it had suffered so much from Confederate conscription that "the absence of the wealthy" was a thing they greatly desired but spoke of "only in whispers." What they had in their favor, declared Reynolds, was "their devotion to the flag of their country."

The abiding question in the minds of all three classes, said Reynolds, simply was "will the Federal army remain in Middle Tennessee?" Or would it advance or even retreat, thus abandoning the civilians to their fate once more? Such insecurity could only be eradicated, in the general's view, by adopting such measures that would convince the loyal populace that the country was to be permanently controlled by the government, that no retreat would be made, and that whatever might be required to "loyalize" a district would be done prior to the army's advance. Reynolds's immediate superior, Major General George Henry Thomas, endorsed this view. A loyal Virginian himself (and spurned by his family for remaining true to his oath as a United States Army officer), Thomas too concluded that "If those who have heretofore been active rebels were invariably put beyond our lines, we should then be able to penetrate and occupy the insurgent territory with much more certainty, as we would not then be under the necessity of keeping up such strong guards in our rear to secure our lines of communication." This may have been wishful thinking on the part of Union officers like Thomas and Reynolds. Still, their view was wisely perceptive of the complexities attending civil matters that were inextricably mixed with military operations in the heartland.[74]

Texan Dunbar Affleck wrote home from Sparta, Tennessee, on May 12, 1863, that Terry's Texas Rangers had been "lying idle here for about three weeks," and they had to haul their corn for food for about fifty miles. "I don't expect the war will last much longer," he told them; "I expect to be home by the first of October next." Twenty-one-year-old Alfred C. Willett of the 113th Ohio wrote his sweetheart on the last day of that month that "the Rebels keep very quiet here at present." Camp life at Franklin, Tennessee, was very pleasant with local farmer's milk, plenty to eat, young contraband boys to carry water, and a round of drill constituting his unit's activity. Picket duty relieved the monotony, and "I still keep in good health," although he had little news to send her.[75]

Yet, if this front-line impasse continued unabated in Middle Tennessee, the growing complexities of wartime civil-military relations had become quite apparent everywhere. The impact of conscription by both Union and Confederacy, the slave-emancipation issue, and the prolonged bloodletting affected attitudes, and hence the war effort. As somewhat paranoid Indiana brigadier Henry B. Carrington quite aptly wired Brigadier General Jacob D. Cox, the Cincinnati district commander, from Cleveland on June 23: "We shall have offensive operations along the border as part of the system of the enemy, to harass the agricultural interests, sunder railroad connections, develop disgust with the war, and distract our attention from more substantial lines of attack." He assured his colleague that such depredations upon the Indiana and Illinois border would come "from men who never had connection with the rebel army." He referred to the copperheads and Knights of the Golden Circle subversives on the northern home front.[76]

Certainly the emancipation issue soured many even in the ranks of northern armies. After reading about an African-American patriotic gathering in Washington that had proclaimed the "Red, White and Blue" should be altered to "Red, White, and Black," Hoosier Arthur B. Carpenter, a lieutenant in the Nineteenth U.S. Infantry, wrote his parents from Murfreesboro quite negatively on the matter. "I have had a sour stomac [sic] ever since, and I fear I shall have to take an emetic," he declared. Blacks had no place in a white man's war for bigots like Carpenter. Still, others in uniform seemed oblivious to racism around them. Tighlman Jones of the Fifty-ninth Illinois nonchalantly referred to one encounter with a rebel contingent where the enemy had "played the tune 'Run Nigger run' so fast that our boys give up the chase. . . ." Later, in the autumn, he would tell his father that blacks freed and fighting for the government that had freed them was inevitable. "I think more of a Negro Union soldier than I do of all the cowardly Copperhead trash of the north," he had decided.[77]

Nevertheless, as spring foliage gave way to summer hues along the river bottoms of the Kentucky and Tennessee war zone, restless youth stirred in camp and garrison. They still battled notorious guerrillas like Dick and George Henson from strategic hamlets like the new Fort Donelson and Dover. Samuel L. McCabe of Company A, Seventy-ninth Ohio, wrote from Gallatin near Nashville to a correspondent in Butler County, Ohio, on May 18 that several "notorious Rebel citizens moved behind the lines of this army" with impunity and that something else should be done with them. "Such men ought to be burnt or something done with them," he advanced bitterly. This summer, he predicted, would see plenty of skirmishing around there for when the river went down, the rebs would cross and "get in around here and bushwack [sic] us."[78]

Yet, the advent of warmer weather brought a lighter note too. The garrison soldiers also gloried in military reviews when the Army of the Cumberland's inspector general paid the post a visit. William H. Dorris again visited his wife's kinsmen in nearby Clarksville and still found them ardent secessionists. But he viewed with greater concern the poor condition of that city's streets and noted that the destroyed east span of the railroad bridge across the Cumberland was evidence of "what war does to any country it destroys rather than builds it up." Why was it that the land of our birth is desolated by the ravages of civil war, he wondered, wishing "to god that our land and country could be in peace once more."[79]

Dorris might declare that "nature seems to be in all her glory in the beautiful valleys of Tennessee and seems to smile upon us," but war continued to spoil that beauty. Cavalryman E. A. Peters wrote his parents from Murfreesboro about the execution of one rebel in early June on the Woodbury Pike about a quarter mile from camp. He was hanged "for the triple crime of murder, spy and guerrilla," observed Peters, as "he is the one that cut the tongues out of the men." The execution was quite spectacular, in fact. There were six thousand viewers, with the prisoner conveyed to the gallows by a wagon team of "six cream colored horses belonging to the Independent Brigade of Cavalry," Peters recounted. The Second Ohio formed an armed square around the scene. William B. Miller of the Seventy-fifth Indiana also witnessed the event. "I never saw a man hung before and I don't care whether I ever do again," he concluded. Yet, one suspects that much of this sort of spectacle was a carefully staged attempt to intimidate people and convey a message both to onlookers and the enemy.[80]

Guerrillas, partisans, and irregulars were little better than felons in the eyes of the Federal government and its agents, the Union soldiers. They would be treated as such. Back on March 5, Alva C. Griest of the Seventy-second Indiana had recorded: "How bad it seems, to be murdered thus in cold blood by an assassin, who, too cowardly to take the field as a manly foe at the side of his brothers of the south, lurks in ravines and thickets and craves to shoot down the first poor soldier who comes that way." Six feet of rope was all such men deserve, "and it is all they will get if caught by us," he suggested. Certainly, Will Dorris's sought-after peace could not occur in a land still so bitterly troubled by such sentiments.[81]

At Nashville, Governor Johnson and his family had returned from their political swing through the North. Speaking to a welcoming crowd before his temporary residence in Lezinka Brown's home on the evening of May 30, Johnson's theme remained that of the olive branch of peace, the Constitution, and the law. But he added: "There can be no peace, except by obedience to the Constitution and the Laws," and those who had prospered and been happy before "ought to submit now, and be happy once more." According to the unionist press, someone in the crowd shouted, "God bless Governor Johnson." Advisedly, the Johnson regime controlled only Nashville and only where the Union army dictated that control. As one historian has suggested, Johnson had enjoyed almost no success in resurrecting civil government at any level "by elective franchise." The Confederacy, in all its raiment, had to be ejected across the upper heartland before that could take place. Even then, the question about the differing loyalties of those classes of people discerned by General Reynolds remained; it was anybody's guess whether they were truly ready for the next political step. Combat had not yet been exhausted as a recourse in the region. The battlefield, not the ballot box, remained the law of the land.[82]

TEN

TO TULLAHOMA AND BEYOND: SUMMER 1863

As summer broke across the upper heartland, the Confederate Army of Tennessee welcomed rumors of northern dissatisfaction with conscription, emancipation, and undiminished casualty lists. The men in butternut and gray watched curiously as Ohio copperhead politician Clement Vallandigham passed through en route to exile abroad. Then, British lieutenant colonel Arthur Fremantle of Her Majesty's Coldstream Guards replaced Vallandigham as an object of interest. This Englishman's whirlwind tour of the South included a review of Braxton Bragg's army, memorialized appropriately in his famous diary entries.

One of Bragg's crack divisions provided the martial display. Parading in the warm breeze before beautifully attired ladies and dignitaries, the marching rebels impressed Fremantle with their battle flags adorned with honors from Belmont, Shiloh, Perryville, and Murfreesboro. The healthy, well-clothed young soldiers seemed "much better workers than I saw in Mississippi," he noted. They personified resolution, confidence, and, in this instance, they were commanded by an ex-British army veteran, Patrick Cleburne.[1]

Frankly, the rebels in Middle Tennessee needed all the élan they could muster. Bragg's estimated fifty thousand effectives around Tullahoma and Shelbyville and Major General Simon B. Buckner's additional sixteen thousand in East Tennessee were all that deterred further Yankee advance on Chattanooga at this point. Their opponent, William S. Rosecrans's Army of the Cumberland, was most anxious to pitch in to its enemy once again. Alanson Rynam wrote his wife on May 12 from a camp near Murfreesboro: "our army here is in fine condition and all they want is another chance at Bragg and they will settle the case with him." He feared that the war might close "without another blow from this army." Washington also worried that Old Rosy's nearly sixty-five-thousand-man field force and Ambrose Burnside's twenty thousand more in Kentucky might idle away the time. But, most assuredly, one way or another the winter impasse was about to end in the early summer of 1863.[2]

Summer 1863

PREPARING A MILITARY RESOLUTION

Union military authorities in Tennessee and Kentucky faced the daunting task of finding sufficient manpower for their multiple responsibilities. In addition to Bragg and his army, they confronted partisan and raider threats, civil disobedience, the difficulties of prison and training camp administration, as well as the problem of managing a vast supply operation. Rosecrans procrastinated because, as he told Washington later, to operate successfully in advance of Murfreesboro ("a point 212 miles from the nearest point of supplies," i.e., Louisville) he had "first to establish and secure a depot of supplies at this point, and, second to organize an adequate cavalry force to combat that of the enemy, protect our own line of communication, and take advantage of the enemy should he be beaten or retreat." Moreover, realizing that his animals had to live off the country, he wanted to allow the corn crop to ripen before advancing. But his delay, coming at the same time as another disturbing Confederate advance north of the Potomac in the East, profoundly unsettled the Lincoln administration. Too much time had been wasted prodding both Rosecrans and Buell about advancing. Washington's mood was therefore quite grim, if not testy.[3]

To make matters worse for Rosecrans, elsewhere Ulysses S. Grant and the navy methodically proceeded toward a decision in Mississippi. Washington also worried that delay would permit possible Confederate transfer of men and equipment against Grant. Indeed, Richmond had directed Bragg to send John C. Breckinridge's six thousand men to bolster John C. Pemberton and Joseph E. Johnston in the Magnolia state. Bragg had planned a major demonstration against Murfreesboro in late April but had faltered. But Grant also searched for reinforcements from his subordinates and enjoined officers like Stephen A. Hurlbut at Memphis to destroy Pemberton's own supply base in northern Mississippi and worry less about chasing partisan shadows in West Tennessee. Hurlbut, of course, remained aware of satisfying Military Governor Andrew Johnson's reconstruction needs in that section, hence emphasizing the need to suppress guerrillas. Little skirmishes and brushes with the rebels took place all over northern Mississippi and West Tennessee so that, like for Buell and Rosecrans, not much had changed in this regard either since the previous year.[4]

Grant directed Hurlbut to strip his district of manpower "to the lowest possible standard," exempting only the Paducah and Columbus base areas in Kentucky. Hurlbut naturally protested, fearing repetition of Nathan Bedford Forrest's December raid. Grant remembered the event only too well, but Forrest was nowhere in sight, and he believed that Colonel Edward Hatch's Union horsemen could handle rebel brigadier James R. Chalmers's scratch force in Hurlbut's immediate front. Places like Salem, Colliersville, La Grange, Antioch Church, and Jackson in West Tennessee, as well as Senatobia and Hernando, Mississippi, became combat flash points in May. Grant also told Hurlbut to keep his men out of citizens' houses, since "they must live as far as possible off the country through which they pass and destroy corn, wheat, crops & everything that can be made use of by the enemy in prolonging the war." Mules and horses could be confiscated and "where it does not cause too much delay, destroy the agricultural implements. . . . Cripple the rebellion in every way without insulting women and children or taking their clothing, jewelry, etc.," instructed the hero of Donelson—fully eighteen months before William T. Sherman would cut his own famous swath across Georgia.[5]

Hurlbut might protest priorities, but he understood orders. Yet, the abandonment of Jackson, Tennessee, in mid-June enabled local Confederates like Colonels Jacob D. Biffle, Jeffrey Forrest (Nathan Bedford Forrest's younger brother), J. F. Newsom, and Chalmers to dash into the breach. Columbus district commander Alexander Asboth complained to Washington that Grant's orders left "the whole country between the Tennessee and Mississippi Rivers—from Paducah to Corinth, over 150 miles in length, comprising about 15,000 square miles, where secessionism prevails and guerrillas are constantly organizing—guarded by only a part of my former force, now not over 4,000 men." His area was clear of partisans, he claimed, since 300 of his cavalry had pursued Colonel Thomas G. Woodward's band near Reynoldsburg. But irregulars under W. A. Dawson on the Tennessee River and Isaac F. Harrison (who had succeeded R. V. Richardson on the Obion River) required attention. He had asked Major General Richard Oglesby (another of Grant's brigade commanders at Fort Donelson the year before) just the previous week to help intercept any of Bragg's raiders from crossing into West Tennessee as Forrest had done before Christmas. Again, the refrain had changed very little over the months.[6]

Asboth also informed Union general-in-chief Henry Halleck that he had reduced but not removed the Fort Heiman garrison, retaining four cavalry companies and an artillery section "to hold the fort at all hazards," since it was "the key to my district from the Tennessee side." Fort Henry, across the river, had been totally abandoned by Rosecrans, he observed, while Colonel William W. Lowe's departure from Fort Donelson had robbed the whole region of veteran counterguerrilla cavalry. Suddenly, various rebel raids knocked down telegraph lines, and even Halleck warned about imminent attack east of Jackson. Only a smattering of Union commanders were positioned to defend places like Columbus, Cairo, Paducah, Fort Pillow, Island Number 10, Hickman, and key points in between. So, the general-in-chief told Asboth to withhold troops from Grant "if there is any real danger." But he added: "I think you will have no forces against you but guerrillas. They will only devastate the country." It was Cairo telegrapher Anson Stager's opinion, however, that Asboth simply "is stampeded."[7]

Indeed, Asboth's dispatches sounded alarmist, and both Halleck and Hurlbut told him to pull himself together. "If you fight half as well as the enemy," noted the former, "you can readily hold your posts against any force with which the rebels can attack you." If Asboth lacked confidence either in himself or his command, "you should ask to be relieved." Still, the Hungarian expatriate persisted, citing reports from Hickman, Clinton, as well as from Lieutenant Colonel Albert P. Henry at Fort Heiman about very active enemy incursions, particularly southward from Paris to Jackson. By June 23, Asboth's communiques had rebels moving from Arkansas on Island Number 10, the USS *Alfred Robb* attacked, and raiders Biffle, Newsom, and others roaming unchecked through Henderson, Madison, and McNairy Counties, "recruiting, conscripting, and organizing," but always eluding pursuit. Lieutenant Colonel Gustav von Helmrich swept the area between Clinton and Lexington, with the help of both local sheriffs and African-American informants, capturing several collaborationists but little else. Affairs soon quieted down, as they usually did in this kind of warfare, but Hurlbut continued to claim that Rosecrans's "strange apathy" permitted such unchecked raids upon the Memphis commander's "entire rear and left." Since the Army of the Cumberland commander "will not believe any reports from this quarter," he told Grant, "I have ceased communicating with him except through Washington." Grant continued his own campaign despite such chaotic conditions among his rear commanders.[8]

THE SUMMER BALL OPENS

An obscure Ohio brigadier who later became president of the republic made the crucial move that sent the Army of the Cumberland finally churning forward again in late June. James A. Garfield, Rosecrans's chief of staff, took comments from the army's senior leaders and crafted an answer to Rosecrans's question of what the army should be doing and when, and forced his commander to a decision. It was an odd way of doing business, this confidential questionnaire Rosecrans dispatched to his commanders. But it worked because Garfield's reply codified the corporate wisdom and then defied the implied caution of that wisdom in personally pushing for an advance. So, the army left winter encampments on June 23, headed for Chattanooga.

Two weeks before, Rosecrans had queried his corps and division commanders about the situation. Did they think Bragg had reinforced Pemberton and should there be an immediate or a delayed advance, or would such an advance actually prevent Bragg from reinforcing the Mississippi front? These queries betrayed a disturbing uncertainty at army headquarters. Solidly conservative, even pessimistic replies came from fifteen of the respondents. All of them cautioned against immediate advance. Eleven were sanguine about successfully fighting a battle by advancing "at this time," while ten thought the rebels along the Duck River had not been weakened thus far by sending reinforcements to Vicksburg. The army's top leaders remained only slightly more divided on whether or not an advance could prevent additional reinforcements from being sent to Mississippi. But at least some of them felt that Bragg would simply fall back behind the Tennessee River at Chattanooga as a result of a Federal advance. "Thus, no battle can be fought either successful or unsuccessful," and the subordinates' wisdom was simply to await the fall of Vicksburg.[9]

Garfield's calculations from the questionnaire replies proved pivotal. He showed that the Federals could advance in overwhelming numbers; "65,137 bayonets and sabers to throw against Bragg's 41,680" was the way the Buckeye described it. Furthermore, the Confederates seemed weaker than at any time since Stones River, or were likely to be anytime in the future. True, said Garfield, the Army

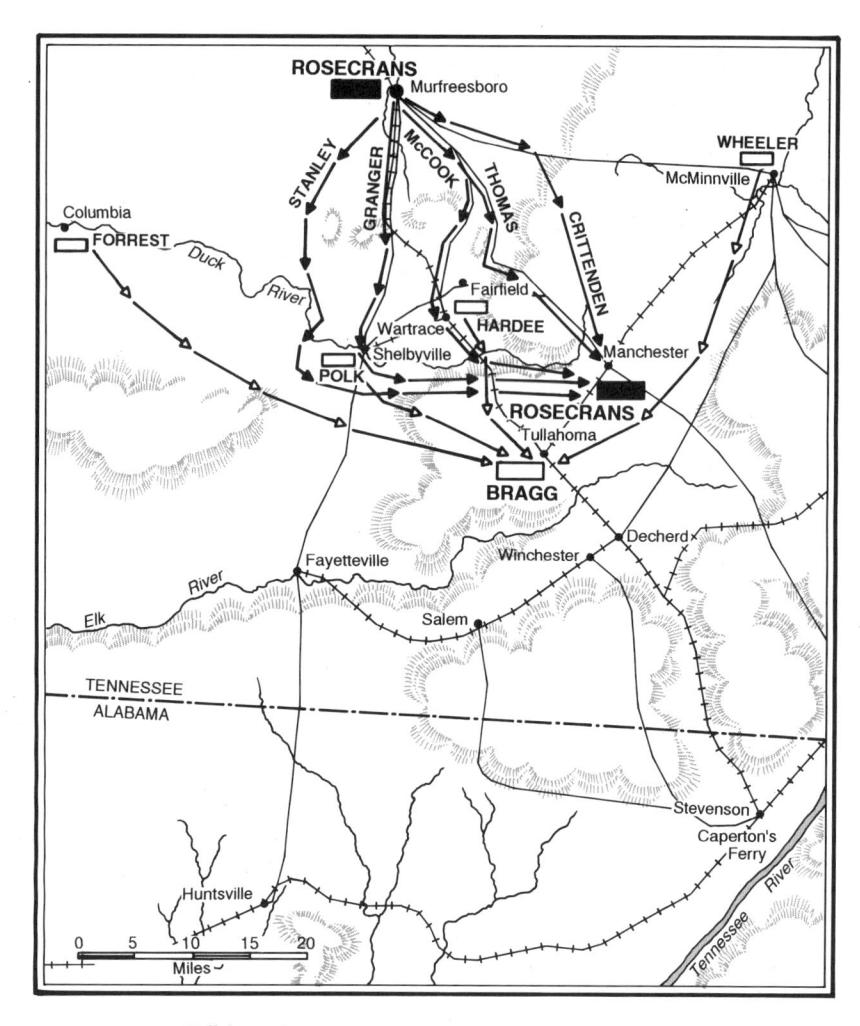

Tullahoma Campaign strategic situation at the end of June 1863.

of the Cumberland could hope for little reinforcement, but awaiting Vicksburg's capitulation seemed fruitless. Bragg would gain help in turn from Johnston's forces elsewhere in Mississippi once the battle for the great river had been lost. Besides, Union arms could simply "overwhelm" Bragg in battle, since they had beaten superior numbers at Stones River. Should Bragg retreat, however, "this could be very disastrous to him." Besides material loss, "and the abandonment of the rich and abundant harvest now nearly ripe in Central Tennessee," the southerners would also lose heavily by desertion, particularly among Kentuckians and Tennesseans in Bragg's ranks. All this would "very materially reduce [Bragg's] physical and moral strength." While Union supply lines might be stretched to their limit in pursuit, such a rebel retreat would directly uncover Chattanooga and East Tennessee.

Garfield championed a sudden and rapid advance that would bring Confederate defeat and prove detrimental to the rebellion to the highest degree. Political uncertainty in the loyal states made such a decisive blow imperative. The national government needed success in upcoming elections as well as in enforcing the conscription law. But Rosecrans's true objective was to annihilate the enemy army, whose last reserves were substantially in the field already. An effective blow would crush the shell of rebellion, followed by collapse of the Richmond government. Rosecrans's delay had been prudent thus far, so that the army could be massed and its cavalry properly mounted. Now, claimed Garfield, a mobile force could be concentrated in twenty-four hours, while the mounted arm, if not numerically equal to the southern horse, "is greatly superior in efficiency and morale." The bottom line, said the Ohioan, was simply that "The Government and The War Department believe that this army ought to move upon the enemy; the army desires it, and the country is anxiously hoping for it." Rosecrans agreed; twelve days later, the Army of the Cumberland advanced.[10]

Frankly, the men in blue knew that an advance was coming all along. On June 1, the signs were unmistakable, the Ninth Ohio's chronicler wrote later. A continual readiness level had been ordered, with provisions for ten days' march. Nonessential baggage and equipment had been sent back for storage in Nashville. Major General Gordon Granger's reserve troops moved forward. "Meanwhile, cannon thundered from the direction of Franklin," as the Ohioans and their comrades engaged in three more weeks of blunting Confederate thrusts at the Harpeth line; the Confederates were "thinking we had abandoned the region." But the soldiers essentially had it correct. In the vernacular of the men in the ranks, "the ball had opened." The campaign season had started with Rosecrans soon gaining the initiative from Bragg.[11]

ROSECRANS OUTWITS BRAGG AT TULLAHOMA

Impatient Washington officials queried Rosecrans point-blank on June 16: was the general going to move forward immediately or not? Ever stubborn, Rosecrans claimed that a movement was being contemplated to begin in a week or so. His timing was off by three days, but, notwithstanding torrential rains, the Army of the Cumberland feinted left and right (toward McMinnville via Woodbury, and toward Shelbyville through Guy's Gap) to outmaneuver Bragg. "I was determined to render useless their entrenchments, and, if possible, secure their line of retreat by turning their right and moving on the railroad bridge across Elk River," Rosecrans observed in his after-action report. This would "compel a battle on our own ground or drive them on a disadvantageous line of retreat." Federal leaders, however, wondered where the ever-dangerous Confederate horsemen were.[12]

Out of position and out of their preferred free-spirited mode of operations was the answer. Major General Joseph Wheeler, unable to abide Nathan Bedford Forrest's attitude, was flamboyant and brave, but inexperienced, and his role was merely to screen Bragg's positions. Earl Van Dorn was in his grave, a victim of a domestic peccadillo, and Bragg had allowed Morgan to ride off to Kentucky, a junket that ended north of the Ohio as the Yankee juggernaut came south. Coupled with irresolute reaction from insubordinate infantry generals William J. Hardee, Leonidus Polk, and others, Bragg's horsemen failed him, allowing Rosecrans to gain the upper hand. The decisive contest for Middle Tennessee (indeed, for the eastern part of the state as a whole) would take place along a curving line stretching some sixty miles or so between McMinnville and Columbia.[13]

Bragg surely had profited by the vigorous mounted activities of winter and early spring. Yet, the local partisans in their respective little fiefdoms probably gained the most from booty taking and disruption of civil comity behind Union lines. Enforcement of the Confederate's 1862 conscription act, and "field recruitment" by Bragg's newly minted chief of the volunteer and conscript bureau, Brigadier General Gideon J. Pillow, dragooned numerous replacements for the ranks. Perpetually a battlefield failure, Pillow always proved his mettle in stimulating recruitment, much as he done during the first year of the war as a Tennessee state general. Now he may have plied his skills too assiduously, for in adding manpower to rebuild the Army of Tennessee during the winter, he had incurred the wrath of manpower bureaucrats in Richmond. His methods resembled European press gangs. He even harassed slave owners into sending their chattel to be employed as army teamsters, thus freeing white men for the privilege of dying on the battlefield in defense of the "peculiar institution." Still, senior rebel generals appreciated Pillow's success at filling their ranks, even if Richmond officials did not.[14]

Colonel William Preston Johnston (Sidney Johnston's nephew and future biographer) claimed that Pillow had netted ten thousand new men for Bragg in early 1863, far in excess of those taken in by the government's own conscript bureau. Pillow, of course, also postured that such approval for his work supported his claim to higher field command and vindication for the Fort Donelson fiasco. A worked-out, fatigued, and demoralized populace from which the levies were drawn, surely disagreed. As it was, Bragg's army probably netted mostly malcontents, raw recruits, and otherwise marginal accruals from Pillow's work. They provided more candidates for the yawning carnal houses of Civil War battlefields, but little else. Worse, Pillow's harvest stripped the home front of labor and stability, a consort to Yankee despoliation and counterpoise to increasing outlawry in the rural South. But Bragg thought he had gained more men for his ranks, at least to fight sufficiently well from defensive positions.[15]

In Rosecrans's words, everything was shielded "by the defiles of Duck River—a deep, narrow stream, with but few fords or bridges—and a rough range of hills which divides the 'Barrens' from the lower level of Middle Tennessee." Bragg's forward positions lay among those hills, breached by colorfully named Hoover's, Liberty, Guy's, and Bellbuckle Gaps. Cedar brakes and clay soil marked the region. Yet, it was considerably more hospitable than the landscape to the rebel rear, where, observed European commentator Comte de Paris: "A species of rough grass, rebellious under the teeth of animals, with here and there tufts of stunted oak trees, cover this desolate region; the wayfarer finds not a drop of water in summer; he runs the risk in fall of losing himself in sloughs, and in winter of disappearing under the snow drifted by the terrible blasts from the north-west." Beyond that lay mountains that shielded Chattanooga, while transiting the more immediate locale were railroad and highway, with branches to McMinnville and Fayetteville for commerce and communication. Bragg planned to defend his position by a variant of his Stones River battle plan. He never had a chance to do so.[16]

Rosecrans aimed his main blow at the hilly country around Manchester, Tennessee. Bragg would then have to fight on the retreat, outside his Tullahoma fortifications. In what even President Abraham Lincoln subsequently admitted was a splendid piece of strategy, the Federal commander simply maneuvered the Confederate army out of Middle Tennessee with minor bloodletting. Commencing on June 23, the Army of the Cumberland advanced on a broad front from Readyville to Franklin. Chaplain W. W. Lyle of the Eleventh Ohio waxed eloquently about the opening moves. "Dense, moving columns on every road, bristling bayonets gleaming everywhere, gay battle-flags streaming out on the morning breeze, or glancing amid the green foliage, as regiment after regiment deployed on the various roads—staff officers and orderlies galloping here and there—the sharp rattle of drums and the shrill sounds of the fife, the confused clangor of countless bugles, and the softer, sweeter, but no less confused notes of brigade bands beating off at the heads of columns—made both scenes and sounds not soon to be forgotten," he noted.[17]

The scenes were different in the rear, but nonetheless indicative of a nineteenth-century army on the move. Anxious quartermasters strained to shift mountains of supplies out of Murfreesboro and into Fortress Rosecrans for safe-keeping. Haste made waste, bristled Captain J. Warren Clark, in a report to quartermaster superiors in Washington. "In every direction could be seen, left and thrown away, Government property that should have been turned into the post quartermaster," he groaned. Axes, spades, shovels, rope, stoves, kegs of horseshoes and nails—in fact, all kinds of property was wasted. All of it could have been stored for future need, he advanced. Instead, soldiers and African-American laborers destroyed or discarded everything and simply moved on. He was especially appalled at the money represented by such waste. Still, this was the way citizen armies did business. It was no different south of the Duck River, for that matter.[18]

The campaign began in almost flawless weather. Then, rain set in within a day, and Major James A. Connolly of the 123d Illinois recalled that from the morning of June 24 until the first of July, "we lived in the rain, slept in the mud and rain and were as wet as fish in the river all that time." Ralsa C. Rice of the 125th Ohio thought that the operation "taxed our powers of endurance" beyond any other experience encountered during his term of service. The mud mired supply trains "so rations ran out, and none could come up," recalled quartermaster

Sergeant Josiah Conzett of the Fifth Iowa Cavalry. It was humorous to see the officers come around the soldiers offering a dollar for hardtack biscuit, he said. The men had little themselves and hung on to what they had, "so Mr. Colonel, Major, Captains and the rest had to go hungry as the men often had to" and received little sympathy from the ranks. Marching on macadam turnpikes and employing superior firepower in early encounters, the blueclad advance ultimately overcame raindrops and rebel opposition. They soon secured hilltops and gaps that commanded Bragg's position. But, as one German American said, "in a word the situation was abominable."[19]

Bragg's remaining cavalry were poorly deployed to cope with the Yankee advance, and Hardee's infantry responded sluggishly when units like Colonel John Wilder's brigade (equipped with new Spencer seven-shot repeating rifles) blasted their way through Hoover's Gap. Brigadier General Richard Johnson's division likewise drove through Liberty Gap the same day, with Guy's Gap falling next to David Stanley and Gordon Granger. Then, the Federals beat back Confederate counterattacks on June 25. Major General George H. Thomas caught the spirit of victory when he commented to young Wilder that the latter's action had saved thousands of lives by one bold stroke. "I didn't expect to get this Gap for three days," he claimed. Despite their success, the Federals were roadbound, and with rain churning the yellow clay into quagmire, the Federals sloshed ahead for the next week, but failed to bag Bragg's now rapidly retiring army. Still, Connolly, for one, recalled sweeping past abandoned fortifications and into Manchester on June 27, catching "citizens at their breakfast tables" before fanning out to occupy the public square and capture stragglers. Tullahoma lay eleven miles ahead, and Bragg had no choice but to withdraw or have his whole army crushed against the flooding waters of Duck River. Dispirited rebels once more took up the retreat in sullen silence.[20]

Bragg's equally wet and bedraggled opponents were sustained by hope of reaching Tullahoma, to "hit the enemy's fortifications (glorified as impregnable)," drive the enemy out of there, and then "thrash him yet another time." Wilder's unit rushed to get on Bragg's line of retreat between Dechard and Cowan, with Brigadier General John Beatty's brigade assuming a flank-covering position at Hillsboro, near the edge of the Barrens and the Cumberland Plateau. Wilder found too many defenders at the Elk River bridge, however, and was unable to truly hamper Bragg's retirement. Connolly recounted how his regiment watched silently from wooded positions as that retreat column passed south of Tullahoma. Outnumbered, they were powerless as they "saw flag after flag pass us and we did not dare attack them." In turn, rebel mounted pursuers never caught Wilder's men as they became preoccupied with protecting the Duck River crossings at Shelbyville and elsewhere. One of Forrest's best brigade commanders, Colonel James "Jake" Starnes, who had been a prewar Williamson County, Tennessee, physician, fell mortally wounded by a sharpshooter's bullet during skirmishing near Bobo's crossroads, about five miles northeast of Tullahoma on the Old Hillsborough and Lynchburg Road. The able George C. Dibrell succeeded him, but one veteran recalled after the war that Starnes's death "cast a gloom over the whole Brigade for no commander ever had a deeper hold upon the affections of his troops than he, they loved him as a child would his father and where he led none hesitated to follow." Starnes's eleven-year-old personal servant wept that he did not know how the Yankees shot his master, but he knew he was "a chargin" when it happened as the "the Cunnel was a powerful brave man."[21]

The confrontation at Shelbyville proved most embarrassing (almost catastrophic) for Confederate fortunes as Stanley and Granger mauled the horsemen of Wheeler and John Wharton in desperate hand-to-hand fighting. Initially steady in their rear-guard role, the gray riders collapsed before repeated onslaughts by Colonels Archibald P. Campbell and Robert H. G. Minty. Campbell and Minty's brigades led a pincer movement against the two bridges still open to Confederate retirement in that sector. Cavalrymen from the Seventh Pennsylvania and Fourth Michigan led the charge against Wheeler's demoralized troopers, their firearms rendered inoperable by the foul weather. "In a short time a complete rout was the consequence," observed South Carolina brigadier Arthur Middleton Manigault. Wheeler tried to rally at the turnpike bridge so that Forrest, retiring fast from the direction of Columbia, might also escape. But poor coordination between them once again produced catastrophe. The Tennessean had found his own crossing, unbeknownst to Wheeler, leaving the Alabamian and fifty of his men to escape by leaping with their horses into the swollen river. Only "Fighting Joe" and thirteen of his men emerged from the raging current.[22]

Quantities of artillery, small arms, equipment, commissary stores, and prisoners fell into Federal hands. The bluecoats reached unionist Shelbyville amid "the waving of flags and cheers of welcome from the inhabitants of this unconquerable stronghold of loyalty," Rosecrans recorded. The retreating Confederates had already impressed or commandeered wagons and teams from nearby residents (many of them unionists) to aid in evacuating supplies and equipage, but apparently had not succeeded in withdrawing everything. The famous Union actress and spy Pauline Cushman was freed from her sickbed arrest in the town. She had been awaiting Bragg's judgment when his "army had to hustle out of town by our rapid approach," remembered Josiah Conzett.[23]

Thus, in just two days time, Bragg's men had been defeated at all three points where they had made a stand. By the end of the month, he had evacuated his lines completely and retired hastily beyond Elk River, burning bridges behind him. Shelbyville citizens turned out to "an old fashioned 4th of July" celebration, while a thoroughly disgusted Harriet Ellen Moore at Edgefield, across the river from Nashville, admitted to her diary how they were received joyfully by "the Union lackeys of Shelbyville." But Alfred C. Willett of the 113th Ohio recalled appreciatively that these were the same townspeople who had served dinner to Don Carlos Buell's liberating Federals the year before and "rejoiced to see us come" again in 1863. Militarily, Gordon Granger claimed, the fight for the town firmly established the Union cavalry's efficiency "beyond a doubt," adding that the enemy could no longer boast of the superiority of their cavalry and its accomplishments.[24]

Rosecrans's pursuit soon became mired in mud and stopped abruptly altogether before the destroyed Duck River bridges. The floodwaters failed to deter some Federals, however. Lieutenant Frederick Nathan Boyer recounted that Brigadier General Jefferson C. Davis's division simply locked arms and waded the stream. Some "fellows who tried it alone, unaided had a hard time getting across," and were swept downstream before gaining passage. Then, the heat and humidity took over while "the pale clay of the barrens turned to veritable mortar." Jesse B. Connelly commented in his diary for July 1: "Eight men have died from overheat today in our division" as he trudged along only midway between Manchester and Tullahoma. "We have driven [the enemy] hard all the time," proclaimed staff officer Alfred Lacey Hough, "but they having the start, destroyed the bridges, and the swollen streams could not be forded, we would have to wait for them to subside, and then another rain before we reached the next stream, we aimed to get into the mountains before they did, but they passed over [Elk River] on the 3d of July, and will be safe in Chattanooga before we get over." As Union cavalry leader David Stanley decided years later, the Tullahoma operation "Failed in its main object—the destruction of Bragg's army—through an act of Providence." He omitted to mention, however, that another objective had been achieved with very low casualties—the rebels had been driven from Middle Tennessee.[25]

The ten-day campaign was over. The dejected Confederates made their way over the Cumberland Mountains, screened by Forrest and Wheeler. They braved rattlesnakes and copperheads and occupied makeshift campsites on the mountainsides. They blocked roads and beat back desultory Yankee pursuit. Captain H. L. Huggins of Freeman's battery, which was with Forrest, remembered later that "we had no rest until everything was safely over the Tennessee River." Yet, signs of precipitous flight were everywhere. Federal observers claimed that "all along the by-paths, in the woods as well as on the highways, over which the fleeing army had gone, were strewed clothing, wagons, blacksmith's tools and corn meal." The graycoats used the meal to fill potholes for passage of artillery. Whole fields of wall tents remained standing in abandoned camps along Duck River, and in them could be found mess chests, trunks, clothing, and thirty-five thousand more pounds of cornmeal. Five sixty-four-pounder siege guns and much miscellaneous ordnance also fell to the victors. By Union accounts, the mountains all over southeastern Tennessee contained single or pairs of rebels either going back toward their units or simply deserting for home.[26]

Some of those Confederates rather ingeniously made their way south. Captain Thomas Fearn Perkins's Company I, Eleventh Tennessee Cavalry, simply headed northward, back to the Murfreesboro and Triune road, capturing Federal and sutler stores, and continuing to skirmish with enemy pickets all the way to Franklin. Still combative, this band, including seventeen-year-old Newton Cannon, sent the pack mules and captured goods to a rendezvous and proceeded on to the Overton woods along the Nashville and Franklin road. There, they culled sixty prisoners from a mixed black and white woodcutting party from Nashville. Now pursued in earnest, these fearless riders departed rapidly to the southwest with captives and booty. They crossed the Tennessee River at Bainbridge, Alabama, and went over Sand Mountain and reached Bragg's army in Chattanooga unscathed.[27]

Harriet Ellen Moore despairingly noted in her diary on June 30 that: "Old Rosey seems to go ahead whether anybody else can or not. I wish Bragg could bring half a million men against him and drive every vestige of Yankeeism from [Nashville]." But Bragg possessed neither the will nor the means. Ailing in health, and thoroughly nonplused by recent events, he wired Richmond from Bridgeport, Alabama, on July 3: "Unable to obtain a general engagement without sacrificing my communications, I have, after a series of skirmishes, withdrawn the army to this river." A more embellished version went that same day to theater commander Joseph E. Johnston in Mississippi explaining that Bragg had found it impossible to attack Rosecrans, that he had been consistently outflanked by the enemy, but that he had succeeded in stymieing pursuit while withdrawing his numerically inferior force and saving supplies. Faced with protecting a long rail line through inhospitable mountains "in a country affording us nothing," he explained, Rosecrans could continue to outflank the Army of Tennessee "and thus secure our ultimate destruction without a battle." Four days later, Bragg wrote Richmond again to say that his army had crossed the Tennessee River, "attended with trifling loss of men and materials." Such information afforded President Jefferson Davis but small comfort, especially following on the heels of General Robert E. Lee's bloody repulse at Gettysburg and even more disheartening news of Vicksburg's surrender on July 4. Bragg's loss of Middle Tennessee, and by implication the road to Kentucky and the Ohio River, was a third staggering blow to the Confederacy's summer hopes in 1863.[28]

THE AUGUST LULL

Many of Rosecrans men simply flopped in the muddy fields and spent July 4 firing salutes, playing games and singing patriotic songs beside the floodwaters of Elk River. The wagons lay on the opposite side, so they had brought nothing across, and foraging offered little aid either. They would pass two weeks here, in a place the men called "Camp Winford," and on the evening of July 9, the German-American Ninth Ohio marched with its new regimental band to serenade corps commander "Pap" Thomas. They hoped he might oblige them with a speech of thanks for their recent work and include some news of the fall of Mississippi fortresses Vicksburg and Port Hudson. But the taciturn general only praised them again as his best unit and then retired to his tent with a simple "well boys, good night." Disappointed, the unit's chronicler noted that the triple cheer they sent after him "was not a thank-you for relevant news about the Mississippi."[29]

The fact that Rosecrans's army had attained the third leg of a triple crown of Union victories (and at considerably less cost than either Grant's forces at Vicksburg or Major General George Gordon Meade's Army of the Potomac at Gettysburg) seemed to pass unappreciated in the nation's capital. Rosecrans had not annihilated the enemy, but neither had Meade—a fact that likewise irked the president. Still, Rosecrans had pursued his foe despite the inclement weather, and his maneuvers won praise from Lincoln. The fact was, however, that by midsummer the administration needed decisive victories, not Pyrrhic ones, and it was growing increasingly impatient with excuses about rain and mud or worn-down troops. Ohio Democrats had nominated the traitorous Vallandigham for governor (in absentia) on June 11, and the winds of negotiated peace were sweeping the North once again. Indeed, waves of consternation swept the ranks of the western armies accordingly. "I can only adequately express my feelings in big sounding 'cuss' words," Major James A. Connolly wrote his wife about the Vallandigham situation. Fellow Ohioan Alfred C. Willett and his comrades actually decried the "butternut" copperheads at home more than the Confederates they faced in battle. "Let them shoulder their musket and come in the field," was Willett's opinion. He promised that these renegades would have to "keep still when soldiers get home from the war." So, the stakes were high, with the Kentucky gubernatorial election looming in August. Administration officials hardly warmed to the notion that Bragg's army had escaped and the Army of the Cumberland was resting on its self-proclaimed laurels after the Tullahoma campaign.[30]

As Rosecrans's army recuperated, its general resumed his telegraphic war of words with Washington. War Department officials fretted about Johnston reinforcing Bragg. "The patience of the authorities here has been completely exhausted," Halleck wrote Rosecrans on July 24, "you are as inactive as was General Buell." Secretary of War Edwin M. Stanton's tone was similar. His dispatch of July 7 had broadcast to Rosecrans: "Lee's army overthrown; Grant Victorious"—an "inexcusably tactless" telegram in one historian's view since it neglected Rosecrans's achievement. "You and your noble army now have the chance to give the finishing blow to the rebellion," Stanton continued, "will you neglect the chance?" Old Rosy's response, in Washington's eyes, seemed to be an uncooperative "yes."[31]

Ever mindful of setting everything in perfect order before moving, Rosecrans knew that his army required rest. Chaplain Lyle observed that, from his perspective, Ohio regiments had "neither rested, slept, nor ate anything, save crackers, for forty-eight hours, standing up or lying down, their muskets never out of their hands, skirmishing with the enemy the whole time, while shell and shot were passing over and around them—all this too, in rain and mud, and after long and fatiguing marches." With all this in mind, Rosecrans fired back at Stanton on July 7 that the War Department seemed unable to appreciate "the fact that this noble army has driven the rebels from Middle Tennessee." He chided Washington politicians not to overlook "so great an event because it is not written in letters of blood." Federal casualties of merely six hundred and Confederate counterparts of possibly sixteen hundred underscored his message. The next day, Rosecrans wrote Ambrose Burnside at Cincinnati that Bragg's disastrous retreat was apparently so demoralizing that some five thousand Tennesseans had deserted into the mountains, and "nothing but the excessive rains and impassable condition of the roads prevented us from overtaking and destroying their entire army." Burnside could appreciate that last remark; his own tour in Virginia had been marred by an abortive January "mud march."[32]

Meanwhile, Rosecrans's army spent most of August around Pelham, Hillsboro,

Wartrace, and Decherd on a front that stretched from Tracy City to Huntsville, Alabama. Alfred C. Willett recalled eating well and enjoying "good times" with his brigade near Shelbyville. The Ninth Ohio returned to Winchester, Tennessee, "where we had camped almost a year before." Ralsa C. Rice and others found time to analyze the region and its inhabitants. He observed that the blacks and poor whites were hardly separated at all by the racial line: both were poor and tilled inhospitable soil. The whole area, in fact, seemed to be growing back into sassafras, pennyroyal, and blackberries due to wartime neglect. He recalled hearing that this area was one of the oldest places of settlement in the hemisphere, but that "the finest of civilization had well nigh burned down" with agricultural attempts "but a mockery." The populace appeared ignorant of the world around it and content with its meager lot in life. Still, "they could drive a bargain equal to a Yankee peddlar," he admitted. Furthermore, the region abounded with rebel deserters and refugees seeking safe passage home.[33]

"The people is all turning to the Union here since the Yankees has got Vicksburg," was the observation of Martha Revis of Marshall, Madison County, North Carolina, in a letter to her husband with the Sixty-fourth North Carolina volunteers, a letter quickly confiscated and passed to Confederate headquarters in Knoxville and on to Richmond in late July and early August. The word of Confederate demoralization spread rapidly back to Union garrisons in Tennessee and Kentucky. John B. Whitcomb, stationed at the new Fort Donelson, wrote his brother on June 26: "There is not any thing of importance going on out here now so there is no news to write." But William H. Dorris, also stationed at Fort Donelson, wrote home later in August: "there is hundreds of deserters from Bragg's and Johnston's army all through Tennessee." Sergeant W. F. Stowell of Company F, Fifty-first Illinois, encamped at University Springs (later Sewanee) in Franklin County, wrote Andrew Johnson that vast numbers of rebel Tennesseans who had left the ranks "seem willing to do almost anything rather than to be forced back again." Whole brigades of them could be formed quickly, he thought. They might garrison forts and rear facilities, thus relieving regular Federal units for front-line duty. Major James Connolly and Brigadier General John Beatty decided that "everything looks favorable now" for concerted movements by all Union forces everywhere. The rebellion was about to fade with the autumn leaves. More worrisome were the post-Gettysburg draft riots in New York City and Confederate raider John Hunt Morgan's summer dash into southern Indiana and Ohio, although the Kentucky cavalier merely "arouses the people" to work harder for the Union, thought Alfred Lacey Hough.[34]

The joy of victory spread elsewhere in Rosecrans's rear guard. The Fifty-seventh Indiana at Murfreesboro fired off its heavy Parrott cannon thirty-four times (the number of states in the Union) in honor of Vicksburg, according to member James I I. Jones. Similar salutes echoed through Nashville, while the oratory of Governor Johnson and fiery East Tennessee unionist preacher William Brownlow droned through Independence Day ceremonies. A brigade of African-American troops paraded in full uniform with burnished arms, causing Mary Ellen Moore to lament, "oh, how humiliating." She would willingly "live on bread and water in the south where there is a liberty and society such as we once enjoyed" rather than dwell in luxury among people who considered former slaves their equal and "raise them up in our midst to kill and destroy."[35]

Morgan's rumored distress during his Ohio raid only added to Moore's displeasure, and she wondered whether eight million "free and chivalrous sothrons" would finally be overthrown in their effort for a separate and national existence. She thought not, citing the American Revolution, in which British redcoats held cities but ultimately had surrendered their army at Yorktown. Should we succumb "to the vilest foe that ever disgraced a national soul," because this foe held the cities, she asked herself. "We will ultimately triumph," she assured herself, "although our sky is for the present overcast by leaden and somber clouds."

Such southern hopes notwithstanding, the hated Yankees held the upper hand as the summer waned. Confident and now rested, the Army of the Cumberland looked for Rosecrans to lead them anywhere in the Confederacy. "Rosecrans in his late movements against Bragg has taken the rebel generals by surprise and completely out-generaled them," wrote Jesse B. Connelly, at the height of the Tullahoma operation. Now, resupply demanded attention, as Alfred Lacey Hough informed his wife on July 5: "What little there is in the country we are taking, but there ain't much left, the people complain as much of the rebel army as they do ours." Trooper Oscar Langworthy of the Fifth Iowa Cavalry told his father that this most beautiful and fertile part of the South was now marred beyond relief. He counted the populace as the losers since "the youngest child will, perhaps, not see the day when this country is brought back to its original greatness."[36]

Brigade commander John Beatty even praised his men's destructive talents, for they had made a clean sweep of hogs, sheep, and poultry along their march. He claimed no sympathy for the rich rebels, but pitied the poor. Even the army's animals lived off wheat still in the sheaf, "and I have seen hundreds of acres of wheat in the sheaf disappear in an hour." Fence rails had been burned unstintingly, while countless fields of growing corn had likewise been stripped clean by the men. Thus, the season's new crop of wheat, corn, oats, and hogs would be of no value to Bragg's army. "When destroyed," Beatty noted, "there will be nothing in middle Tennessee to tempt it back." All of this would have a salutary effect on the rebellious populace, he believed, because it would bring them to a sense of the loss they sustained "when they set aside the protecting shield of the old Constitution and the security they enjoyed in the Union."[37]

Here, then, was war with a vengeance; a "harsh" total war against not merely armies, but also against the populace and their property. No clearer evidence existed that the Civil War long since had passed its conciliatory phase, never to return. Rosecrans's headquarters issued a general order that was a strange combination of pleading with the soldiery to prevent the despoliation of "this beautiful region," and an appeal to help presumably loyal Tennesseans of the area return comity and civil order—in short, to head off anarchy, guerrilla warfare, plunder, and desolation. There could be no negotiated peace in the minds of the Union soldiers, however. Indeed, the Tennessee landscape now resembled more the tableau of Europe during the Thirty Years War. Both Union and Confederate troops spread across the region like a swarm of locusts, eating and destroying everything useful to them. But now this had become officially condoned Union policy; before it had existed as a soldierly perception of necessity. Sergeant Eugene Marshall of the Fifth Iowa Cavalry had addressed the need for total war in late May, with reference to cleaning out partisans northwest of Nashville. It was Rosecrans's intent, he had penned in his diary on the twenty-fourth, "to destroy all sources of supply for the rebel armies in Tennessee." This would "prevent the production of more than will supply the home population." If the general's orders were carried out in good faith, thought Marshall, he would succeed.[38]

Marshall admitted that many people were careless and had no heart for the war; there were those "who look upon treason and armed rebellion as venal offenses only." Two months later, as he and his regiment guarded Rosecrans's rail and highway supply lines, he considered the rebellion an abject failure, although guerrilla activity might still form a residual problem. On August 19, he noted that the war was making a wilderness even of new areas of operations. It seemed strange, he suggested, to ride through a country that "shows no cultivated fields and here and there a house (which shows marks of wealth and taste)," as though it had been "set down in the midst of an uncultivated prairie." Apparently, not every structure or symbol of oligarchy had been destroyed, and whether the rebellion was truly a failure remained to be proven in those areas behind the Federal advance.[39]

The Army of the Cumberland took scarcely a fortnight to maneuver its opponent out of the Duck River country. It would require an additional month to evict Bragg from East Tennessee at Chattanooga. Even then there was no battle. Yet, reopening the Nashville and Chattanooga railroad and the alternate route from Nashville to Decatur, Alabama, ensuring their survival against raiders, or even amassing requisite supplies and wagon trains all took time. Rosecrans never stopped reminding Washington of that fact. In turn, Lincoln and the War Department kept asking why Rosecrans and Burnside could not speed up their coordination and progress. The answer lay with logistics. If Rosecrans perceived that he needed a wagon train of nearly sixty-nine or seventy vehicles per one thousand men, it was because he now had to carry his provender with him. The ease of foraging that his army experienced in Middle Tennessee proved impossible in the Barrens and across the mountains; Bragg's men had seen to that. So, in order to move on Chattanooga, the Union army necessarily would be tied to rail and wagon supply lines, supplemented by what the men carried or might forage on their own.[40]

In the meantime, Union cavalry screened the flank where Burnside's army would fuse with Rosecrans's advance. Rebel irregulars continued to hold out in the Sparta–McMinnville area. Minty's cavalry brigade battled Dibrell's rebel command from Forrest's force to a standstill in running fights all along Wild Cat Creek and the Little Calfkiller River on August 9. "Of course I whipped Dibrell," Minty boasted two days later. "His men scattered about the country like blackberries." But, typically, the Confederates regrouped and came on again to Sparta. They resumed prowling the seam between Union armies until they were simply overwhelmed and withdrawn when Bragg realized that little could be done to stop the Yankee surge northwest of the mountains.[41]

The Lincoln administration allowed Rosecrans about two weeks' respite before beginning a new barrage of orders, comments, and harangues concerning forward movement. Nor was Burnside spared, as Halleck whined: "I do not know what he is doing, he seems tied fast to Cincinnati." Halleck instructed him on July 13 to cover Rosecrans's left flank and to "organize supply parties under your quartermaster and commissaries, and live as much as possible on the country." The bloated supply-train situation had already led to an exchange between Rosecrans and Quartermaster General Montgomery C. Meigs even before Tullahoma. So, Burnside was to take only "hard bread, sugar, coffee, and salt, and push forward rapidly, supplying yourself with forage, bacon, beef, and mutton in the country." Washington grossly misunderstood the now blighted countryside over which its armies operated.[42]

The great object that Rosecrans (and Burnside by implication) "will have in view is to drive Bragg from East Tennessee before he can be reinforced by Johnston," Halleck explained in mid-July. Over the next month, Washington wrangled with its two field commanders about baggage train self-discipline and about the inhospitable country toward Chattanooga ("always barren—with but few fertile spots" that "have been gleaned and scraped by rebels with a powerful cavalry force ever since last winter," noted Rosecrans). Rosecrans peevishly wrote his commander-in-chief on August 22: "I am sure when you consider we have but a single line of railroad from Louisville; that we are 300 miles from that base; that we have crossed by three day's march the formidable barrier of the Cumberland Mountains; that we have in front a swift river from 500 to 800 yards wide, and seventy miles of mountains in front of us to reach the fertile regions of Northern Georgia, you [will] see that few armies have been called upon to attempt a more arduous campaign."[43]

TURBULENCE BEHIND UNION FRONT LINES

The problems confronting Burnside were more than logistical. Grant had failed to return promptly the easterner's own IX corps following the fall of Vicksburg. A large part of Mississippi remained generally untamed, while raiders under Richardson, Biffle, Newsom, and James U. Green kept Grant's own logistical base unsettled by cruising once more through West Tennessee and the Purchase area of Kentucky. In central Kentucky, Burnside also experienced his share of disruption, thanks to Colonel John S. Scott, as well as Captain Thomas C. Hines's eighty-man advance team for Morgan's "Great Raid" across the Ohio. Furthermore, the Department of Ohio also encompassed Copperhead country north of the Ohio, and Burnside's overstretched manpower and administrative officials sensed much unhappiness with the draft and other unpopular measures by Washington. East Tennessee was therefore slow to appear among anyone's priorities despite Washington's sense of urgency.[44]

Summer 1863

Hines was disposed of rather quickly when Yankee pursuers caught his men bathing in Wilson's Creek between Elizabethtown and Bardstown. The rebels fled in disorder, although they had already caused havoc by plundering the area. A rump contingent of Hines's band got across the Ohio, possibly bent upon stirring up a reputed copperhead secret army of ten thousand men. Unsuccessful in their recruitment effort, they returned to create mayhem in Kentucky. One of Hines's lieutenants was John M. Porter, who had ducked imprisonment after Fort Donelson by feigning civilian status. This time, however, he departed for incarceration at Johnson's Island prison camp. Still, Hines's activities were merely prelude to Morgan's memorable strike in July—surely one of the most colorful escapades of the war. It ranked with Abel D. Streight's unsuccessful if well-intentioned Union foray into Alabama the year before.[45]

Yet, Hines and Morgan kept northern officials off guard for weeks, and while Bragg remained blissfully unaware of the Kentuckian's location (thinking that he was merely somewhere in the Bluegrass), the raiders set southern hearts throbbing with renewed dreams of hope and glory. Whether it was undertaken to impress his wife, Mattie, or his brothers, who accompanied Morgan, or to recoup his reputation after the McMinnville disaster in the spring, the two-thousand-rider strike has been interpreted more loftily as an attempt to influence the northern home front. It came at the very moment when Bragg needed his cavalry more at Tullahoma. But Morgan certainly caused "much uneasiness," as Pennsylvania infantryman Frederick Pettit informed his family in August. Moreover, Morgan delayed Burnside's timetable for advancing on East Tennessee, even though it cost the Kentuckian a stint in the Ohio penitentiary for his effort.[46]

In another sense, Morgan's activities enhanced Union army-navy cooperation on the rivers, while destroying the cavalier's reputation for reliability in the eyes of his superiors. After initial delays due to Union colonel William P. Sanders's counterraid toward Knoxville, Morgan surmounted high water in the upper Cumberland and ragged blocking efforts by Grant's old West Point classmate, Brigadier General Henry M. Judah, and Kentucky brigadier Edward Henry Hobson, son of a steamboat captain and himself president of the Greensburg branch of the Bank of Kentucky at the outset of the war. Judah and Hobson also gained the services of Colonel Frank Wolford, an outstanding criminal lawyer from Liberty who would later be cashiered for daring to criticize Lincoln.

Morgan ran into stubborn opposition from a local Tebbs Bend defender on Green River, who bluntly told Morgan that the Fourth of July was a bad day for a Federal officer to surrender and proceeded to snuff out thirty-five rebel lives (including that of Colonel D. W. Chenault) and wound forty more in a nasty little firefight. Morgan then moved on, irritably torching much of the town of Lebanon and the Louisville and Nashville trestle over Rolling Fork. Additional skirmishing became continuous, although plundering better marked the raiders' passage. Burnside assured the War Department on July 6 that, while Morgan had broken through, "as soon as [Morgan] is disposed of, I will start the expedition to east Tennessee." It made no sense to the general to leave the Confederate raiders in his rear "to break up our railroad communications and capture our wagon trains." Before Halleck even received the missive, he had wired Burnside to move promptly and rapidly, "or your opportunity will be lost." He saw "no need at the present time of keeping large forces in Kentucky" and kept hammering Burnside for days about having militia and home guards cope with the raiders.[47]

Along the way, Morgan reneged on his promise to permit Kentucky partisan colonel Adam Rankin Johnson to create a diversion in his old Henderson neighborhood as the whole force crossed the Ohio at Brandenburg, Kentucky, on July 8. The raiders then turned east across the lower end of Indiana and Ohio, vowing retribution for Union military depredations in Kentucky and Tennessee. Morgan made little effort to distinguish between genuine southern sympathizers and copperheads or to use them as guides and scouts. All loyal supporters of the Confederacy belonged in gray uniforms, he thought. So confident that he could elude Hobson and his pursuers and escape to join Lee's army in the east, Morgan failed to account for Union naval control of western rivers. Low water might protect his party as they ranged along just north of the river, but the same torrential rains that deluged the armies at Tullahoma soon enabled the navy, plus an inflated force of militia and other ersatz soldiery, to corner the raiders upriver from Cincinnati.[48]

Indeed, the navy joined the chase soon after Morgan crossed into Indiana. Lieutenant Commander Le Roy Fitch already had interdiction patrols battling contraband traders, and he simply redeployed five gunboats, including his flagship, the six-gun USS *Moose*, to the new mission. Burnside contributed an army gunboat, the *Allegheny Belle*, her boilers protected by southern cotton bales and carrying a rifled Parrott cannon. Fitch proceeded to block potential crossings, although as he stated in his after-action report, "at times Morgan would be, as it were, in the center of a circle, with the river running around him, so that by marching by a few miles in either direction he could strike some six or eight very good fords, while to run by river, these fords were nearly a day's run apart." But the naval officer and his Jack Tars persevered, while army headquarters adeptly coordinated land and river operation that led to Morgan's being brought to ground at Buffington's Island northeast of Portsmouth, Ohio, on July 19. Morgan and eleven hundred of his men escaped from the first clash, only to be blocked again by the navy the next day at Readsville. Eventually, about a week later, Brigadier General James Shackleford (another Kentucky veteran of the Fort Donelson campaign of 1862) and five hundred hand-picked troopers collared remnants of Morgan's band near the village of West Point in Columbian County, about eighty miles from Lake Erie. Morgan's capture came none too soon, as receding water in the Ohio forced Fitch and his gunboats back downstream below Cincinnati.[49]

Morgan and many of his group went off to the state prison at Columbus, while Adam Johnson rallied a smattering of survivors for a retreat across the mountains to safety in Virginia. Late in this episode, Confederate colonel John S. Scott reappeared through Big Creek Gap into southeastern Kentucky, "incidentally to make a diversion in favor of General Morgan," avowed East Tennessee Confederate commander Simon Bolivar Buckner. Frankly, Scott was more interested in raiding for horses, mules, cattle, and arms. Colonel G. B. Hodge was similarly engaged farther north, but was himself stymied in turn by a Union counterraid against southwestern Virginia salt works. At any rate, Scott routed more Yankees near Richmond, Kentucky, and sent another shock wave coursing through the region until Burnside's horsemen got back into position following Morgan's capture. They defeated Scott on the banks of the upper Cumberland; the raider lost an artillery piece plus 350 men as well as pilfered livestock, although he eventually escaped with several hundred Yankee prisoners, two artillery pieces, and some six hundred Enfield muskets. This fiasco supposedly caused many Tennesseans to desert Scott's ranks, and Buckner promised a full investigation. In sum, these Kentucky and Ohio episodes ranked with other rebel setbacks that summer.[50]

Still, Morgan remained the South's paladin, as he cushioned the blows of Gettysburg, Vicksburg, and Bragg's retreat. Robert H. Kean, a Richmond functionary, wrote in his diary that the Kentuckian's work "is the most remarkable smaller event of the war." Remarkable it was, if what counted was a grayclad host temporarily on northern soil, despoiling property, dislocating trade, and forcing imposition of Yankee martial law from Louisville to Indianapolis. Remarkable too was his ride of 926 miles through enemy territory, only to end up as a prisoner of war. Yet, Morgan's troopers' passage produced no outpouring of sympathy or support in the overtly copperhead counties north of the Ohio. If anything, the Indianapolis *Journal* suggested, the raid steeled midwestern patriotism and determination to greater effort for the Union. Morgan's men were brigands to many people, and even normally uninspired militiamen built confidence by chasing them. Good for headlines and raising false hopes in Dixie, John Hunt Morgan caused scarcely a ripple on Rosecrans's agenda and did nothing to help Bragg in his hour of need. Moreover, as Burnside wired Halleck the day after Morgan's capture: "I can now look after the other work you desire done." Five weeks later, he was in Knoxville.[51]

Indeed, Morgan's capture proved to be a particular fillip for Union military morale. Captain Hubbard T. Thomas of the Twenty-sixth Indiana battery wrote home on July 22 that he would have enjoyed seeing his fellow Hoosiers take the fellow. He observed that Basil Duke, Morgan's brother-in-law and second-in-command, was really the "main financier and engineer of the whole force." Morgan was only "bluster and blow," with very ordinary talents, in Thomas's opinion. As for army-navy cooperation, Burnside personally thanked Rear Admiral David Porter for Fitch's help. "The brilliant success which has attended the joint operations of the Army and the Navy in this movement gives abundant evidence of the good feeling between these two efficient arms of the service, and promises much for the future success of all such operations," he wrote. Of course, Burnside was a true believer anyway, a veteran of successful cooperation in coastal operations in North Carolina. But, as at Dover in February 1863, the navy had once more saved the army's fortunes. Morgan might have escaped back across the Ohio if pursuit had been only by land. Army-navy collaboration—the product of Forts Henry and Donelson in early 1862—continued to ensure Union success in the West.[52]

Elsewhere behind the front lines in Tennessee, good reports continued to come from commanders like Colonel Sanders Bruce at Clarksville, who had scouted "with energy and effect" through the range of wild country from the Cumberland to the Duck Rivers. Expiration of enlistment for portions of his cavalry left him with only 210 mounted men among his 1,294 effectives. Still, he managed to seize an estimated "46,000 barrels of flour" and provide an extensive survey for possible restoration of the Edgefield branch railroad (although he lacked the crews necessary to reconstruct the line). Like his counterpart at Fort Donelson, Colonel William P. Lyon, Bruce also recommended transfer of the troublesome telegraph line between the two posts from the guerrilla-prone south bank to the more secure north bank of the Cumberland.[53]

Lyon observed that the telegraph line was cut "three or four times a week," usually about fifteen miles from the fort toward Cumberland City. The guerrillas, claimed the Wisconsin colonel, "must have their headquarters near Waverly, where they were supported and sustained by the whole community." That town, he suggested, was "the nest of the vilest and most pestilential set of traitors that live, and the place ought to be destroyed." Lyon kept Captain Archibald N. Randall's mounted patrols constantly harassing the partisans from Fort Henry to the Duck River and eastward from Dover to White Oak and Indian Mound in the direction of Clarksville. It hardly helped his own soldiers' attitudes when President Lincoln subsequently commuted the July death sentence of a local Dickson County guerrilla captain, Dr. Anson James, for killing an Eighth Kentucky (Union) lieutenant. But, as far as major enemy threats to this sector, Private William H. Dorris of the Eighty-third Illinois judged correctly that "The rebels are mighty afraid of Donelson for here is where they have had bad luck."[54]

Irregulars, especially when teamed with regular Confederate units, proved more contentious in West Tennessee and the Purchase section of southwestern Kentucky. They effectively defied Lieutenant Commander S. L. Phelps's watchful gunboats by conducting ferrying services across the rivers. They infiltrated neighborhoods to rustle cattle and horses, and they seemingly recruited manpower at will. "This part of the South at least is paying dearly for the system of guerrilla warfare which recoils upon themselves with infinitely more harm than it has caused to the national interests," commented Phelps. Then, just as in Middle Tennessee and central Kentucky, the western part of both states received a major jolt in July when they were visited by Biffle, Richardson, Newsom, A. N. Wilson, and yet another of the Forrest brothers, Jesse. Rendezvousing at Jackson, Tennessee, their mission remained unclear, but the August gubernatorial election in Kentucky and abiding concerns for supplies and recruits were factors. Caught in this latest crisis was Memphis commander Stephen A. Hurlbut, who merely wanted to leave the army and return to his comfortable Illinois law practice at this point.[55]

Union raiding expeditions like those of the Third Michigan and Second Iowa cavalry went south from LaGrange, Tennessee, in late June, burning railroad bridges and depots, cotton, and grain as they moved toward Penola and the Tallahatchie River in northern Mississippi in the heart of Chalmers's district. But by mid-July, they were back battling a major rebel counterstrike at Jackson, Tennessee, where a victorious fight on the eighteenth netted the Union cavalry quantities of good firearms and horses—"the rebles [sic] had better horses than we do," Iowan William Wells told his father. "The colonel said that it was the best charge that he ever see," claimed Wells of the four-hour running chase through town. Elsewhere in West Tennessee, the bluecoats fared less well.[56]

Hurlbut was mortified when his Columbus district commander lost the Union City garrison to Biffle's minions on July 10. The garrison surrendered to inferior numbers without a fight. The commander of the relief column, Colonel John Scott of the Thirty-second Iowa, arrived quickly by rail from Columbus only twenty-five miles away, but failed to apprehend Biffle. Scott felt that Major Edward Langen's Fourth Missouri Cavalry garrison, which had only recently moved to Union City from Clinton, had totally neglected "even the ordinary precautions" against such raids. In any case, Alexander Asboth panicked anew, withdrawing outlying units for a close-in defense of Paducah, and he angered the navy by abandoning Fort Heiman and its coal dumps, which serviced the gunboats. Biffle soon departed southward as Hurlbut eventually got Colonel Edward Hatch's pursuit mounted from northern Mississippi. Hatch caught Biffle at Jackson on July 13, killed forty and captured over two hundred of the marauders while freeing four hundred local conscripts and two hundred and fifty horses. Local townsfolk, however, aided the rebels by carrying ammunition to them under fire, while still others attempted to entice Colonel William K. M. Breckenridge's First West Tennessee (Union) Cavalry with liquor. The affair ended with both the Tennesseans and some of Hatch's own Second Michigan looting the town in retaliation.[57]

Hickman, Kentucky, also felt the raiders' wrath about a week later, although it is unclear just who these new interlopers were. Federal commanders too willingly ascribed all penetration in that sector to Forrest, though many of the riders surely belonged to the wizard's organization at some point. At any rate, the Hickman visitors spent July 15–17 ransacking local unionist property and hunting down unionists who were to be liquidated. The Confederates numbered "about 3 companies" or anywhere from 150 to 300 men. Federal reaction proved more sluggish than at Union City, as a waterborne relief column aboard the ram USS *Monarch* never reached Hickman until July 18. Asboth did send Colonel George E. Waring of the Fourth Missouri Cavalry sweeping through Mayfield, Murray, and Feliciana, Kentucky, looking for the rebels from July 22 to 27. Waring, a prewar planner and supervisor of the Central Park drainage system in New York City, found the area along the state line "full of guerrillas and conscripting parties, impressing and robbing Union citizens." But his column never encountered groups in excess of 80 men, although he estimated upwards of 1,000 enemy forces filled the region.[58]

Rumors mentioned Gideon Pillow joining forces with Forrest as part of some vaguely coordinated effort with Morgan's raid north of the Ohio. Hurlbut quickly punctured that myth, but had "so little confidence in Asboth's reports that I am at a loss what to do," he wrote Grant on July 17. Pillow's rumored presence, he decided, was a ruse to help influence the early August election at Mayfield.

{285}

Hurlbut desperately wanted Asboth's removal, and Grant eventually agreed. But Federal spokesmen flatly doubted that the region could ever be pacified. Lieutenant Colonel Edward H. Mix of the Thirty-second Iowa told his superiors that "I think it safe to say that the country about Hickman cannot be protected from Columbus." Fleet Captain A. M. Pennock at Cairo told Porter on July 21: "I hope that the severe chastisement that Morgan's forces have received from the gunboats may deter the guerrillas from active operations." Few signs of that happening surfaced west of the Tennessee River at this point.[59]

Biffle, Wilson, Newsom, and Jeffrey Forrest, along with Colonel A. D. Campbell, remained active in the region. They would be joined on occasion by Colonel P. D. Roddey's command from Mississippi. They now carried distinct orders from exiled Tennessee governor Isham G. Harris "to control the elections on the first Thursday in August, and to enforce conscription." So Hurlbut directed Asboth to send one thousand men from Columbus to work with Hatch at Paris, Tennessee, and drive these bands from the state. He added that "those men who enforce conscription within our lines should not be treated as prisoners of war," the very point that Grant put in a general order issued at Vicksburg on August 1. Two days later the raiders had been dispersed, and on August 5 Grant replaced Asboth with Brigadier General Andrew J. Smith as district commander at Columbus. Hurlbut now settled down to organizing unionist home guards largely in response to Hickman and Fulton County, Kentucky, officials who had suffered from guerrilla persecution during the mid-July visit. Still, some Federals remained skeptical. Waring, for one, suggested on August 12: "I am not disposed to believe 4,000 rebel troops are being spared from Bragg's army for less important work here; yet Morgan's taking away 8,000 at a time when Bragg was in danger, is equally difficult to understand."[60]

Since they lacked manpower to form a line of defense along the high ridge that paralleled the state line from Pine Bluff in the east to just below Hickman on the Mississippi (thus shielding the Purchase from raids to the south), Smith, Waring, and others could only focus on suppressing civil discord and illegal smuggling. Random murders vied with periodic capture of wagon trains loaded with salt, whiskey, and dry goods bound for Confederate customers. Irregulars continued to plague the area, while fretful Union garrisons from Mayfield to Paris dashed about searching anxiously for them. Colonel Isaac R. Hawkins of the Second West Tennessee (Union) Cavalry wrote Military Governor Johnson on August 9: "The Loyal men of that section desire to know if there is any way in which they can be organized so that they can defend their own homes and they think quite a force could be raised for that purpose." People with tepid loyalty to either side now began to believe law and order might be preferable to the zestful credos of high-sounding political causes.[61]

Additional issues confronted Union military officials in the Mississippi valley at this time. Recruitment of black troops, illegal cotton and horse trading, and army-navy bickering over transfer of the infamous, unruly Mississippi Marine Brigade to land duty (thereby freeing transports and gunboats for other missions, according to both Grant and Porter) filled communications with

Washington. The brigade was down to merely five hundred men, far too small for the increasing counterguerrilla requirements, according to Porter. Besides, "I find the Marine Brigade and army do not get along very well together when cooperating," he hinted. Still, the War Department would not allow Grant to turn this special unit into line infantry or cavalry. "This brigade was organized and the men enlisted especially for service as river men," Halleck wired stiffly on August 24. As they already had proven themselves "as valuable auxiliaries," they would continue to engage in sweeps on the lower Mississippi and up the Arkansas and Red Rivers, even though their utility had largely dissipated on the Tennessee and Cumberland. Perhaps the unit's rapacious conduct secretly met favor with "harsh war" enthusiasts in the administration.[62]

A PIVOTAL ELECTION IN KENTUCKY

Perhaps the trickiest issue confronting Union military and political officials behind the front lines at this point was the matter of emancipation and coincidentally the use of blacks in the war effort. These two items fused during the pivotal Kentucky gubernatorial campaign of 1863. In the process, they graphically illustrated the soft state of civil-military relations in the federally occupied upper heartland. Major military operations against East Tennessee, Tullahoma, or Vicksburg aside, the Kentucky election symbolized the impact of new strategic goals, or war aims, and the image of the Lincoln administration concerning defense of the Constitution and private property in the upper South. Kentuckians had suffered through trade restrictions, property losses attending the autumn campaign of Bragg and Kirby Smith (as well as guerrilla incursions and the normal military tramps across the state), and military enforcement of Federal laws and regulations since 1861. However, both preliminary and formal emancipation proclamations and the Conscription Act of March 3, 1863, as it applied to enrollment of blacks proved far more unsettling to the equilibrium of Kentucky unionism.[63]

Historian Victor B. Howard has suggested that the Kentucky election was contested on the issue of slavery (although most of the voters had no interest in the institution), and the enrollment of free blacks into the army was the "most exciting topic of discussion on election day." Certainly Lincoln's emancipation policies had raised Kentuckians' hackles ever since their preliminary expression on September 22, 1862, followed by formal announcement at the beginning of the new year. Military and naval enforcement of the Articles of War of March 13, Confiscation Act of July 17, and War Department General Order No. 139 of September 24 in 1862, insofar as they too involved the issue of slavery in Kentucky, further inflamed the situation. Increasingly stormy confrontations occurred between emancipationist Federal volunteers crossing the state and local Kentucky politicians, soldiers, and civilians. Kentucky unionist officers like Brigadier General Jeremiah Boyle repeatedly warned Washington against enforcing enrollment of blacks as a preliminary to conscription or enlistment in response to the Conscription Act of 1863. In Boyle's view, seventy-five thousand men would take to the field "to keep a miserable few hundreds of slaves from being taken away." Boyle was not adverse to ordering six thousand slave men impressed from selected counties in August to work on military roads, followed within weeks by Burnside's order impressing another eight thousand for railroad construction.[64]

Phrases like "not an honest man in the state" would support placing blacks in combat units, or that it would "meet decided opposition," or that it would "revolutionize the State and do infinite and inconceivable harm," dotted Boyle's communications. Well placed to capture the sentiments of his fellow Kentuckians, Boyle's words represented fears based on economic as well as political grounds. The Bluegrass was fast being overrun with runaway slaves from the deeper South, their bonds unshackled by the Union army and navy or word of Lincoln's proclamation. Many were incarcerated by local sheriffs and sold at auction before authorities stepped in to organize the vagrants as labor gangs for public projects. But enrollment of free blacks imperiled slavery; Kentucky was a slave state—loyal but still slave in focus. As Lincoln's Illinois friend James W. Fell wrote a fellow unionist on February 16, Kentucky's denunciation of the president's emancipationist policy was "bitter and universal," for "Kentucky's loyalty means loyalty to slavery."[65]

Losing property was one thing to loyal Kentuckians. Arming slaves was yet another—an anathema throughout the South before the war, and no different now in wartime. Enrollment was postponed at the time of the election in August. However, the issue was only partially defused in Kentuckians' minds by interpretations that Lincoln did not intend to enroll blacks in order to arm them as soldiers, but rather as a preparatory to employing them as laborers, or that he had only determined to conduct a census, not full-blown registration. In eastern Kentucky, by contrast, many people felt that the proclamation had not gone far enough, since it did not abolish all slavery. So, military enrollment was an additional facet of a highly politicized issue.[66]

Animosity toward Lincoln and his administration concerning emancipation overrode all else, and even produced realignment of political parties in Kentucky. Reemergence of the States' Rights Party (which had been dormant since Governor Beriah Magoffin's resignation the previous August) now provided refuge to those unionists opposed to Lincoln's "radicalism." Staunch unionists who unstintingly supported the war immediately raised the specter that the states' righters really represented the next step to secession. Local garrison commander Colonel S. A. Gilbert used troops to break up the States' Rights Party convention in Frankfort on February 17, calling them traitors, thereby inflaming the situation, since in fact this convocation did not necessarily mean that these Kentuckians were at all ready to forsake the Union. Country folks, despoiled as they were by Bragg's army and guerrillas, hardly leaned toward the Confederate cause. Yet, unionists, particularly those in uniform, took it that way or at the very least worried that states' righters would carry Kentucky out of the war entirely. As the eminent Kentucky historian E. Merton Coulter so sagely understood, Gilbert's action caused both Democrats and Union men to recognize what might be the logical result of military occupation "when an army officer could break up a peaceful political convention and order the party to disband."[67]

Gilbert's attempt to destroy a political party "was a most dangerous interference on the part of the military with civil affairs," Coulter continued. The resulting civil-military friction provided background to the principal political actions of the spring and summer before election day. The party in power—the Union Democracy—held its state convention in Louisville on March 18 and 19, with Boyle an active candidate for governor. The selected nominee withdrew, ostensibly for health reasons, but Coulter suggested that the real reason was "the melancholy situation of the state, dominated by the military authorities." A recently resigned Union officer, Thomas E. Bramlette, became his replacement, presiding over a party concerned about any close identification with Lincoln and the Union military.[68]

In June, discontented Union Democrats broke off and formed the Peace Democrats, nominating Charles Wickliffe for governor. The resulting campaign was "heated and excited," with Union Democrats taking every opportunity to accuse the peace men of advocating secession and treason. Conversely, the Peace Democrats condemned the Lincoln administration for an insane policy of "freedom proclamations, compensated emancipation, and the use of negro soldiers." In effect, the parties in Kentucky reflected their national counterparts—the War versus Peace Democrats. Various subterfuges were employed by the ruling party, including sitting governor James F. Robinson's proclamation disenfranchising expatriated Kentuckians and the army's directives relating to contraband slaves and its intimidation of peace party members and other election dirty tricks. On July 25, Boyle issued an order concerning seizure of secessionist property and indicated that a vote for Wickliffe would be tantamount to admitting the voter was a rebel. Military authorities also intimated that those who attempted to vote, but were unable to establish their right to do so, would be considered rebels. Another strict oath of fealty was demanded of every citizen, and on July 31 Burnside (having succeeded Wright as department commander on the eve of the political campaign back in March) declared martial law throughout Kentucky, citing the possibility of invasion by a rebel force "with the avowed intention of overawing the judges of elections, of intimidating the loyal voters, keeping them from the polls, and forcing the election of disloyal candidates...."[69]

Such strict Federal military control permitted Bramlette to win election by a margin of nearly three and a half to one, and Wickliffe's name was actually stricken off the ticket in many counties. The issues may have been what Howard declared they were, namely, the emancipation and enlistment of black men. But military intimidation and control were the pivotal political actions in the 1863 Kentucky election, claimed Coulter. Some measure of precaution against allowing Confederates and their sympathizers to return had to be made, he admitted. But even the Vincennes (Indiana) *Sun* declared that event "one of the greatest outrages on a free election ever perpetrated on any State," suggesting that it was a victory of "usurpation, terrorism and fraud" over the constitution and laws of Kentucky.

Bramlette's initial zeal for prosecuting the war and for supporting the Lincoln government would change during his term in office. But Coulter, at least, seemed to suggest Kentucky's subsequent wartime tribulation was exacerbated by the unfortunate actions of Union military in the 1863 election. The "course of the military authorities was so exasperating," he wrote in 1926, "as to be later held out against them by all Kentuckians as an additional stinging grievance against the Federal government." Burnside's recent biographer has added that what the Union general feared Confederate raiders like John Scott might do—that is, militarily interfere with the Kentucky election—"he did himself."[70]

Conditions remained unsettled at the end of the summer of 1863. Peace talk vied with that of continuing war in the nation's discourse. J. E. Woodward, a Paducah civilian, advocated the return to normal river commerce until rebuffed by Admiral Porter's August 24 comment that "vessels are not allowed to trade nor steamers to go up the Tennessee River without a gunboat." The navy was not concerned about guerrillas but rather that civilian goods would find their way to the principal Confederate armies. Halleck wrote Hurlbut at the end of July: "If the North were as united as the South, and would fill up our ranks now, we could soon end the war." Local Mississippi Confederate cavalry chieftain James R. Chalmers apprised his own superiors just a week before that Vicksburg's surrender had impacted upon the Magnolia State much as Bowling Green's evacuation had upon Kentucky in the winter of 1862, or Shiloh upon Tennessee in the spring. "It will be some time before much assistance can be expected from [Mississippians]," he decided. On the other hand, Chalmers was heartened by secessionist resurgence in West Tennessee. So he proposed sending a raiding force from Mississippi to round up deserters before returning through Kentucky and Tennessee to disrupt Federal affairs in that quarter. Indeed, that disruption had occurred, but with seemingly little apparent impact on Kentucky elections.[71]

Hurlbut wrote Lincoln personally on August 11 that "the rank and file of the Southern army have begun to awaken to the knowledge that they are not fighting their own battle, but the battle of the officers, the politicians, and the plantation class." He reminded his friend that he had predicted this more than a year before. Moreover, "doubt, fear, and indecision mark the councils of the Southwestern armies." Heavy bodies of deserters, with their arms, held the mountains of north Alabama and defied Confederate conscription. Murmurs of unionism could be heard on all sides, while the terror of arming ex-slaves would hasten war's end. Moral causes would have as much to do with ending the rebellion as physical causes, with battles merely useful for breaking up "the solid array of force" and allowing men to think and act rationally. The days of chivalry had passed, in Hurlbut's view.

As for Tennessee, "this State is ready by overwhelming majorities to repeal the act of secession, establish a fair system of gradual emancipation, and tender herself back to the Union." He admitted to opposing such moves in his own jurisdiction until the eastern counties had been secured. That accomplished, he told the president, the governor should call an election for the legislature, which, in turn, should summon a ratifying convention for a new state constitution. "In sixty days the work will be done," thought Hurlbut, and then "we can use upon the Tennessee troops in Southern service the same tremendous lever of State pride and State authority which forced them into hostile ranks." Whatever Lincoln might have thought of Hurlbut as a soldier, his fellow Illinoisan's political counsel carried weight.[72]

Meanwhile, the men in the ranks merely awaited the pleasure of generals and politicians. Minor triumphs occurred when Private Martin W. Culp captured the notorious guerrilla Major Dick McCann at Weem's Springs on August 19. McCann and fourteen of his brethren joined felons in the Nashville penitentiary. Rosecrans also visited that city, called upon Andrew Johnson, and took stock of the forts and support facilities at the state capital. Movement seemed to be in the air once more, as Private James H. Jones of the Fifty-seventh Indiana watched "several trains of cars loaded with pontoons" passing southward through Murfreesboro. Even garrison troops like the Seventieth Indiana regained their marching legs with long hikes under heavy gear. Sylvester Wills of that unit told his parents about a twenty-one-hour march between Murfreesboro and Nashville in the August heat, with two or three inches of dust covering the men, many without shoes. All of this was designed to prepare the soldiers for the next campaign—the liberation of East Tennessee from Confederate armies and oppression. Meanwhile, Pennsylvania corporal Frederick Pettit observed from Nicholasville, Kentucky, the widespread vice and immorality in the bright and sunny South that was attributable to idleness and slavery. The war itself was fast doing away with the latter. After the war, he prophesied, the whole South "will be a [sic] ruined physically, intellectually, and morally." What a wide field would then be open for those involved in educating the masses.[73]

ELEVEN

VICTORIES BLUE AND GRAY: AUTUMN 1863

In August 1863 Staff officer Alfred Lacey Hough wrote his wife in Philadelphia about mess tables resplendent with summer vegetables. James H. Jones of the Fifty-seventh Indiana similarly mentioned that there were plenty of apples, and the citizenry was selling them for a dollar a bushel, a fact confirmed by Alfred C. Willett of the 113th Ohio. Jones added that, as he wrote, nearly a mile of cattle filled the nearby turnpike, destined for the army. Corporal Frederick Pettit with the One-hundredth Pennsylvania at Camp Nelson, Kentucky, having returned from the Vicksburg campaign, wrote home that he had never eaten so much corn in his life as he had that summer, and he noted the abundance of all sorts of vegetables as well as peaches available by the peck from the populace. To help with housekeeping tasks for the Union soldiers were liberated slaves, who served as cooks, launderers, laborers, teamsters, stewards, and personal servants. They had been "conscripted" into the ranks, as it were, despite headquarters' aversion that it placed an added strain on supplies.[1]

Then, suddenly, "our summer vacation" ended abruptly without warning, recalled Ralsa C. Rice of the 125th Ohio. The date was August 16, and within an hour's time, they were up and away, "going none of us knew where." Rumors said they were headed home; the war over, peace declared. Then, such talk was brutally dashed by reality. Crestfallen, the sunburned veterans turned their faces southward. Ahead lay the arduous climb over the Cumberland Mountains. Beyond lay East Tennessee and the prize of Chattanooga. As the Ninth Ohio chronicler put it: "Our hopes were high that we would cross [the Tennessee River] and strike the decisive blow for the Union in the West."[2]

General-in-Chief Henry Halleck had wired Major General William S. Rosecrans at noon on August 4: "Your forces must move forward without further delay," and he ordered him to report daily progress. Ohio department commander Ambrose Burnside received a similar directive—advance a twelve-thousand-man column immediately on Knoxville and "endeavor to connect with the

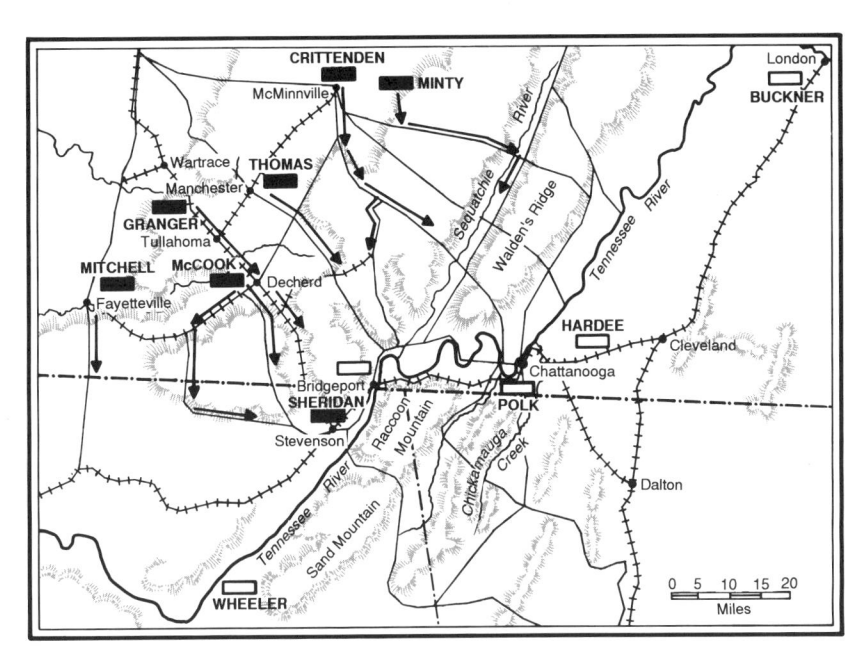

The advance on Chattanooga, August 1863.

forces of General Rosecrans, who has preemptory orders to move forward." Both subordinates had been quibbling for weeks with Washington about lack of high-level understanding of their logistical problems, geographical obstacles, and lack of resources. Tempers became so frayed at one point that Rosecrans had simply telegraphed the War Department from Winchester: "I say to you frankly that whenever the Government can replace me by a commander in whom they have more confidence, they ought to do so, and take the responsibility of the result." His enemies in high places undoubtedly tucked that message away for future use.[3]

The officers and men of the Army of the Cumberland claimed much later that the immense difficulties, "exceeded the comprehension of the critics and cavilers of this war then and since." They justified delay and apparent inertia, and veterans like the Ninth Ohio historian subsequently pointed to a perpetual rations problem, lack of pontoons to bridge the one-thousand-yard-wide Tennessee River in order to quickly occupy Chattanooga, and anticipated enemy opposition to the advance. Rosecrans's force was far from its base, linked solely by thin lines of railroad tracks, supplemented (water permitting) by the western rivers. In his front lay sixty to seventy miles of inhospitable terrain destitute of forage and subsistence and traversed by few good roads. As Old Rosy saw it, "we must so advance as never to recede," for as one flagging southerner had informed him: "'Whip our armies and then, when we no longer fear their return to power, we will show you that we are satisfied to be in the Union; but until you do that, we are not safe from proscription.'"[4]

Burnside's problems differed from those of Rosecrans. After disposing of

Morgan's raid and ensuring positive gubernatorial results, he still had to contend with raiders disrupting the timetable of his forward movement. Ulysses S. Grant tarried in returning IX corps troops from Mississippi. Washington worried that remaining Confederate units in that state would reinforce the defenders of East Tennessee. Rosecrans, for one, discounted such celerity of coordination and suggested that the best thing that Burnside might do in that case was to quickly employ his cavalry and infantry for a Union strike against the enemy's line of communications in north Georgia. "We get him in our grip and strangle him" was Rosecrans's prescription, "or perish in the attempt." But talk was cheap. Washington wanted direct movement into East Tennessee, not a high-sounding repetition of Streight's caper in Bragg's rear. So Burnside remained in a quandary.[5]

TO KNOXVILLE, CHATTANOOGA, AND BEYOND

Rosecrans and Burnside tried hard to convince Washington that they intended to move promptly upon East Tennessee. In a continuing ploy to secure more horsemen, Rosecrans forwarded Kentucky brigadier Lovell H. Rousseau's proposal to the War Department to enlist a special mounted infantry and cavalry corps, with ten thousand mounted on mules, two thousand on horses, all armed with Sharps and Spencer carbines plus sabers, pistols, and accompanied by horse artillery. They would be specially recruited from disbanding eastern units. Rousseau saw this move as a path to higher rank; Rosecrans envisioned it as a device to control the countryside in advance of the army. Such a force, he reasoned, would help restore law and order to the entire region from which "we have expelled the insurgents, a thing now impossible because no one desires to avow his sentiments for fear the rebel cavalry or guerrillas will wreak vengeance upon them." Some 5,000 communications troops would be freed for battle duty too. If the government had only done this six months earlier, he claimed, "an adequate cavalry force would have given us control of all Middle Tennessee, with all its forage, horses, cattle, and mules, driven the enemy from it without the battle of Stones River, and re-established civil order."[6]

Rosecrans liked to dwell upon "might-have-beens." He chided Halleck: "Let it not be overlooked that we lost the corn and all the resources of Middle Tennessee consumed by the rebels, for want of an adequately mounted force." Alluding obliquely to his superior's own highly criticized slowness in reaching Corinth after the Shiloh battle in April and May of the previous year, Rosecrans bristled: "but you know what it is to advance with a great army over twenty-five miles of miry barrens, but when it comes to thirty miles of barrens, seventy miles of mountains, and two small rivers, and, finally, the great Tennessee—as broad here as at Pittsburg Landing—you know the magnitude of the work." Halleck ducked the jibe, however. He was privy to other messages arriving in the capital, such as one from Military Governor Andrew Johnson to the president posturing that even his own meager unionist Tennessee regiments could "enter, take, and hold the country [East Tennessee] without regard to transportation, which has always seemed to be an obstacle [to the principal Union armies]..... Now is the time for an entrance into East Tennessee," concluded Johnson bluntly, but sagely. Washington could not have agreed more.[7]

So Halleck dismissed the Rosseau scheme as simply more of Rosecrans's delaying tactics, and he pointed out that it resembled those independent organizations "which have caused so much discontent and trouble whenever the exigencies of the service required them to be employed in a different way." Both Streight and the Mississippi Marine Brigade came to mind. Secretary of War Edwin Stanton, however, liked the Rousseau idea, but quartermaster deficiencies in mounts and trimonthly army strength returns squelched the scheme. Washington officials knew that Rosecrans claimed to have 80,000 available men with 18 heavy and 273 field guns. Those figures suggested better utilization of existing resources than organizing some exotic special field force. Together, such numbers could fulfill multiple missions, including rear area protection, police and occupation duty, counterguerrilla operations, as well as defeating Bragg's main army, argued the War Department.[8]

So the ponderous Federal buildup continued to run its course. Military railroad superintendent Colonel William P. Innes at Nashville received orders on August 20 to acquire new railroad cars from the Adams Express Company, five additional locomotives, and to standardize more five-foot gauge tracks. "There are also some cars, box and platform, on the Memphis road near Cumberland City," army headquarters informed him, "which Colonel Bruce, at Clarksville, has been directed to secure and bring to the river," where they might be carried to Nashville by boat. In Kentucky, Brigadier General Jeremiah Boyle received authority to impress labor to improve public roads and commence construction of a rail line between Lebanon and Danville, which could aid Burnside's offensive. Rosecrans even wired Grant to ask about any surplus locomotives in his department, and called everyone's attention to the fact that bridging efforts at Bridgeport, Alabama, on the Tennessee would require transfer of lumber and other materials from as far distant as Cincinnati and St. Louis.[9]

Most important of all, perhaps, Rosecrans and Johnson buried their differences long enough to agree almost simultaneously upon completing the prewar Nashville and Northwestern line from Kingston Springs west of the state capital to the Tennessee River. Here was a bold stroke—through the heart of partisan country—designed to circumvent the shoal water and shoreline guerrilla gauntlet on the Cumberland River below Nashville. Reserve corps commander Major General Gordon Granger would supply a protective force (mainly Tennessee brigadier Alvin C. Gillem's contingents), while Innes would corral engineers and rolling stock, and Colonel Charles R. Thompson, a western army engineer and construction expert, would superintend an African-American construction force. Gillem received orders to conscript all available ex-slaves and muster them for this railroad project. The work began in early fall, and by October Stanton had approved Johnson's responsibility for the project by virtue of his military rank.[10]

Moreover, given Rosecrans's need for laborers and Johnson's pronounced preference "that black men work for the Union rather than fight for it" (as Ira Berlin and his co-editors of the emancipation documents volume *Freedom* phrase it), Nashville's quartermaster estimated in August that more than ten thousand contrabands were serving the Union military as teamsters and laborers, cooks and servants, as well as pick-and-shovel men for the engineers in the Department of the Cumberland. Secretary of War Edwin M. Stanton sent northern abolitionist George L. Stearns to Tennessee as a major to recruit fighters for the Union army from the ex-slaves. Blocked largely by Johnson, the two strong-willed unionists were pressured by Lincoln to compromise—with the result that Stearns and his agents recruited black men, but the governor retained authority over their disposition. As such, the recruits clearly freed white soldiers for combat duty. On the other hand, despite Johnson's aversion, a list of United States Colored Troops at the end of October cited 3,995 blacks in uniform in Tennessee units, including the First, Second, and Third infantry (of African descent, said the label), and the First and Second Tennessee Heavy Artillery (African descent). Clearly, then, the landscape involving slavery had changed markedly in the Volunteer State.

Something of an uneasy truce existed between general and governor. Rosecrans wanted weekly status reports about every bridge and other railroad feature, and he instructed workers to remove undergrowth and other obstructions around blockhouses and stockades to improve fields of fire, as well as positioning water barrels to sustain besieged garrisons. President Abraham Lincoln himself wired Johnson on September 8, urging that "you do your utmost to get every man you can, black and white, under arms at the very earliest moment, to guard roads, bridges, and trains, allowing all the better trained soldiers to go forward to Rosecrans." He added quickly: "I mean for you to act in co-operation with, and not independently of, military authorities." Johnson hustled convalescents and nonessential personnel out to help. He also looked desperately for a way to persuade outlying communities like Fayetteville and Winchester to his brand of unionism. Many loyal Tennessee troops offered to help. One second lieutenant in the First Middle Tennessee (First Cavalry) (Union) requested authority to scout in Marion County "so that we may be enabled to visit and provide for our families whom we have not seen for more than twelve months," and who had suffered rebel persecution.[11]

Federal commanders also increased their counterguerrilla sweeps at this time. Fort Donelson commander Colonel W. D. Lyon sent scouts to scour the troublesome Waverly area on August 14 and reported random groups of partisans (their numbers increased by deserters) being carefully monitored by Captain Archibald Randall's mounted infantry. "I think that frequent and vigorous demonstrations on these gangs will deter others from joining them," he told Colonel S. D. Bruce at Clarksville, hoping for more cooperation between their forces. He was very pleased with the mounted troops' performance, and he also mentioned surveying teams at work mapping the roads of the area. Rosecrans directed Bruce on the twenty-fourth to send a regiment to Colonel Daniel McCook at Columbia via Charlotte and to "clear the country of guerrillas as he goes." McCook told his superior, Major General Gordon Granger, that it was time to adopt the same measures at Columbia and Pulaski as Granger had done at Franklin, "to break the necks of the rebels." As far as Granger's scope of influence extended into the countryside, said McCook, "their conduct was perfectly refreshing, but south of Duck River they are impudent and defiant; and must be 'Grangerized.'"[12]

McCook specifically cited one example of a woman and her daughter on Carter's Creek as civilians who should be expelled for openly boasting of bridge burning and vowing to do it again. "All the families you sent from Franklin should be sent south of the Tennessee," he urged, for "they spread wide dissatisfaction." Union soldiers and sailors continued to hold low opinions of the disheveled irregulars and their supporters. An Englishman serving aboard the navy tinclad USS *Silver Cloud* wrote his sister in Liverpool on September 6 to "tell Maggie that if she saw a few of her darling Southerners she would be so disgusted that she'd commit suicide right away." John Swift added that they wore no uniforms but straw or felt hats, old trousers and woolen or coarse white shirts. And, he decided, "they have the most diabolical unshaven countenances you can imagine." On one occasion, he noted standing guard for seven hours over fourteen of the villains and having "the pleasing job of being compelled to shoot one of them and give another a poke with a bayonet."[13]

Granger, however, had a different agenda, as he moved McCook's brigade away from active counterguerrilla operations to railroad repair protection. The Tennessee and Alabama rail line needed attention in order to provide an additional supply route for Rosecrans's advance. Lyon's Thirteenth Wisconsin from Fort Donelson and the Twenty-eighth Kentucky from Clarksville were tapped by the end of the month, as Granger carefully dispersed support units all over Middle Tennessee. The time was ripe for a major Confederate cavalry strike, but none came. Morgan's capture had deflated some of the "Secesch-siding community" spirit, Sergeant Major Vett Noble of the Fourteenth Michigan decided in late August (while he was actively courting a fourteen-year-old Franklin belle who apparently enjoyed youthful flirtation with a Yankee). The railroad work proceeded nicely, ample forage supplied the troops and their mounts, and even the telegraph line south of Columbia was stabilized, as the "citizens will do all in their power to prevent its being destroyed" for fear of Union army retribution. With the absence of major enemy raiding parties, Granger worried more that his sixteen thousand men might succumb to malaria, milk sickness, or general physical breakdown in the garrisoned towns where they were posted. He tried to prevent the Fifth Iowa Cavalry (now led by Major Alfred B. Brackett, as Colonel William Lowe had assumed brigade command) from going forward to the main army, but headquarters overruled him. Rosecrans wanted units like these Hawkeyes to improve relations with the loyal populace while sealing his right flank with Burnside's advance.[14]

In fact, both Rosecrans and Burnside focused on civil-military relations as central to the success of their forward movement. The two generals issued strict orders regarding the citizenry. "Remember that the present campaign takes [the army] through friendly territory," noted Burnside, regarding East Tennessee. Humanity and the best interests of the service required that peaceable inhabitants be treated with kindness. Officers were to enforce strict discipline against "willful destruction of private property" or be held accountable personally. Prisoners would not be paroled but honorably treated nonetheless. "It must be distinctly understood that this war is conducted for national objectives," announced Burnside, "and that any desire which may exist on the part of soldiers to avenge private wrongs must yield to a proper observance of the well-established usages of civilized warfare." He thought his army fairly well disciplined, but still issued a new enjoinder about "the cowardly and infamous practice" of stealing provisions from "defenseless and peaceable inhabitants." Threatened punishment for offensives included head shaving, branding with a large "T" on the left cheek, as well as dismissal from the army. In all, depredations proved slight in Burnside's column, progress was rapid (twenty-five miles a day), and Confederate strongholds like Cumberland and Big Greek Gaps were simply bypassed.[15]

Rosecrans issued similarly stringent orders, but went further by pointing to the accrual of rebel deserters as contributing to lawless bands who engaged in "theft, pillage, and violence under the name of guerrilla warfare." They would be treated as spies or robbers, against whom it was the duty of all military and civilians "to wage a war of extermination," he said. Local property owners who aided such partisans would see their property wasted, while peaceful residents would be counseled to unite in suppressing this lawlessness. They could even enjoy "the freeman's right of bearing arms in self-defense" so long as such arms did not pass to the enemy. Even so, at least one of Rosecrans's division leaders had to reprimand his men about "straggling over the country, foraging, and sometimes pillaging." In the end, the generals were virtually powerless to prevent such occurrences.[16]

Colonel John Foster's blueclad cavalry vanguard clattered into Knoxville on September 2. The march over the mountains was very hard on man and beast but gratifying, since the people flocked to the roadsides, wildly welcoming their deliverers, saluting "the flag of the Republic and the men who had borne it in triumph to the very heart of the 'Confederacy.'" Many of these persecuted unionists gave bounteously of their food and drink to the weary soldiers. The wonder was, said one witness, "where all the 'Stars and Stripes' came from." Burnside's additional reward was capture of a veritable storehouse of supplies at Knoxville. Corporal Frederick Pettit pointed out that there was plenty of grain, mills, and beef cattle here, and Knoxville's mills, bakeries, and car factories were soon "running for the government." Indeed, "we have full possession of East Tennessee except Cumberland Gap," Burnside wired Rosecrans four days later, and the latter surrendered the very next day. Furthermore, according to Pettit, at least two thousand Tennesseans, as well as a number of prisoners and deserters, had enlisted in Burnside's army. "Everything works well," he decided, and Burnside's great movement had been successful thus far.[17]

Major General Simon B. Buckner, the East Tennessee Confederate commander, bowed to superior numbers and retired southward, eventually joining Bragg at Chattanooga. By doing so, however, he yielded control of the vital rail link with Virginia. As for Chattanooga, its residents had been rudely surprised by sudden shelling from Colonel John T. Wilder's advance column on August 21. Nothing resulted that approached the Nashville panic after Fort Donelson's fall. But deserters reported that equipment, military stores, and civilian possessions had departed Chattanooga in every train and wagon. Army of Tennessee medical director Samuel Stout began to transfer patients and facilities to other locations. His successful Chattanooga medical complex of nine hospitals had served Bragg's army well after the Kentucky campaign, Murfreesboro, and the recent Tullahoma affair. Now Stout sought other sites in north Georgia to resume operations. Overall, evacuation proved orderly, but morale plummeted with retreat, as Tennessee troops were much dispirited by this latest turn of events. In fact, Confederate captain Thomas B. Wilson recalled that one of his young First Tennessee cavalrymen had a brother in its infantry counterpart regiment. Heretofore loyal to the Cause, the brother and a comrade simply deserted while on picket duty, went home to the Nashville area, and took the Union oath of allegiance. As had been the case after Tullahoma, Federal accounts reported Bragg's deserters and stragglers wandering freely about the Chattanooga region.[18]

Meanwhile, heavy Federal infantry columns filed over Walden's Ridge or sideslipped past Chattanooga to get on Bragg's line of retreat in north Georgia. Bragg again pulled back and the first ranks of the Army of the Cumberland entered the city without violence or outrage of any kind, recorded local Presbyterian minister Thomas McCallie. Indeed, the Yankees were getting good at this sort of thing. Everyone expected Rosecrans to pause and consolidate his gains. At least, this was the impression that touring War Department assistant secretary Charles A. Dana wired Washington at 5:00 P.M. on September 10. Not so, however, as the general pushed his units to pursue Bragg, permitting only supply and administrative personnel to set up shop in the city. The widely dispersed Union columns promised potential disaster, yet nobody expected Bragg to turn and fight at this juncture. He had not done so after Tullahoma, so why would he now?[19]

ASSESSING THE SITUATION

Meanwhile, Charles Dana kept a steady stream of intelligence flowing back to Washington. He had been sent west to observe and report, but mostly to evaluate Rosecrans and Burnside for Secretary of War Stanton and the White House. "Mr. Dana is a gentleman of distinguished character, patriotism, and ability," Stanton advised Rosecrans at the end of August, "and possesses the entire confidence of the Department." The general should explain "to him fully any matters which you may desire, through him, to bring to the notice of the Department." Soon, Stanton's lackey sent word about the want of arms and horses in Kentucky, quartermaster scandals at Louisville and Nashville, and his meeting with Governor Johnson on September 8. The Tennessee politician "expresses himself in cheering terms," said Dana, for Johnson regarded Knoxville's occupation as "completing the expulsion of rebel power" from his state. Despite a very divisive and unproductive unionist convention in Nashville on July 1 and somewhat farcical gubernatorial contests in Bedford and Shelby Counties thereafter,

Johnson wanted to hold a general election in early October. He would appoint a judiciary himself, he told Dana, and sufficient means would be taken to prevent "all except loyal citizens from voting or being voted for" so that a new state government might take office in December.[20]

Confederate and anti-Johnson unionist attempts to provide an alternative to Johnson failed to shake the military governor. Exiled elected chief executive Isham G. Harris pushed hard, and Tennessee Confederate soldiers as well as Volunteer State refugee voters all across the South selected Judge Robert L. Caruthers of Lebanon as "elected" governor, along with a full congressional delegation to the Confederate national government on August 4. Caruthers wisely decided not to try to take office in Nashville, and the legislators made their way unobtrusively to Richmond. The anti-Johnsonite unionists likewise tried to elect another Lebanon native, William B. Campbell, and placed his name before Lincoln as the duly elected governor of the state. But it was a charade, and none of this disheartened Johnson, who remained optimistic of ultimate success with his reconstruction program. "The great majority of the people of Tennessee are to-day in favor of freedom," he proclaimed in his meeting with Dana, and their only doubts (just as in neighboring Kentucky) were over "the subsequent status of the negro." Even Rosecrans seemed tolerable to Johnson, despite his tardiness and months "wasted in the construction of useless fortifications." Rosecrans's henchman, Nashville army police chief William Truesdail, however, held too much influence with the general and was "deep in all kinds of plunder and has kept the army inactive to enable his accomplices and himself to become rich by jobs and contracts," according to the governor. Still, Dana thought even Nashville's forts signified increasing unionization and control. After making his way to Chattanooga on September 11, he wired Washington enthusiastically: "This army has now gained a position from which it can effectually advance upon Rome and Atlanta, and deliver the finishing blow of the war."[21]

Dana's confidence, Johnson's optimism, and Rosecrans's dogged pursuit of Bragg encouraged Washington. Kentucky and Tennessee had been redeemed for the Union for all intents and purposes, it seemed. Pockets of potential trouble remained in the rear of the army, however. Clarksville, for one, exemplified tenuous Federal control. Daniel W. Nye of Cheatham County wrote Johnson on September 7 about local crime in that city. Bruce's garrison was lax and ineffectual, allowing overflowing jails, he complained. Organized robber bands hovered around the environs, and the distinct possibility of Confederate attack existed, with some mysterious aid of "the free masons and money judiciously applied." On the other hand, the governor received letters from West Tennesseans wanting permission to form home guards or other protection against the brigands and to hold elections to permit the people "to return to their allegiance." Like many Kentuckians, these Tennessee civilians desired some form of uniformed military to deter partisans and criminals, but not necessarily at the expense of their rights.[22]

Kentucky obviously bore close watching. By comparison, however, Lincoln and his officials could congratulate Johnson for purging Tennessee of armed insurrectionists. Press on with emancipation via intended state constitution and government, they urged, failing to realize that Johnson's influence remained fragmentary. Memphis editor James Bingham claimed that local commander Stephen A. Hurlbut thought Johnson "did not care for that part of Tennessee this side of the Tennessee river" and would never openly preach unionism in the western third of his state. Indeed, Johnson remained wedded to reunion and emancipation in the middle and eastern parts. And he increased African-American military recruitment everywhere, suggesting to Lincoln on September 2 that a compensatory scheme was advisable to reward "Loyal Masters" with three hundred dollars in addition to the normal one-hundred-dollar recruitment bounty per enlistee. "It would be an entering wedge to emancipation and for the time paralyze much opposition to recruiting slaves in Tennessee," he thought. Washington responded with a War Department general order on October 3, authorizing the three-hundred-dollar payments.[23]

A Shelbyville wholesale grocer, Robert P. Shapard (who incidentally had two sons in the rebel service), astutely observed to Johnson on August 23 that local citizens were tired of continued thievery and guerrilla depredations. They "feele [sic] a determination to put down bushwhackers and thieves if some plan can be adopted." Allowing citizens to raise a local guard, he suggested, could do the work more effectively than the army. G. C. Jameson of Union City hinted at the same thing, writing on September 14 that since the evacuation of Jackson, Trenton, Humboldt, and even Fort Heiman that summer, "we have been without any protection, and are willing to protect ourselves as State or Home Guards." Here then was a dilemma. If government could not protect citizens against robbers and partisans, then civilians wanted relief from the burden imposed by the legal definition of Tennessee as a rebellious state so that they could create their own state militia. Johnson shrank from the state militia idea, but Hurlbut did not. By mid-September he had told his subordinates to encourage formation of home guards under Kentucky and Tennessee militia laws. "I believe the people of West Tennessee can be trusted to put down the Guerrillas—against regular & organized force I must of course protect them."[24]

Other soldiers were not so sure that conditions merited relaxation of the North's tightening grip. In Mississippi, XV corps commander Major General William T. Sherman told one of Major General Don Carlos Buell's former staff officers (who was seeking to rehabilitate his general's reputation): "I fear the Northern people are again settling back into one of their periodical states of apathy, on the supposition that the war is over, whereas we all know and feel that the leaders of the South are buckling on their armor and preparing for a new, and it may be a more successful, display of desperate physical energy." There should be no idlers now, he proclaimed, declining to intervene with Washington on Buell's behalf. "When the war is over we may have a century in which to scramble for personal fame," he exclaimed prophetically. Sergeant Eugene Marshall of Company K, Fifth Iowa Cavalry, noted in his diary on September 10 from McMinnville that the rebels were at last out of Tennessee, badly demoralized, and in no condition to fight soon. But Tennessee was not quiet; "it is and will be for some time full of Guerrillas and to this war I see no speedy end."[25]

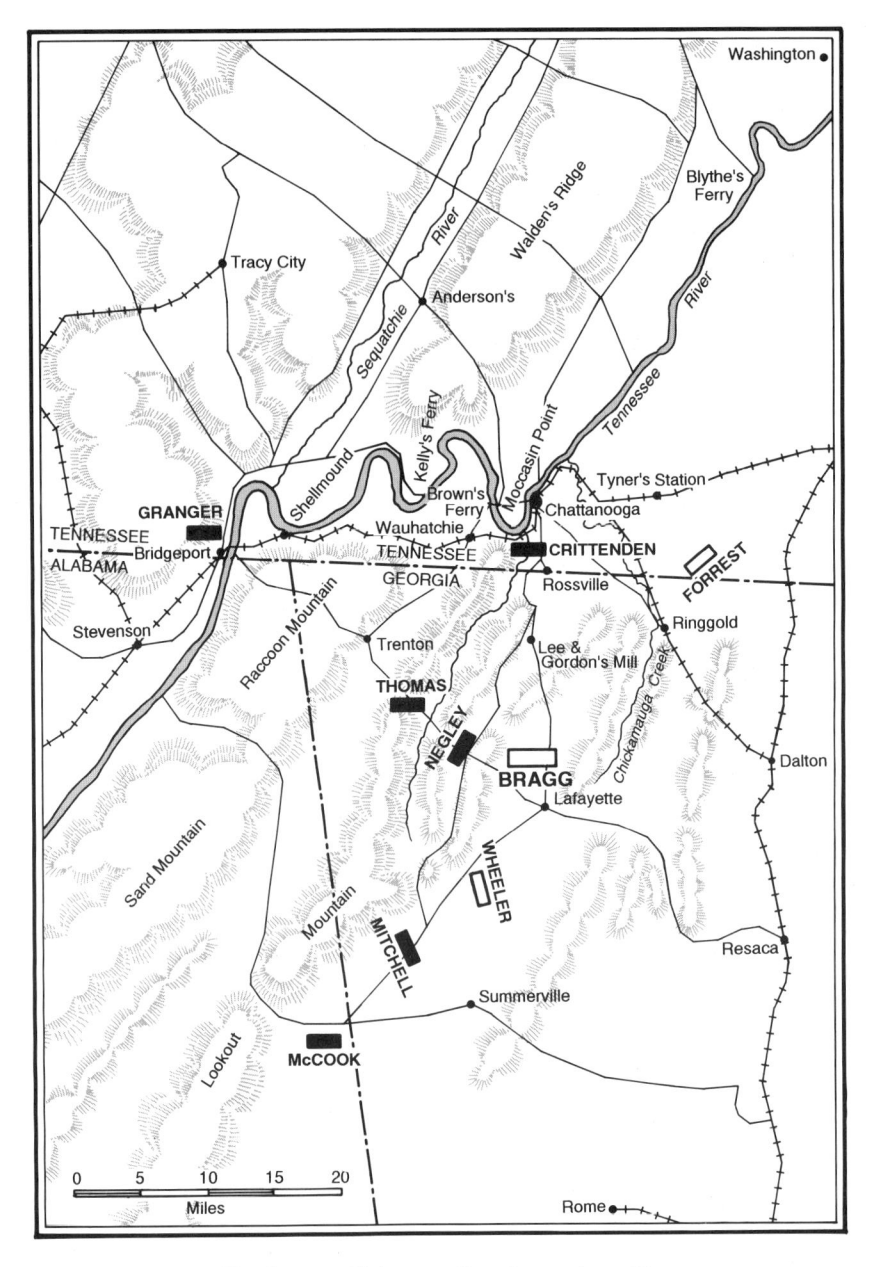

The advance on Chickamauga, September 9 and 10, 1863.

Union control was just shaky as Rosecrans's legions snaked across Raccoon and Lookout Mountains and on down the Rossville road below Chattanooga, looking for rebels. The army was dangerously exposed. Burnside's army could provide little help from Knoxville. Captain Hubbard T. Thomas with the latter force wrote his parents toward the end of September that, since they were surrounded by the enemy, the situation would require fighting or surrender for "we never can make a successful retreat back over those mountains." The same conditions applied to Rosecrans once he reached Chattanooga. Still, Thomas reported never seeing "soldiers put up with privations more cheerfully in my life," and spirits seemed similarly high with their comrades in the Army of the Cumberland. Everything boded a rebel ambush or counterattack. Indeed, that very thought coursed through Confederate command councils as dry autumn winds rustled burnishing leaves on the hillsides of north Georgia and East Tennessee.[26]

GESTATION OF A CONFEDERATE RESURGENCE

The summer's military events had been dismaying for most western Confederates and their sympathizers. On June 21, General Joseph E. Johnston's inspector general, Colonel E. J. Harvie, had penned a lengthy note to Joseph Davis. "In a word," Harvie told the Confederate president's brother, "the Northern Government has made a point on Vicksburg, and has determined it shall fall, and with it, if in their power to accomplish it, the Mississippi Valley." The situation could be saved only if Braxton Bragg's army "was at once ordered to Mississippi." In Harvie's view, Johnston had not addressed the problem. The hour was late, and somebody needed to make a decision. It would require three weeks to transfer the Army of Tennessee to Mississippi. Who better to make that decision than the chief executive himself, argued Harvie. The answer, however, had been silence and no decision. Vicksburg and then Port Hudson had fallen, and the mighty Mississippi flowed "unvexed to the sea." By implication, Jefferson Davis had determined to fight for the upper heartland, not his Mississippi Delta home. Then came Tullahoma, and by August the question no longer hinged on Middle Tennessee but rather on East Tennessee.[27]

Union quartermaster general Montgomery C. Meigs captured the essence of the Confederate quandary when he told Secretary of State William Henry Seward sometime in August that about "50,000 square miles of revolted territory have been recovered." This simple statistic included an estimated 80 percent of Tennessee. The fires of near mutiny burned among Braxton Bragg's senior leaders, and even his men seemed confused. As McMinnville informant R. Henderson told Federal authorities on August 8: "The army may be said to be demoralized, being but little if any better than a mob." The common Johnny Reb, he declared, felt that he could not cope with the relentless Union drive, and "neither officers nor men have any confidence in Bragg's ability, and many doubt his courage." He warned that Johnston's Mississippi force most likely would be sent to East Tennessee "with the intention of making a move into Kentucky." Such a thrust would satisfy Confederate public opinion "that Kentucky and the States north of the Ohio are to be invaded." Indeed, plans for a counteroffensive vied with internal squabbles at Bragg's headquarters.[28]

Confederate corps commander Major General Daniel Harvey Hill might enjoin his men to "occasionally pause and give a day to reflection" after their recent ardors, but others were less willing to break stride. Brigadier General Nathan Bedford Forrest, for one, simply wanted to take his war elsewhere, away from Bragg. The idea of a counterstroke appealed to the cavalryman. Forrest particularly believed that he could procure "a large force now inside the enemy's lines" to seriously, if not completely, obstruct navigation of the Mississippi River. Give him command of forces on that stream from Vicksburg to Cairo, he claimed, and both his firsthand knowledge and that of his subordinates could rally five to ten thousand new men to southern banners. They would come from half-organized, ill-equipped partisans, but they would follow him anywhere, he was convinced. Reluctant though Forrest might be to part with his present command, "a desire to destroy the enemy's transports and property, and increase the strength of our army" induced him to do so, he declared.[29]

Other Confederates, including the ubiquitous General Pierre Gustave Toutant Beauregard (always dreaming of wintering on the Ohio River) and Secretary of War James Seddon, appreciated the need to return to the line of the Mississippi. Seddon wrote Johnston on August 19 to tell him to keep communication with the trans-Mississippi, as "it is not of less importance than the use of the Mississippi River for trade should [it], if possible, be debarred to the enemy." Methods differed, but everyone looked to a cavalry interdiction campaign that "would deprive the North of most of the fruits of their late successes in Mississippi, and perhaps even more effectually than the command of fortified places on the river satisfy the Northwest of the impossibility of ever enjoying the Mississippi as an avenue of trade without peace and amity with the Confederates states."[30]

Bragg was tepid to the idea; Davis embraced it in principle. For the moment, East Tennessee was the focus of their attention. When Bragg's chief of subsistence warned about dwindling supplies without "the most rigid care and economy," and the need for general impressment of stock, the situation assumed still another angle. Ironically, a Federal spy informed superiors that wheat, corn, and oats were "unusually good" this year, and while the hay crop was only average, everything was quickly being consumed around the rebel army because so much less had been planted and poorly tilled than normal. So Bragg and Johnston both fell to arguing with Richmond subsistence chief Brigadier General Lucius B. Northrop about why the Atlanta depot could not supply the western army as it did the Army of Northern Virginia. Yet, Northrop dismissed Bragg's claim that lack of subsistence lay at the root of the Army of Tennessee's morale and desertion problems. He countered that such difficulties stemmed instead from upper heartland residents who had to watch their properties be overrun by the enemy. In the commissary general's view, "an army of men having homes and families not well provided for will be demoralized," while an army with far less rations, "if operating actively, will not become demoralized." His message was clear— "East Tennessee must be recovered and Rosecrans driven from the country."[31]

Other voices were also heard. Major General Joseph Wheeler, the army's cavalry chief, urged blockhouse construction for all the railroads leading into Atlanta (an ominous reversal, since Confederate, not Union, cavalry usually provided the threat to rail lines). One of Bragg's ardent opponents, Major General Leonidus Polk, took the matter even higher. He wrote the president outside of the usual channels of command and urged a general western concentration to fall upon Rosecrans, wrest all of Tennessee from Yankee hands, and concentrate at Memphis before moving on Grant's army still at Vicksburg. Here was another scheme from a rebel general who had never outgrown his river perspective since commanding at Columbus, Kentucky, two winters before. Alabama would be left unprotected, he said, but "this must be risked in the hands of a small force with the State troops, and, if overrun, that calamity could not be compared in importance with the successes indicated elsewhere." A little later, Polk confided to colleague William J. Hardee (another anti-Bragg conspirator) that Johnston, if he commanded such a sortie, could easily redeem Middle Tennessee after crushing Rosecrans. Then, he could recapture the Cumberland–Tennessee River sector, plus Columbus and Island Number 10 as well as Memphis. "In short," said the clergyman in uniform, "place us where we have ever desired and been attempting to be since this war began."[32]

Potential no doubt existed for some grand Confederate resurgence northward. However, neither Bragg's approximately forty thousand men in north Georgia nor Buckner's mere fifteen thousand observing Burnside's advance from Knoxville toward Chattanooga could coalesce for such a move. Buckner, in fact, wanted Bragg to come to him, dispose of Burnside, and then tackle Rosecrans. Johnston realized that his twenty-six thousand effective troops could barely handle responsibilities for Mississippi, Alabama, and Louisiana, much less reinforce Bragg. First, Bragg (whose own health had been bad for over two months) had to draw Rosecrans onto killing grounds of his own choosing, and then nip the Yankee thrust down the railroad toward Atlanta. Furthermore, subordinates like Daniel Harvey Hill remained restive, advising Bragg on September 3: "If we wait until the meshes be thrown around, we may find it hard to break through." He wanted a repeat of the Murfreesboro initiative. But Bragg dawdled with departmental reorganization and other preparation chores while awaiting Johnston's pleasure. Nothing happened as the latter wrangled over the semantics of "authority," "misapprehension," and "serious military offensive" with President Davis. The chief executive rejected suggestions that he simply order Bragg to attack, claiming that it did little good for a pessimistic general to fight. General Robert E. Lee declined to go west from Virginia to take command, but agreed to assist by sending Lieutenant General James Longstreet's veteran corps. Federal authorities even knew about this transfer as early as August, but did little to help Rosecrans brace for the onslaught.[33]

Bragg lured Rosecrans away from Chattanooga while awaiting Longstreet's arrival by rail from Virginia. Then, once the eastern troops had arrived, he turned and savagely struck on the banks of Chickamauga Creek in north Georgia late in September. Two days of bitter fighting along what the Cherokees called "the river of death" gave the Confederacy its most striking victory in the West. A fluke shift in the Federal front line on the second day, recalled the Ninth Ohio chronicler, caused "mistakes, oversights, unauthorized actions, and other aberrations" that needed to be explained, "but probably never will be." In any case, the fortunes of war permitted the bulk of sixty-six thousand fanatical butternut soldiers to sweep most of Rosecrans's fifty-eight thousand Yankees from the field in abject defeat.[34]

Only Major General George H. Thomas's intrepid defense on Snodgrass Hill denied Bragg total victory. Earning the sobriquet "Rock of Chickamauga" for his effort, Thomas's battered ranks subsequently retired to Chattanooga in good order where they joined a besieged Army of the Cumberland. Even then, Bragg missed an opportunity to annihilate his enemy, and, as the postwar chronicler of the Ninth Ohio saw it, whether Chickamauga was judged a victory or defeat for the Union, "the prize of the battle, the city of Chattanooga, remained in *our* hands!" Vett Noble of the Fourteenth Michigan, writing home from garrisoned Franklin, Tennessee, on September 26 suggested that the "great—and to be decisive—battle now on the program, at Chattanooga occupies everybody's attention."[35]

Rosecrans's army was "in a somewhat dilapidated state," decided Ralsa Rice of the 125th Ohio, even as Forrest urged Bragg to pursue the Yankee rabble immediately after the battle and destroy them. But the trauma and irresolution of victory once more descended upon southern fortunes in Tennessee. Thomas sealed off the Chattanooga perimeter, and their combined thirty-seven thousand casualties basically immobilized both armies for a while. James Jones of the Fifty-seventh Indiana wrote home from Murfreesboro on September 27 that every train from the South that particular week had been loaded from end to end with the wounded, and some had died before ever reaching that midpoint on the long ride to Nashville hospitals. He pondered how many more big battles there would be "before this war is over." Still, most of the men in blue retained "faith in the ability of Gen. Rosecrans to hold his position at the very least," said Rice. Noble told his parents in Michigan that the latest telegraph news suggested that Rosecrans "has nearly all the Southern Confederacy to whip and I am as confident of his success as that I am now writing." Even Andrew Johnson offered his help on October 1, telling the general that "the holding of your recent position is looked upon as a great victory and the nation will appreciate it." He asked cordially whether "I can do in your rear that will promote the interests of the Army of the Cumberland."[36]

Another East Tennessean understood the situation accurately when he told the governor that "Rosecrans will not make any further movements for several weeks," but predicted confidently that "we are going to hold East Tennessee." Rosecrans might not have been so sure at that moment. Despite Forrest's desire to obliterate the foe, in spite of Longstreet's ardent advice to strike Burnside "and if he made his escape to march upon Rosecrans' communication in rear of Nashville," and notwithstanding rebel intelligence urging similar bypass of Chattanooga altogether, Bragg resolved to starve out the beleaguered Rosecrans. He placed his army in a semicircular position on the high ground south of town. Commanding most of the access routes into the area, Bragg thought he could simply await the inevitable. Thus, the campaign for Chattanooga continued for another two months, but in reverse to the events of summer. Now the Confederates controlled the situation, and Governor Johnson still lacked the necessary hegemony to ensure restoration of civil authority through free elections. Senior Federal officials pointed to relief of Chattanooga as the focal point for operations from September until November. The situation remained the key to what might happen elsewhere in the occupied heartland.[37]

WHEELER'S RAID

Disharmony among Bragg's immediate subordinates ultimately contributed to his army's undoing. Longstreet joined the anti-Bragg cabal, as he soon communicated to Richmond that the Army of Tennessee commander had done but one thing that he should have done since the Georgian's arrival—Bragg had attacked Rosecrans at Chickamauga. "All other things that he has done he ought not to have done," and only the "hand of God can save us or help us as long as we have our present commander." Longstreet and Polk both voiced a desire for Robert E. Lee to recover Tennessee. As Polk wrote Lee directly on September 27: "If both [Union] armies were driven back to the Mississippi, and Tennessee—not to say Kentucky—freed, and we on Grant's line of communications and in connection with the trans-Mississippi army, we might, by moving south, make short work of the army of the latter." Bragg, however, suppressed the latest mutiny: he arrested Polk, exiled T. C. Hindman and D. H. Hill, agreed to Hardee's departure to Mississippi, dropped Buckner to divisional status, and effected other changes. Still, a petition for his relief went to Richmond, and a dispirited Davis again boarded the rickety southern rail cars for the trek to rally his western army. What came out of all this was Forrest's eventual transfer to independent assignment in West Tennessee, support for Longstreet's offensive idea—which ultimately foundered in the wet fall weather before ever commencing—and no real resolution to the army's command impasse.[38]

To the relief of Forrestphiles ever since, Bragg overlooked a famous confrontation between the two men that occurred during these trying times. There were statements about Forrest slapping his superior's jaw and other general insubordination. Bragg, a martinet professional, nevertheless dismissed the rough-hewn Forrest as ignorant and uncooperative, and as "nothing more than a good raider." Just as Forrest had predicted, Bragg chose not to press charges, and the skilled cavalryman temporarily rode out of the army's life. Of course, Forrest, like Buckner and the others, was too valuable to the Cause. Sending such leaders to other assignments might do some good (and get them away from Bragg), but, in truth, as one of Forrest's staff officers and friends, D. C. Kelley, later admitted, the cavalryman "was unfit to serve under a superior." He likened his idol to a caged lion on the battlefield when he was not personally in charge.[39]

One thing was certain, despite the dissension. Bragg had "the Union Army cooped up in Chattanooga," recorded Frederick Nathan Boyer of the Fifty-ninth Illinois. Just then, Confederate scouts confirmed the vulnerability of Rosecrans's supply lines once more. "Any interference with the Nashville and Chattanooga

Wheeler's attack on a Federal supply train near Jasper, Tennessee. Frank Leslie's Illustrated History of the Civil War *(New York: Frank Leslie, 1895), 383.*

Railroad at this time would materially damage or interfere with [Union] calculations," Captain E. Coleman had advanced even before Chickamauga. So, Major General Joseph Wheeler received orders late in the month to strike for Middle Tennessee. Johnston's cavalry head, Major General Stephen Dill Lee (who while captured at Vicksburg had declared himself properly exchanged according to POW agreements despite Federal protests), promised to cooperate by leading his twenty-five hundred men to attack the Elk and Duck River railroad bridges. Colonel P. J. Roddey, holding the line in north Alabama, would join with Wheeler. Moreover, farther west, Brigadier General James R. Chalmers's hodgepodge assortment of cavalry, partisans, and state troops was to threaten Memphis and the Memphis and Charleston Railroad. All but Wheeler's horsemen reflected inferior arms and equipment, discipline, and organization. "The partisan and State troops are not reliable, being in poor discipline and over one-half the number on the rolls being at their homes," Lee admitted. Most of these contingents were havens for deserters, and "the privilege of raising independent companies is being abused by individuals for their personal advancement and as a shelter to skulkers," he complained. Still, this was the best the Confederacy could offer at that moment.[40]

Wheeler experienced striking initial success. With two of his own cavalry divisions and one from Forrest—a total of five to six thousand men—he dodged Brigadier General George D. Crook's pickets upriver from Chattanooga and crossed on the night of September 29, heading for the Sequatchie Valley–Walden's

Ridge route to Rosecrans's line of communications. The men from Forrest's old command proved badly worn down, but together with Wheeler's fresh troopers they reached the valley and continued unscathed to Dunlap and Jasper. Wheeler divided his command at this point, taking fifteen hundred men in search of a rumored massive Yankee wagon train lumbering to Chattanooga. The rest of the raiders headed for Pikeville and the rich Federal base at McMinnville. In what was the most celebrated exploit of the operation, Wheeler's portion jumped a wagon train—made up of eight hundred to a thousand wagons—near Anderson's crossroads, six miles south of Dunlap in the Sequatchie Valley on the morning of October 2. They pillaged and looted with abandon after overpowering the weak wagon guard. A Union mounted column coming north from Bridgeport finally scattered them, although Wheeler escaped after destroying three hundred to five hundred wagons and countless mule teams. Now, fourteen hours ahead of his main pursuers, he rejoined the rest of the command en route to McMinnville by October 4.[41]

The Confederates frankly carried too much of their booty with them. Yet, they still managed to overawe a raw unionist Fourth Tennessee into capitulation at McMinnville, then looted that town's storehouses and ravaged the railroad. They apparently left the place in shambles, even robbing "the citizens of pretty much all they had," claimed Colonel H. C. Gilbert, commander of a Federal cleanup crew that arrived three weeks later. But, as it turned out, the First East Tennessee (Union) Cavalry, riding in Wheeler's wake, quartered their horses in public buildings and themselves in private dwellings and "were a nuisance hardly inferior to the rebels." Federal officials refused to honor the Fourth Tennessee's parole and set them back to work repairing damage from the raid. Still, Wheeler's rampage produced rumors that preceded his coming, as panicky railroad guards tried to button up their defenses all the way north to Nashville. Colonel William T. Utley, Murfreesboro's post commander, told residents to either join the fortress garrison or move elsewhere to safety, for he planned to shell the town in event of enemy occupation. But Wheeler did not test Utley's mettle. Rather, he contented himself with destroying railroad track, four bridges, and every water tank southward to Wartrace. In this case, communications, not supply facilities, were Wheeler's targets.[42]

A concerned Lincoln wired Johnson for news of the raid. The Tennessean answered cheerfully that everything was in hand, with restoration of facilities expected momentarily. Indeed, the secret to supply-line protection was not in garrison defense at all, but in the Union's quick repair of facilities, according to logistics historian James A. Huston. Then, arrival of new troops from the Army of the Potomac in Virginia (intending to relieve Chattanooga) caused the raiders to swerve off to the west. Shelbyville felt their stern hand of retribution for its unionist sentiment, while local secessionists temporarily frolicked with their deliverers. Of course, they claimed later that no southern soldier pillaged the place, Union assertions notwithstanding. Some families, like that of young Samuel E. Tillman, assisted the escaping rebels, despite his father's avowed unionism. Tillman's mother, however, had a cousin riding with Wheeler. At any rate,

Colonel Robert H. G. Minty, USV. From the Massachusetts MOLLUS Collection, the United States Army Military History Institute.

Wheeler's men now made for Pulaski, riding hard for the Tennessee River crossings. They were overtaken by a near disaster, however, at the Marshall County hamlet of Farmington, when blueclad pursuers finally caught up with them.[43]

Burdened with booty, wagons, and hundreds of mules, the "War Child" (as his admiring assistant adjutant E. S. Burford styled Wheeler) proved no match for the veteran riders of brigadiers Crook and R. B. Mitchell. Two or three cannon, one hundred and fifty dead, and three hundred prisoners all resulted from the fight at Farmington, and the Confederate retreat became disorderly thereafter. Sabered bodies, flotsam of clothing and equipment, and abandoned mounts now marked their retreat. Wheeler's men were hardly capable of another pitched battle when they finally struggled across the Tennessee River near Muscle Shoals on the night of October 9. Roddey's one thousand warriors had barely started on their part of the mission and utterly failed to link up with Wheeler, although small groups hit a few targets, like the railroad tunnel at Cowan. They dropped a few rocks down the air shaft and then faded back south of the Tennessee River near Guntersville, Alabama. Crook could safely wire Rosecrans by October 17 "that the chase is over."[44]

Federal claims suggested Wheeler's foray had cost the rebels one thousand men and five guns and had reduced the overall striking power of Bragg's cavalry. Major General Joseph Hooker's XI and XII corps (arriving from the East) reported restoration of rail and telegraph service on the Nashville and Chattanooga by October 10. Still, Federal pursuit had not gone unblemished. Mitchell was rumored to have been too drunk to prevent the McMinnville capitulation by more rapid pursuit; Crook was similarly remiss in letting Wheeler slip across the Tennessee River at the outset. The ever-popular Colonel R. G. H. Minty was arrested for "alleged disobedience of orders and tardiness of movement in the presence of the enemy" just before Farmington. Unfortunately, he had chosen to rest his jaded command in temporary bivouac outside Shelbyville. Later exonerated, Minty was yet another scapegoat for faulty coordination of the Union pursuit.[45]

Sergeant Eugene Marshall complained to his diary that his skilled regiment had languished on railroad guard ever since arriving from the Cumberland in June and had wasted its time in aimless patrols when it could have helped block Wheeler's path. When Marshall and his comrades were finally thrown into the fray against Wheeler, they quickly overcame a reputation for internal squabbling and mere "distillery-busting." They helped smash rebel barricades in a wild saber charge at Sugar Creek about ten miles from the Elk River. They then led the pursuit through the flotsam of Wheeler's disintegrating command all the way to the Tennessee River. But, like a sister unit, the First Middle Tennessee, they might have helped annihilate the rebels if they had been better positioned earlier in the raid.[46]

Stephen Lee's collaboration also failed. He never reached Tuscumbia, Alabama, and the Tennessee River until the very night that Wheeler recrossed that stream. Deeming his own command inadequate to confront the Union pursuit, Lee subsequently reported that neither he nor Wheeler were in any condition to return north of the river immediately. Rendering excuses, Lee wrote Wheeler on October 17: "I regret that my trip has been of no avail so far as assisting General Bragg, but I did not deem it prudent to cross the Tennessee River alone when with a larger force you had not been able to maintain yourself against a superior force of the enemy." Together, they might have held Middle Tennessee, he ventured lamely, and compelled Rosecrans to retreat, "and [I] regret that you did not deem it prudent to cross with me." Still, Johnston had told Lee from the beginning that "should circumstances now unforseen make the enterprise too hazardous, abandon it." Lee had taken him at his word.[47]

Confederate hopes had once again foundered because of poor coordination and command communications. Closer to the Mississippi, Memphis union general Hurlbut might worry that no fewer than fifteen thousand rebels "all told and of all arms" ostensibly threatened his city, but Chalmers, too, proved incapable of posing a serious threat. He never left Mississippi before October 3, skirmished briefly with a Federal force at Old Salem, Tennessee, then dropped down on the Memphis and Charleston Railroad at Colliersville on the eleventh. At this point, he barely missed perhaps the greatest opportunity of the war. Passing through town at that moment were none other than Major General William Tecumseh Sherman and his headquarters guard—a mere 260 men of the Thirteenth U.S. regulars. Chalmers butted up against the main town garrison (six companies of the Sixty-sixth Indiana—perhaps 240 men), which stopped the attackers. Chalmers's mission of drawing attention away from Lee as well as breaking the rail line evaporated in an enthusiastic little scuffle, as Sherman instructed garrison colonel Dewitt C. Anthony to reject rebel demands for surrender and to fight on. The Union force did so, rallying on the brick depot, a small earthwork, and in a railroad cut and shallow rifle pits nearby. Chalmers blasted them with artillery fire and "knocked to pieces our locomotive," recalled Sherman. But rebel assaults were beaten back. Sherman lost his favorite horse, "Dolly," to the raiders in the bargain. A forced march by Brigadier General Montgomery C. Corse's infantry from Memphis probably saved the defenders, although Chalmers flatly blamed two unruly Mississippi partisan groups for his lack of success.[48]

Sherman, who was beginning to move east to liberate Rosecrans, now recognized the precariousness of his own line of communications. Through Hurlbut, he testily chastised Memphis *Bulletin* editors for publishing "nonsense" and for excessively publicizing the "ridiculous" Colliersville incident, reminding them that freedom of speech and freedom of the press, "precious relics of former history must not be construed too largely." They were to publish "nothing that prejudices the government or excites envy, hatred and malice in a community." In any event, Chalmers withdrew to his Mississippi sanctuary within the week, having lost six killed, sixty-three wounded, and twenty-six captured in the foray. Union losses totaled only sixty men at Colliersville, and Hurlbut soon sent some fifty-seven hundred cavalry after Chalmers (although the Confederates claimed that they were bent more upon preying on helpless civilians than on chasing the raider). Both sides now moved to mere posturing, and cavalry was spread out from south of Memphis to north of Chattanooga. Roddey boasted to Bragg on October 22 that "there is nothing to prevent my making a successful expedition into Tennessee," but he did not do so. Chalmers gathered thirty-seven hundred tattered horsemen (including Richardson's partisans) for new work in West Tennessee and urged Lee to make a strike on Memphis itself—"a move [that] would take them by surprise and strike terror into the enemy." High water in the now rain-swollen Tennessee prevented such a move. Quite frankly, the Confederacy needed a single commander to rally defenders in north Alabama and Mississippi.[49]

Both sides had exhausted their strength during Wheeler's grueling nine-day raid of more than three hundred miles and in the other intense border clashes of Lee, Roddey, and Chalmers. In fact, a very testy Rosecrans wired Burnside on October 5, claiming that the latter's failure "to close your troops down to our left has cost 500 wagons loaded with essentials, the post of McMinnville, and Heaven only knows where the mischief will end.... If you don't unite with us soon, you will be responsible for another catastrophe," he thundered. Still, Yankee troopers stood in higher spirits than before. Josiah Conzett of the Fifth Iowa

Cavalry remembered escorting the unit's sutler back to Nashville as "the finest and best time I had during the war." For Captain Marshall Thatcher of the Second Michigan Cavalry and Lieutenant Joseph Vale of the Seventh Pennsylvania Cavalry, the Wheeler caper "was a losing game to the Confederates," as "the raiding business as a paying institution was a failure." Corps commander George H. Thomas argued that Union pursuit had been "unsurpassed for its energy and the bravery and endurance of the officers and men." At least, he noted, it had prevented "the execution of an extensive plan of destruction to our communications, and plunder, rapine, and murder throughout Middle Tennessee and Northern Alabama," in which Roddey and Lee were to cooperate with Wheeler.[50]

PLAYING THE WAITING GAME

After Wheeler's raid, many Federal mounted units, like the Second Michigan, Ninth Pennsylvania, and Eli Lilly's Indiana battery, spent the final weeks of October and early November recuperating near Winchester. They lived in tents, reblackened their boots, cleaned firearms and clothing, and drew fresh mounts. Overdue after-action reports, receipt of back pay, and other household chores marked this postoperational period. Then, off again in mid-November under a new division commander, Brigadier General Washington L. Elliott, they swung through Shelbyville, Murfreesboro, Sparta, and on to Knoxville. "The country was nearly stripped of livestock," observed Wolverine cavalryman Marshall P. Thatcher, but "our foragers brought in 400 bushels of wheat, 65 head of cattle, 500 to 600 head of sheep, besides horses and mules in one day"—all before even reaching Murfreesboro. Neither army had apparently denuded Middle Tennessee of provender. Moving across the mountains, these Union troops lost some comrades while crossing a flooded Cumberland River and battled past guerrilla chieftains Bledsoe, O. P. Hamilton, and the ubiquitous Champ Ferguson (previously encountered by the Pennsylvanians at Tompkinsville, Kentucky, in the spring of 1862) before reaching Burnside's lines in mid-December. They would then help consolidate Union control over that part of upper East Tennessee.[51]

Meanwhile, the situation had stabilized in West Tennessee except for about three hundred guerrillas who were raiding and conscripting between Paris, Tennessee, and Murray, Kentucky, in September. Elsewhere, in the rear, Rosecrans's needs had steadily drained garrison troops from the lower Tennessee and Cumberland region. The Fifth Iowa had left, soon followed by the rump Seventy-first Ohio and the Thirteenth Wisconsin, with only Flood's battery and the Eighty-third Illinois defending Fort Donelson, for example. Mitchel A. Thompson had told his wife in late August that the Illinois regiment was really the only one that had ever been in pitched battle and that Rosecrans refused one division commander's request for it because "'it would just be the same as taking two Regiments out of the field—the rebels have a wholesale fear of the 83d.'" Such was the legacy of Confederate rebuffs on the Cumberland.[52]

Thus, the situation at the new Fort Donelson had settled into a pattern. Some 120 blacks had been working to perfect the defenses since June, receiving no pay for the services to the Union as opposed to serving their erstwhile owners such as Thomas J. Mumford of nearby Clarksville. Two sets of outlying picket posts now provided early warning of enemy approach. The first defense line lay about one and one-half miles from the fort and comprised three-man posts (each commanded by a corporal). Closer in were two alarm posts, one in camp and one atop a hill about three hundred yards from the fort. Provost and camp guards rotated protection of guardhouse and corral for the garrison. "We are having good times here now," Thompson wrote his wife, even though the regiment was divided between the fort and Clarksville. Cries of "guerrillas" often turned out to be just some of the soldiers off shooting squirrels, although patrols occasionally captured the real thing. George Henson (or Hinson) was one, and his dead countenance "spoke of a reckless spirit engaged in a bad cause" even in death, said William H. Dorris. Mostly, however, the men just awaited the mail boat, stacked winter fuel, and commented on the war elsewhere. By November, Dorris would note that the partisans had "gone home for a few days to warm up around their fires." He supposed they would be back to their old business of stealing and robbing, even though "they are hurting themselves and not us." Indeed, one new scourge would take to the river bottoms in the future—Henson's father, whose hunting rifle would bear numerous notches for Yankee lives snuffed out by the old man in retribution for his sons' lives (for two of his boys would be hung by Lowe's cavalrymen).[53]

Closer to Chattanooga, Colonel Henry Mizner's Fourteenth Michigan, like the Eighty-third Illinois, had been divided between Franklin and Columbia to counter raiders and partisans. Now mounted, most of the Michiganers spent more time impressing horses and parrying irate "old women and men" who arrived at post headquarters seeking recompense for the seizure. The complainants received only receipts for their contributions and the demand that they take the oath of allegiance. Such was the "stability of Tennessee principles," decided Vett Noble, "to take the oath of allegiance to the United States for a poor old blind horse or mule if they think there is any chance of getting it back." Except in cases of extreme necessity, none was returned, he added humorlessly.[54]

Few Federals actually expected to lose East Tennessee back to the rebels. "We are going to hold East Tennessee," unionist Horace Meynard told Andrew Johnson in late September as he urged more loyal Tennesseans to go there to help out. But a worried administration sent Colonel Thomas A. Scott, the Pennsylvania Railroad president, and Quartermaster General Montgomery C. Meigs west to see what could be done to properly organize Rosecrans's relief. Three main routes—the rivers, the Louisville to Chattanooga rail link, and the Memphis and Charleston line provided the means. Hooker had the Nashville to Bridgeport leg in good order, and he was busy scoffing at Wheeler's momentary interruption and indicating that "a much longer time will be required to repair the reputations of some of the officers to whom the defense of our communications had been entrusted." By mid-October, he had the trains running on schedule, and he criticized faulty intelligence reports from Rosecrans about rebel threats to the line.[55]

Reports had the besieged Army of the Cumberland starving inside Chattanooga while their deliverers outside cited verdant cornfields awaiting harvest near Lewisburg, for example. Wheeler's failure to permanently cripple Rosecrans's line of communications and Bragg's inability to reestablish control over agriculturally rich Middle Tennessee ultimately proved costly. But, for the moment in the fall of 1863, Bragg seemed to be close to actually starving out his adversary inside the city. Rosecrans's men laboriously erected necessary fortifications and suffered "the sorest absence of food," and they were reduced to dreaded half rations (in fact, these rations were less than half, since some ingredients of the prescribed army diet were missing entirely). In a word, said the Ninth Ohio historian, Constantin Grebner, "hunger stalked Chattanooga; and it raged into famine after Wheeler's success at Anderson's crossroads." Belts were drawn so tight that "their purpose appeared to be to produce wasp waists." Uncommonly cold nights exacerbated the suffering, as everything in the way of tents, blankets, and clothing had been lost. "We lacked even the everyday garb for the trenches, for the building of fortifications, for picket duty, and for patrols," he observed. Yet, "not an observable trace of demoralization occurred among us," he boasted, "whereas deserters reported plenty of it in the Rebel camp."[56]

In the interim, Washington looked for action while Rosecrans remained strangely inert. Rising waters in the rivers allowed naval convoys to reach Nashville with supplies, where they were then shipped by rail to Stevenson in north Alabama. War Department and Kentucky officials put all their effort into standardizing track gauges to expedite traffic. Midwestern railroads sent additional rolling stock that was reconstituted to accommodate gauge differences, while railroad garrisons neutralized guerrillas like Ferguson, Hamilton, J. Kelly, W. S. Hawkins, and John M. Hughs. Sherman's men trudged eastward from Memphis, living off the land as they went. Governor Johnson searched anxiously for arms and equipment for his Union Guards so that they might "render great and efficient service" in putting down partisans, guarding railroads, and in cooperating with various other operations supporting Rosecrans. Johnson also reported good progress in extending the Nashville and Northwestern to the Tennessee River from Kingston Springs and organizing a Union guard for counterguerrilla operations.[57]

Still, Lieutenant Colonel Theodore Trauernicht's Second United States Colored Troops spent so much time guarding survey engineers, supplying forage guards, and trying to entrench their camps that they found little opportunity to actually protect the construction crews themselves. His officers particularly feared personal guerrilla retribution for commanding black troops, and Alexander Duvall McNairy's partisans were quite active in the area. As far as the laborers themselves were concerned, Federal press gangs ranged the region even as far as Clarksville, snatching field hands from planters, like Joseph Buckner Killebrew, right at the height of tobacco harvest. Killebrew was livid, especially because the husband of his wife's best friend, a John Ivey, led one Yankee gang. Ivey apparently recognized nobody, according to Killebrew, "and he did right for he had turned traitor to all his neighbors and friends and to the cause which they cherished." Ivey and his father-in-law, R. M. House, had been wholesale grocers in Clarksville before the war. "He was never seen after the war" in that city, Killebrew recorded smugly in his later reminiscences.[58]

African-American women made up 20 percent of the railroad construction crews, which included workers from about age twenty-four to fifty-five of both sexes), and men were now in demand for military as well as labor duty. Recruiting bureaus at Nashville—and subsequently at Clarksville, Columbia, Lynneville, Murfreesboro, Pulaski, Shelbyville, Tullahoma, and Wartrace—all furnished soldiers; the one at Clarksville provided two full regiments largely made up of Kentucky refugee blacks. A Gallatin contraband camp contributed the Fourteenth United States Colored Troops, while Alabama freedmen flocked to the Pulaski camp. Such widespread impressment of plantation workers naturally wrought havoc on the agricultural slaveocracy throughout the Upper South, and numerous complaints came from ostensibly unionist slave owners. Finally, on November 10, Nashville officials suspended impressment of more than "one-half of any loyal master's slaves." Federal utilization of heartland blacks for work on forts, logistical facilities, or in the army's ranks not only denied them to their owner's possible clandestine support of the Confederacy by implication, but also impacted adversely upon restoration of stability to local economies disrupted by passage of both armies, raiders, and partisans generally. By November 22, Johnson could at least inform army headquarters that thirty-three miles of the Nashville and Northwestern had been completed, albeit at the expense of stripping iron rail from other lines and dislocating other aspects of Tennessee's economy.[59]

Military Governor Johnson ended his October 12 letter to Rosecrans with a cheery thought: "May the protecting army of a just and Almighty God be suspended over you and your gallant army, and pass you through as it did the children of Israel through the Red Sea." Rosecrans could use divine intervention, it seemed, as his bleak dispatches constantly gave Washington the impression that he had become irresolute and despairing. Assistant Secretary of War Dana fueled pessimism at the nation's capital with caustic comments about Rosecrans. He thought that Rosecrans was "insensible to the impending danger" and dawdling "with trifles in a manner which can scarcely be imagined." Yet, Lincoln continued his own encouragement of his western general, wiring Rosecrans on October 4: "if we can hold Chattanooga and East Tennessee, I think the rebellion must dwindle and die." Only Rosecrans and Burnside acting together could accomplish that task, "hence doing so is your main object," instructed the commander-in-chief. The bottleneck to action at Chattanooga contrasted with Lincoln's continuing impression that his forces had the enemy by the throat and were hanging on. Dana's snide reports about Rosecrans's imbecility hardly helped, for even at that moment, the army commander planned to forge a link with Bridgeport by road across Brown's and Kelly's ferries. Unfortunately, his communiques merely repeated gloomy prospects and increasingly vague references to God's will and grace. Old Rosy's days as army leader were distinctly numbered.[60]

Little wonder that the president concluded that Rosecrans had acted like "a duck hit on the head" since Chickamauga. Many in the ranks agreed. Ill-fed officers and men grew crankier. They penned letters home that at once revealed dreams of desertion from sacrifice and reaffirmed dedication to the Union, even as they continued to sacrifice in the field. "Our confidence in our chief, General Rosecrans, was lost," stated Ralsa B. Rice of the 125th Ohio, and yet "I am sure that our patriotism was unbounded as ever." Staff officer Alfred Lacey Hough told his wife that people in the North "are more extravagant, more luxurious and I am afraid more dissolute to-day, than when their brothers, sons and husbands left them." Morale sagged, as Frederick Boyer of the Fifty-ninth Illinois noted that the picket lines of both armies were so close and in plain view of each other that soldiers could "often converse under a truce with the understanding that 'no shooting' occurs." Here Rosecrans remained, he stated, with food supplies growing shorter, first to half then to quarter rations, with animal forage also quite scarce. "Mules and horses dying of starvation and thrown in the Tennessee River by the hundreds," he added, as the Confederates fired cannon balls and shells into the army's midst. "Matters look very serious indeed," he penned in his diary.[61]

Something obviously had to be done and done quickly. Dana's last dispatch from Chattanooga at 11:00 A.M. on October 18 captured the crisis. "If the army is finally obliged to retreat, the probability is that it will fall back like a rabble, leaving its artillery, and protected only by the river behind it," he wired. Yet, if "we regain control of the river and keep it, subsistence and forage can be got here, and we may escape with no worse misfortune than the loss of 12,000 animals." The War Department finally realized that Rosecrans himself was only part of a bigger problem, dating virtually to the earliest days of the war in the West. What loomed above all was the unworkable notion of three armies and their administrative support elements controlled by a single general-in-chief located 900 miles away at Washington. The need for western unification of command had been patently obvious ever since Halleck had gone east in the summer of 1862 if not the previous winter. Now, some fifteen months later, Ulysses S. Grant, the hero of Vicksburg, was available and really the only choice for resolving both that theater unification and the Chattanooga impasse.[62]

In a meeting with Secretary of War Stanton at the Galt House in Louisville on or about October 16 or 17, Grant was appointed head of the Military Division of the Mississippi and received two options from the administration. He could either retain or replace any or all of his three departmental commanders. Predictably, and to Washington's undoubted relief, Grant sacked Rosecrans and replaced him with Thomas. Here was the same determined Grant who, at the moment of apparent Confederate victory at Fort Donelson, had told subordinates simply, "Gentleman, the position on the right must be retaken!" Now, directing "Pap" Thomas to hold Chattanooga at all hazards, Grant received in reply a simple: "We will hold the town till we starve!" A new spirit and tone set the stage for the final act to Union conquest of the upper heartland in late 1863.[63]

TWELVE

LAST HURRAH AT CHATTANOOGA: NOVEMBER 1863

Ulysses S. Grant put a new command team in place for the heartland by November 1863. While retaining Major General Ambrose Burnside temporarily, Grant sent no particular instructions to the Knoxville general. Grant relied mainly upon his old comrades, Major General William T. Sherman and Rear Admiral David Porter, with whom he had more experience from the river war. Grant's commands to Sherman were simple, however. Rush all possible aid to the new Army of the Cumberland commander at Chattanooga, Major General George H. Thomas. Clean out bloated rear echelon units, like the eight-hundred-man 111th Illinois stationed at Paducah, Kentucky. "A regiment one-third as large would be ample" to garrison that place, he said. Furthermore, Sherman's cavalry should disperse and drive away any lingering Confederate contingents in West Tennessee. Grant then briefly visited Military Governor Andrew Johnson in Nashville as he made his way personally to Chattanooga. He also saw superseded William S. Rosecrans and discovered that Old Rosy had "some excellent suggestions as to what should be done." Grant marveled that "he had not carried them out."[1]

Basically, the situation was this—Confederate besiegement of the Army of the Cumberland at Chattanooga held hostage all other Union moves in the West. In a sense this fact had been General-in-Chief Henry Halleck's perception from Washington when he wired Grant and Sherman on September 13—even before Chickamauga—that "it is quite possible that Bragg and Johnston will move through Northern Alabama to the Tennessee, to turn General Rosecrans's right and cut off his communication." Halleck decreed that Grant's forces should return to Memphis and move via Corinth and Tuscumbia to cooperate with Rosecrans should the rebels make such a move. He repeated the same need to help Rosecrans to both Burnside and Memphis commander Stephen Hurlbut over the next two days.[2]

Of course, Bragg made no such flanking move, although Confederate cavalry in the region hinted at such operations. The important thing is that Union forces

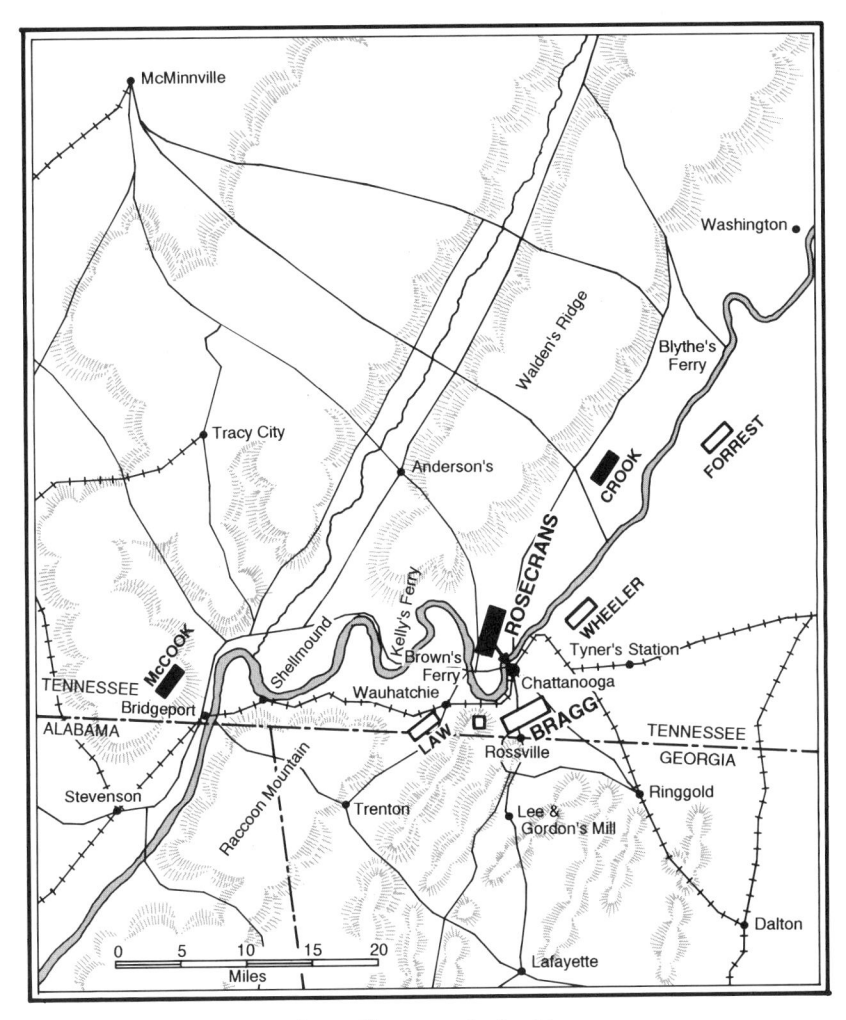

Siege of Chattanooga, October 1863.

from the Mississippi line of advance were already set in motion to help at Chattanooga even before Chickamauga made the move absolutely essential. First Halleck, then Grant, when he took over at Chattanooga, continued to echo concern about some grand Confederate sweep back to Middle Tennessee. When it turned out that Burnside was preoccupied around Knoxville and the Army of the Cumberland could not extricate itself from his own predicament, that left only Grant's trusted lieutenant, Cump Sherman, to save the day. With much urgency, Grant would send his friend the message on October 24 to "drop everything" and speed up his eastward march along the Memphis and Charleston for "the enemy are evidently moving a large force toward Cleveland [Tennessee], and may break through our lines and move on Nashville. This would leave

Sherman's men as the only "forces at command that could beat them there." Therefore, with Vicksburg's victors at Chattanooga before "the enemy cross the Tennessee we could turn their position so as to force them back and save the possibility of a move northward this winter," noted Grant. Of course, that was his prescription after he reached Chattanooga and found the distressing situation there.[3]

A recent riding accident made the overland trek from Bridgeport, Alabama, to Chattanooga most uncomfortable for Grant. But, by October 21, he had arrived and taken hold at the city. He convened an officers' council, sounded out the Army of the Cumberland's top leadership, and listened carefully while his old West Point classmate and crack engineer Brigadier General William F. "Baldy" Smith outlined plans to open a "cracker line" of supply to the railhead at Bridgeport. Smith recited efforts then underway to construct bridges, erect pontoons, and even rehabilitate an old scow for use on the river once passage was reopened. Within days, Thomas and Major General Joseph Hooker had linked up after battles at Browns Ferry and the Wauhatchie. Poorly positioned Confederates under Lieutenant General James Longstreet ineptly tried to impede the meeting in Lookout Valley, but to no avail. Soon, units like the 143d New York of the XI corps encamped in Lookout Valley and learned not only to live on half rations like the westerners, "but to take patiently the amusement of the Confederate artillerists on Lookout Mountain, who practiced, with small charges of powder, dropping shells and pieces of railroad iron in and about the camp." Diarrhea soon became more troubling than the shells, but at least the newcomers had ample firewood, compliments of the rebel shell bursts.[4]

CONFEDERATE FUMBLES

Confederate leaders realized now that they had lost the initiative. President Jefferson Davis, seeking to alleviate General Braxton Bragg's stressful command relationships, agreed to various changes, including Longstreet's independent expedition against Knoxville. Bragg was anxious to rid himself of this eastern general anyway, and with Confederate Tennessee senator Gustavus A. Henry still badgering the Davis regime about a sweeping offensive back to Middle Tennessee and beyond, Bragg found the Knoxville option suddenly attractive. Henry had advanced his scheme as a means "for winding up this campaign gloriously for our army," via a variant of Leonidus Polk's old idea of brushing past the Federal armies and uniting with Joseph E. Johnston's men from Mississippi for a grand advance back to the upper heartland. Wintering near the Kentucky line, "where we can command at moderate rates unlimited supplies," was Henry's desire, with General Robert E. Lee leading the operation. Davis, however, rejected the notion of sending Lee west, and pointedly reminded Bragg that the campaign season was quickly passing. So, the Army of Tennessee commander suddenly decided that Longstreet's advocacy of an offensive could be accommodated and gave him two divisions to defeat Burnside.[5]

The upshot was that Bragg and Longstreet agreed on November 3 to "drive

Burnside out of East Tennessee first, or better to capture or destroy him." Bragg issued the orders the next day. Deceptive phrases followed about eventual Middle Tennessee options. Major General Joseph Wheeler's cavalry would accompany Longstreet, while Brigadier General Samuel "Grumble" Jones would cooperate from southwestern Virginia. Since Johnston had also offered help, Bragg sought to orchestrate some vague cooperation all across the perimeter to northern Mississippi. Brigadier General James R. Chalmers and his cavalry would delay Sherman's eastbound progress. Major General Stephen D. Lee would cover the Tuscumbia corridor, but also move with Brigadier General David Roddey's command into Middle Tennessee and fall upon the enemy's communications. The pair were especially intent on destroying and breaking up the Tennessee and Alabama and Nashville and Chattanooga Railroads.

Lee, however, refused to linger on the Tennessee–Alabama line when his Mississippi base was suddenly threatened by Yankee horsemen. Like the other West Pointers, he did not put have much faith in Brigadier General James R. Chalmers's ragtag regional contingent for base protection. Indeed, parts of Chalmers's force came and went with abandon. Colonel W. W. Faulkner's four hundred irregulars operating from Huntington, Tennessee, for example, wanted to raid northward into the Purchase section of western Kentucky simply to secure hats, blankets, and boots for winter. Mobilized in the summer, they had taken no protective gear from home and impending cold weather, not protection of Lee's Mississippi supply base, drove their effort. Such groups were too freebooting to spawn any confidence from the high command.[6]

Yet, Faulkner promised Chalmers at the end of October that "when I get through I'll show you as fine a looking set of men and the finest mounted command of cavalry you have seen during the war, and they are men who have been forced out by no Confederate law, but who have come out voluntarily sacrificing everything for principles, and will do good fighting." These were just the kind of resources that Tennessee Confederate governor-in-exile Isham G. Harris, Senator Henry, and others anticipated would coalesce around a major Confederate offensive back to the region. Bragg, however, lacked the means and the authority to coordinate such efforts across a long front. Department commander Johnston was too far south in Mississippi, watching Union moves from their new strategic base at Vicksburg. Meanwhile, Bragg battled commissary deficiencies, continuous bickering among subordinates, and disintegration in the discipline and efficiency of his own cavalry. On one occasion he instructed his mounted commanders to stop pillaging and harassing civilians, "which have had an injurious effect on the morale of this army and upon the citizens." His General Order Number 212, issued on November 18, singled out property seizures "under color of the law of impressments" as "unworthy of the Confederate soldier" and as embarrassing "the provisioning of the army." The hated Yankees were not the only perpetrators of crimes against civilians, apparently.[7]

Bad weather, failed military coordination, and the new Federal command team thwarted Confederate operational plans. Burnside pulled back and fortified Knoxville in the face of Longstreet. Floodwaters of the Tennessee in north Alabama, the continuing presence of Union horsemen blocking crossings, and his own poorly equipped command froze Lee in place. Bragg and Davis had also agreed upon an independent command in northern Mississippi for the ever-turbulent Nathan Bedford Forrest, but no one there was sure of Forrest's arrival time or of what was expected from him. Chalmers simply could not prevent Sherman's movement eastward from Memphis to Chattanooga. In fact, Mississippi irregulars lacked both the willpower and strength to inflict major damage. Rumors had Wheeler's outriders threatening distant Paducah and carrying back fifteen wagons of leather, as well as harassing Johnson's black work crews on the Nashville and Northwestern Railroad. Finally, Lee informed Bragg on November 10 that all the bridges from Huntsville to Decatur and from Decatur north to Columbia had been incapacitated. Bragg praised Lee's "noble service" in delaying Sherman nearly a month—"a time of great value to us." In truth, neither Lee nor Chalmers, nor anyone else, accomplished much of consequence. Union land and naval forces adequately controlled river and rail in Middle and West Tennessee. Besides, East Tennessee held the key to the fate of the region.[8]

A FOCUSED UNION EFFORT

A restive Grant now prepared for the inevitable assault on Bragg's hilltop positions around Chattanooga. Thomas's army originally had the mission, but lack of artillery animals stopped the attack. Grant then toyed with having Burnside mount a deep cavalry strike toward Rome or even Atlanta in Bragg's rear to draw attention away from his buildup. That had been Rosecrans's idea some months before. Now, all of Burnside's troops were needed for defense of Knoxville. So Grant returned to logistical matters, ordering his military railroad manager at Nashville, J. B. Anderson, to locate prefabricated bridging to repair the Nashville and Decatur line, then considered indispensable to Sherman's resupplying efforts. But Sherman moved too quickly anyway, and insufficient locomotives and rolling stock proved frustrating. Grant therefore shut down all rear area fabrication and repair facilities (such as those committed to Mississippi Marine Brigade boat repairs) and reallocated their activity to refurbishing the railroads.[9]

Railroad garrisons remained on alert against rebel raiders and actually kept many Union soldiers in the ranks. Sylvester E. Wills of the Seventieth Indiana explained to his parents from Nashville that he had no trouble retaining his sixty-man company in line "as there is no running off home from here." In fact, Grant sent Brigadier General Lovell H. Rousseau back to shape up the Nashville district, while the troops from the Army of the Potomac, together with nearly ten thousand men back in Kentucky, effectively shielded the lines of communication. Local partisans like O. P. Hamilton nonetheless disputed the Glasgow and Bowling Green vicinity, while West Tennessee always remained on edge. But, generally, the autumn passed in missed Confederate opportunities to seriously savage Grant's logistics.[10]

Often these railroad garrisons left a graphic word portrait about war and society in their vicinity. Tighlman Jones of the Fifty-ninth Illinois was stationed

November 1863

Railroad bridge at Whiteside, Tennessee. Note the blockhouse on the near side and the fort beyond the bridge. These elements represent typical Federal bridge and railroad defenses in the Western Theater. National Archives and Records Administration.

ten miles west of Chattanooga at Whiteside Station on the railroad. A unionist family, Jones wrote to his sister, lived in dire poverty close to his camp on the mountain. The father was under constant harassment from secessionists; the children were barefoot and destitute, never having been to school or church. The mountains of East Tennessee were full of such people, he commented, more to be pitied as "it is the education given them by a slaveocracy." All things "have been torn to pieces by this war," he lamented, and "no kind of civil organization exists here." Every man was for himself and the devil was to all, he observed, explaining that the troops had good shelter and plenty to eat. "We are quite contented," he concluded.[11]

In many ways, Sherman bore the spotlight. He left Hurlbut with plenary powers much as he had given to Major General James B. McPherson at Vicksburg. "Viceroys," Sherman styled them to Porter on November 8, while telling them to cooperate fully with the navy. Hurlbut's own subordinates, such as Colonel George E. Waring at Union City, hardly feared raiders like Faulkner or Chalmers; they were more irritating than anything else. Even Sherman deplored "a class of fellows who have avoided the draft and hang about, a nuisance to the army and the country," and, more especially, he disliked the horde of African-American refugees who clung to the army's apron strings for succor. Underrating the potential danger of Forrest (since he had not yet incurred the wizard's wrath),

Sherman contended that as long as Eastport, Mississippi, on the Tennessee River and Memphis on the Mississippi remained in Union hands, no enemy force in strength could penetrate north of the line of the Memphis and Charleston Railroad. "And if they do," he advised Hurlbut on November 9, "they will merely annoy the inhabitants that we are not bound to protect." Sherman captured the essence of a West Point view of war when he stated: "Our duty is to strike and break up the large armies of the Confederacy, which once broken and defeated, the smaller bands will soon be as obnoxious to the people of the South as to us."[12]

Moreover, Sherman told Porter: "I am not going to bother myself about guerrillas and citizens," as long as they "can't do our main arteries harm." The populace would soon tire of their depredations, he felt, and from self-interest combine for their destruction. "Till the Confederacy is shaken to the center," was his conclusion, "we should not bother ourselves with attempts to reconcile people and patch up civil governments." Sherman admitted to the lawlessness of his own soldiers, which he claimed, resulted from the behavior of the citizens themselves. "Our men are full of the idea that all the people are secesh, and would as leave plunder and kill all as not," he observed blandly. In the last analysis, Sherman's movement to aid Thomas depended upon time and nature, not indigenous insurgents or the local populace.[13]

In turn, such celerity involved the weather, since east-west transit meant crossing rivers and streams, at first drought-stricken and then suddenly rain-swollen in quick succession that autumn. Drought had threatened waterborne supplies and even ferrying capabilities at Eastport. Shallow-draft gunboats and transports drawing but three feet of water could not cross the shoals and bars (holding scarcely twenty-six to thirty inches of water in some instances) between Fort Henry and Eastport. The navy even worried that it might not be able to navigate the Ohio River to interdict a rumored relief column sent from East Tennessee to rescue John Hunt Morgan's raiders at Columbus, Ohio. Things were that bad until mid-October rainfall fortuitously raised water levels in the rivers. Porter could then tell a very nervous Sherman that the sea service would meet and resupply his eastbound marching columns.[14]

Sherman was admittedly upset in this period because of the death of his young son from camp fevers contracted while the boy was visiting his father on the Big Black River in Mississippi. "He was my pride and hope of life, and his loss takes from me the great incentive to excel, and now I must work on purely and exclusively for love of country and professional pride," Sherman confided to Porter in mid-October. The general's bitterness and determination toward the South could be seen even earlier in that same letter when he told his friend: "I have no doubt the rebels have every man that is in the Southern Confederacy now armed against us, and the most desperate struggle of the war must be expected. A large proportion of their men are forced; still we know the vindictive feeling that animates this whole people and should not be blinded by any false hopes." He was convinced Porter would soon finish mopping-up operations on the Mississippi and, "with infinite pleasure, help us who must live whilst we penetrate the very bowels of this land."[15]

Turning to his mission, Sherman took no chances. He required the Memphis quartermaster to have a ferryboat sent from St. Louis to carry the army across the Tennessee at Eastport. But when the advance contingents reached that point on October 15, they found Porter true to his word. "I intend to line the Tennessee with gunboats," promised the admiral, so that "your communication shall never be interrupted if there is water in the river." The troops crossed via decked-over coal barges, gunboats like the *Hastings, Key West, Peosta, Tawah, Cricket, Lexington, Paw Paw, Naumkeag, Tuscumbia,* and *Tyler,* as well as steamers *Anglo Saxon, Nashville,* and *Sunny South.* Each army division numbered not only the men but six hundred wagons, four thousand animals, plus artillery. Passage seemed slow to Lieutenant Commander S. L. Phelps and his crews. Nevertheless, by early November, Sherman's expedition had passed the hurdle of the Tennessee River, unstopped by either nature or the rebel army.[16]

"I think our movement up the Tennessee has taken them by surprise," Sherman wrote Porter enthusiastically on the final day of October, "and their cavalry is very much scattered—is powerless for any military purpose, but to molest our communications." Ever alert to dangers of Confederate reoccupation of riverbank positions, "we must never again allow the enemy to make a lodgment on [the Mississippi's bank] with artillery, and therefore Columbus, Memphis, Vicksburg, and mouth of Yazoo must be held with troops," Sherman told Porter on the twenty-fifth. All else would be entrusted to the gunboats and a mobile force at Memphis and Vicksburg, "surplus and available at all times to float to the threatened point to prevent a lodgment."[17]

At this time, General-in-Chief Henry Halleck's monitoring of affairs from Washington intruded on the intentions of local commanders like Grant and Sherman. He simply would not allow them to abandon garrisons along the Memphis and Charleston Railroad. Well aware of that sector where river and rail came together from service there the previous year, Halleck pressured Sherman to position token garrisons like the 122d Illinois in a hilltop fort behind Eastport and to leave guards at Fort Heiman and railroad towns such as Corinth. Nonetheless, claiming "I attach little importance to the railroad from Memphis," Sherman largely abandoned his line of communication much as Grant had done during the Vicksburg campaign that summer. By November, the navy shifted its primary attention back to the Cumberland from the Mississippi and Tennessee Rivers so as to convoy supply boats to railheads more directly linked with Chattanooga or to supply Burnside across intervening mountains at Knoxville. Additional units, including several New Jersey regiments coming from the east, bolstered Hurlbut's political-military control of West Tennessee by stopping off at Eastport and Savannah. They buttressed Union supremacy on the rivers, aided in population and area control, and offered a deterrent against raiders from Mississippi and Alabama.[18]

Small bands of partisans and irregulars continued to harass joint army-navy operations in support of Chattanooga's relief, although they were unable to prevent them. Fitch complained to Porter from the USS *Moose* "below Dover" on November 9 that scatterings of fifteen or twenty such insurgents could be found along the Cumberland. He had uncovered no artillery, he said, but small arms fire had rained upon a steamboat just a mile or two below Fort Donelson. "This is a sample of the energy displayed by the land forces up this river," he fumed, and "if we are not annoyed by batteries soon it will be a wonder." Water-depth fluctuations also plagued the USS *Fairplay* and *Brilliant*, but he still destroyed a distillery rendezvous of guerrillas inland from the burnt-out hamlet of Palmyra near Clarksville.[19]

The Cumberland was even more treacherous to passage upriver above Nashville, and Fitch wanted permission to clear its banks of all habitation in order to keep Burnside's supply route open. "We pass men standing on the banks apparently unarmed and quiet, but no sooner are the gunboats out of sight than they turn around, pick up their guns, and fire into the next steamer coming along," he noted, capturing the essence of the irregular conflict on the western rivers. Therefore, he advocated a scheme that had worked well on the Tennessee. Announce that the navy planned to clear out an area then hold local residents responsible for peace and quiet there. Porter agreed to trying that scheme on the upper Cumberland. Fitch and his mosquito fleet had sufficient firepower to counter the guerrillas. Seven gunboats worked the Cumberland, eight more plied the Tennessee, and still others conducted missions on the Ohio. But Fitch was basically correct about army lethargy in helping prevent guerrilla interference with river traffic. Rosecrans's withdrawal of rear garrisons as reinforcements before Chickamauga had reduced the capabilities of units like the Eight-third Illinois at Clarksville and Fort Donelson for anything more than merely holding their positions.[20]

THE OTHER KIND OF WAR

The troops ashore were no fools for not wanting to chase mounted rebels—regular or irregular. Letters from the Fort Donelson garrison, for example, indicated a certain note of reality. Illinoisan William H. Dorris told his wife in mid-November that irregulars in that area had gone home temporarily to warm themselves before returning to the practice of thievery and molestation. Frankly, for the moment the soldiery was more concerned about the direction of Lincoln administration policies than any guerrilla population. Besides, the army had learned by this time that the elusive irregulars might fire on passing boats and then fade quickly into the forests, defying slow-moving chase columns of Union infantry. Moreover, the need for cavalry at the front had stripped rear garrisons of their only truly effective device for hunting down guerrillas. So the garrisons remained in garrison, while naval convoys again became the most effective method for ensuring that supplies reached distribution points for the field armies. Local "country people," like twelve-year-old Guy Wilbur Jackson helped homesick northern boys desert from the garrison, assisted with "running the blockade" of Yankee river patrols so that neighbors might get provisions at Linton, Kentucky, and in other ways assisted both "our boys" in rebel gray as well as civilian survival under occupation.[21]

Forts Donelson, Dover, and Clarksville again became convoy concentration points for the Chattanooga campaign. The customary ambush places at Harpeth's and Ingrams' shoals, as well as Jackson's woodyard (about a mile and a half downriver from Fort Donelson toward the Kentucky line), claimed new victims. Just about every wooded bluff on the river posed a problem and when not actually sniping at the boats, the partisans prevented local farmers from selling fuel wood to the coal-starved navy. Sensing renewed army-navy cooperation problems, Fitch told Porter that "The army quartermaster seems to forget that there are nearly fifty transports to one gunboat, and sending them down as they do with no regularity, one at a time or perhaps one every two hours, it is impossible always to have a gunboat waiting to give them immediate convoy." Low water, off-loading and reloading issues, congestion at key points, inevitable delays, and army complaints all surfaced anew. As Fitch recounted, "it is certainly very discouraging to work as hard as we have, to aid and assist the army, and to receive, on their part, only complaints in acknowledgement."[22]

Of course, the army had its share of frustration too. In most cases quartermasters, not riverbank garrisons, worried about the need to expedite supplies to Grant and Burnside. One Illinois captain found Fitch unnecessarily wary about working the waters above Nashville without Porter's express orders, so he personally intervened with the admiral in order to secure convoy above the state capital. In all, however, some 108 boats and 24 barges as well as 60 pontoons passed up the Cumberland during November. They were undeterred by irregulars that darted from Waverly or southern Kentucky lairs. This duty forever annoyed Fitch and his sailors, however, and at one point he faced an incipient revolt among Cumberland and Ohio pilots who wanted hazardous duty pay. When a guerrilla party reportedly passed within a mile of Fort Donelson "and nothing was known of them till we got the news from Clarksville, 60 [actually only 30] miles above," Fitch complained, there could be but one remedy. "A bright picket guard must be kept at Dover to let the guerrillas come so near and not know it," he sneered.[23]

The problem seemed to be increasingly universal throughout the upper heartland. Even the south bank of the Ohio contained disloyal towns, while Evansville, Indiana, across the river, said Fitch, "is a place that needs watching, in consequence of contraband trade." Everyone seemed resigned to a certain level of insurgency, keeping it under control by aggressive patrolling rather than complete eradication. Fitch sought to have each of his boats armed with two twelve-pounder howitzers in addition to their main batteries so that he could land these pieces with thirty soldiers or sailors to assail guerrilla parties "forming and encamped two or three miles from the river." They could also be consolidated when necessary into "one division of about twelve or fourteen pieces of artillery, and about 200 small-arms-men or infantry to support them." Of course, this was precisely what the Mississippi Marine Brigade was supposed to be all about. At any rate, Fitch believed that, with such a force, "I can readily break up or disperse any guerrilla band along the Cumberland." Lacking heavy artillery to seriously interdict convoys as they had the previous winter, the partisans merely continued to harass the steamboats as fall moved toward winter in 1863.[24]

The range of clashes between irregulars and Federal authorities was vast—from Cumberland Gap in the Appalachians to Mount Sterling in the Bluegrass; from the Cumberland to the Mississippi River farther west and south. Scouts and expeditions went out regularly after guerrillas from Memphis, Fort Pillow, Union City, Munfordville, the twin rivers forts, Clarksville, even down into north Alabama. Everywhere the results were the same. Union parties battled Champ Ferguson, John M. Hughs, O. P. Hamilton, and Ferdinand H. Daugherty in the foothills of the Cumberlands. They captured Colonel Solomon G. Street and his fifty-five men at Meriwether's Ferry near Union City and killed "the notorious thief and rebel, Captain Belbo" somewhere on the Cumberland. Major J. Morris Young and a portion of the Fifth Iowa Cavalry found the rich bottomland farms of north Alabama from Mayesville to Whiteburg and Decatur still florid with corn and livestock. "Many who had their stock hid out or run across the river had just had it returned or brought out, thinking the Yankees were all out of the country." He netted 150 to 200 fresh mules and horses for his own men and destroyed 9 ferryboats, thereby weakening the guerrilla support structure in this quarter.[25]

Often it proved difficult to determine who the perpetrators of the hinterland turbulence were. Sometimes attributed to Thomas G. Woodward or Adam Rankin Johnson, the raids north into the Jackson Purchase area provided more lore of violence and bloodshed as Faulkner, Richardson, or even one of the Forrest brothers actually led the raids. A Captain Dyer supposedly commanded one party of forty-five or fifty guerrillas that terrorized the Hopkinsville, Kentucky, vicinity before being intercepted in late October near Volney in Logan County by Union colonel Cicero Maxwell. Maxwell's group numbered barely forty hard-bitten troopers from the Third Kentucky and Sixth New Hampshire cavalry plus his own Twenty-sixth Kentucky infantry but gave the raiders a spirited mounted chase. It ended in Tennessee with the rebels dispersed, several civilians dead in the melee, and Maxwell swearing that he was "more than ever convinced of the utter malignity and treachery of the sympathizers with treason in the southern part of Logan County." A similar column from Russellville supposedly caught up with Woodward's main body at its recruiting rendezvous, Camp Coleman on West Fork, near Pembroke, Kentucky, in this same period and wrecked this poorly trained, ill-disciplined, and indifferently equipped mob of insurgents.[26]

Even ambushes of river craft occurred on the Mississippi despite garrisons like Fort Pillow above Memphis. Brigadier General Grenville Dodge informed Hurlbut from Corinth, Mississippi, on October 22 that his scouts from Union City had uncovered a northward march of one thousand men commanded by Faulkner who were apparently planning to raid commissary stores at Murray, Mayfield, and other points in Kentucky. He sent a copy of his dispatch by fast steamboat in order to alert Columbus district commander Brigadier General Andrew Jackson Smith. But, despite this alert, Faulkner's Confederates got into Mayfield, plundered trains, disrupted the telegraph, and then proceeded to use bloodhounds to track local unionists. Numbering only two hundred men in reality, the raiders took eighteen thousand dollars in booty from Mayfield and

View of Paducah, Kentucky, at the confluence of the Ohio and Tennessee Rivers and the northern terminus of the Mobile and Ohio Railroad. Frank Leslie's Illustrated History of the Civil War (New York: Frank Leslie, 1895), 383.

headed toward Paducah. Here, Colonel S. G. Hicks commanding the Fortieth Illinois and gunboat support provided by Lieutenant Commander James M. Prichett's USS *Tyler* thwarted the rebels, so Faulkner retraced his steps back through Mayfield and into West Tennessee via Henry and Carroll Counties unpursued. Few direct military results came from this kind of activity, but the resulting mayhem disrupted civilian life and drastically reduced civilian confidence in Federal occupation as a buffer against banditry and harassment.[27]

Notwithstanding the sentiments of Sherman or other Union generals, the lifeblood of rebellion seethed among the local population. Mary Walker Meriwether Bell of Garretsburg in Christian County, Kentucky, wrote in her journal on October 4 that she had attended a large citizen meeting at Locust Grove and that "if I could have armed all the white men present, there were enough to drive every Yankee out of Hopkinsville and Clarksville." Her husband was with Woodward and she was livid about the presence of shirkers at home who did little to help the Confederacy or even keep the local peace for that matter. She scorned the occupying Federals, who seemed to delight in stealing the trunks of civilians and cavorting about in the pilfered clothing. Failing to realize that most borderstate unionists came largely from the underclass—hence they prized the clothing of the gentry—she sneered, "I would not wear a Yankee's woman's clothes for anything."[28]

Thus, it had become a different war in Kentucky and Tennessee—or actually it had become any number of little (even personalized) wars. Unionists garbed in army blue often used their positions to carry on personal vendettas against their peacetime "betters." Likewise, southerners who became partisans attempted to enforce their belief in separatism in the absence of regular Confederate authority. Brigadier General and Provost Marshal S. P. Carter pointedly complained to Burnside's headquarters in East Tennessee in late October about "the lawlessness of troops in the vicinity of Strawberry Plains" northeast of Knoxville. He cited continuous outrages carried out "upon the persons and property of unoffending citizens for the alleged reason that they have heretofore manifested sympathy with the rebellion." The perpetrators were unionists of the Eighth Tennessee Cavalry. Presumably, these men simply carried out their own brand of sociocultural retaliation against neighbors of a different persuasion—and far from the conventional battlefield. Without military resolution on the battlefield, this internecine conflict could be expected to continue unchecked.[29]

CHATTANOOGA RELIEVED—EAST TENNESSEE REDEEMED

Hard-nosed army and navy professionals now took over operations in the region. Grant wired Hurlbut on November 9 to collect mules and horses—indeed, "all serviceable animals and beef cattle"—in West Tennessee and northern Mississippi, giving vouchers to be paid on nontransferable proof of loyalty. "That country ought to be put in such condition that it will not support Chalmers' command any longer," he decreed. It was only a question "between us and the guerrillas which will get them," he informed the chief quartermaster at Louisville concerning horses and mules still in civilian hands. When local people failed to respond to Hurlbut's tightening grip, the Memphis commander simply closed his picket line to civilian traffic, declared martial law, and told the War Department that he was surrounded by hostile enemies both regular and irregular, "and they are fed and supplied from Memphis" itself. As the army became seasoned or "veteranized," the soldiers assumed harder attitudes. Wilbur F. Hitt of the Eighty-third Indiana told his father while passing through "Old Memphis" in early October, "we have seen so much since we have been out, that places and things loose their novelty the more we circulate."[30]

Sherman became the incarnation of "hard" war as his column marched east to Chattanooga. By the time he reached Fayetteville on the Elk River, he had exhausted his patience for local "secesh," irregulars, execrable roads, swollen streams, and delays. Always worried about the impact of low water on his supply line, he observed to Porter on November 8 that it would be "impossible to use the Tennessee river from this quarter," a sentiment quickly translated for subordinates with respect to civilian property along the line of march. "I find plenty of corn, cattle, hogs, &c. on this route," he told cavalry brigadier George Crook at Maysville, Alabama, on the sixth, but did not expect much to be left once his army had passed. "I never saw such greedy rascals after chickens and fresh meat," he chuckled. This cornucopia had been set aside for Bragg, and "I don't know but what it would be a good plan to march my army back and forth from Florence and Stevenson [Alabama] to make a belt of devastation between the enemy and our country." Here was the forerunner for his famed march through Georgia the next autumn. For now, however, he merely told Grant: "We made large inroads on all such things." Callous to civilian hardship, he told Brigadier General Grenville Dodge, who was trailing the main column at Pulaski: "Let them feel and know that by breaking our communications they force us to eat them out."[31]

Sherman's philosophy of war was made plain to Memphis *Bulletin* editor J. B. Bingham. "I have a right to use every man, every influence, every moral, intellectual, and physical power within my limits to restore order, peace, and finally produce the restoration of the civil power," he claimed. If a man disturbs the peace, "I will kill or remove him; if he does anything wrong and there is no civil power in existence, the military power does exist and must act, for we must have some law." To Dodge, Sherman wrote bluntly on November 9: "Whilst at Pulaski, let your mounted men hunt out the pests that infest that country. Show them no mercy, and if the people don't suppress guerrillas, tell them your orders are to treat the community as enemies." If they remained orderly and quiet, then Dodge should pay for corn, hogs, and other foodstuffs, or provide vouchers, "but eat up all the supplies, grain, hogs, and cattle of Elk River." He passed similar thoughts to the Eastport post commander two weeks later. Sherman added that this officer should clean out a nasty guerrilla base inland from Savannah. "I want them killed and their property destroyed," was Sherman's order, with their families and household goods dispatched to some town on the Ohio River.[32]

Some of Sherman's Vicksburg veterans who now transited back through West Tennessee discovered a changed climate among the citizenry awaited them. Surgeon Jonathan B. Rice of the Seventy-second Ohio wrote his wife from LaGrange on November 16 that the secesh ladies like the one who had refused him a drink of water or to sell him a glass of milk when his unit had first entered the town a year before were now gone. Now, the citizens were obliged to "get their food from us," and while "the town has been sadly, but justly used," the Negroes were gone, "and the white ladies once so proud and haughty, are compelled to do their own work." He was occupied daily in treating the southern civilians, and "of course, I always treat them all kindly," administering to their wants to the best of his ability. "Thus times change, and people change in [*sic*] them," he concluded. Guerrillas lurked about, and "parties of them come within a mile or two of town almost daily," he noted, "but do no other damage than to occasionally pick up or kill some soldier who has inadvertently ventured outside our pickets."[33]

Sherman finished his 250-mile hike from Memphis to Chattanooga by mid-November. By this time, Washington wanted Grant to unleash Thomas against Longstreet's rear guard, as the Confederate general threatened to drive Burnside from Knoxville. But Grant did nothing; his own destruction of Bragg would alleviate the threat to Burnside in due course. Besides, Burnside understood the game very well. He drew Longstreet into a frustrating siege at Knoxville and out of position to help Bragg contain Grant at Chattanooga. Besides, the early winter rains and fog cut deeply into the ardor of soldiers all across East Tennessee, while Longstreet had his own share of problems with independent command, including truculent subordinates, faulty ammunition, and his own inability to drive home a telling assault upon the enemy at a propitious moment.[34]

Elsewhere, Dodge's division took position to survey and complete repairs to the Nashville and Decatur rail line (and shield the mid-state rear from rebel raids out of north Alabama). Indeed, low water in the Tennessee by mid-November permitted Roddey to venture above that river again only to be blocked quickly by alert Union horsemen. "There is a considerable number of rebel bands scattered throughout the country," Dodge wired Sherman, and "they do what damage they can and run." Grant and Sherman continued to press for abandoning Corinth, Mississippi, in order to again combat manpower, but Halleck demurred, claiming that "it would give up the control of all the roads of Northern Mississippi and Alabama, and expose the navigation of the Cumberland, Tennessee, and Mississippi above Memphis."[35]

Then, suddenly, the Confederacy's post-Chickamauga honeymoon in the West ended on November 24 and 25. Bragg's own precarious supply line, the chill winds knifing through the rebels' soft cotton uniforms atop the heights overlooking Chattanooga, and the visible marshaling of a great host below them on the floor of the valley all conspired to foretell disaster. Bragg's force was now a shell of its former self, as Longstreet's departure robbed him of a phalanx of veterans while dissension between Tennesseans and Georgians in the remaining ranks approached the feuds of their generals. On November 22, Bragg wired Longstreet to return, but the easterner remained preoccupied before Knoxville. Two days later, one of Hooker's divisions seized the summit of Lookout Mountain in the famous "battle above the clouds," and the next day, Thomas's half-starved Cumberlanders stormed Missionary Ridge contrary to orders to halt short of that cannon-studded elevation. Only Major General Patrick Cleburne's resolute defense at the north end of Tunnel Hill effectively neutralized Sherman's attack at that point. Then, the stormy Irish American covered the rout of Bragg's army back into north Georgia. "We outwitted Bragg and drove him off Missionary Ridge," Sherman wired Hurlbut on November 27. The whole Midwest went wild with the news of Grant's latest success. "We considered Grant invincible," wrote Ohio veteran Ralsa Rice later in his memoirs.[36]

"If we can catch Bragg before Longstreet, we will make short work of him, and produce a just effect," observed Sherman. Bragg, of course, had neither the means nor the will to join Longstreet after this latest disaster. He could do little to prevent his uncooperative subordinate from dissipating his own strength in a futile attempt to dislodge Federals from Fort Sanders and during other indecisive moments during the siege of Knoxville in late November and early December. True, Longstreet's activities diverted Federal attention from a pursuit of Bragg in Georgia that might destroy his army (and Patrick Cleburne effectively contained a desultory Union force near Ringgold on November 27). Sherman dispatched a relief column to aid Burnside and eventually left Minty's cavalry to pacify other areas north and east of Knoxville. But Minty was back with the main

Knoxville skyline from the parapet at Fort Sanders, looking southeast, with the University of Tennessee in the background, March 1864. Library of Congress.

army by Christmas, and Longstreet's chastened force slipped off to winter quarters around Russellville, Tennessee, and prepared to return to the Army of Northern Virginia. Burnside's jaded army happily watched him go, suffering their own dismal Christmas on short rations and wearing threadbare clothing, but in far better spirits than the previous year after Fredericksburg. "We have beaten the enemy and feel confident of being able to do so still," noted Frederick Pettit of the One-hundredth Pennsylvania. Meanwhile, Bragg was left to puzzle over his defeat. From Dalton, Georgia, he reported only 33,000 rank and file with 2,500 artillerists to service 112 cannon, 3,000–4,000 cavalry, 30 days' rations, 20,000 surplus small arms, plus a reserve augmentation of 3,100 Georgia state troops. Rebel disaster had been complete in East Tennessee.[37]

Bragg himself was gone by Christmas. Bereft of ideas for new campaigns to reverse the trend of defeat in the upper heartland, he relinquished command of the Army of Tennessee. Ironically, another of President Jefferson Davis's old nemeses, Joe Johnston, would succeed Bragg and prepare the army for campaigns in the spring. Grant and his subordinates had missed an annihilative victory. Yet, Chattanooga's consequences could not be slighted. At one strike, the Confederacy's strength was broken at the center; Kentucky and Tennessee had been saved for the Union. Deliverance of a major Union army—the Army of the Cumberland—was itself momentous and helped ease the strain on Burnside's threatened position at Knoxville. By the same token, suggests Burnside's most recent biographer, that general offered his own army as live bait to enable Grant

Chattanooga, Tennessee. Date unknown. National Archives and Records Administration.

to break the Chattanooga siege. Georgia and the Deep South states were now threatened from the rear. The conquest of the upper heartland, begun twenty-two months before on this very river at Fort Henry and continued within days at Fort Donelson on the nearby Cumberland, had finally been accomplished.[38]

FORETASTE OF THE FUTURE

The clash between armies for control of Kentucky and Tennessee had ended. Governor Andrew Johnson had assured Lincoln immediately after Stones River that Tennessee would willingly return to the Union once the principal rebel army had been driven from her soil. The latter was accomplished in November and December; the former remained to be seen. For the moment, the Federal rank and file at Chattanooga continued to suffer from half-rations and lack of supplies, as new uniforms and equipment and full rations "arrived with a beautiful lethargy," recalled German Americans in the Ninth Ohio. Still, duty was easy, "and trouble from the enemy, nonexistent." Recuperation and respite came over time. And it seemed to bode well also for Mitchel Thompson and his mates of the Eight-third Illinois at Fort Donelson. Recounting the news from Chattanooga to his wife on November, he beamed, "Good for Ulysses. He is an old war horse and got a goodly number of good old war horses with him." Thompson thought the rebellion was "fast playing out," and with the favorable northern and border state elections, "I think the time is not far distant that secession views in the south will be as unpopular as it has been popular."[39]

Soaring spirits accompanied this break between battles. Army of the Cumberland brigade leader John Beatty waxed in his journal from atop Missionary Ridge on New Year's Day 1864 about the splendid panorama spread before him. Chattanooga below, the massive mountains around, the silvery ribbon of the Tennessee glistening provocatively, and a huge, white-tented encampment of the national army all around—such things proclaimed their own certain glory, he thought. "The fact that a hundred and fifty thousand men, with all the appliances of war have struggled for the possession of these mountains, river, and ridges," he proclaimed in speaking of the victories at Chattanooga, gave solemn interest to the scene. The future boded well for the army in his view.[40]

Still, another future also beckoned for Beatty's contemporaries. Men such as civilian George Richard Browder, the preacher-farmer in Logan County, Kentucky, had already sensed more ominous portents. Back in September, he had lamented that without Divine (or at least European) intervention, the rebellion seemed doomed to failure. "From the signs of the times," said Browder, "a military power will take the place of our once liberal Republic." He cited suppression of free speech, loss of habeas corpus, press censorship, an ignored Constitution, and the ballot trodden beneath the bayonet as evidence. "Conscription forces us to fight—negroes are armed against their masters—confiscation and exile are common, and a tide of evil is overwhelming the land." He thought sixty days would tell the story of the great revolution or else a war between the United States and France. By December, Browder continued to be dismayed by the decree that signaled the end of slavery, by the indolence and self-will of freed slaves, and by the fact that neither his own governor nor the president of the United States offered any protection to the right of property (i.e., slavery). "If such be the will of God I say Amen," he sighed, "but I cannot so understand the Bible."[41]

Browder's fellow clergyman-farmer, Jesse Cox, residing near Franklin, Tennessee, similarly rejected divine intervention. Despite delivering fourteen sermons and a funeral service around an 187-mile circuit, "I have rode less and preached less than any year since I have been preaching," he exclaimed, blaming the Yankees "who forbid me going from home" as well as ill health. However, Cox admitted that at present his health had never been better nor had his preaching been better received. People like Browder and Cox rejoiced that they were surviving in a war-stricken land. Never before had the Union, and the people of the upper heartland, seen such traumatic change. Emancipation, conscription, violence, national taxes, and long casualty lists dipped deeply into male ranks of society. Copperhead pacifism was by no means stilled north of the Ohio or Potomac Rivers, nor was war weariness banished from hearts and minds of their brethren in the Confederacy, for that matter. Hoosier warrior James H. Jones predicted from Murfreesboro on a soft October evening that "the bigger part of the able bodied men in the north will Smell powder before this war is over."[42]

Even then, rumors of new rebel mischief circulated widely in West Tennessee, for instance. The famed Nathan Bedford Forrest reportedly had arrived in northern Mississippi and together with Stephen Lee's local defenders counted five thousand fresh riders, available for increasing tension north of the Memphis and Charleston Railroad. Central Kentucky was rife with reports of O. P. Hamilton's irregulars preying on the stretch of country between Cave City and Bowling Green. W. W. Faulkner and F. M. Stewart threatened the Fort Pillow neighborhood north of Memphis and disrupted Union work parties removing rails from the Paducah and Hickman line for use elsewhere. Wheeler, Dibrell, and Biffle ravaged Blount County in East Tennessee in support of Longstreet's activities, and then they were reported to be downriver in north Alabama preparing for a raid up through Lawrenceburg toward Nashville. Union garrisons stood on the alert from the Ohio valley to Vicksburg. At Memphis Hurlbut prepared for Forrest's coming.[43]

Forrest, in fact, had gone to northern Mississippi (after lengthy consultations with Jefferson Davis at Atlanta) with scarcely a corporal's guard—little more than three hundred men plus a battery of steel rifled guns. Lee, Forrest's new superior, expressed admiration and fealty, but could provide little else, so Forrest had to recruit his command via an aggressive expedition into Hurlbut's jurisdiction. The response of steadier veterans like Sherman was simple. "Forrest may cavort about that country as much as he pleases. Every conscript they now catch will cost a good man to watch." Still, the West Pointer misread the ardor with which West Tennesseans flocked anew to Forrest's banner.[44]

Colonels Tyree H. Bell and J. F. Newsom led the recruiting vanguard and gathered in many of the local defense or partisan groups. Faulkner's men had been similarly engaged on the Kentucky border and together, using many of Forrest's private funds, were able to amass not only men but provisions for this virtually self-sustaining small army. The distressed town of Jackson rallied to Forrest's call, and within about two or three weeks, Forrest had mobilized about three thousand men despite the onset of winter. If not exactly a repeat of his famous December 1862 raid, Forrest's new operation was just as admirable in raising a new fighting force from a region thought to be reasonably pacified by Federal authorities. Hurlbut eventually deployed four converging columns against him, amounting to fifteen thousand troopers in total under Brigadiers Benjamin H. Grierson, Joseph A. Mower, Andrew Jackson Smith, and William Sooy Smith. "I think we shall cure Forrest of his ambition to command West Tennessee," Hurlbut declared unrealistically. The wizard, in turn, requested reinforcements from Lee, but when the Federals moved too quickly for him, Forrest retired from the state with his recruits, a large wagon train, and nearly three hundred hogs and two hundred cattle.[45]

Forrest made good his escape largely because R. V. Richardson's brigade staged a brilliant rear guard defense near Esenaula on the Hatchie River. Sharp skirmishes and inclement weather also contributed to the rebuff, although Forrest (newly minted as a major general on December 4) led his little army in triumph out of West Tennessee at the end of the year. The command that he gathered around him at Holly Springs, Mississippi, on New Year's Day 1864 numbered thirty-five hundred well-mounted and equipped troopers and two pieces of artillery, and they were well provisioned for active winter service. His passage had inspired West Tennessee secessionists once more. As a young trooper, John Johnston of Denmark in Madison County, Tennessee, recalled, news of Forrest's coming "carried joy and hope and enthusiasm everywhere." The county soon teemed with rebel soldiery, he claimed.[46]

Of course Grant and Sherman remained confident that their subordinates could deal with such disturbances in the Mississippi valley. Dodge, Smith, and Grierson were all veterans and should not be daunted by the likes of Forrest, Lee, or Chalmers, they reckoned. The upper heartland from East Tennessee to Paducah would be protected; the methods were left to these subordinates. Sherman succinctly reflected high-command sentiments when he explained to Hurlbut on November 18 to dispose his forces to protect Memphis and Eastport or Corinth secondarily, since the enemy would only prowl north of the Memphis and Charleston, and "we should so dispose matters that they maraud their own people." The army had no responsibility to protect a people that had sent all its youth, arms, horses, and "all that is of any account to war against us." The people had done all the harm they could do, "so let them reap the consequences." There was little in Sherman's words that spoke to Andrew Johnson's olive branch of reconciliation. Nor was such sentiment evident in the words of Grant about the residents of Paducah, Kentucky—"almost to a man disloyal, and entitled to no favors from the Government."[47]

Such sentiments translated to local subordinates' actions just as the senior military leaders intended. Grenville Dodge, better known for his postwar construction of the transcontinental Union Pacific Railroad, told Colonel Henry R. Mizner, commanding at Columbia, Tennessee, that he regretted any of his soldiers violating the laws of war by their actions. But his own orders demanded that soldiers live off the country in an orderly and legitimate manner. "I propose to eat up all the surplus, and perhaps the entire crops in the country, take all serviceable stock, mules, horses &c., so that when we leave here no rebel army, if it should ever get here, can live a day." In thoughts echoing those of his superiors Sherman and Grant, Dodge underscored that the local populace "are proud, arrogant rebels, who beg our protection, but wish to be allowed at the same time to oppose our armies and our Government." He proposed letting these people know that "we are at war; that we are in a country of rebels, and that they must support my command, respect and obey my orders, and that all they possess belongs legitimately to the U.S. Government." If the civilians brought supplies to the army, claimed Dodge, he would pay for them, not because payment was their right, "but that it is cheaper for us and for the Government." But, he told Mizner, when going after the supplies, never pay for them, never ask the suppliers to take the oath, "but treat them as they act." Every rebel took the oath to save his property was Dodge's view. "I know no Union man in this country unless he openly declares and shows by his acts that he is willing and ready to shoulder a musket in our cause." Here was the clear-cut drawing of lines at the midpoint of an increasingly nastier war.[48]

UNFULFILLED MISSION

On the very first day of the battle of Chickamauga, President Abraham Lincoln had authorized Governor Johnson to exercise such powers as might be necessary and proper "to enable the loyal people of Tennessee to present such a republican form of State government as will entitle the State to the guarantee of the United States therefor, and to be protected under such State government by the United States against invasion and domestic violence." The fourth section of the fourth article of the Federal Constitution provided authority for this move. By the time that Johnson received Lincoln's letter, however, the Chickamauga defeat surely caused him to wonder whether or not the presidential mandate could be carried out. Two months later, that doubt was erased by equally momentous events at Chattanooga. As one Union colonel declared, the appearance of the Stars and Stripes waving in triumph atop Lookout Mountain was "the conclusive evidence to observers for many miles around that one of the grandest feats of the war had been performed by our soldiers." To politicians like Johnson, perhaps anything seemed possible.[49]

Yet, Union armies did not completely control the upper Confederate heartland as a result of their November victories. The pockets of control at Chattanooga and Knoxville hardly indicated hegemony over most of East Tennessee or the Tennessee–Alabama Confederate munitions area, implied one historian of the subject. Furthermore, banditry stalked Union-occupied Tennessee. Rosecrans's post-Tullahoma victory announcement to Burnside on July 8 still echoed with its ominous comment: "Let me know how you are dealing with the robbers, raiders, and guerrillas." Answers to that problem would ultimately decide the question of whether or not Tennessee (and Kentucky) were ready for reunification.[50]

The thoughts and deeds of men from Grant, Sherman, and Dodge to those in the ranks (even citizens on the home front) would ultimately settle this issue. But for the moment, conciliation was hardly in vogue. Corporal Frederick Pettit explained from East Tennessee why his comrades had reenlisted for three years despite intense winter suffering, likened to Valley Forge during the Revolution. The war would be over in less than three years "and we wish to finish what we have begun," he declared. A Hoosier soldier wrote his wife just before Christmas how a poor Memphis ferryman had been brutally murdered and his boat sunk by partisans as he humbly discharged cargo and passengers on the Arkansas shore. Federal authorities worried that Confederate officials intended guerrilla attacks from unprotected shorelines as a new strategy to block a reopened river trade. The major battles seemed to have ended in the west; a civil war of a different stripe continued to engulf the region. James Reed of the Thirty-fourth New Jersey at Columbus, Kentucky, said it about right: "There are plenty of guerrillas in this part of the country and if ever they catch one of our men they hang them right up." Several soldiers of his unit had been taken in this fashion, "and we never heard of them since." The men in blue sensed their work was not done.[51]

Chaplain Alonzo H. Quint of the Second Massachusetts explained to his wife from an Elk River encampment in November how such matters were handled differently in the West than they were in Virginia. "They have a short shrift" in Tennessee, he noted, retelling how one local commander had recently reported an encounter with twenty guerrillas in which his force had killed eight and captured twelve others. "Unfortunately, in bringing his prisoners into camp, they all fell off a log, and broke their necks," Quint quipped unemotionally. He hardly blinked at such retribution, for, he suggested, Tennessee unionists had seen their own lives severely disrupted, often by their own neighbors as much as by strangers in rebel garb. They had a price on their heads from such men, said Quint, so "it is no wonder they are implacable, nor can one pity the murderous guerrilla taken in the act."[52]

On November 27, John Hunt Morgan and his followers broke out of the Ohio penitentiary where they had been incarcerated since summer. That same day his wife, Mattie, gave birth to a daughter in Danville, Virginia, her place of refuge during that ordeal. In Nashville, her desperately ill sister Mary and her husband, the renowned physician Dr. William Cheatham, had endured six months of hell and persecution at the hands of the local secret police and provost marshal—even transportation to Yankee prison (later retracted by the infamous Colonel William Truesdail)—all because of their association with the greatly feared Morgan. Later, they would suffer the indignity of almost losing their residence at the capital to confiscation by Union authorities when Ulysses S. Grant set up headquarters there after defeating Bragg. Since summer, erstwhile partisan leader Adam Rankin Johnson and other Morgan followers had reorganized Morgan's command in southwest Virginia in anticipation of their leader's return. They had rebuffed Bragg's efforts to disband them and had fought under Forrest at Chickamauga as well as riding subsequently with Wheeler. By year's end, however, Morgan's men went again into southwestern Virginia, while Johnson himself (anxious to return to his own little corner of the Confederacy in western Kentucky) discovered that times had changed as far as the status of partisan rangers was concerned—not only with the Yankees, but also an embattled Richmond government.[53]

Secretary of War James A. Seddon told the Confederate president in his annual report on November 26 that the anticipated advantages of a partisan ranger corps "have been very partially realized." Their independent mode of operations had accrued only "license, depredations, [and] grave mischiefs." While under inefficient officers, and operating within Confederate territory, they had "come to be regarded as more formidable and destructive to our own people than to the enemy," he observed. Moreover, the opportunities for profit afforded to them by their captures as well as the light bonds of discipline had upset line soldiers. Seddon admitted some exceptions, but felt that the partisans either needed to be merged with regular troops of the army or disbanded and their members conscripted. The future seemed bleak as far as government action was concerned. However, by this stage of the conflict, most of the partisans operated beyond the limits of regular service or government supervision anyway. Their impact, upon restoration of Union authority or even the peace and tranquillity in the wake of the major Confederate retreat to north Georgia rendered them marginal in Richmond's view. However, guerrilla or partisan warfare as well as renewed regular cavalry raids still offered striking possibilities if Confederate authorities could provide effective coordination.[54]

So conditions quieted for the winter in the Upper South at the end of 1863. Will Dorris wrote his wife from Fort Donelson in early December that "the river is in good order now; boats are continually plying between here and Cairo and up to and from Nashville." The fort served as headquarters for the gunboats patrolling the Cumberland day and night. The guerrillas "are fast playing out here," Mitchel A. Thompson added four days before Christmas, and the weather too cold for them to "lay out." One of the partisans had been caught in his nightclothes, "but was compelled from cold to come back and give himself up." The garrison anticipated a good holiday dinner with "two turkies fattening for the occasion" and "seven-pound cakes to be made" by the commissariat at the post. One of the soldier's wives, Mrs. Artemus Pence, had charge of the kitchen department at Fort Donelson, drawing donations from each soldier of seven dollars per month to provide them with pies, fruit cobblers, jams, and jellies as "toothsome delights to the home-hungry men."[55]

Nonetheless, the heartland remained untamed in many places. Young Sam Davis of Smyrna, Tennessee, and a member of Coleman's Scouts was captured in November, determined to be a spy by Federal authorities, and upon the gallows uttered the words that immortalized his memory to future generations of southerners: "I'd rather die a thousand deaths than betray a friend." Countless others at the time harbored similar feelings as they braved the invaders' rule. As long as such defiance remained—coupled with the threat of cavalry raids and partisan activity—then governors Johnson in Tennessee and Bramlette in Kentucky could not hope to reconstitute normal conditions in their respective states. What Federal armies and gunboats had accomplished by the end of 1863 may have satisfied the military. But for civilians like Browder, Cox, the Cheathams, and others living in the wake of the armies, a new period of conflict beckoned.[56]

Three days before Christmas, Browder jotted once more in his private journal. He noted carefully how a unionist neighbor had survived a robber band and had promptly submitted a bill for five-thousand-dollars' reimbursement under a military order of June 9, 1862, signed by Brigadier General Jeremiah Boyle. The order held that secessionist neighbors should pay such damages. This assessment was two or three times the value of the unionist's property, thought Browder, "but if it were only a part of the value it is unjust and oppressive to require people to pay it who knew nothing of the raid and had no connection with it." Here then were the innocents, caught up in a different kind of civil war from the glorious gore of Shiloh, Vicksburg, or Chickamauga. Yet, the war was real enough to them too, as conflict continued to sweep across Tennessee and Kentucky at the close of 1863. The Union possibly controlled the battlefield; the Confederacy still beckoned to the hearts and minds of many of the people.[57]

November 1863

CODA—THE VARIED LEGACY

United States Army muster rolls enumerated 600,000 men "aggregate and present" at the close of 1863. That same total had been 490,972 on February 15, 1862, when a little-known Illinois brigadier took a mere 15,000 soldiers and a handful of gunboats up two inland rivers and changed the course of the war in the West. Now, almost two years later, Major General Ulysses S. Grant's Military Division of the Mississippi arrayed some 200,000 boys in blue. Even the naval forces on the rivers had grown to a flotilla of 81 craft. Considering losses to battle and disease, the statistics were impressive.[58]

The strategic picture was likewise impressive for Union fortunes at the end of the year. Secretary of War Edwin M. Stanton informed the president that rebel territory had been cut in two, and the trans-Mississippi was no longer able to furnish ample supplies to the rest of the Confederacy. The river's reopening meant that "the national commerce is rapidly and securely returning to that great highway of the continent." This process, begun by Grant on the Tennessee and Cumberland Rivers in early 1862 had been completed. So, too, was the process of eliminating enemy armies from the upper heartland of Tennessee and Kentucky. The continuing success in 1863, said Stanton, "not only shed luster upon our arms," but also meant that "by affording protection to a loyal population they cannot fail to greatly weaken the rebel strength and operate strongly in restoring the authority of the Federal government."[59]

General-in-Chief Henry Halleck further explained the military technicalities in his own annual report. He noted that heretofore the Confederacy had enjoyed great advantages since its generals had operated on short and safe interior lines, "while circumstances have compelled us to occupy the circumference of a circle." The reopening of the Mississippi meant that "we can strike the isolated fragments by operating on safer and more advantageous lines." Halleck also observed how such basic military issues as sustaining armies in enemy territory affected civil-military relations. Confederate armies lived mainly upon the country through which they passed, he asserted. They took food and forage from friend and foe alike, thus enabling them to move "with ease and great rapidity." Federal commanders, by contrast, had generally found no such supplies, and in the border states, "it is difficult to distinguish between real friends and enemies." To live upon the country often produced great distress among the inhabitants, he added, but was "one of the unavoidable results of war and is justified by the usages of civilized nations."[60]

Some military commanders, Halleck declared, had taken advantage of the "right of military appropriation," but others had relied too much upon large supply trains and "have not depended as much as they might have done upon the resources of the country in which they operated." He obviously alluded to Buell and Rosecrans as contrasted with Grant and Sherman. The War Department had authorized reimbursement of local suppliers who proved their loyalty. Still, some Union officers had hesitated, "receipting and accounting for everything taken," mainly because of "mistaken notions of humanity." What was spared by Union troops only ended up in rebel hands, he suggested, to be used then against the national troops. Those same rebel troops manifested "little regard for the suffering of their own people," in Halleck's view, so that women and children had been fed by government troops to save them from actual starvation. At the same time, "their fathers, husbands, and brothers are fighting in the ranks of the rebel armies or robbing and murdering in the ranks of guerrillas."

Soldiers, civilians, logistics, guerrillas—such were the terms relevant to this arch-professional soldier's interpretation of the war in the West; it was, therefore, the view from headquarters in Washington. Accordingly, with the benefit of hindsight, historian James Parton's 1934 assessment that, excepting Confederate general John Bell Hood's raid the following autumn, "Tennessee was permanently freed from the presence of Confederate troops and the process of reconstruction could now be carried on without interruption by the end of 1863" seems incongruous. Nonetheless, national authorities chose to interpret the legacy of success by Grant, Sherman, Thomas, and Burnside as reason enough to try once more to replace carnage with comity. Lincoln issued his proclamation of amnesty and reconstruction on December 8, 1863. Therein, he stated that Confederates generally could be pardoned upon taking the oath of allegiance. When loyal voters in any rebellious state numbered 10 percent of the 1860 voting population and had returned a state government to office that was acceptable to Washington, then that state government could be recognized as legal and entitled to all the guarantees and protection of the Federal Constitution. Again, the perspective came from Washington.[61]

It all seemed quite simple. Little wonder that veterans in the field felt optimism. Chaplain Alonzo H. Quint of the Second Massachusetts wondered from his Elk River, Tennessee, encampment: "Who can help rejoicing at the President's proclamation?" It held out the olive branch "but on terms that preserve our principles," he advanced. It made no treaty with rebels, but "demands unconditional submission," retaining justice, "but tempers it with mercy." It restored forfeited privileges, "but secures the public safety." It assumed that the rebel state regimes were extinct, "but it provides for new ones." Above all, he concluded the day before Christmas, "it demands submission on the very point of issue—slavery."[62]

Few southern heartlanders would have agreed with all of Quint's logic. Yet, most of them had no choice but to accept the underlying theme of submission. The Union had militarily conquered Kentucky and Tennessee by the third winter of war. Admittedly, possession did not necessarily mean political control, much less restoration of peace or social and commercial intercourse. Large cities like Louisville, Lexington, Paducah, Memphis, Nashville, Knoxville, and Chattanooga all lay within the sphere of military supervision. National armies and navies controlled river, rail, and roadways. Nevertheless, rough-hewn men in butternut and gray, shadowy figures and specters of lawlessness, prowled the countryside, often "governing" or at least "ruling" in the absence of duly constituted authority. Economic activity, such as it was, was related largely to the war, with the flow of goods and services dictated by military necessity, not civilian demand.

Kentucky and Tennessee civilians wanted to return to their accustomed life cycle of planting and harvest, birthing and dying as if no conflict raged around them. But physical desolation as well as the breakdown in legal, governmental, religious, educational—even family—institutions and values took over from the military machines that had traversed the region. Historian Stephen Ash's portrayal of "an earthly abyss" where social fabric became "a nightmarish bedlam" with "blind atrocities" routine and unrequited, may seem slightly overdrawn to apply to the end of 1863. Yet, such was a portent of the future. The main armies North and South had gone. But there could be little doubt that the region now passed into a sort of twilight zone in the wake of the mighty battles. Perhaps Ash's pattern of garrisoned town and no-man's-land still obtained, even if the Confederate frontier had faded from the upper heartland.[63]

One hundred miles south of Washington, Confederate president Jefferson Davis also complained bitterly to his congress in Richmond about the war's new turn. Communicating to that political body on December 7, Davis addressed the Yankees' "savage ferocity" that had devastated farms, burned houses, and plundered everything movable in a beneficent slave society. His counterpoise, however, was only grim continuation of the struggle. In point of fact, Confederate authorities had not been able to find a way to surmount Fort Donelson's most immediate legacy. Federal land and naval power controlled the upper heartland. The army and navy had shown that it was possible to work effectively together, no matter how deficient the command structure might be for joint warfare. That legacy had been forged in Grant's twin victories on the Tennessee and Cumberland at Forts Henry and Donelson, and it continued to revolve largely around the attitudes of senior army and navy officers themselves.[64]

Ironically, despite such instant success in February 1862, it had taken Federal authorities those two years to suppress rebellion in the region. Or had they really suppressed rebellion after all? Rather, they had driven Confederate armies from the chessboard of the Upper South. Having dissipated the immediate prospects for decisive military victory in the six months immediately after Henry-Donelson, repeated diversion from mission had permitted a resurgence of Confederate power. Union military and political authorities had become preoccupied with occupation of territory and reconstruction of a political system based on false perception of incipient unionism. Lack of unity of command and the overreach of logistics had thwarted the national cause perhaps enough to permit renewed consolidation of Confederate military fortunes—at least for the moment.

Conciliation had died hard as official policy, and yet a bitter second legacy sprang forth accordingly—one of civil dissidence and partisan warfare. As Union armies drove back their Confederate counterparts, they encountered a rebellious populace, unready in most cases to acquiesce to their invaders' rule. In turn this populace, particularly in the rural areas, spawned what historian Stephen Ash has so quaintly coined "sharks in an angry sea." A fellow student of this hidden side of the Civil War in the upper heartland, James B. Martin, has classified these sharks into more precise groups, including partisan rangers, war-rebels, and outlaws. New

Federal policies—including suppression of civil liberties, the oath-of-allegiance requirement, confiscation of property, and ultimately emancipation of slaves—blended military necessity with political opportunism behind the fighting front.[65]

In fact, intimidation, expulsion, or bloody annihilation became the Federal tools for dealing with this kind of war. Shadow war and simmering anti-administration feelings began to vie with "hard war" policy and stringent military occupation as part of wartime reconstruction in Tennessee and Kentucky. In fact, while Confederate military reaction produced more battles and skirmishes, southern civilians and partisans honed the skill of guerrilla and insurgent against reconstruction authorities. Removed from Richmond's direct oversight by the end of 1863, the shadow war would continue to play out its role in the southern tragedy. Just what that role might be in the new year remained to be seen. At the very least, it would be a different sort of combat from the conventional battles like Forts Henry and Donelson that had initiated the heartland war during that fateful fortnight in February 1862.

In a March 31, 1863 informal letter to Grant, Henry Halleck had effectively summarized a new war policy. It hit upon both the changed character of the war and the position of the government with respect to slaves. Halleck's key points included:

Government policy was to withdraw from the Confederates as much productive labor as possible. As long as the rebels retained and employed their slaves in producing grains and other commodities, they could deploy all whites in the field against Union forces. "Every slave withdrawn from the enemy is equivalent to a white man put hors de combat," Halleck declared.

It was also government policy to use "the negroes of the South, as far as practical, as a military force, for the defense of forts, depots, etc." They certainly could be used advantageously as laborers, teamsters, cooks, and many observers who had examined the issue "without passion or prejudice," held that they could also be used as a military force. It was certainly good policy to use them to the best advantage, Halleck told Grant, and "like almost anything else, they may be made instruments of good or evil." In the hands of the Confederacy, "they are used with much effect against us; in our hands, we must try to use them with the best possible effect against the rebels."

Halleck chided Grant that many officers of his command not only seemed to discourage blacks from coming under U.S. Army protection, but also forced them, by ill-treatment, to return to their masters. "This is not only bad policy in itself, but is directly opposed to the policy adopted by the Government," which was to be obeyed cheerfully and honestly. The measures of the government were not open to debate by the military but to be given a fair trial and carried out by everyone. Halleck thus expected Grant to "use your official and personal influence to remove prejudices on this subject" and to fully and thoroughly carry out the policy now adopted and ordered by the government. In short, that policy was to "withdraw from the use of the enemy all the slaves you can, and to employ those so withdrawn to the best possible advantage against the enemy."

Most important, Halleck also informed Grant about the obvious—"the character of the war has very much changed within the last year." There was now no possible hope of reconciliation with the rebels. "The Union party in the South is virtually destroyed," and "there can be no peace but that which is forced by the sword." We must conquer the rebels or be conquered by them, proclaimed Old Brains. The North must conquer the slave oligarchy or become slaves themselves—the manufacturers mere "hewers of wood and drawers of water" to southern aristocrats, in Halleck's view. So adopted by the government, Halleck told Grant that "we must cheerfully and faithfully carry out that policy."[66]

With that, the initial period of conciliation—of Buell and McClellan, even Halleck himself, as swordbearers of the old Union—had passed into history. The future belonged to Grant, Sherman, and other collective-punishment men, and Halleck sensed that fact of life. They would pursue not merely the defeat of enemy armies or occupation of territory. Rather, they saw the path to peace—to a new Union—lying with subjugation of the people, destroying not merely armies but the will and substance of the people. This very policy now mirrored the desires of officials in Washington as well as the men in the ranks in the field. "Slavery is dead; that is the first thing," Major George L. Stearns, a well-know abolitionist sent to manage black male laborers in Tennessee by the War Department, told the American Freedmen's Inquiry Commission at Nashville on November 23, 1863. Local slaveholders of all types—"the common farmer, the most aristocratic man and the most aristocratic lady—come into this room to talk with me about their slaves, and the most polite people I ever saw," he added.[67] Ironically, Fort Donelson's ultimate legacy, by the end of 1863, was the doctrine of "unconditional surrender"—vaulted from tactical demand to national policy.

NOTES

PREFACE

1. Carl von Clausewitz, *On War*, ed. Michael Howard and Peter Paret (Princeton, 1974), 479–82.
2. Archer Jones, *The Art of War in the Western World* (Urbana, 1987), 416–17; United States Navy Department, *Official Records of the Union and Confederate Navies in the War of the Rebellion* (Washington: Government Printing Office, 1894–1927), series 1, volume 25: 474 (hereafter referred to as *ORN*, series number, volume number, page number).
3. Robert Tracy McKenzie, *One South or Many?* (New York, 1995), 86–87.
4. See Stephen V. Ash, *When the Yankees Came* (Chapel Hill, 1995); Mark Grimsley, *The Hard Hand of War* (New York, 1995); Charles Royster, *The Destructive War* (New York, 1991); also Lance Janda, "Shutting the Gates of Mercy," *Journal of Military History* (Jan. 1995): 7–26; and Everard H. Smith, "Charmbersburg: Anatomy of a Confederate Reprisal," *American Historical Review* (Apr. 1991): 432–55.
5. Moses Wright to S. M. Duncan, May 1, 1869, clipping, Stanford, Kentucky, *Semi-Weekly Journal*, Sept. 12, 1884, Scrapbook, Filson Club, Louisville (hereafter referred to as FCL); Joseph B. Killebrew autobiography, Southern Historical Collection, Univ. of North Carolina (hereafter referred to as SHC/UNC).
6. Edward Dicey, *Spectator of America*, ed. Herbert Mitgang (Athens, Ga., 1989), 174–93.
7. John F. Marzalek, Review of Lee Kennett, *Marching Through Georgia* in *Journal of American History* (Dec. 1995): 1221.

ONE. AFTERMATH OF DISASTER

1. Flavel C. Barber, *Holding the Line*, ed. Robert H. Ferrell (Kent, Ohio, 1994), 32.
2. "The Civil War Diary of Andrew Jackson Campbell," ed. Jill McKnight Garrett, 19, Tennessee State Library and Archives (hereafter referred to as TSLA); J. A. Hinkle reminiscence, 16–7, SHA/UNC.
3. Hugh G. Gwyn to Alice Ready, n.d., in Ready diary, mss. 31/typescript 22, SHC/UNC; W. N. Brown to Jefferson Davis, Aug. 23, 1880, Louisiana Historical Association, Tulane Univ. Library (hereafter referred to as TUL); Nathaniel Cheairs, "Personal Experiences," TSLA.
4. J. A. Haydon reminiscences, Apr. 24, 1862, author's files; Ira Blanchard, *I Marched with Sherman* (San Francisco, 1992), 43.
5. Alice Ready diary, Feb. 11, 1862, mss. 22-23/typescript 15-6, TSLA; George W. Johnson to wife, Feb. 15, 1862, Johnson Papers, FCL.
6. John M. Porter, "War Record," WKL; Sumner A. Cunningham, "Reminiscences of the Forty-First Tennessee Infantry," 6, 13, TSLA.

7. Cunningham, "Reminiscences," 10; Editors of Time-Life Books, *Echoes of Glory: Arms and Equipment of the Confederacy* (Alexandria, 1991), 258; *Virginia Country's Civil War* 3 (1985), 18, 19; Jared C. Frazier diary typescript, 39–41, Confederate Collection, TSLA; Blanchard, *I Marched with Sherman*, 50; Albert D. Richardson, *The Secret Service* (Hartford, 1865), 219.
8. Howard Criswell Jr., "A Conversation with the Past," *Civil War Times Illustrated* (Mar.–Apr. 1990): 57–59.
9. Charles Brown Tompkins to wife, Feb. [?], 1862, Duke Univ. Library (hereafter referred to as DUL); James Drish to wife, Feb. 21, 1863, James F. Drish collection, Illinois State Historical Library (hereafter referred to as ISH); Frank B. Smith to friend, Mar. 17, 1862, in John K. Ross Jr., "Five Civil War Letters," *Journal of Jackson Purchase Historical Society* (June 1990): 29–30; Memphis *Avalanche*, Mar. 31, 1862; Blanchard, *I Marched with Sherman*, 49.
10. Jared Carl Fazier diary, 39–41, TSLA; P. Bishop to father, Mar. 1, 1862, copy, author's files; Drish to wife, Feb. 21, Mar. 3, both 1862, ISH; Patricia M. LaPointe, "Military Hospitals in Memphis, 1861–1865," *Tennessee Historical Quarterly* (Winter 1983–1984): 328, citing Memphis *Daily Appeal*, Feb. 20, 22, and 27, 1862.
11. John Y. Simon, ed., *The Papers of Ulysses S. Grant* (Carbondale and Edwardsville, 1967–91), 4: 245, 264, 276; Richardson, *The Secret Service*, 220.
12. On prisoner experiences, see Benjamin Franklin Cooling, *Forts Henry and Donelson* (Knoxville, 1987), 255–63; George Moorman to William Bayliss, Feb. 24, 1862, W. Rodgers to B. D. Johnson, I. G. Demerest (all M.D.'s) to Henry Halleck, Apr. 2, George W. Gordon to James Adkin, Feb. 23, June 30, Gordon to My Dear Children, Mar. 17, Gordon to My Dear Daughter, Apr. 12, Apr. 30, May 14, May 29, July 5, 9, 11, 17, Aug. 5, 13, 25, Gordon to H. B. Titcomb, July 14, all 1862, all Gordon and Avery collection; T. J. Paine to sister, July 15, 1862, Paine Family Papers; Alfred Harris Abernathy to brother, June 23, 1862; David Clark to uncle, Apr. 25, Clark to aunt, June 30, both 1862, Clark collection, all TSLA; Porter, "War Record," 9–17, WKL; various letters, Frank P. Tryon Papers, FCL.
13. John Henry Guy prison journal, among others, Virginia Historical Society (hereafter referred to as VHS); for parole requests see Leroy P. Graf and Ralph W. Haskins, eds., *Papers of Andrew Johnson* (Knoxville, 1967–), 5: 190, 201, 212–13, 255.
14. Perkins's escapade recounted in Newton Cannon questionnaire in Gustavus W. Dyer and John Trotwood Moore, comps., *The Tennessee Civil War Veterans Questionnaires* (Easley, S.C., 1985), 2: 441–42; Charles M. Cummings, *Yankee Quaker, Confederate General* (Rutherford, N.J., 1971), 207–13; James Kemp Pope to mother, Feb. 24, 1862, Pope-Carter Papers, DUL.
15. Porter, "War Record," 16–23, WKL.
16. For immediate post-battle criticism, see Johnson to wife, Feb. 15, 1862, Johnson Papers, FCL, as well as coverage in Cooling, *Forts Henry and Donelson*, 241–42, 264–67, and Nathaniel C. Hughes and Roy P. Stonesifer, *The Life and Wars of Gideon J. Pillow* (Chapel Hill, 1993), 237–48; Nashville *Daily American*, Mar. 10, 1890.
17. Roger Farquharson to Andrew Buchanan, July 18, 1862, Buchanan-McClellan collection, SHC/UNC.
18. Gideon J. Pillow to William S. Hardee, Feb. 20, Hardee to Pillow, Feb. 23, Pillow to Editor, Memphis *Avalanche*, Feb. 27, Gustavus A. Henry to Pillow, May 6, all 1862, all Pillow Papers, Record Group 109, National Archives and Records Administration (hereafter referred to as NARA); H. C. Burnett to John B. Floyd, Mar. 1, 10, 16, all 1862, Floyd Papers, DUL; Confederate States of American, House of Representatives, *Report of Special Committee* (Richmond, 1862), 1–2; Cunningham, *Nashville Daily American*, March 10, 1890.
19. J. T. Williamson, "Civil War Memoirs," 7, Garrett collection, TSLA.
20. Gwyn to Ready, n.d., in Ready diary, mss. 31/typescript 22, SHC/UNC; Thomas Black Wilson, Reminiscences, SHC/UNC; James Kemp Pope to mother, Feb. 24, 1862, Pope-Carter Family Papers, DUL.
21. Farquharson to Buchanan, July 18, 1862, SHC/UNC.
22. United States War Department, *The War of the Rebellion: A Compilation of the Official Records of the Union and Confederate Armies* (Washington: Government Printing Office, 1880–1901), series 1, volume 10, part 2: 314 (hereafter referred to as *ORA*, series number, volume number, part number, page number).
23. Gustavus A. Henry to Jefferson Davis, Mar. 8, 1862, Confederate collection, TSLA; Magnolia Plantation Journals, Mar. 19, 1862, Henry Clay Warmoth Papers, SHC/UNC; William K. Scarborough, ed., *The Diary of Edmund Ruffin* (Baton Rouge, 1976), 2: 248–49, 277.
24. For Johnston's correspondence, see *ORA*, ser. 1, vol. 7: 130–31, 418–19, 426–27; as well as Headquarters, Western Department CSA, Letterbook, Outgoing Correspondence, Oct. 24, 1861–Mar. 19, 1862, Kuntz Collection, TUL.

25. William M. McKinney to Cousin Abby, Feb. 22, 1862, DUL.
26. Recent analysis may be followed in Steven E. Woodworth, *Jefferson Davis and His Generals* (Lawrence, 1990), especially chaps. 2–6; Archer Jones, *Civil War Command and Strategy* (New York, 1992), 44–49; Thomas Lawrence Connelly, *Army of the Heartland* (Baton Rouge, 1967), chaps. 6, 7.
27. Lucius B. Northrup to Jefferson Davis, Dec. 20, 1879, Louisiana Historical Association Collection, TUL; Charles W. Ramsdell, ed., *Laws and Joint resolutions of the Last Session of the Confederate Congress* (Durham, 1941), 161.
28. J. T. Williamson memoirs, 5, Garrett collection, TSLA; A. P. Merrill, "Health of Our Army," Memphis *Avalanche*, Jan. 30, 1862; David W. Yandell to Lundsford Yandell, Dec. 22, 1861, Yandell Papers, FCL; Nancy Disher Baird, *David Wendell Yandell; Physician of Old Louisville*, "There is No Sunday in the Army"; James O. Breeden, *Joseph Jones, M.D.: Scientist of the Old South* (Lexington, 1975), 125; Harris D. Riley Jr. and Amos Christie, "Deaths and Disabilities in the Provisional Army of Tennessee," *Tennessee Historical Quarterly* (Summer 1984): 132–54.
29. On the impact of illness, ibid.; see also G. W. Gordon to Sons, Sept. 9, 1861, Gordon-Avery Collection; and Williamson, memoirs, 4, 5, both TSLA; Sam House to Brother, Feb. 3, 1862, in Ross, "Five Civil War Letters," *Journal of the Jackson Purchase Historical Society* (June 1990): 28; William C. Davis, ed., *Diary of a Confederate Soldier* (Columbia, S.C., 1990), 23–24.
30. On Polk's dubious performance, see Joseph H. Parks, *General Leonidus Polk, C.S.A.* (Baton Rouge, 1962), chaps. 10, 11.
31. "Willie" to sister, Jan. 25, 1862, FCL; J. E. Bailey to wife, Feb. 6, 1862, Bailey–Lucy Papers, TSLA; Headquarters Western Department, Letterbook, Outgoing Correspondence, Oct. 24, 1861–Mar. 19, 1862, 332, TUL.
32. Headquarters Western Department, Letterbook, 341, see also 305–40.
33. Larry J. Daniel, "'The Assaults of the Demagogues in Congress': General Albert Sidney Johnston and the Politics of Command," *Civil War History* (Dec. 1991): 328–35; see also Charles P. Roland, *Albert Sidney Johnston* (Austin, 1964), chaps. 15, 16.
34. Headquarters Western Department, Letterbook, 342–43, 345, TUL.
35. Ibid., 345–49.
36. Ibid., 356, see also 348–49; Northrup to Davis, Dec. 20, 1879, TUL.
37. Eagleton's daybook entries Feb. 16, 17, 1862, quoted in Alden B. Pearson Jr., "A Middle Class, Border-State Family During the Civil War," *Civil War History* (Dec. 1976): 322.
38. Wilson Reminiscences, 16, SHC/UNC; Headquarters Western Department, Letterbook, 333–62, especially 359–62; Pearson, "A Middle Class."
39. John Beatty, "A Regiment in Search of a Battle," in *Sketches of War History*, ed. Robert O. Hunter (Cincinnati, 1890), 3: 428.
40. P. J. Snyder to sister, Feb. 24, 1862, copy author's files; James F. Drish to wife, Mar. 3, 1862, ISH; Charles Brown Tompkins to wife, Mar. 2, 1862, DUL.
41. Frederick A. Starring to William Bailhache, Mar. 12, 1862, CHS; Drish to wife, Mar. 3, 1862, ISH; P. J. Snyder to sister, Feb. 24, 1862, author's collection; Beatty, "A Regiment in Search of a Battle," 428.
42. On the conservative nature of Union war aims at this point, see Joseph L. Harsh, "Lincoln's Tarnished Brass," in *The Confederate High Command*, ed. Roman J. Heleniak and Lawrence L. Hewitt (Shippensburg, Pa., 1990), 125.
43. Ursula Smith Beach, *Along the Warioto* (Clarksville, 1964), 201–4; *ORA*, ser. 1, vol. 7: 644–45, see also 423.
44. Haskins quoted in Charles M. Waters, ed., *Historic Clarksville*, (Clarksville, 1983), 66; Blanche L. Lewis to Dr. G. W. Jones, Mar. 3, 1894, TSLA.
45. James M. Hoppin, *Life of Andrew Hull Foote* (New York, 1874), 235; Cave Johnson to Andrew Hull Foote, Feb. 20, 1862, copy, author's collection.
46. *ORA*, ser. 1, vol. 7: 423–24, 638; Simon, *Papers of Ulysses S. Grant*, 4: 252–53.
47. Simon, *Papers of Ulysses S. Grant*, 4: 294–97, 300–305, 414, see also 80–81n.; D. L. Phillips to Henry Halleck, Feb. 17, 1862, Department of the Missouri, Letters Received 1861–1867, Box 2, Jan–Mar., A–Q, 1862, NARA.
48. On national policy, see John Cimprich, *Slavery's End in Tennessee* (University, Ala., 1985), chaps. 2, 3; Christopher Mark Grimsley, "'A Directed Severity': The Evolution of Federal Policy Toward Southern Civilians and Property," (Ph.D. diss., Ohio State Univ., 1992), 138–42, published as *The Hard Hand of War* (New York, 1995, especially chaps. 1–3.

49. Simon, *Papers of Ulysses S. Grant*, 4: 267–70, 285, 290–91; Cimprich, *Slavery's End*, 34–35; Grimsley, *Hard Hand of War*, 48–52, 61–63. See also Ira Berlin, et al., *The Destruction of Slavery* (Cambridge, 1982), 194–97, 250–52, 270–74, 519–24; and *Wartime Genesis of Free Labor* (Cambridge, 1993), 368–69.
50. Simon, *Papers of Ulysses S. Grant*, 4: 454–55 n.
51. Section 4 of the Aug. 6, 1861, measure, quoted in Channing Richards, "Dealing with Slavery," in *Sketches of War History*, ed. W. H. Chamberlin (Cincinnati, 1896), 4: 317.
52. Ibid., 315–24.
53. Henry McRaven, *Nashville: The Athens of the South* (Chapel Hill, 1949), 93; Alfred Leland Crabb, "The Twilight of the Nashville Gods," *Tennessee Historical Quarterly* (Dec. 1956): especially 293–94; see also Samuel Hollingsworth, "Some Facts," pts. 12, 24 (Oct. 1902), 566, as recounted in Glenna R. Schroeder-Lein, *Confederate Hospitals on the Move* (Columbia, S.C., 1994), 53.
54. James A. Hoobler, *Cities Under the Gun* (Nashville, 1986), 17–19; F. Garvin Davenport, *Cultural Life in Nashville on the Eve of the Civil War* (Chapel Hill, 1941), especially chaps. 1, 9; Stanley F. Horn, "Nashville During the Civil War," *Tennessee Historical Quarterly* (Mar. 1945): 1–22; and Crabb, "The Twilight of the Nashville Gods," 291–97.
55. John Miller McKee, *The Great Panic* (Nashville, 1862), 29–30; Walter T. Durham, *Nashville, the Occupied City* (Nashville, 1985), chap. 1–3; Rowena Webster, "Memoirs," n.d., Garrett collection, TSLA; Henry R. Slack to wife, Feb. 12, 1862, Slack Papers, SHC/UNC; James A. Hoobler, "The Civil War Diary of Louisa Brown Pearl," *Tennessee Historical Quarterly* (Fall 1979): 308–21; Davis, *Diary of a Confederate Soldier*, 24; Memphis *Daily Appeal*, Feb. 20, 22, 27, 1862; I. G. Harris to P. G. T. Beauregard, Apr. 13, 1880, TUL; H. J. H. Rugeley, ed., *Batchelor-Turner Letters* (Austin, 1961), 21.
56. A. F. Gilbert, recollections, n.d., Garrett collection; Anna Howell diary, 66–69; Wilson Reminiscences, 16–17, A. E. Pope to mother, Feb. 24, 1862, all TSLA; Davis, *Diary of a Confederate Soldier*, 24–25; Stout, "Some Facts," pts. 12, 24, 566–68 in Schroeder-Lein, *Confederate Hospitals*, 53–54.
57. George Washington Matthews journal, Feb. 16–23, 1862, TSLA.
58. Durham, *Occupied City*, especially chap. 2; see also John Fitch, *Annals of the Army of the Cumberland* (Philadelphia, 1864), 630–32.
59. John McGlone, "'What Became of General Barrow?' The Forgotten Story of George Washington Barrow," *Tennessee Historical Quarterly* (Spring 1989): 41.
60. Horace N. Fisher, "Reminiscences of the Raising of the Original 'Old Glory' Over the Capitol at Nashville, Tennessee, on February 27, 1862," *Essex Institute Historical Collections*, 1911, 98–100; Beatty, "A Regiment in Search of a Battle," 440–41.
61. Fisher, "Reminiscences"; Graf and Haskins, *Papers of Andrew Johnson*, 6: 223 n.; Edward S. Park, "Around the Mall and Beyond," *Smithsonian* (July 1993): 12–13, recounts the "Old Glory" story, noting the flag's present location on the third floor of the Smithsonian's Museum of American History.
62. *ORA*, ser. 1, vol. 7: 679, also 671; Simon, *Papers of Ulysses S. Grant*, 4: 276, 284, 286, 288.
63. Convenient coverage of Johnson's appointment appears in Durham, *Occupied City*, 56–61; and Lloyd Paul Stryker, *Andrew Johnson* (New York, 1930), chap. 2; Daniel W. Crofts, *Reluctant Confederates* (Chapel Hill, 1989), 21–22.
64. *ORA*, ser. 1, vol. 10, pt. 2: 47, 56–58, 76, 111, 126, 129, 132; Cincinnati *Commercial*, Mar. 19, 1862.
65. Wilson Reminiscences, 26, TSLA; Mark M. Krug, ed., *Mrs. Hill's Journal* (Chicago, 1980), 69.
66. Statement of Stanton P. McGuire, Feb. 16, 1865, FCL.
67. Entry of Feb. 19, 1862, in *The Civil War Diary of Martha Abernathy*, ed. Elizabeth Paisely Dargan (Beltsville, Md., 1994), 34.

TWO. ASSERTING NATIONAL AUTHORITY

1. Hardy to Martha Ann, Feb. 22, 1862, Book 838-1-433, 242, Douglas-Maney Family Papers, TSLA; Headquarters Western Department, Letterbook, 343–61, TUL; George Eagleton, "Day Book, February 16, 17, 1862," quoted in Alden B. Pearson Jr., "A Middle-Class, Border-State Family During the Civil War," *Civil War History* (Dec. 1976): 322.
2. Schroeder-Lein, "Confederate Army of Tennessee Hospitals in Chattanooga," *Journal of East Tennessee History* (1994): 32–33, 55–57.

3. *ORA*, ser. 4, vol. l: 1008–9; Larry J. Daniel and Lynn N. Bock, *Island No. 10* (Tuscaloosa, 1996): 1–94.
4. Hunter B. Whitesell, "Military Operations in the Jackson Purchase Area of Kentucky, 1862–1865," *Kentucky Historical Society Register* (Apr. 1965): 142–45; Philip Josyph, ed., *The Wounded River* (East Lansing, 1993), 95, 116–26.
5. Arthur J. Carpenter to parents, Mar. 8, 21, Apr. 9, all 1862, quoted in Thomas B. Bright, "Yankees in Arms: The Civil War as a Personal Experience," *Civil War History* (Sept. 1973): 200; H. R. Reckley to brother, Mar. [?], 1862, author's files; for Union command problems, see Williams, *Lincoln Finds a General*, chaps. 11, 12; Herman Hattaway and Archer Jones, *How the North Won* (Urbana, 1983), 146–50.
6. *ORA*, ser. 4, vol. l: , 1018–19, 1001–2, also 1101–2.
7. Matthew Forney Steele, *American Campaigns* (Washington, 1943), 1: 169–71; Thomas B. Van Horne, *History of the Army of the Cumberland* (Cincinnati, 1875), 1: 98–99.
8. Beatty, "A Regiment in Search of a Battle," 443–50; Van Horne, *History of the Army of the Cumberland*, 102–4; on north Alabama, see Mrs. W. D. Chadick, "Diary," Huntsville *Times*, 1934, 3–5, in *The Alabama Confederate Reader*, ed. Malcom C. McMillan (Tuscaloosa, 1963), 154–58; Grimsley, *Hard Hand of War*, 67; on slavery, see Ira Berlin, et al., *Destruction of Slavery* (Cambridge, 1982), 275–76.
9. Stanley J. Folmsbee, Robert E. Corlew, and Enoch L. Mitchell, *Tennessee: a Short History*, (Knoxville, 1969), 256–66; for greater detail see Robert M. Black III, *The Railroads of the Confederacy* (Chapel Hill, 1952), chaps. 1–4; Addie Lou Brooks, "The Building of the Trunk Line Railroads in West Tennessee," in Tennessee Historical Commission, *Tennessee Old and New* (Nashville, 1946), 2: 188, 211; see also L. B. Parsons, "Description of Southern Railroads, Their Condition, Length, Terminus, etc.," accompanying F. M. Colburn–L.B. Parsons, Feb. 15, Letters Received, 1861–1867, Box 2, 1862, Jan–Mar., A–Q, Entry 2593, Record Group 393, Department of the Missouri, (NARA).
10. Bird Douglas, *Steamboatin' on the Cumberland* (Nashville, 1961), chaps. 3, 4; W. P. Greene, ed. and comp., *The Green River Country* (Evansville, 1898), chaps. 1, 2; Louis C. Hunter, *Steamboats on the Western Rivers* (Cambridge, 1949), especially chap. 14.
11. Wooley quoted in William P. Johnston, *Life of General Albert Sidney Johnston* (New York, 1878), 485.
12. For discussions of the resources of the upper heartland, see Connelly, *Army of the Heartland*, intro.; "A.L.C." "Fort Donelson," *The Military Historian and Economist* 1 (Jan. 1916): 55–62; J. W. Killebrew, *Introduction to the Resources of Tennessee* (Nashville, 1874), 1: chaps. 1, 22; Folmsbee, *A Short History*, chap. 17; U.S. Bureau of the Census, *Agriculture of the United States in 1860* (Washington, 1861), 136; U.S. Bureau of the Census, *Manufactures of the United States in 1860* (Washington, 1861), 263–65; and most recently, McKenzie, *One South or Many*, intro. and chap. 1.
13. J. P. Lesley, *The Iron Manufacturer's Guide to the Furnaces, Forges, and Rolling Mills of the United States* (London, 1859), 749, 753, 760, see also 601–10; J. B. Killebrew, *Middle Tennessee as an Iron Center* (Nashville, 1879), 235–42; W. L. Cook, "Furnaces and Forges," *Tennessee Historical Quarterly* 9 (Oct. 1925): 190–92; Corlew, *A Short History*, 87–89.
14. See Redick C. Carnell memoirs, 193, Box 8; Jill Knight Garrett, "A History of Humphreys County, Tennessee," typescript, 1963, Box 18, all in Garrett collection; John E. Duling, "Reminiscences," Dec. 1937; Jesse Cox diary, 480–527, and others; Joseph Buckner Killebrew, 1: 158–65, all TSLA; see also Iris Hopkins McClain, *A History of Houston County* (Columbia, Tenn., 1966), 35–36.
15. Crofts, *Reluctant Confederates*, 46, 134, 144, 149, 152, 156–58, 172, 183–87, 192–93; Robert W. Corlew, *A History of Dickson County* (Nashville, 1951), 84–87, 101; Hughie G. Lawson, "Geographical Origins of White Migrants," author's files.
16. Crofts, *Reluctant Confederates*, chaps. 12, 13; Corlew, *History of Dickson County*, 102; Clarkesville *Leaf-Chronicle*, Aug. 31, 1933; Berlin, et al., *Wartime Genesis of Free Labor*, 368.
17. Duling, "Reminiscences," 11; Killebrew diary, 163–64, both TSLA; Charles L. Lufkin, "Divided Loyalties: Sectionalism in Civil War McNairy County," *Tennessee Historical Quarterly* 48 (Fall 1988): 169–71; McClain, *Houston County*, 35; Garrett, "Humphreys County," 94.
18. Crofts, *Reluctant Confederates*, 329–30, 342–48, quoting Moore to Campbell, May 5, 1861, TSLA; Kermit L. Hall, "Tennessee," in *The Confederate Governors*, ed. Buck Yearns (Athens, Ga., 1985), 188–91; the progression from peace to armed conflict can be followed daily in E. B. Long, *The Civil War Day By Day* (Garden City, N.Y., 1971), 59–83.
19. Oliver P. Temple, *Notable Men of Tennessee* (New York, 1912), 243.
20. Noel Fisher, "The Leniency Shown Them Has Been Unavailing," *Civil War History* 40 (Dec. 1994): 275–77.

21. Ibid., 277–82.
22. Lowell H. Harrison, "Kentucky," in *The Confederate Governors*, 83–87; Thomas Speed, *The Unionist Cause in Kentucky* (New York, 1907), chaps. 1–13; E. Merton Coulter, *The Civil War and Readjustment in Kentucky* (Chapel Hill, 1926), chaps. 2–7; Berlin, et al., *Destruction of Slavery*, 493–95; Whitesell, "Military Operations in the Jackson Purchase," 148–49.
23. Phillip M. Shelton, "Camp Beauregard," *Kentucky Historical Society Register* 61 (Apr. 1963): 148–57; Killebrew, "Reminiscences," 1: 158–63.
24. Christopher Waldrep, "Rank-and-File Voters and the Coming of the Civil War," *Civil War History* 35 (Mar. 1989): 60–63; James E. Copeland, "Where Were the Kentucky Unionists and Secessionists?" *Kentucky Historical Society Register* 71 (Oct. 1973): 344–50; Charles Mayfield Meacham, *A History of Christian County, Kentucky* (Nashville, 1930), 69, 122; Steven E. Woodworth, "The Indeterminate Quantities," *Civil War History* 38 (Dec. 1992): 289–97.
25. Hugh C. Bailey, "Disaffection in the Alabama Hill Country, 1861," *Civil War History* 4 (June 1958): 183–93; Lufkin, "Divided Loyalties," 169–71.
26. Killebrew diary, 1: 164, 166–67, SHC/UNC; on American attitudes toward normalcy in the midst of war, see Charles Royster, *A Revolutionary People at War* (Chapel Hill, 1979), 137; on the rampant rumors about slave uprisings, see John Cimprich, *Slavery's End in Tennessee* (University, Ala., 1985), 12–3.
27. Josephine Covington to father, Mar. 2, 1862, FCL; Richard L. Troutman, ed., *The Heavens Are Weeping: The Diaries of George Richard Browder 1852–1886*, (Grand Rapids, 1987).
28. L. C. Porter diary, 103–8, FCL.
29. Josyph, *The Wounded River*, 56–57, 61–62; Stephen Z. Starr, *Jennison's Jayhawkers*, (Baton Rouge, 1973), 164.
30. Simon, *Papers of Ulysses S. Grant*, 4: 146–47; see also 178–79.
31. Grimsley, *Hard Hand of War*, chap. 1, especially citing Emmerich de Vattel, *The Law of Nations, or, Principles of the Law of Nature Applied to the Conduct and Affairs of Nations and Sovereigns* (London, 1797 edition), and Henry W. Halleck, *International Law; or, Rules Regulating the Intercourse of States in Peace and War* (New York, 1861).
32. Grimsley, *Hard Hand of War*, 21–22.
33. Ibid., 48–52.
34. Ibid., 51–52.
35. Victor B. Howard, *Black Liberation in Kentucky* (Lexington, 1983), intro., chaps. 1, 2; Berlin, et al., *Destruction of Slavery*, 493–95 and *Wartime Genesis of Free Labor*, 368–69; U.S. Cong., 37th, 2d Sess., HR, Ex. Br. Doc. 116, *Preliminary Report on the Eighth Census, 1860* (Washington, 1862), 261, 282; James Welch Patton, *Unionism and Reconstruction in Tennessee* (Chapel Hill, 1934), 4; Coulter, *Civil War and Readjustment in Kentucky*, 442; on soldier views, see Josyph, *The Wounded River*, 73.
36. Cimprich, *Slavery's End*, chap. l; Arthur B. Carpenter to parents, Dec. 5, 1861, Aug. 19, 1862, in Thomas R. Bright, "Yankee in Arms," *Civil War History* 19 (Sept. 1973): 202.
37. R. H. Groves, "Captain Owen Griffith," unpublished mss., 76–78, author files; Josephine Covington to father, Mar. 2, 1862, FCL; ORA, ser. 1, vol. 10, pt. 2: 15; Grimsley, *Hard Hand of War*, 63–64.
38. Gen. Ords. 14, Feb. 26, 1863, Box 2, 1862, Jan–Mar, A–Q Letters Received, 1861–67, Entry 2593, Dept. of the Missouri, 1861–67, RG 293, Dept. of the Missouri, NARA.
39. Richards, "Dealing with Slavery," in *Sketches of War History*, 4: 318–21; Halleck to Morton, Feb. 25, Mar. 3, Halleck to Wright, Mar. 25, both 1862, both Tel. Sent, Nov. 61–July 63; Entry 2587; Wright to Halleck, Mar. 24, 1862, Tel. Recd., Nov. 61–Mar. 62, Entry 2602, vol. 2, all RG 293, Dept. of the Missouri, NARA.
40. "Negroes and Fortifications," Memphis *Avalanche*, Apr. 3, 1862; Berlin, et al., *Destruction of Slavery*, 495–96.
41. Adolphus Meier to Halleck, Feb. 21, N. Ranny to Halleck, Feb. 25, both 1862, Entry 2593, Ltrs. Rec., Jan.–Mar. 1862, A–Q, Box 2, RG 293, Dept. of the Missouri, NARA.
42. ORA, ser. 1, vol. 10, pt. 2: 19, Concerning resumption of river traffic, see W. D. Gallagher to Halleck, Mar. 1; Gallagher to S. P. Chase, Mar. 7; Telegram Chase to Gallagher, Mar. 8; Stanton to Halleck, Mar. 8; Gallagher to Halleck, Mar. 8, all 1862, all Entry 2593, Ltrs. Recd., Box 2, 1862, Jan.–Mar., A–Q, Dept. of the Missouri, 1861–67; see also Halleck to W. T. Sherman, Mar. 8, Halleck to Chase, Mar. 8, Halleck to G. Hamilton, Mar. 20; all 1862, all Entry 2592, Letrs. Recd., 1861–67, Box 3, Jan.–Mar., R–Y, all Dept. of the Missouri; see also Fry to Greene, Mar. 5, 6, Greene to Fry, n.d. [Mar. 6], Sword to Gillem, Mar. 7, all 1862, all Entry 886, Tel. Recd. and Sent, Jan.–Mar. 1862, Dept. of the Ohio; all RG 293, NARA; see also Nashville *Times*, Mar. 4, 5, 10, 11, 23, 1862.
43. Memphis *Avalanche*, Feb. 28, 1862.

44. *ORA*, ser. 1, vol. 7: 669–70.
45. Ibid., 671, 675–76.
46. Grant to Halleck, Halleck to Grant, both Mar. 11, 1862, entries 2602, Tel. Recd., Nov. 61–Mar. 62, and entry 2587, Tel. Sent, Nov. 61–Mar. 62, both RG 393, NARA; *ORA*, ser. 1, vol. 10, pt. 2: 30.
47. Johnston to Jefferson Davis, Mar. 30, 1862, chap. 2, vol. 218, Letrs and Tel. Sent, Sept. 61–Apr. 62, Johnston's Command, RG 109, NARA.
48. Ash, *When the Yankees Came*, 38–39.
49. Peter Maslowski, *Treason Must Be Made Odious* (Millwood, N.Y., 1978), 22–27; McKinney to Cousin Libby, Mar. 27, 1862, DUL.
50. See Johnson's "Speech to Davidson County Citizens," Mar. 22, 1862, Graf and Haskins, *Papers of Andrew Johnson*, 5: 226, 237–38, n. 1; see also 209–212; see also John DeBerry, "Confederate Tennessee," (Ph.D. diss., Univ. of Kentucky, 1967), 162; Durham, *Occupied City*, chaps. 4, 5; Stryker, *Andrew Johnson*, chaps. 8, 9.
51. Ash, *When the Yankees Came*, 45.
52. Ethie Eagleton, "Stray Thoughts," Mar. 17, May 30, both 1862, quoted in Pearson, "A Middle-Class," 323–24.
53. *ORA*, ser. 1, vol. 10, pt. 2: 47, 56, 58 79, 126; Durham, *Occupied City*, 65.
54. *ORA*, ser. 1, vol. 7: 679; vol. 10, pt. 2: 11, 27.
55. Useful portrayals of Nashville's evolution in this regard are Durham, *Occupied City*, chaps. 3, 4, 5; and Hoobler, *Cities Under the Gun*, 107–12.
56. Eagleton, "Stray Thoughts," Feb. 27, 1862, quoted in Pearson, "A Middle-Class," 323; Alice Ready diary, 46, SHC/UNC; Don C. Seitz, *Braxton Bragg* (Columbia, 1924), 82–84.
57. Ready diary, 52, SHC/UNC; Jesse Cox diary, 490, TSLA.
58. *ORA*, ser. 1, vol. 10, pt. 2: 342; see also 338, 343, 350, 362.
59. *ORA*, ser. 1, vol. 10, pt. 1: 4–8, 31–32; James A. Ramage, *Rebel Raider* (Lexington, 1986), chaps. 4, 5, 6, especially 56–60; Dee Alexander Brown, *The Bold Cavaliers* (Philadelphia, 1959), chaps. 1, 2.
60. Ready diary, 53–57, SHC/UNC.
61. Ramage, *Rebel Raider*, 60–61, citing Richmond *Whig*, Apr. 7, 1862.
62. *ORA*, ser. 1, vol. 10, pt. 1: 16–19; Charles C. Nott, *Sketches of War* (New York, 1865), chap. 5; Simon, *Papers of Ulysses S. Grant*, 4: 345–46; AAG to Lowe, Grant to Commd. Gen. Fort Heiman, both Mar. 11, 1862, in Ltrs. Sent, pt. 2, Continental Army commands, RG 393, NARA; Will Kennedy to Sister, Mar. 15, 1862, DUL; Redick C. Carnell memoir, Box 8, No. 2, Garrett collection, TSLA.
63. Nott, *Sketches*, 44–45, 65–66.
64. Ibid., 71–72.
65. Ibid., 67–68. On this phenomenon in the American Revolution, see Royster, *A Revolutionary People at War*, who contends that "Americans' most common escape from their own war, however, was quite open and conspicuous. People tried to live as if there were no war" (137); see also 147, 152–58; and see Ramage, *Rebel Raider*, 78–79.
66. Will Kennedy to sister, Mar. 15, 21, both 1862, DUL.
67. *ORA*, ser. 1, vol. 10, pt. 2: 21, 54–55, 71–72, 110; Simon, *Papers of Ulysses S. Grant*, 4: 374n.; Ezra Warner, *Generals in Blue* (Baton Rouge, 1964), 132–33; John W. Rowell, *Yankee Cavalrymen: Through the Civil War with the Ninth Pennsylvania Cavalry* (Knoxville, 1971), 46–48.
68. See Durham, *Occupied City*, chap. 5; John McGlone, "'What Became of General Barrow?'" *Tennessee Historical Quarterly* (Spring 1989): 42–44.
69. Simon, *Papers of Ulysses S. Grant*, 4: 349–50, 357, 365–66, 373, 374n., 403n., 404n.; 5: 281–82, 349–50; John Nick Barker diary, Mar. 13, 17, 25, 28, 31, all 1862, TSLA.
70. Simon, *Papers of Ulysses S. Grant*, 5: 45–47, 102–7, 137–38, 144, 282n.
71. Bob Avery to William T. Avery, May 25, 1862, Gordon-Avery collection, TSLA; *ORA*, ser. 1, vol. 10, pt. 2: 407–8.
72. Whitesell, "Military Operations in the Jackson Purchase," 150, citing Richard H. Collins, *History of Kentucky* (Louisville, 1924), 1: 106; see also Nott, *Sketches of the War*, 117.
73. *ORA*, ser. 1, vol. 10, pt. 1: 879–83; Nott, *Sketches of the War*, chap. 8; William W. Chester, "The Skirmish at Lockridge Mill in Weakley County, Tennessee, May 6, 1862," *Journal of the Jackson Purchase Historical Society* 15 (June 1987): 51–54; and Lonnie E. Maness, "Captain Charles Cooper Nott and the Battle of Lockridge's Mills," *Journal of the Jackson Purchase Historical Society* 3 (June 1975): 12–20.

74. Dargan, *Civil War Diary of Martha Abernathy*, 38–39, quoting Abernathy diary, May 8, 1862; also John S. Daniel, "Special Warfare in Middle Tennessee," (M.A. thesis, Univ. of Tennessee, 1971), 85–87.
75. Dargan, *Civil War Diary of Martha Abernathy*, see also ORA, ser. 1, vol. 10, pt. 1: 874–76.
76. Robert S. Montgomery diary, cited by Charles R. Gunter Jr., "History of the Civil War in Bedford County," (M.A. thesis, Univ. of Tennessee, 1965), 48; Sallie Florence McEwen diary, May 5, 1862, TSLA; Daniel, *Special Warfare*, 88–91.
77. Ramage, *Rebel Raider*, 84–85; ORA, ser. 1, vol. 10, pt. 1: 884–86.
78. ORA, ser. 1, vol. 10, pt. l: 891; Ramage, *Rebel Raider*, 86–87; Rowell, *Yankee Cavalrymen*, 47–48, 62–64.
79. ORA, ser. 1, vol. 10, pt. 2: 182.
80. Rugeley, *Batchelor-Turner Letters*, 22–23, 25–27.

THREE. CONFEDERATE RESURGENCE

1. Daniel P. Smith, *Company K, First Alabama Regiment* (Prattville, Ala., 1885), chap. 1, especially 17, 18; see also Whitesell, "Military Operations in the Jackson Purchase," 145–47; Daniel and Bock, *Island No. 10*, esp. chaps. 11, 12, 13.
2. Douglas Hale, *The Third Texas Cavalry* (Norman, 1993), 110–12; 121–23.
3. John Houston Bills diary, entries July 1, Aug. 26, both 1862, quoted in McKenzie, *One South or Many*, 94.
4. Brooks D. Simpson, *Let Us Have Peace: Ulysses S. Grant and the Politics of War and Reconstruction 1861–1868* (Chapel Hill: Univ. of North Carolina Press, 1991), 25–35; R. A. Halley, "A Rebel Newspaper's War Story," in Tennessee Historical Commission and Tennessee Historical Society, *Tennessee Old and New: Sesquicentennial Edition* (Nashville: Tennessee Historical Commission and Tennessee Historical Society, 1977), 2: 250–55.
5. William P. Lyon, *Reminiscences*, comp. Adelia Lyon (San Jose, Calif., 1907), 53. Ulysses S. Grant, *Personal Memoirs* (New York, 1885), 1: 368–69; Simon, *Papers of Ulysses S. Grant*, 5: 143; Grimsley, *Hard Hand of War*, 93–94; McKenzie, *One South or Many*, 95–97.
6. Simon, *Papers of Ulysses S. Grant*, 5: 138, 151, 243, 260; ORA, ser. 1, vol. 17, pt. 2: 88, 97–99; Grimsley, *Hard Hand of War*, 99, 120.
7. Grimsley, "A Directed Severity," 113; Simpson, *Let Us Have Peace*, 24–25; ORA, ser. 1, vol. 17, pt. 2: 150.
8. Recent studies illuminating Sherman's role at Memphis include John F. Marzalek, *Sherman: A Soldier's Passion for Order* (New York, 1993), chap. 9, especially 194–95, and Charles Edmund Vetter, *Sherman: Merchant of Terror, Advocate of Peace* (Gretna, La., 1992), chap. 5; on Sherman and slavery at this time, see Berlin, et al., *Destruction of Slavery*, 278–79, 281–82, 285–87, 289–98.
9. ORA, ser. 3, vol. 2: 402, also 349, 350, 382, 454; ser. 1, vol. 17, pt. 2: 158–60, 178–79; Noel C. Fisher, "'Prepare Them for My Coming': General William T. Sherman, Total War and Pacification in West Tennessee," *Tennessee Historical Quarterly* (Summer 1992): especially 78–86.
10. See Daniel E. Sutherland, "Abraham Lincoln, John Pope, and the Origins of Total War," *Journal of Military History* (Oct. 1992): 567–68, especially n. 1, citing James M. McPherson, *Battle Cry of Freedom* (New York, 1988), 490–510, among others; see also Ash, *When the Yankees Came*, chap. 2.
11. Sutherland, "Lincoln, Pope," 570–75.
12. ORA, ser. 1, vol. 12, pt. 2: 50–52.
13. Ibid., also pt. 3: 509; Sutherland, "Lincoln, Pope," 575–78.
14. Graf and Haskins, *Papers of Andrew Johnson*, 5: 569–70, 575–76; see also Sutherland, "Lincoln, Pope," 581; ORA, ser. 1, vol. 12, pt. 3: 515, 573, 577, and ser. 2, vol. 4: 329–30, 830–31, 836–37.
15. ORA, ser. 1, vol. 12, pt. 2: 52.
16. Emory M. Thomas, *The Confederate Nation* (New York, 1979), chap. 7; and *The Confederacy as a Revolutionary Experience* (Englewood Cliffs, N.J., 1971), 51–57, 61–62, 67–68; Paul D. Escott, *After Secession* (Baton Rouge, 1978), 63–64.
17. Ramage, *Rebel Raider*, 67–70.
18. Both the Conscription Act and the Partisan Ranger Act as announced in Confederate General Orders Number 30, Apr. 28, 1862, are found in ORA, ser. 4, vol. l: 1094–99.
19. On guerrillas in history, see Walter Laqueur, *Guerrilla* (Boston, 1974), especially chaps. 1–3; Robert B. Asprey, *War in the Shadows* (Garden City, 1975), especially vol. 1.

20. Allan Millett and Peter Maslowski, *For the Common Defense* (New York, 1984), chaps. 1 and 2; John W. Shy, "A New Look At Colonial Militia," *William and Mary Quarterly* 20 (Apr. 1963): 175–85; John K. Mahon, "Anglo-American Methods of Indian Warfare, 1676–1794," *Mississippi Valley Historical Review* 45 (Sept. 1958) 254–75; Russell F. Weigley, *History of the U.S. Army* (New York, 1967), chaps. 1 and 2; see also Roger Beaumont, "Unconventional Warfare," vol. 3: 1172, Clayton R. Newell, "The Development of Operational Art," vol. 2: 1222, and Michael Pearlman, "Political Objectives and the Development of Military Strategy," vol. 1: 314, all in John E. Jessup and Louise B. Ketz, eds., *Encyclopedia of the American Military* (New York, 1994).
21. On the Revolution, see John Shy, *A People Numerous and Armed* (New York, 1976), chaps. 6, 7, 8.
22. Anne Norton, *Alternative Americans* (Chicago, 1986), chap. 9, especially 243–46; Ramage, *Rebel Raider*, 64–66, 68–70, also citing J. V. Ridgley, *Nineteenth-Century Southern Literature* (Lexington, Ky., 1980), 2, 32–34, 42–43, 48; Nathaniel Beverly Tucker, *The Partisan Leader* (Chapel Hill, reprint, 1972); Peter Horry and William Gilmore Simms, *The Life of Francis Marion* (New York, reprint, 1971).
23. Nashville *Union*, June 19, Nov. 29, both 1861.
24. David Hubbard, Feb. 25, Theodore Harris, June 12, A. O. W. Lattern, June 14, S. J. Rudd, June 15, B. B. Seat, June 17, J. W. McHenry, Aug. 4, all 1861, all to Isham G. Harris, TSLA; Daniel, "Special Warfare in Middle Tennessee," 35–38.
25. Diary of Robert S. Montgomery, cited by Gunter, "History of the Civil War in Bedford County," 48; *ORA*, ser. 1, vol. 7: 4–6; Jill McKnight Garrett, "Guerrillas and Bushwhackers," 22, TSLA; Charles M. Waters, *Historic Clarksville* (Clarksville, 1983), 67.
26. Daniel, "Special Warfare," 143–53; Bromfield Ridley, *Battles and Sketches* (Mexico, Mo., 1906), 24, 522, 524–27; Thurman Sensing, *Champ Ferguson* (Nashville, 1941), 25–26, 55–59.
27. Nashville *Dispatch*, Oct. 22, 1865; Daniel, "Special Warfare," 153–54.
28. *ORA*, ser. 1, vol. 10, pt. 2: 8; see also 25, 29, 30, 80; vol. 16, pt. 2: 124.
29. Ibid., 186; see also vol. 16, pt. 1: 485–91.
30. Memphis *Appeal*, June 19, 1862, quoted in Halley, "A Rebel Newspaper's War Story," 249–50.
31. Thomas B. Wilson Reminiscences, 31, SHC/UNC.
32. Adam R. Johnson, *The Partisan Rangers of the Confederate States Army* (Louisville, 1904), chaps. 1–11.
33. Ibid., chaps. 12, 13, see also 234–53, 344–47.
34. *ORA*, ser. 1, vol. 10, pt. 1: 914–17. Rowell, *Yankee Cavalrymen*, chap. 7; Garrett, "Guerrillas and Bushwhackers," 23–24, 38, 52, 102–12, 156–57; Whitesell, "Military Operations," 154.
35. Garrett, "Guerrillas and Bushwhackers," 23–24; Sensing, *Champ Ferguson*, 80, 89–117.
36. *ORA*, ser. 1, vol. 16, pt. 1: 842–43, pt. 2: 110, 173–74, 194, 195, 199, 212, 228, 233, 242, 252, 261, 268, 282, 283, 300, 305, 310 also vol. 17, pt. 2, 69; Simon, *Papers of Ulysses Grant*, 5: 190.
37. James Negley to Thomas H. Green, June 17, 1862, Misc. Adjutant General files, TSLA.
38. Nashville *Union*, July 8, 12, Aug. 2, all 1862.
39. *ORA*, ser. 1, vol. 10, pt. 2: 183; vol. 16, pt. 2: 173, 178, 228, 232, 233; Fitch, *Annals of the Army of the Cumberland*, 99–100.
40. Blanchard, *I Marched with Sherman*, 58–64.
41. *ORA*, ser. 1, vol. 17, pt. 2: 69; Simon, *Papers of Ulysses Grant*, 5: 190; Grimsley, *Hard Hand of War*, 100–101, 113–14.
42. Simon, *Papers of Ulysses Grant*, 5: 105, 107, 109–11.
43. *ORA*, ser. 1, vol. 10, pt. 2: 162–63, 167, 204, 212–13, 290–95.
44. Ibid., 156–57, 204, 209; for conditions in north Alabama and Tennessee in May and June, see 155–296, among others, and Grimsley, *Hard Hand of War*, 78–85.
45. Mrs. W. D. Chadick, "Diary," Huntsville *Times* (circa 1934), as reprinted McMillan, *Alabama Confederate Reader*, 154–72, especially 172; *ORA*, ser. 1, vol. 10, pt. 2: 257; Grimsley, *Hard Hand of War*, 45, 81.
46. Jacksonville *Republican*, Sept. 25, 1862, reprinted in McMillan, *Alabama Confederate Reader*, 179–80; for Union troop reaction, see, for example, Constantin Grebner, *We Were the Ninth* (Kent, Ohio, 1987), 106–10.
47. Donald W. Disbrow, ed., "Vett Noble of Ypsilanti," *Civil War History* (Mar. 1968): 17, see also 18, 23–52; Virginia Clay-Copton, *A Belle of the Fifties* (New York, 1904), 181–84; Chadick, "Diary," *Alabama Confederate Reader*, 158.
48. *ORA*, ser. 1, vol. 17, pt. 2: 180–84; Stephen Z. Starr, *The Union Cavalry in the Civil War* (Baton Rouge, 1985), 3: especially chaps. 1 and 2, which provide a fuller analysis of problems with the Union cavalry in this period.

49. *ORA*, ser. 1, vol. 17, pt. 2: 656, 657, 662, 663–64, 665, 675–77; Lawrence L. Hewitt, "Braxton Bragg and the Confederate Invasion of Kentucky in 1862," in *Leadership During the Civil War*, 60–63; James Lee McDonough, *War in Kentucky* (Knoxville, 1994), 82–84.
50. *ORA*, ser. 1, vol. 16, pt. 2: 680, 681, 683–85, 701, 706–7, 741, 745–46, 748–49; for general background, see Woodworth, *Jefferson Davis and his Generals*, chap. 9, and Williams, *Lincoln Finds a General*, 3: chap. 15, and 4: chaps. 1 and 2.
51. *ORA*, ser. 1, vol. 17, pt. 2: 681, 683, 685, 687, 690, 691.
52. Ibid., vol. 16, pt. 2: 752–53; vol. 17, pt. 2: 688.
53. Ibid., vol. 16, pt. 2: 755, 764–65, 766–67.
54. Ibid., 758–59, 760–61, 762–63, 765, 784.
55. Ibid., 780, 782–83; Hewitt, "Bragg and the Confederate Invasion," 63.
56. *ORA*, ser. 1, vol. 16, pt. 2: 782–83.
57. Ibid., 726–27, 731, as well as 9, 14; see also vol. 17, pt. 2: 22.
58. Glenn W. Sunderland, *Five Days to Glory* (South Brunswick, N.J.: 1970), 44–45; W. E. Patterson diary, 21, UTL; *ORA*, ser. 1, vol. 10, pt. 2: 630; vol. 16, pt. 2: 22, 129.
59. *ORA*, ser. 1, vol. 16, pt. 2: 15–17, 100–101.
60. Ibid., 18, 54, 102–3, 105, 107, 122–23, 130–31, 161–62, 167, 233, 241; Leland R. Johnson, "Civil War Railroad Defenses in Tennessee," *The Tennessee Valley Historical Review* (Summer 1972): 20–23.
61. *ORA*, ser. 1, vol. 16, pt. 2: 3–4, 10, 11, 15–17, 20, 42, 53, 59, 78, 79, 87–88, 91–92, 101, 131, 160, 165, 299; see also vol. 10, pt. 2: 123.
62. Ibid., vol. 16, pt. 2: 69–70, 74–76, 88–89, 95, 122–23, 145, 147–48, 165–66 also pt. 1: 33–34; vol. 17, pt. 2: 52–53.
63. Ibid., vol. 16, pt. 2: 81–82; vol. 17, pt. 2: 71–72; Stephen E. Ambrose, *Halleck: Lincoln's Chief of Staff* (Baton Rouge, 1962), chap. 5.
64. *ORA*, vol. 10, pt. 2: 128–29; also vol. 16, pt. 2: 36–37, 47, 53, 118, 119, 121, 122, 135, 242–43; see also Maslowski, *Treason Must Be Made Odious*, 39–40; Durham, *Occupied City*, 97.
65. On Washington's analogous position with Nashville, see the author's *Symbol, Sword, and Shield* (Hamden, Conn., 1975), especially chap. 5; and Durham, *Occupied City*, chaps. 5 and 6.
66. Rufus Howell Cook memoirs, TSLA.
67. *ORA*, vol. 16, pt. 2: 118–20, 135, 148, 159, 175–76, 229; Graf and Haskins, *Papers of Andrew Johnson*, 5: 416–17, 429–31, 443–44, 487, 547–48.
68. *ORA*, ser. 1, vol. 16, pt. 2: 122.
69. Ibid., 229.
70. Maslowski, *Treason Must Be Made Odious*, 40–45.
71. *ORA*, ser. 1, vol. 16, pt. 2: 131–33, 136, 137, 142, 143.
72. Ibid., vol. 16, pt. 1: 34–35, 731–84; pt. 2: 19–20, 47, 91, 118–19, 127–28, 131–33, 136, 142–55, 179, 213, 226, 722, 733–34.
73. Ramage, *Rebel Raider*, chap. 9; Rowell, *Yankee Cavalrymen*, chap. 8.
74. *ORA*, ser. 1, vol. 16, pt. 2: 179; also pt. 1: 710–11.
75. Ibid., 809–11; John Allen Wyeth, *That Devil Forrest* (New York, 1959), chap. 5; Thomas Jordan and J. P. Pryor, *The Campaigns of Lieutenant General N. B. Forrest* (Dayton, 1977), chap. 5.
76. Pearson, "A Middle-Class," 327–30; *ORA*, ser. 1, vol. 16, pt. 1: 805–6, 811.
77. Jesse B. Connelly diary, Aug. 5, 1862, 50–1, IHSL; *ORA*, ser. 1, vol. 16, pt. 1: 792–819; pt. 2: 137, 138, 140, 144, 145, 149, 151; Robert Selph Henry, *First with the Most Forrest* (Indianapolis, 1944), 88; James Lee McDonough, *Stones River* (Knoxville, 1980), chap. 1.
78. John A. Berger to parents, Sept. 5, 1862, IHSL; William Henry King memoirs, 25–26, 61–62, SHC/UNC.
79. Connelly diary, Aug. 16, 1862, 53–54, see also 23, 55–57; James F. Fee to brother, Aug. 7, 1862, both IHSL; *ORA*, ser. 1, vol. 16, pt. 1: 815–19; also pt. 2: 154, 163, 167, 169, 171, 192, 202, 205, 207, 208, 220, 239, 241.
80. *ORA*, ser. 1, vol. 16, pt. 2: 197.
81. Ibid., 155, 181, 304, 722, 733–34; while on Negley, see 173–74, 194, 233, and Johnson, 119, 122, 142, 144, 159; see also Ramage, *Rebel Raider*, 71–72.
82. For Kentucky restiveness, see Coulter, *Civil War and Readjustment in Kentucky*, chap. 8; see also Richard Troutman, ed., *The Heavens Are Weeping* (Grand Rapids, 1987), 112–13, 116, 119–20, 121, 122, 123.
83. *ORA*, ser. 1, vol. 52, pt. 1: 263.

84. Troutman, *Heavens Are Weeping*, 114, 119, 122.
85. *ORA*, ser. 1, vol. 52, pt. 1: 264–65.
86. Ibid., vol. 16, pt. 2: 326–27; see also 105, 163, 178, 192, 193, 241, 268–69, also Atlas, plate 124.
87. Durham, *Occupied City*, 104–7; Bobby L. Lovett, "Nashville's Fort Negley: A Symbol of Blacks' Involvement with the Union Army," *Tennessee Historical Quarterly* (Spring 1982): 7–8; Berlin, et al., *Wartime Genesis of Free Labor*, 384–94.
88. *ORA*, ser. 1, vol. 16, pt. 1: 104; also 35–37.

FOUR. HEARTLAND HAVOC

1. Josyph, *The Wounded River*, 114; Grimsley, *Hard Hand of War*, 98–105.
2. Ibid., 108, also *ORA*, ser. 1, vol. 17, pt. 2: 126.
3. *ORA*, ser. 1, vol. 16, pt. 1: 861–62; see also 835, 842–43.
4. Ibid., vol. 16, pt. 1: 843–70, pt. 2: 243, also 232, 254, 257, 273, 279, 294, 301, 309.
5. Ibid., vol. 16, pt. 2: 322; see also pt. 1: 857, and 878–79; Ramage, *Rebel Raider*, chap. 10; Durham, *Occupied City*, 107–11.
6. *ORA*, ser. 1, vol. 16, pt. 2: 763; see also 142–318, among others; pt. 1: 843–57; Mrs. William G. Harding to husband, July 24, 1862, cited in Maslowski, *Treason Must Be Made Odious*, 45.
7. Durham, *Occupied City*, 111–15; Richard P. Gildrie, "Guerrilla Warfare in the Lower Cumberland River Valley, 1862–1865," *Tennessee Historical Quarterly* (Fall 1990): 164–65.
8. *ORA*, ser. 1, vol. 16, pt. 1: 862–70; Gildrie, "Guerilla Warfare," 164; Johnson, *Partisan Rangers*, chap. 15.
9. Wyeth, *That Devil Forrest*, 70, Jordan and Pryor, *Campaigns of Forrest*, 160.
10. Nick Barker diary, Mar. 31, June 11, July 25, 26, all 1862; Sarah Kennedy to Husband, Aug. 16, 1862, both Confederate collections, Box 10, folder 8, TSLA; Richard Gildrie, Philip Kemmerly, and Thomas H. Winn, *Clarksville, Tennessee in the Civil War* (Clarksville, 1984), 10–16.
11. Compare Buell's directive about using river and rail through Clarksville, *ORA*, ser. 1, vol. 16, pt. 1: 629, pt. 2: 129, 243, 281, 331, with Durham, *Occupied City*, 133–34.
12. *ORA*, ser. 1, vol. 16, pt. 1: 866–67n.; see also pt. 2: 243, 281, 319, 331; Simon, *Papers of Ulysses S. Grant*, 5: 107n., 322n.; Graf and Haskins, *Papers of Andrew Johnson*, 5: 628n.
13. Eugene Marshall to sister, July 22, 1862, DUL; *ORA*, ser. 1, vol. 16, pt. 1: 866; pt. 2: 8, 20, 319; vol. 17, pt. 2: 146.
14. *ORA*, ser. 1, vol. 16, pt. 1: 862, 869.
15. W. Williams, "A Reminiscence of Clarksville, Tenn.," *Confederate Veteran* 22 (May 1914): 207.
16. Johnson, *Partisan Rangers*, 112–15; Haskins diary, Aug. 16, 1862, TSLA; Unidentified letter from Amanda, quoted in Beach, *Along the Warioto*, 363.
17. Graf and Haskins, *Papers of Andrew Johnson*, 6: 480–81.
18. *ORA*, ser. 1, vol. 16, pt. 2: 388, 836, 864, pt. 1: 863–70; Simon, *Papers of Ulysses Grant*, 5: 322–33n.; James Taylor Holmes, *Fifty-Second Ohio Volunteer Infantry* (Columbus, 1898), 81–82.
19. *ORA*, ser. 1, vol. 16, pt. 2: 380.
20. M. Jenkins to Col. E. S. Jenkins, Aug. 15, 1862, TSLA.
21. James Buckner Killebrew reminiscences, 170–71, TSLA.
22. Johnson, *Partisan Rangers*, 121–22, chap. 16; *ORA*, ser. 1, vol. 16, pt. 2: 426–27.
23. Troutman, *The Heavens Are Weeping*, 120–33.
24. *ORA*, ser. 1, vol. 17, pt. 2: 53–54, 66–67, 91–94; see also Stephen Z. Starr, *Jennison's Jayhawkers* (Baton Rouge, 1973), chap. 9.
25. Bruce Catton, *Grant Moves South* (Boston, 1960), 289; *ORA*, ser. 1, vol. 17, pt. 2: 150, 154–55, 156–57; Dennis K. McDaniel, "The 12th Wisconsin Infantry Regiment in West Tennessee," *Tennessee Historical Quarterly* (Fall 1974): 255–64.
26. *ORA*, ser. 1, vol. 17, pt. 1: 31–32, 34–38; see also James D. Brewer, "The Battle of Britton's Lane," *Blue and Gray Magazine*, April 1993) 34–38..
27. Ibid., 43–51, and pt. 2: 192, 213; Blanchard, *I Marched with Sherman*, 62–68.
28. Thomas B. Wilson, Reminiscences, 35–41, especially 38, SHC/UNC.
29. *ORA*, ser. 1, vol. 17, pt. 2: 183, 186.
30. *ORA*, ser. 1, vol. 17, pt. 1: 36–38; pt. 2: 179, 180–83.

31. William R. Plum, *The Military Telegraph in the Civil War* (Chicago, 1882), 1: 227; Eugene Marshall, "Narrative of the Civil War," 14–15, MHS; Ronald E. Toops, comp., *The McConnell Letters* (1975, by author), 9–20.
32. Henry Dean to Rock River *Democrat*, Aug. 31, 1862, published in Sept. 9, 1862, edition, quoted in Jim Huffstodt, *Hard Dying Men* (Bowie, Md., 1991), 116–17; T. Lyle Dickey to daughter, Aug. 27, 1862, ISH; George D. Carrington diary, 71, CHS.
33. Barker diary, Aug. 26, 1862, TSLA; *ORA*, ser. 1, vol. 17, pt. 1: 38–39; "Capt. W. B. Allbright," *Confederate Veteran* 10 (June 1901): 275.
34. *ORA*, ser. 1, vol. 16, pt. 2: 447.
35. Simon, *Papers of Ulysses Grant*, 5: 323n.; Marshall, "Narrative," 11, 14, MHS.
36. Eugene Marshall to sister, Mar. 3, Apr. 5, May 18, June 15, July 22, all 1862, also diary 2: 104, 106, 108, 110, 111, all DUL, also "Narrative," 13–15, MHS.
37. John Edgerly to Friend Clark, Sept. 20, 1862, Sword and Sabre Catalog, Item 96 (Gettysburg, Pa., 1991), copy, author's files; also Marshall, "Narrative," MHS.
38. Marshall diary, Sept. 5, 1862, DUL, and "Narrative," 15–17, MHS; on Lowe's units, see *ORA*, ser. 1, vol. 16, pt. 1: 955, as well as Frederick H. Dyer, *A Compendium of the War of the Rebellion* (New York, 1959), 3: 1040–41, 1082, 1161–72, 1678–79.
39. *ORA*, ser. 1, vol. 16, pt. 1: 955; pt. 2: 483–84.
40. Ibid., 16, pt. 1: 955–56, pt. 2: 484–85; Robert McConnell to wife and children, Sept. 11, 1862, in Toops, *McConnell Letters*, 19; Huffstodt, *Hard Dying Men*, 118–19.
41. Toops, *McConnell Letters*, 17; Marshall, "Narrative," 18–19, MHS, and diary, Sept. 7, 18, 1862, DUL; Huffstodt, *Hard Dying Men*, 119–20; Barker diary, Sept. 7, 8, 1862, TSLA.
42. Josiah Conzett reminiscence, 26–27, SHSI.
43. Haskins diary, Feb. 6, 16, 1863; Barker diary, Sept. 6, 7, 1862, both TSLA.
44. Toops, *McConnell Letters*, 19–20.
45. Marshall diary, Sept. 8, 1862, DUL; Huffstodt, *Hard Dying Men*, 120.
46. Clarksville citizens to Grant, Sept. 17, 1862, printed in Beach, *Along the Warioto*, 364; Sarah Kennedy to husband, Sept. 16, 1862, TSLA; Simon, *Papers of Ulysses Grant*, 5: 273n.
47. *ORA*, ser. 1, vol. 17, pt. 2: 730–31.
48. Ibid.; Clarksville citizens to Grant, Sept.. 17, 1862 in Beach, *Along the Warioto*, 364.
49. Ibid., 732, 737–38; vol. 20, pt. 2: 113, 114.
50. Ibid., vol. 17, pt. 1: 62; see also John Edgerly to Friend Clark, 96, author's files; Johnson, *Partisan Rangers*, 346–57.
51. *ORA*, ser. 1, vol. 17, pt. 1: 148; see also 144–47, 150.
52. Ibid., vol. 16, pt. 2: 613–14, 636, 858; Sensing, *Champ Ferguson*, 165–68; Campbell E. Brown, ed., *Tennessee in the Civil War* (Nashville, 1965), 1: 60, 330; Daniel, "Special Warfare," 156–63.
53. *ORA*, ser. 1, vol. 16, pt. 2: 636, 613.
54. Ibid., vol. 17, pt. 1, pt. 2: 237, 246, 250, 270, 294.
55. Ibid., vol. 17, pt. 1: 144–45, 23, also 29–32, 34, 43–55, 138–39, 140–43, 150; pt. 2: 16, 23, 89, 159, 162, 178, 179, 235–36.
56. Elizabeth Avery Meriwether, *Recollections of Ninety-Two Years 1824–1916* (Nashville, 1958), 74–76; PMG Order October 20, 1862, Confederate Collection; Garrett, ed., Campbell diary, 89, both TSLA; *ORA*, ser. 1, vol. 17, pt. 2: 16, 23, 81, 106, 112, 113, 117, 156, 158, 173, 219, 240, 249, 273–74, 276; see also Fisher, "Prepare Them," especially 77–80; Grimsley, *Hard Hand of War*, 114–18.
57. Fisher, "Prepare Them," 84; *ORA*, ser. 1, vol. 17, pt. 2: 261–62; vol. 24, pt. 3: 158, 31; pt. 3: 459, 497–98.
58. *ORA*, ser. 1, vol. 17, pt. 2: 261.
59. Ibid., 273.
60. Johnson quoted in Maslowski, *Treason Must Be Made Odious*, 79–80; see also Coulter, *Civil War and Readjustment in Kentucky*, 150–61; Elizabeth Shelby Kirkhead, *A History of Kentucky* (New York, 1896), 187–88.
61. Mary Bess McCain Henderson, Evelyn Janet McCain Young, Anna Irene McCain Naheloffer, *Dear Eliza* (Ames, Iowa, 1976), 9–10; Eugene Marshall to sister, Sept. 20, 1862, DUL.
62. Long, *Civil War Day by Day*, 241, 270, 306; Patricia Faust, *Historical Times Illustrated Encyclopedia of the Civil War* (New York, 1986), 157; Berlin, et al., *Wartime Genesis of Free Labor*, 19, 28, 33, 35–36, 92.
63. Grimsley, "A Directed Severity," 278–79; Coulter, *Civil War and Readjustment in Kentucky*, chaps. 8, 9; Maslowski, *Treason Must Be Made Odious*, chaps. 4 and 5; Stephen V. Ash, *Middle Tennessee Society Transformed* (Baton Rouge, 1988), chaps. 5, 6, 7.

64. Sunderland, *Five Days to Glory*, 46–47.
65. *ORN*, ser. 1, vol. 23: 309–10, 324; Paul H. Silverstone, *Warships of the Civil War Navies* (Annapolis, 1989), 167, 169, 179; see also *ORA*, ser. 1, vol. 17, pt. 1: 34; pt. 2: 182, 202; Eugene Marshall to sister, Sept. 20, 1862, DUL.
66. *ORN*, ser. 1, vol. 23: 322, 325–26, 330, 331–32, 334, 338–39, 345, 346–47, 354, 355–56, 358, 369, 370, 371, 373, 375, 379–80, 386, 390–91; Silverstone, *Warships*, 166; Eugene Marshall to sister, Sept. 20, 1862, DUL.
67. *ORN*, ser. 1, vol. 23: 346; see also 309–11, 334, 338, 353–54, 358–60, 367–68, 371.
68. Ibid., 451–52, also 348–52, 357, 388–89, 390, 396, 420–21, 427–29, 431–32.
69. Ibid., 434–38; Simon, *Papers of Ulysses Grant*, 6: 151.
70. *ORN*, ser. 1, vol. 23: 390, 451–52, 459.
71. Lufkin, "Divided Loyalties," 176–77.

FIVE. NORTH TO KENTUCKY

1. Garrett, "The Civil War Diary of Andrew Jackson Campbell," 70, TSLA; Smith, *Company K*, chap. 3, especially 26–27.
2. Thomas Rawlings memoir, Mar. 28, 1916, TSLA.
3. Garrett, ed., Campbell diary, 59, TSLA.
4. Nathaniel C. Kenyon, "War Diary," 6, 8, 9, 10, 12, 15, 17, 18, 22, 23, 24, privately owned; Mrs. M. M. Ransom to Dr. Simpson, Dec. 12, 1862, in Lieutenant Frederick Eugene Ransom, Compiled Service Record, NARA, all cited in Huffstodt, *Hard Dying Men*, 130–35.
5. Garrett, ed., Campbell diary, 59–77, TSLA.
6. Ibid., 90; see also 76–79, 82–85, 89–90; *ORA*, ser. 1, vol. 17, pt. 2: 716.
7. Martha Abernathy to C. C. Abernathy, Aug. 18, 1862, in Dargan, *Civil War Diary of Martha Abernathy*, 63–66.
8. Ibid., entry of Aug. 23, 1862, 68–69.
9. "Proclamation of Col. John Hunt Morgan at Hartsville, Tennessee," printed in *The Vidette*, and quoted in ibid., 70–71.
10. Confederate actions should be followed in Woodworth, *Jefferson Davis and His Generals*, chap. 9; Hewitt, "Bragg and the Confederate Invasion," 55–72; Connelly, *Army of the Heartland*, part 5. James V. Murfin, *The Gleam of Bayonets* (New York, 1965); Steven Sears, *Landscape Turned Red* (New York, 1983); and Kenneth Hafendorfer, *Perryville: Battle for Kentucky* (Owensboro, 1981), sufficiently highlight the tactical details of the battles for the borderland. The latest study of the Kentucky campaign is James Lee McDonough, *War in Kentucky* (Knoxville, 1994); while on Price and Van Dorn, see also Ephraim McD. Anderson, *Memoirs* (St. Louis, 1868), chaps. 57–61; and Phillip Thomas Tucker, *The South's Finest: The First Missouri Confederate Brigade* (Shippensburg, Pa., 1993), chaps. 5 and 6.
11. Simon, *Papers of Ulysses Grant*, 6: 44.
12. The subtle factors of failure can be followed in *ORA*, ser. 1, vol. 17, pt. 2: 694, 698, 710–11, 712, 714, 715–16.
13. Porter, "War Record," 39, WKL; Johnson, *Partisan Rangers*, 125.
14. *ORA*, ser. 1, vol. 16, pt. 2: 543–45.
15. Ibid., 877–78.
16. *ORN*, ser. 1, vol. 23, 700, 704.
17. Ross A. Webb, "A Yankee from Dixie," *Civil War History* (Mar. 1964): 89–90.
18. J. B. Cochran to Ben Finnell, Sept. 15, 1862, File 860–64, Civil War Guerrilla correspondence, KAG.
19. McDonough, *War in Kentucky*, chaps. 4, 5; Connelly, *Army of the Heartland*, 214–17; Woodworth, *Davis and His Generals*, 140, 146; Maslowski, *Treason Must Be Made Odious*, 44–47; *ORA*, ser. 1, vol. 52, pt. 1: 451; vol. 16, pt. 1: 906–52; Berlin, et al., *Wartime Genesis of Free Labor*, 387–89, 405–8.
20. Maslowski, *Treason Must Be Made Odious*, 46, citing Tyler Dennett, *Lincoln and the Civil War Diaries and Letters of John Hay* (New York: 1939), 176–77; Ira S. Owens, *Green County Soldiers in the Late War* (Dayton, 1884), 22; *ORA*, ser. 1, vol. 16, pt. 2: 451, 461, 490, and pt. 1: 697–98.
21. Graf and Haskins, *Papers of Andrew Johnson*, 6: 4–6.
22. Lovett, "Nashville's Fort Negley," 7–8; Leland R. Johnson, "Civil War Railroad Defenses in Tennessee," *The Tennessee Valley Historical Review* (Summer 1972): 22; also Berlin, et al., *Wartime Genesis of Free Labor*, 370, 389–94.

23. *ORA*, ser. 1, vol. 16, pt. 2: 470–71, 515; see also pt. 1: 697–98, 713; on defending Washington, see the author's *Symbol, Sword, and Shield*, chap. 5.
24. *ORA*, ser. 1, vol. 16, pt. 2: 476–77, 500.
25. James W. Daniels diary, Sept. 11, 1862, 13, IHSL; *ORA*, ser. 1, vol. 17, pt. 2: 194, 197; Simon, *Papers of Ulysses Grant*, 6: 7n., 11–12n., 18–19, 33.
26. Bergun H. Brown to "Folks at Home," Sept. 7, 23, 1862, IHSL.
27. *ORA*, ser. 1, vol. 16, pt. 2: 515, also 511–12, 516, 524, 563; see also Durham, *Occupied City*, 118–21.
28. Bergun Brown to "Folks at Home," Sept. 5, Oct. 28, 1862, IHSL.
29. Graf and Haskins, *Papers of Andrew Johnson*, 6: 10–13.
30. Ibid., 6: 6–9, 14–23.
31. Entries of Oct. 4, 1862, in June I. Gow, "The Johnston and Brent Diaries," *Civil War History* (Mar. 1968): 49; Johnson, *Partisan Rangers*, 125; Connelly, *Army of the Heartland*, 228–33; McDonough, *War in Kentucky*, chap. 6; *ORA*, ser. 1, vol. 16, pt. 2: 525, 527, 530, 531, 816.
32. Alva C. Griest diary, Aug. 31–Sept. 29, 1862, (typescript, 6–12); Alanson P. Rynam to Jane, Sept. 11, 1862, 12, 13, both IHSL; Robert W. Williams Jr. and Ralph A. Wooster, eds., "With Terry's Texas Rangers," *Civil War History* (Sept. 1963): 309; for strength figures, see Hewitt, "Bragg and the Confederate Invasion," 71n. 41.
33. *ORA*, ser. 1, vol. 52, pt. 1: 479–80.
34. Ibid., 451–52.
35. Jesse B. Connelly diary, Sept. 27, 1862, vol. 1: 55–56; William B. Miller diary, Oct. 5, 7, 1862 (typescript, 20); both IHSL.
36. Griest diary, Sept. 26, 1862, entry, 12; Miller diary, Oct. 5, 7, 1862, 20; Connelly diary, Sept. 27, 1862, vol. 1, 55–56, all IHSL; Grebner, *We Were the Ninth*, 136.
37. *ORA*, ser. 1, vol. 16, pt. 2: 538–39, 546, 549; see also 421, 530; James H. Jones to parents, Sept. 26, 1862, IHSL.
38. *ORA*, ser. 1, vol. 16, pt. 2: 554–55, 557–58; 564, 657; see also Williams, *Lincoln Finds a General*, 4: 119–26.
39. Carpenter to parents, Oct. 5, 1862, quoted in Bright, "Yankees in Arms," 202–3; Miller diary, Oct. 7, 1862, 20, IHSL.
40. McDonough, *War in Kentucky*, chaps. 7, 8, 9; Hafendorfer, *Perryville*, pt. 2; Hewitt, "Bragg and the Confederate Invasion," 66–72n. 45; Grady McWhiney, "Controversy in Kentucky," *Civil War History* (Mar. 1960): 41.
41. *ORA*, ser. 1, vol. 16, pt. 2: 846, 876; Seitz, *Braxton Bragg*, 206–7; Connelly, *Army of the Heartland*, 275; Woodworth, *Davis and His Generals*, 156–59; McDonough, *War in Kentucky*, 308–10.
42. Johnson, *Partisan Rangers*, 118–20, 130; Basil Duke, *Morgan's Cavalry* (Cincinnati, 1867), 292; Webb, "A Yankee from Dixie," 90.
43. McWhiney, "Controversy in Kentucky," 42.
44. *ORA*, ser. 1, vol. 16, pt. 2: 634, also 619, 642; Griest diary, Oct. 7–31, 1862, 15–23; Alanson P. Rynam to Jane, Sept. 27, 1862; Daniels diary, Sept. 17, 23, 24, Oct. 10, all 1862, 12–14, all IHSL.
45. *ORA*, ser. 1, vol. 20, pt. 2: 8, 14; Porter, "War Record," 45–50, especially 49, WKL; Duke, *Morgan's Cavalry*, 292; Charles Mayfield Meacham, *A History of Christian County, Kentucky* (Nashville, 1930), 98–99; Warner, *Generals in Blue*, 40; Hewitt, "Bragg and the Confederate Invasion," 67.
46. Johnson, *Partisan Rangers*, 126–32; S. K. Haycroft journal, entries Oct. 18, 20, 27, 1862 (typescript, 27), FCL; *ORA*, ser. 1, vol. 17, pt. 2: 310, also 303–4, 309; Warner, *Generals in Blue*, 113–14, 389–90.
47. Daniel A. Brooks to John W. Finnell, Oct. 30, 1862, File 860–64, Civil War Guerrilla Correspondence, KAG.
48. *ORA*, ser. 1, vol. 20, pt. 2: 67–68; vol. 16, pt. 2: 646, 652–53.
49. Ibid., 80–83, 101–2.
50. Connelly diary, Oct. 1862, 58–61; Alfred Shields to mother, Oct. 31, 1862, both IHSL; Sunderland, *Five Days To Glory*, 65.
51. Grebner, *We Were the Ninth*, 116; Connelly diary, Oct. 1862, 60.
52. *ORA*, ser. 1, vol. 16, pt. 2: 657, also 619–22, 626–27, 635–38, 640–42, 646–47; vol. 17, pt. 2: 286–87, 307; Carpenter to parents, Oct. 20, 1862, in Bright, "Yankees in Arms," 202–3; Grimsley, "A Directed Severity," 307–9, see also 36–40; Webb, "A Yankee from Dixie," 90.
53. *ORA*, ser. 1, vol. 16, pt. 1: 632–37, also 7–22; Williams, *Lincoln Finds a General*, 4: 143.
54. *ORA*, ser. 1, vol. 16, pt. 1: 632–33.

55. Ibid., 632–35, 636, 639.
56. Ibid., 628–29.
57. Graf and Haskins, *Papers of Andrew Johnson*, 6: 5; see also James Chumney, "Don Carlos Buell: Gentleman Soldier," (Ph.D. diss., Rice Univ., 1964), 131–32, 201.
58. *ORN*, ser. 1, vol. 23: 705.
59. Cartwright quoted in Hale, *The Third Texas Cavalry*, 136, as well as chap. 8; Tucker, *The South's Finest*, chap. 7; *ORA*, ser. 1, vol. 17, pt. 2: 735.
60. Hewitt, "Bragg and the Confederate Invasion," 67–68, quoting Sarah Ridley Trimble, ed., "Behind the Lines in Middle Tennessee, 1863–1865: The Journal of Bettie Ridley Blackmore," *Tennessee Historical Quarterly* 12 (1953): 54; also cited in Grady McWhiney, *Braxton Bragg and Confederate Defeat* (New York, 1969), 1: 53.
61. McDonough, *War in Kentucky*, 321.
62. Compare ibid., chap. 11; McWhiney, *Bragg and Confederate Defeat*, 272–98; Connelly, *Army of the Heartland*, 204–9, 217, 221–46, 262; Stanley F. Horn, *The Army of Tennessee* (Norman, 1941), 170–72; T. Harry Williams, "The Military Leadership of North and South," in *Why the North Won the Civil War*, ed. David Donald (Baton Rouge, 1960), 42.
63. Grebner, *We Were the Ninth*, 117.
64. Berlin, et al., *Destruction of Slavery*, 499–500, 528–46.
65. Ibid., 546–48, 550–64.

SIX. DECISION IN MIDDLE TENNESSEE

1. *ORA*, ser. 1., vol. 16, pt. 2: 636–37, 640–41; vol. 20, pt. 2: 653.
2. Ibid., vol. 16, pt. 2: 760.
3. Ibid., 836–37, also 783, 785, 840, 847, 868–69, 872; on Jones, see Ezra Warner, *Generals in Gray* (Baton Rouge, 1959), 165–66.
4. *ORA*, ser. 1, vol. 16, pt. 2: 867–77, also 856–57, 858, 862, 863; Jordan and Pryor, *Campaigns of Forrest*, 186–87; Wyeth, *That Devil Forrest*, 88–89; Isaac Dunbar Affleck to mother and father, Nov. 1, 1862, in Williams and Wooster, "With Terry's Texas Rangers," 309.
5. *ORA*, ser. 1, vol. 16, pt. 2: 916; see also 907–9.
6. Ibid., pt. 1: 1020–21; pt. 2: 918, 919, 929, 930, 935, 937; Jordan and Pryor, *Campaigns of Forrest*, 187–89; Warner, *Generals in Gray*, 10–11.
7. Bergun H. Brown to "Dear Folks at Home," Oct. 28, Nov. 10, 1862, IHSL.
8. Ibid.; Durham, *Occupied City*, chap. 7.
9. *ORA*, ser. 1, vol. 16, pt. 2: 981–82; see also 937–38, 944–46, 953–58, 967–68, 970–71, 977.
10. Fisher, "The Leniency Shown Them," 285–88; *ORA*, ser. 1, vol. 16, pt. 2: 851.
11. Fisher, "The Leniency Shown Them," 289–90.
12. *ORA*, ser. 1, vol. 16, pt. 2: 980–81, 1003; vol. 20, pt. 2: 25–26; Durham, *Occupied City*, 126–27; Jordan and Pryor, *Campaigns of Forrest*, 188–92; Henry, *First with the Most Forrest*, 106–7.
13. *ORA*, ser. 1, vol. 20, pt. 2: 388, pt. 1: 3–7.
14. Ibid., pt. 2: 5–7; pt. 2: 11, 12, 17, 18, 20, 21, 23; see also Louise Davis, "Box Seat on the Civil War: Rachel Carter's Diary," *The Tennessean Magazine* (Apr. 1979): 6–11; and also Lovett, "Nashville's Fort Negley," 9–10; Berlin, et al., *Wartime Genesis of Free Labor*, 370–71.
15. *ORA*, ser. 1, vol. 20, pt. 2: 25–26; Jordan and Pryor, *Campaigns of Forrest*, 191n.; Brian Steel Wills, *A Battle from the Start* (New York, 1992), 84.
16. *ORA*, ser, 1, vol. 20, pt. 1: 6; Ramage, *Rebel Raider*, 127.
17. *ORA*, ser. 1, vol. 20, pt. 2: 26.
18. Woodworth, *Jefferson Davis and His Generals*, chap. 10.
19. *ORA*, ser. 1, vol. 20, pt. 2: 400, also 389–99, 404, 406–7, 416.
20. Ibid., 412, 418, 420–22, 426–27; vol. 17, pt. 2: 743.
21. Ibid., vol. 20, pt. 2: 416–17, 412.
22. Ibid., 433, also 421–23.
23. Ibid., 415, 422; vol. 17, pt. 2: 755.
24. Ibid., vol. 20, pt. 2; for events in Mississippi at this point, see vol. 17, pt. 2: 758–61, 780, 783–85, 788–92.

Hudson Strode, *Jefferson Davis: Confederate President* (New York, 1959), 342; also McDonough, *Stones River*, 36–37; 46–47; Peter Cozzens, *No Better Place to Die* (Urbana, 1990), 38–45.

25. Ibid., vol. 20, pt. 2: 446–47, also 179; Grainger quoted in McDonough, *Stones River*, 50.
26. Bergun H. Brown to "Dear Folks," Nov. 10, and Amos C. Weaver to Father and Mother, Nov. 14, both 1862, both IHSL; *ORA*, ser. 1, vol. 20, pt. 2: 20–25, 73, 435–36, 440–41, 446–47, 448–49, 453, 459–60; 462–63; Woodworth, *Davis and His Generals*, 182–84.
27. *ORA*, ser. 1, vol. 20, pt. 2: 5, 6, 17, 19–21, 38, 41, 49–50, 50–51, 59, also pt. 1: 9, 14–20, 22–24, 73–85; Van Horne, *History of the Army of the Cumberland*, 1: 207–13.
28. *ORA*, ser. 1, vol. 20, pt. 2: 16, 30, 62–64.
29. Ibid., 65, 73–76, 79.
30. Ibid., 95–96, also 51, 92.
31. Ibid., 76–77, 136; *ORN*, ser. 1, vol. 23: 311, 459, 461–64.
32. Louisville *Weekly Journal*, Nov. 11, 1862 (column dated Nov. 5, 1862).
33. Troutman, *The Heavens Are Weeping*, 136, 138, 139.
34. Mitchel A. Thompson to wife, Nov. 12, 1862, in Henderson, Young, and Naheloffer, *Dear Eliza*, 14–15; see also Thomas Baugh to wife, Nov. 6, 1862, TSLA.
35. Stephen McBide to wife, Nov. 24, 1862, author's files.
36. *ORA*, ser. 1, vol. 17, pt. 1: 463–64; Gildrie, "Guerrilla Warfare," 167.
37. John Nick Barker diary, Dec. 9, 20, 22, 1862, Sarah Kennedy to Husband, Dec. 6, 1862, both TSLA; *ORA*, ser. 1, vol. 20, pt. 2: 51, 53, 90, 99–100, 102–3, 113–14, 126, 127; and vol. 52, pt. 1: 306.
38. *ORA*, ser. 1, vol. 20, pt. 1: 9–40.
39. Graf and Haskins, *Papers of Andrew Johnson*, 6: 97; *ORA*, ser. 1, vol. 20, pt. 2: 113, 116, 120, 125–26, 132–33, 143.
40. *ORA*, ser. 1, vol. 20, pt. 2: 62, 64, 126, 143, 146, 149, 150–51, 155, 165, 187–88.
41. Sara Kennedy to husband, Dec. 6, 11, 23, 29, 1862; Barker diary Dec. 9, 1862, both TSLA; *ORA*, ser. 1, vol. 20, pt. 2: 99, 100, 102–3, 108, 114, 125, 126, 149, 152, 164, 165, 175, 187–88, 194, 197–98, 209.
42. *ORA*, ser. 1, vol. 20, pt. 1: 40–72; pt. 2: 140, 144.
43. Richard Bean, "Recollections of the Battle of Hartsville," 2, FCL; Ramage, *Rebel Raider*, 128–33; Christopher Losson, *Tennessee's Forgotten Warriors* (Knoxville, 1989), 77–79; Walter T. Durham, *Rebellion Revisited* (Nashville, 1982), 117–34; *ORA*, ser. 1, vol. 20, pt. 2:132–33, 136–37, 140; see also "Only a Guidepost of Quirk's Scouts; 'Forty Years Ago Hartsville,' 'Hartsville,' and the 'Christmas Raid,' 1862, General John H. Morgan's Division Kentucky Cavalry," all in Unit File, Quirk's Company, Morgan Scouts, KAG.
44. "Quirk's Scouts," KAG; *ORA*, ser. 1, vol. 20, pt. 1: 40–72, also 9, 14–20, 22–34, 73–85.
45. Ramage, *Rebel Raider*, 133; Williams, *Lincoln Finds a General*, 4: 245–47.
46. Johnson, *Partisan Rangers*, 132–36; Ramage, *Rebel Raider*, chap. 12; "Quirk's Scouts," KAG.
47. Johnson, *Partisan Rangers*, 134; *ORA*, ser. 1, vol. 20, pt. 2: 208–9; ser. 3, vol. 2: 956.
48. *ORA*, ser. 1, v. 20, pt. 2: 272–90.
49. Ibid., vol. 17, pt. 1: 546–99; pt. 2: 389–523, among others; *ORN*, ser. 1, vol. 23: 626–28.
50. Lonnie E. Maness, "Forrest and the Battle of Parker's Crossroads," *Tennessee Historical Quarterly* (Summer 1975): 154.
51. *ORN*, ser. 1, vol. 23: 626–29; see also 311; "Napier's Battalion," 1; and H. L. Huggins to Leroy M. Nutt, Sept. 15, 1866, both SHC/UNC.
52. *ORA*, ser. 1, vol. 17, pt. 1: 61–62, 72, 326–27, 331–32, 336, 405, 410, 445, 451, 465, 490, 505–6.
53. Ibid., pt. 2: 866; see also 321, 335–36, 365–66, 367–77, 380–81, 404–5, 411, 422, 497, 863–65; *ORN*, ser. 1, vol. 23: 627; Graf and Haskins, *Papers of Andrew Johnson*, 6: 51; see also 50, 77.
54. *ORA*, ser. 1, vol. 17, pt. 1: 797–98; pt. 2: 365–66.
55. Ibid., pt. 2: 421–22, 424, 506; *ORN*, ser. 1, vol. 23: 628–32.
56. Ibid., 337, 425–31, 525–27.
57. *ORA*, vol. 17, pt. 1: 592–97; pt. 2: 425–27, 435–36, 441–42, 447, 453–55, 457, 460, 462–63, 493–94; Wyeth, *That Devil Forrest*, 95–97; Bennett H. Young, *Confederate Wizards of the Saddle* (Boston, 1914), chap. 6; *ORN*, ser. 1, vol. 23: 631–32.
58. Krug, *Mrs. Hill's Journal*, 127–43.
59. Huggins to Nutt, Sept. 15, 1866, SHC/UNC.
60. *ORA*, ser. 1, vol. 17, pt. 2: 508–16, also 462–63, 465, 467–68, 469–71, 809; Simon, *Papers of Ulysses S. Grant*, 7: 104, 106–7n.

61. *ORA*, ser. 1, vol. 20, pt. 2: 258; see also vol. 17, pt. 2: 477–79, 481–88, 492–99, 500–9, 880–82; *ORN*, ser. 1, vol. 23: 652–58, 659–64.
62. Huggins to Nutt, Sept. 15, 1862, SHC/UNC; Marshall to sister, Dec. 15, 1866, DUL.
63. *ORA*, ser. 1, vol. 17, pt. 2: 486, 494, 504–5.
64. *ORA*, ser. 1, vol. 17, pt. 1: 546–99; Maness, "Parker's Crossroads," 159–69; "Napier's Battalion," Nutt Papers, SHC/UNC; Wyeth, *That Devil Forrest*, chap. 6; Andrew Nelson Lytle, *Bedford Forrest* (New York, 1931), chap. 9; Jordan and Pryor, *Campaigns of Forrest*, chap. 7; Henry, *First with the Most Forrest*, 116–20.
65. *ORA*, ser. 1, vol. 17: 709; for a succinct statement on the Holly Springs episode, see Hale, *The Third Texas Cavalry*, chap. 9.
66. Jesse Cox diary, Jan. 1, 1863, TSLA; *ORA*, ser. 1, vol. 17, pt. 1: 159, 465–524; pt. 2: 444–46, 448–51, 484–85; Maness, "Parker's Crossroads," 166–67.
67. Graf and Haskins, *Papers of Andrew Johnson*, 6: 92–93, 112–13, 121, 136n., 137, 167n.; Patton, *Unionism and Reconstruction*, 34; Robert H. White, ed., *Messages of the Governors of Tennessee, 1857–1869* (Nashville, 1952–1967), 5: 377.
68. Grant, *Personal Memoirs*, 1: 435; Grimsley, *Hard Hand of War*, 101.
69. Marshall to sister, Nov. 14, Dec. 15, both 1862, DUL; Alva C. Griest diary, Dec. 7, 8, 1862, 34–35, IHSL; *ORA*, ser. 1, vol. 20, pt. 2: 124.
70. Griest diary, Dec. 3, 7, 8, 1862, 34–35; Miller diary, Dec. 6, 7, 1862, 35–37; James Jones to brothers and sisters, Nov. 23, Dec. 6, 12, 16, 20, all 1862; John A. Berger to parents, Dec. 12, 1862; Arthur J. Gates diary, Dec. 24–30, 1862; Mrs. John Lewis Ketcham to Eddie, also Ketcham to William and Frank, both Dec. 23, 1862; James F. Fee to brother, Dec. 10, 1862, all IHSL.
71. Marshall to sister, Dec. 15, 1862, DUL; Griest diary, Nov. 30, 1862; Bergun Brown to George O. Nevins, Dec. 18, 1862, both IHSL.
72. Sunderland, *Five Days to Glory*, 69–71; Grebner, *We Were the Ninth*, 118–19.
73. *ORA*, ser. 1, vol. 20, pt. 2: 108–9, 121–22, 141–43, 152, 154–55, 158–59, 162, 163–64, 173–74, 180–81, 187, 209.
74. Ibid., 309.
75. Griest diary, Dec. 24, 25, 1862, IHSL.
76. *ORA*, ser. 1, vol. 20, pt. 2: 123–24, also 115, 117–18, 141, 179–80; Williams, *Lincoln Finds a General*, 4: chap. 8.
77. For the most recent accounts of the battle, see Cozzens, *No Better Place to Die*, and McDonough, *Stones River*; see also Williams and Wooster, "With Terry's Texas Rangers," 311–15.
78. Grebner, *We Were the Ninth*, 120; John F. Beatty, *Memoirs of a Volunteer*, ed. Henry S. Ford (New York, 1946), 150; *ORA*, ser. 1, vol. 17, pt. 2: 375.
79. *ORA*, ser. 3, vol. 2: 956; ser. 1, vol. 17, pt. 2: 375.

SEVEN. REBELS RETURN TO FORT DONELSON

1. Garrett, ed., Campbell diary, Dec. 31, 1862, TSLA.
2. Dunbar Affleck to Mother and Father, Jan. 7, 1863, in Williams and Wooster, "With Terry's Texas Rangers," 313.
3. Troutman, *The Heavens Are Weeping*, 143, 144, 146; Harriet Ellen Moore (Mrs. Thomas Porter Weakley) diary, Jan. 5, 6, 7, 1863, SHC/UNC; on post–Stones River activities, see McDonough, *Stones River*, chaps. 12 and 13, especially 210–11, as well as Cozzens, *No Better Place to Die*, chaps. 15 and 16.
4. S. K. Haycroft journal, Jan. 9, 15, Feb. [?], 1863, FCL; Troutman, *The Heavens Are Weeping*, 144–47.
5. Troutman, *The Heavens Are Weeping*, 144–47.
6. *ORA*, ser. 1, vol. 17, pt. 2: 332–34, 849–53.
7. Ibid., vol. 20, pt. 2: 317.
8. See Daniel, "Special Warfare," 140, and chap. 6.
9. *ORA*, ser. 1, vol. 17, pt. 2: 858–59.
10. Ibid., 287–88, 860.
11. Kirkhead, *History of Kentucky*, 196; *ORA*, ser. 1, vol. 17, pt. 2: 351–52.
12. Moore (Weakley) diary, Jan. 1, 1863, SHC/UNC.
13. William Henry King memoirs, 31–32, TSLA; Van Horne, *History of the Army of the Cumberland*, 1: 287–88.
14. Grebner, *We Were the Ninth*, 120–22.

15. Van Horne, *History of the Army of the Cumberland*, 1: 288; *ORA*, Atlas, plate 112, number 3; Lenard Brown, "Fortress Rosecrans," *Tennessee Historical Quarterly* (Fall 1990): 136–38.
16. Marshall P. Thatcher, *A Hundred Battles in the West* (Detroit, 1884), 113–22.
17. *ORA*, ser. 1, vol. 23, pt. 1: 6–30; Moore (Weakley) diary, Jan. 18, 1863, SHC/UNC.
18. *ORA*, ser. 1, vol. 24, pt. 3: 8, 20–23; 30–33.
19. Simon, *Papers of Ulysses S. Grant*, 7: 157, 158–59, 160n., 165–66, 167–69, 170, 173, 183, 190–94, 213–14, 251, 514–16n., 519–21; Martha Mitchell Bigelow, "Freedmen of the Mississippi Valley, 1862–1865," *Civil War History* (Mar. 1962): 39–40; Cam Walker, "Corinth: The Story of a Contraband Camp," *Civil War History* (Mar. 1974): 5–7; Cimprich, *Slavery's End in Tennessee*, 49.
20. Simon, *Papers of Ulysses S. Grant*, 7: 236–37, 251–52, 272–73n.
21. Blanchard, *I Marched with Sherman*, 78; Simon, *Papers of Ulysses S. Grant*, 7: 193–94n., 213, 251–52.
22. *ORA*, ser. 1, vol. 23, pt. 1: 7–8; Kincaid Herr, *The Louisville and Nashville Railroad* (Louisville, 1964), 38.
23. *ORN*, ser. 1, vol. 24: 10–11; *ORA*, ser. 1, vol. 17, pt. 2: 541, 543, 544; vol. 23, pt. 2: 3–5.
24. *ORA*, ser. 1, vol. 23, pt. 2: 3–23; *ORN*, ser. 1, vol. 24: 3–24.
25. *ORA*, ser. 1, vol. 23, pt. 2: 23; *ORN*, ser. 1, vol. 24: 18.
26. *ORA*, ser. 1, vol. 23, pt. 2: 9–12, 43.
27. Ibid., 17–18, 20–21, 22–31, 33–34, 62–63.
28. Ibid., 23.
29. Ibid., vol. 23, pt. 2: 7–14, 15, 31, 33, 34, 37–38.
30. Eugene Marshall to sister, Jan. 22, 1863, DUL.
31. Marshall diary, Jan. 1–6, 16, 17, Feb. 1, all 1863, DUL; Mitchel A. Thompson to Eliza, Dec. 5, 1862, Jan. 12, 17, 1863, in Henderson, Young, and Naheloffer, *Dear Eliza*, 17–21.
32. Hughes and Stonesifer, *Life and Wars of Pillow*, 259–63; Woodworth, *Jefferson Davis and His Generals*, 196–99; Craig Symonds, *Joseph E. Johnston* (New York, 1992), 192–96.
33. *ORA*, ser. 1., vol. 20, pt. 1: 979–84; vol. 23, pt. 2: 52–53; Joseph G. Vale, *Minty and the Cavalry* (Harrisburg, 1886), 124; Plum, *The Military Telegraph*, 93.
34. William W. Howard to wife, Feb. 5, 1863, UTL; Holmes, *Fifty-Second Ohio Volunteer Infantry*, 93–95; "Gen. W. B. Wade's Military Achievements," *Confederate Veteran* (Jan. 1906): 17; *ORN*, ser. 1, vol. 24: 19–20, 81.
35. William W. Howard to wife, Feb. 5, 1863, UTL; John B. Lindsley, *Military Annals of Tennessee* (Nashville, 1886), 716–21; *ORA*, ser. 1, vol. 20, pt. 2: 488–89.
36. *ORA*, ser. 1, vol. 20, pt. 2: 275, 289, 315, 344; vol. 23, pt. 2: 15–16; Nick Barker diary, Jan. 1, 1863, TSLA.
37. *ORA*, ser. 1, vol. 23, pt. 2: 16, 20, 24, 35, 38–39; Joseph H. Vanmeter to father and mother, Jan. 24, 1863, IHSL; Ralsa C. Rice, *Yankee Tigers* (Huntington, W.Va., 1992), 35; *ORN*, ser. 1, vol. 23: 15–25.
38. *ORA*, ser. 1, vol. 23, pt. 1: 34–35; Rice, *Yankee Tigers*, 36; Stephen T. McBide to wife, Nov. 24, 1862, author's files; and for a useful recent account of the pivotal battle of Dover, see Terry Wilson, "Against Such Powerful Odds," *Tennessee Historical Quarterly* (Winter 1994): 261–71.
39. Wayne C. Temple, ed., "Fort Donelson in October 1862," *Lincoln Herald* (Summer 1967): 92–96; Dyer, *Compendium of the War*, 3: 1040, 1082, 1162, 1530.
40. Robert McConnell to "Dear Wife and Children," Nov. 24, Dec. 3, 13, all 1862, Jan. 13, 26, 1863, Toops, *McConnell Letters*, 25, 27, 29, 33, 36–37; William H. Dorris to wife, Jan. 14, 26, Feb. 20, all 1863, copies, author's files.
41. Thomas J. Baugh to wife, Jan. 30, 1863, TSLA; Thompson to wife, Sept. 10, 29, Oct. 14, Nov. 12, Dec. 3, all 1862, also Jan. 12, 17, 1863, Henderson, Young, and Naheloffer, *Dear Eliza*, 7–12.
42. Thompson to wife, Sept. 10, 29, 1862, Jan. 12, 17 1863, Henderson, Young, and Naheloffer, *Dear Eliza*, 10–11, 18–19; Joseph A. Latimer to family, Aug. 31; Latimer to father and sisters, Nov. 1, 1862, USAMHI; Thomas M. Eddy, *The Patriotism of Illinois* (Chicago, 1866), 2: 331; Dyer, *Compendium of the War*, 3: 1882.
43. Victor M. Harding to author, May 5, June 17, both 1981, and accompanying biographical information on Harding, author's files.
44. *ORA*, ser. 1, vol. 23, pt. 1: 31–41; pt. 2: 33, 35–36, 37, 38–40; Marshall diary, Feb. 5, 1863, DUL; Charles Alley diary, Feb. 3, 1863, TSLA; Thompson to Eliza, Feb. 4, 1863, in Henderson, Young, and Naheloffer, *Dear Eliza*, 22–23; Plum, *The Military Telegraph*, 52.
45. Jordan and Pryor, *Campaigns of Forrest*, 224, 225; Henry, *First with the Most Forrest*, 123; see also Zeboim Patten diary, Feb. 4, 1863, TSLA.
46. Jordan and Pryor, *Campaigns of Forrest*, 225–26; Wyeth, *That Devil Forrest*, 129n.; R. A. McClellan to father, Feb. 9, 1863, McClellan Papers, DUL.

47. *ORA*, ser. 1, vol. 23, pt. 1: 35, 40.
48. Jordan and Pryor, *Campaigns of Forrest*, 226–27; *ORN*, ser. 1, vol. 24: 25; John B. Whitcomb to Silas C. Whitcomb, June 26, 1863, Fort Donelson National Military Park, Dover, Tenn. (hereafter abbreviated as FDNMP).
49. *ORA*, ser. 1, vol. 23, pt. 1: 39; John A. Hoener diary, Feb. 3, 1863, David A. Fateley diary, Feb. 4, 5, 1863, (typescript pages 33, 34), both IHSL; John B. Whitcomb to Silas C. Whitcomb, June 26, 1863, FDNMP.
50. Robert McConnell to wife and children, Feb. 8, 1863, Toops, *McConnell Letters*, 40; Patten diary, Feb. 4, 1863, TSLA; Wyeth, *That Devil Forrest*, 129; Jordan and Pryor, *Campaigns of Forrest*, 227; Rice, *Yankee Tigers*, 38–39.
51. *ORA*, ser. 1, vol. 23, pt. 1: 40; see also 36–37; Jordan and Pryor, *Campaigns of Forrest*, 228; Marshall diary, Feb. 5, 1863, DUL; Victor M. Harding to author, author's files.
52. McClellan to Father, Feb. 9, 1863, DUL; John Edgerly to Friend Clark, Feb. 9, 1863, excerpt, *Sword and Sabre Catalog* (Gettysburg, Pa., 1991); Whitcomb to Whitcomb, June 26, 1863, FDNMP; *ORA*, ser. 1, vol. 23, pt. 1: 38; see also Wills, *Battle from the Start*, 97–102.
53. *ORN*, ser. 1, vol. 24: 25–28, 46, 57, 239; Edward F. Keuchel and James P. Jones, "Charley Schreel's Book: Diary of a Union Soldier on Garrison Duty in Tennessee," *Tennessee Historical Quarterly* (Summer 1977): 201–2; Lyon, *Reminiscences of the Civil War*, 77–81.
54. B. F. Batchelor to father, Feb. 20, 1862, in Rugeley, *Batchelor-Turner Letters*, 46–47; *ORN*, ser. 1, vol. 24: 28.
55. *ORA*, ser. 1, vol. 23, pt. 1: 32–34; vol. 24, pt. 3: 26.
56. Marshall diary, Feb. 5, 1862, DUL.
57. *ORA*, ser. 1, vol. 23, pt. 1: 33, 38–39, 41; Wyeth, *That Devil Forrest*, 33; Jordan and Pryor, *Campaigns of Forrest*, 129; Fateley diary, Feb. 5, 1863 (typescript, 34), Hoerner diary, memoranda pages, both IHSL; Charles Alley diary, Feb. 3, 1863 (typescript, 15), TSLA; Edgerly to "Friend Chank," Feb. 9, 1863, copy, author's files.
58. *ORN*, ser. 1, vol. 24: 46; McConnell to wife and children, Feb. 8, 1863, in Toops, *McConnell Letters*, 39; Rugeley, *Batchelor–Turner Letters*, 46; Lindsley, *Military Annals*, 717; Edgerly to Friend Chank Feb. 9, 1863, author's files; Charles E. Cort to Dear Friends, Feb. 9, 1863, Helga Tomlinson, comp. and ed., "*Dear Friends*": *The Civil War Letters and Diary of Charles Edwin Cort* (N.p., 1962), 51; Alley diary, Feb. 3, 14, 15, 1863, TSLA; Marshall diary, Feb. 5, 1863, DUL.
59. "The Veteran and the Boy," pamphlet, Garrett collection, TSLA; McClellan to father, Feb. 9, 1863, DUL; Rugeley, *Batchelor-Turner Letters*, 46; Lindsley, *Military Annals*, 717; Marshall diary, Feb. 5, 1863; "History of Napier's Battalion," n.d., 2, Leroy Moncure Nutt Papers, SHC/UNC.
60. *ORA*, ser. 1, vol. 23, pt. 1: 32.
61. Lindsley, *Military Annals*, 717; Henry, *First with the Most Forrest*, 126; Tennessee Civil War Centennial Commission, *Tennesseans in the Civil War* (Nashville, 1964), 1: 43–45; *ORA*, ser. 1, vol. 23, pt. 2: 630.
62. Toops, *McConnell Letters*, 39; Fateley diary, Feb. 4, 5, 1863 (typescript, 33, 34); IHSL; Marshall diary, Feb. 5, 1863, DUL; Patten diary, Feb. 4, 1863; Alley diary, 2: 15, both TSLA; David Coe, ed., *Mine Eyes Have Seen the Glory: Combat Diaries of Union Sergeant Hamlin Alexander Coe* (Rutherford, N.J., 1975), Feb. 4, 1863, 52, *ORN*, ser. 1, vol. 24: 27.
63. Rich, *Yankee Tigers*, 36–39; Marshall diary, Feb. 5, 1863, DUL; William W. Howard to wife, Feb. 5, 1863, UTL; Patten diary, Feb. 4, 1863, TSLA.
64. Regimental Historian, *Ninety-Second Illinois Volunteers* (Freeport, 1875), 68–69.
65. Charles T. Clark, *Opdycke Tigers, 125th O.V.I.* (Columbus, 1895), 25; Patten diary, Feb. 6, 7, 1863; TSLA.
66. Marshall diary, Feb. 5, 1863, DUL; Cort to "Dear Friends," Feb. 9, 1863, in Tomlinson, *Dear Friends*, 51.
67. Thompson to Eliza, Feb. 28, 1863, in Henderson, Young, and Naheloffer, *Dear Eliza*, 26.
68. Major Charles W. Anderson, quoted in Wyeth, *That Devil Forrest*, 131–32.
69. John P. Dyer, *From Shiloh to San Juan: The Life of "Fightin' Joe Wheeler* (Baton Rouge, 1941), 96–97n. 50.
70. Young and Naheloffer, *Dear Eliza*, 24, 50; *ORA*, ser. 1, vol. 24, pt. 3: 35; Vale, *Minty and the Cavalry*, 124.
71. Troutman, *The Heavens Are Weeping*, 147; Moore (Weakley) diary, Feb. 4, 1863, SHC/UNC.

EIGHT. HEARTLAND IMPASSE

1. *ORA*, ser. 3, vol. 3: 65–66; see also Fisher, "Prepare Them," 83–85; Berlin, et al., *Wartime Genesis of Free Labor*, 371–72.
2. Moore (Weakley) diary, Jan. 24, 27; Feb. 4, 6, 14, 23; Mar. 2, 11, 25, 26; Apr. 1, 2, all 1863, SHC/UNC; Sarah Kennedy to Husband, Feb. 2, 1863, TSLA; John Fitch, *Annals of the Army of the Cumberland* (Philadel-

phia, 1864), 564–74, especially 569–71, also Kay Baker Gaston, "A World Overturned," *Tennessee Historical Quarterly* (Winter 1991): 10–11.
3. In addition to Moore, see John Lindsley diary, Dec. 31, 1862, TSLA; Durham, *Occupied City*, chaps. 13, 14, and 16; Maslowski, *Treason Must Be Made Odious*, especially chap. 4.
4. Graf and Haskins, *Papers of Andrew Johnson*, 6: 132.
5. Troutman, *Heavens Are Weeping*, 148.
6. Graf and Haskins, *Papers of Andrew Johnson*, 6: 146–48.
7. Ibid., see 110, 111, 115–16, 121–23, 126–27, 131–32, 134–35, 138, 146–48, 166–68, 205–6n.
8. Ibid., 144–45; see also 123, 135–37.
9. Roy P. Basler, ed., *The Collected Works of Abraham Lincoln* (New Brunswick, N.J., 1953), 6: 149–50, and 187n.; Graf and Haskins, *Papers of Andrew Johnson*, 6: 198–99, 212–13, 218–19, 261–62, 270–71 and n.; on added authority granted in Sept., see *ORA*, ser. 3, vol. 3: 825–26.
10. *ORA*, ser. 3, vol. 3: 115, 122–23.
11. Ibid., 77–78; see also 57–60; William C. Harris, "Andrew Johnson's First 'Swing Around the Circle,'" *Civil War History* (June 1989): 167.
12. *ORA*, ser. 3, vol. 3: 217.
13. Ibid., 99; ser. 1, vol. 23, pt. 2: 105, 174, 191, 207, 208; Graf and Haskins, *Papers of Andrew Johnson*, 6: 205.
14. Graf and Haskins, *Papers of Andrew Johnson*, 6: 137–38; see also 145–46, 148–50, 174–75.
15. Ibid., 194–95; *ORA*, ser. 3, vol. 3: 103, 116, 249–50.
16. Graf and Haskins, *Papers of Andrew Johnson*, 6: 195; see also 175, 194, 198–99.
17. Ibid., 6: 209, 212–14, 216, 222–23, 228, 229–30, 233; Benedict R. Maryniak, "'Pretty Woman' circa 1861–1865," Newsletter of the Buffalo, New York, Civil War Round Table, Sept. 1993, author's files; James Boyd Jones, "A Tale of Two Cities," *Civil War History* (Sept. 1985): 271
18. *ORA*, ser. 1, vol. 23, pt. 1: 146; Graf and Haskins, *Papers of Andrew Johnson*, 6: 114.
19. *ORA*, ser. 1, vol. 23, pt. 2: 41–42; Amos C. Weaver to mother, Apr. 15, 1863, IHSL.
20. *ORA*, ser. 1, vol. 23, pt. 2: 28–29, 30, 93–94, 197–98.
21. Ibid., ser. 3, vol. 3: 196, 209, 229, 242–43, 419–20.
22. Ibid., ser. 1, vol. 23, pt. 2: 162–65; vol. 24, pt. 3: 81, 84–85; William H. Dorris to wife, Feb. 20, 1863, copy, author's files.
23. Dorris to wife, also Dorris to Tabitha, Feb. 20, Apr. 5, 10, all 1863, copy, author's files; Eugene Marshall diary, Feb. 11–Mar. 12, 1863, 18–66, 77, DUL; Henderson, Young, and Naheloffer, *Dear Eliza*, 26–27; Temple, "Fort Donelson in October, 1862," 93.
24. Marshall diary, Mar. 1, 4, 19, 1863, 46, 49, 79, DUL; *ORA*, ser. 1, vol. 22, pt. 2: 152, 153; vol. 23, pt. 2: 99–101, 150; vol. 24, pt. 3, 99.
25. *ORA*, ser. 1, vol. 24, pt. 3: 99; William H. Dorris to wife, Apr. 21, 22, 27, 1863, copies, author's files.
26. Toops, *McConnell Letters*, Feb. 9, 16, 24, Mar. 11, all 1863, 41–22; Henderson, Young, and Naheloffer, *Dear Eliza*, 22–33.
27. *ORA*, ser. 1, vol. 24, pt. 3: 89, 91, 93, 99, 100, 101; see also Whitesell, "Military Operations," 161–62.
28. *ORA*, ser. 1, vol. 22, pt. 2: 152; vol. 23, pt. 2: 150, 151; vol. 24, pt. 3: 93, 99, 100–102, 107–8, 129; William H. Dorris to wife, Apr. 5, 1863, copy, author's files.
29. *ORA*, ser. 1, vol. 23, pt. 2: 195; vol. 24, pt. 3: 74–75, 80, 83, 129, 153; *ORN*, ser. 1, vol. 24: 50–56; Simon, *Papers of Ulysses S. Grant*, 7: 306.
30. *ORA*, ser. 1, vol. 23, pt. 2: 80; vol. 24, pt. 3: 40–41; Hugh Bay to "Dear Companion," Feb. 19; Bay to wife, June 18, both 1863, IHSL.
31. Simon, *Papers of Ulysses S. Grant*, 7: 307–8n., 320n., 348, 349n., 362–64n.
32. Ibid., 371–72n.
33. Ibid., 370–71; *ORA*, ser. 1, vol. 23, pt. 1: 42, and pt. 2: 54–57.
34. *ORA*, ser. 1, vol. 23, pt. 2: 107–9.
35. Grimsley, *Hard Hand of War*, 145, 148–51; Francis Lieber, "Guerrilla Parties Considered with Reference to the Laws and Usages of War," in *ORA*, ser. 3, vol. 2: 301–9.
36. General Orders Number 100 appear in *ORA*, ser. 3, vol. 3: 148–64; Frank Freidel, "General Orders 100 and Military Government," *Mississippi Valley Historical Review* (Mar. 1946): especially 549; Richard S. Hartigan, *Lieber's Code* (Chicago, 1983), 1–26.
37. Hartigan, *Lieber's Code*, 21–23, 60; *ORA*, ser. 3, vol. 3: especially Section IV, Articles 81, 82 on 157.

38. *ORA*, ser. 1, vol. 23, pt. 2: 107–8, 162–64.
39. Simon, *Papers of Ulysses S. Grant*, 7: 401n.; *ORA*, ser. 1, vol. 24, pt. 3: 163.
40. Dunbar Affleck to Mother and Father, Mar. 5, 1863, Williams and Wooster, "With Terry's Texas Rangers," 317; *ORA*, ser. 1, vol. 23, pt. 2: 59, 622, 718, 749, 806, 829, 873, 920, 941.
41. Robert G. Athearn, ed., *Soldier in the West: The Civil War Letters of Alfred Lacey Hough* (Philadelphia, 1957), 87; Paul M. Angle, ed., *Three Years in the Army of the Cumberland* (Bloomington, 1959), 32–33.
42. *ORA*, ser. 1, vol. 23, pt. 2: 53, 57, 59, 68, 71–75, 85, 96, 100, 146–47.
43. *ORN*, ser. 1, vol. 24: 32–34, 42–43; see also vol. 23: 313–14; *ORA*, ser. 1, vol. 24, pt. 3: 101; Beatty, *Memoirs*, 166.
44. *ORA*, ser. 1, vol. 23, pt. I: 63–64.
45. *ORN*, ser. 1, vol. 23: 314–17; vol. 24: 40, 42, 44–45, 46, 57–58.
46. Ibid., vol. 23: 314; vol. 24: 58–60.
47. Ibid., vol. 24: 59–60.
48. Ibid., 63–64; see also vol. 23: 316.
49. Ibid., vol. 24: 74–75; see also 64, 66–68.
50. Ibid., 69–76, 78, 81, 89–90, 668.
51. William Howard to wife, Apr. 6, 1862 [insert to Apr. 5], UTL.
52. Howard to wife, May 6, 18, June 5, all 1863, all UTL.
53. *ORN*, ser. 1, vol. 24: 544–45, also 66–68, 81–87, 636–37.
54. Ibid., 178, 322, 324–25, 544–45.
55. Ibid., 668–70.
56. Ibid., 656–67.
57. *ORA*, ser. 1, vol. 23, pt. 2: 647–49; see also 625–26; on Bragg and his general situation, see Horn, *Army of Tennessee*, 222–23; Connelly, *Autumn of Glory*, 69–92; Symonds, *Joseph E. Johnston*, 189; Hale, *Third Texas Cavalry*, 163.
58. Beatty, *Memoirs*, 166.
59. *ORN*, ser. 1, vol. 23: 318; vol. 24: 56–65, 83–88.
60. *ORA*, ser. 1, vol. 23, pt. 2: 117–19.
61. Ibid., 144–47.

NINE. HEARTLAND DYNAMICS

1. Griest diary, Jan. 30, 1863, 50; Alanson R. Rynam to Jane, Mar. 1, 15, 24, all 1863, IHSL; Beatty, *Memoirs*, 182; G. H. Gates to friend, Feb. 10, 1863, author's files.
2. Rynam, Mar. 1, 24, 1863, IHSL.
3. Frederick Nathan Boyer diary, Feb. 2, 3, 9, 14, and Mar.–May, all 1863, 85, 86, 87, 89, 90–110, copy, author's files; Alfred C. Willett to "Dear Friend," Feb. 23, 1863, in Charles E. Willett, ed., *A Union Soldier Returns South* (Johnson City, Tenn., 1994), 21; Patten diary, Feb. 22, 1863, TSLA; Griest diary, Jan. 10, 1863, 45, IHSL; see also Ash, *When the Yankees Came*, chap. 3.
4. James H. Jones to Father and Mother, Apr. 1; see also Jan. 11, Feb. 6, all 1863, IHSL.
5. Grebner, *We Were the Ninth*, 121; William B. Miller diary, Mar. 18, 25, 26, 29, 31, Apr. 2, 11, 12, May 30, 70, 72–74, 76–77, 92; Rynam to Jane, May 4, all 1863; Griest diary, Jan. 12, 14, 1863, 46, both IHSL.
6. Rice, *Yankee Tigers*, 38; Hudson Alexander, "Trials and Tribulations of Fountain Branch Carter," *Blue and Gray* (Feb. 1995): 30–31.
7. Alexander, "Trials and Tribulations," 31, 33–34.
8. Rynam to Jane, Mar. 15, 1863, IHSL; Alexander, "Trials and Tribulations," 31, 33.
9. Grebner, *We Were the Ninth*, 125, 128, 136; Griest diary, Jan. 18, 20, 22, 23, 24, 28, Feb. 19, 20, 25, 1863, 47–50, 55–57, IHSL.
10. Sunderland, *Five Days To Glory*, 85–86; Frederick Nathan Boyer diary, Feb. 11, May 9, 11, 27, June 4, all 1863, 87, 98, 102, 104, author's files; Rynam to Jane, Mar. 15, 1863, IHSL.
11. Henry Vincent to "Dear Alice," May 5, 1863, excerpt, Number 185, Olde Soldier Books Catalog #47, (Feb. 1991), copy, author's files.
12. Moore (Weakley) diary, Feb. 23, 1863, SHC/UNC; Angle, *Three Years in the Army of the Cumberland*, 37–38; Harry J. Sievers, *Benjamin Harrison* (New York, 1952), chap. 10, especially 223–33; Rice, *Yankee Tigers*, 48.

13. Miller diary, Mar. 31, 1863, 73; Griest diary, Jan. 18, 25, Feb. 8, 22, Mar. 1, all 1863, 47, 49, 51, 53, 56, 57; Connelly diary, Apr. 13, 14, 15, 17, May 5, 7, all 1863, 77–79, 85–87; Arthur Gates diary, Feb. 1–21, 1863, all IHSL; Patten diary, Mar. 24, 1863, TSLA; Hale, *Third Texas Cavalry*, 170.
14. Rynam to Jane, Mar. 15, 1863; Joseph Vanmeter to "Dear Friends," Apr. 6, 1863, both IHSL; Sunderland, *Five Days to Glory*, 84–89.
15. Horn, *The Army of Tennessee*, 229, 459n.; Rynam to Jane, Mar. 24, 1863; Miller diary, Apr. 26, 1863, 81–82, both IHSL; Sunderland, *Five Days to Glory*, 91; Grebner, *We Were the Ninth*, 123; William H. Dorris to wife, Apr. 21, 22, 27, all 1863, copy, author's files; William Gilfillan Gavin, ed., *Infantryman Pettit* (Shippensburg, Pa., 1990), 80, 81, 83.
16. *ORA*, ser. 1, vol. 23, pt. 2: 67–68, 273.
17. Connelly diary, May 5, 1863, 85, IHSL; Grebner, *We Were the Ninth*, 124–25; Sunderland, *Five Days to Glory*, 88–90.
18. Moore (Weakley) diary, Apr. 22, 1863, SHC/UNC; William B. Gordon to daughter, July 22, 1863, and Jesse B. Cox diary, Feb. 10, Mar. 1, 3, 5, 15, 16, 23, 26, 29, Apr. 6, 10, 11, 12, 13, 14–17, 21–26, May 1, June 2, all 1863, both TSLA.
19. William H. King memoirs, 63–70 SHC/UNC; Cox diary, Apr. 6, 23, 1863, TSLA; Moore (Weakley) diary, Apr. 24, 1863, SHC/UNC.
20. Rynam to Jane, May 4, 1863; James Henry Jones to parents, Jan. 22, Feb. 6, Feb. 22, all 1863; Amos C. Weaver to parents, Mar. 6, 1863, all IHSL; Patten diary, Feb. 22, 1863, TSLA; Boyer diary, Jan. 30, 1863, 84, author's files.
21. W. W. Lyle, *Lights and Shadows* (Cincinnati, 1865), chaps. 18 and 19, especially 238; Worthington Davis, *Camp-fire Chats* (Hartford, 1887), 159–60; Williams and Wooster, "With Terry's Texas Rangers," 317; Griest diary, Mar. 4, 1863, 58, IHSL.
22. Williams and Wooster, "With Terry's Texas Rangers," 317; Campbell H. Brown, ed., *Reminiscences of Sergeant Newton Cannon* (Franklin, Tenn., 1963), 28; William C. Davis, *The Orphan Brigade* (Garden City, N.Y., 1980), 160–72; R. Lockwood Tower, ed., *A Carolinian Goes to War* (Columbia S.C., 1983), 72–73; Hale, *Third Texas Cavalry*, 169.
23. Willie Presley to Henrie, Mar. 11, 1863, author's files.
24. Isaac Alexander to sisters, Apr. 18; see also Alexander to brother, Feb. 26, both 1863, in John Alexander, "Letters of Isaac Alexander, 10th S.C., CSA," and Thomas B. Wilson, "Reminiscences," 52–53, 55–57, both SHC/UNC; Nathaniel C. Hughes, ed., *Liddell's Record* (Dayton, Ohio, 1985), 118–24.
25. Hale, *Third Texas Cavalry*, 169–70.
26. Ibid., 163.
27. Beatty, *Memoirs*, 166–67; see also 173–74, 189, 196; *ORA*, ser. 1, vol. 23, pt. 2: 333.
28. Griest diary, Jan. 22, 1863, 48, IHSL; Beatty, *Memoirs*, 187, 189; Athearn, *Soldier in the West*, 88–91.
29. Miller diary, Apr. 1, 5, 9, May 2, all 1863, 73, 75, 83; Connelly diary, May 7, 1863, 86; Amos C. Weaver to mother, Apr. 8, 15, all 1863, all IHSL; Grebner, *We Were the Ninth*, 123–24; Williams, *Lincoln Finds a General*, 5: chaps. 7, 9.
30. Howard, *Black Liberation in Kentucky*, 26–28, 38–40; Webb, "A Yankee from Dixie," 92; Berlin, et al., *Destruction of Slavery*, 570, 565–85.
31. Connelly diary, May 5, 1863, 85; James Henry Jones to father and mother, Jan. 22, 1863; Rynam to Jane, Mar. 25, 1863, all IHSL; John F. Jordan, "Triune in the Civil War," typescript, TSLA; Alfred C. Willett to "Dear Friend," Mar. 28, 1863, in Willett, *Union Soldier Returns South*, 22; see also *ORA*, ser. 1, vol. 23, pts. 1 and 2, among others; vol. 52, pt. 1: 338–40, 342–44, 360.
32. *ORA*, ser. 1, vol. 23, pt. 2: 337, 353–54.
33. Beatty, *Memoirs*, 167; Connelly diary, Apr. 13, 1863, 77, IHSL.
34. The numerous skirmishes can be followed in *ORA*, ser. 1, vol. 23, pts. 1 and 2; see also Ramage, *Rebel Raider*, chap. 13; Young, *Confederate Wizards*, chap. 8; Ridley, *Battles and Sketches*, 165; William Marvel, *Burnside* (Chapel Hill, 1991), 225–27.
35. *ORA*, ser. 1, vol. 23, pt. 2: 96–97; Ramage, *Rebel Raider*, 150–51.
36. *ORA*, ser. 1, vol. 23, pt. 1: 166; see also 50–60, 162–75; pt. 2: 162–64, 202, 210, 225–26, 229, 242, 259, 265, 269, 327, 338, 342–43; Marvel, *Burnside*, 227–28.
37. Gavin, *Infantryman Pettit*, 69, 72.
38. Dyer, *From Shiloh to San Juan*, 78; Samuel Coble diary, Mar. 4, 8, 1863, IHSL; W. H. Whitsitt, "A Year with

Forrest," *Confederate Veteran* (Aug. 1917): 359; Rowell, *Yankee Cavalrymen*, chap. 12, and Rowell, *Yankee Artillerymen: Through the Civil War with Eli Lilly's Indiana Battery* (Knoxville: Univ. of Tennessee Press, 1975), chap. 4; *ORA*, ser. 1, vol. 23, pt. 1: 42–64, 73–126; Hale, *Third Texas Cavalry*, 166.
39. Beatty, *Memoirs*, 178; Buford Cotton, "General N. B. Forrest's Cavalry Raid on Brentwood, Tennessee," *Williamson County Historical Society Publication Number 1* (Fall 1970): 29–35; Patten diary, Mar. 26, 1863, TSLA; Stephen Z. Starr, *The Union Cavalry in the Civil War* (Baton Rouge, 1985), 3: 210–11; Lonnie E. Maness, *An Untutored Genius* (Oxford, Miss., 1990), 123–29; Wyeth, *That Devil Forrest*, chap. 8; Jordan and Pryor, *Campaigns of Forrest*, chap. 8; Henry, *First with the Most Forrest*, chap. 9; Wills, *Battle from the Start*, 102–9.
40. Lytle, *Bedford Forrest*, 146–47.
41. Ramage, *Rebel Raider*, 152; Ridley, *Battles and Sketches*, 165–70; Vale, *Minty and the Cavalry*, 150–52.
42. Miller diary, Mar. 20, 21, Apr. 8, all 1863, 70, 71, 75, IHSL; Beatty, *Memoirs*, 175; Angle, *Three Years in the Army of the Cumberland*, 43–45; John M. Porter, "War Record," 67–68, WKL; *ORA*, ser. 1, vol. 23, pt. 1: 152–60.
43. *ORA*, ser. 1, vol. 23, pt. 1: 266–67; Angle, *Three Years in the Army of the Cumberland*, 50; Vale, *Minty and the Cavalry*, 154–59; Ramage, *Rebel Raider*, 154–57; John Samuel Henry to father, Apr. 27, 1863, and Alanson Rynam to Jane, May 1, 4, both 1863; also Griest diary, Apr. 21, 22, 1863, 69, all IHSL.
44. *ORA*, ser. 1, vol. 23, pt. 1: 152–60, 215–21; pt. 2: 228; Beatty, *Memoirs*, 187; Dyer, *From Shiloh to San Juan*, 80–81; Patten diary, Apr. 7–14, 1863, TSLA.
45. *ORA*, ser. 1, vol. 23, pt. 1: 221–39, 359–62; Jordan and Pryor, *Campaigns of Forrest*, 246–48.
46. Alfred C. Willett to "Dear Friend," Apr. 22, 1863, in Willett, *A Union Soldier Returns South*, 24; Rowell, *Yankee Artillerymen*, chap. 4, and Rowell, *Yankee Cavalrymen*, chap. 12; Whitsitt, "A Year with Forrest," 359; Wilson, Reminiscences, 51, SHC/UNC; Patten diary, Apr. 10, 11, 1863, TSLA; and on activities in Middle Tennessee during this period generally, see *ORA*, ser. 1, vol. 23, pt. 1: 42–200, and pt. 2: 32–200.
47. William G. Piston, *Carter's Raid* (Johnson City, Tenn., 1989), chap. 8, especially 65–66.
48. For official reports on these raids, see *ORA*, ser. 1, vol. 23, pt. 1: 50–59, 162–65 (Cluke); 165–75 (Pegram); 381–84 (Everett); 384–97 (Sanders); 397–98 (Hines); 632–818 (Morgan); Starr, *Union Cavalry*, 3: 95.
49. Starr, *Union Cavalry*, 3: 217–18.
50. *ORA*, ser. 1, vol. 24, pt. 3: 249, 253–55.
51. Jordan and Pryor, *Campaigns of Forrest*, chap. 9, especially 54; *ORA*, ser. 1, vol. 23, pt. 1: 750, 752; vol. 24, pt. 3: 658–59, 685–86, 712–13, 734, 757, 778–79; on the changed Union policy, see vol. 23, pt. 1: 63–64, 194–95, 246–58, 349–52; pt. 2: 373, 381, 382.
52. *ORA*, ser. 1, vol. 23, pt. 1: 280–95; M. H. Clift, "Capture of Streight," in Ridley, *Battles and Sketches*, 171–76; James F. Cook, "The 1863 Raid of Abel D. Streight: Why It Failed," *The Alabama Review* (Oct. 1969): 258–59; Starr, *Union Cavalry*, 3: 215–20; Edward G. Longacre, *Mounted Raids* (South Brunswick, N.J., 1975), 69–73; Maness, *Untutored Genius*, 129–46; Wills, *Battle from the Start*, 109–19.
53. *ORA*, ser. 1, vol. 24, pt. 3: 166, 174; *ORN*, ser. 1, vol. 24: 76–77; Simon, *Papers of Ulysses S. Grant*, 8: 24; Warren D. Crandall and Isaac D. Newell, *History of the Ram Fleet and the Mississippi Marine Brigade* (St. Louis, 1907), 245–65, 268–69; Anne J. Bailey, "The Mississippi Marine Brigade," *Military History of the Southwest* (Spring, 1992): 30–38; and Charles Dana Gibson and E. Kay Gibson, *Assault and Logistics* (Camden, Maine, 1995), 235–50, 277–80, 303–34.
54. Crandall and Newell, *Marine Brigade*, 270–75; *ORA*, ser. 1, vol. 24, pt. 3: 214–15.
55. Simon, *Papers of Ulysses S. Grant*, 8: 15, 16; *ORA*, ser. 1, 24, pt. 3: 189–91, 193; *ORN*, ser. 1, vol. 24: 79–84.
56. Crandall and Newell, *Marine Brigade*, 273, 276–83.
57. *ORN*, ser. 1, vol. 24: 90–91; see also 85–87; for other naval activities, see 61, 67, 76–77, and vol. 23: 317, 396.
58. David S. Stanley, *Memoirs* (Cambridge, 1917), 131–32; also "The Tullahoma Campaign," in Hunter, *Sketches of War History*, 3: 168; *ORA*, ser. 1, vol. 24, pt. 3: 172, 206, 214–15, 237, 271; see also 241–61 (Dodge), 278–80 (Ellet) pt. 1: 33–34, 521–29; pt. 3: 308–9 (Grierson); David Roth, "Grierson's Raid," *Blue and Gray* (June 1993): 12–24, 48–65; Jordan and Pryor, *Campaigns of Forrest*, 278–79; Starr, *Union Cavalry*, 3: 215–20; "History of Napier's Battalion," 3–4, Nutt Papers, SI IC/UNC.
59. *ORA*, ser. 1, vol. 52, pt. 2: 479–83.
60. Jordan and Pryor, *Campaigns of Forrest*, 279–84; Maness, *Untutored Genius*, 247–50; Lytle, *Bedford Forrest*, 177–80; Henry, *First with the Most Forrest*, 160–61; Wyeth, *That Devil Forrest*, 198–99; Clift, "Capture of Streight," 176; *ORA*, ser. 1, vol. 23, pt. 2: 827–28; Hughes and Stonesifer, *Life and Wars of Gideon Pillow*, 266–67.
61. Thatcher, *A Hundred Battles*, 129–31; Miller diary, June 6, 1863, 94; Connelly diary, June 4, 5, 6, 1863, 97–98, both IHSL.

62. Jordan and Pryor, *Campaigns of Forrest*, 289–90; Rice, *Yankee Tigers*, 55; Lytle, *Bedford Forrest*, 181–82; John F. Jordan, "Triune in the Civil War," 16–18, TSLA.
63. Eugene Marshall diary, Apr. 10, 21, 22, 26, May 3, 7, 8, 9, 14, 17, 21, 23, 24, 26, 27, all 1863, DUL; *ORA*, ser. 1, vol. 23, pt. 2: 20–21.
64. Marshall diary, June 8–13, 28, 29, July 3, all 1863, DUL.
65. Ibid., June 8–13, 28, 29, July 3, all 1863.
66. Miller diary, Apr. 29, May 2, both 1863, IHSL; Marvel, *Burnside*, 231–34; *ORA*, ser. 1. vol. 23, pt. 2: 237.
67. Marvel, *Burnside*, 234–38; *ORA*, ser. 1, vol. 23, pt. 2: 142–46, 162–64.
68. Troutman, *The Heavens Are Weeping*, 149–50, 153–54, 156–57, 159; John M. Wilkinson to Uncle, May 12, 1863, quoted in M. C. Garrott, "1863 Letter Tells of Mixed Emotions of the Civil War," Murray (Kentucky) *Ledger and Times*, Mar. 3, 1977; *ORA*, ser. 1, vol. 52, pt. 1: 344, 349.
69. Moore (Weakley) diary, Apr. 24, 1863, SHC/UNC; Durham, *Occupied City*, 258–59; Maslowski, *Treason Made Odious*, 62–64.
70. Moore (Weakley) diary, May 16; see also Apr. 24–28, all 1863, SHC/UNC; Durham, *Occupied City*, 260–61.
71. Durham, *Occupied City*, chap. 16, especially 280–81.
72. Graf and Haskins, *Papers of Andrew Johnson*, 6: 272; see also 255, 256.
73. *ORA*, ser. 1, vol. 23, pt. 1: 269–71; Patten diary, Mar. 26, 1863, TSLA.
74. *ORA*, ser. 1, vol. 23, pt. 1: 271.
75. Alfred C. Willett to "Dear Friend," May 31, 1863, in Willett, *A Union Soldier Returns South*, 26; Dunbar Affleck to parents, May 12, 1863, in Williams and Wooster, "With Terry's Texas Rangers," 318–19.
76. *ORA*, ser. 3, vol. 3: 410.
77. Sunderland, *Five Days to Glory*, 85, 98; Arthur B. Carpenter to parents, May 17, 30, 1863, quoted in Thomas B. Bright, "Yankee in Arms: The Civil War as a Personal Experience," *Civil War History* (Sept. 1973): 205.
78. Samuel L. McCabe to unknown correspondent, May 18, 1863, excerpts, Theme Prints, Ltd., Spring 1995 catalog, author's file.
79. William H. Dorris to wife, June 14; see also Apr. 22, 27, May 18, 25, 26, 27, June 17, 22, all 1863, copies, author's files.
80. Miller diary, June 5, 1863, 93–94, IHSL; E. A. Peters to parents, June 7, 1863, copy, author's files.
81. Griest diary, Mar. 5, 1863, 59, IHSL.
82. Graf and Haskins, *Papers of Andrew Johnson*, 6: 234; Durham, *Occupied City*, 280–81.

TEN. TO TULLAHOMA AND BEYOND

1. Walter Lord, ed., *The Fremantle Diary* (Boston, 1954), 103–37, especially 123–25; Thomas R. Hay and Irving A. Buck, *Cleburne and His Command* (Dayton, reprint, 1985), 125–30.
2. *ORA*, ser. 1, vol. 23, pt. 2: 379, 380, 846, 855; Alanson Rynam to wife, May 12, 1863, IHSL.
3. *ORA*, ser. 1, vol. 24, pt. 1: 403–4; vol. 52, pt. 1; 427–28, 433–34, 439, 442; see also Stanley, "The Tullahoma Campaign," 170–74.
4. *ORA*, ser. 1, vol. 24, pt. 3: 274–75, 751, 788–89, 796–97, 847, 849, 854, 860, 885, 912, 942.
5. Ibid., 274–75; see also pt. 2: 144–45, 424–25, 427–29, 433–34, 443–45, 484–508, 518, 666–67.
6. *ORA*, ser. 1, vol. 24, pt. 3: 414–16; Clark G. Reynolds, "A Hybrid Regiment in Garrison," 15, SHSI.
7. *ORA*, ser. 1, vol. 24, pt. 3: 415, 416.
8. Ibid., pt. 2, 485–88; also pt. 3: 397, 408–9, 416, 420, 424–25, 433–34, 443, 447, 451, 453.
9. Ibid., vol. 23, pt. 1: 394–97, 402–19; Stanley, "The Tullahoma Campaign," 170–74.
10. *ORA*, ser. 1, vol. 23, pt. 1: 420–24; Van Horne, *History of the Army of the Cumberland*, 1: 300–301; Williams, *Lincoln Finds a General*, 5: 213–15.
11. Grebner, *We Were the Ninth*, 129–30.
12. *ORA*, ser. 1, vol. 23, pt. 1: 403–5.
13. Connelly, *Autumn of Glory*, 122–28; Woodworth, *Davis and His Generals*, 224–26.
14. *ORA*, ser. 1, vol. 20, pt. 2: 498; also ser. 4, vol. 2: 305–6; Hughes and Stonesifer, *Life and Wars of Gideon J. Pillow*, chap. 14.
15. *ORA*, ser. 1, vol. 23, pt. 2: 758, 827–28, 844–45; Davis, *Orphan Brigade*, 172–73; Woodworth, *Davis and His Generals*, 212–13; Symonds, *Joseph E. Johnston*, 211–12.
16. *ORA*, ser. 1, vol. 23, pt. 2: 403–5.

17. Lyle, *Lights and Shadows*, 257–58.
18. *ORA*, ser. 1, vol. 52, pt. 1: 453–54.
19. Grebner, *We Were the Ninth*, 130; Stanley, "Tullahoma Campaign," 172, 179–80; Angle, *Three Years in the Army of the Cumberland*, 94, 99; Rice, *Yankee Tigers*, 56; Josiah Conzett reminiscence, 57, SHSI; Boyer diary, June 24, 25, 26, 1863, 108–9, copy, author's files.
20. On the Tullahoma campaign, see *ORA*, ser. 1, vol. 23, pt. 1: 399–627, and pt. 2: 442–522; vol. 52, pt. 1: 365–99, pt. 2: 499–500, all inclusive; see also Williams, *Lincoln Finds a General*, 5: chap. 8; Van Horne, *Army of the Cumberland*, 1: chap. 9; see also Angle, *Three Years in the Army of the Cumberland*, 92, 99; Rice, *Yankee Tigers*, 56; Conzett reminiscence, 58–60, SHSI.
21. H. Gerald Starnes, *Forrest's Forgotten Horse Brigadier* (Bowie, Md.; 1995), 86–90; Napier's Battalion reminiscence, Nutt Papers, SHC/UNC; Maness, *Untutored Genius*, 155–60; Jordan and Pryor, *Campaigns of Forrest*, chap. 10; Beatty, *Memoirs*, 205–27; Grebner, *We Were the Ninth*, 130.
22. Dyer, *From Shiloh to San Juan*, 83–85; R. Lockwood Tower, ed., *A Carolinian Goes to War* (Columbia, S.C., 1983), chap 4, especially 74; Angle, *Three Years in the Army of the Cumberland*, 23; Rowell, *Yankee Cavalrymen*, chap. 5; Vale, *Minty and the Cavalry*, chap. 12; Thatcher, *A Hundred Battles*, chap. 13, especially 133–34; Connelly, *Autumn of Glory*, 130–32.
23. Conzett reminiscence, 63–64, SHSI; *ORA*, ser. 1, vol. 23, pt. 1: 408, 535–37.
24. *ORA*, ser. 1, vol. 23, pt. 1: 535–37; Robert S. Brandt, "Lightning and Rain in Middle Tennessee: The Campaign of June–July 1863," *Tennessee Historical Quarterly* (Fall 1993): 158–69; Alfred C. Willett to Sophia Snyder, July 3, 1863, in Willett, *A Union Soldier Returns South*, 27; Moore (Weakley) diary, June 29, 1863, SHC/UNC; Dwight L. Smith, "Impressment, Occupation, War's End, and Emancipation," *Tennessee Historical Quarterly* (Fall 1990): 177.
25. Stanley, "Tullahoma Campaign," 181, also 178–80; Athearn, *Soldier in the West*, 104; Connelly diary, July 1, 1863, 108, IHSL; Boyer diary, June 26, 1863, 109, author's files; Hughes, *Liddell's Record*, 128–30.
26. H. L. Huggins to J. P. Strange, Sept. 15, 1866 [labeled "Captain Huggins Notes on Operations of Freeman's Battery"], 18, Nutt Papers SHC/UNC; Lyle, *Lights and Shadows*, 264.
27. Brown, *Reminiscences of Sergeant Newton Cannon*, 30–32.
28. *ORA*, ser. 1, vol. 23, pt. 1: 583–84; Moore (Weakley) diary, June 30, 1863, SHC/UNC.
29. Grebner, *We Were the Ninth*, 131.
30. Angle, *Three Years in the Army*, 88–89; Rice, *Yankee Tigers*, 58; Willett, *A Union Soldier Returns South*, 28.
31. *ORA*, ser. 1, vol. 23, pt. 2: 518; see also 552, 555–56; pt. 1: 402–3; Starr, *Union Cavalry*, 3: 250.
32. *ORA*, ser. 1, vol. 23, pt. 2: 522, and pt. 1: 402–3; Lyle, *Lights and Shadows*, 268–69; Athearn, *Soldier in the West*, 103–4; Grebner, *We Were the Ninth*, 130.
33. Rice, *Yankee Tigers*, 60; Grebner, *We Were the Ninth*, 132; Willett, *A Union Soldier Returns South*, 28.
34. Athearn, *Soldier in the West*, 111; Beatty, *Memoirs*, 220; Thatcher, *A Hundred Battles*, 135–36; Angle, *Three Years in the Army of the Cumberland*, 99–100; Graf and Haskins, *Papers of Andrew Johnson*, 6: 287; John B. Whitcomb to Silas C. Whitcomb, June 26, 1863, FDNMP; William H. Dorris to wife, Aug. 14, also June 27, both 1863, copies, author's files; *ORA*, ser. 1, vol. 23, pt. 2: 951–52, 954–56; see also vol. 30, pt. 3: 48–49, pt. 4: 502, 503.
35. Moore (Weakley) diary, July 4, 9, 22, all 1863, SHC/UNC; James H. Jones to father and mother, July 18, 1863, IHSL.
36. Oscar Langworthy to father, July 18, 1863, SHSI; Connelly diary, July 2, 1863, 109, IHSL; Athearn, *Soldier in the West*, 105.
37. Beatty, *Memoirs*, 217–18; see also Athearn, *Soldier in the West*, 106, 107–9, 109–10, 111–14.
38. Marshall diary, May 24, also July 23, 1863, DUL; *ORA*, ser. 1, vol. 23, pt. 2: 184–85.
39. Ibid., Aug. 19, 1863.
40. Edward Hagerman, *The American Civil War and the Origins of Modern Warfare* (Bloomington, 1988), 211–13.
41. *ORA*, ser. 1, vol. 52, pt. 1: 437; see also vol. 23, pt. 1: 846–48, and vol. 30, pt. 3: 21, 79; Vale, *Minty and the Cavalry*, 194–95; Wyeth, *That Devil Forrest*; Henry, *First with the Most Forrest*, 172–73.
42. *ORA*, ser. 1, vol. 23, pt. 2: 531, 552, 554–56, 585–86, and vol. 52, pt. 1: 439.
43. *ORA*, ser. 1, vol. 52, pt. 1: 439, also vol. 23, pt. 2: 110.
44. Ibid., vol. 23, pt. 1: 628–32; Burnside's difficulties are discussed in Marvel, *Burnside*, especially chap. 5.
45. John M. Porter, "War Record," 88–90, WKL; *ORA*, ser. 1, vol. 23, pt. 1: 632; Marvel, *Burnside*, 250–51.
46. Ramage, *Rebel Raider*, chaps. 14, 15; H. C. Weaver, "Morgan's Raid in Kentucky, Indiana, and Ohio," in Chamberlin, ed., *Sketches of War History*, 4: 278–314; for the Union perspective, see Marvel, *Burnside*, 252–63; Gavin, *Infantryman Pettit*, 101.

47. *ORA*, ser. 1, vol. 23, pt. 2: 514, 517, 543, 553, 557, and pt. 1: 633–34 with official reports of the raid, 632–818, inclusive.
48. Johnson, *Partisan Rangers*, 140, 143–46. Ramage, *Rebel Raider*, 171–73.
49. *ORA*, ser. 1, vol. 23, pt. 1: 636, 640–44, 660–61, 666, 668–69, and pt. 2: 552–53; *ORN*, ser. 1, vol. 25: 238–60; Graf and Haskins, *Papers of Andrew Johnson*, 6: 314.
50. *ORA*, ser. 1, vol. 23, pt. 1: 842–43, with the whole operation covered in 828–43; Johnson, *Partisan Rangers*, 148–50; Graf and Haskins, *Papers of Andrew Johnson*, 6: 317; Marvel, *Burnside*, 264–65.
51. *ORA*, ser. 1, vol. 23, pt. 1, 636; Ramage, *Rebel Raider*, 179–82; Weaver, "Morgan's Raid," 323–24; Edward Younger, ed., *Inside the Confederate Government* (New York, 1957), 81; Hattaway and Jones, *How the North Won*, 444–45.
52. *ORN*, ser. 1, vol. 25: 256–57; Hubbard T. Thomas to parents, July 22, 1863, IHSL.
53. *ORA*, ser. 1, vol. 52, pt. 1: 425–26; vol. 23, pt. 1: 518, 533.
54. William H. Dorris to wife, June 22, 1863, and General Orders 396, Dec. 15, 1863, both copies, author's files; *ORA*, ser. 1, vol. 30, pt. 3: 45–46, 71, 204.
55. *ORA*, ser. 1, vol. 24, pt. 3: 563–64, 566–67, and vol. 52, pt. 1: 398–99, 436–37; *ORN*, ser. 1, vol. 25: 332–33, 339.
56. William Wells to father, June 25, July 18, both 1863, author's files.
57. *ORA*, ser. 1, vol. 23, pt. 1: 822–27; vol. 24, pt. 2: 673–80, also 518, 666–67, 682–85, 687, pt. 3: 564–65; see also Whitesell, "Military Operations," 162–64.
58. *ORA*, ser. 1, vol. 23, pt. 1: 825–26, 827; vol. 24, pt. 3: 526, 529, 530, 544; vol. 52, pt. 1: 431–32; *ORN*, ser. 1, vol. 25: 304, 309–10, 315–18, 321–22; Whitesell, "Military Operations," 164–65.
59. *ORN*, ser. 1, vol. 25: 315; Whitesell, "Military Operations," 165–66.
60. *ORA*, ser. 1, vol. 23, pt. 2: 568–71; vol. 24, pt. 3: 556, 560–62, 570, 576, 578–80; vol. 30, pt. 3: 9, 26–27, 66–67, 74, 130–31, 146, 338.
61. Graf and Haskins, *Papers of Andrew Johnson*, 6: 564–65.
62. *ORA*, ser. 1, vol. 30, pt. 3: 24, 25, 144, 183, also vol. 24, pt. 3: 564–65; *ORN*, ser. 1, vol. 24: 293–301, 370–71.
63. See Coulter, *Civil War and Readjustment in Kentucky*, chaps. 8–12; Howard, *Black Liberation in Kentucky*, 31–36, 42, 47, 50.
64. Howard, *Black Liberation in Kentucky*, 31–34, 47; Berlin, et al., *Destruction of Slavery*, 509, 585–87, 592–94.
65. James W. Fell to F. Price, Feb. 18, 1863, quoted in ibid., 41; see also 42–43.
66. Ibid., 41, 49.
67. Coulter, *Kentucky and the Civil War*, 171–72; Howard, *Black Liberation in Kentucky*, 41.
68. Coulter, *Kentucky and the Civil War*, 172–73; Howard, *Black Liberation in Kentucky*, 41–42.
69. *ORA*, ser. 1, vol. 23, pt. 2: 570–72; Coulter, *Kentucky and the Civil War*, 177; Howard, *Black Liberation in Kentucky*, 42–43.
70. Coulter, *Kentucky and the Civil War*, 178–79; Marvel, *Burnside*, 265.
71. *ORA*, ser. 1, vol. 24, pt. 3: 1024–25, also 563–64, 566–67, 570–71, 586, 588–89; *ORN*, ser. 1, vol. 25: 383.
72. *ORA*, ser. 1, vol. 24, pt. 3: 588.
73. Gavin, *Infantryman Pettit*, 101; *ORA*, ser. 1, vol. 30, pt. 2: 647–48; ser. 3, vol. 3: 559–60; James H. Jones to parents, Aug. 21, 1863, Sylvester Wills to parents, Aug. 24, 1863, both IHSL.

ELEVEN. VICTORIES BLUE AND GRAY

1. Athearn, *Soldier in the West*, 101–24; Angle, *Three Years in the Army of the Cumberland*, 89–100; James H. Jones to parents, Aug. 27, 1863, IHSL; Alfred C. Willett to "Dear Friends," Aug. 16, 1863, in Willett, *A Union Soldier Returns South*, 28; Marshall diary, July 15, 1863, DUL; Gavin, *Infantryman Pettit*, 100.
2. Grebner, *We Were the Ninth*, 138; Rice, *Yankee Tigers*, 61, 211–12.
3. *ORA*, ser. 1, vol. 23, pt. 2: 585, 592–93.
4. Ibid., 585; Grebner, *We Were the Ninth*, 138.
5. *ORA*, ser. 1, vol. 30, pt. 3: 406–7; see also vol. 23, pt. 2: 591–94, 597–98, 601–2; Marvel, *Burnside*, especially chap. 6.
6. *ORA*, vol. 23, pt. 2: 594, 595–97, 598–99; Hough, *Soldier in the West*, 123.
7. *ORA*, vol. 23, pt. 2: 559–60, 603; vol. 30, pt. 3: 110.
8. Ibid., vol. 23, pt. 2: 598–99; vol. 30, pt. 3: 62–63, 72, 162, 171, 199.
9. Ibid., vol. 30, pt. 3: 21–23, 64, 79–80, 84, 92–93, 144–45, 297–98, 310.

10. Graf and Haskins, *Papers of Andrew Johnson*, 6: 329, 343–44; *ORA*, ser. 1, vol. 30, pt. 3: 74, 184–85.
11. Berlin, et al., *Wartime Genesis of Free Labor*, 375–76, 396–404, 410–11, 421–24; also Berlin, et al., *The Black Military Experience* (Cambridge, 1982), 123–24, 172–80; *ORA*, ser. 3, vol. 3: 1115.
12. *ORA*, ser. 1, vol. 30, pt. 3: 14–15, 45–46, 54, 67, 111, 131, 156–57, 192–93, 223, 230, 290, 297, 362–63, 440–41.
13. Lester L. Swift, ed., "Letters from a Sailor on a Tinclad," *Civil War History* (Mar. 1961): 49.
14. *ORA*, ser. 1, vol. 30, pt. 3: 168, 223, 238–39, 245–48, 273–76, 290, 309, 313, 328–29; Disbrow, "Vett Noble of Ypsilanti," 26–27.
15. *ORA*, ser. 1, vol. 30, pt. 3: 262, also 30–31, 195; Graf and Haskins, *Papers of Andrew Johnson*, 6: 333–34.
16. *ORA*, ser. 1, vol. 30, pt. 3: 33–38, 189.
17. Gavin, *Infantryman Pettit*, 109–10; Benson J. Lossing, *Pictorial History of the Civil War* (Hartford, Conn., 1868), 3: 129n. 2.
18. *ORA*, ser. 1, vol. 30, pt. 3: 136, 215, 220–22, 433, also vol. 23, pt. 2: 903, and vol. 24, pt. 2: 121–24; Wilson Reminiscences, 57–58, SHC/UNC; Schroeder-Lein, "Confederate Army of Tennessee Hospitals in Chattanooga," 37, 44–45, 49, 55–57.
19. *ORA*, ser. 1, vol. 30, pt. 1: 184; McCallie quoted in Hoobler, *Cities Under the Gun*, 117.
20. *ORA*, ser. 1, vol. 30, pt. 1: 182–83; pt. 3: 229–30.
21. Ibid., pt. 1: 186, also 182–83; see also Patton, *Unionism and Reconstruction in Tennessee*, 38–43; Thomas B. Alexander, *Political Reconstruction in Tennessee* (Nashville, 1950), 15; Dixon Merritt, *History of Wilson County* (Nashville, 1961), 360–61; Halley, "A Rebel Newspaper's War Story," 2: 261–62.
22. Graf and Haskins, *Papers of Andrew Johnson*, 6: 357–59; Coulter, *Civil War and Readjustment in Kentucky*, 170–78.
23. Graf and Haskins, *Papers of Andrew Johnson*, 6: 384, also 311, 315–16, 318–20, 322–25, 327, 334–44, 356–57, 360–68, 376–86.
24. Ibid., 367–69.
25. Marshall diary, Sept. 10, 1863, DUL; *ORA*, ser. 1, vol. 30, pt. 3: 294–95; Williams, *Lincoln Finds a General*, 5: 242–45.
26. Hubbard T. Thomas to parents, Sept. 30, 1863, IHSL.
27. *ORA*, ser. 1, vol. 24, pt. 3: 969–71.
28. Ibid., vol. 30, pt. 3: 48–49, pt. 4: 560; ser. 3, vol. 3: 603–4; Marshall diary, Aug. 3, 1862, DUL; Steele, *American Campaigns*, 1: 492.
29. Maness, *Untutored Genius*, 159–60; *ORA*, ser. 1, vol. 30, pt. 4: 508–9.
30. *ORA*, ser. 1, vol. 30, pt. 4: 503, 505–6, 530; vol. 23, pt. 3: 836–38, 839, 920.
31. Ibid., vol. 30, pt. 4: 547–53, 683–86.
32. Ibid., vol. 23, pt. 2: 909–10, 916, 921–22, 924, 937–38; vol. 30, pt. 4: 494–95, 520.
33. Woodworth, *Jefferson Davis and His Generals*, 230–31; *ORA*, ser. 1, vol. 23, pt. 2: 920, 924–25, 929–30, 952–53, 962–64; vol. 30, pt. 3: 83, 1039; pt. 4: 518–19, 527, 537, 540, 560, 588, 618–19.
34. Grebner, *We Were the Ninth*, 144; *ORA*, ser. 1, vol. 30, pt. 4: 599–600, 610–11; Williams, *Lincoln Finds a General*, 5: 265–67; modern accounts of the battle include John Bowers, *Chickamauga and Chattanooga* (New York, 1993); Peter Cozzens, *This Terrible Sound* (Champaign, 1992); and Glenn Tucker, *Chickamauga* (Indianapolis, 1961).
35. Disbrow, "Vett Noble of Ypsilanti," 28; Grebner, *We Were the Ninth*, 145–46.
36. *ORA*, ser. 1, vol. 30, pt. 4: 10; Rice, *Yankee Tigers*, 72; Disbrow, "Vett Noble of Ypsilanti," 28; Lyle, *Lights and Shadows*, chaps. 32, 33, 34; Marshall diary, Sept. 21, 1863, DUL.
37. Graf and Haskins, *Papers of Andrew Johnson*, 6: 401; *ORA*, ser. 1, vol. 30, pt. 4: 705, 709–10.
38. Horn, *The Army of Tennessee*, 275–90; Connelly, *Autumn of Glory*, 230–56; Symonds, *Joseph E. Johnston*, 246–47; Williams, *Lincoln Finds a General*, 5: 266–67; *ORA*, ser. 1, vol. 30, pt. 4: 708.
39. Kelly quoted in Wills, *A Battle from the Start*, 144, also 142–47; see also Woodward, *Jefferson Davis and His Generals*, 243–46; Losson, *Tennessee's Forgotten Warriors*, chaps. 5, 6.
40. *ORA*, ser. 1, vol. 30, pt. 4: 555, 576–78, 581–82, 587, 593, 609–10, 648–51, 673–74, 678–79, 687–88, 713, 721, 735, 745–46; also pt. 3: 197–98, 224–25, 228–29; Boyer diary, Sept. 22, 1863, 114, copy, author's files.
41. *ORA*, ser. 1, vol. 30, pt. 2: 663–730, inclusive; pt. 4: 32, 37–39, 44, 45–46, 60, 68, 78–79, 84–85, 132–33, 150, 156, 159, 160–65, 174, 176, 187–88, 190–91, 217–18, 223–31, 260–65 268, 273, 279, 291, 441–42; see also Starr, *Union Cavalry*, 3: 292–300; Dyer, *From Shiloh to San Juan*, chap. 5; Rowell, *Yankee Artillerymen*, chap. 8, and Rowell, *Yankee Cavalrymen*, chap. 16.
42. *ORA*, ser. 1, vol. 30, pt. 2: 707–12; pt. 4: 308–9; vol. 31, pt. 1: 847–48; see also Directive, Oct. 4, 1863, Salley Ivie scrapbook, vol. 3, TSLA.
43. Smith, "Impressment, Occupation," 181–82; Walter Durham, *Reluctant Partners* (Nashville, 1987), 7, 8,

citing various newspapers; *ORA*, ser. 1, vol. 30, pt. 4: 78, 87–90, 109–13, 133–37; James A. Huston, "Logistical Support of Federal Armies," *Civil War History* (Mar. 1961): 42.

44. *ORA*, ser. 1, vol. 30, pt. 4: 434–35, also 261–63, 265, 268, 743, 748; James Lee McDonough, *Chattanooga* (Knoxville, 1984), 70–71, 90–95; Conzett reminiscence, 65–66, SHSI.

45. Vale, *Minty and the Cavalry*, 243–50; Starr, *Union Cavalry*, 3: 297–98; *ORA*, ser. 1, vol. 30, pt. 4: 266.

46. Marshall diary, July 23, 30, Aug. 21, 28, Sept. 25, Oct. 1–10, as well as other entries of July–Oct., all 1863, DUL; Conzett reminiscence, 66–67, SHSI.

47. *ORA*, ser. 1, vol. 30, pt. 4: 762, also 140, 156, 158–65, 174–76, 187–91, 217–38, 260–68, 273, 279, 710–11, 713, 724–25, 728–29, 735, 740–41, 743, 746–47, 752, 757–58, 761–67.

48. Ibid., pt. 2: 730–96 for reports; also pt. 4: 30, 53, 74, 119–22, 147–48, 299–305, 326–32, 472; pt. 3: 243–45; Starr, *Union Cavalry*, 3: 362–68; William T. Sherman, *Memoirs* (New York, 1875), 1: 351–53.

49. *ORA*, ser. 1, vol. 31, pt. 1: 747–48, 785; pt. 3: 97–98, 578–83; *ORN*, ser. 1, vol. 25: 468–69.

50. *ORA*, vol. 30, pt. 2: 665; pt. 3: 954–55; pt. 4: 114, 136, 140, 462, 746–48; Vale, *Minty and the Cavalry*, 248–49; Thatcher, *A Hundred Battles*, 155; Conzett reminiscence, 67, SHSI.

51. Thatcher, *A Hundred Battles*, 156–57; Vale, *Minty and the Cavalry*, 260–64; Rowell, *Yankee Cavalrymen*, chap. 17, and Rowell, *Yankee Artillerymen*, chap. 9.

52. Henderson, Young, and Naheloffer, *Dear Eliza*, 48–65.

53. William H. Dorris to wife, Aug. 14, Sept. 6, 18, Oct. 25; Dorris to sister, Sept. 30; Dorris to son, Oct. 2, all 1863, all copies, author's files; Berlin, et al., *Wartime Genesis of Free Labor*, 394–96, 408.

54. Disbrow, "Vett Noble," 28.

55. *ORA*, ser. 1, vol. 30, pt. 2: 712–13, pt. 4: 25, 26, 50–51, 55, 143–45, 262, 270, 288, 290–93, 395, 413, 414, 448–49, 466–67, 469; Marshall diary, Oct. 8–14, 1863, DUL; Williams, *Lincoln Finds a General*, 5: 267; Graf and Haskins, *Papers of Andrew Johnson*, 6: 387; George A. Thayer, "A Railroad Feat of the War," in Chamberlin, *Sketches of War History*, 4: 214–34.

56. Grebner, *We Were the Ninth*, 155–56.

57. *ORA*, ser. 1, vol. 30, pt. 4: 142–43, 150, 193, 195, 306–8, 325–27, 349, 404–11, 449–55, 469–70, 487–88; *ORN*, ser. 1, vol. 25: 465–81, 504–5; Sherman, *Memoirs*, 1: 353; James T. Siburt, "Colonel John M. Hughs," *Tennessee Historical Quarterly* (Summer 1992): 88–91.

58. James B. Killebrew reminiscences, 1: 171–72, SHC/UNC; McClain, *Houston County*, 37–38.

59. Graf and Haskins, *Papers of Andrew Johnson*, 6: 486–94; Lovett, "Nashville's Fort Negley," 15–16.

60. *ORA*, ser. 1, vol. 30, pt. 4: 9–10, 57, 79–80, 150, 306, 401–2, 414–15, 418, 426, 448–49, 455, 477; pt. 1: 142–43, 148–49, 161, 168, and Dana's dispatches particularly, 182–221.

61. Boyer diary, Sept. 23, 1963, 115, author's files; Marshall diary, Sept. 4, 21, 1863, DUL; Athearn, *Soldier in the West*, 166–69; Connelly, *Three Years in the Army*, 133; Rice, *Yankee Tigers*, 72–75.

62. *ORA*, ser. 1, vol. 30, pt. 4: 220–21; Williams, *Lincoln and His Generals*, chap. 11; Bruce Catton, *Grant Takes Command* (Boston, 1968), 33–35.

63. *ORA*, ser. 1, vol. 30, pt. 4: 479, also 404, 430–31.

TWELVE. LAST HURRAH AT CHATTANOOGA

1. *ORA*, ser. 1, vol. 30, pt. 4: 404, 455, 475–76, 485; Grant, *Personal Memoirs*, 2: chaps. 40, 41; McDonough, *Chattanooga*, chap. 5.

2. *ORA*, ser. 1, vol. 30, pt. 1: 36, 161; pt. 3: 592.

3. Ibid., vol. 31, pt. 1: 713, 716; also vol. 30, pt. 1: 37, pt. 3: 840–41, 923.

4. Regimental Association Committee, 143d New York, *A Condensed History* (Newburgh, N.Y., 1909), 22, 27; *ORA*, ser. 1, vol. 31, pt. 3: 207; Lyle, *Lights and Shadows*, 334–40; Guy R. Swanson and Timothy D. Johnson, "Conflict in East Tennessee: Generals Law, Jenkins, and Longstreet," *Civil War History* (June 1985): 104–6; Jeffrey D. Wert, *General James Longstreet* (New York, 1993), 330–38.

5. *ORA*, ser. 1, vol. 30, pt. 4: 742–43, 745–46, vol. 31, pt. 3: 586, 603–4, 609, 650–58, vol. 52, 554–55; McDonough, *Chattanooga*, 97–98; Horn, *Army of Tennessee*, chap. 15; Connelly, *Autumn of Glory*, chap. 10.

6. *ORA*, ser. 1, vol. 31, pt. 3: 597–98, 601, 605, 620–22, 624, 634–35; Symonds, *Joseph E. Johnston*, 245–47.

7. *ORA*, ser. 1, vol. 31, pt. 3: 614–15, 622, 629, 631–32, 710–11.

8. Ibid., vol. 31, pt. 3: 629, 631–32, 635–37, 640–44, 646–47, 650–69, 671–72, 683, 868–67, 700.

9. Ibid., vol. 31, pt. 3: 30–32, 48–49, 58, 64–65, 68–69, 83, 86–87, 91–93, 101–8, 113–15, 123, 130–36, 151, 165–67, 184–85, 195–96, 208, 220, 230, 237.
10. Sylvester F. Wills to father and mother, Nov. 6; N. L. Johnson to parents, Nov. 26, both 1863, both IHSL.
11. Sunderland, *Five Days To Glory*, 99–102.
12. *ORA*, ser. 1, vol. 31, pt. 3: 101, also 90–91; ser. 3, vol. 3: 1006–7; *ORN*, ser. 1, vol. 25: 540.
13. *ORN*, ser. 1, vol. 25: 540–41.
14. Ibid., 469–76, 541.
15. Ibid., 469.
16. Ibid., 469–98, especially 471, 476.
17. Ibid., 482, also 474, 465.
18. Ibid., 482, 487–88, 491, 494.
19. Ibid., 546–47, 553–54.
20. Ibid., 534–35, 548–49, 554–55, 579–80; Henderson, Young, and Naheloffer, *Dear Eliza*, 59–69.
21. William H. Dorris to wife, Nov. 16, Dec. 1, 7, 9, all 1863, author's files; Henderson, Young, and Naheloffer, *Dear Eliza*, 60, 63, 68; also Guy Wilbur Jackson to John Trotwood Moore, June 16, July 16, both 1924, TSLA.
22. *ORN*, ser. 1, vol. 25: 553–57, 579, 582, 592–93; *ORA*, ser. 1, vol. 31, pt. 3: 133–36.
23. *ORN*, ser. 1, vol. 25: 555–57, 594–95, 608–9.
24. Ibid., 508, 579–80, 611.
25. *ORA*, ser. 1, vol. 31, pt. 1: 567–76, 591–94, 601–6.
26. Garrett, "Guerrillas and Bushwhackers," entry Nov. 11, 1863, in "Rebel Atrocities in Kentucky," unpublished typescript, no date, TSLA; Meacham, *History of Christian County, Kentucky*, 198–99; *ORA*, ser. 1, vol. 31, pt. 1: 31–32, 839.
27. *ORN*, ser. 1, vol. 25: 490–91, 530.
28. Mary Walker Meriwether Bell journal, Oct. 4, 1863, TSLA.
29. *ORA*, ser. 1, vol. 31, pt. 1: 829–30.
30. Wilbur F. Hitt to father, Oct. 5, and to sister, Oct. 24, both 1863, both IHSL; *ORA*, ser. 1, vol. 31, pt. 3: 103.
31. *ORA*, ser. 1, v. 31, pt. 3: 100, also 90–91, 98–99, 101–3, 122, 130–31, 152, 160–61, 180; *ORN*, ser. 1, vol. 25: 468, 474, 482–83, 539–40.
32. *ORA*, ser. 1, v. 31, pt. 3: 97–99, 100, 210, 219, 224, 234–35, 237–38.
33. Jonathan Rice to wife, Nov. 16, 1863, author's files.
34. Wert, *Longstreet*, chaps. 16, 17; Marvel, *Burnside*, chap. 6; Swanson and Johnson, "Conflict in East Tennessee," 107–9.
35. *ORA*, ser. 1, vol. 31, pt. 3: 178, also 140–41, 145, 154–58, 161–62, 169–71, 184; Hagerman, *Civil War and Origins of Modern Warfare*, 220–21.
36. Rice, *Yankee Tigers*, 75, 77; Boyer diary, Nov. 27, 1863, 128, copy, author's files, *ORA*, ser. 1, vol. 30, pt. 3: 247, 255, 736, 739; the Chattanooga operation is covered comprehensively in McDonough, *Chattanooga*, especially chaps. 7–13; as well as Peter Cozzens, *Shipwreck of Their Hopes* (Urbana, Ill., 1994); and Wiley Sword, *Mountains Touched with Fire* (New York, 1995).
37. *ORA*, ser. 1, vol. 31, pt. 2: 656–57, 680–84; vol. 52, pt. 2: 567–68, 573, 574; while the Knoxville operation should be followed in vol. 31, pt. 1: 258–550, inclusive, and vol. 52, pt. 1: 484–511, as well as Rice, *Yankee Tigers*, chap. 6; pursuit of Bragg can be followed in McDonough, *Chattanooga*, chap. 14; see also Gavin, *Infantryman Pettit*, 123, as well as chap. 8 generally.
38. Symonds, *Joseph E. Johnston*, 247–48; Connelly, *Autumn of Glory*, 275–78; Marvel, *Burnside*, 324–25; *ORA*, ser. 1, vol. 31, pt. 3: 774–76.
39. Grebner, *We Were the Ninth*, 167; Henderson, Young, and Naheloffer, *Dear Eliza*, 70.
40. Beatty, *Memoirs*, 271–72; *ORA*, ser. 1, vol. 23, pt. 2: 522.
41. Troutman, *The Heavens Are Weeping*, 167, 171.
42. James H. Jones to parents, Oct. 14, 1863, IHSL; Jesse Cox journal, bound volume, 545, TSLA.
43. *ORA*, ser. 1, vol. 31, pt. 3: 172, 180, 184–85, 193–94, 211–12, 224, 242–52, 258, 261, 264, 270–72.
44. Ibid., pt. 3: 187, 242–43, 575, 588–89, 603–4, 641, 646, 730–31, 751, 789, 797, 798; vol. 52, pt. 2: 557, 599–600; Maness, *An Untutored Genius*, 270–72.
45. *ORA*, ser. 1, vol. 31, pt. 3: 443–46, 449–51, 456, 473, 789–90, 853–54.
46. William Alderson, ed., "Forrest's March Out of West Tennessee," *West Tennessee Historical Society Journal*

{375}

(1958): 139, recounted in Maness, *Untutored Genius*, 188–89, also 190–96; Hunter B. Whitesell, "Military Operations," 244; *ORA*, ser. 1, vol. 31, pt. 3: 293, 645, 704–6, 730–31, 743–47.
47. *ORA*, ser. 1, vol. 31, pt. 3: 187, 263.
48. Ibid., 261–63.
49. Sunderland, *Five Days to Glory*, 111; *ORA*, ser. 3, vol. 3: 826–27.
50. *ORA*, ser. 1, vol. 23, pt. 2: 522; Ralph W. Donnelly, "Local Defense in the Confederate Munitions Area," in *Military Analysis of the Civil War* (Millwood, N.Y., 1977), 239–43.
51. Hugh Bay to wife, Dec. 23, 1863, IHSL; Gavin, *Infantryman Pettit*, 124; James Reed to friend Wash, n.d., copy author's files.
52. Alonzo H. Quint, *The Potomac and the Rapidan* (Boston, 1864), 376.
53. Johnson, *Partisan Rangers*, chaps. 20, 21, and 256, 263, 293, 363–93, 438, 467; Ramage, *Rebel Raider*, chap. 16, especially 194–98; Kay Baker Gaston, "A World Overturned," *Tennessee Historical Quarterly* (Winter 1991): 11–13.
54. *ORA*, ser. 4, vol. 2: 1003.
55. Henderson, Young, and Naheloffer, *Dear Eliza*, 72–73, and additional page 1; William H. Dorris to wife, Dec. 7, 9, both 1863, author's files.
56. On Davis, see Edythe Johns Whitley, *Sam Davis, Hero of the Confederacy* (Nashville, 1971), 128–37.
57. Troutman, *The Heavens Are Weeping*, 172.
58. *ORA*, ser. 3, vol. 1: 890–91; vol. 3: 1198.
59. Ibid., 1128.
60. Ibid., 1039–40.
61. Patton, *Unionism and Reconstruction in Tennessee*, 43
62. Quint, *The Potomac and the Rapidan*, 383–84.
63. Ash, *Middle Tennessee Society Transformed*, especially chaps. 5, 6, 7; see also his *When the Yankees Came*, chap. 3, especially fig. 1.
64. *ORA*, ser. 4, vol. 2: 1047–48
65. James B. Martin, "Black Flag Over the Bluegrass: Guerrilla Warfare in Kentucky, 1863–1865," *Kentucky Historical Society Register* (1988): 353; Stephen V. Ash, "Sharks in an Angry Sea: Civilian Resistance and Guerrilla Warfare in Occupied Middle Tennessee, 1862–1865," *Tennessee Historical Quarterly* (Fall 1986): 217.
66. *ORA*, ser. 1, vol. 24, pt. 3: 156–57.
67. Berlin, et al., *Wartime Genesis of Free Labor*, 415.

BIBLIOGRAPHY

MANUSCRIPT COLLECTIONS

Author's Files. Original and Copies from Private Sources.
P. Bishop; James H. Blodgett; Lib Davidson; William H. Dorris; John Edgerly; G. H. Gates; Victor M. Harding; J. A. Haydon; S. C. Lymons; Cave Johnson; Stephen T. McBide; Samuel L. McCabe; George Triplett Moorman; Charles Cooper Nott; C. W. Paris; T. Parvin; Charles Peck; E. A. Peters; Willie Presley; H. R. Reckley; James R. Reed; John B. Rice; P. S. Snyder; Henry Vincent; William Wells; John Wilkinson
Barton, Lon Carter, Mayfield, Ky.
G. W. Hurt
Chicago Historical Society. Chicago (abbreviated in notes as CHS).
William Bailhache; George D. Carrington; Jacob Lauman
Duke Univ. Library. Durham, N.C. (abbreviated in notes as DUL).
John B. Floyd; Will Kennedy; Eugene Marshall; Robert A. McClellan; William M. McKinney; Munford-Ellis family; John C. Pedrick; Pope-Carter family; Hubert Saunders; Helen Shell; C. B. Tompkins
The Filson Club. Louisville (abbreviated in notes as FCL).
Richard Bean, "Recollections of the Battle of Hartsville, Tenn."; Milton Carey; David Clark; Josephine Covington; S. K. Haycroft; Johnson family; Stanton P. McGuire; J. J. Neely; L. C. Porter; Frank P. Tryon; Yandell family
Fort Donelson National Military Park, Dover, Tenn. (abbreviated in notes as FDNMP).
Thomas J. Baugh; John Whitcomb
Indiana Historical Society Library, Indianapolis, Ind. (abbreviated in notes as IHSL).
Hugh Bay; John A. Berger; Bergun H. Brown; Samuel Coble; Jesse B. Connelly; James W. Daniels; David A. Fately; James F. Fee; Arthur J. Gates; Alva C. Griest; J. C. Haddock, "Sketch of Fourth Indiana Battery"; Oliver P. Haskell; John Henry; John A. Hoerner; Wilbur F. Hitt; Andrew Jackson Johnson; N. L. Johnson; James H. Jones; Mrs. John Lewis Ketcham; William B. Miller; A. L. Noble; R. J. Price; Alanson P. Rynam; Alfred Shields; Thomas M. Small; Joseph T. Smith; Henry Strong; Hubbard T. Thomas; Joseph N. Vanmeter; Mathias C. Van Pelt; Amos C. Weaver; John Wilkins; Sylvester Wills
Illinois State Historical Library, Springfield, Ill. (abbreviated in notes as ISH).
James F. Drish; Charles H. Floyd; Douglas Haperman; Wallace-Dickey family
Kentucky Adjutant General, Military and Records Branch. Frankfort (abbreviated in notes as KAG).
Civil War Guerrilla correspondence; Quirk's Company, Morgan Scouts
Minnesota Historical Society. Saint Paul, Minn. (abbreviated in notes as MHS).
Eugene Marshall, "Narrative of the Civil War, 1861–1862"

Murray State Univ. Library. Murray, Ky. (abbreviated in notes as MSL).
    J. P. Cannon
National Archives and Records Administration, Washington, D.C. (abbreviated in notes as NARA).
    Record Group 393, U.S. Army Continental Commands; Department of the Missouri; Department of the Ohio
Southern Historical Collection. Univ. of North Carolina (abbreviated in notes as SHC/UNC).
    John Alexander; Buchanan-McClellan; George Hovey Cadman; Kate N. Carney; J. A. Hittle; Joseph Buckner Killebrew; William Henry King; Harrison C. Lockhardt; Leroy Moncure Nutt; Alice Ready; Henry Richmond Slack; Mrs. Harriet Ellen Moore (Mrs. Thomas Porter Weakley); Henry Clay Warmoth; Thomas B. Wilson
State Historical Society of Iowa. Des Moines, Iowa (abbreviated in notes as SHSI).
    Josiah Conzett; Oscar Landworthy; Clark G. Reynolds, "A Hybrid Regiment in Garrison: Fifth Iowa Cavalry"
Tennessee State Library and Archives. Nashville (abbreviated in notes as TSLA).
    Alfred H. Abernathy; Charles Alley; John Nick Barker; Thomas Baugh; Mary Walker Meriwether Bell; Nathan Brandon; James P. Brownlow; Robert Franklin Bunting; Alexander Jackson Campbell; Nathaniel Francis Cheairs, "Personal Experiences in the War Between the States"; David Clark; Rufus Howell Cook; Cooper family; Jesse Cox; Sumner A. Cunningham; "Reminiscences of the Forty-First Tennessee Infantry"; John E. Duling; Jared C. Frazier; Virginia French; Jill McKnight Garrett collection: (Redick C. Carnell; "Clippings from the Confederacy"; "A History of Humphreys County, Tennessee"; "Guerrillas and Bushwhackers in Middle Tennessee"; A. F. Gilbert, "Recollections of Fort Donelson"; Buford Gotto, "General N.B. Forrest's Cavalry Raid on Brentwood"; "The Veteran and the Boy"; Rowena Webster; J. T. Williamson); Gordon-Avery; Isham G. Harris; Gustavus Henry; Anna Howell; Sallie Ivie; M. Jenkins; Guy Wilbur Jackson; John F. Jordan, "Triune in the Civil War"; Sarah Ann (Bailey) Kennedy; Blanche Lewis; George Washington Matthews; Sallie Florence McEwen; Thomas Rawlings Myer; F. J. Paine; Zeboim Carter Patten; Provost Marshal General Order, October 20, 1862; Provost Marshal Records, Montgomery County, 1862–1864; Spot F. Terrell; Thomas Black Wilson
Tulane Univ. Library. New Orleans (abbreviated in notes as TUL).
    Kuntz collection; Louisiana Historical Association, Confederate
Univ. of Tennessee—Knoxville Library. Knoxville (abbreviated in notes as UTL).
    William W. Howard; M. D. Jenkins; W. E. Patterson
U.S. Army Military History Institute. Carlisle Barracks, Pa. (abbreviated in notes as USAMHI).
    Civil War Times Illustrated Collection; Latimer family
Virginia Historical Society. Richmond (abbreviated in notes as VHS).
    John Henry Guy
Western Kentucky Univ. Library, Bowling Green (abbreviated in notes as WKL).
    John M. Porter, "War Record"

GOVERNMENT DOCUMENTS

Commonwealth of Kentucky. *Message of Governor Bramlette to the General Assembly of Kentucky at the December Session, 1863.* Frankfort: Commonwealth Office, 1863.
United States Bureau of the Census. *Agriculture of the United States in 1860: Compiled from the Original Return of the Eighth Census.* Washington: Government Printing Office, 1861.
———. *Manufactures of the United States in 1860.* Washington: Government Printing Office, 1865.
United States Navy Department. *Official Records of the Union and Confederate Navies in the War of the Rebellion.* Washington: Government Printing Office, 1894–1927, 30 volumes.
United States War Department. *The War of the Rebellion: A Compilation of the Official Records of the Union and Confederate Armies.* Washington: Government Printing Office, 1880–1901. 128 volumes.
———. Adjutant Generals Office. *General Orders, 1861–1863.* Washington: War Department, 1861–1863.

Bibliography

BOOKS

Abdill, George R. *Civil War Railroads: Pictorial Story of the Iron Horse, 1861–1865.* Seattle: Superior Publishing Company, 1961.
Alexander, Thomas B. *Political Reconstruction in Tennessee.* Nashville: Vanderbilt Univ. Press, 1950.
Allardice, Bruce C. *More Generals in Gray.* Baton Rouge: Louisiana State University Press, 1995.
Allen, Hall. *Center of Conflict: A Factual Story of the War Between the States in Western Kentucky and Tennessee.* Paducah: The Paducah Sun-Democrat, 1961.
Ambrose, Stephen E. *Halleck: Lincoln's Chief of Staff.* Baton Rouge: Louisiana State Univ. Press, 1962.
Anderson, Ephraim McD. *Memoirs: Historical and Personal, Including the Campaigns of the First Missouri Brigade.* St. Louis: Time Printing Company, 1868.
Angle, Paul M., editor. *Three Years in the Army of the Cumberland: The Letters and Diary of James A. Connolly.* Bloomington: Indiana Univ. Press, 1959.
Ash, Stephen V. *Middle Tennessee Society Transformed, 1860–1870: War and Peace in the Upper South.* Baton Rouge: Louisiana State Univ. Press, 1988.
———. *When the Yankees Came: Conflict and Chaos in the Occupied South, 1861–1865.* Chapel Hill: Univ. of North Carolina Press, 1995.
Asprey, Robert B. *War in the Shadows: The Guerrilla in History.* Garden City, N.Y.: Doubleday, 1975.
Athearn, Robert G., editor. *Soldier in the West: The Civil War Letters of Alfred Lacey Hough.* Philadelphia: Univ. of Pennsylvania Press, 1957.
Bailey, Fred Arthur. *Class and Tennessee's Confederate Generation.* Chapel Hill: Univ. of North Carolina Press, 1987.
Baird, Nancy Disher. *David Wendell Yandell: Physician of Old Louisville.* Lexington: Univ. Press of Kentucky, 1978.
Barber, Flavel C. *Holding the Line: The Third Tennessee Infantry, 1861–1864.* Edited by Robert H. Ferrell. Kent, Ohio: Kent State Univ. Press, 1994.
Batchelor, Benjamin Franklin. *Batchelor-Turner Letters 1861–1864, Written by Two of Terry's Texas Rangers.* Edited by H. J. Rugeley. Austin: Steck, 1961.
Bate, William B. *Memorial on the Life and Character of Isham G. Harris.* Washington: Government Printing Office, 1898.
Beach, Ursula Smith. *Along the Warioto or a History of Montgomery County, Tennessee.* Clarksville: Clarksville Kiwanis Club and Tennessee Historical Commission, 1964.
Beatley, John. *Memoirs of a Volunteer, 1861–1863.* Edited by Harvey S. Ford. New York: W. W. Norton, 1946.
Beers, Henry Putney. *Guide to the Archives of the Government of Confederate Sates of America.* Washington: National Archives and Records Service, 1968.
Beringer, Richard E., Herman Hattaway, Archer Jones, and William N. Still Jr. *Why the South Lost the Civil War.* Athens: Univ. of Georgia Press, 1986.
Berlin, Ira, Joseph P. Reidy, and Leslie S. Rowland, editors. *The Black Military Experience.* [Freedom: A Documentary History of Emancipation, 1861–1867, Series 2.] Cambridge: Cambridge Univ. Press, 1982.
———. Barbara J. Fields, Thavolia Glymph, Joseph P. Reidy, and Leslie S. Rowland, editors. *The Destruction of Slavery.* [Freedom: A Documentary History of Emancipation, 1861–1867.] Cambridge: Cambridge Univ. Press, 1985.
———. Steven F. Miller, Joseph P. Reidy, and Leslie S. Rowland, editors. *The Wartime Genesis of Free Labor: The Upper South.* [Freedom: A Documentary History of Emancipation, 1861–1867.] Cambridge: Cambridge Univ. Press, 1993.
Black, Robert M. III. *The Railroads of the Confederacy.* Chapel Hill: Univ. of North Carolina Press, 1952.
Blanchard, Ira. *I Marched with Sherman: Civil War Memoirs of the 20th Illinois Volunteer Infantry.* San Francisco, I. D. Huff, 1982.
Bowers, John. *Chickamauga and Chattanooga: The Battles That Doomed the Confederacy.* New York, Harper Collins, 1994.
Boynton, H. V. *Sherman's Historical Raid: the Memoirs in the Light of the Record.* Cincinnati: Wilstack, Baldwin, 1875.
Breeden, James O. *Joseph Jones, M.D.: Scientist of the Old South.* Lexington: Univ. Press of Kentucky, 1975.
Brown, Campbell E., editor. *Tennesseans in the Civil War.* Nashville: Tennessee Civil War Centennial Commission, 1965. 2 volumes.
Brown, Dee Alexander. *The Bold Cavaliers: Morgan's Second Kentucky Cavalry Raiders.* Philadelphia: J. B. Lippincott, 1959.

Bibliography

Brownlee, Richard S. *Gray Ghosts of the Confederacy: Guerrilla Warfare in the West, 1861–1865.* Baton Rouge: Louisiana State Univ. Press, 1958.

Burt, Jesse C. *Nashville; Its Live and Times.* Nashville: Tennessee Book Company, 1959.

Carter, Samuel III. *The Last Cavaliers: Confederate and Union Cavalry in the Civil War.* New York: St. Martins, 1979.

Catton, Bruce, *Grant Moves South.* Boston: Little, Brown, 1960.

———. *Grant Takes Command.* Boston: Little, Brown, 1968.

Cimprich, John. *Slavery's End in Tennessee, 1861–1865.* University: Univ. of Alabama Press, 1985.

Clark, Charles T. *Opdycke Tigers, 125th O.V.I.* Columbus, Ohio: Spahr and Glenn, 1895.

Clausewitz, Karl von. *On War.* Edited and translated by Michael Howard and Peter Paret. Princeton: Princeton Univ. Press, 1976.

Clay-Copton, Virginia. *A Belle of the Fifties.* New York: Doubleday-Page, 1904.

Coe, David, editor. *Mine Eyes Have Seen the Glory: Combat Diaries of Union Sergeant Hamlin Alexander Coe.* Rutherford, N.J.: Fairleigh Dickinson Univ. Press, 1975.

The Confederate Monumental Association of Clarksville. *A History of the Confederate Monumental Association and Roster of "Forbes Bivouac."* Clarksville, Tenn.: The Association, 1893.

Connelly, Thomas Lawrence. *Army of the Heartland: the Army of Tennessee, 1861–1862.* Baton Rouge: Louisiana State Univ. Press, 1971.

Cooling, Benjamin Franklin. *Forts Henry and Donelson: The Key to the Confederate Heartland.* Knoxville: Univ. of Tennessee Press, 1987.

———. *Symbol, Sword, and Shield: Defending Washington During the Civil War.* Hamden, Conn.: Archon, 1975; rev. ed., Shippensburg, Pa.: White Mane, 1991.

Cope, Alexis. *The Fifteenth Ohio Volunteers and Its Campaigns.* Columbus: Privately published, 1916.

Corlew, Robert Ewing. *A History of Dickson County, Tennessee.* Nashville: Tennessee Historical Commission and Dickson County Historical Society, 1956.

Coulter, E. Merton. *The Civil War and Readjustment in Kentucky.* Chapel Hill: Univ. of North Carolina Press, 1926.

Cozzens, Peter. *No Better Place to Die: The Battle of Stones River.* Urbana: Univ. of Illinois Press, 1990.

———. *The Shipwreck of Their Hopes: The Battles for Chattanooga.* Urbana: Univ. of Illinois Press, 1994.

———. *This Terrible Sound: The Battle of Chickamauga.* Urbana: Univ. of Illinois Press, 1992.

Crandall, Warren D., and Isaac D. Newell. *History of the Ram Fleet and the Mississippi Marine Brigade in the War for the Union on the Mississippi and Its Tributaries.* St. Louis: Buschart Brothers, 1907.

Crocker, Helen B. *The Green River of Kentucky.* Lexington: Univ. Press of Kentucky, 1976.

Crofts, Daniel W. *Reluctant Confederates: Upper South Unionists in the Secession Crisis.* Chapel Hill: Univ. of North Carolina Press, 1989.

Current, Richard Nelson. *Lincoln's Loyalists; Union Soldiers from the Confederacy.* Boston: Northeastern Univ. Press, 1992.

Daniel, Larry, and Lynn Bock. *Island Number 10: Struggle for the Mississippi Valley.* Tuscaloosa: Univ. of Alabama Press, 1996.

Dargan, Elizabeth Paisley, editor. *The Civil War Diary of Martha Abernathy, Wife of Charles C. Abernathy of Pulaski, Tennessee.* Beltsville, Md.: Professional Printing Inc., 1994.

Davenport, F. Garvin. *Cultural Life in Nashville on the Eve of the Civil War.* Chapel Hill: Univ. of North Carolina Press, 1941.

Davis, Darrell Haug. *The Geography of the Jackson Purchase.* Frankfort: Frankfort Geological survey, 1923.

Davis, William C. *Diary of a Confederate Soldier: John S. Jackman of the Orphan Brigade.* Columbia S.C.: Univ. of South Carolina Press, 1990.

———, editor. *The Orphan Brigade: the Kentucky Confederates Who Couldn't Go Home.* Garden City, N.Y.: Doubleday, 1980.

Davis, Worthington. *Camp-fire Chats of the Civil War.* Hartford: Park Publishing Company, 1887.

Dennett, Tyler. *Lincoln and the Civil War in the Diaries and Letter of John Hay.* New York: Dodd, Mead, 1939.

Dew, Charles B. *Ironmaker to the Confederacy: Joseph R. Anderson and the Tredegar Iron Works.* New Haven: Yale Univ. Press, 1966.

Dicey, Edward. *Spectator of America.* Edited by Herbert Mitgang. Athens: Univ. of Georgia Press, 1989 edition.

Dodson, W. C. *Campaigns of Wheeler and His Cavalry.* Atlanta: Hudgins, 1897.

Douglas, Bird. *Steamboatin' on the Cumberland.* Nashville: Tennessee Book Company, 1961.

Bibliography

Dugan, James. *History of Hurlbut's Fighting Fourth Division and Especially the Marches, Toils, Privations, Adventures, Skirmishes, and Battles of the Fourteenth Illinois Infantry.* Cincinnati: Published by author, 1863.

Duke, Basil Wilson. *History of Morgan's Cavalry.* Cincinnati: Miami Printing and Publishing Company, 1867.

Durham, Walter T. *Nashville, the Occupied City: The First Seventeen Months, February 16, 1862, to June 1863.* Nashville: Tennessee Historical Society, 1985.

———. *Rebellion Revisited: A History of Sumner County, Tennessee, from 1861 to 1870.* Nashville: Sumner County Museum Association, 1982.

———. *Reluctant Partners: Nashville and the Union, July 1, 1863, to June 30, 1865.* Nashville: Tennessee Historical Society, 1987.

Dyer, Frederick H. *A Compendium of the War of the Rebellion.* New York: Thomas Yoseloff, 1959. 3 volumes.

Dyer, Gustavus W., and John Trotwood Moore, compilers. *The Tennessee Civil War Veterans Questionnaires.* Edited by Colleen Morse Elliott and Louise Armstrong Moxley. Easley, S.C.: Southern Historical Press, 1985. 5 volumes.

Dyer, John P. *From Shiloh to San Juan: the Life of "Fightin' Joe" Wheeler.* Baton Rouge: Louisiana State Univ. Press, 1941.

Eddy, Thomas M. *The Patriotism of Illinois.* Chicago: Clarke, 1865. 2 volumes.

Escott, Paul D. *After Secession: Jefferson Davis and the Failure of Confederate Nationalism.* Baton Rouge: Louisiana State Univ. Press, 1978.

Fellman, Michael. *Inside War: the Guerrilla Conflict in Missouri During the American Civil War.* New York: Oxford Univ. Press, 1989.

Fitch, John. *Annals of the Army of the Cumberland.* Philadelphia: J. B. Lippincott, 1864.

Fleming, Samuel M. *The Reminiscences of Sergeant Newton Cannon.* Edited by Campbell H. Brown. Franklin, Tenn.: The Carter House Association, 1963.

Folmsbee, Stanley J., Robert E. Corlew, Enoch L. Mitchell. *Tennessee: A Short History.* Knoxville: Univ. of Tennessee Press, 1969.

Fuller, Mrs. G. T. *History of Camp Beauregard, Graves County, Kentucky.* Mayfield, Ky.: Tilghman-Beauregard Camp Number 1460, Sons of Confederate Veterans, 1988.

Gallagher, Gary W., editor. *Fighting for the Confederacy: The Personal Recollections of General Edward Porter Alexander.* Chapel Hill: Univ. of North Carolina Press, 1989.

Gavin, William Gilfillan, editor. *Infantryman Pettit: The Civil War Letters of Corporal Frederick Pettit.* Shippensburg, Pa.: White Mane Publishing Company, 1990.

George, Henry. *History of the Third, Seventh, Eighth, and Twelfth Kentucky, C.S.A.* Louisville: C. T. Daring, 1911.

Gibson, Charles Dana, and E. Kay Gibson. Assault and Logistics, Union Army Coastal and River Operations 1861–1866. [Vol. 2—the Army's Navy Series.] Camden, Maine: Ensign Press, 1995. 3 volumes.

Gildrie, Richard, Philip Kemmerly, Thomas H. Winn. *Clarksville, Tennessee, in the Civil War: a Chronology.* Clarksville: Montgomery County Historical Society, 1984.

Graf, Leroy P., editor. *The Papers of Andrew Johnson.* Vol. 7. Knoxville: Univ. of Tennessee Press, 1986.

Graf, Leroy P., and Ralph W. Haskins., editors. *The Papers of Andrew Johnson.* Volume 5. Knoxville: Univ. of Tennessee Press, 1979.

———. *The Papers of Andrew Johnson.* Volume 6. Knoxville: Univ. of Tennessee Press, 1983.

Grant, Ulysses S. *Personal Memoirs.* New York: Charles Webster and Sons, 1885, 2 volumes.

Grebner, Constantin. *"We Were the Ninth": A History of the Ninth Regiment, Ohio Volunteer Infantry April 17, 1861, to June 7, 1864.* Edited and translated by Frederic Trautmann. Kent, Ohio: Kent State Univ. Press, 1987.

Greene, W. P., editor and compiler. *The Green River Country from Bowling Green to Evansville: Its Traffic, Its Resources, Its Towns and Its People.* Evansville, Ind.: J. S. Reily, 1898.

Grimsley, Mark. *The Hard Hand of War: Union Military Policy toward Southern Civilians, 1861–1865.* New York: Cambridge Univ. Press, 1995.

Hafendorfer, Kenneth A. *Perryville: Battle for Kentucky.* Owensboro, Ky.: McDowell Publications, 1981.

Hagerman, Edward. *The American Civil War and the Origins of Modern Warfare.* Bloomington: Indiana Univ. Press, 1988.

Hale, Douglas. *The Third Texas Cavalry in the Civil War.* Norman: Univ. of Oklahoma Press, 1993.

Hall, Clinton R. *Andrew Johnson, Military Governor of Tennessee.* Princeton: Princeton Univ. Press, 1916.

Hartigen, Richard Shelby. *Lieber's Code and the Law of War.* South Holland, Ill.: Precedent Publishing, 1983.

Hattaway, Herman, and Archer Jones. *How the North Won: A Military History of the Civil War.* Urbana: Univ. of Illinois Press, 1983.

Bibliography

Hay, Thomas Robson, editor, and Irvin A. Buck. *Cleburne and His Command and Pat Cleburne.* Dayton, Ohio: Morningside, 1985.

Henderson, Mary Bess McCain, Evelyn Janet McCain Young, Anna Irene McCain Naheloffer. *"Dear Eliza": The Letters of Mitchel Andrew Thompson.* Ames, Iowa: Carter Press, 1976.

Henry, Robert Selph, editor. *As They Saw Forrest: Some Recollections and Comments of Contemporaries.* Jackson, Tenn.: McCowat-Mercer Press, 1956.

———. *"First with the Most Forrest.* Indianapolis: Bobbs-Merrill, 1944.

Herr, Kincaid. *The Louisville and Nashville Railroad, 1850–1963.* Louisville: Public Relations Department, Louisville and Nashville, 1964.

Holmes, James Taylor. *Fifty-Second Ohio Volunteer Infantry: Then and Now.* Columbus: Berlin Printing Company, 1898.

Hoobler, James A. *Cities Under the Gun: Images of Occupied Nashville and Chattanooga.* Nashville: Rutledge Hill Press, 1986.

Hoppin, James M. *Life of Andrew Hull Foote.* New York: Harper and Brothers, 1874.

Horn, Stanley F. *The Army of Tennessee.* Indianapolis: Bobbs-Merrill, 1941.

Howard, Victor B. *Black Liberation in Kentucky: Emancipation and Freedom 1862–1864.* Lexington: Univ. Press of Kentucky, 1983.

Hubert, Charles F. *History of the Fiftieth Regiment Illinois Volunteers in the War of the Union.* Kansas City: Western Veteran Publishing Company, 1894.

Huffstodt, Jim. *Hard Dying Men: the Story of General W. H. L. Wallace, General T. E. G. Ransom, and Their "Old Eleventh" Illinois Infantry in the American Civil War (1861–1865).* Bowie, Md.: Heritage Books Inc., 1991.

Hughes, Nathaniel, editor. *Liddell's Record: St. John Richardson Liddell, Brigadier General, CSA, Staff Officer and Brigade Commander, Army of Tennessee.* Dayton, Ohio: Morningside, 1985.

Hughes, Nathaniel Cheairs, Jr., and Roy P. Stonesifer Jr. *The Life and Wars of Gideon J. Pillow.* Chapel Hill: Univ. of North Carolina Press, 1993.

Hunter, Louis C. *Steamboats on the Western Rivers: an Economic and Technological History.* Cambridge: Harvard Univ. Press, 1949.

Johnson, Adam R. *The Partisan Rangers of the Confederate Army.* Edited by William J. Davis. Louisville: George G. Fetter, 1904; reprint, Austin, Tex.: State House Press, 1995.

Johnston, William Preston. *Life of General Albert Sidney Johnston.* New York: D. Appleton, 1878.

Jolly, Ellen Bryan. *Nuns of the Battlefield.* Providence: Providence Visitor Press, 1927.

Jones, Archer. *The Art of War in the Western World.* Urbana: Univ. of Illinois Press, 1987.

———. *Civil War Command and Strategy: The Process of Victory and Defeat.* New York: Free Press, 1992.

Jordan, Thomas, and J. P. Pryor. *The Campaigns of Lieut. Gen. N. B. Forrest and Forrest's Cavalry.* Dayton: Morningside, 1977 edition.

Josyph, Peter, editor. *The Wounded River: The Civil War Letters of John Vance Lauderdale, M.D.* East Lansing: Michigan State Univ. Press, 1993.

Kennett, Lee. *Marching Through Georgia: The Story of Soldiers and Civilians During Sherman's Campaign.* New York, Harper Collins, 1995.

Killebrew, J. B. *Introduction to the Resources of Tennessee.* Nashville: Tavel, Eastman and Howell, 1874. 2 volumes.

———. *Middle Tennessee as an Iron Centre.* Nashville: Tavel, Eastman and Howell, 1879.

Kinkhead, Elizabeth Shelby. *A History of Kentucky.* New York: American Book Company, 1896.

Kirke, Edmund. *Down in Tennessee and Back by Way of Richmond.* New York: Carleton, 1864.

Krug, Mark M., editor. *Mrs. Hill's Journal—Civil War Reminiscences.* Chicago: R. Donnelly and Sons, 1980.

Lacy, Eric Russell. *Vanquished Volunteers: East Tennessee Sectionalism from Statehood to Secession.* Johnson City: East Tennessee Univ. Press, 1965.

Laqueur, Walter. *Guerrilla: A Historical and Critical Study.* Boston: Little, Brown, 1976.

Lash, Jeffrey N. *Destroyer of the Iron Horse: General Joseph E. Johnston and Confederate Rail Transport 1861–1865.* Kent: Kent State Univ. Press, 1991.

Lesley, J. P. *The Iron Manufacterer's Guide to the Furnaces, Forges and Rolling Mills of the United States.* New York: John Wiley, 1859.

Lindsley, John Berrien. *Military Annals of Tennessee: Confederate, First Series.* Nashville: J. M. Lindsley, 1886.

Long, E. B. *The Civil War Day By Day; An Almanac 1861–1865.* Garden City, N.Y.: Doubleday, 1971.

Longacre, Edward. *Mounted Raids of the Civil War.* South Brunswick, N.J.: A. S. Barnes, 1975.

Lord, Walter, editor. *The Fremantle Diary.* Boston: Little, Brown, 1954.

Bibliography

Lossing, Benson J. *Pictorial History of the Civil War.* Hartford, Conn., 1868, 3 volumes.
Losson, Christopher. *Tennessee's Forgotten Warriors; Frank Cheatham and His Confederate Division.* Knoxville: Univ. of Tennessee Press, 1989.
Lowry, Thomas P. *The Story the Soldiers Wouldn't Tell: Sex in the Civil War.* Harrisburg, Pa.: Stackpole, 1994.
Lyle, W. W. *Lights and Shadows of Army Life.* Cincinnati: R. W. Carroll, 1865.
Lyon, Adelia, compiler. *Reminiscences of the Civil War . . . from War Correspondence of Colonel William F. Lyon.* San Jose, Calif.: Muirson and Wright, 1907.
Lytle, Andrew Nelson. *Bedford Forrest and His Critter Company.* New York: Milton, Balsh, 1931.
Magee, Benjamin Franklin. *History of the Seventy-Second Indiana, Wilder's Brigade.* Huntington, WVa.: Blue Acorn Press, 1992.
Maness, Lonnie E. *An Untutored Genius: The Military Career of General Nathan Bedford Forrest.* Oxford, Miss.: The Guild Bindery Press, 1990.
Marszalek, John F. *Sherman: A Soldier's Passion for Order.* New York: Free Press, 1993.
Marvel, William. *Burnside.* Chapel Hill: Univ. of North Carolina Press, 1991.
Maslowski, Peter. *Treason Must Be Made Odious: Military Occupation and Wartime Reconstruction in Nashville, Tennessee, 1862–1865.* Millwood, N.Y.: KTO Press, 1978.
McClain, Iris Hopkins. *A History of Houston County.* Columbia, Tenn.: Privately published, 1966.
McDonough, James L. *Chattanooga—a Death Grip on the Confederacy.* Knoxville: Univ. of Tennessee Press, 1984.
———. *Shiloh—in Hell Before Midnight.* Knoxville: Univ. of Tennessee Press, 1977.
———. *Stones River—Bloody Winter in Tennessee.* Knoxville: Univ. of Tennessee Press, 1980.
———. *War in Kentucky: From Shiloh to Perryville.* Knoxville: Univ. of Tennessee Press, 1994.
McDowell, Robert Emmett. *City of Conflict: Louisville in the Civil War 1861–1865.* Louisville Civil War Round Table, 1962.
McKee, John Miller. *The Great Panic: Being Incidents Connected with Two Weeks of the War in Tennessee.* Nashville: Johnson and Whiting, 1862.
McKenzie, Robert Tracy. *One South or Many? Plantation Belt and Upcountry in Civil War-Era Tennessee.* New York: Cambridge Univ. Press, 1995.
McMillan, Malcom C., editor. *The Alabama Confederate Reader.* Tuscaloosa: Univ. of Alabama Press, 1963.
McPherson, James M. *Abraham Lincoln and the Second American Revolution.* New York: Oxford Univ. Press, 1990.
McRaven, Henry. *Nashville: The Athens of the South.* Chapel Hill: Univ. of North Carolina Press, 1949.
Meacham, Charles Mayfield. *A History of Christian County, Kentucky from Oxcart to Airplane.* Nashville: Marshall and Bruce, 1930.
Meriwether, Elizabeth Avery. *Recollections of Ninety-Two Years, 1824–1916.* Nashville: Tennessee Historical Commission, 1958.
Merritt, Dixon. *The History of Wilson County: Its Land and Its Life.* Nashville: Benson Printing Company, 1961.
Millett, Allan R., and Peter Maslowski. *For the Common Defense: A Military History of the United States of America.* New York: Free Press, 1984., rev. ed., 1994.
Mitchell, Red. *Civil War Soldiers: Their Expectations and Their Experiences.* New York: Viking, 1988.
Moffatt, Thomas. *A Union Soldier's Civil War: Experience of Thomas William Moffatt Sr. as told to his son Wallace Wilson Moffatt.* Privately published, 1962.
Morton, John Watson. *The Artillery of Nathan Bedford Forrest's Cavalry.* Nashville: Publishing House of the Methodist Episcopal Church South, 1909.
Munden, Kenneth W., and Henry Putney Beers. *Guide to Federal Archives Relating to the Civil War.* Washington: National Archives and Records Service, 1962.
Murfin, James V. *The Gleam of Bayonets: The Battle of Antietam and the Maryland Campaign of 1862.* New York: Thomas Yoseloff, 1965.
Neely, Mark E., Jr. *The Fate of Liberty: Abraham Lincoln and Civil Liberties.* New York: Oxford Univ. Press, 1991.
Ninety-Second Illinois Volunteers. Freeport, Ill.: Journal Stream Publishing House and Bookbindery, 1875.
Norton, Anne. *Alternative Americas: A Reading of Antebellum Political Culture.* Chicago: Univ. of Chicago Press, 1986.
Nott, Charles C. *Sketches of the War: A Series of Letters to the North Moore Street School of New York.* New York: Anson D. F. Randolph, 1865.
One Hundred and Forty-Third New York Regimental Association Committee. *A Condensed History of the One Hundred and Forty-Third Regiment New York Volunteer Infantry.* Newburgh, N.Y.: Newburgh Journal and Printing House, 1909.

Owen, Robert Dale. *The Future of the North-West in Connection with the Scheme of Reconstruction without New England*. Philadelphia: Published by author, 1863.

Owens, Ira S. *Green County Soldiers in the Late War, Being a History of the Seventy-Fourth Ohio Volunteer Infantry*. Dayton, 1884.

Paludan, Phillip Shaw. *Victims: A True Story of the Civil War*. Knoxville: Univ. of Tennessee Press, 1981.

Parks, Joseph H. *General Leonidus Polk, C. S. A.: The Fighting Bishop*. Baton Rouge: Louisiana State Univ. Press, 1962.

Patton, James Welch. *Unionism and Reconstruction in Tennessee*. Chapel Hill: Univ. of North Carolina Press, 1934.

Perkins, Steve L., editor. *Terry's Texas Rangers: Reminiscences of J. K. P. Blackburn*. Austin: Ranger Press, 1979 reprint.

Piston, William Garrett. *Carter's Raid: An Episode of the Civil War in East Tennessee*. Johnson City, Tenn.: The Overmountain Press, 1989.

Plum, William R. *The Military Telegraph During the Civil War in the United States*. Chicago: Jansen, McClurg, 1881. 2 volumes.

Putnam, A. W. *History of Middle Tennessee*. Knoxville: Univ. of Tennessee Press, 1971.

Quint, Alonzo H. *The Potomac and the Rapidan; Army Notes, From the Failure at Winchester to the Reenforcement of Rosecrans 1861–3*. Boston: Crosby and Nichols, 1864.

Ramage, James A. *Rebel Raider; The Life of General John Hunt Morgan*. Lexington: Univ. Press of Kentucky, 1986.

Ramsdell, Charles W., editor. *Laws and Joint Resolutions of the Last Session of the Confederate Congress (November 7, 1864–March 18, 1865; Together with the Secret Acts of Previous Congresses*. Durham: Duke Univ. Press, 1941.

Reed, Rowena. *Combined Operations in the Civil War*. Annapolis: Naval Institute Press, 1978.

Reynolds, Edwin H. *A History of the Henry County Commands*. Jacksonville: Sun Publishing Company 1904.

Rice, Ralsa C. *Yankee Tigers: Through the Civil War with the One Hundred and Twenty-fifth Ohio*. Edited by Richard A. Baumgartner and Larry M. Strayer. Huntington, WVa.: Blue Acorn Press, 1992.

Richardson, Albert D. *The Secret Service, the Field, the Dungeon, and the Escape*. Hartford: American Publishing Company, 1865.

Ridgley, J. V. *Nineteenth-Century Southern Literature*. Lexington: Univ. Press of Kentucky, 1980.

Ridley, Bromfield L. *Battles and Sketches of the Army of Tennessee*. Mexico, Mo.: Missouri Printing and Publishing Company, 1906.

Roland, Charles P. *Albert Sidney Johnston: Soldier of Three Republics*. Austin: Univ. of Texas Press, 1964.

Roman, Alfred. *Military Operations of General Beauregard*. New York: Harper and Brothers, 1884. 2 volumes.

Rowell, John W. *Yankee Artillerymen: Through the Civil War with Eli Lilly's Indiana Battery*. Knoxville: Univ. of Tennessee Press, 1975.

———. *Yankee Cavalrymen; Through the Civil War with the Ninth Pennsylvania Cavalry*. Knoxville: Univ. of Tennessee Press, 1971.

Royster, Charles, *The Destructive War: William Tecumseh Sherman, Stonewall Jackson, and the Americans*. New York: Knopf, 1991.

Royster, Charles. *A Revolutionary People at War: The Continental Army and American Character, 1775–1783*. Chapel Hill: Univ. of North Carolina Press, 1979.

Ruggles, C. L. *The Great American Scout and Spy, "General Bunker." Illustrated*. New York: Olmstead, 1870.

Safford, James M. *Geology of Tennessee*. Nashville: S. C. Mercer, 1869.

Scarborough, William Kaufman, editor. *The Diary of Edmund Ruffin*. Baton Rouge: Louisiana State Univ. Press, 1976. 2 volumes.

Schroeder-Lein, Glenna. *Confederate Hospitals on the Move: Samuel H. Stout and the Army of Tennessee*. Columbia, S.C.: Univ. of South Carolina Press, 1994.

Sears, Stephen W. *Landscape Turned Red*. New York: Ticknor and Fields, 1983.

Sefton, James E. *Andrew Johnson and the Uses of Constitutional Power*. Boston: Little, Brown, 1980.

Seitz, Donald C. *Braxton Bragg: General of the Confederacy*. Columbia, S.C.: Univ. of South Carolina Press, 1924.

Sensing, Thurman. *Champ Ferguson; Confederate Guerrilla*. Nashville: Vanderbilt Univ. Press, 1942.

Shepard, Eric William. *Bedford Forrest: The Confederacy's Greatest Cavalryman*. New York: Dial, 1930.

Sheridan, Philip H. *Personal Memoirs*. New York: Charles L. Webster, 1888. 2 volumes.

Sherman, William T. *Memoirs*. New York: D. Appleton, 1875. 2 volumes.

Shy, John. *A People Numerous and Armed; Reflections on the Military Struggle for American Independence*. New York: Oxford Univ. Press, 1976.

Sievers, Harry J. *Benjamin Harrison: Hoosier Warrior, through the Civil War Years 1833–1865*. New York: Univ. Publishers, 1952.

Bibliography

Silverstone, Paul H. *Warships of the Civil War Navies.* Annapolis: Naval Institute Press, 1989.
Simon John M., editor. *The Papers of Ulysses S. Grant.* Edwardsville: Southern Illinois Univ. Press, 1967–1991. 18 volumes.
Simpson, Brooks D. *Let Us Have Peace: Ulysses S. Grant and the Politics of War and Reconstruction 1861–1868.* Chapel Hill: Univ. of North Carolina Press, 1991.
Simpson, John A. *S. A. Cunningham and the Confederate Heritage.* Athens: Univ. of Georgia Press, 1994.
Smart James G., editor. *A Radical View: The "Agate" Dispatches of Whitelaw Reid 1861–1865.* Memphis: Memphis State Univ. Press, 1976. 2 volumes.
Smith, Daniel P. *Company K, First Alabama Regiment or Three Years in the Confederate Service.* Prattville, Ala.: By Survivors, 1885.
Speed, Thomas. *The Union Cause in Kentucky 1860–1865.* New York: G. P. Putnam's Sons, 1907.
Stanley, David. *Personal Memoirs.* Cambridge, Mass.: Harvard Univ. Press, 1917.
Starnes, H. Gerald. *Forrest's Forgotten Horse Brigadier.* Bowie, Md.:, Heritage Books, 1995.
Starr, Stephen Z. *Jennison's Jayhawkers; A Civil War Cavalry Regiment and Its Commander.* Baton Rouge: Louisiana State Univ. Press, 1973.
———. *The Union Cavalry in the Civil War: Volume III, The War in the West 1861–1865.* Baton Rouge: Louisiana State Univ. Press, 1985.
Steele, Matthew Forney. *American Campaigns.* Washington: Infantry Journal Press, 1943. 2 volumes.
Strode, Hudson, *Jefferson Davis, Confederate President.* New York: Harcourt, Brace, 1959.
Stryker, Lloyd Paul. *Andrew Johnson: A Study in Courage.* New York: Macmillan, 1932.
Sunderland, Glenn W. *Five Days to Glory.* Cranbury, N.J.: A. S. Barnes, 1970.
Sword, Wiley. *Mountains Touched with Fire: Chattanooga Besieged.* New York: St. Martins, 1995.
———. *Shiloh: Bloody April.* New York: Morrow, 1974.
Symonds, Craig L. *Joseph E. Johnston: A Civil War Biography.* New York: W. W. Norton, 1992.
Tapp, Hambleton, and James C. Klotter. *Kentucky: Decades of Discord 1865–1900.* Frankfort: Kentucky Historical Society, 1977.
Taylor, Benjamin. *Pictures of Life in Camp and Field.* Chicago: S. C. Griggs and Company, 1875.
Temple, Oliver P. *Notable Men of Tennessee, from 1833–1875.* New York: Cosmopolitan Press, 1912.
Tennessee Civil War Centennial Commission. *Tennesseans in the Civil War.* Nashville: Tennessee Civil War Centennial Commission, 1964. 2 volumes.
Thatcher, Marshall P. *A Hundred Battles in the West: St. Louis to Atlanta 1861–1865; The Second Michigan Cavalry.* Detroit: Published by author, 1884.
Thomas, Emory M. *The Confederacy as a Revolutionary Experience.* Englewood Cliffs, N.J.: Prentice-Hall, 1977.
———. *The Confederate Nation.* New York: Harper and Row, 1979.
Time-Life Books, editors. *Arms and Equipment of the Confederacy.* Alexandria, Va.: Time-Life Books, 1991.
———. *Spies, Scouts, and Raiders.* Alexandria, Va.: Time-Life Books, 1985.
Tower, R. Lockwood, editor. *A Carolinian Goes to War: The Civil War Narrative of Arthur Middleton Manigault, Brigadier General, C.S.A.* Columbia, S.C.: Univ. of South Carolina Press, 1983.
Troutman, Richard, editor. *The Heavens Are Weeping; The Diaries of George R. Browder, 1852–1886.* Grand Rapids, Mich.: Zondervan Publishing House, 1987.
Tucker, Glenn. *Chickamauga: Bloody Battle in the West.* Indianapolis: Bobbs-Merrill, 1961.
Tucker, Phillip Thomas. *The South's Finest: The First Missouri Confederate Brigade from Pea Ridge to Vicksburg.* Shippensburg, Pa.: White Mane Publishing Company, 1993.
Vale, Joseph G. *Minty and the Cavalry: A History of Cavalry Campaigns in the Western Armies.* Harrisburg, Pa.: Edwin K. Meyers, 1886.
Van Horne, Thomas B. *History of the Army of the Cumberland.* Cincinnati: Robert Clarke and Company, 1875. 2 volumes.
Vetter, Charles Edmund. *Sherman: Merchant of Terror, Advocate of Peace.* Gretna, La.: Pelican Publishing Company, 1992.
Waring, George E., Jr. *Whips and Spur.* New York: Doubleday and McClure, 1897.
Warner, Ezra T. *Generals in Blue: Lives of the Union Commanders.* Baton Rouge: Louisiana State Univ., 1964.
———. *Generals in Gray: Lives of the Confederate Commanders.* Baton Rouge: Louisiana State Univ., 1959.
Waters, Charles M. *Historic Clarksville; The Bicentennial Story, 1784–1984.* Clarksville: Historic Clarksville Publishing Company, 1983.

Weigley, Russell F. *History of the United States Army.* New York: Macmillan, 1967.

Welcher, Frank J. *The Union Army, 1861–1865: Organization and Operations, Volume II: The Western Theater.* Bloomington: Indiana Univ. Press, 1993.

Wert, Jeffrey D. *General James Longstreet: The Confederacy's Most Controversial Soldier, a Biography.* New York: Simon and Schuster, 1993.

White, Robert H., editor. *Messages of the Governors of Tennessee, 1796–1899.* Nashville: Tennessee Historical Commission, 1952–1972. 8 volumes.

Whitley, Edythe Johns. *Sam Davis, Hero of the Confederacy, 1842–1863. Coleman's Scouts.* Nashville: Blue and Gray Press, 1971.

Wilkie, Fran B. *Pen and Powder.* Boston: Ticknor, 1888.

Willett, Charles E., editor. *A Union Soldier Returns South: The Civil War Letters and Diary of Alfred C. Willett, 113th Ohio Volunteer Infantry.* Johnson City, Tenn.: The Overmountain Press, 1994.

Williams, Kenneth P. *Lincoln Finds a General.* New York: Macmillan, 1952–1959. 5 volumes.

Williams, T. Harry. *Lincoln and His Generals.* New York: Grosset and Dunlap, 1952.

Wills, Brian Steel. *A Battle from the Start; The Life of Nathan Bedford Forrest.* New York: Harper Collins, 1992.

Woodworth, Steven E. *Jefferson Davis and His Generals: The Failure of Confederate Command in the West.* Lawrence, Kans.: Univ. Press of Kansas, 1990.

Wyeth, John Allen. *That Devil Forrest: Life of General Nathan Bedford Forrest.* New York: Harper, 1959.

Yearns, W. Buck. *The Confederate Governors.* Athens: Univ. of Georgia Press, 1985.

Young, Bennett H. *Confederate Wizards of the Saddle.* Boston: Chapple, 1914.

Young, J. P. *The Seventh Tennessee Cavalry (Confederate): A History.* Nashville: Publishing House of Methodist Episcopal Church South, 1890.

Younger, Edward, editor. *Inside the Confederate Government: The Diary of Robert Garlick Hill Kean.* New York: Oxford Univ. Press, 1957.

ARTICLES AND ESSAYS

"A. L. C." [Arthur L. Conger]. "Fort Donelson." *The Military Historian and Economist* 1 (Jan. 1916): 55–89.

Alexander, Hudson. "Trials and Tribulations of Fountain Branch Carter and His Franklin Tennessee Home." *Blue and Gray* 12 (Feb. 1995): 30–34.

Andrews, J. Cutler. "The Confederate Press and Public Morale." *Journal of Southern History* 31 (Nov. 1966): 445–65.

Ash, Stephen V. "A Community at War: Montgomery County, 1861–65." *Tennessee Historical Quarterly* 36 (Spring 1977): 30–43.

―――. "Sharks in an Angry Sea: Civilian Resistance and Guerrilla Warfare in Occupied Middle Tennessee, 1862–1865." *Tennessee Historical Quarterly* 45 (Fall 1986): 217–29.

Atack, Jeremy, Erik F. Haites, James Mak, Gary Walton. "The Profitability of Steamboating on Western River: 1850." *Business History Review* 49 (Autumn 1975): 346–54.

Bailey, Anne J. "The Mississippi Marine Brigade: Fighting Rebel Guerrillas on Western Rivers." *Military History of the Southwest* 22 (Spring 1992): 31–42.

Bailey, Hugh C. "Disaffection in the Alabama Hill Country, 1861." *Civil War History* 4 (June 1958): 183–93.

―――. "Reaction in the Tennessee Valley to Federal Invasion." *Bulletin of the North Alabama Historical Association* 5 (1960): 3–9.

Beatty, John. "A Regiment in Search of A Battle." In *Sketches of War History, 1861–1865; Papers Prepared for Loyal Legion of the United States, Ohio Commandery, 1888–1890,* edited by Robert Hunter, 3: 422–52. Cincinnati: Robert Clarke, 1890.

Beaumont, Roger. "Unconventional Warfare." In *Encyclopedia of the American Military,* edited by John E. Jessup and Louise B. Ketz, 3: 1771–1803. New York: Charles Scribner's Sons, 1994.

Bigelow, Martha. "Freedmen of the Mississippi Valley, 1862–1865." *Civil War History* 8 (Mar. 1962): 38–47.

Bowen, Don R. "Quantril, James, Younger, et al.: Leadership in a Guerrilla Movement, Missouri, 1861–1865." *Military Affairs* 41 (Feb. 1977): 42–48.

Brandt, Robert S. "Lightning and Rain in Middle Tennessee: The Campaign of June–July 1863." *Tennessee Historical Quarterly* 52 (Fall 1993): 158–69.

Bibliography

Brewer, James D. "The Battle of Britton's Lane; The Climax of Armstrong's Raid," *Blue and Gray Magazine,* X (April 1993): 34–38.

Bright, Thomas R. "Yankees in Arms: The Civil War as a Personal Experience." *Civil War History* 19 (Sept. 1973): 197–218.

Brooks, Addie Lou. "The Building of the Trunk Line Railroads in West Tennessee, 1852–1861." Tennessee Historical Commission and Tennessee Historical Society. *Tennessee Old and New: Sesquicentennial Edition, 1796–1946.* Nashville: Commission and Society, 1946, 2: 188-211.

Brown, Lenard E. "Fortress Rosecrans: A History, 1865–1990." *Tennessee Historical Quarterly* 50 (Fall 1990): 135–41.

"Capt. W. B. Allbright." *Confederate Veteran* 10 (June 1902): 275.

"The Chattanooga Rebel." Tennessee and Historical Commission and Tennessee Historical Society. *Tennessee Old and New: Sesquicentennial Edition, 1796–1946.* Nashville: Commission and Society, 1946, 2: 273–79.

Cheatham, Gary L. "'Desperate Characters': Development and Impact of the Confederate Guerrillas in Kansas." *Kansas History* 14 (Autumn 1991): 144–61.

Chester, William W. "The Skirmish at Lockridge Mill in Weakley County, Tennessee, May 6, 1862." *Journal of the Jackson Purchase Historical Society* 15 (June 1987): 49–54.

Cook, W. L. "Furnaces and Forges." *Tennessee Historical Quarterly* 9 (Oct. 1925): 190–92.

Cooling, Benjamin F. "The Attack on Dover, Tenn." *Civil War Times Illustrated* 2 (Aug. 1963): 10–13.

———. "The Battle of Dover, February 3, 1863." *Tennessee Historical Quarterly* 15 (Dec. 1956): 143–51.

Copeland, James. "Where Were the Kentucky Unionists and Secessionists." *Kentucky Historical Society Register* 71 (Oct. 1973): 344–63.

Crabb, Alfred Leland. "The Twilight of the Nashville Gods." *Tennessee Historical Quarterly* 15 (Dec. 1956): 291–305.

Criswell, Howard, Jr. "A Conversation with the Past." *Civil War Times Illustrated* 29 (Mar./Apr. 1990): 55–63.

Current, Richard N. "Lincoln, the War, and the Constitution." In *Leadership During the Civil War,* edited by Roman J. Heleniak and Lawrence T. Hewitt, 1–16. Shippensburg, Pa.: White Mane Publishing Company, 1992.

Curry, Richard O., and F. Gerald Ham, editors. "The Bushwhackers War: Insurgency and Counter-Insurgency in West Virginia." *Civil War History* (Dec. 1964): 416–433.

Daniel, Larry J. "'The Assaults of the Demagogues in Congress': General Albert Sidney Johnston and the Politics of Command." *Civil War History* 37 (Dec. 1991): 328–35.

Davis, Louise. "Box Seat on the Civil War: Rachel Carter's Diary," *The Tennessean Magazine.* (Apr. 1979): 6–11.

Disbrow, Donald W., editor. "Vett Noble of Ypsilanti: A Clerk for General Sherman." *Civil War History* 14 (Mar. 1968): 15–39.

Donnelly, Ralph W. "Local Defense in the Confederate Munitions Area." In *Military Analysis of the Civil War: An Anthology,* 239–51. Millwood, N.Y.: KTO Press, 1977.

Fisher, Noel C. "'Prepare Them for My Coming': General William T. Sherman, Total War, and Pacification in West Tennessee." *Tennessee Historical Quarterly* 51 (Summer 1992): 75–86.

———. "'The Leniency Shown Them Has Been Unavailing': The Confederate Occupation of East Tennessee." *Civil War History* 40 (Dec. 1994): 275–91.

Foner, Eric. "The South's Inner Civil War." *American Heritage* 40 (Mar. 1989): 47–56.

Freidel, Frank. "General Orders 100 and Military Government; Rules for Occupying Armies Formulated in the United States Civil War." *Mississippi Valley Historical Review* 32 (Mar. 1946): 541–46.

Garratt, M. C. "1863 Letter Tells of Mixed Emotion of the Civil War," Murray (Kentucky) *Ledger and Times,* Mar. 3, 1977.

Gaston, Kay Baker. "A World Overturned: The Civil War Experience of Dr. William A Cheatham and His Family." *Tennessee Historical Quarterly* 50 (Winter 1991): 3–16.

Gates, John M. "Indians and Insurrectos: The U.S. Army's Experience with Insurgency." In *The Parameters of War: Military History from the Journal of the U.S. Army War College,* edited by Lloyd J. Matthews and Dale E. Brown, 197–208. New York: Pergamon-Brassey's, 1987.

"Gen. W. B. Wade's Military Achievements." *Confederate Veteran* 14 (Jan. 1906): 17–18.

Gildrie, Richard P. "Guerrilla Warfare in the Lower Cumberland River Valley, 1862–1865." *Tennessee Historical Quarterly* 49 (Fall 1990): 161–76.

———. "Woodward's Raid on Clarksville, August, September, 1862." *Cumberland Lore* (Clarksville), Oct. 7, 1985, 3.

Gow, June I. "The Johnston and Brent Diaries: A Problem of Authorship." *Civil War History* 14 (Mar. 1968): 46–50.

Grimsley, Mark. "Burning Down the South." *Civil War Times Illustrated* 34 (Sept./Oct. 1995): 48–55.

Hagerman, Edward. "Field Transportation and Strategic Mobility in the Union Armies." *Civil War History* 34 (June 1988): 143–71.

Hall, Kermit L. "Tennessee." In *The Confederate Congress*, edited by W. Buck Yearns, 185–94. Athens: Univ. of Georgia Press, 1985.

Halley, R. A. "A Rebel Newspaper's War Story: Being a Narrative of the War History of the Memphis *Appeal*." In Tennessee Historical Commission and Tennessee Historical Society, *Tennessee Old and New; Sesquicentennial Edition*, 2: 247–72. Nashville: Tennessee Historical Commission and Tennessee Historical Society, 1977.

Harris, William C. "Andrew Johnson's First 'Swing Around the Circle': His Northern Campaign of 1863." *Civil War History* 35 (June 1989): 153–71.

Harrison, Lowell H. "Kentucky." In *The Confederate Congress*, edited by W. Buck Yearns, 83–90. Athens: Univ. of Georgia Press, 1985.

Harsh, Joseph L. "Lincoln's Tarnished Brass: Conservative Strategies and the Attempt to Fight the Early Civil War as a Limited War." In *The Confederate High Command and Related Topics*, edited by Roman J. Heleniak and Lawrence L. Hewitt, 124–41. Shippensburg, Pa.: White Mane Publishing Company, 1990.

Hewitt, Lawrence L. "Braxton Bragg and the Confederate Invasion of Kentucky in 1862." In *Leadership During the Civil War*, edited by Roman T. Heleniak and Lawrence L. Hewitt, 55–72, Shippensburg, Pa.: White Mane Publishing Company, 1992.

Hoobler, James A., editor. "The Civil War Diary of Louisa Brown Pearl." *Tennessee Historical Quarterly* 38 (Fall 1979): 308–21.

Horn, Stanley F. "Nashville During the Civil War." *Tennessee Historical Quarterly* 4 (Mar. 1945): 3–22.

Huston, James A. "Logistical Support of Federal Armies in the Field." *Civil War History* 7 (Mar. 1961): 36–47.

Janda, Lance. "Shutting the Gates of Mercy: The American Origins of Total War, 1860–1880." *Journal of Military History* 59 (Jan. 1995): 7–26.

Johnson, Leland R. "Civil War Railroad Defenses in Tennessee." *Tennessee Valley Historical Review* (Summer 1972): 20–26.

Jones, James B., Jr. "A Tale of Two Cities: The Hidden Battle Against Venereal Disease in Civil War Nashville and Memphis." *Civil War History* 30 (Sept. 1985): 270–76.

———. "Sam Davis, Boy Hero of the Confederacy," *The Courier* (Publication of the Tennessee Historical Society) 30 (Feb. 1992): 4–5.

Kelly, R. M. "The Secret Union Organization in Kentucky in 1861." In *Sketches of War History, 1861–1865: Papers Prepared for Loyal Legion of United States, Ohio Commandery, 1888–1890*, edited by Robert Hunter, 3: 278–91. Cincinnati: Robert Clarke, 1890.

Keuchel, Edward F., and James P. Jones. "Charley Schreel's Book: Diary of a Union Soldier on Garrison Duty in Tennessee." *Tennessee Historical Quarterly* 36 (Summer 1977): 197–207.

Kutger, Joseph P. "Irregular Warfare in Transition." *Military Affairs* 24 (Fall 1960): 113–23.

La Pointe, Patricia M. "Military Hospitals in Memphis, 1861–1865." *Tennessee Historical Quarterly* 42 (Winter 1983): 325–342.

Lash, Jeffrey. "'The Federal Tyrant at Memphis': General Stephen A. Hurlbut and the Union Occupation of West Tennessee, 1862–64." *Tennessee Historical Quarterly* 48 (Spring 1989): 15–28.

Lovett, Bobby L. "Nashville's Fort Negley: A Symbol of Blacks' Involvement with the Union Army." *Tennessee Historical Quarterly* 41 (Spring 1982): 3–22.

Lufkin, Charles L. "Divided Loyalties: Sectionalism in Civil War McNairy County, Tennessee." *Tennessee Historical Quarterly* 47 (Fall 1988): 169–77.

Mahon, John K. "Anglo-American Methods of Indian Warfare, 1676–1794," *Mississippi Valley Historical Review* 45 (Sept. 1958), 254–75.

Maness, Lonnie E. "Captain Charles Cooper Nott and the Battle of Lockridge's Mills." *Journal of the Jackson Purchase Historical Society* 3 (June 1975): 12–20.

———. "Forrest and the Battle of Parker's Crossroads." *Tennessee Historical Quarterly* 34 (Summer 1975): 154–67.

Martin, James B. "Black Flag Over the Bluegrass: Guerrilla Warfare in Kentucky, 1863–1865." *Kentucky Historical Quarterly* 86 (1988): 352–75.

Marzalek, John F. Review of Lee Kennett, *Marching Through Georgia: The Story of Soldiers and Civilians During Sherman's Campaign* in *The Journal of American History* 82 (Dec. 1995): 1221.

McDaniel, Dennis K. "The Twelfth Wisconsin Infantry Regiment in West Tennessee." *Tennessee Historical Quarterly* 33 (Fall 1974): 255–64.

McGhee, C. Stuart. "Military Origins of the New South: The Army of the Cumberland and Chattanooga Freedmen." *Civil War History* 34 (Dec. 1988): 323–43.

McGlone, John. "'What Became of General Barrow?' The Forgotten Story of George Washington Barrow." *Tennessee Historical Quarterly* 48 (Spring 1989): 37–45.

McPherson, James M. "From Limited to Total War: Missouri and the Nation, 1861–1865." *Gateway Heritage* 12 (Spring 1992): 4–19.

McWhiney, Grady. "Controversy in Kentucky: Braxton Bragg's Campaign of 1862." *Civil War History* 6 (Mar. 1960): 5–42.

"Nashville When in the Confederacy." *Confederate Veteran* 18 (Mar. 1910): 127.

Ney, Virgil. "Guerrilla War and Modern Strategy." *Orbis* 2 (Spring 1958): 66–82.

Nixon, W. M. "Amos Wilson Judd." *Confederate Veteran* 37 (Jan. 1930): 27.

Parks, Edwards. "Around the Mall and Beyond." *Smithsonian* 24 (July 1993): 12–13.

Pearlman, Michael. "Political Objectives and the Development of Military Strategy." In *Encyclopedia of the American Military*, edited by John E. Jessup and Louis H. Ketz, 1: 297–328. New York: Charles Scribner's Sons, 1994.

Pearson, Alden B., Jr. "A Middle-Class Border-State Family During the Civil War." *Civil War History* 22 (Dec. 1976): 318–36.

"PLF" [Patricia L. Faust]. "Confiscation Act of 1862." In *Historical Times Illustrated Encyclopedia of the Civil War*, edited by Patricia L. Faust, 157. New York: Harper and Row, 1986.

Richards, Channing. "Dealing with Slavery." In *Sketches of War History 1861–1865: Papers Prepared for Delivery for the Ohio Commandery of the Military Order of the Loyal Legion of the United States*, edited by W. H. Chamberlin, 4: 315–26. Cincinnati: Robert Clarke, 1896.

Riley, Harris D., and Amos Christie. "Deaths and Disabilities in the Provisional Army of Tennessee." *Tennessee Historical Quarterly* 43 (Summer 1984): 132–54.

Roberts, John C., and Richard H. Weber. "Gunboats in the River War, 1861–1865." *United States Naval Institute Proceedings* 91 (Mar. 1965): 83–99.

Ross, John K., Jr. "Civil War Letters Update." *Journal of the Jackson Purchase Historical Society* 19 (June 1991): 31–32.

———. "Five Civil War Letters." *Journal of the Jackson Purchase Historical Society* 18 (June 1990): 27–30.

Roth, David. "Grierson's Raid: April 17–May 2, 1863: A Cavalry Raid at Its Best." *Blue and Gray* (June 1993): 12–27, 48–65.

Rule, William. "The Loyalists of Tennessee in the Late War." In *Sketches of War History 1861–1865; Papers Read Before the Ohio Commandery of the Military Order of the Loyal Legion of the United States 1886–1888*. 2: 180–204. Cincinnati: Robert Clarke, 1888.

Schroeder-Lein, Glenna R. "Confederate Army of Tennessee Hospitals in Chattanooga." *Journal of East Tennessee History* 66 (1994): 32–58.

Siburt, James T. "Colonel John M. Hughs: Brigade Commander and Confederate Guerrilla." *Tennessee Historical Quarterly* 51 (Summer 1992), 87–95.

Smith, Dwight L. "Impressment, Occupation, War's End, and Emancipation: Samuel E. Tillman's Account of Seesaw Tennessee." *Tennessee Historical Quarterly* 49 (Fall 1990): 177–87.

Smith, Everard H. "Chambersburg: Anatomy of a Confederate Reprisal." *American Historical Review* 96 (Apr. 1991): 432–55.

Stanberry, Jim, editor. "A Confederate Surgeon's View of Fort Donelson: The Diary of John Kennerly Farris." *Civil War Regiments*, 1: 7–19.

Stanley, David. "The Tullahoma Campaign." In *Sketches of War History 1861–1865: Papers for Delivery to the Ohio Commandery, Loyal Legion of the United States, 1880–1890*, edited by Robert Hunter, 3: 166–181. Cincinnati: Robert Clarke, 1890.

Stevens, Guy C. "Iron Again Flows from Old Cumberland Furnace." *Nashville Banner Magazine*, Nov. 21, 1937, 5.

Stevenson, Benjamin F. "Kentucky Neutrality in 1861." In *Sketches of War History 1861–1865: Papers Read Before the Ohio Commandery of the Military Order of the Loyal Legion of the United States 1886–1888*, 2: 44–70. Cincinnati: Robert Clarke, 1888.

Sutherland, Daniel E. "Abraham Lincoln, John Pope, and the Origins of Total War." *Journal of Military History* 56 (Oct. 1992): 567–86.

———. "Getting the 'Real War' into the Books." *Virginia Magazine of History and Biography* 98 (Apr. 1990): 193–220.

Swanson, Guy R., and Timothy D. Johnson. "Conflict in East Tennessee: Generals Law, Jenkins and Longstreet." *Civil War History* 31 (June 1985): 101–10.

Temple, Wayne C., editor. "Fort Donelson in October 1862." *Lincoln Herald* 69 (Summer 1967): 92-95.

Thayer, George A. "A Railroad Feat of War." In *Sketches of War History 1861-1865: Papers Prepared for Presentation to the Ohio Commandery of the Loyal Legion of the United States, 1890–1896,* 4: 214–34, edited by W. H. Chamberlin. Cincinnati: Robert Clarke, 1896.

Waldrop, Christopher, "Rank-and-File Voters and the Coming of the Civil War: Caldwell County, Kentucky, as Test Case." *Civil War History* 35 (Mar. 1989): 59–72.

Walker, Cam. "Corinth: The Story of a Contraband Camp." *Civil War History* 20 (Mar. 1974): 15–22.

Weaver, H. C. "Morgan's Raid in Kentucky, Indiana, and Ohio, July 1863." In *Sketches of War History 1861–1865: Papers Prepared for Presentation to the Ohio Commandery of the Loyal Legion of the United States, 1890–1896,* 4: 278–314, edited by W. H. Chamberlin. Cincinnati: Robert G. Clarke, 1896.

Webb, Ross A. "A Yankee from Dixie: Benjamin Helm Bristoe." *Civil War History* 10 (Mar. 1964): 80–94.

Weller, Jac. "The Logistics of Nathan Bedford Forrest." in *Military Analysis of the Civil War: An Anthology,* 170–78. Millwood, N.Y.: KTO Press, 1977.

Whitesell, Hunter B. "Military Operations in the Jackson Purchase Area of Kentucky, 1862–1865." *Kentucky Historical Society Register* 63 (Apr. 1965): 141–67; (July 1965): 240–67.

Whitesitt, W. H. "A Year with Forrest." *Confederate Veteran* 25 (Aug. 1917): 357–59.

Williams, Robert W., and Ralph A. Wooster, editors. "With Terry's Texas Rangers: The Letters of Dunbar Affleck," *Civil War History* 9 (Sept. 1963): 299–319.

Williams, T. Harry. "The Military Leadership of North and South." In *Why the North won the Civil War,* edited by David Donald. Baton Rouge: Louisiana State Univ. Press, 1960.

Williams, W. "A Reminiscence of Clarksville, Tenn.," *Confederate Veteran* 22 (May 1914): 206–7.

Wilson, Terry. "'Against Such Powerful Odds': The Eighty-third Illinois at the Battle of Dover." *Tennessee Historical Quarterly* 53 (Winter 1994): 260–71.

Woodworth, Steven E. "'The Indeterminant Qualities': Jefferson Davis, Leonidus Polk, and the End of Kentucky Neutrality, September 1861." *Civil War History* 38 (Dec. 1992): 289–97.

NEWSPAPERS

Clarksville *Chronicle.*
Nashville *Times.*
Memphis *Avalanche.*
Washington (D.C.) *National Tribune.*
Dover (Tenn.) *Stewart-Houston Times.*
Paris (Ky.) *Western Citizen.*

UNPUBLISHED MATERIAL

Daniel, John S., Jr. "Special Warfare in Middle Tennessee and Surrounding Areas, 1861–1862." M.A. thesis, Univ. of Tennessee, 1971.

Chumney, James Robert. "Don Carlos Buell: Gentleman General." Ph.D. diss., Rice Univ., 1964.

DeBerry, John. "Confederate Tennessee." Ph.D. diss., Univ. of Kentucky, 1967.

Grimsley, Christopher M. "A Directed Severity: The Evolution of Federal Policy Toward Southern Civilians and Property, 1861–1865." Ph.D. diss., Ohio State Univ., 1992.

Gunter, Charles R., Jr. "History of the Civil War in Bedford County." M.A. thesis, Univ. of Tennessee, 1965.

Lawson, Hughie G. "Geographical Origins of White Migrants to Trigg and Calloway Counties in the Antebellum Period." Unpublished typescript, copy, circa 1981.

Tennessee Valley Authority. "'The Homeplace—1850' Living History Farm in Land Between the Lakes; Historical Documentation and Program Outline." Unpublished typescript, n.d.

Tomlinson, Helga, compiler and editor. *"Dear Friends":* The Civil War Letters and Diary of Charles Edwin Cort. N.p., 1962.

Toops, Ronald E., editor. "The McConnell Letters: The Civil War Letters of Robert McConnell." N.p., 1975.

INDEX

Abernathy, Alfred Harris, 6
Abernathy, Martha, 25, 54–55, 120–21
Acker, Philip, 115
Adams, Wirt, 27, 47
Adamson, Frederick C., 224
Affleck, Dunbar, 176, 222, 223, 240, 260
African-Americans: as freedmen laborers, 126–27, 146, 147, 150, 261, 292, 313–14, 316, 344; as fugitive slaves, 40–41, 42, 67, 114, 158, 183, 190, 243, 244, 259, 267, 288, 301, 323, 345; as slaves, xiv, xvii, 4, 10, 19, 29, 34, 36, 39, 60, 61, 67, 74, 87, 89, 90, 106, 113, 125, 126, 136, 144, 156, 177, 180, 196, 287, 288, 301, 335, 343, 345; as soldiers, 210, 213, 215, 255, 261, 277, 286, 287, 289, 296, 301, 316, 335, 344
Aiken's Landing, Va., 119
Alabama: Jackson County, 76, 84; unionism in, 251, 253
Alabama units, Confederate: Fourteenth Battalion (Malone), 198; Fourth cavalry (Russell), 202; Morgan's cavalry, 146
Albany, Ky., 208
Alexander, Isaac, 241
Alexander, J., 27
Alexander, J. H., 6
Allbright, W. B., 102
Allensville, Ky., 157
Alley, Charles, 203
Alloway, N. E., 85
Alston, R. A., 136
Altamont, Tenn., 86
American-Freedmen's Inquiry Commission, 345
Anderson (?) (guerrilla), 73, 96

Anderson, Charles, 196
Anderson, J. B., 52, 81, 163, 322
Anderson, John G., 129
Anderson, S. R., 147
Anderson's Crossroads, Tenn., 309
Andrews, George W., 95, 96, 98
Anthony, Daniel R., 100
Anthony, Dewitt C., 312
Antioch Church, Tenn., 265
Antioch Station, Tenn., 248–49
Antietam, 122, 143
Appleton's *Railroad Guide*, 30
Armstrong, Frank C., 100, 101, 128, 254
Army-Navy cooperation, xiii, 5, 222–31, 282, 283, 285, 323, 325, 326, 327, 343
Army of Central Kentucky (CSA), 26
Army of the Cumberland (USA), 160, 173, 180, 206, 212, 219, 222, 224, 231, 245, 255, 269, 271, 276, 293, 303, 306, 315, 318, 320, 333, 335
Army of Kentucky (USA), 191
Army of Middle Tennessee (CSA), 149
Army of Northern Virginia (CSA), 304, 333
Army of the Ohio (USA), 10, 80
Army of the Potomac (USA), 127, 180, 238, 275, 309, 322
Army of Tennessee (CSA), 299, 333
Army of Virginia (USA), 63
Articles of War, 18, 287
Asboth, Alexander, 183, 205, 216, 217, 250, 266, 285, 286
Ash, Stephen V., xv, 45, 343
Ashburn, George W., 97
Ashby, Turner, 64, 67

Index

Ashland, Tenn., 73
Athens, Ala., 75, 140
Atkins, Smith D., 144
Atlanta, Ga., 9, 14, 80, 119, 300, 304, 305, 322, 336
Auburn, Tenn., 219, 244

Bailey, James Edmund, 6
Bainbridge, Ala., 274
Baird, J. P., 249
Bankhead, S. P., 110
Barber, Flavel C., 1
Bardstown, Ky., 135, 281
Barker, John "Nick," 84, 102, 160, 190
Barren River, 30, 31
"The Barrens," 270, 271, 272
Barron, Samuel, 123, 141
Barrow, George Washington, 22, 52
Batchelor, Benjamin Franklin, 56–57, 58, 201, 202
Baton Rouge, La., 253
Battle, A., 28, 58
Baugh, Thomas J., 193
Bay, Hugh, 218
Bayliss, William, 5, 6
Bean, Richard, 161
Bear Creek, Tenn., 245
Beatly, "Tinker Dave," 68
Beats (Betsy) Town, Tenn., 226
Beatty, John F., 15, 22, 29, 174, 230, 242, 245, 247, 272, 277, 278, 335
Beauregard, P. G. T., 8, 9, 13, 27, 37, 46, 48, 49, 51, 54, 58, 59, 78, 123, 124, 178, 207, 304
Beersheba Springs, Tenn., 86
"Belbo, Captain" (guerrilla), 328
Belisle, W. T., 184
Bell, John, 16, 17, 33
Bell, Mrs. John, 21
Bell, Mary Walker Meriwether, 329
Bell, Tyree H., 336
Bell Buckle, Tenn., 241
Bellbuckle Gap, Tenn., 270
Belle Meade Plantation, 37, 46
Belmont, battle of, 264
Benjamin, Judah P., 26, 27, 64
Benton, Ky., 217
Benton Barracks, Mo., 97
Berger, John A., 88, 171
Berlin, Ira, 296
Biffle, Jacob, 14, 67, 72, 73, 150, 267, 280, 284, 285, 286, 336
Big Barren River, 22
Big Black River, 324
Big Creek Gap, Ky., 282, 298
Big Hill, Ky., 156

Big Sandy River, 244
Bingham, J. B., 301, 331
Bingham, J. D., 141
Bishop, Michael P., 5
Blackburn, George W., 129
Blackmore, Betty Ridley, 143
Blanchard, Ira, 2, 3, 74, 184
Blanton, Major (CSA), 217
Bledsoe, Willis Scott, 54, 68, 86, 313
Bloodgood, Edward, 247
Bobo's Crossroads, Tenn., 272
Bock, Lynn, 13
de Boernstein, Carl Schaffer, 54
Bolivar, Tenn., 100, 110 165
Bon Aqua Springs, Tenn., 202
Boone, William P. 74
Bowen, Berry S., 33
Bowles, James, 68
Bowles, Theodore C., 131
Bowling Green, Ky., 7, 8, 10, 11, 12, 15, 30, 32, 33, 36, 40, 47, 52, 55, 56, 72, 82, 127, 131, 137, 156, 159, 160, 179, 234, 243, 248, 322
Boyer, Frederick Nathan, 239, 274, 307, 317
Boyle, Jeremiah, 73, 86, 89, 92, 93, 112, 113, 122, 128, 136, 137, 138, 140, 144, 155, 160, 163, 165, 185, 214, 231, 245, 246, 287, 289, 295, 340
Brackett, Alfred B., 297
Braden, Daniel P., 209
Bradyville, Tenn., 180, 245
Bragg, Braxton, 47, 78, 79, 80, 81, 86, 94, 107, 121; and Chattanooga/Chickamauga, 277, 278, 280, 294, 298, 299, 303, 304, 305; and fight for Middle Tennessee, 160, 165, 168, 169, 172, 176, 185, 188, 191, 207, 214, 219, 223, 230, 234, 240, 241, 244, 247, 249, 250, 251, 254, 255, 264, 265; and Kentucky campaign, 123, 124, 126, 128, 129, 130, 134, 135, 139, 141, 142, 143, 145, 146, 148, 151, 152, 153, 287; and Tullahoma campaign, 266, 267, 268, 269, 270, 271, 272, 273, 275; and siege of Chattanooa, 306, 307, 311, 312, 218, 320, 321, 322, 330, 331, 332, 333, 339
Bramlette, T. E., 215, 289, 340
Brandenburg, Ky., 282
Breckenridge, William K. M., 229, 285
Breckinridge, John C., 9, 33, 122, 146, 148, 150, 151
"Breckinridge Guards," 72
T. M. Brennan Company (Nashville, Tenn.), 32
Brentwood, Tenn., 247, 248, 249
Bridgeport, Ala., 29, 131, 295, 309, 316, 320
Bringhurst, Mrs., 97
Bristow, Benjamin Helm, 125, 135, 139, 243
Britton's Lane, Tenn., 100
Brooks, Daniel R., 137

Index

Brott, E. C., 158
Browder, Richard George, 37, 89, 90, 99, 157, 177, 206, 209, 257, 258, 335, 340
Brown, Bergun, 129, 147, 154
Brown, Lenard, 182
Brown, Lezinka, 262
Brown, W. N., 1
Brownlow, William G., 237, 277
Brown's Ferry, Tenn., 316
Bruce, E. M., 9
Bruce, Sanders D., 113, 155, 156, 159, 160, 161, 190, *191*, 195, 200, 214, 224, 227, 242, 256, 296
Bruch, Samuel, 130
Bryantsville, Ky., 135
Buckner, D. P., 13
Buckner, Simon Bolivar, 2, 3, 4, 7, 8, 49, 79, 80, 122, 241, 264, 282, 283, 298, 305, 307
Buell, Don Carlos: and civil-military policy, 24, 38, 39, 40, 43–44, 50, 69, 85, 91, 109, 111, 140, 141, 151–52, 301, 345; and 1862 operations, 8, 10, 13, 15, 22, 27, 28, 32, 44, 45, 46, 52, 69, 74, 75, 78, 79, 81, 82, 83, 84, 88, 89, 91, 94, 95, 98, 101, 109, 110, 117, 123, 142, 145, 241, 265, 273; and Kentucky campaign, 127–30, 132–38, 144
Buffalo Creek, Tenn., 73
Buffington's Island, Ohio, 282
Buford, N. B., 221, 222
Bull Run, battle of First, 25, 64
Bullis, Robert E., 50, 51
Bunting, Robert F., 21
Burford, E. S., 310
Burkesville, Ky., 156
Burnside, Ambrose E.: and civil-military relations, 222, 342; and departmental conditions, 230, 246, 257, 264, 276, 280, 289, 290, 342; and East Tennessee, 180, 185, 292, 293, 294, 297, 298, 302, 312, 325, 326, 327, 331, 333, 338, 342; and Morgan, 281, 282, 283

Cadiz, Ky., 156, 255, 257
Cage's Ford, Tenn., 155
Cairo, Ill., 9, 30, 114, 118, 185, 193, 266, 286, 304, 340
Camp Beauregard, Ky., 11, 36
Camp Coleman, Ky., 135, 136, 328
Camp Dick Robinson, Ky., 246
Camp Nelson, Ky., 292
Camp Winford, Tenn., 275
Camp Zollicoffer, Tenn., 67
Campbell, Alexander J., 1, 84, 118, 119, 120, 176
Campbell, Archibald, P., 273
Campbell, Lewis D., 83
Campbell, William B., 34, 140, 300
Caney Fork, 223

Cannon, Newton, 240, 274
Carlin, W. P., 158
Carpenter, Arthur P., 28, 40, 134, 261
Carrington, Henry B., 261
Carrollsville, Tenn., 230
Carter, Franklin Branch, 235
Carter, George W., 109
Carter, S. P., 232, 249–50, 330
Carter, Tod, 235
Carter's Creek, 297
Carthage, Tenn., 129, 161, 170, 226
Cartwright, Lon, 142
Caruthers, Robert, 300
Caseyville, Ky., 67, 115, 137
Castalian Springs, Tenn., 162, 170
Catton, Bruce, 100
Cave City, Ky., 56, 130
Celina, Tenn., 72
Central Army of Kentucky (CSA), 10, 12
Centreville, Tenn., 202
Cerro Gordon, Tenn., 229
Chadick, Mary Jane, 76
Chalmers, James R., 13, 250, 265, 266, 284, 290, 308, 311, 312, 321, 322, 323, 330, 337
Chaplin River, 134
Charlotte, N.C., 123
Charlotte, Tenn., 73, 98, 158, 161, 187, 202, 216, 255, 296
Chase, Salmon P., 42, 212
Chattanooga, Tenn., 13, 14, 15, 21, 26, 28, 75, 78, 80, 82, 83, 86, 89, 91, 125, 138, 146, 242, 243, 264, 267, 269, 271, 279, 292, 293, 298, 299, 300, 302, 303, 305, 306, 308, 309, 312, 315, 317, 318, 319, 322, 331, *334*, 338, 342; battle of, xiv, xvii, 332, 333
Chattanooga *Daily Rebel*, 235
Cheairs, Nathaniel, 1
Cheatham, Benjamin Franklin, 161, 162
Cheatham, Mary, 208, 339, 340
Cheatham, R. B., 21, 22
Cheatham, William, 339, 340
Chenault, D. W., 281
Chestnut Mound, Ky., 12
Chicago *Times*, 216
Chicago *Tribune*, 221
Chickamauga, battle of, xiv, 305–6, 307, 317, 319, 338, 339, 340
Church, Benjamin, 65
Cincinnati, Ohio, 102, 120, 123, 124, 128, 185, 280, 282, 295
Cincinnati *Enquirer*, 216
Civil-Military Relations, 18–19, 22–24, 25, 29, 35, 36, 37, 38, 42, 43, 51, 52, 53, 54, 60, 67, 69, 71, 72, 75, 76, 79, 84, 86, 88, 89, 90, 97, 100, 107, 112, 113, 120, 121, 128, 129, 134, 156, 163, 164, 166, 169, 171,

{393}

Index

Civil-Military Relations, *cont.*
210, 211, 212, 213, 215, 219, 234, 235, 236, 239, 245, 257, 258, 259–60, 262, 287, 289, 290, 297, 298, 300, 314, 329, 331, 334, 335, 337, 338, 340, 341, 342, 343, 344, 345
Claiborne, Thomas, 54
Clark, Charles T., 204
Clark, J. Warren, 271
Clark River, 30
Clarksburg, Tenn., 168
Clarksville, Tenn., xv, 7, 12, 13, 16, 17, 18, 33, 34, 36, 41, 44, 52, 53, 67, 75, 89, 102, 103, 136, 146, 157, 158, 159, 160, 162, 166, 172, 187, 189, 191, 193, 208, 214, 215, 224, 226, 242, 255, 256, 257, 262, 295, 297, 300, 314, 315, 316, 326, 327, 329; Union recapture of, 105–7; Woodward's capture of, 94–98, 108
Clarksville Female Academy, 34
von Clausewitz, Karl, x–xiii
Clay, C. C., 76
Clay, Thomas H., 90
Cleburne, Patrick, 264, 332
Cleveland, Tenn., 319
Clift, M. H., 254
Clift, William, 109
Clifton, Tenn., 164, 168, 184, 201, 223, 224, 253
Clinton, Ky., 217, 250, 266, 267, 285
Cloud, B. F., 212
Cluke, Roy S., 245, 250
Coble, Samuel, 246
Coburn, John F., 246
Cockran, J. B., 124
Coldwater, Mich., 168
Coleman, E., 308
Coleman's Scouts, 340
"Collective Punishment," 62, 91
College Grove, Tenn., 245
Colliersville, Tenn., 265, 312
Columbia, Ky., 156
Columbia, Tenn., 14, 33, 72, 73, 74, 88, 92, 158, 160, 163, 187, 196, 201, 202, 215, 243, 270, 297, 314, 322, 337
Columbus, Ky.: as Confederate post, 8, 9, 12, 26–27, 30, 36, 67, 123, 136; as Union post, 75, 100, 108, 164, 166, 168, 169, 179, 183, 206, 216, 265, 266, 285, 286, 305, 325, 338
Columbus, Ohio, 324
Commercial Trade, 122, 177–78, 222, 341
Como, Tenn., 54
Conciliatory Policy, 60, 75, 139–41, 149, 220, 343
Confederate River Defense, 11, 123–24, 142, 156, 223, 224, 230, 325
Confiscation Acts, 18, 62, 113, 287
Connelly, Jesse B., 87, 88, 131–32, 138, 239, 244, 274, 278

Connolly, James A, 237, 271, 272, 276, 277
Conscription: Confederate, 50, 78, 147, 148, 149, 270, 286; Union, 209, 238, 257, 335
Continental Army (Revolution), 44, 278
Contraband Trade, 160, 187, 218, 231, 326, 330
Conzett, Josiah, 105, 272, 273, 312
Cook, Rufus Howell, 84
Cooper, Duncan B., 72, 129
Cooper, Samuel, 123, 146, 151, 153
"Copperhead" Movement, 174, 207, 238, 261, 276, 280, 335
Corinth, Miss., 13, 27, 36, 54, 58, 60, 61, 76, 78, 83, 162, 165, 183, 225, 250, 252, 266, 294, 318, 325, 328, 337; battle of, 122, 142, 148, 168
Cornyn, F. M., 224, 250, 251
Corse, Montgomery C., 312
Cotton: cash crop, 28–29, 81, 286; trade in, 42–43, 59, 60, 61, 116, 231
Coulter, E. Merton, 288
Counter-Guerrilla Operations, 103, 157–59, 165, 183, 187, 216, 244, 255, 287
Covington, Josephine, 37
Covington, Ky., 123
Cowan, Tenn., 272, 310
Cowen, Ed and Dorsey (Waverly, Tenn.), 33
Cox, Jacob D., 261
Cox, Jesse, 169, 238, 239, 335, 340
Cox, N. N., 302
Crab Orchard, Ky., 156
Crittenden, George, 12, 47
Crittenden, John, 87
Crittenden, Thomas T., 87
Croft, J. F., 50
Crofts, Daniel, xv, 33
Crook, George D., 308, 310, 311, 330
Crosby, George B., 247
Cuba Ford, Tenn., 164
Cullum, George W., 232
Culp, Martin W., 291
Cumberland City, Tenn., 295
Cumberland, Department of, 130, 214, 296
Cumberland Gap, Ky., 28, 79, 80, 85, 91, 93, 109, 126, 135, 143, 148, 298, 328
Cumberland Iron Works, 102, 195, 216
Cumberland Mountains, 274, 280, 292
Cumberland Plateau, 68, 272
Cumberland River, 1, 7, 8, 12, 20, 22, 27, 30, 31, 33, 35, 44, 53, 82, 93, 97, 101, 102, 103, 104, 105, 114, 115, 116, 122, 142, 148, 153, 155, 159, 162, 163, 164, 166, 171, 180, 181, 183, 185, 187, 188, 189, 190, 191, 204, 208, 223, 225–26, 227, 229, 230, 242, 253, 255, 256, 268, 295, 305, 313, 325, 326, 341
Cumberland Rolling Mill, 201
Cumming, Kate, 26

Index

Cunningham, Sumner Archibald, 3
Curtis, Samuel R., 168
Cushman, Pauline, 273
Cynthiana, Ky., 136

Dalton, Ga., 333
Dana, Charles A., 299, 300, 316, 317
Daniel, Larry, 13
Daniels, James W., 128
Danville, Ky., 85, 295
Danville (Tenn.) Railroad Bridge, 16
Danville, Va., 339
Daugherty, Ferdinand H., 328
Davies, Thomas A., 110, 136, 137, 166, 167, 168, 183
Davies, Thomas T., 144
Davis, Charles H., 114, 115
Davis, Jefferson, 1, 9–10, 13, 27, 36, 51, 79, 107, 137, 152, 154, 238, 254, 275, 303, 307, 322, 336; and East Tennessee, 35, 148, 149, 249, 320, 333; and hard war, 343; and Kentucky, 133, 134; and partisans, 64
Davis, Jefferson C., 133, 202, 274
Davis, Joseph, 303
Davis, Sam, 340
Dawson, W. A., 266
Dean, Henry, 102
De Bow's Review, 64–65
Decatur, Ala., 14, 21, 54, 88, 279, 322, 328
Dechard, Tenn., 76, 272, 277
Denmark, Tenn., 100, 337
Dent, Henry, 156
Department Number 2 (CSA), 78
Dibrell, George C., 150, 251, 272, 279, 336
Dicey, Edward, xvi
Dickey, T. Lyle, 102
Dickinson, Daniel, 237
Dillahunty plantation (Savannah, Tenn.), 226
Dodge, Grenville, 75, 77, 100, 166, 167, 183, 225, 227, 252, 253, 328, 331, 332, 337, 338
Dorris, William H., 193, 216, 262, 277, 284, 314, 326, 340
Douglas, D. C., 302
Douglas, Hugh, 209
Dover, Tenn., 1, 4, 5, 6, 15, 19, 33, 43, 52, 74, 95, 99, 101, 102, 104, 108, 158, 160, 224, 226, 256, 261, 325, 326; August 1862 skirmish, 101–2; February 1863 battle, 188–206, 283
Dover (Bufford) Hotel, 4
Drake, Isaac, 33
Dresden, Tenn., 54, 167
Drish, James, 5, 16
Driver, William, 23
Duck River, 30, 31, 49, 52, 98, 114, 146, 160, 177, 182, 183, 187, 188, 202, 214, 219, 226, 230, 244, 252, 253, 270, 271, 272, 273, 274, 279, 308

Duke, Basil, 78, 94, 122, 163, 283
Duling, John, 34
Dumont, Ebenezer, 52, 53, 55, 56
Dunbars Cave, 95
Dunham, Cyrus L., 168
Dunlap, Tenn., 309
Dunn, Martin, 226
Dutton's Hill, Ky., 246
Dwyer, C., 105
Dyer, Captain (guerrilla), 328
Dyersburg, Tenn., 100, 108

Eagleton, Ethie, 46, 53
Eagleton, George E., 15, 26, 87
Eagleville, Tenn., 245
East Burlington, Ill., 193
East Tennessee, 34, 35, 90, 126, 185, 232, 294, 303, 304, 323, 337; Department of (CSA), 76, 147
East Tennessee and Georgia Railroad, 152
Eastport, Miss., 252, 324, 325, 337
Eaton, John, 183
Eddyville, Ky., 44, 67, 68, 92, 122, 156, 223
Edgefield, Tenn., 13, 19, 21, 52, 149, 151, 159, 180, 206, 207, 237, 273
Edgefield and Kentucky Railroad, 30, 94, 98, 105, 155, 187
Edgefield Junction, Tenn., 158
Edgerly, John, 104, 108
Eighth Brigade (Turchin) (USA), 75
Elizabethtown, Ky., 136, 162, 177, 257, 281
Elk River, 30, 82, 269, 272, 273, 275, 308, 311, 330, 331, 339, 342
Elkins, Spencer, 3
Ellet, Alfred, 252, 253
Elliott, Washington L., 313
Ellsworth, George, 86, 102, 162
Emancipation Proclamation, 144, 149, 177, 180, 207, 235, 245, 287
Enrollment Act of 1863, 238
Evansville, Ind., 166, 327
Everett, P. M., 250
Ewen, Mrs. Andrew, 21
Ewing, Thomas, 156
Ezell, Calvin S., 169

Fairfield, Tenn., 240
Farmington, Tenn., 310, 311
Farquharson, Roger, 7, 8
Fateley, David A., 203
Faulkner, W. W., 72, 321, 323, 328, 329, 336
Fayetteville, Tenn., 29, 33, 46, 330
Feliciana, Ky., 285
Fell, James W., 288
Fellman, Michael, xv

{395}

Index

Ferguson, Champ, 54, 55, 68, 72, 73, 86, 313, 315, 328
Finnell, Ben, 124
Finnell, John, 137
Fisher, C. G., 253
Fisher, Horace N., 23
Fisher, Noel, 62, 149
Fisk, Clinton B., 168
Fitch, John, 258
Fitch, Le Roy, 114, 115, 156, 163, 192, 199, 200, 201, 203, 223, 224, *225*, 226, 227, 229, 230, 231, 253, 282, 325–26, 327
Fitzpatrick, James, 227
Flood, James P., 102
Florence, Ala., 201, 251, 252, 331
Floyd, John B., 3, 6, 7, 8, 10, 12, 13, 14, 15, 22, 70
Foote, Andrew Hull, 5, 16, 114
Foraging, 170–71, *181*, 222, 238, 239, 248
Force, Manning, 170
Ford's Station, Tenn., 105
Forked Deer River, 30, 166
Forrest, Jeffrey, 266, 286
Forrest, Jesse, 284
Forrest, Nathan Bedford: chasing Streight, 251, 253, 254, 255; Chickamauga/Chattanooga, 306, 307, 309; Dover, battle of (1863), 192–206; partisans' rise, 67, 68; post-Fort Donelson, xiv, 6, 8, 14, 22, 52; raiding, summer 1862, 70, 77, 79, 80, 85, 86, 87, 88, 89, 90, 91, 94, 96, 98, 101, 120, 135, 142; Spring/Summer 1873, 259, 270, 279, 304; target Nashville, 146, 148, 149, 150, 152, 153, 154, 155, 159, 160; West Tennessee, 163–70; West Tennessee 1863, 322, 335, 336–37, 339; Winter 1862/1863, 173, 178, 183, 185, 188, 208, 214, 215, 224, 231, 241, 245, 246, 247
Fort Defiance (Bruce), 17, 190, *192*
Fort(s) Henry/Donelson Campaign, 1862, xiii, xiv, xvi, xvii, 1–13, 15, 16, 17, 24, 25, 27, 28, 32, 36, 44, 58, 67, 72, 79, 104, 107, 118, 123, 127, 192, 206, 228, 234, 246, 254, 266, 270, 282, 283, 299, 317, 331, 334, 343–45; prisoners, 114, 118, 129
"Fort Donelson" (U.S. post at Dover), 43, 46, 52, 53, 73, 92, 94, 96, 101, 108, 110, 112, 157, 158, 159, 160, 179, 186, 193, 203
Fort Donelson (Second, U.S.), 205, 216, 224, 250, 253, *256*, 261, 266, 277, 284, 296, 297, 313–14, 326, 327, 328, 334, 340
Fort Granger, 235, 249
Fort Heiman, 50, 52, 84, 92, 95, 101, 104, 110, 158, 170, 179, 188, 193, 195, 216, 217, 266, 285, 301, 325, 328
Fort Henry (Confederate), 1, 2, 7, 16, 24, 25, 27, 67, 79, 118, 120, 123, 127, 184, 334
Fort Henry (Union), 44, 52, 73, 92, 95, 104, 110, 160, 179, 186, 188, 192, 197, 200, 204, 216, 226, 230, 251, 252, 266, 324, 328
Fort Negley, 127, *151*
Fort Pillow, 165, 250, 266, 328, 336
Fort Sanders, 332
Fortress Rosecrans, 182, 234, 271
Foster, John, 99, 231, 298
Fouke, Philip, 19, 53
Fountain Head, Tenn., 125
Foutty, George W., 227
Fowler, Al, 99
Fowler, Peter, 101, 189, 195
Fowler, Wiley P., 54
Fox, Gustavus, 165
"Frank" (mascot), 3
Frankfort, Ky., 122, 124, 130
Franklin, Ky., 243
Franklin, Tenn., xvi, 33, 52, 169, 180, 187, 196, 202, 234, 235, 243, 244, 245, 246, 261, 269, 271, 274, 297, 306, 314, 335
Fraser, P. A. (Miss), 179
Frazier, Jared Carl, 5
Fredericksburg, battle of, 332
Freeman, S. L., 146, 249
Fremantle, Arthur, 264
Fremont, John C., 216
Fry, James R., 69, 81, 85, 86, 127, 215
Fry, Speed, 74
Fuller, John W., 168

Gaddis, M. P., 189
Gainsborough, Tenn., 155
Gallatin, Tenn., 33, 52, 74, 98, 151, 155, 156, 161, 170, 180, 227, 316; Morgan's Raid at, 93–94
Galloway's Switch, Tenn., 165
Galt House (Louisville), 317
Galveston, Tex., 173
Gano, R. M., 86
Garfield, James A., 267–69
Garretsburg, Ky., 193, 329
Garth, H., 94, 99
Gates, G. H., 233
Geiger's Lake, Ky., 108
General Orders (CSA): Number Two Hundred and Twelve, 321
General Orders (USA): Number Eleven, 64; Number Thirty-Eight, 257; Number Sixty, 75; Number One Hundred, 221–22, 257; Number One Hundred and Thirty-Nine, 287; Number One Hundred and Sixty-Eight, 186–87
Georgia units: First Partisan Rangers, 86; Second Cavalry, 87; Fourth Cavalry, 198
Gettysburg, battle of, 275, 283

{396}

Index

Gilbert, A. F., 21
Gilbert, H. C., 309
Gilbert, S. A., 288–89
Gillem, Alvan C., 84, 85, 295
Gilmer, Jeremy, 10, 123, 124
Gillmore, Quincy A., 144, 214, 245, 246
Glasgow, Ky., 72, 86, 322
Goodlettsville, Tenn., 94
Goodpasture, Jefferson, 68
Gordon, William B., 238–39
Gould, Dr., 33
Grainger, Gervis D., 154
Grand Junction, Tenn., 168, 183
Granger, Gordon, 132, 160, 187, 191, 203, 214, 225, 254, 269, 273, 297
Granger, Richard, 160
Grant, Julia, 24, 53
Grant, Ulysses S.: after Chattanooga, 337, 338, 339, 341, 342, 344, 345; and Chattanooga relief, 317, 318, 319, 320, 322, 325, 327, 330, 331, 332, 333, 334; and conciliatory civil policy, 23, 24, 38, 39, 40, 44; and Forts Henry and Donelson, 3, 4, 5, 7, 12, 16, 18, 19, 25, 33, 94, 196; and hard war policy, 60, 61, 68, 75, 77, 110, 111, 114, 117, 221; and Mississippi campaign, 145, 153, 154, 158, 163, 164, 165, 166, 167, 168, 169, 170, 178, 183, 185, 217, 218, 221, 250, 251, 252, 253, 265, 267, 285, 286, 294; in West Tennessee, 27, 28, 52, 53, 54, 78, 91, 95, 99, 100, 102, 103, 105, 122, 136, 137, 139, 142
Graves, Rice E., 150
Great Britain, 173
Grebner, Constantin, 315
Green, James U., 280
Green Bottom, Tenn., 229
Green River, 15, 22, 30, 31, 37, 82, 130, 155, 156, 163, 231, 281
Greene, Oliver D., 84
Greensburg, Ky., 281
Greenville, Miss., 252
Grenada, Miss., 58
Grierson, Benjamin, 251, 336, 337
Griest, Alva C., 130, 132, 171, 172, 233, 240, 243, 262
Griffin, R. B., 92
Griggs, Chauncey, 217, 226
Grimsley, Mark, xv, 38, 39, 60, 113, 169, 220
Guerrillas, 54, 55, 60–64, 67–70, 72–78, 86–92, 99, 100, 102, 104, 107–11, 114–16, 122, 129, 130, 137, 155, 156, 165, 170, 172, 179, 183, 184, 188, 189, 212, 217, 218, 220, 221, 224, 225, 226, 227, 231, 232, 242, 256–58, 261, 262, 266, 279, 284–86, 295, 298, 300, 302, 313–15, 326–28, 331, 338, 340, 342
Guild, Josephus Conn, 52
Gunter's Landing, Ala., 69

Gurley, Frank, 76
Guthrie, James, 139, 173
Guy, John Henry, 6
Guy's Gap, Tenn., 269, 270, 272
Gwinn, William, 68
Gwyn, Hugh, 1

Hagen, James, 247
Hale, Douglas, 242
Hall, Albert S., 247
Hall, Allen A., 212
Halleck, Henry W.: and civil-military policy, 18, 38, 39, 40, 41, 42, 43, 44, 46, 61, 62, 63, 132, 138, 179, 184, 211, 219–22, 255, 257, 290, 341–42, 344–45; and military operations, 5, 16, 27, 28, 60, 77, 78, 80, 81, 82, 83, 84, 89, 100, 102, 103, 117, 127, 135, 139, 155, 164, 172–73, 175, 185, 186, 187, 222, 246, 250, 280, 282, 292–93, 317, 318, 319, 325
Hamilton, Andrew, 25, 97
Hamilton, Charles S., 184, 217
Hamilton, O. P., 72, 73, 313, 315, 322, 328, 336
Hanson, Roger, 150
Hard War Policy/Practice, xv, 60–64, 76, 92, 100, 101, 103, 107, 110, 111, 112, 113, 129, 136, 138, 148, 164, 167, 170, 172, 177, 179, 180, 183, 184, 207, 210, 225, 227, 228, 233, 235, 239, 240, 243, 251, 255, 265, 266, 278, 279, 291, 297, 324, 330, 331, 337, 343–45
Hardee, William, 10, 12, 47, 152, 238, 241, 270, 272, 305
Harding, Abner, 107, 113, 188, 192–205, *194*, 206, 215
Harding, Elizabeth, 37, 129
Harding, William, 37, 46, 52, 129, 172
Harland, John Marshall, 163
Harper, Ellis, 72
Harpers Ferry, Va., 143
Harpeth River, 30, 52, 55, 230, 235, 249, 269
Harpeth Shoals, 158, 189, 190, 195, 225, 226, 227, 327
Harrington, Tenn., 68
Harris, Isham G., 13, 21, 23, 33, 34, 35, 47, 67, 86, 142, 286, 300, 321
Harris, James "Calico Jim," 33
Harris, Theodore, 67
Harris, Thomas W., 165
Harris, William C., 211
Harrison, Benjamin, 236
Harrison, Isaac F., 266
Harrodsburg, Ky., 86
Harsh, Joseph L., 16
Hart, James H., 101, 193
Hartsville, Tenn., 74, 161–62, 170, 248
Hartt, Edward, 115
Harvie, E. J., 303

{397}

Haskins, Nannie, 97, 106
Hatch, Edward, 265, 285
Hatchie River, 30, 110
Hawes, Richard, 130
Hawkins, Alvin, 169
Hawkins, Isaac R., 286
Hawkins, W. S., 315
Haycroft, S., 136, 163, 177, 257
Haydon, J. A., 2
Hazel Green, Ky., 245
Heiman, Adolphus, 20
Helm, Ben Hardin, 94
Helm, Charles J., 28
Helm, Mary Todd, 26
von Helmrich, Gustav, 267
Henderson, Ky., 70, 71, 72, 99, 137, 231, 282
Henderson, R., 303
Henderson's Switch, Tenn., 165
Henry, Albert P., 266
Henry, Gustavus, 9, 320, 321
Henry, John Samuel, 248
Henryville, Tenn., 73
Henson (Hinson), Dick, 261
Henson (Hinson), George, 261, 314
"The Hermitage," 171
Hernando, Miss., 265
Hewitt, Lawrence L., 143
Hickman, Ky., 167, 250, 266, 285, 336
Hicks, S. G., 329
Hill, Daniel Harvey, 303, 305, 307
Hill, Sara Jane, 24, 166–67
Hillsboro, Tenn., 276
Hillsborough and Lynchburg Road, 272
Hindman, Thomas C., 14, 307
Hines, Thomas C., 250, 280–81
Hinkle, J. A., 1
Hitt, Wilbur F., 330
Hobson, Edward Henry, 281
Hodge, G. B., 282–83
Holden, William, 251
Hollingsworth, Samuel, 26
Holloway, Junius, 150, 151
Holly Springs, Miss., 163, 167, 168, 169, 184, 336
Holman, D. W., 190, 201, 202
Holmes, Theophilus, 152, 153
Holston River, 249
Hood, John Bell, 251, 342
Hooker, Joseph, 311, 314, 320
Hoover's Gap, Tenn., 270, 272
Hopkinsville, Ky., 33, 44, 67, 70, 94, 125, 135, 136, 155, 156, 158, 161, 255, 328, 329
The Horse Soldiers, 251
Hoskins, William A., 163
Hough, Alfred Lacey, 223, 274, 277, 278, 292, 317

House, R. M., 316
Howard, Victor, 243, 287
Howard, William, 190, 203, 228, 253
Hubbard, David, 67
Huggins, H. L., 167, 274
Hughs, John M., 68, 315, 328
Hull, J. B., 115
Humboldt, Tenn., 165, 166, 301
Hume, B. M., 107
Hume, William, 107
Huntington, Tenn., 321
Huntsville, Ala., 14, 28, 69, 75, 76, 277, 322
Hurd, Jacob S., 115, 227
Hurlburt, Stephen A., 16, 164, 167, 169, 183, 184, 210, 213, 217, 250, 252, 253, 265, 266, 267, 284, 286, 290, 291, 301, 311, 312, 318, 323, 324, 328, 330, 336
Hurlburt, Valerie, 166, 179
Hurst, Fielding, 117
Huston, James A., 309

Illinois Artillery units: Second Light, Battery C (Flood), 102, 104, 158, 192, 193, 196, 197, 201, 313; Battery H (Stenbeck), 104, 200, 201
Illinois Cavalry units: Second, 108; Seventh, 165
Illinois Central Railroad, 30
Illinois Infantry units: Eleventh, 104, 105, 184, 204, 250; Sixteenth, 150; Twentieth, 74, 184; Twenty-Eighth, 158; Fifty-First, 277; Fifty-Fourth, 165; Fifty-Seventh, 239; Fifty-Ninth, 171, 234, 236, 261, 307, 317, 322; Seventy-Second, 108, 243; Eighty-Third, 104, 108, 157, 158, 188, 192, 193, 194, 195, 197, 203, 215, 216, 284, 313, 314, 326, 334; Eighty-Fifth, 246; Ninety-Second, 240; One Hundred and Fifth, 209; One Hundred and Ninth, 184; One Hundred and Eleventh, 217, 318; One Hundred and Fifteenth, 203, 234; One Hundred and Twenty-Second, 168, 325; One Hundred and Twenty-Third, 237, 242, 271
"Independent Provisional Brigade" (Streight), 251–54
Indian Mound, Tenn., 284
Indiana Infantry units: Fifteenth, 45; Twenty-Ninth, 148, 171; Thirty-First, 131; Thirty-Third, 203; Fifty-Seventh, 132, 171, 233, 277, 306; Fifty-Eighth, 233; Sixty-Fourth, 312; Sixty-Eighth, 130; Seventieth, 291, 322; Seventy-First, 162; Seventy-Second, 132, 171, 233, 262; Seventy-Fifth, 132, 170, 233, 257, 262; Eighty-Third, 330; Eighty-Fifth, 249; Eighty-Ninth, 218
Indianapolis Journal, 283
Ingersoll, Robert G., 166
Ingrams Shoals, 327
Innes, William B., 81, 295
Iowa Cavalry units: Second, 77, 284; Fifth, 50–51,

Index

54–56, 77, 101, 103, 104, 105, 106, 112, 158, 167, 188, 192–93, 195, 203, 204, 215, 255, 272, 278, 279, 297, 301, 312, 313, 314, 328
Iowa Infantry Unit: Thirty-Second, 286
Iron Industry, 16, 32
Iron Manufacturer's Guide to the Furnaces, Forges, and Rolling Mills of the United States, 32
Island Number Ten: as Confederate post, 27, 58, 67, 79, 118; as Union post, 108, 167, 250, 266, 303
Iuka, Miss., 81, 122
Ivey, John, 315–16

Jacinto, Miss., 81
Jackman, John S., 11
Jackson, Andrew, 88, 171
Jackson, Guy Wilbur, 326
Jackson, William H. "Red," 53, 54, 100, 184, 284
Jackson, Tenn., 165, 166, 183, 210, 265, 266, 284, 285, 301, 336
Jackson Purchase (Ky.), 30, 33, 35, 36, 37, 39, 72, 74, 108, 216, 251, 280, 284, 321
Jackson's Woodyard, 327
Jacksonville *Republican*, 76
James, Anson Dr., 284
James, Thomas C., 84
Jameson, G. C., 301
Jamestown, Ky., 156
"Jake" (mascot), 3
Jasper, Tenn., 308, 309
Jenkins, M., 98
Johnson, Adam Rankin, 70, 71, 72, 88, 94–98, 99, 100, 101, 104, 106, 108, 109, 115, 122, 125, 130, 135, 136, 137, 155, 157, 162, 178, 215, 231, 282, 328, 339
Johnson, Andrew, xvi, 24, 35, 52, 80, 95, 103, 301, 314, 340; and hard war policy, 64, 112, 140, 259, 262; and Lincoln, 24, 212–13, 257, 294–95, 296, 309, 334, 338; and military, 141, 255, 257, 272, 291, 296, 307, 316, 318; and Nashville's protection, 53, 83–84, 85, 93, 98, 126–27; and secessionists, 29, 140, 259, 262; and soldier recruitment, 109, 210, 211, 255, 296; and Tennessee reconstruction, 45, 140, 163, 165, 169, 178, 209, 211, 262, 265, 299, 301, 334, 338; and unionists, 56, 84, 120, 140, 262
Johnson, Bushrod, 5, 6, 8
Johnson, Cave, 17, 107
Johnson, Eliza, 213
Johnson, George W., 3, 7
Johnson, Richard, 93, 272
Johnston, Albert Sidney, 3, 7, 8, 9, 10, 11, 12, 13, 14, 15, 20, 21, 22, 26, 35, 44, 45, 47, 48, 49, 57, 58, 64, 85, 241
Johnston, John, 337
Johnston, Joseph Eggleston, 14, 152, 178, 188, 214, 230, 251, 265, 268, 275, 276, 303, 311, 320, 321, 333

Johnston, William Preston, 270
Jones, Archer, xiv
Jones, James H., 132, 171, 234, 239, 277, 291, 292, 306
Jones, Samuel, 146, 147, 148, 149, 321
Jones, Tighlman, 81, 113, 138, 236, 261, 322–23
Jordan, John A., 255
Jordan, Thomas Jefferson, 56, 86, 109
Judah, Henry M., 281

Kansas Cavalry unit: Seventh, 37, 99–100, 103, 184, 253
Kean, Richard, 283
Kelley, D. C., 307
Kelly, J., 315
Kelly's Ferry, 316
Kennedy, D. H., 94
Kennedy, Sarah, 94, 107, 159, 160–61, 208
Kennedy, Will, 52
Kennett, John, 49, 50
Kennett, Lee, xvi
Kentucky: Campaign of 1862, 121, 122, 123–26, 130–37, 140–41, 142, 144, 145, 147–49, 151, 152, 153, 173, 245, 287, 289; Coal Fields, 30; Confederate Counteroffensive of 1863, 303–5, 319, 321; Confederate Occupation of 1861, 36–37; Defense Line (U.S.), 155–56, 214, 215; District of, 136; and Emancipation, 89, 287–89; Home Guards, 156; and Lincoln, 288–89; Neutrality, 35–36, 42; Political Situation, 35–36, 86, 89–90, 92–93, 98, 102, 124, 130, 137, 144, 209, 243, 244, 245, 285, 286, 287–90, 343
Kentucky Counties: Benton, 188; Bourbon, 156; Boyle, 134; Caldwell, 36, 137; Christian, 36, 94, 155, 157, 329; Clark, 156; Clinton, 73, 208; Crittenden, 137; Cumberland, 73; Fulton, 286; Gallatin, 67; Graves, 169; Henry, 156; Hickman, 73, 74, 286; Hopkins, 73, 137; Livingston, 137; Logan, 37, 89, 99, 335; Madison, 156; Montgomery, 156; Nicholas, 156; Todd, 155, 157, 159, 209; Trigg, 32, 137, 155, 257; Union, 72, 89, 115, 137; Wayne, 248
Kentucky River, 125
Kentucky units (Confederate): First Partisan Rangers, 71, 72, 94, 135; Second Partisan Rangers, 245; First Cavalry, 86, 94; Graves Battery, 150
Kentucky units (Union) Cavalry: First, 55; Third, 73, 77, 328; Fourth, 55, 77, 155; Eighth, 108, 124, 125, 135, 155, 190, 243, 245, 284; Fifteenth, 244, 250
Kentucky units (Union) Infantry: Eleventh, 209; Seventeenth, 155, 160, 190; Twenty-Third, 55, 109, 140; Twenty-Sixth, 328; Twenty-Eighth, 155, 190, 297

{399}

Index

Kenyon, Nathaniel C., 119
Ketcham, Mrs. John Lewis, 171
Killebrew, Joseph B., xv, 34, 36, 37, 98–99, 315
Kinderhook, Tenn., 73, 96
King, H. Clay, 50
King, James Moore, 88
King, James Moore (Colonel), 180, 239
King, William Henry, 88
Kingston Springs, Tenn., 295, 315
Kirk, Lewis, 72
Knights of the Golden Circle, 261
Knoxville, Tenn., 78, 86, 93, 123, 277, 283, 292, 298, 299, 302, 305, 313, 320, 325, 330, 331, 332, 333, 338, 342
Kogier, Elijah, 68

La Grange, Tenn., 168, 265, 284, 331
La Vergne, Tenn., 146, 147, 149, 159, 180, 181
Lancaster, Ky., 139
Langen, Edward, 285
Langworthy, Oscar, 278
Latimer, Joseph A., 194
Lattern, A. O. W., 67
Lauderdale, John Vance, 37, 92
Lawrenceburg, Tenn., 131, 336
Lawton, W. J., 87
Lebanon, Ky., 86, 162, 281, 295
Lebanon, Tenn., 54, 55, 56, 72, 140, 180, 300
Lee, Robert E., 63, 121, 128, 142, 143, 265, 275, 305, 307, 320
Lee, Stephen Dill, 308, 311, 313, 321, 322, 336, 337
Lesley, J. P., 32
Lewis, Blanche L., 17
Lewisburg, Tenn., 315
Lexington, Ky., 49, 54, 85, 90, 124, 126, 134, 135, 160, 245, 246, 342
Lexington, Tenn., 167, 267
Liberty, Ky., 281
Liberty, Tenn., 180, 248
Liberty Gap, Tenn., 270, 272
Licking Creek, Ky., 135, *136*
Liddell, St. John Richardson, 15, 241
Lieber Code, 221, 257
Lieber, Francis, 219, 221
Lincoln, Abraham, 174, 238, 239; and conciliatory policy, 44, 62; and defending Washington, 127–28; and emancipation, 149, 177, 180, 207, 243, 245; and General Burnside, 280, 292, 316; and General Hurlburt, 291; and General Rosecrans, 271, 279, 280, 316; and hard war policy, 62, 63, 111, 113, 257, 284; and Johnson, 24, 127, 212–13, 296, 309, 338; and Tennessee Reconstruction, 24, 212–13; and Tennessee Secession, 33–34; and Virginia war, 62–63, 82, 83–84

Linden, Tenn., 229
Lindsley, John, 208
Linton, Ky., 326
Litchfield, Ky., 131
Little Calfkiller River, 279
Little Harpeth River, 247
Liverpool, England, 297
Lockridge, Marshall, 54
Lockridge Mill, Tenn., 54
Locust Grove, Ky., 329
Logan, John A., 19, 111
Logistics, 12, 14, 22, 80, 81, 82, 83, 86, 93, 130, 140, 145, 153, 155, 162, 163, 166, 167, 169, 178, 180, 187, 189, 190, 222, 230, 239, 250, 265, 271, 280, 293, 294, 304, *308*, 315, 317, 321, 322, 341
Longstreet, James, 305, 307, 320, 331, 332, 333, 336
Lookout Mountain, 302, 320, 332, 338
Lookout Valley, 320
Louisiana unit: First Cavalry, 49
Louisville, Ky., xvi, 5, 73, 123–25, 131, 132, 133, 142, 160, 175, 180, 230, 242, 244, 248, 265, 283, 299, 317, 342
Louisville and Nashville Railroad, xvi, 18, 30, 31–32, 52, 55, 72, 82, 89, 90, 95, 130, 145, 155, 162, 163, 173, 180, 185, 214, 236, 243, 281, 314
Louisville Journal, 49, 157, 179
Louisville Weekly Journal, 156
Lowe, William, 53, 54, 92, 95, 101, 102, 103, 105–7, 113, 137, 158, 160, 166, 168, 172, 183, 192, 193, 199, 200, 201, 202, 214, 255, 266, 297
Lowry, Robert, 48
Lubbock, John, 70
Lyle, W. W., 240, 271, 276
Lynnville, Tenn., 316
Lyon, William P., 60, 200, 284, 296, 297
Lyons, Ky., 155

Mackall, W. W., 10, 58
Madisonville, Ky., 72, 99, 125
Magdeburg, Tenn., 164
Magoffin, Beriah, 288
Mallory, Stephen R., 124
Malone, James C. Jr., 198
Mammoth Cave, Ky., 93
Manchester, Ky., 139
Manchester, Tenn., 180, 248, 257, 271
Manigault, Arthur, 240, 273
Marable, Dr., 33
Mario, Ky., 54
Marion, Francis, 66, 86
Marshall, Eugene, 95–96, 101, 103, 104, 112, 168, 170, 171, 188, 201, 203, 204, 215, 216, 256, 279, 301, 311
Marshall, Humphrey, 79, 245
Marshall, N.C., 277

{400}

Index

Martin, James B., 343
Martin, Robert M., 70, 71, 108
Martin, William, 55
Mason, Rodney, 53, 94–98, 162, 200
Massachusetts unit: Second Infantry, 339, 342
Massey and Atkins (Waverly, Tenn.), 33
Matthews, Stanley, 84
Matthews, Washington, 21
Mattson, Hans, 244
Maverick, Samuel, 200
Maxwell, Cicero, 328
Maxwell House (Nashville, Tenn.), 20
Mayfield, Ky., 33, 54, 217, 285, 286, 328, 329
Mayfield Creek, 30
Maysville, Ala., 328, 330
McBide, Stephen, 158, 192
McCabe, Samuel L., 261
McCallie, Thomas, 299
McCann, Dick, 72, 94, 178, 183, 233, 248, 291
McClanahan, John, 197, 215
McClellan, George B., 24, 39, 43, 63, 64, 83, 84, 127, 142, 199, 345
McClellan, Robert Anderson, 202
McClelland, John S., 159
McClernand, John A., 17, 19, 169, 175, 177–78, 222
McConnell, Robert, 105, 106, 193, 200, 203, 216
McCook, Alexander, 91, 154
McCook, Daniel L., 296–97
McCook, Edward M., 213
McCook, Robert L., 76
McCord, David, 255
McDonough, James, 143
McGee, James, 33
McGowan, John P., 123
McGuire, Stanton B., 25
McHenry, John H. Jr., 160
McKee, David, 158
McKenzie, Tenn., 30, 166
McKenzie, Robert Tracy, xiv
McKibbin, J. C., 132, 133
McKinney, William M., 10
McMillan (guerrilla), 86
McMinnville, Tenn., 87, 125, 239, 243, 248, 259, 269, 270, 271, 279, 281, 303, 309, 312
McNairy, Alexander Duvall, 315
McNairy, Frank, 198, 201, 204, 206, 233
McNairy, J. W., 68
McPherson, James B., 323
McPherson, James M., 62
McWhiney, Grady, 134
Meade, George Gordon, 275
Medon, Tenn., 100
Meier, Adolphus, 42
Meigs, Montgomery C., 280, 303, 314

Mellen, W. P., 259
Memphis, Tenn., 11, 27, 33, 59, 60, 86, 92, 110, 111, 114, 119, 164, 165, 166, 169, 179, 184–85, 210, 215, 218, 250, 253, 305, 308, 311, 312, 315, 318, 322, 324, 325, 328, 330, 331, 336, 337, 338, 342
Memphis and Charleston Railroad, 28, 29, 30, 59, 80, 91, 184, 308, 312, 314, 319, 324, 325, 336, 337
Memphis and Ohio Railroad, 28, 30, 75
Memphis *Appeal*, 59, 60, 69, 205
Memphis *Argus*, 60
Memphis *Avalanche*, 4, 41, 43
Memphis *Bulletin*, 312, 331
Memphis, Clarksville and Louisville Railroad, 30, 53, 157, 226, 295
Mercer, S.C., 120
Meriwether, Elizabeth Avery, 110
Meriwether's Ferry, Tenn., 100, 328
Mexican War, 38–39
Meynard, Horace, 314
Michigan Cavalry units: Second, 182–83, 254, 285, 313; Third, 284; Fourth, 273
Michigan Engineers unit: First Regiment of Engineers and Mechanics, 81, 82, 155
Michigan Infantry unit: Fourteenth, 297, 306, 314
Mickley, J. E., 33
Middle Tennessee, District of (CSA), 147
Middleburg, Ky., 237
Middletown, Tenn., 240
Militia Act of 1862, 62, 113
Mill Creek, Tenn., 14, 183
Mill Springs, battle of, 2, 35, 181
Miller, William B., 132, 134, 170, 234–35, 237, 243, 248, 257, 262
Milton (Vaught's Hill), Tenn., 245, 247
von Minden, Henning, 192–93, 195, 196
Minnesota units: Second Infantry, 244; Third Infantry, 87, 95, 217, 250; Twenty-Third Infantry, 74
Minty, R. G. H., 189, 202, 247, 248, 273, *310*, 311, 332
Missionary Ridge, battle of, 332, 335
Mississippi Central Railroad, 30
Mississippi (CSA) units: Fifteenth Infantry, 13; Twenty-Sixth Infantry, 48
Mississippi, District of (USA), 75
Mississippi, Division of the (USA), 341
Mississippi Marine Brigade, 229–30, 252, 286, 295, 322, 327
Mississippi River, 9, 27, 28, 78, 111, 118, 122, 174, 178, 185, 222, 223, 286, 303, 324, 325, 328, 332, 341
Missouri (CSA) First Infantry unit, 22
Missouri (USA) Artillery unit: First, Battery I, 50
Missouri (USA) Cavalry unit: Fourth, 285
Missouri (USA) Infantry unit: Thirteenth, 41, 95

{401}

Index

Mitchel, Ormsby McKnight, 28–29, 46, 69, 75
Mitchell, Robert B., 100, 113, 183, 214, 255, 258, 310, 311
Mitchellville, Tenn., 94
Mix, Edward H., 286
Mizner, Henry, 314, 337
Mobile, Ala., 123
Mobile and Ohio Railroad, 28, 30, 100, 104, 166
Monmouth, Ill., 193
Moody, Granville (Rev.), 83, 126
Moore, Absalom B., 161, 162
Moore, Harriet Ellen, 177, 180, 183, 206, 208, 237, 239, 273, 275, 277–78
Moore, R., 43
Moore, Tennie, 97
Moorman, George Triplett, 5
Morgan, George Washington, 56, 80, 86
Morgan, J. T., 146, 202
Morgan, John Hunt: after Fort Donelson, 14, *48*, 49–50, 52, 53, 54, 55, 56; Kentucky Campaign, 1862, 120, 122, 124, 125, 129, 135, 137, 142; Middle Tennessee, 149, 150, 160, 161, 162–63, 170, 171, 173, 178, 180, 192, 193, 208, 222, 231, 243, 244, 247, 248, 259; Ohio Raid, 277, 278, 280, 281–83, 285, 297, 324, 339; Summer Raids, 1862, 64, 67, 68, 70, 72, 73, 76, 77, 78, 85, 86, 88, 89, 91, 93, 94, 98, 101, 109
Morgan, Mattie Ready, *48*, 49, 154, 162, 173, 208, 248, 281, 339
Morgantown, Ky., 136
Morse, S. B., 34
Morton, James St. Clair, 82, 90, 126, 148, 150, 182
Morton, Oliver P., 41, 135, 139, 163, 175
Moscow, Tenn., 166
Mount Pleasant, Tenn., 93
Mount Sterling, Ky., 245, 328
Mower, Joseph A., 336
Muhlenburg, Ky., 155
Muldraugh's Hill, Ky., 162, 163
Mumford, Thomas J., 314
Mundy, Marcellus, 55, 109, 140, 144, 244
Munfordville, Ky., 10, 130, 143, 153, 328
Murfreesboro, Tenn., xiv, 13, 15, 22, 26, 29, 33, 49, 52, 55, 74, 79, 84, 85, 87, 96, 125, 146, 147, 149, 153, 154, 161, 171, 172, 173, 176, 180, 182, 183, 200, 205, 219, 230, 235, 237, 242, 243, 254, 256, 264, 265, 271, 274, 291, 305, 313, 335
Murphy, R. C., 167
Murray, Ky., 33, 217, 285, 313, 328
Muscle Shoals, Ala., 224, 310
Myer, Thomas Rawlings, 118

Nabers, Benjamin D., 210
Napier, T. Alonzo, 7, 73, 92, 158, 160, 164, 165, 168, 178, 201, 202

Nashville, Tenn., xvi, 1, 5, 8, 10, 11, 12, 13, 14, 15, 16, 17, 19, 20, 21, 22–23, 25, 26, 33, 43, 46, 47, 49, 52, 68, 74, 85, 95, 97, 98, 105, 111, 113, 119, 125, 131, 158, 159, 170, 172, 173, 174, 176, 180, 183, 185, 188, 189, 190, 206, 208, 209, 213, 214, 225, 226, 231, 233, 236, 237, 242, 251, 256, 259, 274, 277, 279, 291, 295, 297, 299, 313, 319, 322, 327, 340, 342; as Confederate Objective, 78, 83–84, 90–91, 93, 146, 147, 154, 177, 255; Protection for, xvii, 83, 84, 90–91, 126–30, 141, 142, 145, 146, 147, 148, 149–53, 155, 175, 181, 258, 300
Nashville and Chattanooga Railroad, 15, 21, 30, 32, 52, 81, 85, 152, 183, 187, 279, 307, 311, 314, 321
Nashville and Northwestern Railroad, 187, 295, 315, 316, 322
Nashville *Daily Post*, 259
Nashville *Daily Union*, 259
Nashville Penitentiary, 291
Nashville *Union*, 67, 142, 206
Nashville "Union Guards," 85
Neely's Bend, Tenn., 130
Negley, James S., 73, 74, 92, 129, 146, 147, 149, 150, 155, 158
Negro Head Cut, Ky., 243
Nelson, T. A. R., 149
Nelson, William, 22, 86, 87, 88, 126, 128, 132, 143
New Albany, Ind., 167
New Albany, Miss., 184
New Hampshire unit: Sixth Infantry, 328
New Jersey unit: Thirty-Fourth Infantry, 338
New Madrid, Mo., 27
New Market, Ala., 76
New Orleans, La., 9, 49, 88, 100, 179
New Orleans and Ohio railroad, 30
New Portland, Tenn., 226
New Providence, Tenn., 105, 190
New York Draft Riots, 277
New York unit: 143d Infantry, 320
Newsom, Ella, 26
Newsom, J. F., 266–67, 280, 284, 286, 336
Nicholasville, Ky., 291
Nix, R. M., 86
Noble, Vett, 77, 297, 306, 314
North Bridgewater, Mass., 170, 188
North Carolina unit: Sixty-Fourth Infantry, 277
North Moore Street School (New York City), 50
Northrop, Lucius B., 11, 14, 22, 304
Norton, Anne, 66
Nott, Charles Cooper, 50–51, 52, 54, 104
Nye, Daniel, 300

"Oak Hill Rangers," 94
Obion River, 30, 100, 266

Index

Oglesby, Richard, 266
Ohio Artillery unit: First, Battery D, 236
Ohio Cavalry units: Second, 262; Fourth, 49, 155
Ohio Counties: Butler, 271; Colombian, 282
Ohio, Department of the (USA), 128, 185, 214, 245
Ohio Infantry units: Third, 174; Ninth, 139, 143, 175, 181, 182, 231, 236, 238, 269, 275, 277, 292, 293, 305, 306, 315, 334; Eleventh, 240, 271; Twenty-Second, 52; Thirty-First, 155; Thirty-Fifth, 181; Seventy-First, 53, 95, 97, 101, 105, 193, 200, 201, 203, 216, 313; Seventy-Second, 331; Seventy-Ninth, 261; One Hundred and Second, 190; One Hundred and Thirteenth, 234, 249, 261, 292; One Hundred and Twenty-Fifth, 271, 292, 306, 317
Ohio River, xv, 30, 72, 78, 99, 114, 115, 118, 123, 131, 144, 156, 174, 187, 223, 231, 248, 250, 275, 283, 324, 326, 327, 331, 335
Okolona, Miss., 67
Old Salem, Tenn., 311
Ord, Edward O. C., 109
Owen, Frank Amphilias, 72
Owensboro, Ky., 155
Oxford, Miss., 168, 169, 170

Paducah, Ky., 7, 9, 30, 33, 38, 54, 102, 114, 165, 168, 217, 224, 226, 250, 265, 266, 285, 290, 318, 322, *329*, 336, 337, 342
Paine, E. A., 156
Palmer, J. B., 150
Palmer, John McAuley, 129, 147
Palmyra, Tenn., 190, 195, 226, 227, 251, 326
Paris, Comte de, 271
Paris, Ky., 86, *125*, 245
Paris, Tenn., 33, 44, 50, 68, 103, 266, 286, 313
Parker's Crossroads, Tenn., 168
Partisan Ranger Act (1862) 64, 65
Partisan Rangers, xv, 64, 70, 78, 108, 179, 312, 339–40
Partisan Warfare, 44; American Revolution, 65–66; Civil War, 66, 343–45 (*see also* guerrillas); Colonial Period, 65; Napoleonic Era, 65
Parton, James, 342
Patrick, Mathewson T., 105, 158
Patriot, Tenn., 14
Patten, Zeboim Carter, 203, 234, 259
Patterson, E. W., 81
Paxson, Len G., 67
Payne, Andrew S., 3
Pea Ridge, battle of, 216
Pearlman, Michael, 65
Pegram, John, 245, 246, 250
Pelham, Tenn., 276
Pemberton, John C., 152, 153, 154, 164, 167, 218, 250, 251, 254, 265, 267, 276

Pemberton, William, 115
Pembroke, Ky., 328
Pence, Mrs. Artemus, 340
Pendicord, Harry, 125
Pennock, Alfred M., 114, 163, 167, 185, 186, 223, 286
Pennsylvania Cavalry units: Seventh, 55, 77, 87, 189, 273, 313; Ninth, 55, 72, 77, 84, 86, 313
Pennsylvania Infantry unit: One Hundredth, 237, 246, 292, 332
"People In Arms" concept, xiii
"Peoples War," xi–xv
Perkins, Charles G., 115
Perkins, Thomas Fearn, 6, 274
Perryville, Tenn., 217, 164
Perryville, battle of, xiv, 122, 134, 138, 141, 143, 153
Persimmon Branch, 73
Peters, E. A., 262
Petersburg, Tenn., 245
Pettit, Frederick, 237, 246, 281, 291, 298, 333, 338
Phelan, James, 153–54
Phelps, Samuel, 192, *228*, 229, 230, 284, 325
Philadelphia, Pa., 58, 292
Phillips, D. L., 18
Piatt, Donn, 140
Pickins, Andrew, 66
Pikeville, Tenn., 309
Pillow, Gideon J., 3, 6, 7, 10, 13, 15, 22, 36, 122, 188, 189, 254, 270, 285
Pioneer Brigade, 182
Piston, William, 250
Pitts Brothers (Waverly, Tenn.), 33
Polk, Leonidus, 8, 9, 12, 36, 67, 152, 202, 238, 241, 270, 305, 307, 320
Pope, John, 62–64
Port Hudson, La., 142, 176, 275, 303
Port Royal, Tenn., 160
Porter, David Dixon, 113, 115, 116, 163, 164, 166, 179, 186, 217, 218, 223, 224, 225, 228, 229, 230, 252, 283, 286, 290, 318, 323, 324, 325, 326, 327, 330
Porter, John M., 3, 6–7, 122, 136, 248, 280
Porter, L. C., 37, 84
Potomac River, 335
Prattville, Ala., 240
Prentice, George D., 49, 179
Presley, Willie, 240–41
Price, Sterling, 78, 79, 81, 100, 120, 121, 122, 128, 141, 142, 153
Prison Camps: Alton, 119; Camp Butler, 118; Camp Chase, 119, 138; Camp Douglas, 118; Camp Morton, 118; Fort Warren, 6, 7; Johnson's Island, 2, 6, 53, 72, 84, 118, 119, 281
Prisoners of War, 5, 6, 7, 114, 118, 138
Proctor's Station, Ky., 130
"Proto-Ruhr" (Ky./Tenn.), 31, 32

{403}

Index

Pulaski, Tenn., 54, 67, 74, 109, 120, 140, 297, 310, 316, 331

Quarles, J. M., 19
Quinby, Isaac F., 75, 109
Quinby and Robinson Manufacturing Company (Memphis), 32
Quint, Alonzo H., 338, 342
Quirk, Tom, 162

Raccoon Mountain, 302
Railroads, 8, 11, 13, *14*, 16, 20, 21, 28, *29*, 30–32, 46, 52, 55, 56, 74, *77*, 81, 82, 90–91, 93, 94, 95, 98, 105, 117, 130, 145, 146, 148, 149, 152, 157, 162, 163, 164, 166, 209, 230, *242*, 243, 246, 279, 281, 284, 293, 295, 298, 304, 305, 307, 310, 311, 314, 315, 321, 322, *323*, 336, 337
Ram Fleet, 252
Randall, Archibald, 284, 296
Randolph, George W., 58, 137, 145
Randolph, Tenn., 110
Randolph Furnace, 216
Ranny, N., 42
Ransom, T. E. G., 104, 105, 157
Rawlins, John, 40
Ray, Andrew, 71
Ready, Alice, 2, 47–48, 49
Ready, Charles, 47
Ready, Mary, 339
Readyville, Tenn., 271
Reckley, H. R., 27
Red River, 17, 97, 105, 160, 256
Reed, James, 338
Reedyville, Tenn., 240
Renaeau, Isaac T., 208
Revis, Martha, 277
Reynolds, A. E., 48
Reynolds, Joseph J., 163, 219, 237, 248, 259–60, 263
Reynoldsburg, Tenn., 266
Rice, Jonathan B., 331
Rice, Ralsa C., 235, 271, 277, 292, 306, 317
Richards, Channing, 19, 41
Richardson, R. V., 165, 183, 218, 250, 266, 280, 284, 312, 328, 336
Richland Station, Tenn., 245
Richmond, Ky., 86, 126, 143, 153, 283
Ridley, Bromfield, 245
Riggin's Hill, Tenn., 105, 106
Ringgold, Ga., 332
Rinker, John I., 168
Rivers, Thomas, 184
Roberts, Franklin, 150
Robinson, James F., 245, 289
Rochester, Ky., 136

Roddey, P. D., 184, 286, 308, 310, 312, 313, 321
Rogers, Ethridge, 103
Rogers, Monroe, 33
Rogers, Robert, 65
Rogers Rangers, 65
Rolling Fork Creek, 163, 281
Rome, Ga., 300
Rome's Mill, Tenn., 68
Rosecrans, Williams S.: Chattanooga Campaign, 275, 276, 278, 291, 294, 297, 299; Chickamauga and Siege of Chattanooga, 302, 303, 304, 306, 311, 314–18; Protecting Nashville, 139, 145, 151, 154, 155, 158–64, 172, 173, 175, 176, 180–90, 200, 206, 209–11, 214, 217–20, 223, 231, 232, 237, 239, 242, 246, 248, 250, 252–53, 255; Tullahoma Campaign, 264, 265, 267, 269, 270–75, 338; in West Tennessee, 78, 80, 100, 109, 117
Rousseau, Lovell H., 294, 295, 322
Rover, Tenn., 244, 245
Rudd, S. J., 67
Ruffin, Edmund, 9, 13
Russell, A. A., 150, 202
Russellville, Ky., 7, 12, 33, 35, 92, 121, 135, 156, 157, 159, 160, 161, 255, 257, 328
Russellville, Tenn., 333
Rutherford Creek, 52
Rynam, Alanson R., 130, 233–34, 235, 237, 239, 244, 248, 264

Saint Louis, Mo., 114, 195, 325
Salem, Tenn., 245, 265
Salt River, 89
San Antonio, Tex., 200
Sand Mountain, Ala., 274
Sanders, Q. C., 68
Sanders, William P., 250, 281
Savannah, Tenn., 27, 52, 68, 253, 325, 331
Sayers, Edward B., 123
Scantlin, J. M., 115
"Scarborough Hill" (Dover, Tenn.), 205
Scott, (?) (Marion, Ky.), 67
Scott, John, 285
Scott, John S., 14, 49, 52, 246, 280, 282, 283, 290
Scott, Thomas A., 314
Scott, Sir Walter, 66, 208
Scott, Winfield, 39
Scottsville, Ky., 72
Scranton, L. S., 247
Seat, B. B., 67
Seddon, James A., 304, 339
Senatobia, Miss., 265
Sequatchie Valley, 308
Seward, William H., 144, 303
Shackleford, James M., 99, 108, 124, 125, 282

{404}

Index

Shafter, William R., 246
Shapard, Robert P., 301
Shawneetown, Ky., 114
Shelbyville, Tenn., 13, 14, 29, 33, 55, 173, 180, 182, 202, 241, 246, 255, 264, 269, 272, 273, 277, 301, 309, 313, 316
"Shelbyville Rebels," 3
Sheliah, George, 10
Sherman, William T.: and Civil-Military Relations, xiv, 61, 62, 100, 110, 111, 115, 164, 165, 179, 207–8, 222, 301, 312, 324, 329, 330–32, 345; and Operations, xvii, 27, 60, 61, 62, 80, 91, 117, 156, 266, 312, 336, 338, 342; and relief of Chattanooga, 315, 320–25
Shiloh, battle of, xiv, xvi, 13, 17, 28, 29, 47, 52, 53, 48, 64, 67, 71, 95, 101, 184, 235, 264, 294, 340
Shipp, Eb, 34
Shipp, Stump, 34
Shirk, James H., 217
Shorter, John Gill, 254
Shy Family (Franklin, Tenn.), 234
Siddell, W. H., 98
Sills, Joshua, 131
Simms, William Gilmore, 66
Simpson, Brooks D., 60, 61
Slack, Henry Richmond, 21
Smith, A. A., 197
Smith, Andrew Jackson, 286, 328, 336, 337
Smith, B. F. Cloud, 212
Smith, Charles Ferguson, 17
Smith, Daniel P., 58
Smith, Edmund Kirby, 76, 78, 80, 93, 121, 124, 126, 128, 129, 134, 137, 139, 143, 148, 152, 287
Smith, George, 17
Smith, Green Clay, 237, 247
Smith, Robert E., 150
Smith, William F., 320
Smith, William Sooy, 336
Smithland, Ky., 54, 92, 102, 137, 155, 185
Smyrna, Tenn., 67, 340
Snow Hill, Tenn., 248
Somerset, Ky., 156, 246
Somerville, Tenn., 165, 184, 218
South Tunnel, Tenn., 243
Spalding (guerrilla), 188
Spanish-American War, 246–47
Sparta, Tenn., 86, 260, 279, 280, 313
Spencer, Tenn., 109
Spring Hill, Tenn., 237, 240, 241, 243, 245, 247, 249, 255
Springfield, Ill., 180
Springfield, Tenn., 33, 52, 159, 209
St. Cloud's Hill (Nashville, Tenn.), 150
Stager, Anson, 266

Stanley, David B., 247, 249, 253, 254, 273, 274
Stanton, Edwin M., 24, 42, 46, 74, 75, 77, 83, 112, 163, 210–11, 213, 223, 276, 295, 296, 299, 317, 341
Starnes, Jake, 150, 169, 247, 254, 255, 272
Starr, Stephen, 250
Starring, Frederick A., 16, 108, 117
States' Rights Party (Ky.), 288
Steadman, James, 162
Steamboats, 30, 62, 142, 203, 218, 222, 325; *Anglo-Saxon*, 325; *Callie*, 114; *Catahoula*, 179; *Choutan*, 118; *Connelston*, 204; *Continental*, 110; *Cordelia Ann*, 114; *D. A. January*, 37, 92; *Dunbar*, 184, 185, 223, 224; *Eugene*, 110; *Gladiator*, 179; *Hastings*, 189, 190; *Hazel Dell*, 115; *I. Raymond*, 92; *J. H. Baldwin*, 25; *J. H. Dickey*, 110; *John A. Fisher*, 5, 6; *Mary Crane*, 190; *Minnetonka*, 49; *Nashville*, 325; *New York*, 204; *Parthenia*, 189; *Skylark*, 114; *Sunny South*, 325; *Trio*, 189; *Uncle Sam*, 6; *W. B. Terry*, 114; *Wild Cat*, 195, 197, 199
Stearns, George L., 296, 345
Stenbeck, Andrew, 104
Stevenson, Ala., 29, 76, 79, 125, 315, 331
Stevenson, Carter, 154, 218
Stevenson, V. K., 21, 32, 84, 85
Stewart, F. M., 336
Stewart College (Clarksville, Tenn.), 96
Stokes, William B., 109, 129
Stones River, 155, 243
Stones River, battle of, 173, 175, 176, 177, 178, 180, 181, 182, 213, 223, 235, 238, 264, 268, 271, 334
Stout, Samuel, M. D., 298
Stowell, W. F., 277
Strawberry Plains, Tenn., 330
Street, Solomon G., 328
Streight, Abel D., 76, 251–54, 281, 294, 295
Strickland, William, 20
Sugar Creek, 311
Sullivan, Jeremiah, 166, 168, 183, 210
Sumter, Thomas, 66, 86
Sutherland, Daniel, 62
Swift, John, 297
Swords, Thomas, 81

Tallahatchie River, 284
Taylor, Sam, 99
Tebbs Bend, Ky., 281
Telegraph, role of, 159, 162, 167
Temple, Oliver P., 34
Tennessee: Election of 1863, 299–300; morale of people in: after Fort Donelson, xiv–xv, 9, 15, 17, 18, 19–20, 21–22, 23–25, 28, 29, 37, 39; Summer 1862, 40, 41, 43, 46, 47–48, 49, 50–52, 53, 54, 58, 59, 60, 61, 62, 69, 70, 74, 79, 84, 87, 91, 94, 97, 99, 103, 110, 111, 112; Autumn 1862, 119, 120, 122, 127,

{405}

Tennessee, *cont.*
128, 129, 143, 152, 159, 160, 161, 164, 167, 169, 172; Winter/Spring 1863, 176, 177, 179, 180, 208, 213, 219, 226, 227–28; Spring/Summer 1863, 234, 235, 236, 239, 246, 258, 260, 262, 273, 275, 277–78, 279, 286, 290–91, 297, 314; Fall 1863, 315, 323, 329, 335, 337, 340, 343; Secession, 33–34, 35, 36, 37, 51; Wartime Reconstruction, 23–25, 37, 38, 43–45, 54, 55, 60, 74, 83, 84, 87–88, 90, 100, 103, 105–7, 110, 111, 112, 113, 121, 126, 140, 163, 165, 169, 178, 183, 208, 211, 212, 213, 219, 220, 222, 227, 233, 239, 259, 262–63, 290–91, 297–98, 301, 334, 341, 343–44, 345

Tennessee and Alabama Railroad, 30, 81–82, 246, 279, 321, 322, 332

Tennessee Counties: Bedford, 55, 241, 299; Benton, 244; Blount, 336; Carroll, 168, 244, 329; Cheatham, 159, 300; Davidson, 70, 94; De Kalb, 212, 248; Decatur, 244; Dickson, 159; Dyer, 100, 169; Fayette, 165, 169, 184; Fentress, 68; Franklin, 180; Giles, 54, 67; Hardiman, 165, 169; Haywood, 165, 169; Henderson, 267; Henry, 50, 51, 103, 244, 329; Humphreys, 33; Lawrence, 72; Lincoln, 189; Macon, 212; Madison, 267; Marshall, 310; Maury, 72, 74, 98, 125; McNairy, 233, 267; Montgomery, 33, 94, 97, 160; Obion, 165; Perry, 229; Putnam, 212; Robertson, 159, 209; Rutherford, 88, 208; Shelby, 165, 169, 299; Smith, 212; Stewart, 32, 73; Sumner, 125; Tipton, 165; Van Buren, 109; Weakley, 36, 103, 167, 244; Williamson, 272; Wilson, 212

Tennessee Iron Works, 16

Tennessee Ridge, Tenn., 74, 215

Tennessee River, 11, 16, 27, 28, 30, 31, 50, 53, 68, 72, 100, 101, 103, 114, 115, 116, 123, 142, 164, 167, 168, 187, 204, 216, 223, 225, 226, 229, 230, 244, 266, 267, 274, 290, 293, 301, 310, 311, 315, 322, 324, 325, 326, 330, 332, 341

Tennessee units (CSA) Artillery: Freeman's Battery, 146, 150, 274; Roberts' Battery, 150; White's Battery, 196

Tennessee units (CSA) Cavalry: First, 299; First Partisan Rangers, 165; Fourth, 150; Eighth, 150, 251; Ninth, 150; Tenth, 202; Eleventh, 202, 274; Thirteenth, 251

Tennessee units (CSA) Infantry: Fourteenth, 107; Twenty-Fifth, 68; Forty-Fourth, 87; Forty-Eighth, 176; Forty-Ninth, 107; Fiftieth, 107; Fifty-First, 129

Tennessee units (USA) Artillery: First, 190; First Heavy (African Descent), 296; Second Heavy (African Descent), 296

Tennessee units (USA) Cavalry: First East Tennesseee, 309; First Middle Tennessee, 296; 311; First West Tennessee, 285; Second West Tennessee, 285; Sixth, 117; Seventh, 109; Eighth, 330

Tennessee units (USA) Infantry: First, 46; First (African Descent), 296; Second (African Descent), 296; Third (African Descent), 296; Fourth, 309; Union Guards, 315

Texas, units (CSA) Cavalry: Sixth, 253; Eighth (Terry's Texas Rangers), 37, 86, 130, 176, 197, 200, 201, 222, 240, 260

Thatcher, Marshall P., 182–83, 254, 313

Thayer, William A., 195

Thirty Years War, 278

Thomas, Emory, 64

Thomas, George H., 127, 128, 129, 132, 139, 161, 219, 237, 260, 272, 306, 317, 318, 322, 331, 342

Thomas, Hubbard T., 283, 302

Thomas, Lorenzo, 213

Thomas, Mrs. R. W., 19

Thompson, Charles R., 295

Thompson, Jake, 64, 67

Thompson, Mitchel Andrew, 112–13, 157–58, 193, 204, 206, 216, 313, 334, 340

Thompson's Station, Tenn., 246, 249

Tilghman, Lloyd, 7, 13, 80, 120

Tillman, Samuel E., 309

Tiptonville, Tenn., 53

Tisomingo Hotel (Corinth, Miss.), 77

Tod, David, 207

Tompkins, Charles Brown, 5

Tompkinsville, Ky., 73, 86, 109, 158, 313

Tracy City, Tenn., 277

Trauernicht, Theodore, 315

Trenton, Ky., 159

Trenton, Tenn., 53, 165, 166, 301

Triune, Tenn., 244, 245, 249, 255, 274

Troy, Tenn., 165

Truesdail, William, 191, 209, 258, 300, 339

Tucker, Beverly, 66

Tucker, Joseph T., 68

Tullahoma, Tenn., 125, 147, 152, 155, 182, 264, 271, 272, 274, 276, 281, 287, 299, 316, 338

Tunnel Hill (Chattanooga, Tenn.), 332

Tupelo, Miss., 58, 79

Turchin, John B., 75, 140

Tuscaloosa, Ala., 118

Tuscumbia, Ala., 13, 99, 167, 224, 252, 311, 318

Tyree Springs, Tenn., 94

Underwood, J. R., 40

Union City, Tenn., 33, 166, 285, 301, 323, 328

Union Democracy Party (Ky.), 289

Union Pacific Railroad, 337

Unionism, 33, 34, 35, 45, 51, 68, 73, 74, 76, 90, 99, 111, 117, 122, 128, 135, 137, 149, 148, 158, 167, 177, 179, 184, 185, 210, 212, 226, 250, 272, 259–60, 286, 287, 289, 296, 298, 300, 301, 325, 330, 337, 343

Index

Uniontown, Ohio, 114
Unionville, Tenn., 245
United States Army (Corps): IX, 246, 280, 294; X, 301; XI, 311, 320; XII, 311; XIV, 219; XVI, 183, 250; XVII, 183
United States Army Regiments (Cavalry): Fourth, 249; Fifth, 150; (Infantry): Thirteenth, 312; Nineteenth, 134, 261; (Colored Troops): 62, 296; Second, 315; Fourteenth, 316; (Gunboat): *Allegheny Belle*, 282
United States Army, Military Division of the Mississippi, 341
United States Navy, 2, 13, 16, 18, 27, 32, 49, 69, 113, 114, 115, 116, 156, 163, 169, 185, 186, 190–200, 203, 217, 324; convoys, 186, 191, 203, 223, 327
United States Navy Warships: *Alfred Robb*, 114, 186, 190, 200, 224, 266; *Argosy*, 229, 252; *Brilliant*, 115, 186, 190, 200, 203, 217, 224, 227, 253, 326; *Carondelet*, 5; *Covington*, 229, 252; *Cricket*, 325; *Eastport*, 229; *Fairplay*, 114, 166, 186, 190, *199*, 200, 224, 227, 326; *General Pillow*, 114, 137, 186, 188; *Hastings (Emma Duncan)*, 229, 253, 325; *Key West*, 325; *Lexington*, 186, 190, 191, 200, 224, 226, 252, 325; *Little Rebel*, 114; *Monarch*, 285; *Moose*, 282, 325; *Naumkeag*, 325; *New Era*, 167; *Paw Paw*, 325; *Peosta*, 325; *Queen City*, 229, 252; *St. Clair*, 115, 186, 190, 200, 224, 227, 229; *Siddell*, 189, 190; *Silver Cloud*, 297; *Silver Lake*, 186, 190, 200, 225; *Springfield*, 225; *Tawah*, 325; *Tuscumbia*, 217, 325; *Tyler*, 68, 114, 325, 329
United States Sanitary Commission, 18
University Springs (Sewanee), Tenn., 277
Utica, N.Y., 194
Utley, William T., 309

Vale, Joseph G., 189, 205, 313
Vallandigham, Clement, 238, 257, 264, 276
Valley Forge, Pa., 338
Van Dorn, Earl, 78, 79, 100, 121, 122, 142, 153, 163, 167, 184, 185, 202, 215, 223, 224, 230, 240, 241, 244, 246, 247, 249, 253, 254, 270
Van Dorn, William, 190
Van Horne, Thomas B., 28
Vanmeter, Joseph, 237
de Vattel, Emmerich, 38
Vernay, James, 119
Versailles, Ky., 135
Vicksburg, Miss., xiv, 78, 114, 118, 138, 145, 170, 174, 175, 185, 217, 222, 224, 228, 236, 251, 267, 268, 275, 276, 283, 287, 290, 303, 304, 308, 317, 320, 321, 325, 331, 336, 340
Vidette, 136
Villipigue, John p., 128
Vincennes *Sun*, 289

Vincent, Henry, 236
Virginia: Powhatan County, 146
Volney, Ky., 328
Volunteer and Conscript Bureau (CSA), 188

Walden's Ridge, 86, 298, 308
Walke, Henry, 5
Walker, John H., 230
Walker, Leroy Pope, 36, 73
Wallace, Lewis, 4, 139
Wallace, William H., 17
Ward, W. T., 214
Waring, George E., 285, 323
Warren, Stanford L., 117
Wartrace, Tenn., 277, 309, 316
Washburn, Elihu B., 5, 38
Washington, D.C., defending, 84, 127–28, 142
Washington, George, 44, 208, 209, 237
Watauga River, 249
Waterman, Luther D., 189
Watson, P. H., 56
Wauhatchie Creek, 320
Waverly, Tenn., 33, 50, 74, 158, 187, 188, 216, 230, 253, 255, 284, 296, 327
Waverley (Sir Walter Scott), 208
Wayne, John, 251
Waynesboro, Tenn., 164
Weaver, Amos, 239
Webster, Joseph D., 16
Webster, Rowena, 21
Weem's Springs, Tenn., 291
Welles, Gideon, 115, 164, 185, 186, 224
Wells, William, 285
West Point, Ky., 131
West Point, Ohio, 282
West Tennessee, 72, 73, 74, 77, 78, 83, 86, 100, 103, 104, 108, 109, 117, 183, 184, 251, 280, 284, 318, 322, 329, 336; Forrest's Raid in, 153, 163–70
Western Kentucky, District of (USA), 185
Western Military Institute, 6
Wharton, John A., 87, 152, 192, 196, 201, 205, 222, 244, 247, 273
Wheeler, Joseph, 142, 152, 161, 162, 164, 173, 181, 189, 208, 214, 215, 224, 245, 247, 248, 254, 273, 304, 308, 309, 310, 312, 313, 314, 315, 321, 322, 336, 339; and Battle of Dover, 190, 192–98, 201, 205–6
Whitcomb, John B., 197, 277
White, B. F., 196
White, D. H. and Brothers (Waverly, Tenn.), 33
White, Robert M., 253
White Oak, Tenn., 284
Whiteburg, Ala., 328
Whitfield, James Wilkens, 247
Whiteside Station, Tenn., 323

Index

Whitthorne, W. C., 21
Wickliffe, Charles, 289
Wild Cat Creek, 279
Wilder, John, 237, 272, 299
Wilkinson, John M., 257, 258
Willett, Alfred C., 235, 249, 261, 273, 276, 292
Williams, Edward C., 73, 109
Williams, Kenneth P., 139, 162, 243
Williams, Thomas J., 72, 73, 93
Williamson, J. T., 8, 11
Williamsport, Tenn., 98, 163
"Willie" (CSA), 12
Wills, Sylvester, 291, 322
Wilson, A. N., 284, 286
Wilson, Thomas Black, 8, 15, 25, 70, 100, 299
Wilson's Creek, Ky., 281
Winchester, Ky., 86
Winchester, Tenn., 277
Wisconsin units: Eighth Infantry, 167; Thirteenth Infantry, 102, 106, 200, 284, 297, 313; Fifteenth Infantry, 158; Twenty-Second Infantry, 40
Wolf River, 30
Wolford, Frank, 55, 281
Wood, Ben, 196
Wood, Robert C. Jr., 47
Woodbury, Tenn., 245, 269
Woodlawn, Tenn., 105
Woods, Lewis and Company (Clarksville, Tenn.), 107
Woodward, J. E., 290
Woodward, Tom, 89, 90, 94–98, 99–108, 136, 137, 155, 156, 159, 160, 161, 178, 193, 201, 215, 227, 231, 245, 266, 328, 329
Wooley, Robert W., 31–32
Worth, W. E., 93
Wright, Crafts J. , 18–19, 41, 53, 95
Wright, Horatio, 102, 128, 132, 138, 144, 155, 156, 185, 186, 187, 214, 230, 232, 245, 249, 289
Wright, Moses, xv, 13, 14

Yancey, Thomas L., 97
Yates, Richard, 139
Yazoo River, 142, 325
Yorktown, Va., 278
Young, J. Morris, 328

Zollicoffer, Felix, 2, 35

Fort Donelson's Legacy was designed and typeset on a MacIntosh computer system using PageMaker software. The text is set in Centaur, chapter titles are set in Aurea Titling and Aurea Inline, all-caps alphabets based on inscriptions on ancient Roman buildings. This book was designed by Todd Duren, composed by Wolf Song Design, and printed and bound by Thomson-Shore, Inc. The recycled paper used in this book is designed for an effective life of at least three hundred years.